D0679159

A LITERARY HISTORY OF FRANCE

A LITERARY HISTORY OF FRANCE

General Editor: P. E. CHARVET
Fellow of Corpus Christi College, Cambridge

THE SEVENTEENTH CENTURY 1600–1715
by P. J. YARROW
Professor of French at the University of Newcastle upon Tyne

THE EIGHTEENTH CENTURY 1715–1789
by ROBERT NIKLAUS
Professor of French at the University of Exeter

THE NINETEENTH CENTURY 1789–1870
by P. E. CHARVET

THE NINETEENTH AND TWENTIETH CENTURIES 1870–1940
by P. E. CHARVET

A LITERARY HISTORY OF FRANCE

THE EIGHTEENTH CENTURY

1715–1789

A LITERARY HISTORY OF FRANCE

The Eighteenth Century 1715–1789

ROBERT NIKLAUS
Professor of French, University of Exeter

LONDON · ERNEST BENN LIMITED

NEW YORK · BARNES & NOBLE INC

LIBRARY
EISENHOWER COLLEGE

First published 1970 by Ernest Benn Limited
Bouverie House · Fleet Street · London · EC4
and Barnes & Noble Inc. · 105 Fifth Avenue · New York 10003
Distributed in Canada by
The General Publishing Company Limited · Toronto
© Robert Niklaus 1970
Printed in Great Britain
ISBN-0-510-32231-X
SBN-389-03996-9 (U.S.A.)

PQ
103
L5
v.3

FOREWORD BY THE GENERAL EDITOR

IN HIS QUEST for the past, the historian proper deals with a variety of evidence, documentary and other, which is of value to him only for the light it sheds on events and on the men who played a part in them. The historian of literature has before him documents in manuscript or print that exist in their own right, books and ever more books, as the centuries unfold. Within the space allotted to him, his first task must be to give the maximum amount of relevant information about them, but if he is to avoid producing a mere compilation of unrelated and therefore meaningless facts, he is bound to organise his matter into some sort of pattern.

Time itself does this for him to some extent by keeping alive the memory of those writers and books that retain their relevance, and, often enough, setting one school of writers against another, as successive generations seek to establish their own originality by revolt against their immediate predecessors.

At whatever point in time the historian of literature may stand, he is bound to adopt as a basis of his work the patterns time gives him, although he knows well enough that, just as the tide and the waves may alter the patterns they themselves are for ever imprinting on the sands of the sea shore, time, bringing with it changing tastes and values, will alter these patterns, at least in detail or emphasis.

Within these broad natural patterns come problems of arrangement. Here inevitably a degree of arbitrariness creeps in. Some writers are dubbed precursors, as though they themselves had consciously played the role of prophet in a wilderness, others are marked down as 'epigoni' – poor fellows! Had they but known! – others again are lumped together because they are seen to have in common the characteristics of an age, though they may have had no relations with each other; chronology must often be sacrificed to the need of tidiness. Thus does the historian of literature try to create from the vigorous and confused growth he is faced with, at least on the surface, an ordered garden, where the reader may wander and get an impression to store away in his memory, of neatness and controlled change, an impression helpful, indeed indispensable, as a preliminary to the study of the subject, but not to be confused with the reality.

Nor is this all. Should the historian of literature, need he, smother his personal responses? And if he should (which we doubt and indeed have not tried to do), is this really possible? Within the kindly Doctor Jekyll, recording in detached tones his literary history, seeking to give an objective picture of an age, explaining, elucidating, lurks Mr Hyde, the critic, ready to leap out at the reader on the slightest provocation and wreak his mischief. As in all of us, the levels of his personality that may respond to stimuli are numerous: intellectual, emotional, moral, spiritual; more numerous still the sources of interest whence the stimuli may come: historical and social, psychological, linguistic and stylistic, aesthetic. Literature is a vast catchment area all these streams flow into; a book, a great book is like a burning glass that concentrates the rays of human experience into one bright point; it burns itself into our memories and may even sear the soul.

If he be wise, Mr Hyde the critic will use as his criterium of judgment only the degree to which he feels his own experience has been enriched, his own perceptiveness extended. Thus will he avoid being too rigid or narrow in his attitudes and avoid the temptation of for ever seeking some underlying principle that controls the whole mechanism. Since the corpus of a writer's work is the expression of his experience, since the writer belongs to a given age, a given people, the works may easily become the pretext for an exercise in individual or national psychology. Conversely, the idea of race, the age, the accumulated legacy of history – its momentum, in a word – may be invoked as cause and explanation of the works. Or again, since the works have their place in one or more given art-forms, they may be seen as no more than moments in the evolution of these.

Such ideas and unifying theories have their value no doubt; the people, the society, the age, the art-forms all bear on the question, but who is to assess their impact? They leave the mystery of individual genius and of artistic creation intact; to emphasise them at the expense of the latter is really using the history of literature for other ends. Admittedly books do not spring from nothing, but whether we consider them historically or critically, in the last resort they stand, as we observed at the outset of this foreword, in their own right, and their value depends upon their impact on the individual; every book has three aspects: what the author meant to express, what the book contains, and the image the reader carries away with him; this latter changes with every reader of the book and depends as much upon himself as upon the book and the author.

From its early beginnings in the ninth century down to the present day, French literature can claim a continued existence of 1100 years. What country, besides our own, can boast such literary wealth, such resource, such powers of renewal? The authors of this history, the first of its kind in English, have been only too well aware of the difficulties attendant upon so vast an enterprise. Their hope is that it may give to all readers of French literature a coherent background against which particular periods or writers may be studied and enjoyed in greater depth.

P. E. C.

PREFACE

THE PRESENT VOLUME differs in some respects from others in the series, partly because of the character of eighteenth-century literary works, with their emphasis on ideas, and their desire to extend the frontiers of literature whilst uneasily accepting the classical canons of the previous age; and partly because of the dominance of a few outstanding writers who were primarily thinkers and not littérateurs. Inevitably, considerable space has been allocated to such outstanding figures as Montesquieu, Voltaire, Rousseau, and Diderot, who broadened the concept of literature to include law, philosophy, and science. They will be seen against a complex background – historical, intellectual, and artistic – which has been dealt with in some detail, and which will provide also a general introduction to the life, manners, and literary activity of the period. The vast output of lesser writers, who all played a not insignificant part in the cultural life of their own day, is cursorily reviewed, among them those who deserve mention either for the intrinsic interest of their work, or for their possible significance in the light of later developments.

In the chapters on the novel and on the theatre the main currents of change are brought out, with emphasis on the more interesting experiments in technique, or on the theories explicitly formulated or implicitly revealed in the works of novelists and dramatists alike. Poetry presented a special problem, for the very conception of poetry has changed since the eighteenth century. The contemporary assessment of the qualities of the poetry as such had to be borne in mind, and in view of the vast number of poets of equal, if relatively small, intrinsic merit, information has been provided which serves to link them with the society in which they played their minor part. In this way we have sought to present a clear picture of the pattern of literary and social life of the age, which has its own peculiar flavour, as specific as that of rococo art (with which it has close affinities).

From a vast, if not exhaustive, panorama such as that here attempted, the recognised works of major consequence to French and world literature, and to the history of ideas, will emerge with greater clarity and with their true originality. In an age as rich in colour and variety and as distinctive as the French eighteenth century, no part can be properly divorced from the whole with which it is invariably linked, whatever the genius and personal circumstance of the individual writer. It is to be regretted that the necessary limitations imposed by the subject of this volume have not allowed for more than passing mention of contemporary literary activities in other lands. *Le siècle des lumières, the Age of Enlightenment, Die Aufklärung, e illuminismo*, if related to their original meaning and usual context, are as different in spirit as the words used would suggest; but they nevertheless serve to bring out the overall cosmopolitan outlook of its leaders and their common objective. For those who feel prompted to pursue the study of individual writers, as well as of currents of thought, short bibliographies have been appended, and these invariably include works which provide in turn extensive booklists for still further reading.

I should like to express my appreciation to all those who have given help and encouragement in a difficult and protracted undertaking: to my publishers, for their courtesy and forbearance over inevitable delays in completing my task; to the General Editor, P. E. Charvet, for moral support and much practical advice, as well as for reading the draft of this volume; to Professor W. Barber and Dr M. H. Waddicor, for suggesting improvements to the chapters I submitted to them; To Dr Vivienne Mylne, for expert help in dating the novels listed; to Mrs M. G. Singh, for compiling the Index; lastly to my wife, for her assistance over matters concerning the theatre – in particular Italian comedy, of which she has a detailed knowledge – and over questions of presentation and style.

I wish also to thank the large band of eighteenth-century scholars from many countries who have helped me with criticism and advice, including those whose names appear in my bibliographies. Whenever necessary, I have embodied the fruits of their research into the pattern of my argument, for which I must remain solely responsible. If I have not always acknowledged in my text or in my notes my indebtedness to them, it was to avoid burdening the general reader with a critical apparatus running counter to the spirit in which the series of volumes has been conceived.

I have received assistance from many librarians and their staffs, and from many libraries, among which mention must be made of the British Museum, the Bibliothèque Nationale, the Bodleian, the Taylorean, the Library of Congress, the library at Berkeley, University of California, and the University Library, Exeter.

I have unhesitatingly drawn on a number of my own articles published at various dates in the course of the last decade. I wish to thank various journals and their editors, as also the publishers of French texts which I have edited, for permission to utilise, rework, and, where thought advisable, incorporate ideas which were first formulated in their pages or under their imprint.

Among many articles on Diderot, mention should be made of those in the following: *Diderot Studies* (IV, 1963; VI, 1964; VIII, 1966); *The Romanic Review* (April 1952; February 1963); *Europe* (Jan.–Feb. 1963); *Filosofia* (LVI, Nov. 1963); *Saggi e Recerche di litteratura francese* (vol. II, 1961); *Cahiers de l'Association Internationale des Etudes Françaises* (No. 13, 1961; No. 18, 1967); *French Literature and its Background*, vol. 3, 'The Eighteenth Century' (ed. J. Cruikshank, London, Oxford University Press, 1968); also of my introduction to editions of Diderot's *Pensées Philosophiques* and *Lettre sur les aveugles*, both published by E. Droz. For Rousseau, I have drawn on my introduction to the translation of the *Confessions* published by Dent in Everyman; and on that to an edition of the *Rêveries du promeneur solitaire*, published by the Manchester University Press; for Marivaux, on the introduction to

Arlequin poli par l'amour, which I wrote in collaboration with my wife for the University of London Press, and from an article 'La Comédie Italienne et Marivaux' which appeared in *Studi in Onore di Carlo Pellegrini* (*Studi Francesi*, 2, 1964); for Beaumarchais, from 'La Genèse du Barbier du Séville', in *Studies on Voltaire and the Eighteenth Century* (ed. T. Besterman, vol. LVII, 1967) and from *Beaumarchais: Le Barbier de Séville* (*Studies in French Literature*, 13, ed. Dr W. G. Moore, London, Edward Arnold, 1968). In particular, mention should be made of signed contributions to the *Encyclopaedia Britannica* on E. B. Barthélémy, Mme du Deffand, Diderot, Mme Geoffrin, Lamettrie, Mlle de Lespinasse, Restif de La Bretonne, Mme Riccoboni, the preparation of which involved me in acquiring data and information now utilised in full; to *Chambers' Encyclopedia*; and to the *Encyclopedia of Philosophy* (Paul Edwards editor-in-chief, copyright Crowell Collier and Macmillan Inc., 1967) on Henri, Comte de Boulainvilliers (vol. I, pp. 114–18) and 'Clandestine Philosophical Literature in France' (vol. II, pp. 114–18), which I have largely incorporated into the early part of my chapter on the general background to the philosophic movement, and which is here reprinted with the kind permission of the publisher. Two articles of mine have proved especially useful to my purpose: 'La propagande philosophique au siècle des lumières', in *Studies on Voltaire and the Eighteenth Century* (vol. XXVI, 1963), which Dr Besterman has graciously allowed me to incorporate, and 'The Age of the Enlightenment' in *Studies presented to Theodore Besterman* (St Andrews University Publications, No. LVII, Edinburgh, Oliver & Boyd, 1967), which the editors and the University of St Andrews have very willingly authorised me to reproduce in the present modified form. The latter seemed to be particularly apposite in its present context, as a conclusion to my work, since it reviews current critical opinion and offers a perspective based on new interpretations put forward in the light of present research on the main features of the Enlightenment and on its contribution to the history of ideas.

The interpenetration of the arts, and the fundamental connections between art, philosophy, literature, and science and the political and social background of the period, are increasingly stressed nowadays. This revolution in thought is to be found throughout Europe in the eighteenth century and offered in France the manifestation of a vital intellectual force and of a fresh understanding of human experience, which brought about a record of literary activity that is without parallel.

Exeter R.N.
March 1970

CONTENTS

Chapter 1

HISTORICAL SURVEY

THE death of Louis XIV in 1715 brought to an end an epoch remarkable for its splendour and its misery; and one illumined, even in its darkest corners, by the powerful and extravagant personality of the monarch. Louis came to the throne at the age of five, under the regency of his mother, Anne of Austria, and later under the dominance of Mazarin. The latter died in 1661 and the king, who had then been on the throne for eighteen years, wasted no time in declaring himself absolute monarch of France. From the age of twenty-three, therefore, and for the next fifty-four years, he implemented his pronouncement so thoroughly that he achieved for himself the status of God upon earth – the title of 'the Sun King', and an unassailable position of total power at the heart of an illustrious court, whose glory shone throughout all Europe, and over the whole of a nation that worshipped and obeyed their king without question (in theory if not always in fact), even while they suffered under him.

By the end of his reign, Louis had achieved for France the widespread national misery that stems from extravagance and indifference in high places at home; religious intolerance; perpetual wars abroad; and alienation from the rest of Europe. The paradox was that none of these things – the failure of his foreign policy, the impoverishment of the nation through endless wars that brought in neither victory nor plunder, the known corruption at his court – served in any way to dim his glory. The ageing monarch, even in the gloom of his last years, when everything at court was submitted to the austere control of Mme de Maintenon, whom he married secretly after the death of Queen Marie-Thérèse in 1683, still wore the trappings of greatness with extraordinary panache. He remained to the end the monarch of absolute power, characterised in the remark: 'L'Etat, c'est Moi', who believed himself to be the representative of God upon earth; and who, since his glory was the glory of God and of France, had dedicated his life to his own aggrandisement.

During his long reign, literature and art reached a peak of perfection, power, and beauty, with a pleiad of brilliant writers, poets, and artists, among them Corneille, Racine, Molière, La Fontaine, Boileau, Bossuet, Fénelon, La Bruyère, La Rochefoucauld, Pascal, and Descartes. Louis XIV was himself an expert artist in living, patronising the arts that embellished his court and the artists who added lustre to himself and his nation. During his life the arts flourished, and when he died he left a double legacy to France, and it is one of these with whose effects this volume is concerned.

His people worshipped him, but by the end of his reign, their misery, and their total lack of redress in their misery, brought about a disillusion that caused the crowds to stand in sullen angry silence as his magnificent funeral cortège passed them by, or in some instances to utter curses and obscenities at the golden bier of their defunct monarch. This was one part of his legacy to France: he left behind a nation of oppressed and starving peasants, deprived of their human dignity and their stake in the future, seething with hidden rancour and despair. The other part of his legacy was due to the great artists and writers of his time, encouraged by him and by the splendour of his court to develop their great gifts to their highest pitch, so that the golden rays of the Sun King shine undimmed down the corridors of time.

Both legacies of Louis XIV – the misery of France and the glory of her writers and artists – were to bring about a dangerous fermentation throughout the whole course of the eighteenth century, where political, social, and literary factors born and bred in the reign of the Sun King grew and multiplied until exploding point was reached at the end of the century. It is true, as P. Hazard has pointed out,[1] that a great intellectual revolution was already taking place during the period 1680–1715; that the tradition of freethinking continued unbroken from the time of the Renaissance, gaining momentum with the passing years; that the quarrels of the Jansenists and the Jesuits had seriously weakened the authority of the Church, one of the pillars of the state; and that the *parlements*, judicial bodies, were becoming politically conscious. The seeds of decay were growing beneath the tarnished mantle of glory.

The Sun King was succeeded in 1715 by his great-grandson, the third son of Louis, duc de Bourgogne, whose father, the Dauphin, had died four years before Louis XIV. As did his predecessor, Louis XV ascended the throne when he was five years old, with Philippe, duc d'Orléans, as regent, appointed to preside over the Council, while executive power resided in the duc du Maine.

The child Louis received his double legacy, of national misery and private splendour, and with it the ferment that arose from opposition to the previous régime. Parliamentarians, Jansenists, and the aristocracy of France were opposed to the exercise of

[1] P. Hazard, *La Crise de la conscience européenne (1680–1715)*, 1935.

absolute power vested in the monarchy, as were the freethinkers and writers, philosophers and wits – particularly those who frequented the salons and the academies of the day, where universal problems were freely discussed at the highest intellectual level. The Société du Temple was already well established as the focal point of a group of freethinkers of distinction, both young and old; a group in which the young Voltaire could enter and shine at an early age, and where he met the notorious courtesan Ninon de Lenclos. Here it was that the sober Montesquieu, determined to make his career in law, was able to discuss and to entertain seriously the idea of publishing his daring, and to some minds indecent, *Lettres persanes*. There was also the mass of the peasantry, politically insignificant, without representation, without power, but a redoubtable mass, suffering, listening, waiting.

Philippe d'Orléans, on whom the hopes of these several factions were pinned, wasted no time, in conjunction with the Parlement de Paris, in setting aside the testament of Louis XIV, and assuming absolute power. So armed, he examined a situation which could not have been worse. The Treasury was empty, with an astronomic National Debt to face, and a virtually non-existent national income, since the revenues for 1716 had been spent in advance. Abroad, France was isolated by the actions of the English who, following the Treaty of Rastadt (1714), had robbed her of both naval and trade supremacy, and surrounded her with apparently neutral, but in fact hostile, states.

Faced by these intractable problems, the regent embarked upon a programme that reversed all the earlier decisions, and which therefore promised the liberal reform dear to those who opposed absolute monarchy.

Through wily and intelligent diplomacy, he reached an understanding with England, one of Louis XIV's bitterest enemies. The Sun King had been devout, even while self-worshipping; so Philippe, charming and corrupt, released and indulged his own libertine predilections, and encouraged *libertinage* in those who surrounded him.

Life at court and in Paris changed overnight, revealing all too clearly the hypocrisy of countless courtiers who affected to be devout, whilst in fact they were self-seeking and cynical, longing for total release and freedom. The regent and his friends, known as *roués*, set the tone and the pace for a new life of frivolity and pleasure. They indulged in loose-living and gambling, and patronised the theatre. This gay, licentious period was thus acclaimed by Voltaire:

> Voici le temps de l'aimable Régence
> Temps fortuné marqué par la licence.

Montesquieu's *Le Temple de Gnide* has the same inspiration. With the craving for immorality and indecency went a growing desire for money as a means to enjoyment, greater comfort, and luxury. The social standing of the financier was greatly enhanced, the aristocracy grew impoverished, and the pitiful condition of the peasantry, as also the poor rewards of the artisans and the writers, became more apparent.

The strength of this violent reaction to the official moral code of behaviour of the previous age was so great that it outlived the regency and may be detected during the more sober years of the mid-century and right up to the French Revolution, not only in the writings of Voltaire and Montesquieu, but in those of Diderot, Crébillon *fils*, and Beaumarchais, to name only a few.

The regent, moreover, gained popularity and support on the more narrow political front by freeing the Jansenists, whom Louis had put in gaol, and giving new powers to the *parlements*, whose prerogatives Louis had curtailed.

The financial and economic impasse clearly demanded strong measures. Philippe brought in the Scots banker Law. Law evolved the brilliant scheme of issuing vast quantities of paper money, to increase the flow of wealth and to activate trade, hoping by these means to diminish the National Debt and reorganise the state budget.

This liberal beginning to the regency soon changed, however, to absolutism. Certain of the *Conseils* appointed by the regent to replace the *Contrôleurs des finances* had to be disbanded for reasons of incompetence, if not corruption; certain of his Secretaries of State disappeared overnight, for similar reasons; and the wider powers of the Parlement de Paris were withdrawn the moment they were used to oppose the régime.

The débâcle was assured when Law, still overhauling the sorry finances of France, decided to establish the *Compagnie du Mississippi* to exploit the French colony of Louisiana in America. This soon became the *Compagnie des Indes*, borrowing enormous sums to repay debts incurred by the state. Law was then appointed *Contrôleur-général des finances*. His scheme was highly speculative, but would have held great possibilities, had it not been grossly mismanaged. Shares changed hands too rapidly, with speculators making and losing fortunes at such speed that the shareholders panicked and demanded repayment. There were riots and demonstrations, so that the bubble burst and Law was declared bankrupt. His few years at the helm had led to the development of trade, but they had also destroyed public confidence in banks for many a long year, and achieved ruin and despair for those who had invested in the *Compagnie*. The net result of Law's machinations was to bring about a social upheaval begun by the wealth of the *fermiers-généraux* in the previous century; for after Law, the hitherto despised bourgeois was to be of greater consequence than the titled aristocrat. Saint-Simon offers an authentic account of these few but important years of French history, with a wealth of detail concerning the events and vicissitudes of those dramatic days, and a vivid presentation of those who played leading roles in them. For many French writers, the years of the regency, 1716–23, provided a formative period that left its mark upon them in later years. Montesquieu's *Lettres persanes* (1721) is at one level a satire of contemporary French customs, institutions, and manners.

With the death of the regent in 1723 came Louis XV's personal rule, which lasted, with a preparatory period under Fleury as Minister, until 1774, covering the golden age of the century in matters of art and literature, of philosophy and fine writing; but concealing the worm in the bud, the decline of the monarchy in France.

Louis XV, who was to earn and to lose the title of 'the Well-Beloved', was declared to have reached his majority at the age of thirteen, a few months before the regent died. Timid, well-meaning Fleury was appointed, at the age of seventy, as tutor to the king, becoming in 1726 Minister of State, replacing the duc de Bourbon, whose increasing unpopularity made it impossible for him to continue in that post. Fleury was next made Cardinal, and remained in effective control of government until his death in 1743. It was natural for him to follow a policy of appeasement, remaining on good terms with Walpole in England, but at the same time drawing closer to Spain: no mean feat of diplomacy, since that country had been totally alienated when, during the regency, their Infanta, destined to marry the boy King Louis XV, had been promptly sent back to her own land.

Louis, now married to Marie Leczinska, was persuaded by Fleury to uphold his father-in-law's claim to the throne of Poland, and to sign a treaty which established the Bourbons in Naples. He had also every reason to hope that Lorraine would shortly be annexed to France.

Fleury's policies of appeasement received a setback when, in 1739, England went to war with Spain; and another in 1740, when the War of the Austrian Succession began. France joined with the King of Prussia and with Spain against Maria-Theresa, and by so doing involved herself in major wars that lasted throughout the greater part of the century.

Backed by the financier Orry, Fleury succeeded in balancing his budget in 1739. Economic development and increased trade were leading to a new prosperity, and to the establishment of a wealthy bourgeois class, eager to secure for themselves fine houses filled with *objets d'art*, which had hitherto been the prerogative of the aristocracy.

The Minister was able to deal intelligently, if deviously, with the Jansenists, doing nothing to alter their condemnation by the papal bull *Unigenitus*, yet nothing specifically to arouse their anger or protest. Even when confronted with the extraordinary problem of an extreme and fanatical sect among them, Fleury was still able to apply his panaceas. The sect in question was known as the *Convulsionnaires*, because of their writhings in the St Médard cemetery, upon the tomb of the Deacon Pâris, whom they claimed to be working miracles; a belief they demonstrated with increasingly disquieting scenes of mob hysteria. They had achieved a considerable following, as well as a considerable nuisance value, when Fleury took over and applied the same mixture of public authority and private negotiation that he had brought to those other problems with which he had been assailed.

In the event, the *Convulsionnaires*, with their degrading behaviour and false claims, served in the end to discredit the Church, whose belief in miracles as a demonstration and proof of the Christian faith was to sustain heavy attack throughout the century under review. Diderot refers to the sect in his *Pensées philosophiques* (1746), and further allusions are to be found in the *Refutations* to which that work gave rise. Diderot was living fairly close to St Médard and it is thought that he witnessed the *Convulsionnaires* in action, condemning them as manifestations of religious fanaticism.

The result of Fleury's policies of appeasement at home and abroad, in spite of their partial failure, was the generation in France of a reasonable confidence in the future, and the belief that a better world was slowly but surely evolving.

This confidence, which was quite general and is reflected in numerous plans for the betterment of mankind, and in faith in reason and human progress, was soon destroyed by Louis the Well-Beloved, a title that owed much to the gentle policies of Fleury. When the latter died, in 1743, at the age of ninety, Louis decided not to appoint another Minister but to keep the reins of government in his own hands. In this he resembled his predecessor, the illustrious Sun King; but there the comparison ends. Louis XV pronounced himself absolute monarch without making any effort to implement his pronouncement. Intelligent, charming, blasé, he preferred hunting and family life to power politics, a select and intimate society to the splendours of a lavish court, and the company of his mistresses to that of his courtiers and advisers. Not even the duchesse de Châteauroux, in the three years of her intimacy with the king, was able to interest him in affairs of state, though she made every effort to do so. Madame Lenormand d'Etioles, the enchanting young bourgeoise whom he created marquise de Pompadour, was able to turn herself into a patron of the arts and a brilliant leader of society; but she was not able to turn her king and lover into a statesman and a monarch actively concerned with the duties and responsibilities of his position. Moreover, her lavish expenditure and freedom with the privy purse aroused hostility not only against herself, but against the monarch who permitted and encouraged her to squander the revenues of a nation impoverished by war.

Because of Louis' lazy indifference, she was in a position to meddle with politics, which she did without much success. Three extremely able Ministers were appointed: the marquis d'Argenson, Secretary of State for Foreign Affairs from 1744 to 1747; his brother the comte d'Argenson, Secretary of State for War from 1743; and Machault d'Arnouville, Chancellor of the Exchequer from 1745 to 1756, and Secretary of State for Naval Affairs from 1751 to 1757. They made a valiant attempt to reorganise the policies of the nation, but their combined intelligences and expertise could not put back the tide of affairs, which had been running against France even under Louis XIV.

The War of the Austrian Succession flared up again, in a pattern of shifting and dissolving alliances. In 1743, England, together with Holland and Saxony, signed the Treaty of Worms in alliance with Austria against France and Spain, thus provoking Louis XV to take up arms against them. Maria-Theresa's forces had crossed the Rhine and pressed on into Alsace before Frederick II of Prussia, who had every reason to fear the success of Austria, restored the balance of power and checked the invasion in 1744. In spite of his defection in the same year, he concluded a separate treaty with Maria-Theresa, and, largely owing to the brilliant generalship of Maurice of Saxony, Louis XV was victorious in his attempted conquest of the Netherlands at Fontenoy (1745), Rancoux (1746), and Lawfeld (1747). He speedily concluded a peace treaty at Aix-la-Chapelle in 1748, one that displeased all those who had enjoyed the taste of victory, or who believed the treaty to have given every advantage to the King of Prussia, who had abandoned their side three years before and had taken no part in the victorious campaign. Otherwise, it seemed to have achieved nothing, but had put everything back as it was before the wearisome and costly eight-year war.

Meanwhile, affairs at home had reached crisis point. D'Arnouville, in view of the desperate situation, attempted to withdraw some part of the exemptions and privileges of Church and aristocracy by imposing a tax of one-twentieth of their revenue, in order to establish a sinking-fund to bolster up the National Debt. He met with total resistance, and in 1757 Louis XV yielded to the pressure of this powerful opposition and exempted the Church from taxation, destroying in one blow the reform in national finance so urgently required. Louis, consulting as always with Mme de Pompadour, was no more successful in maintaining the small degree of religious tolerance that Fleury had earlier been successful in achieving, albeit with difficulty. In the three years following his death, Church and state grew steadily opposed, until in 1746 matters came to a head over the affair of the *billets de confession*. In a determined effort to stamp out the Jansenist heresy, bishops instructed their clergy to insist upon a confession of orthodox Catholicism before administering extreme unction. The result of this instruction was a series of outbursts culminating in mob violence and outcry against the Church, and the intervention of the Parlement de Paris against the directives of the bishops. Louis XV pursued once more his inconsistent policies, first by reacting strongly against the archbishop, insisting on the papal bull *Unigenitus* being followed to the letter, and by condemning those who opposed him to prison or to exile; then making his accustomed *volte-face* by calling upon the Pope for intervention – which in the event proved insufficient to quell the dissidents. In 1757, Louis was therefore forced to compromise, setting his seal upon the diminished authority of the monarchy and the increased power of the opposition within the Church.

Louis betrayed himself on all fronts, at home and abroad. The peace treaty signed at Aix-la-Chapelle was rendered useless by the alliance of Prussia and England against France and Russia (Treaty of Whitehall, 1756). This was counteracted by a pact between Maria-Theresa and Louis, signed at Versailles in the same year, and joined a year later by several German princelings, who had viewed with misgivings Frederick II's unheralded attack upon Saxony. This marks the beginning of the Seven Years War, which served to complete abroad the disasters engendered by the monarchy at home, and which was to yield India and Canada to Great Britain.

However depressing her foreign affairs, France was more deeply concerned over the public and private life of her monarch. The mood of the people grew increasingly unfavourable, and military defeat served only to feed the flame lit by philosophic propaganda. Montesquieu's *Lettres persanes* and his *Considérations sur les Romains* had achieved an ever-widening popularity; and Voltaire's *Lettres anglaises* were reaching an even larger public. There was an atmosphere of intelligent survey and keen criticism in the air;

forms of possible government other than a monarchy tended to be discussed wherever groups of intelligent men congregated. Voltaire's satire, Montesquieu's exegesis, the knife-edged comment of writers generally, the increased dissemination of pertinent pamphlets,[2] the frequency of popular uprisings – all contributed to a spirit of unrest.

The king's Ministers had already striven to stop the flood of philosophic and subversive ideas by condemning and publicly burning Voltaire's *Lettres anglaises* in 1743 and Diderot's *Pensées philosophiques* in 1745, but these works continued to be printed abroad and circulated by hawkers and pedlars, and even, in manuscript form, in the cafés, and wherever men met together to discuss the questions of the day. These attempts on behalf of the monarchy to halt the spread of subversive ideas served only to increase popular discontent, and also the circulation of the condemned works, particularly since the monarchy was never consistent in its policies, as is revealed to the full in the story of the publication of the *Encyclopédie*. In 1752 the Council of State, alerted by the Faculty of Theology of Paris University, brought out an injunction against publication of the *Encyclopédie*. But there was so much dissension among members of the Council and the theologians, so much hesitation about a final commitment, that while matters were still under discussion, Mme de Pompadour entered the lists. She had given her favour to the *philosophes* from the beginning, partly to help rid herself of the Jesuits, who were wholly hostile to her, partly to gain allies among those who clearly had increasing influence over the mood and temper of the times, and therefore of the people, and partly perhaps from her own taste and conviction. Now she emerged triumphantly on the side of the Encyclopædists against the Jesuits and the bigots, and the *Encyclopédie* was published, ironically enough, largely through her intervention, and through the inability of the monarch ever to make up his mind on major, or even minor, issues.

In 1757 a fanatic, Robert-François Damiens, attempted, and failed, to assassinate the king by stabbing him. In himself, Damiens is of little importance, but his action symbolises the growing unpopularity of Louis XV and the frustration and blind anger deeply felt by the people of France. The repercussions of his attempt were varied, and some of them surprising. In spite of general hostility to the monarchy, the intended assassination outraged public opinion, for there was never a century more repelled by violence and the

[2] See Ira O. Wade, *The Clandestine organisation and diffusion of philosophic ideas in France from 1700 to 1750*. Princeton University Press, 1938; J. S. Spink, *French free-thought from Gassendi to Voltaire*, 1960; our article on 'Clandestine literature in France' and on 'Boulainvilliers' in *Encyclopedia of Philosophy*.

shedding of blood than the age of Louis XV, a century that ended in one of the major bloodbaths of all history. The anger and shock aroused by Damiens led to action being taken against opponents of the régime, who were sent to the galleys. Mme de Pompadour was able to rid herself of Machault and d'Argenson, with whose policies she had long disagreed, and who had shown scant respect for her opinions.

In October 1758, the duc de Choiseul was made Secretary of State for Foreign Affairs, and subsequently for War and Naval Affairs. He took over a situation at home and abroad that in the end defeated his most gallant, able, and determined efforts. He did everything in his power to rally public opinion to the throne. Aware of the long-continued and dangerous struggle between the Jesuits and the Jansenists, the latter being supported by the *parlements* of Paris and of the provinces, he came down firmly on the side of the *parlements,* and in 1764 secured the suppression of the Society of Jesus by the king, and their banishment from France in 1767.

Abroad, the Seven Years War had brought little success to France after her first minor victories. Neither Soubise nor Richelieu, France's generals of the first rank, were competent enough to stand out against the brilliant military tactics of Frederick II. In spite of Choiseul's firm attempts to limit the participation of France, inferior tactics and jealousy among her military leaders led to the loss in 1763 of some of her most valuable colonies – Canada, Senegal, and India – to England; and in the same year the Treaty of Hubertusburg restored the *status quo* in Germany, thus negating years of struggle on the part of the French army. The Seven Years War ended in a stalemate that had proved, and was to prove, costly to France.

Choiseul was forced to spend large sums of money on the reorganisation of the army, which had shown itself inadequate in the field. He improved artillery units, built new arsenals, and, turning to the navy, built new battleships.

In 1766 Lorraine was annexed, following the death of King Stanislas, according to the Fleury treaty, and Corsica was annexed in 1768; but these successes were offset by public indifference to foreign affairs, and concern at home over rising taxation. New fiscal measures, made necessary by the ruinous costs of war and of the reorganisation of the army and navy, had already led to renewed opposition to the monarchy, and to Choiseul as the king's Minister. In 1763 the Parlement de Paris demanded that the States-General be convened; in 1765 rebellion flared up in Rennes over local parliamentary hostility, leading, after several years of disturbance, fanned by the chronic indecision of Louis XV, to a strike of parliamentarians in 1770. Choiseul, in spite of his intelligent diplomacy and long-continued attempts to restore unity to France and re-establish her security at home and abroad, was attacked on all sides for the failure of his policies, particularly by those privileged classes who had taken a major part in bringing about those failures, and also for the concessions he had made in his last desperate bid to call an end to the parliamentary stalemate. The death of Mme de Pompadour in 1764 deprived him of his most powerful ally and protector, and he was dismissed in disgrace in 1770.

The duc d'Aiguillon, Governor of Brittany, and known opponent of the Jesuits, was appointed to succeed Choiseul as Secretary of State for Foreign Affairs; and together with Maupeou, made Chancellor in 1768, and the Abbé Terray, *Contrôleur-général* since 1769, he formed the triumvirate which was to govern France until the death of Louis XV from smallpox in 1774. The relations between the king and the *parlements* underwent many changes in the course of the century and their significance can only be understood in an historical context. The Parlement de Paris had acquired the right to scrutinise the king's edicts, with a view to determining whether they were in conformity with the fundamental laws of the kingdom. It was a purely judicial body and since it was in no wise representative, it could not have the status of the *Etats-Généraux*; but it was nevertheless in a position to oppose the will of the king by declining to endorse its signature on his bills. Its challenge dated back to the time of the regency. In 1751 it refused to support the demand for increased taxation to meet the costs of the Seven Years War. In 1753 it was replaced, but was reinstated in 1754, after the attempt by Damiens on the life of the king, which gave it a new importance, since the people, deeply shocked, turned to justice for reassurance. From the first it was of Jansenist persuasion, and opposed the Vatican over the bull *Unigenitus* (1713) of Pope Clement XI. The bull, which strongly condemned Jansenism, was, however, enforced till the expulsion of the Jesuits in 1764. The Parlement de Paris, closely associated with the provincial *parlements*, also Jansenist in persuasion, became popular as the upholder of civil liberty; yet it often stood out against necessary reforms urged by the king or his Ministers, and lost in public esteem over the cases of La Barre and Lally-Tollendal, which were taken up by Voltaire as grave miscarriages of justice. It aspired to a political role for which it was not constitutionally fitted. In the quarrel over the bull *Unigenitus*, which set the magistrature against the clergy, Maupeou had intervened, with the support of the duc de Choiseul and Mme du Barry. He deprived the Parlement of its rights, and in 1771, by a *coup d'état*, he swept away the old *parlements*, promising reforms of civil and criminal justice. An abortive attempt at constitutional reform had been made under the regency, when *Conseils* had been set up.[3] Maupeou was concerned only with the establishment of a new reformed Parlement, which he defended in his *Code des Français*. The venality of the system, however, was too deep-rooted to allow his scheme to prove effective. His Parlement became discredited, and the old Parlement was called back in 1776, Maupeou having been sent into exile in 1774, after the death of Louis XV. The *parlements* were for long a valuable check on the arbitrary power of the monarchy, but were swept away by the Revolution, when the liberties they had fought for were secured by other means.

The *parlements*, and men such as Turgot, Malesherbes, Robert Saint-Vincent, and the *philosophes*, were all agreed on efforts to improve the conditions of the Protestants, who stayed on in France after the Edict of Nantes, and who are said to have numbered one million. A very severe *ordonnance* of 1724, called by Abbé Careivac 'le chef-d'oeuvre de la politique chrétienne et humaine', denied them all civil and religious rights, and imposed very heavy penalties on them for failure to profess the Catholic faith. They went underground, or conformed outwardly whilst preserving their liberty of conscience, and their tenacious opposition was an important factor in the feeling of general unrest leading more specifically to the ultimate secularisation of the state.[4]

In the last years of his reign, Louis' unpopularity was so great that he no longer dared to show himself in Paris. A succession of industrial crises, poor harvests, corruption among the governing classes, increasing hatred of the magistrature, and continued opposition to fiscal reform led to popular uprising. D'Aiguillon's inability to prevent the partition of Poland, France's ancient ally, by Austria, Prussia, and Russia, set the seal upon the failure of Louis' diplomacy abroad; and France faced the grievous situation of realising that she no longer had any voice or influence in foreign affairs. The monarchy seemed to have reached its lowest ebb when the jeers and catcalls of the mob followed Louis the Well-Beloved to his tomb. But Louis XVI had yet to finish the work of his ancestors.

The brilliance and splendour of the Sun King had been powerful enough to shed a golden light even over the darker side of his régime. His great-grandson, intelligent but blasé, pleasure-loving, indifferent, and with much less personal lustre, inherited both the splendour and the misery, and was a central factor in the decline

[3] See above p. 4.

[4] See H. Hughes, *Histoire de la restauration du protestantisme en France au dix-huitième siècle*, 2 vols., 1872.

of the monarchy. With Louis XVI, the decline reached its nadir, and the great light that had bathed France in its splendour at the beginning of the century was finally extinguished.

Louis, grandson of Louis XV and married to Marie-Antoinette, daughter of Maria-Theresa, four years before he ascended the throne at the age of twenty in 1774, received a legacy that would have daunted Louis XIV himself, inheriting as he did all the problems of his predecessor, with even less capacity to deal with them. He came to the throne enjoying a well-founded reputation for virtue and clean living, and was welcomed with relief and enthusiasm by all those who were heartily sick of the corruption and immorality of the court, the law, and the Church, and who believed themselves to be at the beginning of a new age. But a good heart in a virtuous man cannot make a fine monarch without the strength and the ruthlessness that were entirely lacking in his person. Physically impressive, intelligent, well educated, and with the personal charm that was part of the family strain, he raised great hopes in France, which were soon destroyed by the revelation that, behind that impressive façade, lurked a weak and vacillating spirit, timid, uncertain, full of good intentions but without the personal dynamism to put them into practice. His careless dress, his speech defect, and his gaucherie, combined with his lack of drive, caused his own queen, Marie-Antoinette, to describe him as 'un pauvre homme'.

He was singularly unfitted to inherit the throne of France in the state to which his predecessor had reduced it. All his virtues – honesty, humility, gentleness, and plain goodness – were of no use to him in the complex affairs of state, at home and abroad, with which he was confronted. He did, in any case, prefer hunting to presiding over councils and, in this, he followed in his family's footsteps.

Yet he began well, with one decisive action. He dismissed the infamous Maupeou triumvirate, whose Parlement had become increasingly notorious, and made Maurepas Minister of State, who in turn appointed Vergennes as Minister for Foreign Affairs, and Turgot as Chancellor of the Exchequer. These were all statesmen of proven ability and integrity, and Maurepas completed his cabinet with men of similar political and ethical standards, all concerned with public good – Malesherbes, Sartine, and Saint-Germain.

Turgot had contributed to the *Encyclopédie*, for the *philosophes* thought highly of him, as did the intellectual élite of France. The prospect of his proposed reforms aroused great hopes, for he was a magistrate of the Parlement de Paris and had specialised in political economy. He had studied the theories of the Physiocrats, whose two main principles were respect of natural order and of net produce. He shared most of the opinions of Quesnay, Gournay, and Adam Smith, whose work had aroused great interest in France.

Turgot sought to reduce expenditure at court, which had for years been in excess of all revenue, and to replace the several and various levies by a single tax, the *subvention territoriale*, to be paid by all landowners. He pinned his hopes for the future on a general increase in national productivity and wealth, which would necessarily bring increased revenues to the state; and he believed that by abolishing minor levies and irritating regulations, he would offer an incentive to productivity and trade. He worked for an understanding between the king and his people, intending to establish a number of local authorities responsible to a national assembly, with access to the king's Ministers.

In 1774 Turgot proclaimed internal free trade in corn, abolishing provincial jurisdiction over its barter. Two years later, he replaced the *corvée* (or forced labour) by his land tax, and suppressed the corporations, which had gained a stranglehold over their various trades and professions.

It cannot be supposed that such radical reforms were easily achieved. Turgot was opposed by the queen and by her courtiers, who objected wholeheartedly to any curb upon expenditure at court; and by the Parlement de Paris who feared exposure and loss of power, and who issued *remonstrances* against every move Turgot made. The unhappy Louis, harried by his wife, his courtiers, and his Parlement, and seeking only a peaceful life, was unable to stand up against the pressures put upon him. Only two years after his brilliant beginning on necessary reform, Turgot was dismissed. Malesherbes who, in the same brief period, had achieved some degree of prison reform, had reduced the application of torture, and improved the lot of the Protestants, went with him. So did Saint-Germain, who had aroused the hostility of the militarists by his discipline of the army, his refusal to allow or exercise favouritism, and his overhauling of equipment.

Louis, having shamefully dismissed Ministers in whom he himself had every confidence, called upon Necker, a Swiss banker and well-known philanthropist, to take over finance. Forewarned by the fate of his predecessors, Necker met immediate obligations by loan, but did not attempt the major reforms that were urgently required. He managed to cover the expenditure due to French intervention in American affairs in 1778, and to create Municipal Assemblies that were a less powerful form of local government than Turgot had intended. Then he, in turn, was defeated by the fanatical self-interest of the privileged classes and the vacillation of the king, and, with his resignation in 1781, all attempts at reform came to an end.

Abroad, France had made an alliance with the American rebels seeking to break away from England. In 1779, an expeditionary force under Rochambeau landed in America, and with the help of General de La Fayette and the fleet of Admiral de Grasse, the rebels forced the British general Lord Cornwallis to capitulate on 19 October 1781. Two years later, after other skirmishes, England was forced to sign the Treaty of Versailles, which marks the foundation of the United States.

France gained immensely in military and diplomatic prestige from these successful campaigns, but their vast cost led to greater financial difficulties at home, with the same determination on the part of the court and the aristocracy, now formed into an *Assemblée de Notables*, to yield nothing to any Minister who might be appointed.

When two successive Ministers resigned without achieving any amelioration of a rapidly worsening situation, and riots broke out in the provinces, Louis at last exerted himself, to the extent of convening the States-General on 1 May 1789 and recalling Necker, the only man in France capable of securing urgently necessary bank loans.

Louis XVI opened the States-General at Versailles on 5 May 1789, the first time they had met since 1614; and the three elements concerned – the aristocracy, the Church, and the *Tiers Etat* (the bourgeoisie) – became embroiled one with the other in such bitter and insoluble conflict that on 17 June the *Tiers Etat* broke away to form a separate National Assembly, with powers to control taxation. Two days later, certain representatives of the Church seceded and joined the National Assembly. The king, totally unable to deal with what was, in effect, a rebellion against his authority, after much hesitation, ordered the aristocracy and the Church to join with the *Tiers Etat* to form an *Assemblée Nationale Constituante*.

This last pathetic attempt to force irreconcilable elements together under an all-embracing title failed lamentably in its purpose. The monarchy had reached its nadir and was soon to be submerged beneath the avalanche that had been slowly gliding downwards throughout the century. Within a few months, anarchy had come to France, with troops massing outside Paris, popular risings all over the country, the power of the mob unleashed from a vast powerhouse fed on repression and starvation to sweep away the monarchy, the aristocracy, and the privileges of the Church. The People's Government was established and a national militia of 12,000 men recruited. On 14 July 1789 the enraged mob, after looting the Hôtel des Invalides, stormed the Bastille, the hated symbol of the injustices and abuses of the society they were about to destroy. The king yielded, with no option to do anything else, to the infinitely more dangerous pressures now put upon him, dismissed his troops, and accepted the formation of the revolutionary municipality and of the *gardes nationales*. The National Assembly, prompted by certain liberal-minded aristocrats, pronounced all men equal before the law on 4 August; and on 26 August the Declaration of the Rights of Man, embodying the concepts of liberty, equality, fraternity, was proclaimed. This was the cornerstone of the social and juridical revolution that had taken place, and of a government that was seeking now to draft its constitution.

The problem of finance remained insoluble, and an attempt on the part of the *Constituante* to meet the swollen National Debt, by confiscating the property of the Church and using it to guarantee the value of the paper money called *assignats* put into immediate circulation, was defeated by the excessive amount of such money irresponsibly printed and circulated. There was an attempt to establish a constitutional monarchy, with power in the hands of the people through their elected representatives, but voting power was still kept to landed gentry. It was insisted that France be decentralised, with separation of the powers of the monarchy and the state. Reform of the Church released the clergy from their obedience to the Pope in civil law; a measure which the majority of churchmen refused to admit, and which was condemned by the Pope himself in April 1791.

Throughout this turmoil, Louis XVI, increasingly aware of the parlous situation of the monarchy in France, determined to regain power, with the help of European monarchies and foreign troops. He secretly left the Tuileries; but since he left with his wife, family, and retainers, with the full panoply of a monarch, it was not surprising that he was caught at Varennes on 21 June and brought back to Paris.

The emergent leaders of the extremists, Danton, Marat, and Desmoulins, who had formed the Club des Cordeliers, and the similar republican Club des Jacobins, both with headquarters in former convents, were unable at this juncture to sway the moderates, who held the majority vote. Louis XVI was therefore restored to his constitutional monarchy, and set up residence once more in the Tuileries; and in September 1791 the *Assemblée Constituante* was dissolved, its mission accomplished.

With the formation of the Legislative Assembly in October came the next phase of the conflict, with the newly assembled deputies falling into three parties, right, left, and moderate. Louis XVI, unable to believe that the monarchy was in jeopardy, did his best to assure its extinction by refusing to accept the decrees of the Assembly, and by constant appeals to foreign powers. The outbreak of war in 1792 between Austria and France caused further manifestations of hostility to the king, when the Assembly declared the country to be in danger. Inflamed by the revolutionary extremists, incited to action by federal groups converging upon Paris – one from Marseilles entered the city singing the new marching song afterwards known as the *Marseillaise* – the people broke out in a new series of riots and disturbances, flaring into open rebellion when the duke of Brunswick, on behalf of Leopold II of Austria, threatened reprisals if the person of the king or the queen should be put in jeopardy. The mob stormed the Tuileries, forcing the Assembly to suspend the king, and to elect, by popular vote, a new Constituent Assembly, to be known as the Convention, and one which marked the end of the monarchy and the beginning of a new régime. On 21 September 1792 the newly elected Convention voted for the abolition of the monarchy and the establishment of a French republic.

The situation had hardened, and the leaders of the republic were divided into hostile camps, each determined to secure victory for their own extreme policies, with Robespierre, Danton, Marat, and the Montagnards on the left, bitterly opposed to Condorcet, Brissot, and the Gironde. The Montagnards, determined to establish the republic in absolute power by whatever means at their disposal, accused Louis XVI of collusion with the enemy abroad, and brought him before the Tribunal, where he was condemned by an overwhelming majority and executed on 21 January 1793. The unhappy monarch, who had reaped not only his own harvest but that of his forebears, died with dignity; and his death unleashed the horrors of the worst excesses of the revolution, and the struggle, literally to the death, among the leaders, against enemies within and without France. The reign of terror had begun, and with it the long procession of fanatical extremists who, one by one, met their death upon the guillotine, a death to which they had condemned thousands, the innocent together with the guilty, until the bloodbath subsided, and an essentially republican France emerged, to be followed by the Empire and the Restoration.

Chapter 2

SOCIAL AND ARTISTIC SURVEY

THROUGHOUT the century, the causes of the French Revolution were made manifest: they stemmed from the absolute powers of the monarchy, a system of centralised despotism dependent upon the king's Council; from the position of the privileged classes, wherein the nobles kept many of their old feudal rights, which pressed heavily upon the poor, monopolised the chief appointments in Church and state, and often were exempted from taxes. The higher clergy owned one-fifth of the land, were not liable to taxation, and controlled the leading journals. Many among the upper-middle classes held government appointments, and obtained exemption from taxes and military service, while the survival of the trade guilds in the towns favoured the masters at the expense of the craftsmen.

The grievances of the lower classes, arising from these conditions, were manifold. Taxation, so largely evaded by their social superiors, fell heavily upon the lowest classes, especially upon the peasantry, who found the *corvée* (the duty of repairing the high roads), the *taille* (a heavy property tax), and the *gabelle* (the old feudal salt dues) a burden too great to bear in lives that scarcely reached subsistence level. Out of every hundred francs he earned, the peasant was fortunate if he could keep eighteen for himself.

The consequence of this inequitable system of taxation was an economy that was bound to end disastrously; particularly when it had to contend with the extravagance of Louis XIV, who spent 30 million livres in building Versailles, and was reputed to have squandered over a million francs on ornate and jewelled buttons alone. His personal bodyguard is known to have worn buttons of solid gold. Louis XV lavished 3 million livres upon one of his favourites; and the assistance given to the United States added to the deficit under Louis XVI, as did the extravagances of his queen.

Despite such a background, the century under review becomes one of extraordinary growth,[1] change, and expansion, covering as

[1] From an estimated population of 15 million in 1715, France rose to 24 million in 1789, a fact which, taken in conjunction with a greater expectation of life, created its own problems. A series of poor harvests between 1773 and 1789 had inevitable political repercussions.

it did all the stages of political transformation from an absolute monarchy to a republic, that, in its earlier stages, bore a strange resemblance to a series of dictatorships.

So violent an upheaval brought with it fundamental changes in behaviour, and in the social and literary patterns of the age. One of the several paradoxes contained within its framework is that, while the monarchy fell from its zenith through a sharp decline to a nadir unimaginable at the beginning of a century resplendent under a Sun King, the social and artistic, if not the literary, history of that same period is one of preparation and growth towards an apogée of brilliance that reached its peak with the downfall of Louis XVI and the dissolution of the monarchy.

Voltaire's ironic condemnation of Church and state exposed the *ancien régime* in all its inadequacies; Rousseau's assertion in his *Contrat Social* that 'man was born free and is everywhere in chains' released a consciousness of the sovereignty of the people that fed the smouldering fires of rebellion; Diderot and the Encyclopaedists fanned the flame with their examination of social systems and the rights of man.

Under Louis XIV artists and writers of stature were to some degree enmeshed in the ponderous pomp and splendours of a gold-encrusted court. The brief eight-year-long regency of Philippe d'Orléans, whose tastes were for all that was light, graceful, and facile, in people as in the arts, offered a breathing-space.

The regency left behind a great restlessness, that led in turn to a need to challenge all preconceived ideas, and to a desire for material wealth and wellbeing. It weakened immeasurably the hold of the Church by setting up a new conception of earthly happiness here and now, in opposition to that of a putative eternal bliss hereafter. It shook the social fabric in ways that the debonair Philippe could not have foreseen, led to an intellectual freedom he would have abhorred, and to a general instability that provoked the greatest minds of a great century to close examination of man and his environment.

The regency was in some sort a sigh of relief, marked by a determination to indulge in light and frivolous pleasures. A universal desire for escape, for liberation, for freedom, which flowed through dark undercurrents for the mass of the people of France, still powerless and poverty-stricken, was translated by the privileged classes into their *fêtes galantes*, those highly sophisticated festivities organised by a polished society, court entertainments in a pastoral setting, imaginative make-believe with no expense spared. There were endless masked fancy-dress balls, symbolising this same desire to escape, from oneself and from reality, by assuming another personality, and hiding behind a mask, firework displays to dazzle eyes that did not wish to see things as they were. The court, and we should include such large gatherings as that at Sceaux, indulged in a perpetual game of love, and was enamoured of all its manifestations throughout the century. The licence engendered provoked the current of hedonism, immorality, and perversion associated with the name of Philippe d'Orléans; but it also gave rise to new writings, which revealed the civilised refinement and the seeds of decadence in a régime which had firmly turned its back upon the majestic and ponderous extravaganzas with which it was sated, after fifty-four years ending in austerity and gloom.

This pursuit of pleasure, this playing at life by a generation bent upon the total enjoyment of everything that was light and gay, graceful and unreal, profoundly influenced the art of the century, so that painters, architects, writers, sculptors, and musicians left behind an exact record of their times. The paintings of Watteau, Lancret, and Fragonard first conveyed this atmosphere of elegance and urbanity, at once fleshy and illusory, a poetic dream filled with sensuous overtones. Marivaux's plays enter the same enchanted landscapes, where exquisite lovers play out the graceful formal pattern of their game in sunlit gardens.

Dress expressed the change in desire by becoming simpler, as though the courtiers of Louis XIV were in haste to declare allegiance to the regent and to the new monarch by stripping themselves of the excessive frills and furbelows, incrustations and ornamentations, of the Sun King. The *fêtes galantes*, the alfresco picnics, led to an informality in dress that was more apparent than real, with the wearing of pseudo-pastoral gowns and rustic suits made from the finest silks and satins. Women wore gowns with low-cut tight bodices and fully pleated skirts falling in ample folds to the feet, sometimes worn over hoops or paniers, with short or elbow sleeves trimmed with vertical pleats and falling lace ruffles that sometimes came to the wrists. Demure *fichus* often veiled the low-cut neckline, and the hair was worn 'undressed' in long curls, or pinned closely to the head with a jaunty lace cap perched on top, the whole giving the impression of an artless yet highly sophisticated milkmaid, matching in simple elegance the wilful, careless, and untidy dress of her pastoral lord, who left his shirt collar open, neglected to button his waistcoat, and wired the skirts of his coat only upon very formal occasions.

Antoine Watteau has left an immortal record of this enchanting regency dress, so well fitted to the pursuit of pleasure and the *fêtes galantes*. Since his name was given to the pleats at the shoulders of the dresses, he may even have influenced fashion, and may be responsible for the *cartouche*, the full and graceful overdress gathered at the shoulders to envelop the hoops of the dress beneath, and tied in front with one or two ribbon bows, which figures in several of his paintings. This was the period when noble lords and ladies first took pleasure in looking like shepherds and shepherdesses, rustic swains and serving wenches, as they set out on their *embarquement pour Cythère*, so long as they were still dressed in the finest of silks and satins, lawns and laces. They retained therefore, and in spite of their best endeavours, their elegance, the sophistication of their status and their way of life, their courtly aura, and their extravagant follies; and this dichotomy added the final charm to their unreality.

Voltaire's *mondain* expressed this determination to achieve terrestrial happiness when he exclaimed: 'Le Paradis terrestre est où je suis'; Rousseau's idyllic *La Nouvelle Héloïse* may well be seen as the testament of this escapist society in its purest form. Diderot's Tahiti, in his *Supplément au Voyage de Bougainville*, is another manifestation of the enchanted isles all men were seeking, an implementation of a poetic vision.

Natural man, free man, 'the noble savage', to use Dryden's words, is a major character in the writings of the eighteenth century, projected perhaps in the first instance by Montesquieu in his 'Histoire des Troglodytes' (*Lettres persanes*), incarnated by Rousseau, and developed in his own ironic manner by Voltaire when he created 'le bon Huron' in *L'Ingénu*.

The social structure seemed virtually the same as under Louis XIV. Yet, insensibly, the magistrates and the *noblesse de robe* were gaining in power, and the development of the wealthy bourgeois class brought about the beginning of the rule of wealth, as the unstable financial conditions brought about the impoverishment of some noble families, whose estates and heirlooms fell into the hands of astute and wealthy traders, bankers, lawyers, and financiers with ambitions to take their place in high society.

Marriage in the upper classes was still a matter of conventional and financial arrangements, and young girls twelve years of age were leaving the convents where they had been carefully reared to marry men they had never met, in accordance with dynastic plans or material family gain. Married women enjoyed a social consequence and respect that to most minds justified the manipulations necessary to that end.

Liberty was still no more than a word. Both men and women could be deported with no reason given, and with no opportunity of presenting their case. It was common for men to be recruited into the army for six to eight years' service by press gangs, a point made by Voltaire in the third chapter of *Candide*, where he satirises

Russian recruiting officers in a manner relevant to the French.[2] The police were brutal and harshly disciplined, and one of the major judicial methods was the extortion of confession by torture, with the mob crowding to witness such scenes.

Yet the wind of change was blowing through the land and a new sensibility was awakening; beneath the apparently frivolous pursuit of pleasure and escape the voice of reason was beginning to be heard, the more serious demand for a new way of life. The thinkers of the age recognised the deep-rooted malady beneath the surface fever, and sought its causes: they realised that it demanded remedies that were in effect revolutionary, in the realms of government and finance, and through these, in the status and freedom of man.

There was a rallying of intellectuals and men committed to the social upheaval they saw taking place. Paris became the centre, rather than Versailles. Academies were founded there and in the provinces, while salon society came back into favour. All the brilliant young men, all the artists, poets, and thinkers of the day crowded in turn into the salons of Mme de Lambert, Mme de Tencin, Mme Geoffrin, and the marquise du Deffand, for intellectual stimulus, open discussion, and the meeting of free minds. Nothing here was sacred, except polished manners and an original, unprejudiced approach to all issues.

The stranglehold of Louis XIV upon the artists of his day, released upon his death, and the liberation of the court under Philippe d'Orléans, led to their desertion of Versailles in favour of Paris and other towns throughout France. Men of genius, of talent, and experience in all media of the arts, stimulated the whole country. Facilities in Paris and other major towns were greatly improved. There were still bad roads and stinking open drains, but there was improved street-lighting, to the dismay of the cutthroats, and the delight of those who thronged gala performances at the Théâtre Français, the Opéra, and Théâtre des Italiens.[3]

Some quarters of the capital, notably the *grands boulevards*, the Palais Royal, the Jardin des Tuileries, assumed new graciousness. Private building created residential areas of great beauty, and the houses reflected the new demand for simple elegance, intimacy, comfort, and luxury. Architecture began to embody some part of the poetic vision that marked the early part of the century and continued into the reign of Louis XV.

Flowing lines and curves, ornamental sculpture, and windows, varied in size and shape, added to the exterior of these private

2 There was a legal obligation on French villages to supply a specific number of men each for military service.

3 Sébastien Mercier in his *Tableau de Paris* (1781, increased to 12 vols. 1783–88) and Restif de La Bretonne in his novels have given a particularly vivid account of conditions of life in the heart of the capital.

houses, and made them remarkably different from the classical regularity of the earlier buildings that surrounded them. Family and social life based upon a court pattern of large state rooms for general purposes, changed with the dispersal from court. Rooms became smaller and more specialised, and each house boasted its dining-room, drawing-room, and bedrooms; a new and cosier way of life. The first recorded transformation of this kind was at the Palais Bourbon in 1722, by L'Assurance,[4] and the fashion spread swiftly, reaching even Versailles, where the smaller private apartments began to resemble those found in private houses, with light and airy colours and painted woodwork or *boiseries* often picked out in gold, creating an intimate family atmosphere, with a plethora of exquisite boudoirs, elegant drawing-rooms, and charming dining-rooms, all furnished with delicate draperies and simple pieces that entirely lacked the ponderous dignity of an earlier age. These houses, these rooms, held within them the atmosphere of fragile gaiety, the poetic charm of the age; light, airy, insubstantial, they expressed the longing for an immediate paradise on earth, in which to feel secure or to escape to.

Yet almost at once, and in spite of Robert de Cotte (1656–1735), brother-in-law of J.-M. Mansard, who wished to continue in the traditional style of Louis XIV, the simplicity and purity of the new fashion in architecture were destroyed by the increasing desire for luxury and ostentation. The clean lines were obscured by overloaded ornamentation, incrustation, gilt, convolutions, garlands, walls, and ceilings weighed down with a proliferation of pastoral and mythological scenes, panels of carved fruit and flowers in supernatural abundance – all the absurd joys and glories of the rococo, in building, in décor, and in art.

The fashion spread to churches; witness, among others, Saint-Germain l'Auxerrois in Paris, with its wrought-iron rails delicate as lace, its sumptuous woodcarvings and magnificent canopies over the altars; and to public buildings, like the Military School founded by Louis XV. Jacques-Ange Gabriel (1710–82), the architect responsible for this edifice, as for the Petit Trianon, was certainly the first in all France, and his life spans the major part of the century, whose creative abundance he recorded in several superb buildings. He was appointed leading architect to the king in 1742, and with his preoccupation with balance and harmony, with perfect proportions – to which the façade of the Military School bears full witness – he escaped from the worst excesses of

[4] L'Assurance l'Aîné (1690–1751) was the son of J. Cailleteau, called L'Assurance, an architect responsible for the Hôtel d'Argenson among others. L'Assurance l'Aîné undertook the work at the Hôtel d'Evreux, now the Palais de l'Elysée, for Mme de Pompadour, and was responsible for the Hôtel des Réservoirs at Versailles.

the new ornamental fashion. To some degree he continued along the line laid down by his father, who was responsible for the royal squares of Rennes and of Bordeaux, with their splendid symmetry; yet his work foreshadows the sober elegance of the *style Louis XVI*.

Gabriel, in fierce competition with the leading architects of the day – Boffrand, Blondel, Contant d'Ivry, Servandoni, L'Assurance – was successful in having his plan for the Place Louis XV (known after the Revolution as the Place de la Concorde) accepted by the monarch, who had chosen the site himself. This was, and remains, the greatest and most famous square in the world, one of the most artistic realisations of the eighteenth century, along with the Garde-Meuble de la Couronne, now the Ministry of Marine, which was perhaps his masterpiece, and remains a model of public building, as well as showing him once more to be a forerunner of the 1780s.

After Gabriel, architecture grew heavier, more massive, dominated by decorative effects and generally modelled upon Roman antiquity. Most architects of the latter part of the century drew upon classical sources without having any real feeling for classical antiquity, so that the results lacked true form. Nicolas Servandoni (1695–1766), who was in charge of the *décorations de l'Opéra*, indulged in a theatrical style; while Germain Soufflot (1714–80), who had lived in Rome for many years, designed the Law School and the Church of Sainte-Geneviève (now known as the Panthéon); and Victor Louis was responsible for the Grand Théâtre de Bordeaux, as for the *galeries* surrounding the gardens of the Palais Royal, basing his design upon Herculaneum and Pompeii. Lesser artists and architects, though still of considerable stature, designed châteaux, country and town houses of size and style, where people of quality and wit tended to forgather.

The construction of public and private buildings, which was one of the major activities of the age, changed the face of Paris, and of major towns throughout France, in a remarkably short space of time, beginning with the simple elegance of the *rocaille*, soon exaggerated into the rococo, flanked by gardens much given to 'follies' and fountains, gazebos and statuary, winding alleys, copses, natural growth where before there had been formal flower-beds, straight paths, and avenues of trees. Mystery and a gentle melancholy hung about these parks and gardens, imported perhaps, as some have said, from England, but most fitting to the temper of the times. Rococo, driven to change by its own excesses, gave way to sober elegance; flower motifs yield to geometrical designs, the airy and the frivolous to the solid austerity of Greek, Roman, and Etruscan influences; until the century which began with a distillation of sunlight and air and ephemeral values into its architecture and décor, ends with the massive portentousness of the imperial style, so named after the Emperor Napoleon I. Paris became the prestige city, with Casanova stating categorically: 'On ne vit qu'à Paris, on végète ailleurs.'

Changes in costume followed equally closely the spirit of the age. The elegant simplicity of the pseudo-pastoral dresses soon became elaborate. Women wore paniers, then hooped skirts, increasingly larger and fuller until they became too unwieldy and whalebone was removed from the paniers and set into the fashionably tight, low-cut bodices or into the corset worn beneath. Watteau pleats remained fashionable for the greater part of the century, and so did Watteau cloaks – full pleated full-length capes with large hoods. As with decoration in rococo architecture and décor, so costume was loaded with ribbons, laces, frills, encrusted jewels, and embroidery and made in the most sumptuous satins, velvets, and brocades. Men soon discarded their mock peasant clothes, and wore richly puffed breeches, silk stockings, elegant shoes, richly embroidered and bejewelled waistcoats, with coats fitting close to the body, swelling out into a semicircular shape over the hips. In the course of the century breeches grew longer, to just below the knee; the coat was also longer, with a flared or pleated skirt stiffened with whalebone and lined to match the waistcoat. A variety of lace ruffles, silk cravats, black silk ties, and white muslin scarves superseded each other as neckwear; in fact, the noble lord vied with his lady in the superb complexity and ornamentation of his dress.

As rococo in art and architecture sometimes led to excess, so there were excesses in dress to be found among certain more than usually exhibitionist or eccentric members of the nobility or the emerging wealthy bourgeoisie; but perhaps the most rococo element was to be found in the amazing hairstyles that proliferated throughout the century, as soon as the early simplicity of regency days was abandoned for more complex manifestations of the pursuit of pleasure and the unreal world. In fact, it would not be an exaggeration to discover architectural influences, for hair was built, erected, loaded with artificial hair, towering aloft in a multitude of shapes, fixed by pomade over wicker-work constructions and lavishly powdered, bestrewn with a plethora of veiling, artificial flowers, birds, butterflies, jewels, feathers, until hairstyles became the most important factor in eighteenth-century female dress. They changed continuously, according to the dictates of the fashionable hairdressers, and specific styles were given special names that were largely descriptive of their charms – *à l'Inconstante*, *à la Magicienne*, *à la Capricieuse*, *à la Tracassière*, even *à Inoculation*, a style invented by the celebrated Léonard when the wife of the British ambassador in Constantinople brought back the news that inoculation against smallpox was widely practised in Turkey.

Both Mme de Pompadour and, later, Marie-Antoinette profoundly influenced the fashion of their time, the former by prolonging the life of the style that suited her most, the latter by her elegance and her adaptation of current fashions to her own good taste and requirements, reducing the rococo element with new trends introduced from England, tending once more towards simplicity, towards the natural and flowing lines that suited the young queen, who loved nature so well; she enjoyed the nostalgic country life of her Austrian childhood in the Petit Trianon, whenever she could escape to this reconstitution of a childhood dream, putting on her light muslin gown with its frilled *fichu*, and a shady straw hat adorned only with pastel-coloured ribbons. Architectural hairstyles gave place to softly falling, natural-seeming curls, often left unpowdered on informal occasions. White became the fashionable colour, a forerunner of the move towards neo-classicism, with simple inexpensive fabrics, often cottons and muslins, replacing the brocades and velvets.

Elegant accessories of all kinds accompanied and shared the convolutions, the scrolls and the encrusted ornamentation, the subtle play of curves and curlicues, the free-flowing and asymmetrical line that marked the rococo style in whatever medium it appeared. Jewels, fans, handkerchiefs, purses, little boxes, ornaments, cosmetic bottles, and flagons followed the flow of fashion, ebbing into simple elegance with Louis XVI and neo-classicism. Both men and women enjoyed the acquisition and the use of this *bijouterie* with all its charm, its exaggeration, and its sumptuous beauty. Fine porcelain from Chantilly, Limoges, Saint-Cloud, Sèvres, Vincennes, or Strasbourg, or *faïences* from Lunéville, Nevers, Moustiers, set on newly designed furniture, in keeping with the changes in fashion, were seen as the ultimate refinements in wall-panelled rooms richly adorned with tapestries from the Gobelins or Beauvais. André-Charles Buhl (or Boule; 1641–1732), who brought inlay in furniture to the level of art, was remarkable for the intricacy of his work, a method of overlaying wooden surfaces with a veneer of tortoiseshell dyed red and finely inlaid with brass. He often constructed pairs of cabinets and tables, apparently identical, in which one was composed of brass inlay on a tortoiseshell ground (Boulle) and the other tortoiseshell inlay on a brass ground (counter-Boulle), a subtlety much appreciated in his own time and subsequently. Other furniture-makers followed the changing stylistic patterns of the century, from the ornate and gilded splendour of what is still known as 'Louis XIV' through the curlicues and extravagant curves of 'Louis XV' rococo, to the increasingly severe and balanced lines, with elegantly restrained upholstery and garnishing, of 'Louis XVI'. Never, too, were books so finely printed and bound, enriched by engravings of exceptional quality made by such artists as Eisen, Gravelot, Cochin, Prud'hon (who illustrated *Paul et Virginie*), and countless others.

Painters, sculptors, and musicians were equally involved in the evolution of their century. Among those painters who most faithfully reflected the new era is Antoine Watteau; this is the more remarkable in that, born in 1684, his brief life was over by 1721, and he did not in fact see the evolution of the century he foresaw so accurately in the 200 canvases and 300 sketches he left behind.

Consumptive, quarrelsome, hypochondriac, he was not a pleasant character, and the self-portraits he delighted to paint in odd corners of his romantic-seeming canvases show a malicious, sardonic pixy. He was a pupil and friend of Claude Gillot (1673–1722), who delighted to paint the masks of Italian comedy of his day – particularly of Arlequin in his many poses – and whose later work, more 'devil-may-care' in atmosphere, may have been to some extent determined by his serious financial losses due to the Law bankruptcy. Watteau in his turn was stimulated to put these masks to different use. Inspired by their strangeness and their unique fantasy, the gaiety of their improvised comedy, he painted his own vision of them in the poetic and pastoral décor of his misty parks, with delicate tracery of trees and shrubs among fountains and broken masonry, and fluted pillars overgrown with a tangle of riotous blossom. Along with these fragile Columbines, romantic Arlequins, and wan Pierrots, he created an unreal crowd of disguised figures to people his astonishing *fêtes galantes*, to bring gaiety and strangeness and a necessary element of fantasy to his exquisite and fragile paintings, which embodied the dreams of an era he never lived to see.

The astonishing aspect of his paintings, as original in their genre as were the plays of Marivaux in theirs, is that beneath the surface charm, the romantic nostalgia, the enchantment of the idyllic scene, there lurks the divine unrest that thrust the century forward into unimaginable change. Yet Watteau imagined it all. He painted, with a heightened awareness of colour, the new discovery of sensitivity and graciousness, of the charm and beauty of nature; and, with all this, he translated the uneasiness that characterised the new generation, their rejection of reality, of themselves, and of the real world, symbolised by so many of his groups and figures whose backs are turned to the painter as they set off on their search for an unknown land, as in his 'L'Embarquement pour

Cythère' (1717);[5] or by the languid groups in shot-silk garments, wearing masks or fantastic disguises to conceal their own identities, playing at amorous dalliance, strumming on musical instruments, playing games, dancing or sleeping – anything to avoid knowing or being. His parks are filled with the longing for an unrealistic dream, with the evanescent and frivolous atmosphere, nostalgic and melancholy, enchanted and lost, of the century to come. There is, as the Goncourt brothers discovered in the nineteenth century, an unbearable and enduring sadness beneath the gay surface of his paintings. His famous 'Gilles' in the Louvre is a profound study in melancholy. His strange figures, graceful and remote, bore a striking resemblance to the company of Italian players brought to Paris in 1716 by the regent, and whom Watteau could have seen only after he had painted most of his canvases showing scenes typical of their comedy, which had been banished from Paris since 1679, by a decree of Louis XIV. His paintings had a deep and lasting influence upon fashion in the reign of Louis XV, and brought about modifications in the theatrical costumes of Riccoboni's players. But the subtle and troubling charm of his figures is that they were not simply cardboard stands for future fashions, but were also an expression of all that was unquiet, confused, and disturbed in the emergent spirit of an unsatisfied society bent upon release. His lightly done painting of a girl on a swing – 'L'Escarpolette' – is the forerunner of many others on the same theme, but none has the same charm.

He was the chief inspiration of Pater (1695–1736) and Lancret (1690–1743), a pupil of Gillot. Chardin, Boucher, Greuze, Fragonard, however different their subjects and their treatment, all belong among those painters who were for the first time concerned with the dream world of the *fêtes galantes*, with nature and sensibility. They share a delicacy and fragility that for the first time drew painters and connoisseurs into awareness of aesthetic values. Art became a valuable commodity for amateurs and collectors, and its history became of interest; picture galleries were needed to exhibit the treasures of a nation, and experts found themselves in great demand. Art also became a necessary part of everyday life, for those who could afford it – and these included the new wealthy bourgeoisie, eager to fill their new town and country houses with painting and sculpture, porcelain and bibelots of quality.

Portraits, landscapes, and still-lifes were still painted, but now artists were freed from the Academy, they thrust themselves eagerly into new fields, and new genres evolved – scenes of everyday life, idealised and gracile, were painted, as well as *fêtes champêtres and fêtes galantes*.

[5] Inspired by a play by Dancourt.

Boucher (1703–70) continued in the Watteau tradition, but where the latter had been fascinated by *commedia dell'arte* and its masks, Boucher drew upon *opéra-comique*, and peopled his canvases with the gods and goddesses of classical mythology, or with the bucolic types and the rustic scenes, stylised by their passage through this sparkling new form of opera, generated in the great fairs as one of the by-products of the struggle for supremacy between the Comédie Française and the fairground Italian comedy. Venus, Diana, Cupid, shepherds and shepherdesses (often with the features of his patrons), sensuous and insubstantial, recline against gentle pastel landscapes, shadowed vast-seeming parks, and broken pillars, garlanded with flowers; or they are grouped against embroidered hangings in rooms whose muted colours bring the delicate pink and white of their complexions into relief, the whole framed in rococo embellishment of shells and leaves. He was a painter of fantasy, whose delicate modulations of colour matched his inspiration. Like his contemporaries, he studied nature, but his vision was so personal that his landscapes seem to us far from realistic and have the appeal of a mirage. Already in 'L'Offrande à l'amour' (1757), there is a romantic sensibility akin to the mood of Fragonard and Prud'hon. On the pedestal of the statue portrayed in this work is inscribed the revealing words: *aimer, c'est le bonheur.*

There is in Boucher an element unknown to Watteau, 'une pointe de libertinage équivoque' as it has been called, so that his nudes, dappled with light and shade, are delicately lewd, just as the postures and groupings of his rustic swains are faintly suggestive. There is, in his painting, a decadence, an exhalation of debauchery that was in keeping with his time, and also indeed with his own gay and orgiastic life. The politeness of his eroticism is well illustrated in 'La Toilette' (1742). He is a superlative painter of light and shadow, of delicate flesh tints, of enchanting nudes, touched with lascivious promise. He offers, moreover, a witty commentary on the life of the period and carries the genre inaugurated by Watteau further into the expression of an age. His versatility is shown by the fact that he was successively a book illustrator, a designer for tapestry and the theatre, and a portrait painter – his chalk and pastel portrait of Mme de Pompadour (1752) being noteworthy.

This revolution in style in painting, and in attitudes to painting, spread disarray among artists like A. Coypel (1661–1722), J.-Fr. De Troy, Le Moyne, J. Restout, and C.-J. Natoire, who were accustomed to great religious, mythological, or historical canvases. The wall of Versailles and the Louvre were covered with paintings of gods and goddesses; mythological scenes which, lacking the pagan enthusiasm of the Renaissance, grew ever more rigid and dull, and became essays in technique. Similarly, in the churches, huge canvases of the life of Christ and of the Apostles hung upon the walls, betraying the same frozen attitudes, the same rigid technique, the same lack of interest. Historical canvases depicted horror and violence without heart or understanding, compulsion or enthusiasm. There can be no surprise, then, that people turned to the new painters. J.-Fr. De Troy, Subleyras, and Carle Van Loo all abandoned academic painting for the new genre, and painted masterpieces alive with colour and wit and grace. Some were based on the fables of La Fontaine, some were entitled 'Déjeuner des Huîtres' or 'Halte de Chasse'; new pretexts for *fêtes galantes* in pastoral settings. Baudouin carried on the libertine love games of Boucher in paint, and his *gouaches*, beautifully engraved, provide us with an invaluable series of scenes from everyday life. There was, in France and abroad, a predilection for the new gaiety and charm in painting, and those artists who were unable to change from academic to new techniques lost prestige and often their livelihood, while F. Le Moyne (1688–1757) was even brought to suicide.

Nothing was to check the rococo painters. Captivated by the East, and by the *Mille et une nuits* of Galland, Boucher, Van Loo, J.-B. Huet, and Desportes sought the unrealisable dream in an exotic mirage, dressing their figures as Persians or Turks, painting *chinoiseries*, taking Watteau's fantasies into the Orient. Fragonard (1732–1806) is one of the greatest of these painters; he had originality, yet kept within the rococo, though he did experiment with all genres and was influenced by Tiepolo and Rembrandt as well as Boucher. He had received a sound academic education in painting, but he early turned his back on models from antiquity and in some measure epitomises the eighteenth century in art. He was a pupil of Chardin and of Boucher. His training gave him a sound technique, which he was able to adapt equally well to the requirements of his early historical paintings, or to those of his gay *scènes galantes*, loaded with the suggestiveness of Boucher, filled with the charm and sensibility of the period. Though his paintings, whether portraits, landscapes, or *fêtes champêtres*, express a poetic sensuality, there is no trace of vulgarity or excess. His sources are literary and theatrical; his own vitality and exuberance, his personal dynamism, glow from his canvases and his bold and brilliant technique never fails to bring out the emotional content of his chosen theme; this no doubt is why his *fêtes galantes* are more alive than those of his predecessors. He is the acknowledged master of *sensibilité* and the 'Fountain of love', in the Wallace Collection, reveals clearly how he idealised love, its hopes and its frustrations.

Portraitists were also caught up in the new vitality and new forms of expression. Chardin (1699–1779) chose simple, humble people for his subjects – a child at play, a woman returning from the market. Perronneau and especially La Tour (1704–88) specialised in pastels. La Tour, a friend of Voltaire and disciple of Rousseau, was particularly successful at capturing facial play, expressive eyes, and natural gesture (his pastel of the Italian actor Thomassin is a *tour de force*). He made the pastel, a medium introduced by the Venetian Rosalba, truly his own. There were some, like Largillière (1656–1746) and Rigaud (1659–1743), who retained the pompous, heavy, formal style of the seventeenth century, even though they continued to paint well into the eighteenth. Yet on occasion Largillière could display a luscious paint quality, as in his portrait of Philippe d'Orléans with Mme de Parabère, and his portrait of the young and handsome Voltaire is worth recalling as a corrective to those who can only visualise the very old man seen by Houdon. J.-M. Nattier (1685–1766), who painted the noble ladies at court as Flora, Aurora, Diana, and the like, was more typical of his century, together with Aved (1702–66) and Tocqué (1696–1772).

Chardin, whose portrait of himself and of his wife are unexcelled masterpieces of their kind, was skilled also in landscapes, which he painted with greater realism than others. Mountainous or rural, and with leafy foliage, they are filled with emotion and a deep sincerity, with nothing in them of the artifice of the *fêtes galantes*. The son of a carpenter, he painted for the bourgeoisie in terms recognisable to them, giving life and meaning to interior scenes – a table laid for a meal reveals the character of the absent owner of house or room or table by the manner in which it is painted, just as he caught the essential character of his models, 'La Mère laborieuse', 'L'Econome', 'La Pourvoyeuse', 'Le Bénédicité', and the like. His still-life suggests Rembrandt. He ranks with the greatest masters for his unerring sense of proportion and perfect manipulation of tones.

Greuze (1725–1805) followed in a way in the footsteps of Chardin, but was more influenced by literary sources. He turned away from domestic scenes painted realistically, after the Dutch manner. There is in him a certain sentimentality, a reaching-out for solid conventional virtues, that combines with strong sensuality to achieve a flavour of hypocrisy. Diderot and Jean-Jacques Rousseau were major influences in his life, and he adopted the latter's form of sensibility, eager to bring tears to the eyes of those who look upon his dramatic canvases of 'La Malédiction paternelle', 'Le Retour du fils maudit', 'Lecture de la Bible', etc. He often expressed the emotional force of a situation by a telling gesture, and his treatment of his subject is always sophisticated. Technically, Greuze is one of the finest of painters – witness the delicacy of his

'L'Enfant et l'oiseau mort' – but his work is frigid, as though his bourgeois melodramas with their suspect sensibility and pseudo-morality stemmed from a cold heart. They have the same dead presentation as the early pseudo-classical tragic canvases of Coypel and Van Loo, and their coldness is accentuated by the faded bluish tints he favours. Yet his work is graceful, and his remarkable technique earned him a prodigious reputation in his lifetime. He is at present coming back into favour in a smaller way, largely for historical record, and for his sheer capacity in paint.

Mention should also be made of the deep perspective landscapes of Hubert Robert (1773–1808), often incorporating long avenues of trees and waterfalls. He is also known as the designer of the *jardin anglais-chinois*, but his Roman ruins hold a special appeal, indicating a new, pre-Romantic emotion and inviting melancholy.

The Moreau brothers, L.-G., and especially J.-M., called Moreau le Jeune (1741–1816), also gave a more direct account of the last years of the age: the latter produced a 'Couronnement de Voltaire', which subject also inspired Gabriel de Saint-Aubin. C.-J. Vernet (1712–89) deserves special mention for the theatrical quality of his seascapes and ports, well observed, sophisticated in presentation, and greatly admired by Diderot. J.-P. de Loutherbourg (1740–1812), a pupil of Casanova who settled in London in 1771, where he designed sets for operas, is known for his landscapes, battle scenes, and decorative and animal pieces.

J.-B. Oudry (1686–1755), director of the tapestry factory at Beauvais and at the Gobelins, was animal painter to Louis XV. We have by him a sketch of Louis XV hunting. His acute powers of animal observation and sensitivity are well brought out in his painting of a gazelle with three white hounds, and a still-life of pheasants, as well as in that of a dead duck casually placed between a silver candlestick and a bowl of pudding, constituting a *tour de force* based on subtle tones of white. These remarkable paintings stood out at the Royal Academy of Arts Winter Exhibition, 1968, and enhanced the growing reputation of this talented artist. His illustrations of the Fables of La Fontaine, a subject which also inspired Subleyras, Lancret, and Fragonard, are particularly fine. François Desportes (1666–1743) is best remembered for his hunting scenes such as 'Le Cerf aux abois', and C. Parrocel (1688–1752) for his landscapes and battle scenes; Amédée Van Loo (1715–73) for his Italianate historical scenes and his portraits; J.-B. Van Loo (1684–1745) for his equestrian portrait of the king (1723) and his mythological scenes; Carle Van Loo (1705–65) was made *Premier Peintre du Roi* in 1763, for portraits such as that of the actress Mlle Clairon; but they were all versatile artists, as was De Troy (1679–1752), until recently neglected, except by biographers interested in pointing out that he died of a broken heart. He is increasingly studied for his genre pictures, which provide a vivid image of conversation in the salons, of preparations for the ball, of love-making, and of the music lesson, and for his mythological and historical canvases, such as the 'Rape of the Sabines', which pave the way for Boucher's rich decorative style.

With Louis XVI and the return to neo-classicism, portraits grew simpler and even more vigorous. Madame Vigée Le Brun and Mme Labille-Guiard both followed the new mode with elegance, but the change from rococo to neo-classicism is best exemplified in the work of Louis David (1748–1825), whose return to classic purity in his line demonstrated his return to conventional art. He follows after Vien, his teacher, and his work can be seen as illustrating the passage from rococo to neo-classicism by a process of evolution and reaction. His 'Serment des Horaces', shown at the salon of 1785, his splendid equestrian portrait of Count Potocki, which had already made a mark in 1781, reveal the talent and inspiration that led him to paint Marat dead in his bath and to become the official painter of Napoleon I. He was exiled to Brussels during the Restoration and died there in 1825.

Sculptors did not break away from traditional form as early as did painters and architects, in fact not until the middle of the century. The Versailles school, with Girardon, Coysevox, Coustou, Bouchardon, Falconet, J.-B. Le Moyne, and Pigalle continued to produce the great ornamental sculptures of an earlier age. Changing tastes, however, swept them eventually into the new forms of expression, largely blending the rococo with the more realistic art of the second half of the century. The fashion of decorating salons in town and in country with busts of the owner and his family, or with those of distinguished contemporaries, led to a greater concern with psychology and the realistic expression of recognisable faces – witness Houdon's exquisite and revealing bust of Voltaire – much as portraitists like Chardin were painting real people. Freer expression was sought in terms of tortured, convulsed bodies, locked in battle or in love, in flowing draperies, in implicit movement; yet these efforts towards liberation were still somewhat stilted, reaching out to the rococo through ornate bacchantes, satyrs, nymphs, and mythological deities bearing cornucopias spilling an abundance of flowers and fruit, yet without the gaiety and *galanterie* that was the mark of rococo in painting and in architecture.

The strength of the sculptors of the period, and their unique contribution to it, was to be found in the portrait busts which were the closest parallel to other developments in art. J.-J. Caffiéri (1725–92), Jean-Baptiste Le Moyne (1704–78), with his skill in catching fleeting expressions, Pigalle (1714–85) and the realism of his child portraits, Falconet (1716–91) and his allegorical models so much to the taste of contemporary society, were all masters of the portrait bust, as was Pajou (1730–1809), who, under the patronage of Mme du Barry, was accredited official sculptor to Louis XVI, and brought to the newly developed form the classical simplicity that marks the reign of that monarch.

The highest and most perfect form of the portrait bust, however, is to be found in the work of Jean-Antoine Houdon (1741–1828), which covers the second half of the century. He has left a vast gallery of incomparable portraits, not only of great kings and princes, noble lords and ladies, literary figures, artists and writers – all the great ones of his time – but also of simple souls, ordinary people. Bringing a fine technique and sensitivity and an awareness of psychological truth to this art, his busts – witness those of Louis XVI, Mirabeau, and Voltaire – are each a study in depth of personality and character. He entered into his creative world at a time when baroque and neo-classic art, the ideal and the real, fused into classic purity, and each of his portraits, in marble, bronze, or terracotta, is a revelation of the inner life of the subject, built upon an anatomical realism that was one of the most conscious bases of his work.

Another aspect of the changes in sculpture during the course of the century arose from the desire for small and frivolous objects, decorative, fragile, and charming, to embellish the dainty boudoirs and elegant salons that were such a feature of the rococo houses of the century. Falconet, for example, who was made director of the royal Sèvres factory, created smaller models of the huge allegorical and mythological pieces of the early years, and with them achieved an enormous success, since their exquisite delicacy and miniature charm exactly suited the taste for fragility and daintiness. His figurines became known throughout all Europe. Clodion (1738–1814) was called 'the Fragonard of sculpture', for his terracotta sketches and statuettes of nymphs and bacchantes showed the same sensuality. From Bouchardon (1698–1762) to Clodion these decorative pieces, based upon antiquity yet drawn into the gaiety and frivolity of baroque art, were to be found in every home that prided itself upon its modernity, and reflected the contemporary insistence upon light airy surroundings for fragile furniture, and a décor insubstantial as a dream, a further expression of the *galanterie* of the age, which persisted right up to the time of the Revolution.

Music was an essential part of the delight and enjoyment of the century. Welcomed as a diversion by a pleasure-loving throng, open to all classes of society, secure in the patronage of the king and the interest of the intellectuals, music flourished in the eighteenth century. The first public concerts were given in 1725 in the Palais des Tuileries, under the auspices of F. A.-D. Philidor (1726–1795), a composer who was one of the first to write *opéra-comiques* in France. He launched a fashion, and it became customary not only to give and to attend public concerts, but also for amateurs to join together in playing pastoral airs on flute and harpsichord, in tune with similar manifestations in other arts.

The clarinet made its first appearance in France in 1750, and this was followed by the addition of other wind instruments – flute, horn, oboe, bassoon – under the influence of German music brought to Paris by the Mannheim orchestra.

Religious music lost interest for composers, who flung themselves with ardour into the creation of pieces expressing the sentiment, the sensibility, the grace, charm, and nostalgia of the age.

By the time of the Revolution, music, as an art, had ceased to exist, and was used to serve political ends – marches and popular or patriotic songs, of no great value, destined to arouse the mob.

Yet paradoxically, it was the eighteenth century that saw the birth of the modern orchestra. By 1777 there could be as many as seventy-seven musicians employed in playing a variety of wind and string instruments, a number and variety that account for the complexity of instrumental music at that date, and the evolution of the symphony, the concerto, and the sonata. The violinist Leclair (1697–1764) was largely responsible for bringing the French sonata to its more perfect form, no doubt because of his extensive travels abroad and contact with Italian musicians and music generally. Later in the century the clavichord, the harpsichord, and an early form of the modern pianoforte became more popular, and interest in the violin and similar stringed instruments dwindled. Rameau (1683–1764), who had composed memorable pieces for the harpsichord, turned his talents to opera, a form of theatre that held a particular appeal. He followed in the footsteps of Lully, but introduced many innovations, including the thorough bass theory in harmony. In his operas, music is the dominant art, thus centring the attention of the audience as much, if not more, upon the score as upon the libretto. In the middle of the century a controversy arose over French and Italian music, focused by the Querelle des Bouffons, Italian players who performed in Paris. Rousseau and the Encyclopaedists strongly supported the Italians in an endeavour to renew the art, and the public, still bent upon extracting all possible pleasure from every aspect of social life, grew dissatisfied with the music of tragic opera. The vacuum was filled by *opéra-comique*, which offered simple and tuneful music interspersed with dialogue, and a sentimental theme at the level of ordinary understanding, expounded by ordinary people with whom each member of the audience could identify – a genre that has been quite properly described as a 'drame bourgeois lyrique'.[6] The genre, which owed a great deal to Italian influence, corresponded so exactly to the atmosphere and spirit of the age, offered so exactly the realisation of public desire, that it enjoyed a fantastic success. It became so typically French that its name cannot be translated into any other tongue, a fact which by itself illumines a particular phase in the long history of the development of sensibility in France. So rapidly did it grow in public favour that in 1781 the celebrated dramatic poet Favart (1710–92), author of several *opéra-comiques*, and husband of a famous actress, was made director of the newly-created Théâtre de l'Opéra-Comique. With the new theatre in view, composers lent themselves to this popular form of entertainment, which, though never to achieve the status or prestige of great art, nevertheless threw up some little masterpieces, as, for example, *Le Déserteur* by Monsigny, and certain others by Favart, Laruette, Grétry, much applauded in their time.

Arts, major and minor, flourished throughout the eighteenth century and in all their manifestations exactly reflected the wit and elegance, the bravura, the aristocratic good taste and sophistication, and the growing scepticism of a troubled age, the final flowering of a civilisation about to disappear for ever. Religious faith was shaken, the core of social life removed from court and palace, to centre round the intimate salons. As if it foresaw its own imminent doom, society sought distraction and entertainment at all levels, intellectual, artistic, frivolous, and vulgar, as it sought escape in its *fêtes galantes*, its masks and disguises, from a reality not wholly understood yet wholly rejected. And David, in his self-portrait (1791), for instance, seems to point the way to a romanticism which Diderot and especially Rousseau had already announced. But it is a far cry from Watteau to Houdon's bust of the aged Voltaire and to the neo-classicism and crypto-romanticism of David. The range of French eighteenth-century art is wide and reflects clearly the successive moods of the people. We move from the *fête galante* of Watteau to the luxurious and rococo Boucher, from the intimacy of the domestic, homely middle classes depicted by Chardin to the more melodramatic and moral scenes of Greuze which in their turn reflected the political and social realities behind the aristocratic veneer of the salons depicted by Boucher, realities well appreciated by men who had suffered from the disasters of the Seven Years War and from the crippling taxation. The serious,

[6] J. Thoraval, *Les Grandes Etapes de la civilisation française*, 1967, p. 245.

moral paintings of Greuze were in tune with the philosophic propaganda of Diderot and his fellow-Encyclopaedists. Greuze and Aubry (1745–81) endorsed Rousseau's conception of natural man uncorrupted by civilisation, and Chardin's lesson, in so far as his canvases contain an implied admonition, is in accord with them. It may be that it is only because their work shows too much eighteenth-century charm that it failed to be politically effective. The most representative painter of the period is undoubtedly Fragonard, who ranged from the frivolous 'The Swing' (Wallace Collection) to intimate genre painting. He serves, too, to show the overriding unity of the art of the period, by a technical skill handed down to him through the years, by moving fluently, and as by some natural evolution, from the flowing rococo style to political and moral statements. And David, through seemingly innocuous classical compositions, gave expression to a new and threatening message. So neo-classicism itself, which was conceived by Vien as an added titillation to an abused rococo art, whose force had become spent through excessive reiteration, can be seen as an inevitable development.

This feeling of evolution rather than revolution in style is also partly due to the exceptional gathering of talents which took place. The arts in France were more centralised than anywhere else in the world. The *Directeur-général des Bâtiments du Roi* sought the advice of the *Premier Peintre du Roi*, usually the mouthpiece of the Académie, whose power was seldom challenged, and he was in a position to give his orders to the French Academy in Rome, to the tapestry works at Gobelins, to the state porcelain factories at Vincennes or Sèvres, to the *Menus Plaisirs* and the *Garde-Meuble de la Couronne de France*. Eighteenth-century French art is the success of a team and of a definite taste.

Until recently it was customary for critics to recognise the talent of the *petits maîtres* whilst stressing the dichotomy between their inspiration and the grim social background. Today we emphasise the close links between the two and see more clearly the psychological explanation. The French artists now appear greater. Watteau is no longer seen as providing an admirable prelude to the regency, but as a man who was also able to depict real love, which in turn retained the attention of all his successors up to and including Fragonard, and which, upon reflection, Greuze alone was to falsify. Behind the apparently frivolous and artificial, we see the serious with its parallel, and sometimes simultaneous, development of sensibility and reason, fantasy and realism. The artists were in their several ways the original interpreters of their age and bore the stamp of its intellectual sensuality. Their work complements the work of the great writers of their times. It is the lesser artists who confined themselves to a mere accurate transcription of what they saw: Gabriel de Saint-Aubin, so beloved of the Goncourt brothers,[7] who captured the flickering gaiety of Paris before the Revolution, the mad race for pleasure before the final catastrophe; or Lépicié, Aubry, and Jeaurat, who depicted realistic scenes of ordinary life. They provide us with an invaluable record, but their somewhat photographic art fails to convey the depth and truth of a more personal vision. Perhaps Hubert Robert's drawings of Parisian scenes have the added quality of an artist's original interpretation, and, paradoxically, a greater truth.

The great flowering of art spread from France to England, where collectors eagerly vied to obtain examples of fine French work, and to Prussia, Russia, Poland, and Sweden, in whose courts the prestige of French art was second only to that of the French mind. The influence of French art has been studied with care. What, however, remains to be investigated in depth is the relation between art and literature. Painting, architecture, and music illustrate multiple aspects of the age, but certainly not all its facets. We need to turn to Montesquieu, Voltaire, Rousseau, Diderot, Laclos, and Sade for a fuller and more telling analysis. The writers, for their part, speculated on aesthetic problems in a way until then unknown. With Diderot's *Salons*, art criticism was born, or so it has been said. At all events, sensitivity to colour and to form, philosophical disquisitions on the beautiful, the good, and the true, and an effort to understand the purpose of artists and to feel their emotions, become more widespread. In art, as in literature, the main drive is towards seeking enjoyment, but, underlining this search for pleasure, so ably brought out by R. Mauzi in his monumental thesis,[8] there is a feeling of terror and impending doom. Hubert Robert's poetic vision of classical ruins seems in this context to be prophetic. And in the very age of reason there are forebodings of the irrationality to come, for those who had the eyes to see as well as to read.

Every medium of art and literature combined to form a framework for an exquisite aristocracy; and the same media helped to destroy it, in the course of the same century. The descendants of Watteau's elusive Arlequins and Pierrots and Columbines died upon the guillotine, young and old alike. Those artists who survived the Revolution – Fragonard, Moreau le Jeune – found themselves in a lost world, among strangers who had no appreciation of their work, and with whom they could have no communication.

The year 1789 brought to an abrupt and dramatic end a whole

[7] Cf. P. E. Charvet, *A Literary History of France, The Nineteenth and Twentieth Centuries, 1870–1940*, 1967, pp. 8 et seq.

[8] *L'Idée du bonheur dans la littérature et la pensée française au XVIIIe siècle*, 1960.

way of life, as decisive in society and in art as in history and in politics. A few months sufficed to see the disintegration of social patterns, the ideals and conceptions of artists, the dispersal and loss of techniques, of talent, purpose and grace, to make way for a new and more rugged society, with its own robust art forms and fundamentally different social rhythms.

Yet in a strange foreboding, the seeds of change were already present in the minds and work of the great artists and writers of the age; witness, at opposite extremes, the paintings of Watteau and the writings of Jean-Jacques Rousseau, and in Rousseau's case, the presentiment of a new world.

Chapter 3

FRENCH SOCIETY, COFFEE-HOUSES, CLUBS, AND SALONS

THE art of conversation has always been notable in France, and its practice a feature of national life. From earliest times, society sought occasion for gatherings at which the topics of the day could be discussed at the highest level of intelligence and wit. Those meeting-places once established, writers, philosophers, artists, and politicians descended upon them in great number, eager to enjoy an open forum of debate and analysis of issues and ideas of major importance.

The eighteenth century offers abundant witness, not only to the nature and number of these groups, but also to the profound and lasting influence they exerted upon the evolution of their time, similar to that exerted today by the press and other forms of general communication.

As the retreat from Versailles began under the regency, and the court ceased to be the core of social and artistic life, the élite of the nation sought other centres. In Paris, cafés became fashionable, and the coffee-houses, largely around the Pont-Neuf, were thronged with courtiers and notables. The most popular was the café Procope, established in 1689 by the Sicilian Francesco Procopio dei Cotelli opposite the site where the Comédie Française stood (until the Odéon was built), 13 Rue des Fossés-Saint-Germain, now Rue de l'Ancienne Comédie. A brilliant throng filled this coffee-house, including Boindin, the Abbé Terrasson, Fréret, Fontenelle, Duclos, Dumarsais, Piron, Voltaire, Diderot, Marmontel, and La Chaussée. There were also the café Gradot, Quai de l'Ecole, frequented by La Motte, Saurin, and Maupertuis; and that of the widow Laurent, at the corner of the Rue Dauphine and the Rue Christine, where J.-J. Rousseau, La Motte, Saurin, La Faye, Maupertuis, and Crébillon were often to be found.

The coffee-house clientèle included the major literary figures of the day, with a sprinkling of politicians, wits, and philosophers, and the inevitable hangers-on, who, having no specific talents themselves, nevertheless enjoyed the brilliant discussion, the vigorous debate, and fiery argument that took place. A number of other cafés, of less literary influence or social standing, offered similar scope at a less important, but still lively, level. Coffee had become popular in Paris only in 1667, through the Turkish ambassador Soliman-Aga; yet it became the source of new social customs, and provided in the early eighteenth century a reason for centres of free and open discussion and the exchange of news, in a manner impossible elsewhere. This new café-society has been sardonically described by Montesquieu, who wrote in a passage dated 1717 [in his *Lettres persanes* (xxxvi)],

Le café est très en usage à Paris. Il y a un grand nombre de maisons publiques où on le distribue. Dans quelques-unes de ces maisons, on dit des nouvelles; dans d'autres on joue aux échecs. Il y en a une [probably the Procope] où l'on apprête le café de telle manière qu'il donne de l'esprit à ceux qui en prennent; au moins de tous ceux qui en sortent, il n'y a personne qui ne croie qu'il en a quatre fois plus que lorsqu'il y est entré.

This is no doubt related to the fact that, although coffee-drinking was less harmful than alcohol, the medical profession warned against excess. When Fontenelle was informed by his doctor that coffee was a poison, he replied 'Il faut avouer que le café est un poison lent, car j'en bois plusieurs tasses par jour, depuis près de 80 ans!'

At a later date, Delille celebrated the drink in a gay couplet:

Il est une liqueur au poète plus chère
Qui manquait à Virgile et qu'adorait Voltaire.

Whilst, in his *Mémoires*, Duclos describes a metaphysical disputation between Fréret and Boindin; and Mme d'Epinay, in a letter written in 1765 to M. de Lubière, describes the extension of the meaning of the term café in high-society circles:

Vous ne savez peut-être pas ce que c'est qu'un café? C'est, en deux mots, le secret de rassembler chez soi un très grand nombre de gens sans dépense, sans cérémonie et sans gêne; bien entendu qu'on n'admet que les gens de sa sociéte; et voici comment on s'y prend –

Le jour indiqué tenir pour café, on place dans la salle destinée à cet usage plusieurs petites tables de deux, trois ou quatre places au plus; les unes sont garnies de cartes, jetons, échecs, dames, trictracs, etc.; les autres de bière, vin, orgeat, et limonade. La maîtresse de la maison qui tient le café est vêtue à l'anglaise; robe simple, courte, tablier de mousseline, fichu pointu, et petit chapeau; elle a devant elle une table longue en forme de comptoir, sur laquelle on trouve des oranges, des biscuits, des brochures et tous les papiers publics. La tablette de la cheminée est garnie de liqueurs; les valets sont tous en vestes blanches et en bonnets blancs; on les appelle garçons, ainsi que dans les cafés publics; on n'en admet aucun d'étranger; la maîtresse de la maison ne se lève pour personne; chacun se place où il veut et à la table qu'il lui plaît. Mais ce n'est pas tout; il y a tout plein d'accessoires charmants à tout cela; on y joue des pantomimes, on y danse, on y chante, on y représente des proverbes . . . .

It was surely a 'café' of this kind which was held by Marie-Antoinette at Marly in 1778; and it is clear that, as the century began with its pseudo-pastoral, its simulated rusticity, *fêtes galantes*, *dîners à l'herbe*, *fêtes champêtres*, and *pastorales*, so later society played at keeping cafés, with renowned hostesses pretending to be café-keepers, and their guests acting the part of café society; yet another form of the play-acting and love of disguise that runs like a thread through the whole century.

The real coffee-house grew increasingly popular as the century progressed, and its frequenters dominated by literary groups. M. Roustan, in his article on 'Les cafés littéraires' (*Revue de Lyons*, 1906), considered their literary significance, in the age in which they flourished.

Writers were still to some extent dependent upon patronage, and, with few exceptions, their financial positions lamentable. Lesage is said to have been the first writer to live – and only at subsistence level – by his pen. Voltaire was a wealthy man, but through careful and clever investment, not through the publication of his books. When he went to Potsdam, at the invitation of Frederick the Great, it was not for reasons of financial gain; but Diderot was glad to receive badly needed financial help from Catherine II of Russia, who in 1765 bought his library, and then appointed him curator for life. Montesquieu earned nothing from his *Esprit des lois*. Rousseau, with his fierce desire for solitude and independence, tried to live by writing, but the only two works that brought him monetary reward were *Le Devin du village* and his *Dictionnaire de musique*. Buffon was fortunate to receive 15,750 francs for his *Histoire naturelle*; but this did not constitute a fortune, since it had to be shared among his collaborators.

It must be remembered that copyright was established only in 1777 (confirmed by a decree in 1791). The readers belonged to the cultured élite and their number remained small. Most first editions numbered less than 3,000 copies; the *Encyclopédie* itself had at first only 4,300 subscribers. With no protection (apart from an uncertain *privilège*), a small public, and poor returns, the writer was hard put to it to make ends meet, without financial aid.

This dependence upon worthy (or unworthy) patrons was offset by the writer's growing influence in society and in affairs of state. He was king in the café society of his time, his ideas paramount, his works read and discussed, and a band of eager disciples clustered about him, ready to admire and to spread his word. In the cafés, as in the salons, that other fertile source of social intercourse, he was the focal point of the centres where public opinion was formed.

The writer and philosopher was no longer the literary entertainer, brought in to amuse and stimulate the leisured classes clustering around the monarch and the court. He existed in his own right as a man of influence in society, able and ready to discuss art, politics, religion, philosophical ideas, and new scientific discoveries, with more energy, wit, understanding, and expressiveness than was common to his fellows. Nor was he above an interest in gossip concerning the characters and actions of notable men and women, or enjoyment of scandal in high places. The eagerness with which both Frederick the Great and Catherine of Russia, both noted for their intellectual interests, set out to attract abroad the great literary and philosophical figures of the age testifies to the increased importance of such men. It was Frederick who established in Potsdam an Academy of greater importance than his own Berlin Academy (to which he appointed the French geometer, naturalist, and philosopher Maupertuis as president), and where he gathered men like Formey, the materialist La Mettrie, and for a time Voltaire himself.

It is true that Voltaire was beaten up by servants outside the doors of the duc de Sully for his insolence, and when he sought to fight a duel with someone of a higher social class in order to obtain redress, he was imprisoned in the Bastille (1726), and then virtually forced into exile to England, a series of humiliations which left him with a deep sense of grievance, from which he never fully recovered. It is equally true that such treatment of a writer and philosopher had become unthinkable by the latter part of the century.

To some degree the arbitrariness of authoritarian power, illustrated again in the vicissitudes of Beaumarchais following upon the Goëzman affair,[1] is illustrative of a vacillation due to the complex patterns evolving, the turmoil of a new way of life. And when Beaumarchais, the victim, was disgraced, it is significant that the prince de Conti and other notables hastened to invite him into their great houses, and to express publicly their sympathy and solidarity with him. Both censorship and police were weakened, wherever writers were concerned, by the sympathy exercised towards them by officials in key positions, like Malesherbes, d'Argenson, and Sartine. Their policies are only intelligible in terms of their general awareness of the importance of major literary figures, and of the progress and tendencies of philosophical thought.

The cafés, which had helped to establish the great, and make them familiar to a wider public than their books would ever reach, were frequented also by lesser literary luminaries, hack-writers, artists, and would-be artists; young sons of noble families in search of stimulus or adventure; the *nouveau-riche* wishing to be seen in

[1] See below, p. 324.

fashionable surroundings; and an always increasing number of foreigners – Englishmen, Germans, Spaniards, and Italians – bringing with them the revelation of foreign customs and speech, a breath of a wider world outside the confines of France; horizons enlarged still further by travellers like La Hontan, La Condamine, and later Bougainville, who brought back fascinating tales of life on the distant coral shores of Tahiti – a whisper of strange customs, and stranger religions. Café society became cosmopolitan.

Cafés were frequented also by actors, who enjoyed congenial company in informal surroundings. Thomassin, the Arlequin of Riccoboni's Italian Company, brought to Paris by the regent, is known to have entertained the café crowd. It is very possible that Marivaux, who wove the essence of Thomassin into the incomparable Arlequin of his plays, often saw him dancing and improvising upon a table in one or other of the famous cafés, as well as in the more conventional settings of the theatre.

Coffee-houses were established also in the provinces; as were clubs similar to that of the celebrated Club de l'Entresol (1720–31), where more restricted groups met, in this case in the hôtel of the Président Hénault in the Place Vendôme, for intellectual and political discussion. Montesquieu was one of the regular members of the Entresol, together with the abbé de Saint-Pierre, who expounded his plan for everlasting peace. These clubs were similar in kind to the academies set up in suitable places in the provinces, to which belonged scholars, writers, artists, and philosophers, who met to discuss topics of interest to them all; and also the *cénacles*, meetings of like-minded men, sharing the same ideas and the same way of life, or pursuing the same ends. These several forms of discussion offered the greatest possible scope to young and ardent men destined to play their part in the troubled destiny of their century, and offered fertile ground for the formation of a public opinion that grew increasingly powerful.

All these were masculine strongholds; and in their different ways engendered an atmosphere in which men were entirely free to discuss any subject they chose, in whatsoever manner they chose, without fear of offending more delicate sensibilities. The cafés, clubs, academies, and *cénacles*, and perhaps too the numerous masonic lodges which supported the Encyclopaedic movement and disseminated its ideas, created a male society that bore no relation to social life in general, nor was it in any way influenced by female company.

It is the more interesting, therefore, to realise that the driving force in the formation and dissemination of public opinion, and the most effective centres of discussion, were the salons, each presided over by a gracious and formidable hostess, who insisted upon courtly behaviour, according to the usages of the time, and manipulated to some degree the discussions taking place. Salons of one kind or another had existed whenever women held a paramount place in the society of their time; but Mme de Noailles is probably right in stating that 'c'est avec l'Hôtel de Rambouillet que commence véritablement l'histoire des Salons'.

The 'Salon de Madame de Rambouillet' was the name given to a society of witty and elegant men and women of the seventeenth century, who met at her house in Paris for purposes of discussion and the reading aloud of literary works. It exerted a happy influence upon the purification of the French language and upon the development of literature.[2] Under the aegis of the superb marquise (1588–1665), society had reacted strongly against the coarseness and grossness in tone and manner of the court of Henri IV, and brought about a revolution in the customs and habits of her age.

The salons of the eighteenth century gave coherence and considerable unity to a movement that would otherwise have been too diffuse and too undisciplined. The ferment at work throughout the century, the great intellectual upheaval and the political and social unrest, threw up many demagogues. The clubs and coffee-houses allowed free rein, not only to discussion, but also to acrimony, internecine warfare, and abuse among a squabbling army of writers and thinkers, united only by their common hatred of *L'Infâme*, understood in terms of the Church, the state, the law, or any other form of authority. Voltaire was probably right in calling the philosophers whom he believed to be his followers *la séquelle encyclopédique*, to whom his ironic 'Mes enfants, aimez-vous les uns les autres, si vous le pouvez' was probably directed.

Those concerned with the burning questions of the day, spread around in clubs and coffee-houses as they were, nevertheless had their leaders, few in number, it is true, but in constant contact one with another. These were men who had their differences but seldom quarrelled (apart from the schisms in their movement brought about by the defection of Rousseau). They spoke the same language, dovetailed their activities, and took it upon themselves to spread the word.

These were the men who met in the salons and discovered there that a curb was put upon the freedom of behaviour, speech, and violent argument which was tolerated and encouraged in the coffee-houses and other male preserves. Here, in the salons, they were required to become civilised members of a sophisticated social system ruled by intelligent and socially adroit women, some of whom had served their apprenticeship in the Hôtel de Rambouillet.

[2] See P. J. Yarrow, *A Literary History of France, The Seventeenth Century, 1600–1715*, 1967.

The three most important salons of the first half of the century were literary. The first was that of the duchesse du Maine (1676–1753), a grand-daughter of the Grand Condé, and married to Louis-Auguste de Bourbon (1670–1736), legitimised son of Louis XIV and Mme de Montespan. Here the poets Chaulieu, La Fare, La Motte, Fontenelle, and the young Voltaire met frequently. From 1699 onwards the duchess organised splendid fêtes at her Château de Sceaux, a small version of Versailles, very often held at night in the park by the light of torches; and her sixteen *grandes nuits* became famous. From literature she turned to politics, dragging her husband into the abortive Cellamare conspiracy of 1718. When the conspiracy failed, she was incarcerated in the Bastille, so horrific an experience that, when she was freed in 1720, she held only a literary salon. But in its heyday, the Château de Sceaux not only gave the most fabulous *fêtes galantes* and *champêtres*, but offered a centre for freethinkers, libertines of all kinds, serving as a focus for the wits and intellectuals of the early part of the century, as did the Société du Temple and the Salon of Ninon de Lenclos at a still earlier date. The memoirs of the Président Hénault (1685–1770), and those of Mme de Staal de Launay, offer vivid images of life at the château.[3]

The marquise de Lambert (1647–1733), daughter of Mme de Courcelles and possibly Bachaumont, first opened her salon in 1690, but its importance as a literary salon dates only from 1710. She held her receptions on two days, in her house in the Rue de Richelieu; Tuesdays for men of letters, and Wednesdays for persons of quality, but in the event suitable people were often invited to both. Among her guests were to be found La Motte, Fontenelle, Montesquieu, Marivaux, the marquis d'Argenson, the Président Hénault, and the abbé de Saint-Pierre. In the early years of the eighteenth century she revived the *préciosité*[4] she had enjoyed in her youth, in the salon of Mme de Rambouillet, and was instrumental in refining taste and language. She was interested in general topics of conversation, in human nature, and in love. She herself wrote a number of books, including two treatises on education – *Avis d'une mère à son fils* (1726) and *Avis d'une mère à sa fille* (1728) – both of which show the influence of Fénelon and demonstrate the growing interest in new methods of education, which was to culminate in Rousseau's *Emile*.

Her salon, her values, and her outlook, as well as the refined and inbred language spoken there, exerted a strong influence over

[3] They form the main source of works such as A. de Julien, *La Duchesse du Maine et les Grandes Nuits de Sceaux*, n.d.; and A. Maurel, *La Duchesse du Maine*, 1928.

[4] See Yarrow, op cit., pp. 75 et seq. and F. Deloffre, *Une préciosité nouvelle: Marivaux et le marivaudage*, 1954.

Marivaux, who felt more at home in her salon than in any other. Certain elements of his style, such as his dialogue and the delicacy of the love intrigue of his plays, as well as its courtesy and formalism, were forged in the salon of Mme de Lambert.[5]

After her death in 1733, all the habitués of her Tuesday gathering turned to the salon of Mme de Tencin (1682–1749), who had kept open days since 1726, but had been overshadowed by the marquise. New members were added: Duclos, Marmontel, Piron, Helvétius; and Bolingbroke and Chesterfield from England. A remarkable woman, Mme de Tencin would seem to have sought success as a leader of society to compensate for failure in other spheres.

She was a sister of the powerful bishop of Grenoble, who was later made archbishop of Lyons and then Cardinal. It was he who secured the election of Dubois as Cardinal, and of Benedict XIV as Pope. He is known to have encouraged the Pretender Charles Edward to make a landing in Scotland, only to disavow him when the invasion failed. His whole life was given to duplicity, intrigue, and a long line of scandalous affairs. As a young girl, Mme de Tencin, whether through religious conviction or the pressure of her parents, became a nun; but her brother, as soon as it served his purpose to make use of her abundant charm, released her from her vows and from her convent. It is for this reason that Mme de Noailles refers to her as *une religieuse défroquée.*

During the regency, Mme de Tencin made full use of her attractions, sustaining rewarding affairs with the English diplomat Matthew Prior, and also with d'Argenson, the future Garde des Sceaux, and Lieutenant de Police. She failed, however, to seduce the regent, who sent her away with the remark: 'Je ne cause pas politique entre deux draps.' Madame de Tencin was never a woman to waste time repining, and she then, as Saint-Simon pointed out, 'retomba du maître au valet'. She plunged into affairs with both Dubois and Destouches. Her child, born in 1717 and reputed to have been fathered by Destouches-Canon, was abandoned on the steps of the Church of Saint Jean-le-Rond.[6] Adopted by the wife of an impoverished glazier, he later became known as Jean le Rond d'Alembert, enjoying a distinguished scientific and literary career. Mme de Tencin, unlike Destouches, never evinced the slightest interest in the fate of her son, and never met him. Once he had become famous she did make one attempt to see him, but understandably d'Alembert declined her invitation.

[5] See Arvède Barine, *Princesses et Grandes Dames*, 1890, pp. 215 et seq.; see also Ch. Giraud, 'Le Salon de Mme de Lambert', *Journal des Savants*, 1880.

[6] See below, p. 241.

Her life provoked scandal even in an age notoriously lax, and included a spell in the Bastille in 1726, as a result of the death of one Laffresnaye immediately after bequeathing all his possessions to her. Laffresnaye was said to have committed suicide; but Mme de Tencin was suspected of having shot him with her own pistol. Yet in spite of suspicion strong enough to have brought her to the Bastille, she was released without trial, owing to the efforts of powerful protectors. She was, after all, on intimate terms with most of the leading figures of her time. Both Cardinal Dubois and the regent himself advanced her fortunes at court, and gave substantial aid to her brother, not yet elected Cardinal; and this in spite of a suspected incestuous relationship between brother and sister. Both grew inordinately rich by speculating during Law's period of office.

By that time there was such widespread corruption, both moral and social, that even her excessive intrigues and her endless *galanteries* no longer aroused scandal or gossip, and she enjoyed a peaceful old age, surrounded by friends who were the intellectual élite of the time, and whom she called her *ménagerie*, or her *bêtes*. She became an arbiter of taste, indulged in a lengthy correspondence with Pope Benedict XIV, and late in life became a writer. She was the author of at least two books: *Le Comte de Comminge* (1735) and *Le Siège de Calais*, which she allowed to be attributed to her nephew Pont-de-Veyle; of an autobiography, *Les Malheurs de l'amour*; and of *Les Anecdotes d'Edouard III*, published posthumously in 1776. She left behind a number of letters, of which her correspondence with her brother, Cardinal de Tencin, is the most significant. Her style is elegant and the substance of her work licentious.[7]

Her salon, like that of Mme de Lambert, was a centre for men of learning and culture,[8] for witty conversation and the discussion of literature, science, fine art, and politics; but Mme de Tencin, herself an exhibitionist, encouraged debate with the express intent of scoring a point or indulging in cerebral fireworks. With her private licentiousness and her public sobriety, Mme de Tencin's salon had an ambivalence that was one of its several attractions.

The salons had become dynastic; for, just as Mme de Tencin took over from the marquise de Lambert, so upon the former's death in 1749, the habitués of her lively and sparkling open days transferred to the salon of Mme Geoffrin (1699–1777) in the Rue Saint-Honoré, with a subsequent shifting of emphasis on the sub-

[7] Her works were first published in 1786 in seven volumes. See P. M. Masson, *Une Vie de femme au XVIIIe siècle*, 1909.

[8] As compared with seventeenth-century salons, their gatherings, which included Fontenelle, Marivaux, Montesquieu, Maupertuis, and Clairant, reflected more serious intellectual and scientific interests.

ject and nature of the discussions that took place. Madame Geoffrin was not of noble birth. Daughter of a *valet de chambre* of the Dauphin, married in 1713 to a kindly rich manufacturer who was also lieutenant-colonel of the national guard, she was a notable member of the new and increasingly influential bourgeoisie. From the beginning, she received persons of high quality in her salon; but it was only with the death of Mme de Tencin that she really came into her own. Marivaux, Saint-Lambert, the Abbé Morellet, Helvétius, Diderot, d'Alembert, and Caylus thronged her house, together with the artists Falconet, Van Loo, Soufflot, Vernet, Boucher, and La Tour, and later Grimm, d'Holbach, and many distinguished foreigners, among them the Abbé Galiani, Horace Walpole, and Prince Stanislas-Auguste Poniatowski, who became King of Poland in 1764. She, like Mme de Tencin, kept to special days – Monday for artists, Wednesday for writers, philosophers, and other men of letters; but that was the only point of resemblance, for she received her close friends every day. Increasingly, her salon in the Rue Saint-Honoré became the centre for the Encyclopaedists, and it was clear that she delighted to have them around her, in conversation and in action, so that she could enjoy feeling that she was involved in the launching of that major work which covered the second half of the century, the *Encyclopédie*. She did in fact subsidise the mammoth undertaking to the tune of 300,000 francs; and it is certain that she offered generous financial help to many of her guests and protégés, to whom she also extended motherly advice and friendly criticism. She was not well educated – she never learnt how to spell – nor was she pretentious; but she had warmth and generosity of mind and spirit, and a fund of good commonsense, of inestimable value to some of the hotheads who surrounded her. She was an experienced and able hostess, who knew how to listen, and had the wit to speak only about matters she thoroughly understood, or when conversation was flagging; and with inborn courtesy, tact, and patience, she excelled at presiding over her disparate guests, keeping discussion under control, intervening only when necessary, or to formulate a wise maxim, and then calling the assembly to order by witty anecdotes and sudden *bons mots*, or a 'Voilà qui est bien', meaning 'that is enough'. Marmontel, who lived in the same house, bore witness to the perfection of her technique, and Horace Walpole referred to her in his letters as a model of stability and commonsense. In spite of her advanced views and her profound attachment to the Encyclopaedists and their work, she continued to observe the forms of religion;[9] and did not fail to criticise nonsensical attitudes, or to

[9] While she lay dying, her daughter, the marquise de la Ferté-Imbault, sought to reconcile her with the Church and to keep her Encyclopaedist

become extremely displeased with any of her friends who incurred open disgrace, for whatever reason.

Not only did her salon become the leading one of the day, but she herself enjoyed a personal celebrity throughout the whole of Europe. She was essentially Parisian, with no desire to leave the city; but in 1766, at the age of sixty-seven, she did travel to Poland to visit the king, Stanislas Poniatowski, being received by monarchs throughout her journey. Upon her return, Marie-Antoinette, remembering her passage through Vienna, asked to see her; and it is reported that Mme Geoffrin stoutly announced that she was glad she had been born French.

Mme du Deffand (1697–1780), whose salon dated from 1730, was in some measure the rival of Mme Geoffrin, but never achieved a similar degree of celebrity or influence, even though it was attended by the same leading spirits. As Mlle de Vichy and niece of the duchesse de Luynes, she enjoyed the privileges of noble birth; she was educated in a convent, and married at twenty-two a kinsman whom she found a bore and from whom she separated four years later, having by that time plunged with gaiety and abandon into the extremely dissipated life at the court of the regent, whose mistress she had fleetingly become. She lived for a time in a brothel of the Palais Royal. Beautiful, well-educated, and witty, but shameless, she was known for her scepticism and for her materialism. She formed a long-lasting liaison (or rather a *mariage sans amour*) with the Président Hénault, which continued, with divers storms and tempests, until his death in 1770. She can hardly be said to have had even a general feeling of sympathy for him, and said to him: 'Vous m'êtes un mal nécessaire.' But to her friends she declared: 'Pour ce qui est du rouge et du président, je ne leur ferai pas l'honneur de les quitter.'

In early days she was a frequent visitor at Sceaux, enjoying the brilliant company there, and well able to hold her own in it. An avowed unbeliever from her earliest days,[10] her scepticism remained unshaken in spite of attempts to bring her back into the fold. When the Cardinal de Polignac referred in her presence to the miracle of Saint Denis who is said to have walked two miles with his severed head in his hands, she answered him: 'Je n'ai pas de peine à le croire, Monseigneur, il n'y a que le premier pas qui coûte!'

Her salon in the Rue Saint-Dominique attracted scientists, writers, wits, and philosophers – Montesquieu, Fontenelle, Turgot,

friends at bay. 'Que voulez-vous,' she said, 'ma fille est comme Godefroy de Bouillon, elle veut défendre mon tombeau contre les infidèles,' and her final testament shows her faithfulness to d'Alembert.

[10] Even as a child she failed to respond to the blandishments of Massillon, who strove to resolve her religious doubts.

Marmontel, La Harpe, Marivaux, Sedaine, and Condorcet. Unlike Mme Geoffrin, she was never drawn to the Encyclopaedists, although she was fond of d'Alembert. She detested Rousseau, who gave her short shrift in his *Confessions*. She belonged in spirit more to the seventeenth century, and enjoyed the conversation of her guests, often without sharing their ideas.

She grew lonely and disillusioned: 'Je sens que je m'ennuie, ça fait toujours plaisir', she wrote, but finally her despair knew no bounds: 'Le néant (dont je fais grand cas) n'est bon que parce qu'on ne le sent pas. Je ne trouve en moi que le néant, et il est aussi mauvais de trouver le néant qu'il serait heureux d'être resté dans le néant.'

In 1752 she began to lose her sight, and two years later she took Mlle de Lespinasse into her house as companion, and to help her entertain at her salon. In 1764 a quarrel took place, when Mme du Deffand discovered that some of her guests, including d'Alembert, were so taken by the charm and wit of Julie de Lespinasse that they were coming an hour earlier to enjoy her company alone. She was dismissed, and the salon finished, for Mlle de Lespinasse took with her d'Alembert, Turgot, and most of the literary men. The Président Hénault, incensed by Mme du Deffand's obduracy, offered to marry Julie on the spot. Julie would have welcomed a reconciliation, but Mme du Deffand remained acid and adamant. Mme du Deffand spent her last years in sadness and neglect, rarely receiving any distinguished men of letters. She, the dry, disillusioned rationalist, became infatuated with Horace Walpole at the age of sixty-eight, when she had been blind for eleven years, and for the first time she knew true love and emotional suffering.

Her claim to fame relies not upon her salon, but upon her correspondence; letters written in her later years to the duchesse de Choiseul, with whom she enjoyed close friendship, and to Horace Walpole; and to Voltaire over a span of forty-three years. Her earlier writings gave little promise of the style and eloquence she developed in her correspondence and the ease with which she suited her manner to the different recipients. Her letters to Voltaire are brilliant, dazzling with wit, ironic, and informed; those to the duchesse de Choiseul are charming, lively, the letters of one highly sophisticated woman addressed to another of similar tastes. The last letters she wrote to Walpole are among her best, and reveal the deepest secrets of her heart, her loneliness, and her ultimate nihilism. The whole correspondence forms a lively, valuable, and fascinating chronicle of events at court and at home.

Julie de Lespinasse earns her own niche in the gallery of the remarkable women who opened salons in Paris and by so doing exerted major influences upon the manners, customs, art, and politics of their day. The illegitimate daughter of the comtesse d'Albon, and, as was rumoured, of the Cardinal de Tencin, she was brought up as the child of Claude Lespinasse of Lyons. She left her convent school to become governess in the house of her mother's legitimate daughter, the marquise de Vichy, sister-in-law of Mme du Deffand. Her relationship with the latter, to whom she became companion after consultation had taken place with the Cardinal de Tencin, seemed to have been agreeable for ten years, although her lot cannot have been enviable. Mme du Deffand never rose before 6 p.m., so Mlle de Lespinasse formed the habit of meeting her friends an hour or so earlier. By the age of thirty-two she had developed into a personality who attracted the leading spirits of the day in her own right; a situation intolerable to the egocentric Mme du Deffand.

Following the break with her patron, Julie de Lespinasse opened her own salon in the Rue Saint-Dominique, where she welcomed most of the men who had frequented Mme du Deffand, including d'Alembert, Marmontel, Turgot, Condorcet, Condillac, Mably, and Suard. She was a superb hostess, and one able to provoke and sustain brilliant conversation and lively debate. Possessing neither beauty, rank, nor good health, her abilities made her reunions the most popular in Paris.[11] D'Alembert was particularly attracted to her and for eight years he lived in her home, tending her most lovingly, but she did not return his feelings and finally broke his heart.

She was, however, a deeply passionate woman, disproving the masculine statement that passion and intellect cannot dwell together in the same woman. Even more than Mme du Deffand, she bore living witness to the fact that the apparent cold rationalism of the age concealed strong, deep currents of sensibility and passion. If she made d'Alembert suffer and break his heart over her, she suffered intensely herself in the course of her own *amours*. She first fell in love with the marquis de Mora, son of the Spanish ambassador, and ten years her junior, who died two years before her; and then with the comte de Guibert (1743–90) – author of several tragedies and an *Essai général de tactique* that was heralded as a masterpiece in its own day – whose indifference led indirectly to her death at the age of forty-four.

She, like Mme du Deffand, owes her lasting fame to her correspondence, published in two volumes in 1809. Her letters are self-revelation of a most moving kind, for they show how totally she was the victim of her own emotions, her desire to live through passion alone. She was torn apart by her lingering affection for

[11] She figures in Diderot's *Rêve de d'Alembert*, a work which she asked him to suppress.

de Mora, and her intense but unrequited love for Guibert. Her letters describe her remorse; her useless efforts to check her own nature, to dim down the ardour through which and by which she lived; her selflessness in her attempts to help on Guibert's marriage; her partial disillusion; and her final despair. The last irony was that she handed over to the faithful d'Alembert, who had been most sympathetic and helpful over the Mora affair, the letters she had addressed to Guibert, just before she died. D'Alembert never recovered from the shock of her revelations.

In the second half of the century, countless salons were established by ladies of birth and breeding, following the fashionable cult and receiving specialised guests: the Hôtel de Villars for the most aristocratic nobles of France; the salons of the maréchale de Luxembourg and the maréchale de Beauvau, faithful to Choiseul, Necker, and Brienne; that of the maréchale d'Auville, devoted to Turgot; of the duchesse d'Aiguillon, a refuge for philosophers who were being persecuted; of the princesse de Robecq, for those who were mainly interested in the past; and that of the comtesse de La Marck, sister of the duc de Noailles, for the devout. There were also an increasing number of a more social and frivolous kind, like those of Mme de Ségur, an illegitimate daughter of the regent; the comtesse de Noisy; Mme de Brionne, frequented by Marmontel; Mme de Mazarin; the princesse de Bouillon; the duchesse de Villeroy; the duc de Choiseul, who gave resplendent dinners that often cost the whole of his 800,000 livres of income; Mme de Grammont; the beautiful duchesse de Brancas – an almost inexhaustible list of the great ladies of France.

Several among those salons established throughout the century were only slightly less celebrated than the major ones referred to above. Madame d'Epinay (1726–83), who received Rousseau at L'Ermitage, held the salon most favoured by the critic Grimm after 1762. Like Mme de Lambert, she wrote two works on education – *Lettre à mon fils* and *Conversations d'Emilie* (1774). She figures largely in Rousseau's *Confessions*, and in Diderot's letters. Rousseau's refusal to accompany her to Geneva was one of the reasons for the break between him and the rest of the group. The critic Grimm was destined to become the centre of Mme d'Epinay's world, and to replace Rousseau as Diderot's closest friend, an ambivalent situation which led Diderot to dislike Mme d'Epinay until Grimm's growing indifference to her, and his removal to Germany, brought Diderot and Mme d'Epinay into a close friendship which lasted until her death in 1783. Her pseudo-memoirs, or *Mémoires de Mme de Montbrillant* written in collaboration, are a truly fascinating document, totally biased against Rousseau, but serving, with the latter's letters and

Confessions, and with the letters of Diderot and Voltaire, to illuminate the ramifications of the social and literary, personal and amorous, life of their society. She was related to Mme d'Houdetot, who figures largely in the Rousseau saga, and whose share in the genesis of *La Nouvelle Héloïse* offers rewarding study.

Madame Necker (1739–94), wife of a Swiss banker who became Finance Minister during the last years of the reign of Louis XVI, follows in the footsteps of Mme Geoffrin as a wealthy bourgeoise who opened a successful salon in 1764. She received, among others, Raynal, Morellet, Suard, Buffon, Marmontel, La Harpe, and Grimm. She wrote a *Mémoire sur l'etablissement des hospices*; but perhaps her greatest claim to fame is that she was the mother of the future Mme de Staël, who had every opportunity to develop her brilliant wit, intelligence, and intellectual gifts at an early age, in her mother's salon.

There were also the remarkable Tuesdays of Helvétius (1715–1771), whose widow continued to receive in their house at Auteuil, which became a centre for the Encyclopaedists; and the even more famous Thursdays of baron d'Holbach (1723–89), known as *le maître d'hôtel de la philosophie*. Of German origin, he had lived in France since the age of twelve, and became a popular figure in French society because of his generosity, his love of learning and of the arts, and his complete honesty, which made him a living demonstration of Bayle's statement that it was possible to be both an atheist and an honest man. His *Système de la nature* (1770) created a scandal, which endeared him to the freethinkers; and the nature of the meetings and discussions that took place in his house have been recorded in Diderot's letters, for it was here that Diderot found his most congenial company, and a freedom of mind and spirit that stimulated him most.

The salons were clearly coteries, and some had no other than social interest. Voltaire, most of whose life was spent outside Paris, viewed them with suspicion –

> Il y a dans Paris un grand nombre de petites sociétés où préside toujours quelque femme qui, dans le déclin de sa beauté, fait briller l'aurore de son esprit. Un ou deux hommes de lettres sont les premiers ministres de ce petit royaume. Si vous négligez d'être au rang des courtisans, vous êtes dans celui des ennemis, et on vous écrase. Cependant, malgré votre mérite, vous vieillissez dans l'opprobre et dans la misère. Les places destinées aux gens de lettres sont données à l'intrigue, non au talent . . .

This was no doubt true in some measure, but Voltaire himself held court at Ferney, and for his own part took care to keep on good terms with Mme du Deffand for example, whom he made a point of visiting when he paid a last visit to Paris in 1778, the year of his death.

The salons certainly made or marred literary reputations; but they also successfully challenged the verdicts of governmental censorship, encouraged young writers such as Delille, Chamfort, and Rivarol, the author of a *Discours sur l'universalité de la langue française* that was awarded a prize by the Academy of Berlin.

The salons played an important role in elections to the Académie Française; they formed the real public of most leading writers, who depended for reputation and reward upon their verdict; and in the absence of newspapers as we understand them today, and other modern forms of communication, they were a centre for the collection and spreading of news, and the dissemination of theories and ideas. They also ensured a high standard of literacy and an ability, even among lesser authors, to write with clarity and intelligence on general topics, and to carry learning lightly. In another sense they were sometimes regressive, remaining attached to classical formulae, and tending sometimes to block the way to innovations of a decisive kind. But, considered in general terms, their contribution to the whole rationalist upheaval of the age, to the new freedom of thought and the growth and development of the equally important currents of the new sensibility, was of paramount importance. They remain a product of an age curiously unaware of the contradiction implicit in the spreading of philosophical ideas running counter to the cherished prejudices and way of life of a society soon to disappear.

Chapter 4

POETRY IN THE EIGHTEENTH CENTURY

THE art of conversation and all the graces of social life, coupled with interest in science and philosophy, are the hallmark of the century. They were not conducive to great poetry as we generally understand the term. There were very few authors who did not indulge in writing some verse at one time or another, and the sheer quantity of poetry published was enormous. Never had there appeared a greater number of odes, idylls, eclogues, elegies, and satires, but only the epigrams, and perhaps the *amphigouris* (or nonsense verses), are outstanding. Most writers composed verse so as to cut a figure in society, and to enter the French Academy, a much criticised body, which nevertheless conferred a considerable social *cachet* on its members. It should, however, be remembered that the output of the poets of the age, which to us appears quite secondary, and which we subordinate frequently to their other literary productions, represented in their eyes and in those of their contemporaries a major contribution to letters.

The most representative and, by general consent, the finest poet of the age was Voltaire, whose *Henriade* was destined to be for France what the *Æneid* had been for Rome. Yet it is Voltaire's epigrams and *pièces fugitives*, together with his philosophical poems, that are still read; and his whole poetic work has been relegated to a lowly position in the order of merit of his total output.[1] One of the greatest of poets – the only true poet of the French eighteenth century – is André Chénier, whose work has close affinities with the poetry of the following period, on which it exercised considerable influence (and thus is traditionally studied in that context). It should be pointed out, however, that apart from his genius, which is of all time, he is essentially a man of the eighteenth century, as recent critics such as F. Scarfe[2] have demonstrated. It is the accident of history, even more than his poetics, which has made of him in certain respects the forerunner of the Romantics.

[1] For an account of Voltaire's poetry, see below pp. 164 et seq.
[2] *André Chénier, His Life and Work, 1762–1794*, 1965.

It would be difficult to single out a small number of poets as the best, when so many proved to be competent without ever being outstanding. It is then tempting to embark on the study of the poets by classifying them according to the genres they adopted, grouping separately the authors of odes, idylls, and eclogues and so forth, but it happens that most poets attempted all the genres, and only a few were more successful in one than in the other. The general standard strikes one as surprisingly consistent. It seems therefore most satisfactory to review briefly, and under general and somewhat arbitrary headings, a relatively large number of writers, relating where possible their poetic activity to their other known literary work, and situating them, when relevant, in their own milieu. In this way, it will be seen how closely interconnected was the world of letters; and it is mainly as expressions of the social scene of their time that their work is of interest today. Certainly the poetry of the eighteenth century is closely linked with the historical and artistic development of the period. It is characteristically *ancien régime*, and is open to the same phases of rococo and neo-classicism that we have found in the other arts; and the rumblings of the new Romantic revolution can be clearly heard as the century draws to a close. But the picture is more blurred, and the interweaving more complex. There is a lavish use of mythology, increasing representation of idylls in Arcady; which, coupled with a growing discontent and need of innovation, fomented by new influences from overseas, brought fresh impetus to a flagging inspiration and bring a new awakening; but, owing to the diversity of production, the message is not so clear, and the groupings of poets, such as they are, are very loose if compared with the schools of the nineteenth century.

I. POETIC THEORY AND TRADITION

Close ties with the seventeenth century are everywhere manifest. Classical aesthetics, as expressed by Malherbe and Boileau, was accepted with little question, and the majority of poets wrote in the same vein and on similar themes. Echoes of the controversy between the Ancients and the Moderns lingered on. The flame was rekindled dramatically by Houdar de la Motte (1672–1731), the author of a successful tragedy *Inès de Castro*, but a mediocre poet. He took exception to Mme Dacier's reasonably faithful translation of the *Iliad*. He believed that any of the Moderns excelled the best of the Ancients in poetic skill, and to prove his point published his own version of the *Iliad* in French verse, adding embellishments of his own invention – such 'improvements' as changing Achilles' imperfect shield for a better one, and modifying the circumstances of Hector's death. He also cut down Homer's twenty-four cantos by half. His adaptation was then dedicated to the king and introduced as an example of what Homer might have written had he lived in 1713. Madame Dacier published a rejoinder in 500 pages, *Des Causes de la corruption du goût* (1713), and Fénelon, who supported the Moderns in principle, wrote a guarded *Lettre sur les occupations de l'Académie* (1714), in which he criticised mere versification. The Abbé Terrasson and abbé d'Aubignac then gave useful support to La Motte by questioning the very existence of Homer. Further publications by the chief antagonists in this little drama led to a climax in 1716; but on Palm Sunday of that year, La Motte and Mme Dacier were reconciled, through the intercession of a mutual friend, M. de Valincourt. Houdar de la Motte, however, was not to be won over. He developed his argument still further, and questioned the very use of poetry, which he deemed to be quite artificial. In his view, poetry was a matter of technique and difficulty overcome, of the acceptance of arbitrary rules and restrictions. Finally he wished rhyme to be proscribed, since poetry obscured man's judgement by piling up images which veiled pure thought. This attack on rhyme is already to be found in the works of Pascal and Fénelon, and was to be taken up again by Montesquieu, and by Vauvenargues who, in *Sur la poésie et l'éloquence* (1746), asked whether poetry can be considered beneficial to mankind; by Fontenelle, a friend of La Motte, who went so far as to forecast the disappearance of rhyme; by Buffon, who was convinced that prose was a finer instrument of expression; by abbé de Pons who, in his *Fragment sur l'art d'écrire*, judged poetry to be frivolous and its disappearance as quite immaterial. As for Duclos, on hearing some particularly fine verse being declaimed, he solemnly stated: 'Cela est beau comme de la prose.' Most of these critics, as M. Allem has pointed out, were men who did not write verse. This can hardly be said of La Motte, who, in addition to numerous critical works on poetry, proved to be a prolific versifier. He wrote odes, mostly in prose, and fables, the last lines of *Les Amis trop d'accord* being worthy of quotation as illustrating his flat style:

> C'est un grand agrément que la diversité:
> Nous sommes bien comme nous sommes.
> Vous ôtez tout le sel de la société.
> L'ennui naquit un jour de l'uniformité.

All his opinions spring from his conception of poetry as a technical exercise. He wrote his odes in prose, to prove his main contention, and when his first play *Œdipe*, which he had written in verse, met with no success, he rewrote it in prose.

Poetry, however, had its champions, and first among them was Voltaire, who had indulged in rhyme from the age of twelve, and excelled in light verse. In the preface to his own *Œdipe*, he established a clear distinction between versification and poetry. La Faye (1674–1751), an amiable patron of the arts and author of madrigals, epigrams, and much *poésie badine*, wrote an *Ode en faveur des vers*, and pointed to the value of verse as a discipline. Nivelle de La Chaussée, too, in an *Epître de Clio á M. de B . . . au sujet des opinions répandues depuis peu contre la poésie* (1732), spoke in favour of poetry, which had a beneficial effect on mankind; and he acknowledged being sensitive to its glorious history. It can be seen how greatly the writers were preoccupied with theory, questions of form, experimentation with metres, devices of style, by the very nature of the controversy; technical accomplishments were to figure largely in their theory and in their practice. Their approach was superficial, but it was also intellectual; and Fontenelle, for instance, in discussing imagery, rated above all others images that appealed to the mind and conveyed thought, placing low in his scale of values fables and images drawn from mythology. Even André Chénier, who at the close of the century heralded a new poetic sensibility, wrote in verse clothed in classical garb. 'Sur des pensers nouveaux faisons des vers antiques' (*L'Invention*) stresses the need for new themes. Paradoxically, the real novelty in Chénier's work lies not in the novelty of his subject matter but in his gift for poetic expression.

The classical inspiration, from which oddly enough La Motte's theories are derived, is constant throughout the century. The taste for antiquity was fostered by Fénelon's *Télémaque*, innumerable translations in verse of Greek and Latin originals, Winckelmann's *Histoire de l'art chez les anciens* (the French translation appeared in 1766), and Abbé Barthélemy's very popular *Voyage du jeune Anacharsis en Grèce* (1788). But in the particular case of André Chénier, the fact that his own mother was Greek may have contributed to a greater feeling for Greek art and culture, and for the greater depth of Greek influence.

The classics as a source of poetic inspiration gained support from the type of education provided in the schools. A very large number of translations of, or adaptations from, the classics continued to appear throughout the century. Mention has been made of Mme Dacier's rendering of the *Iliad*, and of La Motte's adaptation of the same work. La Motte also adapted the *Æneid*. Saint-Lambert, in his poem *Les Saisons*, borrowed from Virgil and Lucretius, though he was chiefly indebted to the English poet Thomson. Richer (1685–1748) started his literary career by translating Virgil and Ovid; Diderot wrote a free translation of the beginning of Horace's first satire; the duc de Nivernais (1716–98) was known by his verse imitations or adaptations of Virgil and Ovid, as well as of the Italian poet Metastasio and the English poets Pope, Gray, and Milton. Turgot (1727–81) translated Virgil and Horace, as well as Pope and Gessner. Malfilâtre (1733–67) translated Virgil. Barthe (1745–80) published an *Art d'aimer*, imitated from Ovid. Delille, encouraged by Louis Racine, wrote a translation of the *Georgics* and embarked on a translation of the *Æneid*, as befitted the Professor of Latin at the Collège Royal, now Collège de France. Florian wrote a novel *Numa Pompilius* (1786), inspired by Tacitus. But all these translations and adaptations are little more than academic exercises, which served their purpose of refining the command of language of the poets concerned, and contributing to the prevailing poetic idiom.

II. SALON POETRY AND 'VERS LÉGERS'

The majority of writers, from the end of the seventeenth century right up to the time of the Revolution, and even up to the Restoration, indulged in light verse or *poésie badine* as a form of entertainment. The writing of verse was a favourite pastime and *de rigueur* in certain circles, such as the Société du Temple, the salon of Mme de Lambert, and at the court of the duchesse du Maine at Sceaux. Men moved easily from one milieu to the other, and carried with them their style, thereby establishing a continuous tradition. The poets wrote chiefly madrigals, epigrams, and *amphigouris*, or tissues of nonsense, to charm the *bureaux d'esprit*, as the salons were soon called. The style was light, the wit pretty, and the prevailing tone that of the inveterate libertine. Fontenelle was an acknowledged master of salon poetry. He wrote a *Description de l'empire de la poésie*, rather as Mlle de Scudéry had written the *Carte de Tendre*, and also a *Discours sur la nature de l'églogue*; but, for the most part, he was content to write brief uncomplicated poems, in which his shepherds were renowned for their idleness. The Société du Temple had its own devotees. The abbé de Chaulieu (1639–1720), friend of the *grand prieur* of Vendôme, who obtained many benefices for him, was a wealthy priest without vocation, a hedonist bent on social pleasures. He lived within the precincts of the Temple, seeking no other fame than to be known as its Anacreon. Influential in his own day, his production, in the style of Chapelle, is that of a very minor poet, hardly deserving the place assigned to him by Voltaire in his *Temple du goût*, as *le premier des poètes négligés*. He had verve, but was too facile. When nearing eighty years of age, he fell in love with Mlle de

Launay, the future Mme de Staal, but it was presumably too late for him to add sincerity to his other accomplishments. He wrote *Ode sur l'inconstance*, *La Retraite*, *La Goutte*, and *La Solitude de Fontenay*. His friend, the marquis de La Fare (1644–1712), a fellow-hedonist, who died of a surfeit of cod, modelled his style on that of the abbé de Chaulieu, and on Horace. He assumed the well-chosen name of M. de la Cochonnière. His *Poésies* were first published in 1755, and he left some curious *Mémoires*. The marquis de Saint-Aulaire (1648–1742), a friend of Fontenelle, shone for forty years in the Temple, in the salon of Mme de Lambert, and at the court at Sceaux, and in his ninetieth year continued to write *vers galants*, having started to write poetry at the age of sixty. The following *élégie* is in his best manner:

Où fuyez-vous, plaisirs? où fuyez-vous, amours?
De mon printemps, compagnons si fidèles,
Vous sembliez à mes pas attachés pour toujours.
Commencez-vous à déployer vos ailes
Pour m'enlever votre secours
Lorsque le reste de mes jours
Est menacé d'ennuis et de langueurs mortelles?

He was elected to the French Academy in 1706. These authors were already well established in the earlier period, and pointed the way for Grécourt (1683–1743), the graceful poet who wrote *Les Quatre Ages des femmes*, to be found in many anthologies of verse;[3] Gentil-Bernard, Bernis, Lattaignant, and Baraton; Du Cerceau (1670–1730), the long-winded author of *La Valise du poète*, and of some uninspiring *Réflexions sur la poésie française*; and Boufflers, who continued to write light poetry up to the Restoration. Of greater interest is the Président Hénault (1685–1770), who was *Conseiller au Parlement de Paris* at twenty-one and *Président de la Chambre des Enquêtes* at twenty-five, but who from the age of thirty devoted his whole life to society. He moved on from Sceaux to the salon of Mme de Lambert, then to Mme de Sully, and finally to Mme du Deffand. He was elected to the French Academy as early as 1723. His chief work is, however, an *Abrégé chronologique de l'histoire de France* (1744). He was a friend of Voltaire, yet in later years he turned to religion. His *Mémoires*, first published in 1854, are of consequence because of his wide circle of friends and acquaintances; poetry for him was merely an occasional pastime. Moncrif (1687–1770), the trustworthy secretary of the comte d'Argenson, was a free-living rake who wrote short stories and a novel, *Les Ames rivales*, but is best remembered for his most original *Histoire des chats*. He too was elected to the French Academy (1733). He wrote light verse in the

[3] Cf. *Anthologie poétique française*, edited by M. Allem (1966 ed.), p. 84.

contemporary style, but his best poetry is of Christian inspiration as, for instance, *Le Véritable Bonheur*, which opens with the following lines:

De tous les biens que tu nous donnes,
Le bien qui sait le mieux charmer
Ce n'est ni l'or, ni les couronnes,
Mon Dieu, c'est le don de t'aimer.

Gentil-Bernard (1710–75) had the name Gentil given him by Voltaire. He was also known as the Anacréon of France. A libertine famed for his discretion, he wrote an *Art d'aimer* in a ponderously cold style, and the libretto of an opera *Castor et Pollux*, with music by Rameau (1737). Bernis (1715–94) was elected to the French Academy at twenty-nine, appointed ambassador in Venice in 1753 through the influence of Mme de Pompadour, Minister of State for Foreign Affairs in 1757, and elected Cardinal in 1758. He lost favour for a time but succeeded in recovering some of his credit, and became archbishop of Albi in 1764 and ambassador in Rome in 1769, a post which he retained till 1791. His early verse in particular is in the manner of salon literature. Vadé (1719–57), famous as a mime and *diseur*, was a prolific writer of verse which became the rage in Paris. He wrote *amphigouris*, songs, fables, epistles, comedies, comic operas, vaudevilles, pastorals, and probably a story entitled *Lettres de la Grenouillère*. His best-known poem is *La Pipe cassée*. His chief claim to attention is, however, as originator of a new type of burlesque based on *le style poissard*, a language borrowed from the Halles of Paris. Desmahis, who wrote five comedies, also wrote an *Epître à Voltaire* and a *Voyage à Saint-Germain*. Piron and Gresset are both better remembered as playwrights; while Voisenon (1708–75), an industrious abbé and friend of Voltaire, wrote plays, operas, and oratorios, as well as short stories and *poésies fugitives*, few of which are remembered. Voisenon refused a bishopric and a diplomatic post, so as to continue his social and literary life without hindrance. He was duly elected to the French Academy in 1763. Lattaignant (1697–1779) is best remembered as the probable author of *J'ai du bon tabac* . . . Dorat (1735–80), who started life as a musketeer, became one of the most prolific writers in all genres. His volume of verse entitled *Fantaisies* brought him to public notice, but he is now best known as a minor playwright. He was, however, much admired as a poet by Cubières de Palmézeaux (1752–1820), who assumed the name Dorat-Cubières, but later changed it to Marat-Cubières because of his great admiration for Marat. He too was a prolific writer, and with advancing years his verse became increasingly macabre. Guichard (1731–1811) wrote light poetry; as did Panard, Desforges-Maillard, called 'La Muse bretonne', Pons de Verdun (1759–1844),

Desmoutiers (1760–1801), Augustin de Piis (1755–1832), Collin d'Harleville (1755–1806), and others. The number of these more or less competent minor poets is legion, and their poetry, known only from samples found in anthologies, is certainly the most voluminous and perhaps the most characteristic of the age.

III. FABLES

This genre was long popular. Florian (1755–94) wrote the best fables of the century, and they are commonly re-edited for the use of children to this very day. Florian visited Ferney at the age of ten, when he was presented to Voltaire. He had from the first a facile, pleasant style and justified the nickname of *Florianet* which Voltaire gave him, as also the words of M. de Thiard: 'Dans les bergeries de Florian il manque un loup.' He wrote a novel, *Galatée*, borrowed from Cervantes, the *Numa Pompilius*,[4] a pastoral idyll *Estelle et Némorin*, a Spanish tale *Gonzalve de Cordoue* (1791), and an abridged version of *Don Quichotte*. His numerous plays were mainly written for the Théâtre Italien. They all have charm and wit, and show an excellent sense of theatre. His *Fables*, published in 1792, are indubitably his best work. Their quality stands out by comparison with the fables of Richer (1685–1748), Boisard (1744–1833), Pesselier (1712–63), Le Bailli (1756–1832), who wrote four books of them, and those of Barthélemy Imbert (1747–90), a most prolific writer, and the Abbé Aubert (1731–1814), Professor at the Collège Royal and from 1774 director of the *Gazette de France*. Imbert's fables, much admired by Voltaire, were rated by the author as better than those of La Fontaine, for, as he pointed out, he had himself invented his subjects, whereas La Fontaine had found it necessary to borrow his from Aesop and others. His poem *Psyché* is a poor effort and his drama entitled *La Mort d'Abel* and imitated from Gessner is equally feeble.

IV. LYRIC POETRY

Pride of place naturally went to lyric poetry in the grand classical manner. Jean-Baptiste Rousseau (1671–1741) was held in very high esteem as a poet in his day. He received encouragement and advice from Boileau and wrote in the tradition of Malherbe and Racan. His life was an unhappy one. He was born in Paris, the son of a shoemaker, and educated by the Jesuits. His talent enabled him to enter literary circles and he wrote five comedies in verse, *Le*

[4] See above, p. 60.

Flatteur (1696) being the most successful, and two operas. He wrote several cantatas, which paraphrase the psalms, and poems of a serious meditative kind, such as the *Ode à La Fare*, as well as more frivolous verse. In 1712 he was banished from France for an alleged slander contained in some scurrilous verse circulating under his name, which he denied having written, and which he attributed to the poet Saurin. Apart from a secret visit to Paris in 1738, he lived in exile in Brussels, lonely and in poor health till he died, still protesting his innocence. His odes, the finest of which is perhaps his *Ode à la Fortune*, have a rhetorical flourish, but in spite of harmonious lines, suffer from a monotonous style. One of his sacred odes, inspired by Psalm XLVIII (lib. I, ode 3), ends on this note:

> Justes, ne craignez point le vain pouvoir des hommes;
> Quelque élevés qu'ils soient, ils sont ce que nous sommes,
> Si vous êtes mortels, ils le sont comme vous.
> Nous avons beau vanter nos gloires passagères,
> Il faut mêler sa cendre aux cendres de ses pères,
> Et c'est le même Dieu qui nous jugera tous.

In his day he was known as *Le grand Rousseau* for his skill in clothing commonplace subjects with the full prestige of classical oratory. He was much admired by Lefranc de Pompignan (1709–1784), who adopted the same conventional grand style and the same frigid manner, and who began his literary career with a tragedy, *Didon* (1734), then turned to poetry, writing four books of *Odes*, two books of *Allégories*, twenty *Cantates*, two books of *Epîtres*, four books of *Epigrammes*, and one book of *Poésies diverses*. His *cantate* on Circe is notable, though the one on the death of Jean-Baptiste Rousseau is perhaps better known. J.-B. Rousseau had inspiration and a good lyrical style, but his work was unequal, and he became the butt of Voltaire's relentless satire. Nevertheless, he entered the French Academy in 1759. Some of his religious poems are very fine, and his work as a whole deserves more sympathetic treatment than it has hitherto received. Ecouchard-Lebrun (1729–1807), called Lebrun-Pindare, wrote eloquent odes, imbued with classical taste and modelled on those of J.-B. Rousseau, and, as in the case of Lefranc de Pompignan, there are some less worthy passages side by side with some excellent stanzas. His father was the prince de Conti's *valet de chambre*, and it was the prince who had him educated at the Collège Mazarin. One of his odes drew Voltaire's attention to the plight of Corneille's niece, whom he decided to adopt. Among the better known are: *Ode à M. de Buffon sur ses détracteurs*, *Ode au vaisseau Le Vengeur*, and *Ode sur la ruine de Lisbonne* (1755). His correspondence with Voltaire was subsequently published. He was severely criticised by

Fréron, and published two brochures by way of rejoinder, *La Wasprie* and *L'Ane littéraire*. He left six volumes of epigrams and numerous satires. His *Elégies*, which are feeble, are addressed to his wife, whom he calls Fanny. Later he quarrelled with her, to the point of beating her; this action led to a judicial separation, his own mother and sister testifying against him (1781). He was now in financial straits, and the bankruptcy of the prince de Guéménée, to whom he had entrusted the remainder of his fortune, completed his ruin. He was reduced to living in one small room, became a revolutionary, and later a Bonapartist. During the Directoire, he married a much younger woman, who had been his servant. He lived out his unhappy life, penniless and blind, in a room in the Palais Royal. He was elected to the French Academy in 1803. He was a friend of Buffon, the chevalier de Pange, Mme Chénier, and her son André, whose talent he had noticed. The following epigram illustrates his kind of wit:

Sur une dame poète

Chloé, belle et poète, a deux petits travers:
Elle fait son visage, et ne fait pas ses vers.

Ecouchard-Lebrun's main trouble lay in the artificiality of his verse as in the neat lines that follow:

On vient de me voler . . .
—Que je plains ton malheur!
—Tous mes vers manuscrits.
—Que je plains le voleur.

Louis Racine (1692–1763) was the second son of Jean Racine, and studied the classics, Hebrew, and Italian at an early age. In 1720 he wrote a poem *La Grâce*, which met with some success, perhaps thanks to the advice given him by Boileau. *La Religion* (1748) reveals a Jansenist faith, which deepened after the death of his son in the Lisbon earthquake, without, however, redeeming an essentially didactic manner and a monotonous style. In addition to a number of lyrical poems and some epistles, he translated *Paradise Lost*, and wrote interesting *Mémoires sur la vie de Jean Racine*, as well as *Réflexions sur la poésie*.

Reference may perhaps be made here to Delille (1738–1813), who received some encouragement from Louis Racine. He may more properly be classified as a descriptive poet. He became Professor of Latin poetry at the Collège Royal. He was elected to the French Academy in 1774. His best-known work is *Les Jardins ou L'Art d'embellir les paysages* (1782), which could be called didactic. It reveals considerable competence and a certain feeling for nature, but the style is cold and artificial, as in his poem *Versailles*, which opens in this manner:

O Versailles! ô regrets! ô bosquets ravissants!
Chefs d'œuvre d'un grand roi, de Le Nôtre, et des ans!

His *Tableaux de la nature* are placed one after the other with no effort at composition. In 1780 he had published *L'Homme des champs* in London. Blind and paralysed, he finally succumbed to a stroke, and was given one of the most impressive funerals of the century. Marie-Joseph Chénier, a younger brother of André, wrote a *Petite Epître à Jacques Delille* and the following *Epigramme sur L'Homme des champs* is hard but just:

Ce n'est donc plus l'abbé Virgile:
C'est un abbé sec, compassé,
Pincé, passé, cassé, glacé,
Brillant, mais d'un éclat fragile.
Sous son maigre et joli pinceau
La nature est vaine et coquette:
L'habile arrangeur de palette
N'a vu sous son petit tableau
Les champs qu'à travers sa lorgnette
Et par les vitres du château.

V. DIDACTIC AND PHILOSOPHICAL POETRY

A number of poems reflected the new philosophical and scientific outlook, and Voltaire was the most successful in this type of poetry. In *Le Mondain*, he had voiced his epicurean views clearly and in a lighthearted manner. The tone became more serious in *Discours en vers sur l'homme* (1738), and especially in *Poème sur le désastre de Lisbonne* and *Poème sur la loi naturelle* (1756), but also in *A l'Auteur du livre des trois imposteurs*, in which occurs the famous line: 'Si Dieu n'existait pas, il faudrait l'inventer', so often quoted out of context and misunderstood. He considered with some care the problem of evil, and expressed with clarity his own deism, which he associated with his philosophical propaganda and with the new science. Even when striving to express in verse the laws of gravitation and the implications of the new physics, he managed to convey a sense of drama. Thus he writes:

Le compas de Newton, mesurant l'univers
Lève enfin ce grand voile et les cieux sont ouverts.

Denis Diderot, who was a *poète galant* on occasion, did compose *Le Code Denis*, the general message of which is crystal clear, but this was for a select company and on a social occasion. It begins thus:

Dans ses Etats, à tout ce qui respire
Un souverain prétend donner la loi:
C'est le contraire en mon empire;
Le sujet règne sur son roi.

But such directness on political issues is rare, outside Voltaire's plays and the *drames*, where the plot chosen could be held to dictate the statements made, thereby offering the author some protection.

The moralising attitude found in other literary productions is common in much of this poetry. Early in the century (1707), La Motte had written odes on *l'amour-propre*, *l'enthousiasme*, *la variété*, *la colère*, *le goût*, *la nouveauté*, and *l'aveuglement*. Later the definition of virtue became more blurred, and sometimes turned into a lachrymose emotional concept, at once superficial and conventional. As a general rule, the more complete the break with Christianity, the greater the insistence on a general morality based on social or civic virtue. This, too, is manifest in Voltaire's verse. But Louis Racine, as well as other poets of religious inspiration and those who combine the sacred and the profane, reflects the same tendency. Helvétius, in a poem *Le Bonheur*, which was left unfinished, and Fontanes, in his *Fragment d'un poème sur la nature et sur l'homme* (1777), both show a blend of philosophical, scientific, and moral attitudes. Fontanes took up and developed Fontenelle's idea of universal solidarity and his view that the planets were possibly inhabited. In his *Essai sur l'astronomie* (1757) he writes:

> Tandis que je me perds en ces rêves profonds
> Peut-être un habitant de Vénus, de Mercure,
> De ce globe voisin qui blanchit l'ombre obscure,
> Se livre à des transports aussi doux que les miens . . .

Only Diderot, however, in the prose of *Lettre sur les aveugles* and of *Le Rêve de d'Alembert* captured something of Lucretius' *De rerum natura*. The term didactic is better than that of propaganda for very much of this kind of literature. Polignac entitled his work *Anti-Lucrèce*, and Malfilâtre his best-known poem *Sur le soleil fixe au milieu des planètes* (1759), both of which would answer to this definition. There is also C.-H. Watelet's *Art de peindre* in four cantos, Lemierre's *La Peinture*, Gentil-Bernard's *Art d'aimer*, and C.-J. Dorat's *La Déclamation théâtrale*. The term didactic could also be applied to much in Saint-Lambert's *Saisons*, as to Delille, who wrote an *Epître à M. Laurent à l'occasion d'un bras artificiel qu'il a fait pour un soldat invalide*, which may be held up as a tribute to the progress of technology rather than to human sympathy. Here is how Delille explains in poetic language the decomposition of light:

> Avant que de Newton la science profonde
> Eût surpris ce mystère et les secrets du monde
> La lumière en faisceaux se montrait à nos yeux;
> Son art décomposa ce tissu radieux.
> (*Les Trois Règnes de la nature*, chant I).

VI. ENGLISH AND GERMAN INFLUENCES, AND PRE-ROMANTIC VERSE

Translations from the English abound. Feutry (1720–89) imitated Thomson and Pope (his rendering of Pope's *Epistle from Heloisa to Abelard* is earlier than that of Colardeau), and popularised Young. He wrote a gloomy poem which leads up to the conclusion:

> Tout n'est qu'illusion d'illusions suivie
> Et ce n'est qu'à la mort que commence la vie.

And it is not surprising to learn that the unfortunate man hanged himself in a fit of insanity. There appeared many translations of Pope's *Essay on Man*, which was much read in philosophical circles. Letourneur translated in full *The Complaint, or Night Thoughts* by Young, and Macpherson's *Ossian* (1777), but the influence of both these poets was not fully felt before the nineteenth century. Delille and others translated Milton's *Paradise Lost*. Shakespeare became increasingly known through La Place's translations (1745–49), and through those which Letourneur produced somewhat later (1776), when Ducis' adaptations had brought him to the stage. Madame Bontemps translated James Thomson's *The Seasons* (1759). The marquis de Saint-Lambert (1716–1803), author of some good madrigals, wrote his own *Les Saisons* (1769) over a period of some twenty years, in an elegant style in which the expression of his feeling for nature is too often marred by philosophical disquisitions, manifestations of *galanterie*, and superficiality. Saint-Lambert's love affair with Mme du Châtelet, whom he met at the court of the King of Poland, Stanislas I Leczinski, at Lunéville, is well known, as are his relations with Voltaire, which were at first very cold,[5] but improved with time; in 1770 Voltaire went so far as to second Saint-Lambert's efforts to enter the French Academy. Saint-Lambert's liaison with Mme d'Houdetot, which began three years after the death of Mme du Châtelet, lasted until his death. He left some *Fables orientales*, some prose tales, and an *Essai* on the life and works of Helvétius. *Les Saisons* has counterparts in *Les Mois* (1779) by Roucher, *Les Fastes* by Lemierre, and *Les Jardins* by Delille. Roucher, a friend of J.-J. Rousseau, died on the scaffold on 25 July 1794, on the same day as André Chénier. The duc de Nivernais (1716–98), as well as adapting Virgil and Ovid, translated or adapted Pope, Milton, and Gray. Colardeau coined the word *héroïde* to define Pope's *Epistle from Heloisa to Abelard*, which term has since been applied to letters in verse form.

[5] See below, p. 159.

The dominant Germanic influence was that of Gessner, a Swiss poet, whose *Idylls* were translated by Haller in 1762. Gessner's influence can be traced in the *Idylles* by Berquin (1747–91), and in the poetry of Léonard (1744–93), who was born in Guadeloupe, but studied in France and told in his novel *La Nouvelle Clémentine ou Les Lettres d'Henriette* the story of his own misfortune. He had fallen romantically in love with a young girl, who returned his affection, but owing to her parents' objection to his poverty, the match did not take place. The girl was sent into a convent, where it is said that she died of grief. This experience is at the source of Léonard's inspirations, and he sang his melancholy in moving, harmonious verse which he published as a sequel to his *Idylles*. The end of his poem *Les Regrets* is characteristic:

> Dans cette triste inquiétude
> On passe ainsi la vie à chercher le bonheur.
> A quoi sert de changer de lieux et d'habitude
> Quand on ne peut changer son cœur?

He exercised a certain influence on Lamartine. He wrote also an imitation of Montesquieu's *Temple de Gnide*, a poem on *Les Saisons*, another on Hero and Leander, a tragedy, *Œdipe roi ou La Fatalité*, a pastoral novel, *Alexis*, and a novel in letter-form, *Lettres de deux amants habitants de Lyon*. Thomas (1732–85) also influenced Lamartine. In particular his *Ode sur le temps* has phrases which Lamartine utilised. The last lines of this ode recall a famous passage in *Le Lac*:

> O Temps, suspends ton vol, respecte ma jeunesse,
> Que ma mère, longtemps témoin de ma tendresse,
> Reçoive mes tributs de respect et d'amour;
> Et vous, Gloire, Vertu, déesses immortelles,
> Que vos brillantes ailes
> Sur mes cheveux blanchis se reposent un jour.

At the age of fourteen he had written *Jumonville*, a poem in four cantos (1759), which is of little interest apart from its precocity. His *Eloges* are declamatory in style, but were highly successful. His *Essai sur les éloges* appeared in 1773, and he also wrote an epic in six cantos on the voyages of Peter the Great in Holland, England, France, and Thuringia. His early *Réflexions philosophiques et littéraires sur le poème de la religion naturelle* is an attack on Voltaire. He was deeply religious and enjoyed the reputation of being a good man.

No doubt the most considerable poet of a group born in the Ile Bourbon, now the Ile de la Réunion, was Evariste Parny (1753–1814). Educated at Rennes, he moved on to Versailles where he made friends with his compatriot Bertin. He returned to the Ile Bourbon in 1773, hoping to marry the woman he loved, but he was unsuccessful, and she eventually married someone else. He sung her praises under the name of Eléonore in *Poésies érotiques* (1778), and his unhappiness is recorded in the fourth book of the 1784 edition of these poems. His *Chansons madécasses* appeared in 1787. He wrote a heroic-comic poem *La Guerre des dieux*, which met with success, and *Le Portefeuille volé*, a parody of *Paradise Lost*. The volume contains also *Les Déguisements de Vénus, pièces galantes*. At the time of the Revolution he faced ruin, but managed to live through the period and in 1802 he married, entering the French Academy in 1803. He was now famous, and the melancholy mood he had captured so well endeared him to Lamartine and to a widening public. The following poem, *Vers sur la mort d'une jeune fille*, translates his melancholy in a manner which Lamartine adopted in his own verse:

Son âge échappait à l'enfance;
Riante comme l'innocence
Elle avait les traits de l'Amour.
Quelques mois, quelques jours encore,
Dans ce cœur pur et sans détour
Le sentiment allait éclore.
Mais le ciel avait au trépas
Condamné ses jeunes appas.
Au ciel elle a rendu sa vie,
Et doucement s'est endormie
Sans murmurer contre ses lois.
Ainsi le sourire s'efface;
Ainsi meurt, sans laisser de trace,
Le champ d'un oiseau dans les bois.

Another poet, Ginguené (1748–1816), who was born in Rennes and educated with Parny, shares some of his pre-Romantic sensibility. Parny's compatriot Bertin (1752–90) started his literary career as a disciple of Dorat, but drew closer to Parny who had become his friend. He contributed to the *Almanach des Muses*, and in 1783 *Les Amours* appeared, inspired by two women he loved. These poems combine a certain *libertinage* with considerable grace and charm. Bertin had a real feeling for nature, and knew how to express his jealousy and his suffering, but his verse has not the quality of Parny's. His end was tragic: he became engaged in the year of his death, but fell ill as he was about to get married and died a few weeks later. Bonnard (1744–84) is yet another poet friend of Dorat and of Parny.

Gabriel Legouvé (1764–1812) is a quite different poet, whose best work, *La Mélancolie*, ending *Werther à la main*, points to a certain romanticism through its author's predilection for gloom and for funereal scenes. He wrote a pastoral tragedy inspired by

Gessner, *La Mort d'Abel*, and a few melodramas. His most commonly quoted poem, entitled *Le Mérite des femmes*, has the following closing lines:

> Et, si la voix du sang n'est point une chimère,
> Tombe aux pieds de ce sexe à qui tu dois ta mère.

Examples of this kind of rhetoric are all too common in the *drames* of the period.

Gilbert (1751–80) has left an *Ode sur le jugement dernier*, which has quality but was not appreciated, and two satires, *Le Dix-huitième siècle* and *Mon Apologie*. It is certain that he was poor and lived on a very small pension, but it is untrue to say, as Alfred de Vigny did in *Stello*, that he died of hunger. In fact he fell from a house and had to be trepanned, dying from the effects of the operation soon after. Shortly before his death he wrote an ode, inspired by a number of psalms, which is extremely moving. It is called *Adieux à la vie*, and is one of the finest lyrical poems of the century:

> J'ai révélé mon cœur au Dieu de l'innocence.
> Il a vu mes pleurs pénitents;
> Il guérit mes remords, il m'arme de constance:
> Les malheureux sont ses enfants.

The whole poem is reminiscent of Lucretius, La Fontaine, Chénier, and Millevoye, but the over-all impression is one of sincerity and original beauty. Gilbert's satire was pungent, as one would expect from a friend of Fréron, whose dislikes he shared. His comment on his age is sarcastic, all-embracing, and virulent:

> Eh! quel temps fut jamais en vices plus fertile?
> Quel siècle d'ignorance en beaux faits plus stérile,
> Que cet âge nommé siècle de la raison.

VII. POETRY AT THE TIME OF THE FRENCH REVOLUTION

Under this heading may be considered Fabre d'Eglantine (1750–94), who entered Holy Orders and taught for a time at Toulouse, before turning actor and playwright. His best-known comedy is *Philinte de Molière ou L'Egoïste*, which he conceived as a sequel to *Le Misanthrope*. He called himself d'Eglantine after receiving the award of a golden eglantine as prize at the *Jeux floraux* in 1775. He joined the revolutionaries, became a member of the Paris Commune, and a deputy to the Convention. He was guillotined with Danton and Desmoulins on 5 April 1794. His poetry does not reflect his politics. He is responsible for a number of odes, *Le Triomphe de Grétry*, a long poem *Châlon sur Saône* in four cantos, and some stories and songs, the best known beginning:

Il pleut, il pleut, bergère,
Presse tes blancs moutons;
Allons sous ma chaumière,
Bergère, vite allons;
J'entends sur le feuillage
L'eau qui tombe à grand bruit;
Voici, voici, l'orage
Voilà l'éclair qui luit.

He wrote also a *poème-sirvente* (a form of Provençal lay) entitled *Le Berger Martin*, and a poem *L'Histoire naturelle et son étude dans les cours des saisons.*

Marie-Joseph Chénier (1764–1811), younger brother of André, wrote chiefly for the theatre. He admired Voltaire's tragedies, and composed an *Epître à Voltaire*. He wrote also a *Petite Epître à Jacques Delille* and a *Discours sur la calomnie*, which he addressed to those who said he was responsible for his brother's death, and a number of elegies and revolutionary hymns. He was elected deputy to the Convention, from which eventually he accepted a pension and which invited him to continue his work on his *Histoire de France*. His revolutionary hymn *Le Chant du départ* is his best known. The following stanza is headed *Un représentant du peuple*:

La victoire en chantant nous ouvre la barrière
La liberté guide nos pas,
Et du Nord au Midi la trompette guerrière
A sonné l'heure des combats!
Tremblez ennemis de la France,
Rois ivres de sang et d'orgueil;
Le peuple souverain s'avance,
Tyrans, descendez au cercueil!
La République nous appelle,
Sachons vaincre ou sachons périr!
Un Français doit vivre pour elle,
Pour elle un Français doit mourir!

VIII. OTHER AND OCCASIONAL POETS

It will be seen by the wealth of names put forward, and even from the few quotations given, that French eighteenth-century poetry has a greater range and variety than is usually thought. In fact, all writers seem to have indulged in verse-writing at one stage or another in their careers. Mention has been made of Florian, perhaps better known as a playwright, and of Piron, the author of *La Métromanie*, who wrote a poem, *Ode à Priape*, the indecency of which he never lived down, and also a famous epitaph –

Ci-gît Piron qui ne fut rien
Pas même académicien.

Many other poets were primarily playwrights. Lagrange-Chancel (1677–1758) is best remembered as the author of *Jugurtha* (1694) which he wrote at fourteen and which gained him the favour of the court, and some useful advice from Racine; and of a number of tragedies, among them *Ino et Mélicerte*, which was stolen from him by his friend the duc de La Force. This led to a quarrel in which the regent took sides with La Force. Lagrange-Chancel then published a stinging satirical ode against the regent, called *Les Philippiques*, in which he went so far as to accuse the regent of having attempted to poison the young Louis XV. Not unnaturally this led to his arrest, but he contrived to escape and fled to Sardinia, and thence to Holland. Returning to France in 1729, he renounced the theatre, following the failure of his *Orphée* and *Pygmalion*, and turned to historical works. Lagrange-Chancel had some talent, and much natural facility. He said of himself: 'Je ne savais pas lire que je savais rimer.'

Panard (1694–1765), whom Marmontel called the 'La Fontaine du vaudeville' and who wrote one hundred plays, published a great variety of poems in his *Œuvres diverses* (1763). Collé (1709–83) was the favourite poet at the court of the regent,[6] and a great purveyor of plays, vaudevilles, parodies, *amphigouris*, and songs; his style and tone are quite uninhibited. He wrote one good and successful play, *La Partie de chasse de Henri IV* (1764; performed at the Comédie Française, 1774), and his *Journal historique* has much useful information on contemporary authors. Vadé (1719–1757), equally prolific, also wrote poetry in all the genres. Gresset (1709–77) had his hour of poetic glory; his pretty wit led him to write *Vert-Vert* (1734), a long narrative poem about a parrot, well trained in the Convent of the Visitation at Nevers, who was sent to Nantes for the delight and edification of the Visitandines who dwelt there, who could appreciate his talents. Unfortunately, he was sent by boat down the river Loire, where he picked up some shocking language. He was therefore returned in shame to Nevers, where he was restored to grace and finally died of a surfeit of dragées. The style of this very long poem is light, gay, and well sustained, and the general tempo is fast:

Vert-Vert était un perroquet dévot,
Une belle âme innocemment guidée;
Jamais du mal il n'avait eu l'idée,
Ne disait onc un immodeste mot . . .

[6] He was appointed reader and Secretary to the duc d'Orléans after Louis XV had reached his majority.

The work delighted Voltaire and his contemporaries. Gresset then wrote *Le Lutrin vivant* and *Le Carême impromptu*, which are not in the same class. He entered the Académie Française in 1748. He wrote a number of plays, one, *Le Méchant*, rated as among the best of the century. In later years he became devout and retracted his early work, much to the disgust of Voltaire, who satirised this return to the faith in *Le Pauvre Diable*.

Sedaine (1719–97), who is only remembered for his excellent plays *Le Philosophe sans le savoir* (1763) and *La Gageure imprévue* (1768), published in 1752 some undistinguished verse, including eclogues, fables, cantatas, and epistles. His *Epître à mon habit*, however, attracted much attention, although it ends in this characteristically pedestrian manner:

> Ici l'habit fait valoir l'homme,
> Là l'homme fait valoir l'habit.
> Chez nous, peuple aimable, où les grâces, l'esprit
> Brillent à présent dans leur force,
> L'arbre n'est point jugé sur ses fleurs, sur son fruit,
> On le juge sur son écorce.

Lemierre (1733–95), a professor at the Collège d'Harcourt, who was known to the circle of the *fermier-général* Dupin, wrote plays: *Hypermnestre*, which had a resounding success, *Guillaume Tell* (1768), and *La Veuve du Malabar* (1790), but he also published two long poems, *La Peinture* and *Les Fastes*. La Harpe (1739–1803) wrote verse, as well as eleven tragedies; he is best remembered as a critic who reviewed for the *Mercure*, and as the author of a famous course on literature, which he started to give in 1786. Beaumarchais himself indulged in some verse of his own in the *Barbier de Séville*, and in the *Mariage de Figaro*. Desmahis wrote a number of comedies, some of which are in verse. Marmontel (1723–99), who began his career with a poem which he sent to Voltaire, who gave him some encouragement, wrote academic poems as well as tragedies, which all failed – *Denys le Tyran* (1749), *Aristomène*, *Cléopâtre*, *Les Héraclides*, *Egyptus* (1753) – ballets, *opéras-comiques*, *contes moraux*, and *Bélisaire* and *Les Incas*, the last two works taking up the question of toleration; and also *Eléments de littérature* and *Mémoires*. He was elected to the French Academy in 1763 and became its *secrétaire perpétuel* in 1783. He was also appointed Royal Historiographer, and in 1776 he married a niece of the Abbé Morellet. During the Revolution he retired to the country. He was the author of the following epigram against Piron, which is unduly severe:

> Le vieil auteur du Cantique à Priape,
> Le cœur contrit s'en allait à La Trappe,
> Pleurer le mal qu'il avait fait jadis.

Son directeur lui dit: 'Bon métromane,
C'est bien assez de ton *De profundis.*
Rassure-toi: le bon Dieu ne condamne
Que des vers doux, faciles, arrondis,
Et faits pour plaire à ce monde profane;
Ce qui séduit, voilà ce qui nous damne:
Les rimeurs durs vont tous en paradis.'

Marmontel was for some years director of the *Mercure*, which gave him a position of some importance in the world of letters. Fréron (1718–76), who had worked with the Abbé Desfontaines on two journals, *Observations sur les écrits modernes* and *Jugements sur les ouvrages nouveaux*, became Director of the *Année Littéraire* (1754–76). He was thus in a position to criticise freely his contemporaries, to whom he preferred the writers of the seventeenth century, and his independent critical approach incurred the wrath of Voltaire, who wrote epigrams at his expense, and satirised him in *L'Ecossaise*. With the support of M. de Malesherbes, he was able to hold out until 1776, when his enemies at last succeeded in getting the *privilège* for publication of the journal revoked. Fréron died in the same year. He wrote a number of odes, and some epistles and epigrams, one of which is here quoted:

Au fond d'un bois, assez près de Paris
J'errais, lisant l'admirable Racine;
J'entends crier: 'Au meurtre! on m'assassine!'
Je vais au lieu d'où s'élançaient les cris.
Que vois-je, ô ciel? quelle surprise extrême!
Le dieu du goût assassiné lui-même.
'Ami, dit-il, je cède au coup mortel,
A mes tyrans je voulais me soustraire.
Mais par malheur, dans ce bois solitaire,
J'ai rencontré R xxx [Raynal] et M xxx [Marmontel].'

Chamfort (1741–94) is better known for his epigrams and maxims than for his plays and *éloges*. Rivarol (1753–1801) started his career by criticising Delille's *Jardins* (1782). He wrote a *Discours sur l'universalité de la langue française* (1784), which was crowned by the Academy of Berlin, and in 1785 he translated Dante. He was recognised as a wit, and wrote a number of epigrams, some of which were in verse. Montesquieu is known to have written verse. J.-J. Rousseau wrote *Le Verger des charmettes* in rhetorical style, loaded with exclamation marks. His bitter epitaph for Voltaire has force:

Plus bel esprit que beau génie,
Sans foi, sans honneur, sans vertu,
Il mourut comme il a vécu
Couvert de gloire et d'infamie.

IX. PROSE POETRY

Poetic prose is to be found in *Télémaque*, in *Manon Lescaut*, even in *Le Temple de Gnide*, and has one source in the tradition of pulpit oratory. It is Rousseau, however, without doubt, who is the greatest poet of the eighteenth century, if the word poet be given its widest connotation and allowed to include the writer of prose poems. In his *Rêveries*, more especially in the *Cinquième Rêverie*, passages of pure poetry can be found. There are alexandrines, and octosyllabic lines of great musicality, but above all there is a harmonious flow of language, a balance of parts, and a power of expressing *nuance* of feeling and depth of human experience, which rank second to none in French literature. It is as if the veil that separates words from experience had been lifted; Rousseau in a subdued minor key has greater penetration and more magic than most other writers of prose-poems. This is perhaps because he did not write literature as an exercise in style, nor for the pleasure of his possible readers. Never has the form adopted been better suited for the expression of the feelings he experienced, and above all of the whole man, of the very core of his being. Whilst alexandrines may be found in *La Nouvelle Héloïse*, as also is a feeling for nature and, above all, the experience of romantic love, there are great differences of style between this book and the *Cinquième Rêverie*. A comparison of the passage in the *Confessions* where Rousseau describes his experience in the Ile de Saint-Pierre and the passage in the *Dialogues* where he comments on and explains his ecstasies, with that in the *Cinquième Rêverie*, again serves to demonstrate Rousseau's sense of poetry in the latter. The added truth poetry can bring to experience nowhere stands more clearly revealed. As for the famous *Prosopopée de Fabricius* (*Discours sur l'inégalité*), given as a model of style to countless generations of French schoolchildren, it reads to many ears as little else but an exercise in Latin rhetoric. Fine style and real poetry need to be distinguished, and a qualitative distinction can only be satisfactorily achieved by relating the form of expression to the very core of the artist's being. Then alone will style emerge in all its purity, as if part of some ideal equation.

Buffon in his finest passages retains too much that is rhetorical and self-conscious to rank in the same class as Rousseau; but there is one other great poet in prose in the century – Diderot. It would be difficult to find in his works sustained passages of poetic prose as well characterised as those in Rousseau's, but lyricism does exist. Diderot, like Rousseau, had a deep understanding of nature and was able to convey this. But it is his remarkable insight and combination of intellect and emotion, his natural enthusiasm, and the lyrical movement of his phrase when he sees, as in a vision, the full implications of the new religion of science, which justify most fully his claim to the title of poet. He knew what real poetry was about, and dreamt of a poetry unknown in his own day, using the word poet not only to define the creative artist – the dramatist with him is always the *poète dramatique*, whether he writes in verse or in prose – but the creative interpreter of life and nature. He sensed that a new intensity of feeling was required, as when he wrote: 'La poésie veut quelque chose d'énorme et de barbare.' He heralds here the Romantic poet, but he also holds theories that later characterised the poetry of Baudelaire and the Symbolists. Arguing from the invention by Père Castel of a clavichord of ribbons with which he played symphonies of colour, by virtue of his sensualist philosophy he believed in the correspondence of different sense-impressions and, without denying the particular role of any given sense, he saw that they could be combined to advantage, and that on occasion one sense could take over the function of the other, so that the poet's task was to relate sense-impressions, and note the affinities existing between the messages from all our five senses. Thus he favoured the creation of new hybrid arts, like opera and ballet, and, like Rousseau, occasionally indulged in *correspondances*, to borrow Baudelaire's term,[7] for his conviction that 'les parfums, les couleurs et les sons se répondent'. Marcel Raymond has heralded Rousseau as the progenitor of surrealism, if not of existentialism; whilst Diderot, for his part, strove to restrict the creative experience of man and his intellectual pursuits to the boundaries of our universe. With both writers the field of poetry is incomparably broadened, and makes even the best of the acknowledged poets of the age seem very puny. The latter were, for the most part, too concerned with pleasure to experience deep passion, and too much with intellectual ideas to produce original images. The use of traditional forms led to eloquence of a kind, but at the expense of sincerity, and simplicity in expression. These poets did experiment with rhymes and metres, and used all known devices of style, but, by equating fine poetry with difficulty overcome, they lapsed into mere versification, and many became tightrope walkers of great ability, with little else to commend them.

[7] Cf. *Les Fleurs du Mal*, Sonnet IV, *Correspondances*.

Chapter 5

LESAGE – MARIVAUX – PRÉVOST

IN THE first half of the century, three names stand out among the literary figures, as distinct from the *philosophes*, for the intrinsic interest of their works and the influence they exercised both on their immediate and their more distant successors. Lesage and Marivaux each have a place in the history of the theatre and of the novel, and Prévost, mainly considered as a novelist, had a varied output which does not readily fall under any one heading. These authors will therefore be reappraised in the chapters dealing with the novel and the theatre as genres, but their works need first to be judged in relation to the pattern of their life and to their literary activity as a whole.

I. LESAGE

Alain-René Lesage was born on 8 May 1668 at Sarzeau, near Vannes, in Brittany, and he retained many Breton characteristics, including a love of independence that led him to accept poverty rather than to forfeit his freedom of action and his integrity. He was the only son of Claude Lesage, barrister, solicitor, and recorder of the royal court of Rhuis, who died in 1682; since his mother, Damoiselle Jeanne Brenugat, had died in 1677, he was made the ward of two uncles, Gabriel Lesage and Blaise Brenugat. His mother was of an old Breton family, and his early childhood, unlike his later life, was spent in reasonable affluence. About 1686 he was sent to the Jesuit college of Vannes, where he received a good education, and developed his taste for the theatre. In 1690 he was sent to complete his education in Paris, where he studied first philosophy, then law, and was ultimately called to the Bar. He made the acquaintance of the poet and librettist Danchet, and the friendship which followed was to last sixty years.

In order to earn his living he became a notary's clerk and clerk to a financier and led a free and easy existence; he was well liked in the salons and frequented the Société du Temple, the home of the Vendôme family, and that of the duchesse de Bouillon. He met Dancourt, who befriended him and urged him to become a dramatist; it is believed that he had a liaison with a lady of quality, but soon became interested in a poor and beautiful girl, Marie-Elisabeth Huyard, the daughter of a carpenter, whom he married in 1694. He had three sons and one daughter, and is known to have enjoyed a happy family life. By 1695 Lesage lost interest in his legal career, and turned to writing. On Danchet's advice, he translated the *Lettres galantes d'Aristénète* (probably from a Latin version of the Greek original), from which he derived no financial profit. The abbé de Lyonne took him under his protection in 1698, securing for him an income of 600 livres. He advised Lesage to learn Spanish, and to seek inspiration in the picaresque novels, suggesting that he translate the plays of Calderón and Lope de Vega. In 1700 he published two five-act comedies under the title *Théâtre espagnol, Le Traître puni* (imitated from Rojas) and *Don Felix de Mendoce* (imitated from Lope de Vega). In February 1702, Lesage presented on the stage of the Théâtre Français *Le Point d'honneur,* a three-act play adapted from Rojas. This skit on duelling was not well received, and ran for only two nights. Lesage then published a free translation of Fernández de Avellaneda's continuation of Cervantes' work under the title *Nouvelles Aventures de l'admirable Don Quichotte de la Manche* (1704, 2 vols.). In 1707 he met at last with literary success. The Théâtre Français performed a five-act comedy, *Don César des Ursins,* an adaptation of a Calderón play, which proved a failure; but the performance included a one-act play, inspired by Hurtado de Mendoza's *Los Empeños del mentir,* with the title *Crispin rival de son maître,* which proved extremely popular outside court circles (15 March). In the same year he published his first great prose work, *Le Diable boiteux,* which he was subsequently to expand. This work is once more drawn from Spanish sources (Guevara's *El Diavolo coivelo*), but is in fact a satire aimed at Parisian society, only the framework being truly Spanish. We find in it anecdotes about Ninon de Lenclos, Dufresny, Baron, and other contemporaries. The character of the devil Asmodée has been transformed. In 1708–9, Lesage offered a one-act play, *La Tontine,* to the Théâtre Français, which declined to put it on, probably for political reasons, and it was only much later that it was performed at the Théâtre de la Foire, under the title *Arlequin colonel,* and later still, in 1732, on the stage of the Comédie Française. *La Tontine* was a public loan to which individuals subscribed according to their age group, in order to qualify for an annuity which increased as their numbers in the same age group died off. The second of these loans had been raised in 1696 and the whole scheme became the object of heated discussion in 1708. This accounts for Lesage's interest in the subject, and also for the criticism he evoked. With characteristic persistence, Lesage then offered a new one-act comedy, *Les Etrennes*, in 1708, which was again turned down by the *Comédiens français*. He expanded this play into five acts, but *Turcaret ou Les Etrennes*, as it was now called, did not fare any better. The *traitants*, a group of vulgar, newly rich financiers whom Lesage had satirised in his play, were successful in getting the play suppressed, largely through their connections with the actresses of the Théâtre Français.

Lesage read his play in the salons to rouse interest in it, and the circulation of a story that financiers had offered him 10,000 francs to keep the play off the stage proved to be excellent publicity. *Turcaret* was eventually put on at the Théâtre Français, thanks to the intervention of Monsieur, but it was withdrawn after seven performances (14 February 1709), as a result of which Lesage became involved in a quarrel with the *Comédiens*.

His abortive experience with *La Tontine* and *Les Etrennes* led him to turn away from the Théâtre Français and towards the more popular, if less exalted, Théâtre de la Foire. The winter fair of Saint-Germain and the summer fair of Saint-Laurent attracted mountebanks and strolling players, supplemented after the expulsion of the Italian players from Paris in 1697 by companies performing so-called *commedia dell'arte* scenarii in the Italian manner and others containing lesser players from the expelled company who fled to the fair booths rather than return to Italy or tour the provinces. From these bastardised forms of Italian comedy a genre including acrobatics and dancing, to fit the requirements of players and audience, evolved with great rapidity and popular success. These *forains* were further stimulated by a lively and continued struggle waged with the Théâtre Français, which continued until the Revolution broke out. Throughout the century the *Comédiens du Roi* strove to exert their own monopoly and to deprive the *forains* of their right to perform, by any means which came to hand, fearing a rivalry that might, and did, rob them of their audiences. Throughout the century, the *forains* evaded every edict, and avoided destruction; they continued to evolve a form of theatre based upon Italian comedy, and which developed despite all the stresses imposed upon it by the *Comédiens*. They enjoyed an increasing popularity, drawing their patrons from among the workers, the bourgeoisie, and the aristocracy. Their struggle for survival made them alert and adaptable, revolutionised stage technique, and as time went on offered the possibility of satiric drama of a direct, ebullient, and often virulent kind.

From 1712 until 1734 Lesage wrote for this theatre, which offered better financial reward as well as greater artistic freedom.

Eighty-eight of his plays are to be found in the *Théâtre de la Foire* (10 vols., 1737).

Twenty-nine of the plays appear under the name of Lesage alone, twenty-three in collaboration with d'Orneval, thirty-two with d'Orneval and Fuzelier, one with d'Orneval and Autreau, one with d'Orneval and Piron, and one with Lafont and Fromaget. His first are: *Arlequin empereur dans la lune*[1] and *Arlequin baron allemand, ou Le Triomphe de la folie* (in three acts with *vaudevilles*[2] and *écriteaux*[3]), in collaboration with Fuzelier and Dominique. The following titles give some idea of Lesage's output:

1713 *Arlequin, roi de Serendib* (three acts).
1714 *La Foire de Guibray* (prologue), followed by *Arlequin Mahomet* (one act) and *Tombeau de Nostradamus* (one act).
1715 *La Ceinture de Vénus* (two acts)
La Parodie de l'opéra de Télémaque (one act)
Le Temple du Destin (one act)
Les Eaux de Merlin (one act, with a prologue).
1716 This is the year in which the *Comédiens de la Foire* were freed from some of the restrictions imposed upon them by the *Comédiens Français*, but they still had to contend with the Opéra.
Le Temple de l'Ennui (prologue), followed by *Tableau du mariage* (one act), and *L'Ecole des amants* (one act)
Arlequin Hulla ou La Femme répudiée (one act).
1718 *La Querelle des théâtres* (prologue), followed by *La Princesse de Carizme* (three acts)
Le Monde renversé (one act)
Les Amours de Nanterre (one act)
L'Ile des Amazones (one act)
Les Funérailles de la Foire (one act).
1720 *La Statue merveilleuse* (three acts).
1721 *Le Régiment de la Calotte* (comedy in one act)
La Fausse Foire (prologue), followed by *La Boîte de Pandore* (one act)
La Tête noire (one act)
Le Rappel de la Foire à la vie (one act)
La Forêt de Dodone.

[1] Collaborators Rémy and Chaillot.

[2] Topical or satirical songs with refrain. Later the word was used to define light comedies with occasional song.

[3] Scrolls on which couplets were written, carried by the actors of the fairground theatres, and exposed to the audience when all forms of spoken dialogue had been forbidden to them by the Parlement de Paris.

1722 *L'Ombre du cocher* (one act)
Le Rémouleur d'amour (one act)
Pierrot Romulus ou Le Ravisseur poli (one act)
A prologue followed by *La Force de l'amour* and *La Foire des fées* (comedies in one act).
1723 *Les Trois Commères* (comedy in three acts).
1725 *Le Temple de Mémoire* (comedy in one act)
Les Comédiens corsaires (prologue), followed by *L'Obstacle favorable* (comedy in one act) and *Les Amours déguisés* (one act).
1728 *La Pénélope moderne* (comedy in two acts)
Achmet et Almanzine (three acts).
1729 *Les Spectacles malades* (prologue), followed by *Le Corsaire de Salé* (one act) and another prologue, *Les Couplets en Procès.*
1730 *La Reine de Barostan* (one act)
L'Industrie (prologue), followed by *Les Routes du monde* (one act) and *L'Espérance* (one act).
1732 *Les Désespérés* (prologue)
Sophie et Sigismond (one act).
1734 *La première représentation* (prologue) and *Les Mariages du Canada* (one act).

This considerable output is in addition to the ill-fated *La Tontine* (one act), given without success at the Théâtre Français in February 1732, and the following novels: *Le Diable boiteux* (1707); *Gil Blas de Santillane* (Books I–VI of which appeared in 1715, Books VII–IX in 1724, and Books X–XII in 1736); *Roland amoureux*, a novel in verse, taken from the Italian Boïardo (1717–1721, two vols.); *Entretiens des cheminées de Madrid*, added to the third edition of *Le Diable boiteux* (1726); *Histoire d'Estevanille Gonzalès* and a dialogue entitled *Une Journée des Parques* (1734); and *La Valise trouvée* (1740). Finally there is the *Mélange amusant de saillies d'esprit et de traits historiques des plus frappants* (1743).

Lesage is one of the most prolific writers of *comédies-vaudevilles* or *comédies mêlées d'ariettes*, genres considered to be the forerunners of comic opera. The form of these plays resulted from the prohibition of dialogue and singing on all stages except that of the Théâtre Français and that of the Opéra, imposed by the *Comédiens* and circumvented by the *forains*.

Even this long list of works is incomplete, for in the year in which he brought out the first part of *Gil Blas*, Lesage also wrote the adventures of Marie Petit, who kept a Paris gaming-house in the early years of the century, and in 1703 *M. Fabre, 'envoyé extraordinaire de Louis XIV en Perse'*, a work which he later abandoned. He also undertook adaptations and translations. His *Histoire de Guzman d'Alfarache nouvelement traduite et purgée des moralités superflues* (1732) is an abridged version of Mateo Alemán's romance, which had also inspired Chapelain (1621), Gabriel de Brémon (1696), and others.[4] *Les Aventures de Monsieur Robert Chevalier, dit de Beauchêne*, which has been held to be an authentic autobiographical document, is from the work of Vicentio Espinella. *Le Bachelier de Salamanque ou Les Mémoires de don Chérubin de la Ronda* (1736–38), is also based on a Spanish manuscript. Lesage in the course of his work in the theatre developed a strong dislike of all actors, and bitterly resented his own sons' desire to go on the stage. His eldest son, René-André, became an actor of repute under the name of Montménil, and on 28 May 1726 he played Mascarille in Molière's *L'Etourdi* with great success; he then toured the provinces, returning two years later to Paris, acting the part of Hector in Regnard's *Le Joueur*, of Davos in Terence's *Andria*, and of La Branche in *Crispin rival de son maître*, and finally Turcaret. But his father remained unreconciled and the news that his third son was to take up a stage career in Germany, under the name of Pittence (1730), only added to his grief and anger. This third son eventually returned to Paris, where he put on two comic operas, *Le Testament de la Foire* and *Le Miroir véridique*, at the Foire Saint-Germain. The second son, the Abbé Julien-François Lesage, who lived at Boulogne-sur-Mer, was successful in arranging a temporary *rapprochement* between his father and his brothers, but only after Lesage had been induced to see Montménil's performance in the role of Turcaret; and his last years were saddened by the death of his eldest son in 1743. Too old to work, extremely deaf, and quite poor in spite of his prodigious output, he went to Boulogne with his wife and daughter, Marie-Elisabeth, to live in the home of the abbé, his second son. He dined almost every day with the Abbé Voisenon, who wrote of his kindly wit. He had quiet obstinacy and the independence of the Breton. His deafness at the age of forty obliged him to use an ear trumpet, which he referred to as his 'bienfaiteur'.

Two plays and two novels stand out from this vast output. *Crispin rival de son maître* is generally considered to be one of the best-constructed one-act plays ever to be staged. The plot is unoriginal, borrowed from a Spanish play by Hurtado de Mendoza, in which an adventurer tries to marry the sister of a man whose life he has saved by posing as her fiancé. Professor T. E. Lawrenson[5]

[4] Mateo Alemán's work, of which the second part appeared in 1604, is considered to be the quintessential example of the picaresque novel.

[5] See his edition of the play, 1961, p. 14.

has reminded us that there is in fact a close resemblance between Mendoza's play and the adventure of Jérôme de Moyadas in *Gil Blas*. The play provides a social document of interest. It heralds the regency and the new social confusion, underlined by the language spoken by both servants and masters, and also the rise of men of intrigue. The milieu is bourgeois; M. Oronte, father of Angélique, is a tax-farmer, and Valère a *chevalier d'industrie* (an adventurer or card-sharp). Lesage gives to his valets exuberance of temperament and speech and the ability to cope with situations, before Beaumarchais ever created Figaro. He has what Lintilhac called *le mot qui ramasse*, an ability to use telling short-cuts. His style of writing owes nothing to the preciosity of the salons. Lawrenson rightly speaks of its drama of the outspoken, as opposed to the drama of half-statements which characterises the theatre of Marivaux. Minor scenes lead naturally and logically into major ones. There is great dramatic economy, and the structure of the play allows for rapid movement, which creates a sense of speed and suspense, and the possibilities of discovery are piled on at an increasing rate as the play reaches its finale.

Crispin is a brilliant comedy of intrigue, to be compared in this respect with the plays of Regnard. Lesage developed his technical skill by learning how to modify the action of Spanish dramas to suit French taste. By cutting out monologues and tirades, he speeded up the action and promoted a new liveliness on the stage.[6] Crispin himself is interesting from another point of view, for he belongs to a long line of *valets de comédie* bearing that name (1654–1853). Lawrenson has traced him from Scarron's *L'Escolier de Salamanque* through plays by Poisson, Hauteroche, Champmeslé, Montfleury *fils*, La Thuillerie, Lesage's own Crispin in *Le Point d'honneur* (1702), Lafont, Regnard, Delon, Mayet, Pessey, and Leclercq. He was incarnated by three generations of actors belonging to the same family, the Poissons, which partly accounts for the surprising degree of consistency in playing the part of this cunning and very self-confident valet. Lesage changed a popular stock character into a Crispin unique in that he becomes his master's rival, and in this he is clearly differentiated from the valets who preceded him, the Mascarilles, the Jodelets, the Scapins, the Frontins, and from his Italian counterpart Arlequin, who was dominating the Théâtre de la Foire at that time. The full story of the *valet de comédie* is as long as that of comedy itself. Comedy was born in a society based on slavery, and the *servus* of Plautus and Terence (whose *Andria* Lesage had translated) survived the passing of time, albeit in a new guise. The servant–master relationship changed with evolving social patterns, but ultimately

[6] Ibid, pp. 18–20.

became conventional in the theatre, the servant always concerned with his freedom or his wages first and the interests of his master second. With Lesage he is for the first time solely concerned with his self-advancement and usurps the function of the master. The bold title of this short and often acted play was to resound throughout the century, for the spectators were able to witness the rise of a servant in a society now primarily concerned with money, and no longer with aristocracy of birth. *Crispin rival de son maître* is essentially a comedy of intrigue, with a character title, a plot, and some repartees that were to gain in significance with the passing years. Certain slogans taken out of their context, such as 'La justice est une si belle chose qu'on ne saurait trop l'acheter', and individual expressions of opinion, such as Crispin's 'Que je suis las d'être valet! . . . je devrais présentement briller dans la finance', presage Beaumarchais, but Crispin himself belongs to a world that still hopes for reform and does not foresee revolution. Crispin is less dangerous than Frontin in *Turcaret.*

Turcaret is the second play under review, and the social background it reflects needs to be borne in mind if the work is to be properly understood.

France was enduring military defeat from all quarters. In 1708 the British and their allies took Lille and in 1709 the French were seriously defeated at Malplaquet. Court life had long since lost its golden glitter. The ageing Louis XIV and Mme de Maintenon had turned to religion, the cost of living had gone up, and the nobility were in a changed position, one in which it was increasingly difficult to cut a figure in Paris and at the same time maintain their estates in the provinces. At Versailles and in Paris fortunes were lost by the nobles at the gaming tables. The bourgeoisie, on the other hand, was growing in power; the prevailing mood was a desire to enjoy life to the full. Tragedy had become unpopular and comedy, especially farce, was welcome, provided that it had vitality and movement. Perhaps the most peculiar social change at that date was the rise of the *financier*, also called *commis*, *agent de change*, *sous-fermier*, *fermier*, *traitant*, *partisan*, and *maltôtier*. These were in fact tax-collectors, and went back to the time of Colbert who, in 1681, had established a *Compagnie de quarante financiers*, required collectively to pay the government 670,000 livres per annum, but entitled to recoup themselves by levying customs, *traites*, *aides* (on drink), and *gabelle* (on salt). The lease or *traite* (hence the word *traitant*) to collect certain taxes in specified areas was ceded for six years to a financier embodied by Lesage in *Turcaret*, who received 4,000 livres per annum for his services. A whole world of *directeurs*, *inspecteurs*, *contrôleurs*, *ambulants*, *vérificateurs*, and *commis buralistes* gravitated around them, exempt from paying taxes and hoping for preferment to the nobility. Around them flocked *agioteurs*, or speculators, and usurers. All these men were disliked by the nobility, for they amassed enormous fortunes as the aristocracy were losing them. Some set themselves up as patrons of the arts, as did Crozat, who helped Watteau, and others later became publishers, who favoured the *philosophes*. The peasants, like the aristocrats, hated them and generally held them to be responsible for the bad state of the country. In his play *Turcaret* Lesage drew on contemporary conditions and on *libelles*, or satirical pamphlets, as also on varied works such as *Les Agioteurs* by Dancourt, and *Factum de la France* (1707) by Boisguillebert; on Giton in La Bruyère's *Les Caractères*, Harpagon in Molière's *L'Avare*, Dorante in his *Le Bourgeois Gentilhomme*, and La Rapinière in Jacques Robbe's play of that name (1682), in which there is a scene similar to that between Rafle and Turcaret; on *Le Mercure galant* by Boursault (1683) and *Esope à la cour, Esope à la ville, and La Coquette*, by Baron; and on *L'Eté des coquettes* by Dancourt, *Le Banqueroutier* by N. de Fatouville (1687), to be found in Gherardi's collection of Italian plays, *La Foire de Besons* (1695), and *La Foire Saint-Germain* (1696). The name Turcaret has been linked with that of the lackey Cascaret, to be found in the *commedia dell'arte* and in Dancourt.[7] In Gherardi's collection, Lesage could find Regnard's *Arlequin, homme à bonne fortune*, and could also draw on his *Le Joueur* and his *Critique du 'Légataire universel'* (1708). Lesage borrowed from Dancourt's *Le Chevalier à la mode*, *La Folle Enchère* (1690), *Les Fonds perdus* (1686); also from Dufresny's *Les Bourgeoises à la mode* (1692); and finally from his own *Diable boiteux* and *Crispin rival de son maître*. But these varied and general sources merely add to the contemporary relevance of the play. Turcaret himself stands out as a character and his name has become a byword.

The play is often said to be gloomy. It is not realistic in the modern sense, for the décor is virtually non-existent. It is not as well constructed as *Crispin rival de son maître*. The tempo is fast, especially in the last two acts, and owes something to the movement of *commedia dell'arte*. This prevents the mood from becoming too serious. The technique has much in common with the narrative technique utilised in *Gil Blas*, which is essentially a picaresque novel. We find a similar discontinuity in the episodes of the play, and we move from comic scene to comic scene. 'Le jeu de l'argent et de la surprise' has been suggested as a sub-title.

The plot revolves around the question of whether the financier will succeed in marrying the young widow, but the fifth act vindi-

[7] Or from the cruel Turk, or the worm which attacks pear-trees called *turic*, confused with the parasitic blood-sucking *tique*!

cates arbitrary justice, rather than providing a solution. The return of Mme Turcaret, and the intervention of the king's justice, which bring the play to an end, are external factors; and the demise of Turcaret is a kind of *dénouement postiche*, or contrived ending, which has been likened to that of *Tartuffe*. The final triumph of the servant Frontin is full of irony. Frontin summed up very adequately the subject of the play in the following words: 'Nous plumons une coquette; la coquette mange un homme d'affaires; l'homme d'affaires en pille d'autres: cela fait un ricochet de fourberies le plus plaisant du monde.' Over the years we see that critics have questioned the comic element in the play. Today, however, through a better understanding of *commedia dell'arte*, and a close examination of other plays of the time, it has been possible to present a gayer interpretation of a comedy which has *lazzi, or* gags, and fantasy as well as realism, though the characters should be taken seriously; even when highly stylised they belong to professions which have determined their nature and their actions. The Chevalier is a melancholic yet passionate gamester, full of vanity; Turcaret is bold, careless, libidinous; the Baronne, a widow and a coquette, is clearly a stock character; Frontin is in the tradition of Arlequin, Scapin, or Crispin; and Lisette is a variant of Colombine. Lesage extends sympathy to none of them. His cold detachment, his quick wit, and his feeling for sharp repartees and well-timed ripostes, coupled with his unfailing ability to construct a scene, would have sufficed to establish his claim to distinction among French dramatists. It is, however, his satire of the world of finance and money, and his presentation of a vast and corrupt society unredeemed by a single example of a good man, which have won him a special place in the history of the theatre. If Turcaret was not the first financier to be put on the stage, he was the first character of the kind to be studied in depth against his social background, in his relations with others, and especially as he had evolved through the exercise of his profession. There are therefore serious undertones to this comedy which leave a sour taste in the mouth – a fact which enhances Lesage's moral condemnation of the characters. *Turcaret*, although now judged more comic than has hitherto been thought, does nevertheless serve as a pointer to the *drames* of the latter half of the eighteenth century, and contains many biting remarks that are worthy of Voltaire's pen in their sophisticated wit.

Frontin now belongs to the same social class as his master; he has grown in power since Crispin, who had merely confined himself to hopes of a great financial future. Frontin has a better technique, an abler assistant, and more real power, and the triumph of this *valet de comédie* heralds that of Figaro. The closing lines of the play show a mastery of nuance and a felicity of language which all alert spectators will relish, and which has only been equalled by Voltaire:

Lisette: Et nous, Frontin, quel parti prendrons-nous?
Frontin: J'en ai un à te proposer. Vive l'esprit, mon enfant! Je viens de payer d'audace: je n'ai point été fouillé.
Lisette: Tu as les billets?
Frontin: J'en ai déjà touché l'argent; il est en sûreté; j'ai quarante mille francs. Si ton ambition veut se borner à cette petite fortune, nous allons faire souche d'honnêtes gens.
Lisette: J'y consens.
Frontin: Voilà le règne de M. Turcaret fini; le mien va commencer.

The proposal of marriage is unusual in its form and the real implications are clear. Love for the likes of Frontin and Lisette is a very special thing, as their choice of words and form of persuasion reveal. Lesage can say all in a few words, and with crystal clarity, by compression and implication. A rascally financier as the essential theme of a play will be found in Balzac's *Mercadet* (1851), O. Mirbeau's *Les Affaires sont les affaires* (1903), E. Fabre's *Les Ventres dorés* (1905), and especially H. Becque's *Les Corbeaux* (1882).

The same qualities of style are to be found in Lesage's *Histoire de Gil Blas de Santillane*, which is a long comedy of manners presented in the form of a picaresque novel. Voltaire thought that Lesage had borrowed his episodes from Vicente Martínez Espinel, whose partly autobiographical novel *Relacions de la vida del escudero Marcos de Obregón* was published in 1618 and soon translated into French, under the title *Relation de la vie de l'écuyer Marcos Obregon*; in fact Lesage did borrow ten passages from this work. The Jesuit priest P. Isla thought that Lesage had translated a Spanish manuscript since lost, so he retranslated *Gil Blas* into Castilian with some success. An academic controversy over Lesage's originality ensued. It must be obvious that Lesage, like Molière, borrowed from all and sundry, but that the essence of *Gil Blas*, its style and tone, its realism and fantasy and satire, is original. The Spanish setting mainly lends piquancy to an unmistakably French scene, and contemporaries of Lesage had the added pleasure of experiencing a slight if somewhat bogus sense of *dépaysement*, such as was exploited, among others, by Montesquieu in the *Lettres persanes*, and Beaumarchais in the *Barbier de Séville*. In *Gil Blas* Lesage shows his ability to portray characters which seem to have the authenticity of the theatre rather than that of ordinary life, and offers a wealth of realistic details which lead us to accept inconsistencies in the plot. The work abounds in brilliant scenes and stylised dialogue which call for production on the stage. The same rapid movement carries all before it and the structure of each episode – but not of the work as a whole – is as taut as in his plays.

We witness a series of *tableaux* owing something to the literary technique of La Bruyère, conjuring up haphazardly a whole world of people of all ranks and characters, with their peculiar manners, tastes, and foibles. There are petty thieves and canons, doctors and writers, prelates and actors; there are old men in love with young girls of dubious morals laying snares for the old and rich; there are Ministers, dukes, and servants. Dr Sangrado with his hopeless remedies, Fabrice the poet, Raphaël and Laméla, who, weary of their role of penitents, abscond with the monastery funds, and many other characters stand out in one's memory. They come and go and reappear in very different moods. Both Smollett (who translated *Gil Blas*) and Walter Scott were filled with admiration at the richness and vitality of Lesage's *comédie humaine*.

The hero, Gil Blas, is on the high road at the age of seventeen. He is gay and full of illusions, and is bent on social advancement, financial success, and, above all, personal happiness. He moves through life without any strong moral principle, concerned mainly with personal advancement and survival in the jungle of society. He is an *arriviste* who only succeeds late in penetrating into high society. He becomes *intendant* of Don Alphonse, and then secretary to the duc de Lerme. But his success leads to his corruption. A further twist of fortune leads him to end his days at home, in the role of the good father. Gil Blas is Everyman, neither more nor less moral than most ordinary men, whose behaviour and standards are determined by events. He is neither vicious nor moral, but natural, somewhat naïve, and disarming. He is without prejudice and humorously self-centred. He grows in maturity with the author himself who worked on the novel over a period of more than twenty years. He may be likened to Candide; Lesage's rapier thrusts, anti-clerical wit, and use of irony bring home the similarity.

Lesage, like all the novelists of the period, who were constantly being attacked for immorality or uselessness, is at pains to stress the moral benefit to be derived from his tale, as well as the enjoyment. He can be placed in the moralist tradition of La Bruyére. In fact it is his restraint in the use of moral lectures that commends the book to us today; and nineteenth-century criticism, centred on an attempt at moral justification for the novel, leaves present-day readers indifferent. His fictional technique is of greater consequence. Lesage lacked the creative power and the penetration of Cervantes, who incarnated in Don Quixote and Sancho Panza two opposite yet complementary aspects of mankind. We have to wait for the dialogue between Jacques le Fataliste and his master in Diderot's last novel to rediscover, in a very different setting and intellectual climate, something of the dichotomy of man and his mind. But Lesage recorded faithfully and in a straightforward, incisive manner his own more limited experience; the picture of his times which he gives us may be over-dramatised, yet it strikes one as exceptionally vivid, illuminating, basically accurate, and often penetrating.

II. MARIVAUX

Pierre Carlet de Chamblain de Marivaux (1688–1763) is one of the enigmatic figures of literary history, largely because of his diffidence and because his role in the society of his time was that of spectator rather than actor. In spite of his predilection for the theatre, there was nothing dramatic about his life or personality: his impact upon the circles in which he moved impelled very few to comment upon it. We gather that he was known to be a kindly, generous man of great sensitiveness, extremely unwilling to criticise the behaviour or literary work of his contemporaries. His innate fastidiousness was revealed, not only by his reluctance to be drawn into the artistic or political quarrels of his day, but by his scrupulous cleanliness and elegance – his friends remarked upon the white satin, gold braid, and snowy ruffles he wore to attend performances by the Italian players – his delight in fine wines, exquisite meals, and witty conversation. Crudity and violence jarred upon him, and throughout his life he sought urbane and civilised society.

He was born in Paris on 4 February 1688. His father, a Norman and a member of a family highly distinguished in law, was appointed *Directeur de la Monnaie* at Riom soon after the birth of his only child: and later the family moved to Limoges. His background – wealthy, cultured, and intelligent – nurtured his particular talent for aristocratic living, even in the provinces.

At nearly twenty he wrote his first play, a one-act comedy in verse entitled *Le Père Prudent et équitable* (1706). It was the work of a young dilettante with a gift for writing, and was performed in one of the *théâtres de société* of Limoges. He was at that time engaged in legal studies. It is certain that law courts offer a splendid dramatic training, and Marivaux's concern with lawsuits and marriage contracts in his subsequent plays may well be due as much to his early association with the law as to the later influence of Italian comedy, of which many scenarii were concerned with legal imbroglios.

He soon abandoned the law, without, however, turning definitely to literature or the theatre, contenting himself with the life of a wealthy man of leisure, leavened occasionally by a little light journalism, which did not weigh too heavily upon his urbane search for pleasure. It was inevitable that when he came to Paris, at a date as yet untraced, he should be immediately welcomed into the fashionable and literary circles of the day. He had the habits and manners of a man of quality and, until he lost his entire fortune in the bankruptcy of Law (1720), was wealthy enough to take his place naturally among them.

It is typical of Marivaux that he accepted without bitterness or resentment the sudden reversal of his fortune in 1720: and in spite of his impoverishment, he continued to behave with unfailing generosity to all those in need who sought him out, often at great cost to himself. He was, however, forced to overcome his natural indolence. It was inevitable that he should turn to writing – for which he had already shown some flair – to secure his necessary luxuries. Without undue effort, he had written enough to have acquired apprenticeship status in the art of letters. His first play had been followed at intervals by three rambling narratives – *Pharsamon ou Les Folies romanesques* (in the manner of Cervantes' *Don Quixote*); *Les Aventures de * * * ou Les Effets surprenants de la sympathie*; *La Voiture embourbée*; two parodies – *L'Iliade travestie* (1716), in which is to be found an engraving of the Greek gods in the shape and costume of Arlequin and Pierrot, and one of Fénelon's Télémaque; and a series of articles on the different social classes of Paris. This sporadic output is of interest today only in so far as it throws light on the genesis of Marivaux's talent. Many of the adventures in his narratives are borrowed from other picaresque novels. The parodies, resembling those of Fielding, as well as Cervantes, are exercises in a conventional style then much in vogue. When Marivaux ridiculed Homer, or transposed his long-drawn-out and unfinished parody of *Télémaque* to the end of the reign of Louis XIV, he was merely following a trend. The success of this genre owes much to the Quarrel of the Ancients and the Moderns. Fontenelle, La Motte, and members of the salon of Mme de Lambert used parody to undermine the supporters of the classical tradition. Fénelon, however, was able to combine considerable art as a storyteller with his fancies. Marivaux did little else than show his own originality in occasional flashes of humour, touches of realism, and subtle psychology.

For Marivaux, on the threshold of sustained effort, these long but minor works presented exercises in writing that prepared him for the next and urgent stage of his career. It was at this moment that certain factors of his life came into new focus. From the moment of his arrival in Paris, Marivaux had found his spiritual home in the salons of his day. It is quite clear, from the pattern of his life, that he could not live without the frequent opportunity of moving in congenial society, and he was fortunate in that by the early eighteenth century salon society had reached its zenith, eclipsing in intelligence, polish, and spontaneity even the celebrated salons of the reign of Louis XIV.

Every Tuesday Marivaux was a welcome guest in the Hôtel de Nevers where, since 1710, Mme la marquise de Lambert held her 'at home', and into whose circle he had been introduced by Fontenelle and La Motte. Conversation sparkled and ranged widely under the patronage of the intelligent and sensitive marquise, who had the enviable gift of stimulating her guests to offer of their best.

At ease among the kindred spirits gathered together by the marquise, Marivaux the born spectator noted the delicacy of feeling, of manner, of movement, and of verbal interchange that prevailed in that society. He, the born dramatist, absorbed the minute change of stress or intonation in the expression of a subtle idea, the ability to convey a complex experience by the inflection of a voice or the movement of a hand, and the lilting *badinage* that covered a multitude of emotional reflexes. So exactly was Marivaux the artist identified with the life of the salons that it was believed until recently that Marivaux's style was an exact transcription of the formal language spoken in the salons: but a recent critic, F. Deloffre, after an exhaustive examination, has convincingly reported: 'le marivaudage fait survivre un art de la conversation tel qu'il n'en avait peut-être jamais existé.'[8]

It is certain that he found the manner and being of his characters in the salon, but the stage upon which he placed them was created from another source. Part of his pleasure as a young man of wealth and leisure had been, typically enough, frequent attendance at the theatre. As the latent dramatist within him stirred, he turned more frequently, and with deepening interest, to the Italian theatre, established in Paris under the patronage of the regent, Philippe duc d'Orléans. It is interesting to note in passing that Marivaux, who was revolted by the corruption of the Orleanists and the decadence of the court, nevertheless had one thing in common with the regent – a wholehearted appreciation of Italian comedy. He wrote several plays for the Théâtre Français, among them a five-act tragedy in verse, *Annibal* (1720), but, with the possible exception of *La [Seconde] Surprise de l'amour* (1727), none was as successful as the comedies he wrote for the Italian players, from *Arlequin poli par l'amour* (1722) to *Le Jeu de l'amour et du hasard* (1730) and *L'Epreuve* (1740). He needed, for his finest work, to write for a specific company and particular actors, and it is significant that he did not find the conditions he was seeking among his compatriots. It was a curious amalgam of salon society and Italian comedy that nourished his original genius.

[8] F. Deloffre, *Marivaux et le marivaudage*, 1955, p. 500.

The salons exerted as beneficent an influence upon his private as upon his professional life. His views upon religion, politics, art, literature, and matters of taste were shared by his friends: and they were at one with him in their attitude towards the great controversies of the age. One of his close associates was Fontenelle, nephew of the great Corneille and permanent secretary of the Académie des Sciences, a playwright of little distinction, but a considerable thinker and a notable social figure of his time. In Mme de Lambert's house he frequently met Montesquieu, and also La Motte, champion of the progressives against the traditionalists. With the death of Mme de Lambert in 1733, he lost this perfect setting for his growing talent, and although he frequented other salons in subsequent years, he never again found a social background so exactly to his taste. He was welcomed, however, by Mme de Tencin, into whose circle he was drawn from 1730, and, after 1753, by Mme du Deffand, and also Mme Geoffrin, whose salon had opened in 1749.

As the years flowed by, Marivaux found himself in the isolated position of a man who had outlived his reputation in the worlds of theatre and literature and his own generation of distinguished men and women. His wife, Colombe Bologne, whom he had married in 1717, had died in 1723, and the daughter of that marriage, their only child, had in 1746 taken her vows and entered a nunnery (perhaps because he was then too poor to provide her with an adequate dowry), so that he was without close family relations. Madame de Tencin had obtained a pension for him through Mme de Pompadour, and he had been unanimously elected to the Académie Française in 1742, in preference to Voltaire. In 1759 he was elected Director of the Académie Française by ballot, but official honours did not disguise his isolation and loneliness. In 1744 he was fortunate in being invited to set up house with Mlle de Saint-Jean, first in the Rue Saint-Honoré and later in the Rue de Richelieu. They took out a joint annuity of 2,800 livres. D'Alembert, whose *Eloge de Marivaux* is one of our main sources of information on the author, and a penetrating appreciation of the man and his work, wrote that their association, which had obvious practical advantages, 'remplit ses dernières années de douceur et de paix'. In 1761 Marivaux received from the publisher Duchesne 500 livres, for a volume of *pièces détachées* and for *Félicie*, *Les Acteurs de bonne foi* (pub. 1757), and *L'Amante frivole* (now lost). He died on 12 February 1763, aged seventy-five.

The curve of his creative output shows clearly the significance of the salon of Mme de Lambert. Not only were several of his major plays, including his masterpiece, *Le Jeu de l'amour et du hasard*, written during the years when he frequented Mme de Lambert's, but his novels, *La Vie de Marianne* (1731–41) and *Le Paysan parvenu* (1734–35), are so impregnated with the atmosphere of her milieu, and so typical, in their different form, of the work of Marivaux the playwright, that they may properly be described as a memorial to the salon which, more than any other, answered his needs as man and artist.

Yet there are other dates that mark turning-points in his literary career. The year 1717 is important, since it shows Marivaux feeling his way in different directions. He wrote his *Réflexions* on the world around him, mostly in the form of sketches and in a style recalling La Bruyère, for the *Nouveau Mercure* (1717–19). His *Lettres contenant une aventure*, published in the *Norveau Mercure* (1720), are held to show Marivaux's early insight into feminine psychology. The year 1720 is of quite outstanding significance. Marivaux seems to have tested the reaction of his public to very different forms of literary production. In October 1720, at the age of thirty-two, he produced for the Théâtre Italien a short one-act play, *Arlequin poli par l'amour*. In December he presented his tragedy *Annibal* at the Théâtre Français. This five-act play is in competent, but undistinguished and flaccid, verse. It had three performances only, and its failure probably led Marivaux to abandon this genre, and to write all his comedies in prose. On 3 March he had offered *L'Amour et la Vérité*, written in collaboration with the chevalier de Saint-Jorry, a play of which only the prologue has survived. It was *Arlequin poli par l'amour* which appealed to the public and determined the evolution and style of his plays. It is in the tradition of the *commedia dell'arte*, and not that of Molière, that his work may best be judged.[9]

From the ferment of the Renaissance in Italy there sprang a form of popular theatre that bore strange resemblances to the farces and mime-shows of the ancient Roman theatre, and which was known as *commedia dell'arte*. During the 400 years it was in vogue it gradually developed into a sophisticated group-theatre, of a wholly creative kind. It soon grew roots in France. Essentially non-scripted, it had stimulated Molière in the seventeenth century, and the return to Italy in 1697 of a well-established Italian company had left a void which the theatre of the fairgrounds at Saint-Laurent and Saint-Germain had only partially filled. In 1716, however, a new company, led by Luigi Riccoboni, better known as Lelio, was settled by the regent in the Hôtel de Bourgogne. This company, formed under the distinguished patronage of Antonio Farnese, duke of Parma, was of outstanding quality. It retained at

[9] See X. de Courville, *Luigi Riccoboni, dit Lelio*, 1942–45; and R. Niklaus 'La Comédie italienne et Marivaux', *Studies in Honour of Carlo Pellegrini*, vol. II, 1963.

first its Italian *repertorio*, representing in traditional manner plots involving Pantalone, Il Dottore, Isabella, Lelio, Arlecchino, and Colombine, and other masks such as Pulcinella, Scaramuccia, and so on, and indeed continued to do so until 1762. But to meet the taste of its public it had to do more than refine the stock characters and the traditional masks. It turned increasingly to renderings in French of an Italian scenario, and finally, when the actors had acquired the language, presented scripted plays in French. In this theatre, Arlecchino was the key figure. Sometimes loutish and crude, sometimes witty, intelligent, and cunning, he was a protean character and held a special fascination for Marivaux, as is evidenced by the fact that Arlequin figures in fourteen of the eighteen or nineteen plays he wrote for the Italian players.

Marivaux found all the elements of his creative vision already present in the Italian theatre, the gracious lovers with their elegant courtesy and the family of masked clowns bringing laughter and relief to the romantic tension. He noted their technique: their stylised gestures, expert mime, active pattern of movement, intimacy in playing together, and their exact timing. He found there plot, characters, and stagecraft to realise his own dramatic powers. Riccoboni himself, besides being an actor, was a writer of some distinction, a scholar, and a linguist, and had made his name as a tragic actor before becoming the Lelio of *commedia dell'arte*. He led a lifelong crusade against the licentiousness and profligacy that marked the theatre of his day. His wife, Elena Balleti, who played the Lady under the name of Flaminia, also belonged by birth and training to the distinguished line of traditional Italian players, and was herself a scholar, linguist, and musician. Thomassin (Tomasso Antonio Vicentini) was the Arlequin of Lelio's company. He was a gentle, sensitive, complex, and highly intelligent man who might almost have been created by Marivaux to play a family of Arlequins so exquisitely different from all the others. Largely through him Marivaux achieved the final transformation of Arlecchino. In a succession of remarkable plays:

Arlequin poli par l'amour (1720)
La Surprise de l'amour (1722)
La Double Inconstance (1723)
Le Prince travesti (1724)
La Fausse Suivante (1724)
L'Ile des esclaves (1725)
L'Héritier de village (1725)
Le Triomphe de Plutus (1728)
La Colonie (first performed in 1729 in a text subsequently lost)
Le Jeu de l'amour et du hasard (1730)

Le Triomphe de l'amour (1735)
L'Heureux Stratagème (1733)
La Méprise (1734)
Les Fausses Confidences (1737)

the different elements added to Arlequin over the years by the great actors that played him were fused and polished, to release the core of poetry he had always carried within him. Marivaux gave Arlequin a subtlety and a delicacy of spirit that were his own, and the Bergamask[10] clod emerges from the comedies as an exquisite *galant*, intelligent, sensitive, gracious, and elegant, the poetic creation of an original genius. Not the least striking factor in this transformation is the manner in which these radical changes were established in Marivaux's first comedy for the Italian players, *Arlequin poli par l'amour*.[11] At the opening of the play we see, for the last time, the original Arlecchino of early *commedia dell'arte*, brutish, crude, and stupid. Within the brief space of the play's single act we watch his transformation by the power of love into an enchanting creature of mythology, witty and elegant enough to find his spiritual home in the salon of Mme de Lambert. Thomassin, in his own person, was Marivaux's clown, humour made flesh – gentle, subtle, graceful, agile, mischievous, fantastic, enchanting, and unexpected. With his technical and traditional training added to his natural qualities, he was able to play each one of the several Arlequins created by Marivaux – the mature Arlequin of *La Surprise de l'amour*, the primitive one of *Le Jeu de l'amour et du hasard*, and the dolt of *Les Fausses Confidences* (1737) – with as much apparent ease and certain success as he had covered the whole history of Arlecchino from his rustic Bergamask days to his witty eighteenth-century elegance in *Arlequin poli par l'amour*; he later sustained that transformation in *La Double Inconstance*. But important as was the influence of Thomassin upon Marivaux the dramatist, that of Silvia, the *seconde amoureuse*, brought to Paris in 1716 at the age of fifteen to capture the heart of Parisian theatregoers, was even greater. She incarnated the *ingénue* of Marivaux's comedies. It has been recorded that her radiance was so undimmed by age that even at fifty she was able to create upon the stage the illusion of youthful beauty. Inspired by her personality and by her special accomplishments as an actress, Marivaux created his iridescent heroines, those graceful and disturbing young girls over whom lies a golden enchantment. Silvia, with her mobile face, her natural charm and studied grace, her gaiety and her

10 Adjective frequently applied to Arlecchino, who came from Lower Bergamo.

11 See *Arlequin poli par l'amour*, edited by Thelma and R. Niklaus. University of London Press, 1956.

vitality, was for him the quintessence of enchantment. For over 200 years, *commedia dell'arte*, however laden with farcical acrobatics and humorous sub-plots to please a popular audience, had been romantic in inspiration and its characters suffered, however superficially, all the vicissitudes and triumphs of love. The magically remote world in which Isabella worked out her love-plots, among a crowd of extraordinary masked clowns, was the world of fantasy into which Marivaux's characters could enter most naturally. The *repertorio* of the Lovers, by this time refined and polished by the generations of distinguished men and women who had played these parts, by proximity to court circles, and by the literary self-consciousness of the time, was already within the orbit of Marivaux's natural idiom. Lelio's company completed professionally and socially the liberation of the artist, begun by force of circumstances – the bankruptcy of Law, that compelled Marivaux after 1720 to engage upon earning his own living – and by the influence of the salons of Mme de Lambert and her successors.

In Marivaux's plays there is little characterisation in the sense in which Molière understood the term. He does not deal with people so much as with stock types, yet he gives his characters personality and life. He excels at presenting a gallery of *amoureuses*, ranging from the *ingénue* to the *coquette*, usually clever and witty, temporarily deceitful but ultimately sincere. His Silvie is at once naïve and sophisticated, innocent and worldly, the victim of chance and of temperament. The heroes are from the start caught up in the *jeu de l'amour*, for love has taken them by surprise. Marivaux, in his brilliant, sophisticated dialogue, now called *marivaudage*, is as terse as in his novels he could be diffuse and explicit. The essence of his comedy is not to be found in the written word alone, although the imaginative reader can conjure up the *jeu de scène*, and the talented actor is given all the directions he needs. No other playwright has been able to stage the love relationship as Marivaux saw it. It is never purely gratuitous, never essentially sensual, although the awakening of sensuality attends its birth. It is not cerebral, nor romantic, nor libertine, the terms in which it was largely understood in the society of the time. For Marivaux, the core of interest in the *jeu de l'amour* lies in the delicate nuances of feeling liberated, the fine shades of emotional experience, the conveying of inexpressible relationships between two people in love, and in the approach and withdrawal, avowal and retraction, discovery and concealment, misunderstanding and revelation, leading always to the point of truth. In his plays the curtain comes down when the protagonists have recognised and confessed their love, overcome any vicissitudes engendered by it, and met together in their moment of complete sincerity. His comedy never derives, as Molière's so often does, from ill-matched couples, from the contrast between the romantic ideal and the sad reality; nor does his drama ever arise from a conflict of emotion and personality in love relationships which will either cause the lovers to fret each other into irritation and separation, or to achieve, after severe tribulation, a relationship akin to their first recognition, but essentially deeper and more lasting. Aware that in all men there is more than a germ of self-love, he tempered the moment of truth by the reflection that, for each protagonist, love is a personal emotion, based upon personal need heightened by imagination, so that in most cases the moment of truth is also the only moment of selfless love.

There is another recurring character in Marivaux's plays that has only recently aroused interest and curiosity. It is that of Trivelin, first found in *Arlequin poli par l'amour*, who is used to further the plot and act as a kind of chorus. It is he who opens the play with the Fairy, helps to expose her unpleasant character, and finally brings about the right dénouement. As the Fairy's valet, he plays his part in shaping the destinies of those around him; as chorus, he is the intelligent spectator presiding, sometimes invisibly, over events, helping the audience to draw correct inferences from the situations presented, and to foresee others. It is almost as if Trivelin represented Marivaux himself, present on stage and elaborating his play as he goes along. Such a spectator-character, commonly found in Marivaux's plays, offers an interesting glimpse of the man who works the puppets. Much of the subtlety of the comedies is derived from ambivalent viewpoints presented as cross-patterns, on the one hand by intelligent, understanding underlings, and on the other by the highly tensed, emotionally charged antagonists, too self-absorbed to be able to assess the situation objectively. Trivelin is the basic design for characters more fully developed in *La Surprise de l'amour La Double Inconstance*, *Les Serments indiscrets* (1732), *Le Petit Maître corrigé* (1734), *Le Legs* (1736), and *L'Epreuve*, who add enormously to the artist symmetry of the play.[12]

In these later plays, the love ploys of valet and *soubrette*, subordinated to those of their masters, yet following a similar, though less distinguished, pattern, form a counterpoint to the major plot, offering another perspective, one that allows even more scrupulous analysis of the birth of love. The valet presents a simplified anticipation of his master's experience, forewarning and so heightening the awareness and understanding of the spectator, at a moment when the major protagonists are themselves blinded by love and

[12] Cf. J. Rousset, 'Marivaux et la structure du double registre', *Studi Francesi*, Jan.–April 1957, pp. 58–68.

unable to see the implications of their situation. The term *marivaudage* was coined in the eighteenth century and used to characterise the form of *préciosité* in vogue between 1720 and 1730. The word first appeared in a letter written by Diderot to Sophie Volland on 16 October 1760, and Diderot makes similar use of it in another letter dated 6 November of the same year. In both letters, it is meant to express at once the endless speculation on minor points common to salon society, and also the excessive refinement of moral analysis in which it indulged; and in spite of an expressed admiration for Marivaux, there is a pejorative note in Diderot's usage of the term. Its meaning was soon extended to define a literary style, as used by the critic La Harpe in the following definition:

C'est le mélange le plus bizarre de métaphysique subtile et de locutions triviales, de sentiments alambiqués et de dictons populaires. (*Lycée*, 1797, 3e partie, I, p. 5.)

Later, in the nineteenth century, the critic Sainte-Beuve equally withheld praise:

Qui dit 'marivaudage' dit plus ou moins badinage à froid, espièglerie compassée et prolongée, pétillement redoublé et prétentieux, enfin une sorte de pédantisme sémillant et joli. (*Causeries du lundi*, IX, 1854.)

On the other hand, both the poet Théophile Gautier and the critic Jules Janin highly approved of 'ce style vif, ingénieux, subtil', and it is interesting to note that, since its inception, the word has been used in a pejorative or a complimentary sense according to the taste of the user.

Like all terms that become part of a living tongue, *marivaudage* acquired new meaning as time went on. In our day, the Larousse Dictionary offers this definition: '*Marivauder* – Imiter le style, l'afféterie de Marivaux. Faire des galanteries raffinées.' Within these terms of reference, the word is a synonym for lighthearted, sophisticated *badinage*, and is commonly used, for example by French film critics, in referring to the love dialogue of certain American films, which has only a distant relationship to the charming *badinage* of *Le Jeu de l'amour et du hasard*. Yet for the more informed literary critic, *marivauder* is to indulge in light and graceful word-play with serious intent. The complex dialogue of Marivaux's plays is conditioned by his sincerity, and by his desire to give full expression to hitherto inexpressible aspects of emotion. Language was one of the instruments of his design, and with his unique blending of salon conversation, the *repertorio* of the lovers of Italian comedy, and his idiosyncratic speech,[13] he forged an

[13] Noted by his contemporary d'Alembert, who frequented the same salons, in these terms: 'Il croyait être naturel dans ses comédies, parce que le style qu'l prête à ses acteurs est cclui qu'il avait lui-même' (*Eloge de Marivaux*).

instrument fitted to his purpose, enabling him to exploit the ambiguity of words to underline the ambiguity of the love relation in its early stages, and their clarity at the moment of truth. His flexible and original dialogue has inspired others, among them Beaumarchais and Musset, to such a degree that contemporary French comedy is haunted by its echoes. *Marivaudage*, then, used by Diderot in a fit of exasperation, serves to cover almost any aspect of Marivaux's work or its total values, and by extension any literary style having some connection with the dialogue of his plays. The persistence of the term bears unwitting tribute to the unique quality of Marivaux's creative genius and its strength under a deceptive appearance of fragility.

His creativeness can in fact be assessed at two levels, the one superficial and emotional, the other intellectual. At the first level, he offers a delightful medley of fantasy, graceful *badinage*, romance and farce, and song and dance, blended into the typical eighteenth-century *divertissement* and expressed in a language both naïve and *précieux*. There is not one element here that could not be found in the scenario of late Italian comedy, but Marivaux had fused these elements into a pattern rich and strange, and previously unknown. His characters are set among delightful vistas, in a fairy's garden, an enchanted meadow, an eighteenth-century salon, or on a far distant island, shimmering in some never-never land of his own invention. His plays have the charm of a *fête champêtre*, and over them hangs the impalpable beauty and promise of Watteau's 'Embarquement pour Cythère' (1717).

Under Marivaux's spell, we enter the kingdom of perpetual youth and beauty, where lovers meet in that breathless flash of recognition, moving gracefully towards their moment of truth, and disappearing in all their radiance towards Cythera. Beneath this golden and poetic creation is another, more enduring, without which Marivaux's kingdom could not exist. It is supported by skilful play-structure, and by the serious content of each comedy underlying its first frivolous appearance. Each scene leads inevitably to the next, building towards the climax, the moment of truth; swept along on the tide of the *surprise de l'amour*, each character, knowingly or unknowingly, contributes to the climax, and after the revelation reacts in such a way as to compel the spectator to understand and accept the importance and value of that moment.

The dialogue is a potent instrument in this classical scene development. Attention is caught and held by its unusual quality; the impact of phrases of deceptive simplicity, laden with undertones given by the play of voice, facial expression, gesture, and movement, and by the lively repartee in which the antagonists indulge with the skill of the born duellists, parrying thrust and counter-thrust with rapier flash of witty epigram. The interest of the spectator, already aroused, is quickened by subtle variations in the tempo of speech and movement cleverly adjusted to the context, by the alternation of mime and the spoken word, dialogue and soliloquy, and by the symmetrical patterns of Mistress and Lover, Maid and Valet. The structure supports the enchantment, and both contribute to Marivaux's love theme, which is the core and essence of all his best comedies, as it is of his genius. With an almost feminine perception, he was able to describe the birth and awakening of love. Marivaux, a man of penetrating lucidity and infinite tenderness, probed deeply into the moral and psychological implications of love, and his discoveries were set down against a radiant background of fantasy, in a love pattern that is never completed; we never know whether Silvia lived happily ever after. We have a new comedy of love – the double game of love; an exteriorisation, on the one hand, in quarrels, approaches, repulses, and reconciliations, nicely calculated to foster and cherish the delicate growth of love; and its subconscious quickening, betrayed by a half-gesture, an intonation, an unexpected phrase, an apparent inconsequence of mood or speech. In *Arlequin poli par l'amour* we find the genesis of Marivaux's highly individual talent, just as we find there also in germ the reasons for the coining of the term *marivaudage*, its multiple use, and its persistent identity with Marivaux himself.

It is with *Le Jeu de l'amour et du hasard* that his genius reaches its maturity. It is a comedy of love, the love of Dorante and Silvia, paralleled by the love of Arlequin and Lisette, their servants. Silvia disguises herself as a serving wench to test her lover, but, with the connivance of her kindly father Orgon, Dorante has recourse to the same stratagem. The servants, although intelligent, witty, and sensitive, have not the polish of their masters and provide subtle comic effects within a general framework of seemly decorum. The lovers share a romantic outlook, and cherish the mirage of an ideal marriage founded on perfect love. Silvia has the normal feminine vanity, but she is also sincere and full of charm and vitality, a perfect match for the elegant Dorante. Marivaux brings out clearly in this play that truth must prevail and the mask which hides our deepest feelings must ultimately fall. The play, with its simple plot, has been worked out with consummate skill. Never has the awakening of love been studied in such detail and with such success on any stage. Here, as in *Les Fausses Confidences*, which deals with a young widow about to fall in love, love inevitably conquers prejudice. The subtlety and diversity of Marivaux's portrayal of the love game is well expressed

LIBRARY
EISENHOWER COLLEGE

by d'Alembert in the following passage concerning the comedies:

> C'est tantôt un amour ignoré des deux amants; tantôt un amour qu'ils sentent et qu'ils veulent se cacher l'un à autre; tantôt un amour timide et qui n'ose se déclarer; tantôt un amour incertain et comme indécis, un amour à demi-né, pour ainsi dire, dont ils se doutent, sans en être bien sûrs, et qu'ils épient au dedans d'eux-mêmes, avant de lui laisser prendre l'essor.[14]

His characters wish to love but cannot allow themselves to, and are in a state of bewilderment. Chance has played them a strange turn. 'J'aime, mais je n'aime plus ce que j'aimais', discovers one lover, whilst with equal lucidity another declares: 'Maintenant, je vois clair dans mon cœur.' Marivaux focuses our attention, as G. Poulet has pointed out,[15] on the distance that separates immediate emotion from its recognition by the conscious mind. This 'distance' is the duration of the comedy in which the characters 'se hâtent lentement'. As Voltaire has said, Marivaux's plays are 'une conversation sous un lustre', but in a deeper sense than he believed. But this conversation, which might have been full of anguish, is, miraculously, happy and gay.

There are comedies of Marivaux that may be classified under headings other than *comédies d'amour*. M. Arland distinguishes *comédies d'intrigue, de moeurs, de caractère, comédies sociales ou philosophiques*; *comédies, allégoriques, comédies héroïques* (*Le Prince travesti*), *fantaisies exemplaires*, and *drames bourgeois*. These classifications are arbitrary and in one sense all his comedies are *comédies d'amour*, the domain he excelled in. *La Surprise de l'amour*, *La Double Inconstance*, *Le Jeu de l'amour et du hasard*, *Les Fausses Confidences*, and *L'Epreuve* are masterpieces in this vein, but Arland's detailed classification[16] brings out the range of Marivaux's talent and the experimental nature of much of his drama, which his contemporaries wrongly considered repetitive because they failed to appreciate delicate variations on a theme.

L'Ile des esclaves is an enlightened piece of satire set on an island inhabited by the descendants of former slaves, who had established a model community there. Four Europeans, two masters and two slaves, are shipwrecked nearby and the ensuing adventures allow Marivaux to satirise social privilege. *L'Ile de la raison* (1727) presents European society through the eyes of foreigners endowed with the light of reason. Both these plays are satirical in tone. *La Nouvelle Colonie ou La Ligue des femmes* (1729; a three-act comedy, later redrafted in one act under the title of *La Colonie*) is a drama of ideas. It deals with the question of equality between

[14] Cf. *Œuvres complètes*, vol. II, 1967, p. 584.
[15] Cf. *Etudes sur le temps humain*, vol. II, 1952, pp. 1–34.
[16] Cf. *Marivaux*, 1950, pp. 97–194, esp. pp. 188–92.

the sexes and there are some deft touches of satire couched in gentle and gracious language, which do not obscure Marivaux's rationalist approach to his subject and his advanced views. *L'Ecole des mères* (1732) and *La Mère confidente* (1735) are a study of the relationship between mother and daughter. Marivaux shows his awareness of the social and economic problems of his day, and of the various forms of inequality and injustice from which his contemporaries suffered, themes he developed more fully in his novels and in *Le Spectateur français*. We have noted that Marivaux, although relatively poor, was extremely charitable, and his statement in *Le Jeu de l'amour et du hasard*: 'Va dans ce monde il faut être un peu trop bon pour l'être assez' (Act I, scene 2), with its careful qualifications and happy nuance, reflects the author's approach to life as well as any other. He was a careful and charitable observer of his age, and sympathetic to the underdog. He used social barriers, real or fictitious, as elements in plot structure, as in *Le Jeu de l'amour et du hasard*, *Les Fausses Confidences*, *La Double Inconstance*, etc., and *Le Préjugé vaincu* could serve as a subtitle for many of his plays. *L'Héritier de village* brings out well the relationship between money and rank, but he does poke fun at the newly rich. He was certainly no revolutionary. Although he painted an unflattering picture of court life, and raised some significant political questions, as for instance in *La Double Inconstance*, in which Arlequin says: 'Allez, vous êtes mon prince, et je vous aime bien, mais je suis votre sujet, et cela mérite quelque chose' (Act III, scene 5), he was a moralist, indirectly urging reforms, rather than a politician. In this he reflects the prevailing mentality in the salon of Mme de Lambert, and something of that of the *grand siècle*, the *préciosité* of a La Rochefoucauld, and the intelligent detachment, slightly disillusioned yet kindly, of Fontenelle. He retains the discretion, the sensitive but restrained emotion, and the deep humanity of an earlier age, but he moved away from the religious inspiration of a Fénelon, to a secular conception of *bienfaisance*, and shared the new philosophical outlook. *La Mère confidente* in some respects anticipates the philosophical *drame bourgeois* of Diderot. His feminism may be linked with that of Mme de Lambert, who published in 1737 a *Traité de l'éducation des filles*, and with Fénelon's work with the same title (1687); but also with that of the later Diderot, on whom he exercised a greater influence than has yet been acknowledged. Although Marivaux was a believer and one who accepted the doctrine of original sin, which the *philosophes* had rejected, he based his moral philosophy on natural reason and instinct rather than on dogma, and saw men bound together by a *contrat de justice*, to use his own phrase, spontaneously acknowledged by all. In his journals, he indulged in sentimental moralising and philosophising. But these one-man journals, which were on the model of Addison's *Spectator* – *Le Spectateur français* (1722), *L'Indigent philosophe* (1728), and *Le Cabinet du philosophe* (1734) – reflect Marivaux's own tastes and attitudes as well as the general spirit of the age, and they contain a wealth of anecdotes and short stories, and penetrating observations of great inherent interest.

The same understanding of life is to be found in his major novels, *La Vie de Marianne* and *Le Paysan parvenu*. F. Deloffre points out[17] that the isolation of Marivaux's plays from the rest of his work, and from their historical background, has preserved their poetry for us intact, but he also notes the close connection between works such as *La Vie de Marianne*, begun when Marivaux was thirty-nine and finally abandoned unfinished when he was over fifty, and *Le Paysan parvenu*, with *Le Cabinet du philosophe* and plays such as *L'Heureux Stratagème*, *Le Jeu de l'amour et du hasard*, *Les Serments indiscrets*, *Le Legs*, *Les Fausses Confidences*, and *L'Epreuve*. In his book *Marivaux par lui-même*, P. Gazagne has in like manner underlined the connection between the psychology of love in *La Vie de Marianne* and that in the plays. In the plays, the presentation is subtle, suggested by a few, well-chosen words and half-sketched gestures, since Marivaux could rely on his actors for an appropriate interpretation. In the novels, it is equally subtle but more explicit, developed in such detail that a modern reader thinks of Proust. The background, consisting of a wealth of social detail, *tableaux de mœurs* and *portraits à clé*, provides a historical record of considerable value.

Marivaux underwent a long apprenticeship in the art of fiction. By the age of twenty-five he had written a satirical tale, *Le Bilboquet*, a story, *La Voiture embourbée*, and three long novels each consisting of two volumes, *Les Effets surprenants de la sympathie* (1712–13), *Pharsamon* (1713), and *Le Télémaque travesti* (1714). *Pharsamon*, *La Voiture embourbée*, and *Le Télémaque travesti* belong to the Spanish and French picaresque tradition and may be considered as essays in parody and the burlesque. This vein was exploited most successfully in *Le Paysan parvenu* (1734–35), but also, with less success, in the earlier *L'Indigent philosophe* (1726–27). On the other hand, *Les Effets de la sympathie*, certain passages in *La Voiture embourbée*, and *Pharsamon* are in the tradition of the sentimental novel, harking back to Spanish and French sources, namely *Los Trabajos de Persiles y Sigismunda, historia septentrional* (1617) and *Novelas ejemplares* of Cervantes, and the novels of D'Urfé, La Calprenède, Gomberville, Mlle de Scudéry, Mme de La Fayette, and Mme de Villedieu. The highlight in this distinctive form of

[17] In his edition of *La Vie de Marianne*, 1957, pp. ii, xxxix.

novel was reached with *La Vie de Marianne*, very different in tone from *Le Paysan parvenu*.

If it is to be properly understood, *La Vie de Marianne ou Les Aventures de Madame la comtesse de* *** needs to be seen in the context of the *genre romanesque ou galant*. Marivaux's initial theme is to be found in *Les Effets surprenants de la sympathie*, as is the curious detachment from his work and its conventions noted also in plays such as *Arlequin poli par l'amour*, *Le Prince travesti*, and *Les Fausses Confidences*. Marianne is a young girl of unknown but probably noble parentage who is brought up by villagers. Her early misfortune and the mystery surrounding her birth and person arouse interest and sympathy, and there is the sense that a great destiny lies before her. The self-analysis, the commentary on life, and much of the general moralising come from her pen, and not that of the author. But the narrator is an older Marianne than the one whose experiences are being retold. Marivaux's debt to Courtilz de Sandras' *Les Mémoires de Monsieur de B.* (1711), first pointed out by André Le Breton in *Le Roman au XVIIIe siècle*, has been underlined by F. Deloffre. Sandras taught Marivaux how to mingle truth and fiction whilst preserving verisimilitude, and to pay attention to *minutiae* in depicting the background of his characters. Many of the themes and fictional techniques of *La Vie de Marianne* are therefore to be found, albeit in embryonic form, in his earlier and little-known work, and in that of contemporary and earlier writers. Parallels may be drawn between passages in *La Vie de Marianne* and in *Le Spectateur français*. Again, a character such as Climal in *La Vie de Marianne* can be compared with Tartuffe in Molière's play, and Onuphre in La Bruyère's *Caractères*. Yet in the very first pages of *La Vie de Marianne* Marivaux's own genius stands out, as again in the highly original scene in which the libertine and the *ingénue* are confronted. If we examine the love story as such, the main source is no doubt *Les Illustres Françoises* (1713) by Robert Chasles, which may also have inspired Prévost and Richardson..[18] In particular the story *L'Histoire de M. de Contamine et d'Angélique* held his attention. But Marivaux relied chiefly on his own great powers of observation. He drew on Mme de Lambert for the character of Mme de Miran, and perhaps for some episodes in the work. He depicted Mme de Tencin under the name of Mme Dorsin. Names of real people have been put forward for Mlle de Fare, for the Minister in the sixth part of the novel, and for the officer who proposes to Marianne in the eighth part. Some episodes are so developed that they stand apart from the novel, as for instance the

[18] Cf. H. Roddier, 'Robert Challes, inspirateur de Richardson et de l'abbé Prévost', *Revue de Littérature comparée*, 1947, t. XXI, pp. 5–38.

story of the nun without vocation, consumed by passion in her convent, a story which left its impression on Diderot's *La Religieuse*. Here his main source of inspiration may have been the famous *Lettres d'une religieuse portugaise* (1669) by G. de Lavergne, sieur de Guilleragues, attributed to Mariana Alcoforado.[19]

La Vie de Marianne ou Les Aventures de la comtesse de *** is the autobiography of a young girl who escaped from an accident on the road to Bordeaux, in which her parents were killed. She is now alone in the world and is taken in by the sister of an old *curé*, upon whose death she finds herself, at the age of fifteen, left once again to her own resources in Paris. She becomes a *lingère*, and is exposed to the machinations of an old hypocrite, M. de Climal. She meets the comte de Valville, whom she would no doubt have married in the end, had the novel been brought to a conclusion, in spite of being locked up in a convent and in spite of Valville's infidelity. Marianne is a coquette, but retains much of the principles inculcated in her by the sister of the *curé*. She is even capable of courage, as when she declines to marry Valville, whom she adores. The secondary characters, from M. de Climal to Mme de Miran, the generous grand lady, are well depicted. The last three books recount the story of a certain Tervire, a girl forsaken by her mother and succoured by strangers, and that of a mother abandoned by her favoured son and comforted by the very daughter whom she had sacrificed, an edifying tale which Marivaux had not the heart to finish. The interest of the novel as a whole is not in the story itself but in the picture of a woman's life it offers. It is a full life which, however, cannot be brought to its logical conclusion, since the narrator can hardly describe her own death. But if Marivaux left his novel unfinished it is scarcely for this simple reason, but rather that he grew tired of his heroine or that he felt his public had done so. Certain features of the work have held the attention of critics, such as Marivaux's emphasis on destiny rather than chance determining events and giving life its meaning. Fate, which is seen as both helpful and unkind, is constantly referred to as 'mon étoile'. As a result, the protagonists remain strangely passive. Marianne, unlike Jacob in *Le Paysan parvenu*, never loses faith in her destiny, and is not constantly endeavouring to shape events, although she is quick to take advantage of any favourable circumstance. It has been pointed out that Marivaux is not interested in dramatic scenes as such, but rather in pathos, so that *La Vie de Marianne* has therefore been hailed as the first *roman sensible*. There are many moving scenes,[20] but

[19] See introduction by F. Deloffre and J. Rougeot to *Lettres Portugaises, Valentins et autres œuvres de Guilleragues*, 1962.

[20] Cf. R. K. Jamieson, *Marivaux, a study in eighteenth-century sensibility*, 1941.

nothing horrific, nor are there any long-drawn-out scenes of physical suffering, illness, or death, as in the works of Prévost. Marivaux's view of life is perceptive and kindly, yet ironical. He is without illusion, but also without bitterness. The analysis of feeling becomes the very essence of life itself and Marianne's own observations, instead of impeding the development of the novel, enrich its fabric and justify its rhythm.[21] The events of the narrative inevitably arise from the need to unfold the psychology of the characters. It is for his ability to describe in depth, and with infinite care and subtlety, mature feelings and their evolution that Marivaux may be included among the small band of truly original novelists. He starts from careful introspection, using memory and intuition in his plausible reconstruction of past emotions, and in his effort to bring out the real motivation of human action and conduct. His sincerity is never in doubt.

Until recently, critics have deplored Marivaux's style, failing to understand that what at first sight appeared to be contrived was natural to him and necessary for the expression of his own peculiar sensibility. He had to make do with a vocabulary that did not as yet include *sentimental*, *intuitif*, *mental*, *amical*, *fortuit*, *fictif*, *affectif*, *affectivité*, and so on. He coined new words and expressions: *fictivement*, *amicablement*, *finesse de sentiment* (for *intuition*), and *effusion de coeur* (for *sentimentalité*). He is led to qualify his terms so as to make his precise meaning clear, and his sentences become involved, long, and sinuous phrases, not unlike those of Proust. He uses the tentative approach. Thus: 'pour enchanter, pour apprivoiser jusque là, comment dirai-je'; 'pour jeter dans de pareilles illusions . . .' He makes subtle use of rhythm to translate the stirrings of a human heart. Depth is obtained by skilful transpositions in time. Marianne, who tells her story, is sometimes the older woman she is supposed to be at the time of writing, sometimes the young person whose experience she is reliving: and the story gains from the alternation between the greater clarity of the retrospective mind and the occasional immediacy of the present tense. Sometimes Marianne is the mouthpiece of the author, sometimes she is indistinguishable from the reader. At times she is innocent and naïve, and at times retrospectively cunning. She is thus always complex and her unique personality is composed of a subtle blend of very diverse elements.

Le Paysan parvenu was composed during the interval that separates the drafting of the second and the third parts of *La Vie de Marianne* (1734–early 1735), no mean feat in view of the great difference between the two novels. But the five books of *Le Paysan parvenu* were also written at the same time as the draft of eleven

[21] Cf. C. Roy, *Lire Marivaux*, 1947, p. 87.

numbers of *Le Cabinet du philosophe* and two comedies, *La Méprise* and *La Mère confidente. Le Paysan parvenu* is in certain respects the antithesis of *La Vie de Marianne.* It is the story of a poor peasant, son of humble wine-growers, who starts off as a valet. Jacob leaves his village at the age of eighteen to seek his fortune in Paris. Thanks to his good looks, he is favoured by the ladies and through their good offices becomes a *fermier-général* (but only in the anonymous final section of the book). He finally returns to his home town and becomes the benefactor of his fellow-men. Jacob is in a way another Cliton, a character who appeared in *Pharsamon,* and parallels may be found in the novel with passages in *L'Indigent philosophe. Le Paysan parvenu* is in the tradition of *Lazarillo de Tormes,* of *Don Guzman de Alfarache,* and of *Francion.* Moving away from the burlesque vein, Marivaux concentrated on an objective observation of ordinary people, as Lesage had done in *Gil Blas.* Jacob needs to be studied with care. His rapid rise in fortune depends far more on chance than did that of Marianne, as one would expect in a novel derived from the picaresque tradition. He succeeds in integrating himself into successively higher levels of society and shares with Marianne a social consciousness very different from *Gil Blas'* mere observations of such levels. He recounts his adventures with an acceptance of experience and a great deal of moralising. He is a hedonist, unscrupulous in his actions and consequently incapable of sincere moral indignation. His standards are lower than those of Marianne, who has more heart and belongs to a higher social class. Some have asked whether Jacob was not in fact Marivaux. But we know too little of Marivaux's life story and inner feelings to warrant such an assumption. He has some of the physical attributes of Marivaux, and the *gros brunet,* or country bumpkin, is a recurring type in his novels and plays – one, moreover, that was fashionable during the regency. Jacob, as indeed Marianne, owes much to his creator, whose intuition, turn of mind, and powers of analysis he shares. It would have been strange if Marivaux had not given his characters something of his own personality and outlook. But one may be more greatly struck by his sheer creative genius, manifest in the bringing together of so many facets of personality with varying emphasis. F. Deloffre has suggested that Jacob is a forerunner of Versac in *Les Egarements du coeur et de l'esprit* by Crébillon, and of Valmont in *Les Liaisons dangereuses* by Laclos. But Jacob is not just the seducer or the libertine. Jacob is also an 'âme sensible', whose virtue is suspect; Marivaux shares his fellow-novelists' realism, not to say pessimism, and his picture of the society of his time is unflattering. All his characters are convincing, on account of a physical and mental portrait closely linked with their social background, and because of their individual way of experiencing and expressing their feelings. Jacob stands out from among a long list of self-seekers, of tax-gatherers and others of the kind, by the depth of the analysis, which is Marivaux's own contribution to the novel in general, and also by the unexpected complexities he reveals. He has his own brand of insolence, his personal dignity, and a feeling for independence. *Le Paysan parvenu*, like *La Vie de Marianne*, is unfinished. The last three parts are apocryphal[22] and of poorer quality than Mme Riccoboni's conclusion to *La Vie de Marianne*: they are quite different in conception, tone, and style. In both of Marivaux's great novels, the psychological commentary slows down the pace, but the halting and inconclusive movement and structure, which some consider to be an aesthetic blemish, have not dimmed the favoured position held by these works among the great novels of the century. Marivaux as playwright and novelist is a figure of consequence in world literature, whose stature is still growing.[23]

III. ABBÉ PRÉVOST

The life of the Abbé Antoine-François Prévost d'Exiles (1697–1763) reads like an adventure story, in which the picaresque blends with the romantic in a manner that is not usually associated with a monk or priest; and one, moreover, in which many important pages are still missing. He left fifty volumes of novels, twenty volumes of *Le Pour et Contre*, a journal he edited from 1733 to 1740, seventeen volumes of an *Histoire générale des voyages*, the first seven volumes of which are translated from English, and many volumes of translations, chiefly from English.

He was educated by the Jesuits at Hesdin in Artois, where his precocious intellect was noted and seemed to destin him for a career in the Church. At sixteen, however, he joined the army to fight in the War of the Spanish Succession (1712), but he soon became disillusioned with military life, and after pursuing his studies at the Collège d'Harcourt in Paris, he moved on to La Flèche (1717), where the Jesuits received him as a novice. He continued to show exceptional aptitude for study, but his temperament, his love of society and pleasure, and a persistent wish for freedom, soon led him to wish for another career. It is possible that he rejoined the army (1718–19) and also paid a first visit to

22 They were written by a Dutchman or a Frenchman living in Holland.
23 It is reported that *La Vie de Marianne* in a Japanese translation proved to be a Japanese best-seller and that Marivaux's plays draw packed audiences throughout the world, being received with quite exceptional enthusiasm in Latin America.

Holland; but the Church claimed him again, and was never to lose altogether its hold on his mind. His long association with the Jesuits and later with the Benedictines, who forgave him much and frequently saved him from the worst effects of his follies, was due to his religious conviction and sensibility, and his personal charm and plausibility when undertaking his own defence, at least as much as to the Church's natural reluctance to lose a man whose gifts might shed lustre on the order. Prévost would seem to have been involved in an unhappy love affair (1720), which may have led to his break with the Jesuits, for on returning from Holland he entered the Benedictine monastery of Saint-Wandrille. In December 1721 he took his vows at Jumièges, in the Benedictine congregation of Saint-Maur. He moved from abbey to abbey, studying theology and teaching the humanities, and occasionally becoming involved in religious controversies, such as that waged with the Jesuit Le Brun. He was ordained by the bishop of Amiens, and preached for a year at Evreux, where his eloquence won him recognition, then at the fashionable Blancs-Manteaux in Paris, moving on in 1728 to Saint-Germain-des-Prés, the principal centre of the Congrégation de Saint-Maur. He won a second prize for an *Ode sur Saint-François Xavier, apôtre des Indes* in a competition organised by the Academy (published in the *Mercure*, May 1728). He was now working on the monumental collective Benedictine publication *Gallia Christiana*, being himself responsible for a whole volume.

It was during this period that he regaled his fellow monks with stories, and began work on the *Mémoires d'un homme de qualité qui s'est retiré du monde* (published 1728–31, 7 vols.). He was fully aware of his own incompatibility with the monastic life, and requested his transference to the less rigid discipline of the general Benedictine order. He assumed that his request would be granted, and all would no doubt have been well, had he not left without formal permission, leaving behind him a letter of protest to his superiors. The latter ordered his arrest, the papal brief on which his hopes depended was not fulminated, and on 6 November 1728 a *lettre de cachet* was issued against him. Prévost, now at Amiens, was in an impossible and highly dangerous position. He fled to England, where he was introduced to the archbishop of Canterbury as a new convert to the Anglican faith. He remained in England from November 1728 to November 1730, acting as tutor to Francis, the only son of Sir John Eyles, a former Lord Mayor of London and Governor of the Bank of England, a Member of Parliament for the City of London (1727–34), and a director of the South Sea Company. In Sir John's house he met many distinguished writers, read widely in English literature, and made frequent visits to the theatre. He translated Congreve, Farquhar, Vanbrugh, Dryden, Otway, Shakespeare, Milton, Spenser, Prior, Addison, and Thomson. He became involved with Francis's sister Mary, and was planning to marry her secretly when Sir John, discovering this, ordered him to leave the country. He went to Holland, taking with him a number of manuscripts on which he had been working in England, including a translation into English of *Histoire du Président de Thou* (announced as a forthcoming publication 23 January 1731, published 1733), and especially *Histoire de M. Cleveland, fils naturel de Cromwell ou Le Philosophe anglais* (vols. I and II appeared early in 1731, vols. III and IV in October 1731, last vols. 1738–39). *Cleveland*, much admired by Rousseau and Diderot, was by far the most popular of his novels in his own lifetime. It is given as a translation from the English, and part of its originality is derived from his English experience, although the work as a whole was completed in Holland. Cleveland's character, in particular, struck his readers as interesting and new, for he is a melancholy, romantic hero, cast in the mould of the phlegmatic Briton, without strong faith, whose philosophy cannot cure the ills of love – to some degree an incarnation of Prévost's personal despair. Cleveland is brought close to suicide, but in the end religion triumphs, even though his religion rests on little else than sentimental yearning. The sombre, pre-Romantic hero, the plot with its romantic theme, elopement, duels, deaths, and burials, made a lasting impression on its readers and helped to fashion a new taste. Prévost now continued the *Mémoires d'un homme de qualité*, the first two volumes of which had caused a stir at Saint-Germain-des-Prés in February 1728. Drawing on his own or his vicarious experience, and demonstrably interpolating incidents from his own life, he described tellingly and with pathos the sufferings of persons carried away by passions of which their reason disapproves.

The work has little unity; and volume VII, first entitled *Histoire du Chevalier des Grieux et de Manon Lescaut*, was issued in 1733 as a separate volume, and is today universally acclaimed as Prévost's masterpiece. The first edition of this work is dated 1731, and was thought by many critics to have been misdated, yet today expert opinion increasingly favours 1731. The point is of more than academic interest, for we know that in Amsterdam Prévost made the acquaintance of a fascinating young Protestant, Lenki Eckhard, a woman said by Prévost to be of good family and reputation, but whom one of his friends called a 'leech' and who is reputed to have had a child by some other man before becoming Prévost's mistress. Prévost's known liaison with Lenki recalls in many particulars that of des Grieux and Manon in the novel

Manon Lescaut. It is therefore of particular interest to discover whether Prévost drew upon his real experience with Lenki to create *Manon*, or, as is more generally believed today, first wrote the novel, and subsequently lived through his fictional adventure in fact. For anyone interested in the connection between fact and fiction the problem posed has peculiar significance.[24] Prévost was criticised by Lenglet-Dufresnoy for his relationship with Lenki, and replied by drawing his own portrait under the name of Médor in *Le Pour et Contre*, a journal after the fashion of Addison's *Spectator*, which served to prolong the influence of Voltaire's *Lettres philosophiques*, and promoted Anglo-French relations. It reviewed scientific as well as literary publications, and was published in Paris by Diderot, although directed from London, to which city Prévost had now returned, this time accompanied by Lenki, and leaving behind him substantial debts, chiefly to publishers. *Le Pour et Contre* took over from the *Nouvelliste du Parnasse*, edited from 1731 until 1738 by the Abbé Desfontaines, which had ceased publication. It appeared first as a fortnightly, then in view of its success, as a weekly. The journal was to vary in its quality, but as a whole is a tribute to Prévost's sound judgement. It provides a mine of information on events in London, and its many numbers appearing over a period of years certainly accustomed a large French public to English manners and literary taste, and the influence of Shaftesbury, as well as that of Addison, can be discerned. Prévost naturally dwells on the eccentricities of the English, thereby frequently challenging the prejudices of his compatriots. *Le Pour et Contre*, which Lefèvre de Saint-Marc took over from 1739 until 1740, introduced its readers to Pope, Chesterfield, Swift, and Dryden, whose *All for Love or The World Well Lost* contributed to a better understanding of Shakespeare. *Antony and Cleopatra* was Prévost's favourite play. He admired, too, *The London Merchant*, by Lillo, which had thirty-eight consecutive performances on the stage of Drury Lane; and he translated *The Conscious Lovers* by Steele in numbers 110–18 of his journal, as well as writing favourable articles on Voltaire's plays.

Prévost is known to have travelled in England, in particular visiting the south-west. M. E. I. Robertson[25] has discovered that he became involved in a curious incident that might easily have led to his being hanged. He wrote in a promissory note for £50, in a blank space above the signature of Francis Eyles, which he had cut off from a genuine letter addressed to him, and had used this

[24] See below, p. 116.

[25] See her preface to a critical edition of *Mémoires d'un homme de qualité*, V, 1927.

forgery to pay a bill or obtain cash. He was prosecuted and gaoled in the Gate House Prison in London, for five days (15 December 1733), but the charge was not pressed by Francis Eyles, possibly on the intervention of Sir John. Prévost, who used the name d'Exiles while he was in England, was now anxious to return to France, where he had paid a clandestine visit in 1734. The Cardinal de Bissy and the prince de Conti interceded on his behalf, asking that he be permitted to return to France as a secular priest. The Pope, Clement XII, granted him absolution, and had him transferred to a less austere branch of the order of St Benedict. He is known to have frequented the salon of Mme de Tencin in 1734. From September to December 1735 he underwent a second novitiate in the Benedictine abbey of La Croix-Saint-Leufroy, near Evreux. He was then appointed chaplain to the prince de Conti, and devoted most of his time to his literary activities. *Le Doyen de Killerine, histoire morale* (1734–40, 6 vols.) is not unworthy of the author of the *Mémoires d'un homme de qualité*, containing as it does moving passages couched in a fine, simple style. It had also the historical realism notable in *Cleveland* when dealing with the death of Henriette d'Angleterre – the passage may be profitably compared with that in Bossuet's famous *oraison funèbre*.[26] In *Le Doyen de Killerine*, Prévost describes the entourage of James II and his court at Saint-Germain as a background to his story. The Doyen, a well-meaning, interfering, and ineffectual priest, is conspiring in Ireland, together with his brothers, on behalf of James II. His tragedy is that, though he is filled with benevolence, he can never successfully fulfil his duties as a priest through his incapacity to understand. He wins a grudging respect for his honesty and his good intentions. Prévost's imaginative writings seem to reflect attempts at solving human and personal problems, which all prove to be abortive. Pity and good intention, as the Doyen demonstrates, are not enough. H. Roddier[27] has suggested that *Le Doyen de Killerine* foreshadows *The Vicar of Wakefield*, which appeared some thirty years later.

In 1741 Prévost published *L'Histoire d'une Grecque moderne* (2 vols.), which recounts the true story of a pretty Greek slave, Mlle Aissé. The action takes place in Turkey. The heroine is fascinating and is more inscrutable to her lover than Manon is to des Grieux. Prévost leaves the reader guessing as to the real nature of her conduct and feelings. Prévost's life became increasingly that of a man of letters, until he was unwittingly compromised through correcting some proofs for a clandestine publication (January 1741), and had to take refuge in Brussels. Through the good offices

[26] See Yarrow, op. cit., pp. 318–22.
[27] *L'Abbé Prévost, l'homme et l'œuvre*, 1955, p. 137.

of Bachaumont he was allowed by Maurepas to return and was soon reinstated in his chaplaincy. The Chancelier d'Aguesseau charged him with the task of writing an *Histoire générale des voyages* (1745–70, 21 vols.) which began as a translation from an English original, being published by weekly instalments. Prévost published the first seventeen volumes, and the rest were corrected and published by La Harpe. It is this work which helped to establish Prévost's reputation. He improved on the English edition by providing better maps, and fine engravings by Cochin *fils*. He offered his readers the history and geography of a new world that was only then being discovered. The work is a mine of information on the customs and way of life of people in foreign lands, with particular reference to instruments or implements used by natives. It paved the way for Buffon's *Histoire naturelle*, and its plates have the precision of some of those to be found in the *Encyclopédie*. Rousseau drew on this work to illustrate ideas he expressed in his *Discours sur l'inégalité*, and it has its place in the early development of a science later to be known as sociology. Prévost's *Voyages du capitaine Robert Lade* (1743), which mixes fact with fiction, was less interesting than his factual work.

Prévost is best remembered in his later years as the translator of Richardson, sacrificing his own creative work to this task. He is said to be responsible for part, if not the whole, of the translation of *Pamela* (1742), but for stylistic and other reasons this seems to be highly improbable. *Pamela*, a bourgeois, realistic novel of a servant girl who marries her master, certainly made a strong impact on contemporary minds.

In 1751 Prévost's translation of *Clarissa, or the History of a Young Lady* (1747–48, 7 vols.) appeared under the title *Lettres angloises ou Histoire de Miss Clarisse Harlove*, with engravings by Eisen. The title recalled the famous *Lettres portugaises* and the *Lettres péruviennes*, and the subject was one dear to the author of the *Homme de qualité* and of *Manon Lescaut*. Both the translation and the illustrations enchanted Rousseau, and the triumph of virtue and sentiment seemed to open up new modes of behaviour. In 1753–54 the *History of Sir Charles Grandison* appeared in seven volumes. Prévost translated it under the title *Nouvelles lettres angloises ou Histoire du Chevalier Grandisson* (1755–56). As with *Clarissa*, he made many cuts and toned down scenes of emotional and physical violence so as to render Richardson more acceptable to the French, and *Grandison* ran into many editions. It exercised an influence on Rousseau, as *Clarissa* had done previously. As a result of Prévost's translations, Richardson became widely known in France, and his type of novel was imitated and integrated into the French and European novel. Diderot's *Eloge de*

Richardson, and his aesthetic conception of realism, are the fruit of a careful consideration of Richardson's works.

Prévost ultimately acquired a small property near Chantilly, where he lived the life of a monk until his macabre death. He had a stroke, and was presumed to be dead. An autopsy was decided upon and as the surgeon opened his abdomen Prévost uttered a cry and died, presumably from shock.

Others of his works include the following: *Histoire de Marguerite d'Anjou, reine d'Angleterre* (1740, 2 vols.); *Campagnes philosophiques ou Mémoires de M. de Montcalm* (1741, 2 vols.); *Mémoires pour servir à l'Histoire de Malte ou Histoire de la jeunesse du Commandeur de**** (1741, 2 vols.); *Histoire de Guillaume le Conquérant duc de Normandie et roi d'Angleterre* (1741–42, 2 vols.); *Mémoires d'un honnête homme* (1745), which might be described as a sequel in novel form of *Le Pour et Contre*; *Manuel lexique ou Dictionnaire portatif des mots français dont la signification n'est pas familière à tout le monde* (1750, revised and enlarged edition, 1754, 2 vols.), a translation of the English dictionary of T. Dyche; *Le Monde moral ou Mémoires pour servir à l'histoire du cœur humain* (1760), which was left unfinished; *Mémoires pour servir à l'histoire de la vertu, extraits du journal d'une jeune dame* (1762, 4 vols.), adapted from the *Memoirs of Miss Sidney Biddulph*, a novel by Frances Sheridan (née Chamberlaine), mother of the well-known dramatist Richard Brinsley Sheridan; *Almoran et Hamet* (1763), a translation of a work by J. Hawkesworth; *Lettres de Mentor à un jeune seigneur* (1764), published posthumously, is a translation of *Letters to a Young Nobleman*. He contributed many articles to the *Journal encyclopédique*, founded by P. Rousseau, and to the *Journal étranger*, which he edited between 1754 and 1755, but handed over to Fréron in September 1755. This journal included among its contributors Rousseau, Diderot, d'Holbach, and Grimm. England figures less prominently in this journal than in *Le Pour et Contre*, for room was found for reporting on Russian, German, and Spanish news items. In addition to translating Richardson, he translated Dryden's *All for Love* (1755) and brought out an *Histoire de Cicéron* (1743, 4 vols.) translated from the English, and *Lettres de Cicéron à M. Brutus et de M. Brutus à Cicéron* (1744) and *Lettres de Cicéron qu'on nomme familières, traduites en français* (1745), for which Prévost claims to have turned to the Latin original. In 1743 he had translated from the Dutch a work by G. van Loon. In 1760 he published in three volumes a translation of David Hume's *History of the Stuarts*, which led Rousseau to form a favourable opinion of the great philosopher.

Prévost was too versatile and too facile to play more than a secondary role on the literary stage of his day. He excelled as a journalist, and as a promoter of anglophilia. Had he resided longer in England, his comments might have greatly enriched *Le Pour et Contre*, which, however, does give a valuable picture of cosmopolitan life.

His real claim to universal fame rests on one short work, *Manon Lescaut* (1731, revised in 1753 and again in 1759),[28] the quality of which his contemporaries failed to see. There has been much speculation on the genesis of the work. If indeed *Manon* was published in 1731 and not antedated, it becomes impossible for Prévost to have derived his inspiration from his actual relationship with Lenki. The ring of truth in the novel is so great that attention has then been focused on his love affair of 1720. Perhaps greater concentration on the general frame of mind of Prévost in 1730 would prove more profitable. This might explain why, having written *Manon*, it was inevitable that he should live through a strangely similar experience; but the authenticity of the book is in the truth of the emotion portrayed and not in that of the events.

The quality and drawing power of the novel stems from the obvious sincerity of the author in expressing feelings, and in the poetic, mellifluous, and uniform style of the writing. There is a classical, Racinian purity of style, and an avoidance of local colour, even in the latter part of the book, where the action takes place in the New World. There is a deep sense of a destiny being unfolded, and the gradual degradation of des Grieux through his love for Manon is seen as inevitable. The atmosphere of pessimism is tainted with Jansenism. The disaster which overwhelms the two lovers is prepared long in advance, and the novel reads like a tragedy by Racine. Both lovers are involved in a passion so excessive that, like Tristan and Isolde, or Heloïsa and Abelard, they have to be condemned and necessarily brought to retribution. Ironically enough, this retribution overtakes them just as they are about to seek the blessing of the Church on their union, and to develop their lives into something possibly finer and less destructive. In the eyes of the Church, human love must never be confused with divine love, and must always stop short of worship, and Manon's death brings home the fact that ultimately profane love cannot usurp the place of sacred love in the heart and the spirit of a man without destroying him. The story is unfolded by des Grieux, a fact which explains the presentation of Manon as an enchanting,

[28] M. E. I. Robertson in her edition of 1943 has reproduced photographically the text of 1753, which is the basic text of F. Deloffre and P. Picard's edition with variants (1965). C. King, in his edition with variants (1963), has reproduced the text of 1759. G. Matoré in his edition (1953) has based his work on the 1731 text.

wilful, and loving girl whose physical portrait is never clearly defined.

The content of the novel is certainly moral, and its condemnation on the grounds of immorality is absurd. The danger may lie in the reader, remembering that Manon is only sixteen and des Grieux seventeen at the beginning of the story, tending to react overmuch in favour of the 'sinners', who have confused the love of man with the love belonging properly to God. Manon has the complete authenticity of a creature vividly present in des Grieux's mind and heart. Both des Grieux and Manon develop their character as the action unfolds, and this fact enhances the realism of the novel. Des Grieux has been described as a romantic hero, and is said to prefigure Saint-Preux in *La Nouvelle Héloïse*. As a narrator he is more moral than as a participant, thus enabling Prévost to present his character at two levels, and the retrospective shame of the narrator, punctuated by such recurring expressions as 'à ma honte', prevents the reader from condemning the young lover, even while he is impelled to condemn his actions. The sense of fatality, or indeed predestination, serves as a further excuse.

Prévost is above all concerned with man's lasting happiness. This is why *Manon Lescaut* is very much more important than Robert Chasles' *Les Illustres Françoises*, so often read between 1721 and 1731, which has been cited as a source for Richardson, Marivaux, and Prévost.[29] There are moral and religious undertones which have prompted H. Coulet to write: '*Manon Lescaut* est le plus tragique cri d'angoisse qu'ait arraché à la charité humaine le mystère de la volonté de Dieu.' On the one hand, the love of des Grieux for Manon is innocent, natural, and good, and as such can be justified, according to F. Deloffre and R. Picard, by the 'morale de l'intention',[30] and would be acceptable in a New World free from social prejudice – this before *La Nouvelle Héloïse* and *Paul et Virginie*. On the other hand, it is an 'amour physique idolâtre'. Des Grieux, caught in his snare, never renounces love as a *raison d'être* of his existence. And after Manon's death, he lives in a vacuum, without any real repentance. From the Jansenist standpoint, he is a man untouched by the grace of God. Secondary characters in the novel, Tiberge in particular, who is des Grieux's friend, are well drawn, as is the social background, which characters such as Lescaut bring into relief. The successive rivals up to and including Synnelet have only episodic significance. There are lengthy but vivid descriptive passages: the opening pages, for

[29] Cf. the *Histoire de des Frans et de Sylvie*. Manon has been compared with Moll Flanders, and Defoe's influence can be detected in vol. III of the *Mémoires d'un homme de qualité*.

[30] *Manon Lescaut*, ed. Picard, 1965, p. cix.

example, with the deportation to the New World of women of easy virtue, and a death scene managed with remarkable economy; but there are also pages of close-knit argument, such as that between Tiberge and des Grieux on divine and human love, which Prévost's training as a monk helped to make both disturbing and convincing.

The novel as a whole is exceptionally tightly knit, short, and dramatic. Incidents are brought in to illustrate certain aspects of the characters, and especially to hasten the development of the novel. They are so briefly sketched in and passed over that an impression of speed, economy, and understatement is preserved throughout. There is virtually no commentary by the author or the characters on events, and few moral judgements. The value of the work lies not only in the presentation of characters, but in the presentation of human problems: that of human free-will and fatalism, of Providence and the Grace of God, and of the relative validity of human love. The work gains from being loosely connected with the *Mémoires d'un homme de qualité*, in that des Grieux, addressing himself as he does to the *homme de qualité*, can express greater personal indignation or impatience than he could if addressing the common reader. The general framework of the novel rests basically on four episodes, each involving a rival of des Grieux for Manon's affections. The symmetry is deliberate and unmarred, according to H. Coulet, by the addition of the story of the Italian prince in the 1753 edition. Three basic movements may be discerned: movements to and away from love, ups and downs of fortune, and alternating violence and moments of peace.

Des Grieux's degradation is marked step by step, as is also his groping towards a higher ideal. In the last resort he would seem to be dedicated to the single-minded pursuit of a unique love, which destroys him.

The story of the fallen woman being redeemed by a pure love was to have a long line of successors in the nineteenth century, from Dumas' *La Dame aux camélias* to Zola's *Nana* and A. France's *Thaïs*. Manon herself was to be effectively portrayed in one of Massenet's best operas. More significantly, *Manon Lescaut* renews the tradition of the psychological *nouvelle* so well illustrated by Mme de La Fayette's *La Princesse de Clèves* in the seventeenth century, and B. Constant's *Adolphe*, Fromentin's *Dominique*, and Gide's *Ecole des femmes* in the nineteenth and twentieth centuries. These novels each present an analysis in very great depth of a specific relationship, to the exclusion of almost all else. The art-form perfected, sometimes called *réalisme moral*, is one of the main French contributions to the history of the novel.

Manon Lescaut, which was published in the same year as the early chapters of *La Vie de Marianne*, shares with the latter a pre-occupation with feminine psychology and the mechanism of the human heart, a new sensibility associated with a new realism very different from that of *Gil Blas*, and both novels manifest analytical powers equalled only by the greatest of their successors.

Chapter 6

THE GROWTH OF SCEPTICISM AND RATIONALISM

HISTORICAL dates are often misleading; and it would be particularly difficult to date the dawn of the new epoch that triumphantly declared itself throughout the eighteenth century. The *grand siècle* died hard. Louis XIV at Versailles outlived his glory, and already, beneath the glittering trappings, the absolute majesty, and the religious austerity of his final years, a brave new world struggled to break free.

The desire for freedom of thought, and the determination to achieve that freedom, had been growing since the sixteenth century, despite persecution and severe restrictive measures, religious and political. Signs of the increasing ferment were manifest towards the end of the seventeenth century, a quarter of a century or so before the death of the Sun King in 1715.[1]

Louis de Rouvroy, duc de Saint-Simon (1675–1755) has left in his *Mémoires*, the work of his lifetime, an unparalleled record of the years of urgency and transition. It was his evident intent to draw his readers into such communication that they would seem to share his experiences, and examine with him the causes of the events he was relating. He was well placed for his purpose: an officer and a courtier, he was a close friend of the powerful duc de Beauvillier, on intimate terms with the regent, Philippe d'Orléans, and a member of the Council of the Regency. To these social assets he added personal ones – a lively and enquiring mind, a vivid idiosyncratic style, a wit spiced with malice, and an absorbed interest in people, in life at court, and in matters of policy, etiquette, and the army.

In style and outlook he belonged to the seventeenth rather than the eighteenth century, and brought therefore to his skilled and detailed dissection of the time a detachment that adds to its value. In his chronicle of daily life at the court of Versailles, he removed the mask of hypocrisy normally worn by the entourage, and through the speech and action, personality and conflict of the

[1] See P. Hazard, *La Crise de la conscience européenne*, 1935.

vast number of major and subsidiary characters that throng his *Mémoires,* he revealed the arrogance, venality, and greed, the concupiscence and corruption, of the courtiers among whom he lived in close association for more than a quarter of a century, under Louis XIV, and later under the regency.

The fact that he wrote his memoirs well into the eighteenth century accounts perhaps for the strength of his urgent criticism of Louis XIV, as man and as monarch. His critical analysis of the court of Versailles, and his chronicle of the history of France in the years of her decline from greatness, no doubt serve in part to explain why his vast work was not published in its entirety until the nineteenth century (1829–31). The *Mémoires* in their totality, in spite of inadequate social coverage, give a vivid and deeply felt picture of the authentic background against which the great struggle for freedom took place throughout the century; they express the new feeling of enquiry in the air, and they are a preparation for more virulent criticism to come.[2]

Fénelon (1651–1715), in his *Lettre à Louis XIV*, a direct attack on the monarch, and in *Les Aventures de Télémaque, fils d'Ulysse* (1699), a didactic tale, criticised the administrative and financial policies of the monarch, and in the latter work depicted an ideal, primitive Utopia in a kind of pre-social Golden Age, comparing favourably the happiness of the noble savage with the misery of the ultra-civilised man, thereby influencing Rousseau, Chateaubriand, and others.[3] Through his attack on despotism, his quietism in religious matters, and especially through his style, with its mythological trappings and pungent, if oblique, criticism, Fénelon influenced Voltaire, as evidenced by a number of borrowings to be found in some of his *contes.*

Vauban (1633–1707) and Boisguillebert (1646–1714), in their observations on the state of France and the impoverishment of her people, and La Bruyère, in his *Caractères,* had already manifested a critical spirit and pointed to the need for social and moral reforms. But during the reign of Louis XIV, other men, atheists and freethinkers, known indiscriminately as *libertins,* concentrated on the religious issue, which they commonly linked with the political. They grew in numbers and spread their word secretly and well, until they came to be counted in thousands: and this in spite of the efforts of the government to suppress their activities. The *libertins* had a long background: incredulity, which may be traced back to antiquity, owes much in its modern form to Boccaccio, and the new spirit, which developed in the Italian

[2] See Yarrow, op. cit., pp. 393 et seq.

[3] See G. Chinard, *L'Amérique et le rêve exotique dans la littérature française au XVIIe et au XVIIIe siècle*, 1934.

universities during the Renaissance, which was more firmly rooted in the medical teaching of Aristotle than in theology. The intellectual approach of Pomponazzi (1462–1525), the experimental philosophy of Campanella (1568–1639) and Cardano (1501–76), lead directly to the scientific speculations of Bruno (1550–1600) and philosophies of science of Francis Bacon and Gassendi. By a similar development the humanism of Erasmus, Bodin, Rabelais, and Montaigne also paved the way for the *libertin*, who was essentially a pagan *honnête homme*. It was Gassendi (1592–1655), however, who was the strongest representative of the new philosophy. In the empirical sciences he turned to Leucippus, Democritus, and Lucretius, and evolved a doctrine which, by implication, postulated motion as an integral part of matter, a point which John Toland later brought out very clearly. Gassendi's *Life of Epicurus* was the first vindication of the ethics and philosophy of that philosopher. He opposed Descartes' extreme rationalism, as well as Bacon's extreme empiricism. One of his disciples was Cyrano de Bergerac (1619–55), whose work in three parts, *L'Autre Monde*, *Les Etats et empires de la lune*, and *Les Etats et empires du soleil*, satirises existing institutions and attacks prejudice and conventional morality, whilst stressing the importance of the future role of science. Other *libres-penseurs* who came under the influence of Gassendi were Molière, Chapelle, La Mothe le Vayer *fils*, and Bernier. Gassendi also inspired Locke and Bayle, and through them reached the scientists and philosophers of the eighteenth century. Mention may be made also of Saint-Evremond, a lifelong friend of Ninon de Lenclos,[4] for his general scepticism, for his light, bantering wit, and for his mastery of innuendo as a means of conveying his thought effectively.

The quarrel between the Jansenists and the Jesuits, which was carried into the eighteenth century, and the discussion around Pascal's attractive method of converting *libertins* by inviting them to wager on the existence of God, did much to discredit the Church; the gradual propagation of Spinoza's biblical criticism and of what John Toland was the first to call pantheism; the disturbing effect of the Quarrel of the Ancients and the Moderns; all these factors contributed to undermine orthodoxy in all fields. But special mention needs to be made of the anonymous critical pamphlets which have only recently become an object of detailed study, and whose historical importance is now seen to be great. Towards the close of the seventeenth century, an active and vigor-

[4] Ninon de Lenclos (1620–1705) was a famous *femme galante*, with a recognised place in high society, who held her own salon, and was a friend of Mme de Maintenon. Her last lover was the abbé de Châteauneuf, whose friend Gédoyn introduced to her Voltaire, then eleven years old; she was eighty-five.

ous trade in clandestine literature, often in manuscript form, was already paving the way for the writings of Montesquieu, Voltaire, Rousseau, Diderot, and d'Holbach, who became the giants of the ideological upheaval of their age.

There is an impressive body of clandestine literature[5] in seventeenth- and eighteenth-century France dealing with aspects of philosophy, religion, ethics, and social questions. This literature, which could never have found a publisher or a printer through the normal channels, was designed to circumvent the censorship. It was widely circulated, in the form of essays, throughout the period 1710–40, during which time copyists, *colporteurs*, and the police were all particularly active in their different spheres. Having found their way into print, these essays were subsequently impounded, and then were copied and distributed secretly – a practice that continued right up to the Revolution. Voltaire, Dulaurens, d'Holbach, and Naigeon, driven by their desire to foster deism or atheism, were responsible for prolonging the life of certain anonymous tracts by including them at a later date in collective volumes – *Nouvelles libertés de penser* (1743, 1770), *Recueil nécessaire* (1765, 1766, 1768, 1776), *L'Evangile de la raison* (1764, 1765, 1768), *Recueil philosophique* (1770), and *Bibliothèque du bon sens portatif* (1773). The treatises are an important record of intellectual activity between the publication of Bayle's *Dictionnaire historique et critique* (1697) and Montesquieu's *Esprit des lois* (1748); they provided scholarship and one of the main sources of information and ideas on which the *philosophes* drew for their polemics.

Records now in the Bibliothèque Nationale, and the contemporary sources, offer valuable data concerning the organisation and diffusion of these manuscripts. Those of Henri de Boulainvilliers, for example, were copied and distributed thanks to Le Coulteux, Charles Bonnet, Lépine, and a certain Mathieu or Morléon (who was incarcerated in 1729). These works were distributed, often in the vicinity of the Procope and other cafés, to listed patrons and initiates, including members of the clergy and the Parlement. Copies such as those of Meslier's *Testament*[6] were made by professionals, occasionally the personal secretaries of men like the comte de Boulainvilliers, the comte d'Argenson, and Malesherbes, and the practice of employing copyists was continued throughout the century. The price of such copies varied greatly. A sum as prohibitively high as 20 *pistoles* (220 livres) is known to have been asked for Mirabaud's *Examen critique du Nouveau Testament*.

[5] For the period 1700–50, Professor I. O. Wade listed 392 MSS. extant, of 102 different treatises, including 15 translations from other languages. Many more are known to have been in circulation.

[6] See below, p. 130.

The clandestine movement, fed by new discoveries in science, reflected the climate of European opinion, an attitude to life and society, man and his welfare, God and the universe, which, although not new, was reinforced by new arguments and gained an ever-increasing audience. Although the tracts appeared sporadically, and were mostly anonymous, they share a few common characteristics.

The *Theophrastus Redivivus* (1659) is significant in that it establishes a link between the atheism of men of the Renaissance and that of men of the seventeenth century (it refers, for example, to Lucilio Vanini and Cyrano de Bergerac) and also of the eighteenth century, when it was secretly circulated. The author developed the arguments that, if God exists, he is the sun and that the world is eternal. For him all religions are false, and miracles, oracles, prophecies, and revelations are man-made. The resurrection of the dead and the immortality of the soul are absurdities; happiness is to be found only in living according to nature, which is revealed to us through experience; there is no absolute good or evil, as we may deduce from the multiplicity of customs and laws; man is a species of animal endowed with speech and reason. Animals, however, are not totally devoid of these faculties. The author referred neither to Gassendi nor to Descartes, but he did mention the treatise *De Tribus Impostoribus*, attributing to the Emperor Frederick II the proposition that Moses, Christ, and Mohammed were three remarkable impostors.

Throughout the seventeenth century, the *libertins*, in the wake of Rabelais and Montaigne, became erudite sceptics, radical naturalists, associating freedom of morals with freedom of belief. As freethinkers they were prompted more by a feeling of revolt against ascetism and scholasticism than by any convincing argument. Gassendi contributed to the rehabilitation of Epicurus and Lucretius. Emmanuel Maignan, too, in his *Cursus*, evolved a philosophy that bridged Aristotle and Epicurus, linking matter and thought, sensationalism and the spiritual world, and developing the idea of a chain of being. But it was from Descartes that the movement of free-thought gained its greatest impetus. Cartesian rationalism and mechanism provided freethinkers with a new certainty, and their systems with a new coherence. Long after his philosophy had been adopted by the Jesuits and had consequently grown unpopular, Descartes continued to exercise a determining influence on free thought through the method he advocated. His philosophy, however, was commonly misunderstood by freethinkers, and with La Mettrie it culminated in an extreme mechanistic materialism that Descartes would have decried.

Spinoza's influence on the clandestine literature was considerable but rather indirect. His work was largely known through the writings of other thinkers, like Bayle and Boulainvilliers, and his philosophy was commonly distorted by Cartesian misrepresentation. The *Ethics* was little known, and frequently its views were reconstituted through refutations. The *Tractatus Theologico-politicus* was of interest on account of its biblical criticism, and in Holland, Jean Leclerc, professor of philosophy and Hebrew at the University of Amsterdam, was allowed to carry on this critical work. In France, however, the uncompromising attitude of Bossuet stifled biblical criticism. Richard Simon, a well-known teacher at the Oratorian school at Juilly, who had admitted in his *Histoire critique du Vieux Testament* (1678) the truth of much of Spinoza's exegesis while recognising the authority of the Bible, succeeded in offending both Catholics and Protestants and was expelled from the Oratorian congregation in 1678. He retired to continue his rational critique in two *instructions pastorales* (1702, 1703), in *Histoire critique du texte du Nouveau Testament* (1683), *Histoire critique des versions du Nouveau Testament* (1690), and *Histoire critique des principaux commentateurs du Nouveau Testament* (1692).

Disputes that reached the general public – such as those over the authorship of the Pentateuch, in which La Peyrère, Hobbes, Spinoza, Simon, Jean Leclerc, and others held different views – led to much perplexity. The body of anonymous treatises that continued such discussions, and in many cases rejected revelation, is naturally large. These include the *Examen de la religion*, the *Analyse de la religion* (written after 1739), and the *Militaire philosophe* (composed between 1706 and 1711).

Hobbes's *Leviathan* (1651) seems to have been little known in France and his influence, often indirect, is to be detected at a later date; Bayle's *Dictionnaire*, however, enjoyed great authority. The anonymous writers also read Fontenelle and knew something of the English deists, whose thoughts developed along parallel lines. There were translations of works by Bernard Mandeville, Lord Bolingbroke, John Toland, Anthony Collins, and Thomas Woolston, but it was only after the publication of Voltaire's *Lettres anglaises* (1734), which discussed Newtonian physics and philosophy and the ideas of Locke (the latter known through P. Coste's translation in 1700), that the English influence became significant. Leibniz's influence, too, was felt only at a late stage, partly because he was known primarily through Bayle and also through Maupertuis, whose ideas served to link the *Monadology* with Diderot and materialism.

The only group of writers known to have been involved in concerted action was that centred round the comte de Boulainvilliers, and closely linked with d'Argenson, the duc de Noailles, and the Académie des Inscriptions. This coterie included Nicolas Fréret, Jean-Baptiste de Mirabaud, César Dumarsais, and J.-B. Le Mascrier. Voltaire, in his *Dîner du comte de Boulainvilliers* (1767), bears witness to the important influence of this group, which was especially responsible for the diffusion of Boulainvilliers' *Esprit de Spinoza* (known to have existed by 1706 and first published in 1719 in Holland).

Henri, comte de Boulainvilliers (1659–1722) or Henry, comte de Boulainviller, as he preferred to spell his name, historian, philosopher, astrologer, and *savant*, first took up military service, as befitted a member of an old aristocratic family. After leaving the army, he developed an interest in history, first studying his own family tree and then the social and political institutions of the Middle Ages. He approved of feudalism, which he envisaged as a kind of federal republic governed by independent aristocratic families, whom he considered to be the inheritors of the Franks, conquerors of Gaul. He deplored the increase in the power of the central authority – the king – and in the liberties of the people as encroachments on the rights of the nobles. He favoured a patriarchal society. Many of his reforms, submitted to the regent, recommended the fostering of trade, proportional taxation, the suppression of tax-farmers, and the calling of the *Etats-Généraux*.

Boulainvilliers is best known as the probable author of parts of the *Essai de métaphysique*, which was published in 1731 under the title *Réfutation des erreurs de Benoît de Spinoza*. He became interested in Spinoza through reading the *Tractatus Theologico-politicus*, which he annotated copiously, and also the *Ethics*, which he read in 1704. The first part, or *Vie de Spinoza*, of the *Essai de métaphysique* has been attributed to J.-M. Lucas. The second part, or *Esprit de Spinoza*, has been attributed by I. O. Wade and others to Boulainvilliers himself. Both parts are commonly coupled together in the manuscripts and in the editions, under the title *La Vie et l'esprit de Spinoza*. Boulainvilliers correctly presents Spinoza's doctrine that God and the universality of things are one and the same, then proceeds to argue that Spinoza's 'attributes' are in fact 'modes' of something he terms existence.

In this work he has evolved an original philosophy. Starting from the Cartesian principle that he knows himself to be a thinking being, he infers that other beings exist, some endowed with thought, others only with feeling, and others with neither feeling nor thought. All things, whether living or non-living, thinking, feeling, or merely extended, have one property in common: existence. From such premises, he proceeds to a universal Idea or Being, more all-embracing than matter. He stresses the degrees of being, and claims that sensations are the source of all experience. He concludes by asserting that at death the body returns to universal matter, while the soul remains as an idea in the infinite mind, and is, therefore, capable of being restored to the body. Boulainvilliers' exposition of Spinoza is curiously based on Cartesian assertions, and incorporates ideas borrowed from Locke.

He strove to harmonise the notion of a single substance with a sensationalist psychology and a naturalistic ethical system. He believed in a 'chain of being', in the capacity of animals to think, and in evidence or intellectual coherence and clarity (as opposed to verifiable observation) as the only criterion of truth; he also helped to discredit Christian revelation. In an *Abrégé d'histoire ancienne*, he expressed his belief in the primacy of natural laws, denying the possibility of miracles. These points were later taken up by Diderot in the article 'Certitude' of the *Encyclopédie*.

Figuring as part of the *Essai de métaphysique*, sometimes entitled *L'Esprit de Spinoza*, is to be found a treatise, commonly known as the *Traité des trois imposteurs*, under which title it was published in 1719.[7] Polemical and concise, it provided freethinkers with valuable ammunition. Its aggressive title helped to ensure its success, and may have been chosen by the Dutch printers as the last and profitable stage of an elaborate hoax. It is an allusion to a lost treatise, *De Tribus Impostoribus* (1230), supposedly written by the Emperor Frederick II (Hohenstaufen) for the edification of his friend, Otto. Interest in this Latin work, evidenced in *Theophrastus Redivivus* (1659), had been revived at the close of the seventeenth century and the beginning of the eighteenth.

The author of the *Traité des trois imposteurs*, believed by Voltaire to be Boulainvilliers, launched a virulent attack on the prophets and apostles; he expressed his disbelief in heaven or hell, rewards or punishments, his faith in natural law as enshrined in the hearts of men, and in the soul as the expression of the principle of life. The system of religion is, according to him, the work of false legislators, among whom are Moses, Christ, and Mohammed. Moses was nothing more than a magician and a charlatan. Christ, who may be likened to Genghis Khan, was a casuist in his discussions with the Pharisees and in claiming to be the son of a god; his religion owes much to Greek mythology and his ethics compare unfavourably with those of Epictetus and Epicurus. Mohammed differs from the other two imposters in having recourse to violence in the establishment of his kingdom. Voltaire, among others, seized on these points to bolster his polemics against

[7] 2nd ed., 1721; numerous others throughout the century. Since printed copies were commonly impounded and consequently hard to find, manuscript copies continued to circulate both before and after publication.

the Church. He, too, saw the advantage of an oblique attack on the Church by an onslaught against Islamic fanaticism, coupled with the claim that all religions are equal. The treatise marks an early, if crude, attempt to consider religion from the comparative standpoint.

Boulainvilliers is best remembered as a confirmed 'spinoziste', and his views on the subject of nature and matter, the relationship of matter and thought, and the origin and nature of government, won him a place as a forerunner of the *philosophes*.

Nicolas Fréret (1688–1761), a student of law, joined the coterie of Boulainvilliers at the age of nineteen. Fréret appended to copies of the *Histoire ancienne* an account of Boulainvilliers' life and works. In 1714 he was admitted to the Académie des Inscriptions; in 1715 he was imprisoned for some months in the Bastille, where he read Bayle's *Dictionnaire* and wrote a Chinese grammar. From 1720 to 1721 he was preceptor of the duc de Noailles.

The *Lettre de Thrasibule à Leucippe* (written *c.* 1722 and published in London, probably in 1768; also published in *Œuvres de Fréret*, vol. IV, London, 1775) is generally attributed to him. Systematic and Cartesian in its presentation, this treatise combines sensationalist psychology and naturalist ethics. Thrasibule, a Roman, describes the early Christians as combining Jewish beliefs with Stoicism, and as influenced by both monotheist and polytheist currents. He argues that knowledge is acquired through our senses and has only relative validity. Only the truths of mathematics and reason are universal. Religious beliefs, however, do not spring from reason; it is reason alone that should guide man in regulating his life, in establishing society and laws, and achieving happiness. This work can be seen as an early essay in comparative religion, and it sharply reflects the growing interest in the science of law and social philosophy. It perhaps influenced Montesquieu, and Rousseau annotated it while engaged in writing the *Discours sur l'inégalité*. Echoes of the *Lettre* are to be found in Voltaire's *Traité de métaphysique*, and in parts of Condillac's works.

Fréret is also reputed to be the author of an *Examen critique des apologistes de la religion chrétienne* (composed after 1733), which introduces the historical method adopted by Voltaire in, for example, the *Essai sur les mœurs* and the *Dictionnaire philosophique*, in which Voltaire acknowledged his debt. Fréret was held in high esteem as a *savant*. He was a chronologist, a geographer, an orientalist, and a philologist as well as a philosopher, and he delivered papers on a wide variety of subjects to the Académie des Inscriptions, becoming its permanent secretary in 1743. These *Mémoires de l'Académie* outline new methods for the study of pre-history and geography as well as history. Fréret specialised in mythology, opposing the *évhéméristes,* who believed that all myths had a basis in historical fact. A pioneer in comparative philology, he made known the Chinese linguistic system. His *Oeuvres complètes* were published by Leclerc de Septchênes in Paris during 1796–99.

Jean-Baptiste de Mirabaud (1675–1760) was educated by the Oratorians and embarked on a military career. He then became secretary to the duchesse d'Orléans and preceptor of her two youngest daughters. In 1724 he translated *Gerusalemme liberata* by Tasso. He was elected to the Académie Française in 1726, becoming its secretary in 1742. Mirabaud read his manuscripts to select groups of friends. He was probably the author of four essays (described below), often to be found together, that threw new doubts on biblical chronology and promoted Fontenelle's method of oblique attack on miracles. Many of Mirabaud's notes recall ideas expressed in *La Religion chrétienne analysée* (a popular post-1742 tract, attributed by Voltaire and Claude-François Nonnotte to César Dumarsais). The *Opinion des anciens sur le monde* (*c.* 1706–22) challenges the story of Genesis. In the *Opinion des anciens sur la nature de l'âme* (composed before 1726, published in *Nouvelles Libertés de penser*) Mirabaud pointed out that the Jews, the Greeks, and the Romans envisaged the soul as material and that the Egyptians introduced the belief in the immortality of the soul as a restraining influence on public morals. The *Opinion des anciens sur les Juifs* (c. 1706–22), based on Jacques Basnage's *Histoire des Juifs* (1706), tries to prove that the Jews had no right to claim to be a 'chosen' people. The *Examen critique du Nouveau Testament* (c. 1706–22), which deals with the canonical and the non-canonical gospels, stresses that neither Philo nor Josephus mentioned Christ, and that Christian morality conflicts with natural morality.[8]

César Chesneau Dumarsais (1676–1756), a grammarian, was personally known to Fontenelle and Voltaire, and was associated with the *Encyclopédie* until his death. For a time he was preceptor in the family of John Law. Dumarsais edited, with Le Mascrier, some of the deistic works of Mirabaud and wrote a defence of Fontenelle's *Histoire des oracles,* and probably the deterministic essay *Le Philosophe.*[9] He was probably responsible for *La Religion chrétienne analysée* (also known as *Examen de la religion* and *Doutes*), in which inconsistencies in the Bible are shown up, the doctrine of original sin is attacked, and the doctrine of the Trinity is stated to be contrary to reason. It is argued that God should be worshipped

[8] For further information, see *Notice sur Jean-Baptiste de Mirabaud* (Paris, 1895) by Paul Mirabaud.
[9] Written before 1728; edited by Herbert Dieckmann in 1948.

without ceremony and that man must follow his reason, which is his *lumière naturelle*, and adopt a social morality rather than Christian dogma.

The most interesting of the clandestine authors was no doubt Jean Meslier (1664–1729), a priest who was directly or indirectly influenced by Spinoza. (Reading Fénelon's *Démonstration de l'existence de Dieu* and R.-J. de Tournemine's *Réflexions sur l'athéisme* helped Meslier clarify his ideas.) He identified nature with matter, which he saw as eternal and as endowed with movement. He favoured a mechanical interpretation of nature, rejecting the arguments of those who believed in chance and in a divine design. In his manuscript of 716 pages in three volumes, which he called *Mémoire*, and Voltaire restyled *Testament*, Meslier listed the errors, illusions, and impostures of Christianity. His attack on Christianity is one of the most detailed and comprehensive ever written, and his materialistic system is particularly interesting in that it foreshadows many aspects of Diderot's thought. His social ideas are of particular interest.

Voltaire is known to have acquired a copy of the *Testament* and to have made extracts of the first half of the *Mémoire* from a manuscript *abrégé*, which he dated 1742 and published in 1761 or 1762 under the title *Extrait*. The first edition sold out immediately, and was followed in the same year by an edition of 5,000 copies; in all fifty-five editions were made. In 1772 d'Holbach published so-called extracts under the title *Le Bon Sens*, only appending the name of the Curé Meslier in 1791. This work has nothing in common with the writings of Meslier.[10] In 1789 Sylvain Maréchal published *Le Catéchisme du curé Meslier*.

Meslier's social ideas were remarkable for the time. He claimed in very general terms that all men are equal and have the right to live, to be free, and to share in the fruits of the earth. He divided mankind into workers and parasites, and saw in revolt the best hope of better conditions. He dreamed of a class struggle, not reconciliation. He has been heralded as the first atheist communist.

Among other anonymous works that cast doubts on the proofs of the truth of Christianity and allege contradictions in the Bible are five manuscript volumes of the *Examen de la Genèse* and the *Examen du Nouveau Testament* (probably written in the late 1730s or early 1740s), which are attributed to Mme du Châtelet, Voltaire's mistress. She purports to have proved that the stories of the Bible relate barbarous and cruel events and cannot have

[10] See p. 249. A critical edition of the *Mémoires des pensées et des sentiments de Jean Meslier* by J. Deprun, R. Desné, and A. Soboul is shortly to appear. Cf. R. Desné, 'Les œuvres complètes du Curé Meslier', *Revue de l'université de Bruxelles*, 1–2, Nouvelle série, 22e année, pp. 135–50.

been inspired by God. No doubt she received some help from Voltaire, but she relied chiefly on the work of Jean Meslier and Thomas Woolston, and especially on the *Commentaire littéral sur tous les livres de l'Ancien et du Nouveau Testament* (23 vols., Paris, 1707–16) by the orthodox Benedictine Augustin Dom Calmet.

Among other manuscripts whose authorship is now known is *Le Ciel ouvert à tous les hommes* (also entitled *Le Paradis ouvert* and *Nouveau Système de la religion chrétienne*), by the priest Pierre Cuppé, which must have been in draft in 1716. The tract never assails orthodoxy, but Cuppé submits the Scriptures to scrutiny and preaches toleration and brotherly love, concluding that all men are saved by God's love. Cuppé's stress on his respect for reason, as well as his deistic beliefs, led to his being considered a forerunner of French deism.

The author of *Le Militaire philosophe* (*c.* 1710; given as published in London, but probably printed in Holland by M.-M. Rey for Naigeon in 1767) is unknown. It is first a commentary of Malebranche's views on religion. It gives a frank exposition of deism which won Voltaire's commendation. After a strongly worded criticism of the Old and New Testaments, the work rejects Christianity and develops the doctrine of natural religion, stressing the roles of reason and instinct. Man, who is both body and soul, is free and immortal, and his behaviour should be governed by reason and by conscience. Man must worship God and abide by the golden rule. The author foreshadowed Montesquieu in his insistence on the absolute character of justice and the relative nature of civil laws, and in his treatment of chance, which he rejected as an explanation of events. He anticipated Voltaire in his use of the figure of a watchmaker to explain the function of God. His idea that truth is to be found in the individual soul was later developed by Rousseau. The real title of the work is *Difficultés sur la religion* and it is in fact the first coherent French exposition of deism. It was substantially cut and modified by d'Holbach and Naigeon to suit their propaganda in favour of atheism.[11]

A widely disseminated treatise was *Israël vengé*, by Isaac Orobio, a Spanish Jew who escaped from the Inquisition to France and then to Holland, and died in 1687 or 1688. His originally unpublished critical attack on the Christian religion was translated by Henriquez and published in London in 1770. It was circulated by Lévesque de Burigny.

The *Jordanus Brunus Redivivus* is a materialistic compilation. The author believed in the Copernican system (and the existence of other solar systems with living beings) and in the eternity of

[11] R. Mortier has prepared a critical edition of this work, which is in the press. See Desné, op. cit., pp. 60–71; below, p. 249.

matter. There are no innate ideas, no objective good or evil. Man is motivated by pain and by pleasure. Experience can deceive us. Reason alone is valid but must not be thought infallible. The laws of nature are eternal, but everything is in a state of flux. Certain passages of this work bring to mind Diderot's *Rêve de d'Alembert*. Other manuscripts whose authorship is uncertain include *Lettre d'Hypocrate à Damagette* (1700 at latest); *Recherches curieuses de philosophie* (1713); *Suite des Pyrrhoniens: qu'on peut douter si les religions viennent immédiatement de Dieu ou de l'invention des politiques pour faire craindre et garder les préceptes de l'homme* (*c.* 1723); *Traité de la liberté* (a determinist and materialist tract, probably by Fontenelle, *c.* 1700); *Essai sur la recherche de la vérité*; and *Dissertation sur la formation du monde* (1738), which was inspired by Lucretius and formulates transformist theories while upholding the conception of fixed species.

It will be seen that the clandestine tracts fall into two main categories, those written from the standpoint of critical deism and those that are atheistic, deterministic, and materialistic. The outstanding eighteenth-century literary works based on them can be similarly characterised. Montesquieu's adoption of the letter-form for *Les Lettres persanes* (1721) may owe something to the *Lettre à Damagette*, and the views expressed in *Lettre persane* xlvi reflect those expressed in *La Religion chrétienne analysée*. Voltaire, who also adopted this form for his *Lettres philosophiques*, published anonymously in 1734, wrote in the same year a *Traité de métaphysique* (which Mme du Châtelet kept under lock and key), which embodied his own deism as well as many of the ideas expressed in the clandestine literature.

Towards the middle of the century, atheism gained ground, no doubt encouraged by such treatises as *Lettre sur la religion, sur l'âme et sur l'existence de Dieu*. Diderot's *Pensées philosophiques*, published anonymously in 1746, allegedly at the Hague, but actually in Paris, and condemned to be burned by the Parlement de Paris, is characteristic of this tendency. Although based on a translation of Shaftesbury, the work succeeds in presenting an original and vividly expressed atheism, side by side with more commonplace arguments in favour of natural religion. In particular it challenges Christian belief in miracles, outlining the principles of the new biblical criticism. In the eighteenth century alone the *Pensées philosophiques* ran to twenty editions (some with crude interpolations) and reprints. It was translated into German, Italian, and English and was the subject of long and heated controversy. Twelve signed or anonymous refutations by Protestants, Catholics, parliamentarians, and others were published, often accompanied by the text of Diderot they purported to refute. We know that manuscript copies of the printed text of the *Pensées* were made and distributed.

As government policy wavered and censorship grew slack, an increasing number of the manuscripts of earlier date were published, and anonymity became a thin veil, if not a mere convention. Clandestine literature, which many have identified with the tradition of free thought, reached its apogée with the advent of Montesquieu, Voltaire, Rousseau, and Diderot. In their works it found its finest literary expression, and thanks to them it became integrated into coherent patterns that have won it a place in the history of ideas.

Among the better-known writers who may properly be regarded as forerunners of the philosophic movement, two great names stand out: Pierre Bayle (1647–1706), whose *Dictionnaire historique et critique* (1697, enlarged edition 1702) was to become the Bible of the *philosophes*; and Bernard le Bovier de Fontenelle (1657–1757), whose *Entretiens sur la pluralité des mondes habités* (1686) and *Histoire des oracles* (1686) exerted a definite and lasting influence on the evolution of thought in the eighteenth century.

Pierre Bayle, a Protestant forced into exile in Holland when the academy at which he taught was closed down in 1681, was misunderstood in the eighteenth century, when the complex nature of his apparent scepticism led the *philosophes* to assume that he was a freethinker of their own kind. Recent critical work has revealed more clearly his indebtedness to the Protestant theology in which he was reared, and has established his position as a rationalist who sought clarification of dogma to strengthen, not to destroy, belief; his assertion that morality is of greater importance than doctrine was the essence of his Protestantism, not of any deism or atheism. But if his views were those of a Protestant, his argument was such that his articles could easily be used to develop anti-Christian ideas. It is to his erudite dictionary, from which only scientific data seem to have been excluded, that a whole generation of thinkers turned for evidence of human folly and ignorance, and for a lesson in scepticism. Freedom of conscience, the critical spirit of the new epoch, are to be found in Bayle; and his manner of stating and suggesting the truth disarmed his avowed critics, whilst encouraging his sympathisers to read between the lines even more than he himself intended.

Bayle's dictionary, which provided arguments both for and against most doctrines and beliefs, was chiefly used in search of arguments against the uncritical acceptance of the Bible and of miracles. Bayle may not have been, as Joseph de Maistre later stated, 'le père de l'incrédulité moderne', but he was undoubtedly a promoter of the concept of humanity and of freedom, of the idea that man on earth should be judged by his actions, and that religion and morality may be divorced. He popularised the idea that the conception of Providence did not rest on rational premises, and that atheists could be good men. As he expressed it in the first part of his *Pensées diverses sur la comète* (1682): 'Néron était dévot: en fut-il moins cruel? . . . Les Soldats qui pillent, violent et tuent sont-ils déistes ou philosophes?' Bayle exacerbated the latent conflict between the champions of religion and the champions of reason, and although he asserted that there might be merit in holding to a faith that ran counter to reason – he in fact distrusted a reason that can readily be swayed by prejudice – he became in practice a potent force in the rationalist movement. His account in the *Dictionnaire historique et critique* of the ideas of the early English deists was widely read.

His general attitude led him to argue convincingly in favour of toleration, especially in his *Commentaire philosophique sur ces paroles de Jésus-Christ: Contrains-les d'entrer* (1686). His plea is bolder and more broadly based than that in Locke's *Letters on toleration*. Until about 1750 Bayle was much hated by the French political and religious authorities and all references to him had to be expressed in very guarded tones. Diderot's praise of him in the *Encyclopédie* was suppressed.

Fontenelle was from the start much involved in the intellectual and social life of Paris, and, by his contributions to literature, philosophy, and science, may be viewed as a representative figure of the circles he frequented. A nephew of Pierre Corneille, sponsored by Thomas Corneille, he was led to seek success as a dramatist, but his real talent lay elsewhere. He entered the Académie Française in 1691, and remained a member for sixty-six years. In 1699 he became *secrétaire perpétuel* of the Académie des Sciences, whose history he wrote (1702–40). He frequented in turn the Château de Sceaux and the salons of Mme de Lambert, Mme de Tencin, and Mme Geoffrin, whom he made the executor of his will; and right up to the time of his death, in his hundredth year, he was famed for his brilliant conversation, his wit, and the charm of his manner. His literary works include *Histoire du théâtre français* (1742), *Vie de Corneille*, *Réflexions sur la poétique*; he played an important role in the Quarrel of the Ancients and the Moderns, in which he sided with the Moderns; but it is as a thinker that he is chiefly remembered today. He combined with his 'bel esprit' a scientific detachment and a remarkable independence of judgement. His absence of prejudice, and his disillusion with life, proved singularly attractive to men of a younger generation, creating a personality which became typical of many of the *philosophes* of the age. His *Histoire des oracles* (1686), an adaptation of

Van Dale's *De Oraculis Ethnicorum*, embodied potentially dangerous ideas first expressed in *De l'Origine des fables* (1680, but only published 1724). It was widely read, and its criticism of oracles extended to Christian miracles. His *Relation de l'île de Bornéo* (1676) is a guarded defence of the Protestants before the Revocation of the Edict of Nantes.

'L'esprit philosophique', Grimm wrote in the *Correspondance littéraire* (1 February 1757), 'aujourd'hui si généralement répandu, doit ses premiers progrès à Fontenelle'; and the most recent critic to write at length on the *Encyclopédie*, Professor J. Proust, called him 'le premier des Encyclopédistes'.[12] He certainly exercised an intellectual dominance before Voltaire. It would be wrong to limit him to the period up to 1697. His philosophy, of which scepticism is the key, varied more than has been hitherto thought and its evolution may be closely related to the political and social scene, and to the needs of his polemics. His clandestine publications, which have not yet been fully explored, would probably confirm this view. Before Montesquieu and Voltaire, he saw in history a record of human folly, which nevertheless holds the key to the understanding of man.

He rejected political and military history in favour of a history of the people, and he early adopted a sound critical approach. He noted the mechanism of human error, denied revelation, and saw in the invention of the gods a first attempt at a rational explanation of the universe. His position drew close to that of the deists. In *Sur l'histoire* (published in 1758), a treatise on the origins of religion, he developed these ideas, holding that all mythologies are equal, and that Greek myths have no rational validity. This work has been dated 1678–80 by J.-R. Carré[13] and 1685–90 by M. Roelens,[14] whilst J. Dagan[15] has suggested 1720. It certainly takes the reader further than *De l'Origine des fables*, and may have been reworked at different dates. His stress on the laws that govern the working of the human mind impressed his contemporaries, and, whilst he believed in the greater perfectibility of man, he expressed reservations about an uncritical acceptance of the idea of human progress.

In the field of science he upheld Descartes' physics and his theory of *tourbillons*, which led to his being attacked by Voltaire, who had become converted to the Newtonian system, thanks to Maupertuis. As a *savant*, he illustrated well the new scientific

[12] *Diderot et l'Encyclopédie*, 1962, pp. 179, 239.
[13] *La Philosophie de Fontenelle ou le sourire de la raison*, 1932.
[14] Introduction to Fontenelle *Textes choisis*, in 'Les classiques du peuple', 1966.
[15] 'Pour une histoire de la pensée de Fontenelle', *Revue d'histoire littéraire de la France*, 1956, pp. 619–41.

method, and his *Eloges* of Malebranche, Leibniz, and Newton, which are masterpieces of clear exposition, as well as his annual volume from 1699 on scientific developments, did much to enhance the status of the men of science; whilst his *Histoire de l'Académie* from 1666 to 1679 enhanced the status of the French Academy. In his most famous work, *Entretiens sur la pluralité des mondes habités*, he popularised the Copernican system, but he also provided a model of didactic technique that has not been excelled. He showed himself to be at once a scientist and a littérateur, and by mingling philosophical and scientific discussion at a high level with *badinage*, set a precedent which Diderot in particular adopted and developed with success.

His general scepticism falls short when confronted with scientific facts. It is possibly his conception of the solidarity of science and of the fundamental unity that governs the physical world which is Fontenelle's chief contribution to the history of ideas. This notion may not have been new, but he succeeded in making it his own and in popularising it. It was to underpin the *Encyclopédie*, and the creation of modern universities in the nineteenth century. By awakening curiosity in science and in its methods, he extended the field of literature, which was henceforward to embrace science as well as philosophy; and he may be said to have effectively bridged the gap between the arts and the sciences, which the Encyclopaedists were to attempt to close.

Other influences, besides that of Bayle, Fontenelle, and clandestine philosophical literature, were sapping the foundations of orthodoxy. The Huguenot refugee circles abroad had created centres of publication for prohibited works and provided a constant reminder of the value of intellectual liberty and the advantages of personal freedom. The English deists proved themselves to be even more valuable allies in the intellectual struggle for emancipation, offering a respectable alternative to Roman Catholicism. The word *deist* was first used by P. Viret, a disciple of Calvin, in 1564; but it was Herbert of Cherbury in *De Veritate*, first published in Paris in 1624, who formulated the general principle of deism: *recta communisque ratio*. Essentially deism involves a rational belief in the existence of God, with the rejection of the Church and its ministers, of all ceremonies and ritual, and of faith as a basis for religion. For the deists, the spectacle of nature, and the need of a divine architect and a prime mover to set the world in motion, are proof of the reality of God. Unlike the theists, they held that God never intervenes in the affairs of man. All mystical or transcendental experience is held to be absurd. Deism in practice becomes little else than social ethics, and the good deist is in fact the good citizen. Voltaire and d'Alembert held consistently to this view, basing themselves on the physics of Newton; and for the first half of the eighteenth century their 'natural religion' was in keeping with the known facts of science.

Later, however, a younger generation turned away from deism to a still more natural atheism. The chief English deists: Lord Herbert of Cherbury; Blount; Toland, who was a pantheist and who fiercely opposed the 'machinations' of the priests; Collins, whose *Discourse of Free-thinking* (1713) owes something to Locke; Shaftesbury,[16] who attacked religious extravagance, false prophets, asceticism, and persecution as contrary to natural religion; Woolston; Chubb; Bolingbroke; and others were closely studied by Voltaire[17] and the Encyclopaedists, and were freely translated into French by d'Holbach in support of his own atheism. This English influence, which has been closely studied and variously assessed, led to developments of great consequence for the history of ideas. Whereas deism could be almost considered as an acceptable variant of Protestantism in England,[18] in France such toleration was unthinkable, and there a limited religious controversy became a desperate conflict between faith and reason. The uncompromising attitude of the Roman Catholic Church, which would not allow the individual the right to think for himself, led to a confrontation which brought the deists close to the atheists in an ideological conflict of great magnitude.

The high mark of English deism is between 1689 and 1742, when men such as Newton and Robert Boyle remained Christians, holding on to the argument of design as proof of the existence of God. Yet Boyle's lectures were rationalistic, and such as to convert Benjamin Franklin to deism. All deists treated the scriptures as history, and attacked miracles and the literal interpretation of the Bible. It was only with the emphasis on the new sciences, physiology and biology, that firm basis for a more advanced thought became possible, and that we see in France, most clearly in the case of Diderot, the movement away from deism and natural religion to an avowed materialism. D'Alembert, whose philosophy was conditioned by his mathematical studies, clung to deism, as did Voltaire, chiefly bent on believing in what would lead to the

16 Shaftesbury was freely translated by Diderot, who popularised his ideas in France. Diderot adopted Shaftesbury's deism until he developed his own materialism.

17 Voltaire also claimed as a deist Samuel Clarke, the rationalist Anglican theologian.

18 There had developed in England broad movements of dissent such as anti-Trinitarianism, Unitarianism, secularism, Erastianism, Arminianism, Socianism, and sects of various kinds, which, however, were primarily within the Church of England; but Quaker pietism and 'latitudinarian' nationalism as expressed by Samuel Clarke may be cited in support of the general contention about the nature of English deism.

betterment of man's lot on earth, and also Rousseau, for whom deism is natural religion revealed through conscience, a sentimental, primitivist conception which comes close to that of Herbert.

Diderot, through the impact of new scientific discoveries, and by means of inspired conjectures on the origins of life and the evolution of the species, moved on to a form of dialectical materialism which the nineteenth century was to perfect. In retrospect, the English deists helped the French *philosophes* to uphold the right of the individual to think for himself, and reinforced the humanist tradition, as also the sense of the oneness of mankind. Their influence, extended to other countries, but at a later date than in France – to Germany where it was felt by Lessing, Moses Mendelssohn, and Kant; to America, where their influence merged with that of the French, as in the cases of Benjamin Franklin, Jefferson, Washington, Thomas Paine, and Ethan Allen.

Another rich source of inspiration of the Encyclopaedists was the literature of Greece and Rome. Education was based on the classics, and the humanists of the Renaissance had strengthened ties with a civilisation that was essentially pre-Christian. Little wonder if the young educated men of France, who were not invited to turn to the Bible as a basic text for enlightenment, as they were in Protestant countries, should seek in antiquity the first examples of a Golden Age they sought to recreate in their own time. The Pantheon, which comfortably housed so many gods, became a kind of temple for modern deists, in which moral realism was most highly prized. The Stoics and Epicureans, Seneca, Democritus, Epicurus, and increasingly Lucretius, were studied and reinterpreted. Peter Gay has given as subtitle to his book *The Enlightenment: an Interpretation*, vol. I: *The Rise of Modern Paganism* (1966) and laid great stress on this important aspect of the Enlightenment. He sees the Enlightenment as a paganism directed against the Christian inheritance, and dependent upon the paganism of classical antiquity; but also as a modern paganism emancipated from classical thought as much as from Christian dogma. It is certain Rousseau saw himself as a modern Plutarch and Diderot as Diogenes, Socrates, or Seneca. Reminiscences of the classics are constantly to be found in the works of the *philosophes*. The Greeks had moved from myth to reason, thereby setting an example for modern times. In spite of efforts to evolve a critical method, sources were most often used in a highly individual manner. Rome attracted the *philosophes* more than Greece, and in this respect Montesquieu set a pattern that Gibbon and Ferguson were to follow. Cicero is preferred to Aristotle for his conception of *humanitas*, a major concept the *philosophes* wished to promote, to deepen, and to make their own.

Other influences were at work besides the intellectual forces that have been described. As D. Mornet pointed out in *Les Origines intellectuelles de la Révolution française* (1933), social, political, and economic factors were no doubt more important from the standpoint of the political historian. Many have stressed the part of the impoverished peasantry, whilst others have stressed the rise of the artisan class. The *philosophes* were, consciously or not, sensitive to the basic needs and aspirations of the less as well as the more enlightened people of the period. In the intellectual climate that was specifically theirs, they selected and integrated all data serving their purpose.

Each one turned to those sources of inspiration compatible with his temperament, his upbringing, and the special circumstances, often of an accidental kind, which prompted him to write. The interplay of personalities in high places or with high reputations, the conflicting ambitions and policies of members of the Establishment or of the Encyclopaedists themselves, all played a part in the moulding of new ideas. Intelligent reactions to events that seemed to be solely dictated by the whim of kings, mistresses, Ministers, prelates, and other *religionnaires*, or by the *parlements*, led to fundamental revision of main theories as the century progressed. The Encyclopaedists became bolder as political and economic crises grew worse. They adjusted their thinking to a world that was growing vaster through new discoveries, yet smaller through trade and easier communications, and the knowledge of foreign lands and foreign ways for which they were responsible.

One minor and yet important focal point of social and political unease, and one which illustrates the combination of factors working in the minds of thinking men, was the Club de l'Entresol, founded in 1720 by the Abbé Alary, with the help of the abbé de Saint-Pierre (1658–1743). This *club à l'anglaise* gathered together about twenty members under the presidency of the Abbé Alary, and with the marquis d'Argenson, future Minister for Foreign Affairs, as secretary. They met on Saturdays between 5 and 8 p.m., either in Alary's rooms in the house of the Président Hénault, or in the Tuileries. The members read papers on historical subjects, or on the administration of foreign countries, and freely discussed the news of the day. Each member made himself a specialist in certain aspects of their general interests. To this club, the first of its kind, the abbé de Saint-Pierre contributed as many papers as all the other members combined. It was there, in 1722, that Montesquieu read his *Dialogue de Sylla et d'Eucrate*. The club was virtually an academy of social and political science, and it flourished until 1730, when Cardinal Fleury, who headed the government at the time, became suspicious of its motives. The members, who were in no way revolutionary, wisely decided to disperse. D'Argenson attempted to revive the club in 1734, but without success.

The abbé de Saint-Pierre, one of the two founder members, showed both ingenuity and tenacity in the schemes he put forward for the greater well-being of the world. It is said that the neologism, *bienfaisance*, which was to become a key word of the century, is due to him. He wrote an important work which illustrates his kindly idealism: *Projet de paix perpétuelle* (2 vols., 1713; 3rd vol., 1717; his own *abrégé* appearing in 1729). In his *abrégé*, he claimed that he was merely reviving a scheme first propounded by Henri IV, in a letter addressed to Queen Elizabeth I (1595), by which a federation of European states could be established. Later Henri IV's Minister Sully, in his *Economies royales* (published in 1638), proposed a Supreme Council, or League of Nations, to ensure perpetual peace; a further scheme on similar lines was put forward by Emery Cruce in 1623. Saint-Pierre's system, however, was worked out in very great detail, and is very close indeed to that adopted by the League of Nations in the twentieth century. In another work, *Discours sur la Polysynodie* (1718), for which he was dismissed from the Academy, in spite of Fontenelle, the only member to vote for him, he sought to establish committees or councils of competent men in place of the usual governmental Ministries. The regent, who befriended him, wished to see this scheme implemented, but the experiment was not a success. The untiring abbé wrote a large number of papers, some highly idealistic, others with practical objects in view; the following titles show his range of interests: *Projet pour perfectionner le commerce en France*; *Projet pour rendre les chemins praticables en hiver; Mémoire pour l'établissement d'une taille proportionnelle ou taille tarifée*; *Projet pour perfectionner la médecine; Observations politiques sur le célibat des prêtres*; *Projet pour perfectionner l'éducation*; *Projet pour rendre les spectacles plus utiles à l'Etat*, etc. In his effort to secure universal peace he insisted on the maintenance of the *status quo* between nations and not on the ideal concept of right. J.-J. Rousseau followed up these ideas, publishing an *Extrait du projet de paix perpétuelle* in 1761, as did the German philosopher Kant; and in the nineteenth century the French socialists Fourier and Saint-Simon, and the French writers Victor Hugo and Michelet.

The *philosophes* for a long time centred their hopes of perpetual peace on the increase in trade between countries, and on the growing power of 'enlightened' merchants, whose interest, in every sense of the term, lay in peace. Voltaire in addition popularised the idea of a vast 'république des lettres', cutting across traditional political boundaries. The Enlightenment, which took on different forms in England, in Germany, and in Italy, and which spread to all other countries, was a cosmopolitan phenomenon. Outside France men such as Gibbon, Franklin, Jefferson, Beccaria, Lessing, and Kant all made outstanding contributions to the new movement; and it may be claimed that Hume, for whom religion had lost all authority, epitomised the scepticism that underlined all efforts towards intellectual emancipation and greater personal liberty. In France it had the deepest political significance, largely through the unity achieved by undertaking a common work, the *Encyclopédie*. In practice, the Encyclopaedists were a body of men who knew one another and were drawn together by common interests. They did not constitute any rigid political party, but fully justified the term 'la séquelle encyclopédique' which Voltaire liked to use. They were in fact rather like the members of the Club de l'Entresol, but formed a larger group, representing the élite of the nation, who had undertaken a task of outstanding importance. Each preserved his individuality intact, and was capable of argument with his fellows; but they all moved ultimately in the same direction through a general purpose in common. No doubt part of their strength lay in their personal freedom to work within a broad framework of which they all approved.[19] Much of their success may be attributed to the many parallel lines of reform they offered, and their encouragement of experimentation in ideas as well as in science: but the necessary changes in the intellectual, social, and political life of France, as of the rest of the thinking world, would have been inconceivable without the growth of scepticism during an earlier period. The confrontation of the Christian and pagan heritage, the interpretation of the new facts of science, the application of rational methods to the study of religion and of man, and the glorification of increasingly well-informed criticism, all played a part in making the Enlightenment a 'science of freedom'. [20]

19 The one *philosophe* to be ostracised was J.-J. Rousseau, after his break with Diderot and other Encyclopaedists. Until then he had been a member of their inmost circle, and cognisant of their policies, and they had cause to fear the development of his own thought on lines often at variance with their own on fundamental issues.

20 See Peter Gay, *The Enlightenment: An Interpretation*, vol. II: *The Science of Freedom*, 1969.

Chapter 7

MONTESQUIEU

CHARLES-LOUIS DE SECONDAT, baron de La Brède et de Montesquieu, was born in 1689 in the Château de La Brède, near Bordeaux, the second son of Jacques de Secondat, an active soldier and president and chief justice of the Parlement de Guyenne, and of Marie-Françoise de Pesnel. When his mother, a wealthy and devout woman with English as well as French forebears, died in 1696, the barony of the wine-producing property of La Brède, which she had owned, was inherited by Charles-Louis, then aged seven. This family background of wealthy and distinguished landowners holding high parliamentary office serves to explain much of Montesquieu's ultimate views on politics and society.

At the age of eleven he was sent to the Collège de Juilly, in the diocese of Meaux, a school belonging to the priests of the Oratory, and one which provided tuition in science as well as a sound classical education, including philosophy and law, on unusually enlightened lines. He left school in 1705 to study law at the University of Bordeaux, and in 1708, after graduation, he was admitted advocate, and moved to Paris in order to gain practical experience. In 1714, one year after the death of his father, he became *conseiller* to the Parlement of Bordeaux; and on the death of his uncle, who left him all his estates, including the barony of Montesquieu, near Agen, he was made *président à mortier*, or deputy president.

In 1715 he married Jeanne de Lartigue, a wealthy Protestant, who came to him with a dowry of 100,000 livres and subsequently bore him two daughters and a son. He was by now socially and financially unassailable, engaged in the administration of his property and the exercise of his judicial functions, and at the same time pursuing a careful study of Roman law and acquiring a considerable knowledge of contemporary science, mainly in the fields of geology, physics, and biology.

Scholarship proving more attractive than parliamentarianism, he sold his office in 1726 and at the age of thirty-seven decided to devote himself solely to the pursuit of knowledge. Between the years 1716 and 1721 he had read a number of papers, drafted in his leisure hours, to the Academy of Sciences in Bordeaux, among them a *Dissertation sur la politique des Romains dans la religion* (1716), treatises, or rather *résomptions* of other people's work, on the cause of echoes, the weight and transparency of bodies, the use of renal glands, the tides, and motion; but he abandoned experimental research, either because of his defective eyesight or because he felt more drawn to other fields of activity.

His *Discours académiques* were not in any case destined to bring him world renown, which came to him through the *Lettres persanes*, published anonymously in 1721 and achieving an immediate success. The revelation of the author's name and status added enormously to the early surprise and scandal aroused by the anonymous publication, ensuring an even wider circulation for this very provocative work.

Montesquieu's *Lettres persanes* are a landmark in the history of the novel and of satire, as well as a social document vividly presenting his world. Through the eyes and pens of two Persians, Usbek and Rica, writing to each other and to family and friends over the period 1711 to 1720, Montesquieu was able to present a satirical portrait of contemporary life in Paris, and to deride French society, as he observed it at the end of the reign of Louis XIV and during the regency. The creation of two characters enabled Montesquieu to present different but complementary standpoints, which together with the alienation effect of making them Persian and not French, enlarged both the scope of the satire and its objectivity. Moreover, the inclusion of harem stories, of Persian incident and comment to be expected in the circumstances, served to illumine the attitudes to the society of the time, by contrast or unexpected similarity, and by a dichotomy of atmosphere and experience. The Persians set the scene: Paris with its café and salon society, life in the Tuileries, the bustle in the streets, description of buildings and institutions – the Hospice des Quinze-Vingts, the Académie Française; references to current events, the death of Louis XIV, political disturbances, the Revocation of the Edict of Nantes; echoes of celebrated controversies, like that of the Ancients and the Moderns; comment on the system of John Law and on the intricacies of social pattern; all presented through the eyes and minds of two Persians, and interpreted through their own background.

The letters are studded with character sketches that call to mind a kindlier La Bruyère: the *fermier-général*, the nobleman, the lackey, the starving poet, the old warhorse, the hack writer, the *directeur de conscience*, and the *homme à bonnes fortunes*; through them Montesquieu is able to shed new light upon the problems of his time – divorce, depopulation, colonialism, slavery, and certain dubious laws. Moreover, the apparently objective attitudes of his Persians permit new and ironic assessments: of the king, seen as an oriental despot and 'un grand magicien; il exerce son empire sur l'esprit même de ses sujets, il les fait penser comme il veut'; of the Pope, 'un autre magicien, plus fort que lui (le prince) ... Ce magicien s'appelle le pape: tantôt il lui fait croire que trois ne sont qu'un; que le pain qu'on mange n'est pas du pain, ou que le vin qu'on boit n'est pas du vin; et mille autres choses de cette espèce' (Lettre xxiv).

The new iconoclastic mordant spirit of the times is reflected throughout the *Lettres persanes*, notably in barbed commentary on the bull *Unigenitus*,[1] in mockery of Roman Catholic doctrine and of the Spanish Inquisitors; this factor accounts in no small measure for their immediate and resounding success. The allegory of the Troglodytes (Lettres xi–xiv) made a particularly strong impact upon contemporary minds, for this symbolic tale of the development of modern society is the dream of a rationalist magistrate, based on an intellectual reconstruction of history rather than on any empirical knowledge of early society. Admirably written, effectively phrased, it leads inevitably to an objective reappraisal of political and social systems, and in many respects foreshadows Montesquieu's later *Esprit des lois*.

Throughout this lengthy interpolated tale, society is seen to rest upon solidarity of interests, and religion has only a social context. A free society can thrive only if civic virtues are encouraged, as was true of the republics of antiquity, since happiness in a lawless social pattern must depend upon the perfection of each and every one of its members. When individual citizens find total virtue a burden too great to be borne, an endurance test under which they falter, then laws are required: and inevitably, the individual feels free to act with what may well be dubious morality, provided he respects the letter of the law.

This preoccupation with happiness and morality is a characteristic of the century. It was already to be found in Fénelon's *Télémaque*, one of several works that profoundly influenced Montesquieu. As presented by Montesquieu, the Troglodyte story reveals his main preoccupations through the recurrence of certain words, typical of a man of law, that run like a *leitmotiv* through his narrative – justice, equity, humanity – the last a lay ideal, given new

[1] The bull *Unigenitus* was promulgated by Pope Clement XI in 1713. It condemned 101 propositions in Père Quesnel's *Réflexions morales*, which the Jesuits had branded as Jansenist heresy. In 1752 the archbishop of Paris, Christophe de Beaumont, ordered priests in his diocese to refuse Holy Communion to all persons failing to produce a signed statement of endorsement of the bull *Unigenitus*. Only the expulsion of the Jesuits in 1764 put an end to this requirement.

emphasis in contemporary thought, and one which the *philosophes* were later to adopt. And running like a golden thread through the whole story is the idyllic, Virgilian picture of a man in his simplicity happily living his primitive life, imbued with the austere virtues of Roman civilisation at its zenith. This concept, ideal or illusory according to taste, was expressed by many eighteenth-century rationalists, including Rousseau in his two *Discours*, and in *Julie ou La Nouvelle Héloïse*, Diderot in the *Supplément au Voyage de Bougainville*, and Bernardin de Saint-Pierre in *Paul et Virginie*.

Another element contributing to the popularity of the *Lettres persanes* is to be found in the oriental tale that runs side by side with the more serious content of the work. The Orient was very much in fashion: already the *Voyage de Tavernier en Turquie, en Perse, et aux Indes orientales* (1676–79) had enjoyed a vogue.

In 1704–17 the celebrated translation of the *Mille et une nuits* by Galland had appeared; in 1711 the *Journal du voyage du Chevalier Chardin en Perse et aux Indes orientales* appeared; and *L'Espion dans les cours*, a translation of Giovanni Paolo Marana's *L'Esploratore turco* (1684) of which Montesquieu is known to have possessed the 1717 edition by Marana, together with the *Amusements sérieux et comiques d'un Siamois* (1707), by Dufresny, is generally thought to have been the springboard for Montesquieu's work, which fitted so admirably into the fashionable literary atmosphere of his day. The *intrigues de harem* taking place while the Persian Usbek was abroad titillated the contemporary reader by their open impropriety and indecency. The harem story, with its revelations of an unsatisfactory way of life, which balances the Paris experience of the two visiting Persians, is not extraneous, but designed to point the triumph of natural instinct and justice over despotism, for this was Montesquieu's intention. It is possible that Montesquieu deliberately pandered to the taste of his readers, indulging in his particular brand of dry and humorous salacity, in his ribald account of the pleasures of the harem, the sufferings of the women enclosed in it, and the troubles of the Great Eunuch during his master's absence. It is certain that his work stands out for its originality and wit by reason of his new incisive and ironical style, his treatment of his theme, which makes abundantly clear the relativity of our conventions and judgements, and above all the form in which it is presented.

His narrative, developed in the form of letters passing between a group of people, makes full use of one of the most interesting kinds of imaginative writing, equal in importance to that of the pseudo-memoirs that were a feature of the age. The epistolary form had a long posterity, including Voltaire's *Lettres philosophiques*, which proved its suitability for the presentation, discussion, and propagation of ideas, as well as for satire; it included works of astonishing variety, from Rousseau's *La Nouvelle Heloïse* to Laclos' *Les Liaisons dangereuses*: for Diderot it offered greater freedom to digress and a greater intimacy with his reader; the use he made of these factors deserves special study.

Montesquieu demonstrates the advantages of the form, in presentation of diverse but closely linked themes, in helping to awaken the reader's mind and force him to examine his prejudices, and in allowing the author a simulated ambiguity of expression, an alienation from the core and content of his work that in some measure protected him from criticism. It was not he but others, and these others reared in the exotic Orient, who expressed their astonishment at the social, political, and moral pattern prevailing in Paris and in France.

The sharp, elegant style, the sardonic wit, the literary devices implicit in the letter-form still bring enjoyment to present-day readers no longer interested in detail concerning the daily life of a period now dead and gone. There may have been, for Montesquieu's first readers, the added malicious pleasure of putting exact names to all the characters in the book, but it is doubtful whether the book really falls into the category of the *roman à clé*. It is more likely that, given such barbed detail and such satiric comment on known events, descriptions and attitudes could be made to fit personalities of the day chosen at random by different readers. The work was, and remains, unparalleled in a way peculiar to Montesquieu.

In it, moreover, are to be found his fundamental political thoughts as later developed in the *Esprit des lois*. We have the same notion of law, the same distinction between republic, monarchy, and despotism. Most pertinently, and through his social criticism, we sense his gnawing fear that France was in the process of decline from monarchy to despotism owing to the policy of Louis XIV, 'tant il fait cas de la politique orientale'. Montesquieu found *parlements* in decline, an idle nobility, and talent widely diverted into vacuous frivolities, whilst female influence was paramount at court.

He moved to Paris, where he enjoyed a great social success, and gained admission to court circles through the duke of Berwick, whom he had known as military governor of Bordeaux. He became a prominent visitor to the salon of Mme de Lambert; and frequented the Club de l'Entresol, where the marquis d'Argenson, Andrew Michael Ramsay, and Bolingbroke were to be met, and where in 1722 he read his *Dialogue de Scylla et d'Eucrate*, which was published in the *Mercure de France* in 1745.

He still, however, spent much of his time in Bordeaux, and frequently read papers to the Academy of Bordeaux, including part of a *Traité général des devoirs* (1725), a serious work written from the standpoint of Stoic philosophy. He also wrote a prose poem, in quite another vein, entitled *Le Temple de Gnide* (1725), intended mainly for the entertainment of court circles. It is an odd work to have come from his astringent pen, a novel written in the first person, and in an artificial and mildly indecent manner, expressing an equally mild eroticism, and purporting to satirise life at the court of the young Louis XV.

Having incurred certain debts, Montesquieu sold his legal office in the Parlement of Bordeaux in 1726, in order to improve his financial position, and came to settle in Paris, where he hoped to be elected to the Académie Française. A vacancy occurred in October 1727, but Fleury, who had taken exception to certain passages in the *Lettres persanes*, blocked Montesquieu's election. Fleury, however, was in the course of time placated, and Montesquieu duly became a member on 24 January 1728.

In April of that same year, he set off in the company of Lord Waldegrave on a prolonged tour of foreign parts, leaving his wife behind. He visited Vienna, where he met the famous general Prince Eugene, and went on to visit the mines of Hungary, and to examine the constitutions of Hungary and Poland. He then moved on to Venice to meet the financier John Law, now living in poverty and exile; and formed a close friendship with Lord Chesterfield. In Rome he studied art, and was received, very cordially, by the Pope. There are references both to Pietro Giannone and to G. B. Vico in Montesquieu's works, and considerable evidence of a profitable time spent in Italy. His travels took him next to Switzerland, and he then followed the Rhine to Holland.

In October 1729, in the company of Lord Chesterfield, he went to England, where he stayed until the spring of 1731. This lengthy visit proved to be a milestone in his education and in his intellectual development. His own account of that year and a half of his life was unfortunately destroyed by his grandson. We know, however, from other evidence, that he moved in a wide circle which included Tories and dissident Whigs, and that he became a freemason. He was presented at court, attended parliamentary debates, bought many books for his own library, and read contemporary journals, among them *The Craftsman*. He studied the political writings of Locke with extreme care, and strove to understand the workings of the English constitution. He became, and remained, a great admirer of that constitution and of the English political system.

Upon his return to La Brède, he consecrated two years to the furtherance of his literary pursuits. A short treatise on *La Monarchie universelle* (1734) was quickly withdrawn, and only his own copy survives. He also wrote an interesting essay on the English constitution, which appeared in 1748 as part of his major work, and is in itself one of the most remarkable of the early contributions to the study of history to offer a modern interpretation.

Montesquieu's *Considérations sur les causes de la grandeur des Romains et de leur décadence* was published anonymously in 1734. It was not at first well received, and is in some ways less finished than his previous work, for there is some uncritical documentation in it, a disregard of the findings of archaeology, and a certain mishandling of evidence: yet it was soon acclaimed as a work of major importance.

Montesquieu was not the first modern historian of Roman antiquity. He had been preceded by Machiavelli, Balzac, Saint-Evremond, and above all by Bossuet, whose particular account of the grandeur of Rome had inspired Montesquieu. The latter's originality lay in his analysis of the decadence of Rome, the quality of his observations, and their implication for the understanding of current events and adumbration of the basis of future reforms in France.

If Montesquieu failed to apply Bayle's strict criteria in the assessment of sources, he adopted the right general method for the study of history, the principle of historical causation. He was not, however, a determinist, but one who strove to reconcile free-will and historical determinism through the distinction he made between cause and occasion:

> Il y a des causes générales, soit morales, soit physiques, qui agissent dans chaque monarchie, l'élèvent, la maintiennent, ou la précipitent: tous les accidents sont soumis à des causes; et si le hasard d'une bataille, c'est-à-dire, une cause particulière a ruiné un Etat, il y avait une cause générale qui faisait que cet Etat devait périr par une seule bataille: en un mot, l'allure principale entraîne avec elle tous les accidents particuliers.

Here he states the modern scientific approach to history, and shows himself the precursor of Voltaire and all subsequent historians. D'Alembert, in his preface to the fifth volume of the *Encyclopédie*, gave the best brief account of this notable work, under the title of *Eloge de M. le président de Montesquieu*.

Montesquieu's analytical method leads him to seek the deep general causes of events leading to the decadence of Rome, to note all the intermediary stages, starting without preconceived ideas. His examination enables him to expose the strength of specific institutions, particularly military institutions, and the advantages of evolving sound laws and a system based upon the Roman soldier's self-interest as a landowner, and of establishing a powerful

Senate as head of the structure of government. He then demonstrates his own belief that the seeds of decay are present in Rome at her very zenith and brilliantly stresses the growing decadence under Tiberius and Caligula, and the ultimate tyranny of the régime. He portrayed in detail and highlighted the several overlapping aspects of Roman civilisation, continually expressing by direct statement or by implication his own detestation of despotism, and his love of liberty, which must be achieved as the greatest political benefit to be bestowed upon mankind. The work is a mature expression of Montesquieu's whole philosophy. It is written in fine and dignified prose, coining new and striking formulae; and his vigorous, firm, Latin style is enriched by images, comparisons, and antitheses, which nevertheless avoid all over-emphasis or ostentation.

From 1734 onwards his time was divided between Paris, where he frequented the salons of Mme de Tencin, Mme Geoffrin, and Mme du Deffand, in whose gatherings he met d'Alembert and the Président Hénault, and the Château de La Brède where he prepared his great work, *De l'Esprit des lois*, which may be said to be the application to law of the methods he used in the *Considérations sur les causes de la grandeur des Romains et de leur décadence* for the analysis of Roman history.

De l'Esprit des lois (Geneva, 1748) is a major work on law and politics; with it sociology enters into the field of literature. It met with instant success, due partly no doubt to its excellence, and partly to its apposite appearance. Twenty editions were brought out in as many months, and it was translated into most known languages. To prepare this, his major work, Montesquieu had embarked upon an extensive reading programme embracing law, history, geography, and political theory. Ten secretaries at least were employed to act as readers, research assistants, and general amanuenses: and his notes filled a number of volumes, of which only one survives, *Geographica t.II.* By 1740 the main part had been drafted, and the book was virtually finished by 1743, whereupon Montesquieu began the first of two very thorough revisions, which took him until December 1746. Even after J. Barrillot of Geneva had been selected as publisher, Montesquieu undertook further emendations, and added several new chapters: and the work was finally published in November 1748 in two quarto volumes running to 1,086 pages, divided into thirty-one books. The full title of the work was: *De l'Esprit des lois, ou du rapport que les lois doivent avoir avec la constitution de chaque gouvernement, les mœurs, le climat, la religion, le commerce, etc.*

Montesquieu defined laws as *les rapports nécessaires qui dérivent de la nature des choses*, and it is through the study of these *rapports* that we are able to perceive *l'esprit des lois*, that is, the rational principles underlying scientific, moral, and positive laws. Surprisingly in a man of Montesquieu's temperament and training, the work was long, rambling, and ill-arranged, within a loose framework:

I–VIII Laws in general, their relationship with nature, and principles of government.
IX–XIX Relativity of laws to military force, political constitution, civil state, taxation, climate, and customs.
XX–XXVI Relationship of laws with commerce, currency, population, and religion.
XXVII–XXXI Study of Roman laws on succession, French laws, and feudal laws.

Broadly speaking, Montesquieu moves from a consideration of man in the state of nature (anticipating here Rousseau) with pre-rational, pre-moral 'lois de la nature' to that of the positive laws of man in society. It is at this point that the kind of government adopted, and a study of physical and other factors determining needs, becomes relevant.

The whole work, which draws on Montesquieu's long years of study, was designed to embody acquired knowledge and to make it readily accessible to minds that were open to receive it: and it was received with open acclaim, though, perhaps because of the imperfections of presentation, it took a little while for the general public to realise that here was a political treatise comparable to the *Politics* of Aristotle.

The work contained, moreover, some important and original ideas. The method of examining the reasons for existing laws, and the relation of laws, by applying principles of historical and comparative studies on a universal basis, was new. Montesquieu was more lucid than Vico and he ranged more widely in his efforts to understand the reason for laws and the principles underlying historical causation and natural and social conditions. He saw the immutable character of the mechanical laws governing the universe, and of moral or natural law, but he showed himself to be more of an empiricist than Locke in his general approach, and combined more effectively his abstract concept of natural law with empirical considerations drawn from his reading and his observation.

He was also original in his classification of forms of government, to each one of which he assigned an animating principle. A republic – democratic if the government is by a whole people, aristocratic if only by a section of the people – is founded upon *vertu*, i.e. public spirit, a monarchy upon honour, and despotism upon fear. He condemned despotism as wholly bad and feared that without vigilance oriental tyranny might govern France. He personally favoured monarchy, as most likely to achieve political and civil liberty in the absence of true virtue and self-restraint in the majority of citizens; for it rested on fundamental laws which limited the power of the monarch. The nobility, the Church, and the *parlements* are intermediate powers which should prevent monarchy degenerating into despotism. As for the republic, it is an admirable form of government, but for another and better age. His theory of the separation of powers, which should, in a well-organised state, lead to political liberty, was equally new. A certain mingling of powers was in fact acknowledged by Montesquieu as being inevitable, but the legislative, the executive, and judicial powers must rest in the hands of different individuals, or groups of individuals, so as to ensure the maximum amount of liberty for those who are governed. The model government, for Montesquieu, is exemplified in the English pattern, as seen through the eyes of the Tory opposition to Walpole, and in the writings of Bolingbroke.

These ideas are set out in Book XI, chapter 6, which may therefore be regarded as one of the most important on political theory in the whole of the eighteenth century, and which had first been drafted in 1734. Montesquieu's analysis, now seen to be imperfect, was long held to be authoritative, even in England, where it was held to be an advance on Locke's views because of its emphasis on the role of the judicial element in politics.

The principles laid down in *L'Esprit des lois* were carried into effect at the time of the French Revolution, and since that time have been regarded as a safeguard against anarchy or arbitrary rule, because of the balance established, and the allowance for intermediary powers.

The presentation given of the British constitution may well be challenged today: it should be remembered nevertheless that the constitution of that time inspired the Declaration of the Rights of Man and the constitution of the United States of America.

Montesquieu's theory of climate, adumbrated in the *Lettres persanes* as exercising an influence on population, customs, and religion, is extended to the political field in *L'Esprit des lois*. From the effect of climate on man's physique, he passes to its influence on shaping the mind of society. In primitive communities this influence is paramount, in more sophisticated societies it may be counteracted by legislation. The theory of climate had many exponents before Montesquieu, among whom may be cited Fontenelle, Fénelon, and the Abbé Dubos: but for Montesquieu it was of such primary importance that the emphasis he placed upon it led him to take up a conservative position. For, in effect, if the character of a people is determined by climate, each nation must have the form of government which suits this character, even if it is not ideally the best form of government. 'S'il est vrai', he writes, 'que le caractère de l'esprit et les passions du coeur soient extrêmement différents dans les divers climats, les lois doivent être relatives et à la différence de ces passions et à la différence de ces caractéres, (XIV, ch. I).

It should, however, be made clear that Montesquieu was not a true determinist, for he believed in man's free-will, and in his moral responsibility: it was because of this that he could allow for a wise legislator with powers for good, and one who could educate public opinion.

In more general terms he aligns himself with the sensationalist philosophy: 'C'est d'un nombre infini de petites sensations que dépendent l'imagination, le goût, la sensibilité, la vivacité' (XIV, ch. 2). Montesquieu's own observations at Bordeaux in support of his theories proved inconclusive. His general ideas on the influence of climate, and of milieu in general, were nevertheless taken up by Mme de Staël, and fully developed later in the nineteenth century by H. Taine, who extended them to cover literary criticism. They are the basis of Montesquieu's quasi-determinist philosophy, echoes of which may be found to this day.

There are, of course, other influences besides climate, which are increasingly effective as civilisation becomes more complex; and in this context Montesquieu studies laws, maxims of government, and religion, considered from the standpoint of a sociologist concerned more with the utility of a belief than with the truth of a doctrine. Montesquieu believed in God and free-will, as did Locke, and accepted the simple dogmas of God's existence and His benevolence and the part both must play in his political system. He believed that a good political order must be based upon Christian principles; and that Catholicism was the right religion for France. But he was opposed to religious intolerance, as he was opposed to all forms of despotism, and never, for example, seems to have suggested to his wife that she should give up her Protestant faith. His views on religion and religious institutions were those of a magistrate concerned with equity rather than those of a man of faith, and he experienced no difficulty in avoiding the religious experience.

R. Shackleton's examination of successive drafts of *L'Esprit des lois*[2] has shown that with the passing years Montesquieu grew increasingly wary in his criticism of religious institutions; but his alleged repentance upon his death-bed, after the visit of Bernard

[2] *Montesquieu, a Critical Biography*, 1961.

Routh, an Irish Jesuit, seems improbable, and is certainly irrelevant. As one writer has stated, with truth, Montesquieu was a deist at heart and an Erastian in politics.

The final book of *L'Esprit des lois* may be regarded as an appendix to the whole work. It deals with the history of law, both written and customary law; with sound commonsense and the help of philological evidence, it examines the origins of French aristocracy; and expresses a preference, shared with Saint-Simon and his friends, for a revival of feudalism. Montesquieu was a member of the *noblesse de robe*, and he would have liked to have, in France as in England, a powerful aristocracy as a check on the despotism of the monarch or the people. He cannot be described as a conservative, but rather as a reformer with conservative tendencies. He is known to have exerted an influence on Edmund Burke.

Montesquieu would have welcomed the re-establishment of the power of the nobility, and the *parlements*, and of the French Estates, General and Provincial; and he showed remarkable insight in passages where he expressed the view that in a democracy, equality can lead to despotism. Throughout his work, a spirit of criticism of the established order reigns supreme; and concrete proposals for change are inherent in his analysis of existing structures and his discussion of political theories, including both their causes and their effects.

The *philosophes* welcomed his constant attack upon despotism in all its manifestations – *lettres de cachet*, torture, judicial interrogation, poverty, and war – and on intolerance and slavery, even as they shared his preoccupation with freedom and civil liberty. For Montesquieu, freedom, however, must be limited to what is allowable by law, and it is therefore of paramount importance to have good legislators, to protect the common interests of the people, to bring law into harmony with economic, social, and political conditions, and to examine the penal system in closest detail. Both justice and behaviour must be based upon reason, and upon an exact appreciation of the development of social and political institutions.

It is interesting to note that Montesquieu's methods and whole approach to the problems of man in society, involving as they did an awareness of evolution in social patterns, and the relativity and interdependence of laws, foreshadow Emile Durkheim, the founder of sociology. Montesquieu was also a pioneer in the philosophy of history: his political and legal thought influenced J.-J. Rousseau, and also led to modifications in governmental institutions, and in existing laws. It had direct bearing on the constitution of 1791, and led to some of the reforms of the Constituent Assembly, the Restoration, and the July monarchy; and no doubt to the increased emphasis on the *séparation des pouvoirs* in the constitution of the Fifth Republic.

In spite of Montesquieu's own moderation, his work must be considered as one of the most important milestones along the road to the French Revolution, as he is a forerunner of nineteenth-century liberalism. His work is not without faults – inadequate documentation, inaccuracies, confused dates, oversimplification here and there, too great a reliance on early histories, and certain intellectual limitations, as, for example, his belief that republics are suitable only for small states, or that despotism was evolved only by the Turks. But through him a great step forward had been taken, new avenues of thought opened up; and political theory was henceforward to be seriously considered as a science worthy of close study.

Denunciatory articles were soon forthcoming from the Sorbonne and the general assembly of the French clergy. The attacks came from the Jansenists, who accused him in the *Nouvelles Ecclésiastiques* of being a deist, and by the Jesuits, who could not stomach religion considered from the humanist standpoint, in the *Journal de Trévoux*. In 1750 Montesquieu published his brilliantly written and finely argued *Défense de L'Esprit des lois*, to which the opposition could find no equally brilliant and succinct reply. One year later, *L'Esprit des lois* was placed on the Index.

Thereafter Montesquieu rested upon his fame, leading an unpretentious, kindly life, affable, willing to assist any who called upon his help, a trifle absent-minded in society: 'Je suis un bon citoyen; mais dans quelque pays où je fusse né, je l'aurais été tout de même.' He continued with his double life, a feudal lord at La Brède, a *philosophe* of recognised wit and intellect in Paris; and in both lives a rationalist with humanitarian ideals. He also continued to write, in spite of failing eyesight, and in 1748 published *Lysimaque*, a dialogue on despotism, addressed to the Académie de Nancy, which elected him to membership in 1751. This was followed by a novel, *Arsace et Isménie*, and finally by an *Essai sur le goût*, requested by d'Alembert, and destined for publication in the *Encyclopédie*. He died, exhausted and totally blind, in Paris on 10 February 1755, leaving behind a number of unfinished projects. His *Notes de voyage*, which have for the eighteenth century the significance of Montaigne's *Essais* in the sixteenth, and his correspondence, were published posthumously. He wrote, in a sense, his own epitaph: 'L'étude a été pour moi le souverain remède contre les dégoûts de la vie, n'ayant jamais eu de chagrin qu'une heure de lecture ne m'ait ôté.'

Chapter 8

VOLTAIRE

I. LIFE AND WORKS

FRANÇOIS-MARIE AROUET (1694–1778) was born on 21 November, of a family that had resided in Paris for two generations. His mother died when he was seven years old, and he was left with a feeling of alienation from his father, which increased some years later when the young Arouet wanted to devote himself exclusively to literature, and was forced instead to study law.

He was educated at the Collège Louis-le-Grand, where he remained for seven years, revealing an early aptitude for poetry. The abbé de Châteauneuf, his godfather, sponsor, and friend, was equally responsible for his education, introducing him to *belles-lettres*, to deism, and into society. While he was still a child, he frequented the dissipated, libertine group of intellectuals known as the Société du Temple, meeting Ninon de Lenclos while he was still at school, shortly before her death in 1705. In her will, she left the child 2,000 francs with which to buy books, proof of the impression he had made upon her.

In 1713, the brother of the abbé de Châteauneuf, who was an ambassador, took the young Arouet with him to the Hague. There he met Olympe Dunoyer, whom he called Pimpette, and with whom he fell in love. She was a young girl of excellent character, poor but well connected, whose mother enjoyed a dubious reputation; and the boy of nineteen was eager to marry her. The affair led to his dismissal from the service of the ambassador, and his father even went to the length of procuring a *lettre de cachet*, which in the event he did not use.

François returned home in no enviable frame of mind, was set to work in a lawyer's office, and amused himself writing libellous poems. His father, with whom relations were now strained to breaking-point, sent him into the country, in the care of Louis de Caumartin, marquis de Saint-Ange. On his return, he was introduced to the duchesse du Maine and the court of Sceaux. Influenced by the duchess's dislike of the regent, Philippe, duc d'Orléans, he wrote two lampoons concerning him, and as a result in 1716 he was exiled to Tulle, and then to Sully-sur-Loire. Two further lampoons took him to the Bastille on 16 May 1717, where he was imprisoned for eleven months. It was with this unlikely background that he began his literary career.

While he was in the Bastille he redrafted his first play, *Œdipe* begun in 1715, and also worked on the *Henriade*, his great epic poem which he was to publish in 1723 under the first title of *La Ligue*. In April 1718 he was freed from the Bastille, and assumed the name of Arouet de Voltaire, a supposed anagram of *Arouet le jeune*. He was exiled to Châteney, but after an audience with the regent his exile was rescinded and a better atmosphere was engendered, although there was never to be complete mutual trust between them.

Œdipe was performed on 18 November 1718, and ran for forty-five nights, a phenomenal run for a new play in that century. The play was not only well received, but also made a profit, with which Voltaire began those financial speculations that were to prove highly successful. He was then suspected of lampoons in fact perpetuated by Lagrange-Chancel, and found himself once more in exile. He returned to Paris in the winter of the same year, and in 1729 his second play, *Artémire*, was presented, without success.

In December 1721, or early in 1722, his father died, leaving him some property, and revenue of 4,000 livres annually, which the regent supplemented with a pension of 2,000 livres. He then offered his services as secret agent to the Cardinal Dubois, chief Minister of Philippe d'Orléans. His diplomatic missions took him to Cambrai, Brussels, and The Hague, but in the year 1722–23 he was back in Paris, with the tide of fortune running against him. Thus, in November 1723 he contracted smallpox; his play *Mariamne* was a failure; and the regent, who had treated him with generosity after his initial hostility, had died. On the other hand his friendship with Adrienne Lecouvreur dates from this time, and the patronage of the regent was replaced by that of the duc de Richelieu, with whom he stayed in 1724–25 while he reshaped *Mariamne*, which in its new form met with considerable success. It was through him and other school friends that he frequented high society.

Towards the end of 1725 came the incident which radically changed his life. He was insulted by the chevalier de Rohan, to whom he made a sharp Voltairean reply. Later, while he was dining with the duc de Sully, he was called out and soundly beaten by the lackeys of the chevalier de Rohan, who stood by watching while it happened. Three months later he challenged the duc de Rohan to a duel; and on the very morning on which it was due to take place, he was arrested by *lettre de cachet* and sent to the

Bastille, where he remained for a fortnight until, at his own request, he was shipped off to England.

His resentment concerning the whole incident, and his sense of outrage and of injustice, were enduring, and provided a background of personal involvement to his subsequent political activity. Voltaire stayed in England for nearly three years, and was made welcome by Walpole, Bubb Dodington, Bolingbroke, Congreve, Sarah, duchess of Marlborough, and Pope; he was presented to George I in 1727; and he frequented members of Huguenot society, mainly merchants in silk, then in London. He acquired a good working knowledge of English, which he continued to speak and to write throughout his long life, and a great and lasting admiration for England.

He learned much about the English way of life at first hand, its values, its literature, science, and philosophy, its developing trades, and its religious sects, among which he was particularly fascinated by the Quakers. An English edition of the *Henriade*, dedicated to Queen Caroline, earned him thousands of pounds. During this period, he paid a few unofficial visits to Paris, and was finally allowed to return in the spring of 1729. His play *Brutus*, performed in 1730, in which there was no love interest nor female characters, owes something to the influence of Shakespeare. The death of Adrienne Lecouvreur in that same year led to his writing an *Ode sur la mort de Mademoiselle Lecouvreur*, destined to become famous; and he had already begun work on *La Pucelle*, an indecent poem in scurrilous language recounting the life of Joan of Arc, which deeply gratified his own sense of humour, but which he had to keep hidden for fear of reprisals by the authorities. He worked on this burlesque epic on and off for years, with manifest enjoyment, and certain knowledge of retribution if he were found out. In 1732 *Eriphile* was presented, followed by *Zaïre*, usually acknowledged to be his best play, on 13 August of the same year. His *Lettres philosophiques*, or *Lettres anglaises*, appeared in English in 1733 and in French simultaneously in London and Rouen in 1734. Although they were written chiefly with France in mind, and are by implication as effective a criticism of French life and manners as Montesquieu's *Lettres persanes*, they nevertheless formed an excellent introduction of England to France. A little later he published the *Temple du goût*, a treatise that is a satire on J.-B. Rousseau and contemporary English literature.

On 10 June 1734, the *Lettres philosophiques* were condemned, extant copies seized and burnt, a warrant issued against the author, and his house searched. Voltaire, however, was safe in or on the borders of the independent duchy of Lorraine, in the company of Emilie de Breteuil, marquise du Châtelet, with whom he had been on intimate terms since 1733. Voltaire and Mme du Châtelet led a passionate life in the Château de Cirey, renovated largely at Voltaire's expense; but this did not prevent them from maintaining their prolific literary output. In 1735 the ban on Voltaire's return to Paris was lifted, but he seldom availed himself of his restored privilege. He worked indefatigably at Cirey, where he wrote the seven *Discours en vers sur l'homme* (1734–37); several plays – *Adélaïde du Guesclin* (1734), *La Mort de César* (1735), *Alzire* (1736), and *L'Enfant prodigue* (1736), a comedy in five acts in octosyllabic verse; and treatises on Newtonian physics in collaboration with Mme du Châtelet. He was still working on *La Pucelle*, and had drafted an unorthodox *Traité de métaphysique*, which Mme du Châtelet kept safely under lock and key. In addition to this very considerable literary activity Voltaire also indulged in a vast correspondence, and performed his own plays, with the co-operation of willing or unwilling visitors, in his own theatre at Cirey.

In March 1736 he received his first letter from the Crown Prince of Prussia, the future Frederick the Great. Shortly afterwards the publication of a poem entitled *Le Mondain* led to trouble because of its impiety and its satirical aspects, so he moved to Brussels; but he returned to Cirey in March 1737, spending some time in his large laboratory experimenting in physics, concerning himself with iron-founding, and writing an essay on the nature of fire.

In 1740 Frederick ascended the throne, and invaded Silesia. He met Voltaire for the first time in the September of that year, at Moyland, and established a friendship based on mutual respect that was to last for many years.

Voltaire finished two plays, *Mahomet* and *Mérope*, in Brussels in 1741. *Mahomet* was presented first in Lille in that same year, and in 1742 in Paris, where it was withdrawn after three performances, owing to the action of various cabals; and *Mérope* was presented only in 1743, by which time Voltaire was involved in abortive diplomatic ventures. He had also written most of his *Essai sur les mœurs* and *Le Siècle de Louis XIV*.

He became *persona grata* at court, through the good offices of d'Argenson, with whom he had been at school, and who was now Minister for Foreign Affairs. Through the duc de Richelieu, he became involved in the preparations for the marriage of the Dauphin; and on New Year's Day 1745 he was appointed Historiographer Royal, through the grace and favour of Mme de Pompadour. In that year he wrote a *Poème de Fontenoy*, received a medal from the Pope, to whom he had dedicated *Mahomet*, and wrote several *divertissements* for the court. In the spring of 1746 he was elected to the Académie Française, and made *Gentilhomme*

Ordinaire de la Chambre du Roi. This enabled him to offer a measure of protection to Marmontel, d'Alembert, and Vauvenargues; and he was probably inspired to write two *contes* – *Babouc ou Le Monde comme il va* and *Memnon.*[1]

Then in 1747 his fortunes suffered a reversal. His enemies gained favour at court; and his mordant wit and biting tongue led him into difficulties. For a time he judged it prudent to go into hiding at Sceaux, the home of his old friend the duchesse du Maine, where he wrote *La Prude* and the tragedy *Rome sauvée,* and wrote or finished *Zadig.* He went on to stay with Mme du Châtelet at Lunéville, at the court of King Stanislas, and discovered that she had become the mistress of Saint-Lambert, an officer of the King's Guard. She died in 1749 bearing his child. Voltaire endured great suffering during this period of his life. With the death of Mme du Châtelet he lost a woman he had loved, an intelligent friend with whom he had shared many interests, and a protectress of high standing with whom he had been on intimate terms for over fifteen years.

He dared not settle in Paris, where his satirical tale *Zadig* had aroused the zeal of the bigots, and where he had become involved in a prolonged rivalry with Crébillon *père,* the author of *Rhadamiste et Zénobie,* who had supplanted him in the favour of Mme de Pompadour. Voltaire, determined to show his greater gifts as a playwright, deliberately chose the same themes as Crébillon for his own plays: in the event, this rivalry was responsible for *Sémiramis* (1748), *Oreste* (1750), as well as *Rome sauvée.*

Frederick the Great had showered frequent invitations upon Voltaire, who at last set out to visit him on 15 June 1750, arriving in Berlin on 10 July. He was most warmly welcomed; honours, and a sum of 20,000 francs a year, were showered upon him, with a further 4,000 francs annually on condition that Voltaire's niece, Mme Denis, kept house for him. It has only recently been discovered that there was a deep and lasting love affair between Mme Denis and her uncle.[2]

Voltaire stayed three years with Frederick, as his Chamberlain, and for the first few months everything enchanted him. Soon, however, he grew jealous of Maupertuis, president of the Berlin Academy, and of Baculard d'Arnaud, the twin stars of Frederick's Potsdam Academy. He showed himself restless, self-important, and grasping. He contrived d'Arnaud's exile, and quarrelled with Lessing. He became involved in financial transactions with Hirschel,

[1] The dating of the composition of the *contes* is very difficult. It is now thought that *Le Songe de Platon* (1737) and *Voyage du Baron de Gangan* (1739), which later developed into *Micromégas,* are his two earliest *contes.*

[2] Cf. *Lettres d'amour de Voltaire à sa nièce,* ed. T. Besterman, 1957; and T. Besterman, *Voltaire,* 1969, p. 261.

a Dresden Jew, and was accused of forgery. This led to an open scandal, and Frederick was on the point of ordering Voltaire to leave the country when the matter was arranged by his Secretary of State, Longchamps. Voltaire grew increasingly irascible at having to correct the king's French verse, and also at the theft of some of his manuscripts. He did, however, finish *Le Siècle de Louis XIV*, and began work on what was to be known as the *Dictionnaire philosophique*. Meanwhile his relations with Frederick worsened. Already in 1751 La Mettrie had reported to Voltaire Frederick's statement: 'Quand on a sucé l'orange on jette l'écorce.'

Maupertuis now quarrelled with Koenig,[3] who visited Berlin in 1750, over a letter by Leibniz and Voltaire took sides with the latter. Maupertuis wrote some biting *Lettres*, and Voltaire replied with his still more celebrated *Diatribe du Docteur Akakia*, asking the king to endorse it. Frederick very much enjoyed having the *Diatribe* read to him, then ordered the manuscript to be burned. Copies were nevertheless printed and circulated, and Frederick placed Voltaire under arrest. There were several attempts at reconciliation, but on 26 March 1753 Voltaire left Potsdam. Three months later he and his niece were arrested in Frankfurt, without warning; but after the intervention of the civic authorities, they were allowed to leave for Colmar on 7 July.

Voltaire, now in his sixtieth year, was refused permission to settle in France; and his enemies were in no way appeased when they heard that he had attended confession and partaken of the Eucharist at Colmar, with all due solemnity, and that he stayed with the Benedictine historian Dom Calmet.

He spent the summer at Plombières and then returned to Colmar, moving from there to Lyons, and on to Geneva (1754). He was very deeply moved by an earthquake which occurred in Lisbon on 1 November 1755, killing 10,000 people, and it shook his faith in a beneficent providence. 'On est bien embarrassé de dire comment les lois du mouvement opèrent des désastres si effroyables dans le meilleur des mondes possibles . . . tandis que quelques sacrés coquins brûlent quelques fanatiques, la terre engloutit les uns et les autres', he wrote to the banker J.-R. Tronchin on 24 November 1755. He also wrote his elegiac *Poème sur le désastre de Lisbonne*, and *Poème sur la loi naturelle*, both published in 1756.

It was also in 1755 that he decided to buy Les Délices, a prop-

[3] Koenig, a disciple of Wolff, had been mathematics tutor to Mme du Châtelet at Cirey. He became Professor of Natural Law at The Hague and was elected to associate membership of the Berlin Academy in 1749, thanks to Maupertuis. He visited Berlin in 1750.

erty just outside the city gates of Geneva, and close to four frontiers (at present the Musée et Institut Voltaire); and in his search for greater security, he went on to acquire other property. He kept open house at Les Délices, and had his own private theatre there, and his own printers. His play *L'Orphelin de la Chine* was well received in Paris in 1755, and *La Pucelle* was finally published the same year.

In the following year, his *Essai sur les mœurs* appeared, and in 1759 he produced his masterpiece, *Candide*.

Geneva decided to uphold a ban on theatrical performances, for moral reasons; so Voltaire insisted that d'Alembert should censure this prohibition in his article 'Genève' for the *Encyclopédie*. Rousseau then published his *Lettre à d'Alembert sur les spectacles*, attacking the theatre; and Voltaire, who had previously been in friendly correspondence with him, never forgave him for it.

In 1758 Voltaire acquired considerable property at Ferney, on French soil, not far from the lake; and another property at Tournay, 4 miles away. He lived at Ferney like a king, receiving homage from his numerous and most distinguished visitors, writing voluminous letters to his friends and acquaintances, and to Frederick the Great, with whom he was now on reasonably good terms again.

In 1759 besides *Candide* he published an *Histoire de l'empire de Russie sous Pierre le Grand*. Many of his works were published anonymously, and his *pistolets de poche* became increasingly virulent, as he amused himself by denying authorship even before they appeared, so that everyone knew who had in fact written them, but no one could prosecute him for them. The suppression of the *Encyclopédie* led to his lampoons against 'L'infâme', and against personal enemies like Lefranc de Pompignan, Palissot and Fréron, an excellent writer and critic who had dared to attack Voltaire, and whom he had satirised pitilessly in his play *L'Ecossaise*.

It was some time later that Voltaire began actively to concern himself with the oppressed, and in particular with men wrongly condemned to death. Voltaire's name is for ever associated with that of Jean Calas, a Protestant merchant who, on 9 March 1762, was found guilty at Toulouse of murdering his son, a supposedly prospective convert to Catholicism, who had been found hanged. He was condemned to be broken on the wheel, and died courageously, in spite of appalling torture. Voltaire, at the instigation of another Protestant merchant from Toulouse, who claimed that Calas had been the victim of religious prejudice, personally investigated the case, determined that there had been a miscarriage of justice, and rallied his friends to rehabilitate Calas. Three years after he had been found guilty, and owing to Voltaire's unyielding determination and tireless pen, Calas was vindicated, and justice prevailed in spite of the prejudice of judges, the state, and the Church.

This was followed by a similar case, in which a man called Sirven, also a member of the Reformed Church, was accused of the murder of his daughter, who had in fact drowned herself following her escape from a convent in which she had been detained, in 1765. This case led to Voltaire defending Sirven in his *Avis au public sur les parricides*, which he published in 1766. And he was equally stirred to play an active part in the rehabilitation of a young man of eighteen, La Barre, accused in 1765, with a friend d'Etallonde, of having mutilated a wooden cross, and denounced his uncle, who had a private score to settle with him. D'Etallonde prudently disappeared, but La Barre was summarily executed in 1766; and it took Voltaire and others twelve years to establish his innocence. It is interesting to note that Frederick II, Catherine the Great, and the King of Poland all contributed generously to the funds needed in these protracted struggles. His efforts on behalf of the comte de Lally, son of an Irish-French commander in India, executed in this same year, 1766, for surrendering Pondicherry, were equally successful, and news of his rehabilitation was brought to Voltaire just before his death. There can be no doubt that this series of men wrongly condemned and executed crystallised Voltaire's total opposition to injustice, religious persecution, and oppression, and outraged his sense of the dignity, the liberty, and the rights of man. His sense of outrage was no doubt further increased by learning that, in the brutal execution of the young La Barre, his decapitated body was burned with a copy of Voltaire's *Dictionnaire philosophique*. He was profoundly disturbed also by the cases of Espinasse – sent to the galleys for harbouring a Protestant minister – Montbailli, and others. In 1766 he published *Le Philosophe ignorant*, urging tolerance, and destined to provide useful ammunition for the defence of the persecuted and the oppressed.

During this same period Voltaire's break with Rousseau became irrevocable. They had been in touch, largely by correspondence, since December 1745, when they collaborated on the ballet *Fête de Ramire*. Serious disagreement began in 1760, following upon acidulous discussion concerning the theatre in Geneva; and by 1764 their hostility was open, made public by Rousseau's *Lettres écrites de la montagne*, and Voltaire's counter-attack, *Sentiment des citoyens* (December 1764).

In 1766 he adopted, in a semi-official manner, a girl of impoverished but noble family, Reine-Philiberte de Varicourt, whom he rescued from a convent and married to the marquis de Villette. He called her affectionately 'Belle et Bonne', and she brought a breath of freshness and delight to his last years.

In 1767 he published his *conte*, *L'Ingénu*, and in 1768 *L'Homme aux quarante écus*. In 1769 Mme Denis returned to Ferney after an exile of eighteen months. Voltaire, in great anger, had sent her away when he discovered her complicity with La Harpe in the theft of some of his manuscripts. A year later he started work on *Questions sur l'Encyclopédie*, completing this in 1772, and it was subsequently published in nine volumes. At Ferney, apart from his increasing writing of tracts, treatises, brochures, letters, and a diversity of major works, he led the life of a country squire, looking after his property, and encouraging the establishment of regional crafts, such as watchmaking, within his boundaries; he also took time off to write a refutation of d'Holbach's materialism.

The death of Louis XV in 1774 led him to hope that he could return to Paris, but the Minister Turgot offered him no encouragement. And it was not until 1778 that he decided to visit Paris, to see his play *Irène*, finished in 1777 or early 1778, performed on the stage of the Théâtre Français. Voltaire's return to Paris after an absence of twenty-eight years, at the age of eighty-four, was a triumph. He was surrounded by an atmosphere of adulation, interest, success, and celebrity, and warmly received by the Academy. He revisited old friends, among them Mme du Deffand, but, no doubt partly because of the excitement engendered, fell ill a fortnight after his arrival, and, in view of his age and fragility, a confessor was sent for. But he rallied in time to witness his own apotheosis, when his bust was crowned upon the stage of the Théâtre Français. He attended several meetings of the Academy, and was so stimulated that he worked on a new play *Agathocle*; it was at this time that he learned of the rehabilitation of the comte de Lally, for which he had striven so long. By the middle of May he was seen to be failing. His nephew, the Abbé Mignot, and other priests closed in on the dying man, but on 30 May 1778 he refused to receive them, and died that same night. He was hurriedly interred at the Abbey of Scellières, in Champagne, for fear of an interdiction by the bishop, which did in fact arrive, but two hours too late. On 10 July 1791 his body was moved to the Panthéon, but disinterred and concealed on a piece of waste land during the Hundred Days. Upon his death, his heart was removed from his body, embalmed, and given to Mme Denis, who passed it on to 'Belle et Bonne', Mme de Villette, preserved in a silver case.

II. POETRY

In his own day, Voltaire's international reputation was largely based upon his greatness as a poet. Academic circles are today witnessing a revaluation of his poetry, following a long eclipse due to changes in aesthetic taste. He had no equal for variety of subject, diversity of rhythm, vivacity and wit, and competence of technique, the whole exactly embodying his dramatic genius. Yet it is doubtful whether the present reassessment will do more than restore him to his rightful place in the history of poetry, since poetic preoccupations have changed fundamentally since his day. He inherited the great classical tradition, and demonstrates his inherent classicism in *Le Temple du goût* (1733) and the *Commentaire sur Corneille* (1764).

Apart from his dramatic poetry, which will be considered when dealing with his theatrical works, he is best remembered for his epigrams, among them one on Fréron:

> L'autre jour, au fond du vallon,
> Un serpent piqua Jean Fréron
> Que pensez-vous qu'il arriva?
> Ce fut le serpent qui creva.

and another inspired by Le Jay's unfortunate frontispiece to *La Henriade*, which showed a portrait of Voltaire placed between La Beaumelle and Fréron:

> Le Jay vient de mettre Voltaire
> Entre La Beaumelle et Fréron:
> Ce serait vraiment un calvaire
> S'il s'y trouvait un bon larron. (1774)

He also wrote odes, elegies, epistles, satires, narrative poems, madrigals, and epic poetry with verve, wit, and a fine sense of language.

His well-known *Stances à Madame du Châtelet* beginning:

> Si vous voulez que j'aime encore
> Rendez-moi l'âge des amours;
> Au crépuscule de mes jours,
> Rejoignez, s'il se peut, l'aurore.

are typical, in their conventional presentation and their grace, charm, and sincerity, of much of his general work. The criticism that he wrote facile verse, however expert and harmonious, rather than poetry, is not wholly true, but the stately alexandrines of his plays seldom compare with those of Corneille and Racine, largely because of Voltaire's technical limitations as a dramatist. He wrote at great speed, and no writer has ever found it easier to write in verse, a facility that, together with an undeniable lack of depth, prevented him from becoming a great poet. It is possible that great dramatic poetry was out of harmony with an age that sought for clarity, thought, logic, and scientific exploration, and turned aside from complex imagery and the lyrical expression of emotion or atmosphere. *Le Mondain* is best remembered for its satirical ideas. The *Henriade*, his great epic poem, is considered a failure today, in spite of Voltaire's high critical intelligence, his knowledge of history, and the skill with which he overcame the technical problems of the genre: there are few who read more than a few chosen passages, but these serve to reveal the range of Voltaire's intellect, and of his style. He shows his philosophical preoccupation in his *Poème sur la loi naturelle*, and *Poème sur le désastre de Lisbonne*; but he is best remembered for his vitriolic quatrains against Fréron, Pompignan, and others who incurred his enmity. The series *Les Pour, Les Que, Les Qui, Les Quoi, Les Oui, Les Non*, showed how effectively Voltaire could retaliate against his enemies; but he could also be very moving when he allowed his feelings to take over, as in *La Mort de Mademoiselle Lecouvreur*, which gains from his profound indignation, and from the inevitability of his broadening of his subject into an attack on the prejudice against actors, which robbed them of Christian burial.

Individual lines in *épîtres* and *stances* are beautiful enough to recall the poets of the *Pléiade* and foreshadow the Romantics with their preoccupation with death, time passing, love, and melancholy. Voltaire's poetry is marked by a surprising sense of freedom and a particularly successful use of the octosyllabic line. Matthew Arnold accepted him as a major poet; yet there must be reservations. Taken as a whole his verse lacks the passion, mystery, imagination, vivid metaphors, and images that are generally associated with great poetry, and which has been called the 'plastic sense'.[4]

V. W. Topazio has singled out *La Pucelle* as Voltaire's finest single poetic effort.[5] It is an epic deliberately patterned upon Ariosto's *Orlando Furioso*, and intended to expose the sham pretensions of the epic form, and to ridicule Chapelain's treatment of the same theme. The mythological aspects of Joan of Arc irritated the rationalist in Voltaire, and in his work on *La Pucelle*, continued over many years, he gave free rein to his delight in *badinage*, bawdy, and salacity, his gift for irreverence, his sense of the grotesque and the outrageous, and his whole immoral and irreligious attitude to convention. At times the burlesque surpasses that of Rabelais; in other parts all but the most devoted addicts of Voltaire's work were shocked by his vulgarity and his obscenity.

[4] Richard Aldington, *Voltaire*, 1925, p. 138.
[5] *Voltaire, a critical study of his major works*, 1967, p. 122.

Voltaire's particular form of pornographic humour was here unchecked, and *La Pucelle* must be read, even though it is not to all tastes, if the nature and character of Voltaire are to be fully understood, since he reveals in this mock-epic a fundamental aspect of his being. In its own way *La Pucelle* is a masterpiece, containing real poetry and much lyrical verse, with every evidence of high technical skill; but the humour is too personal to be generally enjoyed, somewhat reminiscent of a precocious French schoolboy with a greater gift of literacy than is usual.

III. PLAYS

Voltaire the dramatist is no longer considered to be in the same class as Corneille, Racine, and Shakespeare, but his reputation for dramatic excellence lasted a long time, and he is still placed next after Corneille and Racine in France as a writer of tragedy. His best play, *Zaïre*, was performed at the Théâtre Français 488 times between 1732 and 1936, more often than either *Rodogune* (Corneille) or *Bajazet* (Racine), and the leading role of Orosmane has tempted great actors from Le Kain in 1734 and 1742 to Mounet-Sully in 1874, when the title role was played by Sarah Bernhardt.

His first play, *Œdipe* (1718),[6] was a resounding success, at a time when *Athalie* alone of Racine's plays was appreciated by the public, for its spectacular effect. *Œdipe* was performed 336 times up to 1852, the date of its last performance, and probably still holds the record for the greatest number of performances given to any French writer's first play.

It was after his prolonged visit to England, and the enlarging of his talent through appreciation and understanding[7] of Shakespeare, that he wrote in swift succession a number of interesting, if not major, plays. The first act of *Brutus* he originally wrote in English prose, close to the French verse of the final draft, yet it shows in fact little sign of English influences. *Eriphyle* has a ghost somewhat reminiscent of the one in *Hamlet*, but of less importance to the plot. The play was intended to depict strong passions, but its interest lies mainly in brilliant criticisms of the court and of courtiers. Its real claim to notice is that it is the first play by Voltaire to give clear evidence of Shakespearean influence, and that it fore-

[6] Its lines:

> Nos prêtres ne sont pas ce qu'un vain peuple pense
> Notre crédulité fait toute leur science . . .

were immortalised by being frequently quoted out of context.

[7] We may not think his understanding to be very great, but it seems penetrating when set by the side of eighteenth-century English criticism of Shakespeare.

shadows his later *Sémiramis*. *La Mort de César* shows a greater Shakespearean influence; it has no love interest, and provides a spectacle remarkable for its liberty and audacity. The work, however, fails to provide a great dramatic tableau, as Shakespeare had done. Voltaire is closer to Suetonius and Plutarch. Brutus is killed off stage, no moral conclusions are offered, nor is the historical end of the plot made clear. The play is written with vigour and skill, but suffers by comparison with Shakespeare's earlier version, or even with Voltaire's own *Mahomet*, in which a son kills his own father. It has always enjoyed success in performance at boys' schools, because of its theme and its all-male cast.

Zaïre is indubitably Voltaire's best play, both in quality and in popular success. He claimed to have written it in about three weeks, from 29 May to 25 June 1732. The historical background of the play, set in the time of St Louis, is accurate, but the plot is of his own invention. It was a relative innovation to take a theme from the history of France; it is related to the conquest of Jerusalem by the crusaders, and one inspired perhaps by Shakespeare's seeking and finding of plots in strange historical records. He embroidered known facts, for example, by lengthening Lusignan's captivity by twenty years to suit his dramatic convenience; by inventing Orosmane's love for the Christian-born Zaïre, and her brother Nérestan's efforts to ransom his companions; also the reunion of Zaïre with her father and her brother, and her dilemma; and the jealousy of the Sultan Orosmane, who finally kills Zaïre, and then himself.

There is considerable artificiality and excessive theatrical convention in the play, typical of the age in which it was written – fortuitous meetings, unlikely coincidences, the accident of fate – but the play is successful in conveying unusual tenderness combined with fanaticism. The character of Zaïre is most engagingly drawn, the style is noble but not over-exalted, and there are masterpieces of understatement, strangely modern in tone, that reveal the playwright's sense of theatre: as when such simple phrases as 'Zaïre, vous pleurez' (IV. 2); 'Zaïre, vous m'aimez' (IV. 2); 'Sa soeur? . . . J'étais aimé' (V. 10) are, in their context, laden with pathos, and become deeply moving. The play is artistically well made, with no didactic nor polemic purpose in favour of the Muslim at the expense of the Christian, and as a result the message is more successful, because obliquely conveyed. There is, however, a clarion call for tolerance, which foreshadows *Mahomet* and is singularly effective. Religion is presented chiefly as a matter of upbringing, and therefore of only relative importance, while Voltaire's humanity and his deism are revealed the more profoundly because he avoids easy and cheap effects.

Généreux, bienfaisant, juste, plein de vertus
S'il était né chrétien, que serait-il de plus?

is a typically Voltairean couplet, summing up both the character of Orosmane and the attitudes of his creator. With *Zaïre*, Voltaire helped to show that plays based upon the dramatic opposition of conflicting principles can be as effective as those based upon characters and the human situation. *Zaïre* is primarily a drama, a tragedy of love and jealousy. Voltaire never specifically acknowledged any debt to *Othello*; and critics have tended to link the play with Voltaire's own *Hérode et Mariamne*, and with Racine's *Bajazet*, *Andromaque*, and even *Britannicus*. Zaïre is, however, a unique character, the victim of a causeless jealousy and of her brother's fanaticism, and she ends her life leaving the main intellectual problem unresolved: she has not had time either to accept or to reject baptism, or to accept or reject Orosmane. Corosmin, close to Orosmane, is as fanatical a Mohammedan as Nérestan is a Christian. The play is wonderfully well constructed. Even Rousseau was compelled to call it 'une pièce enchanteresse' and Condorcet described it as 'la tragédie des cœurs tendres et des âmes pures'.

The play marked a turning-point for Voltaire the dramatist, who used is henceforward as a model. *Adélaïde du Guesclin* has a plot of a similar kind. *Alzire ou les Américains* (1736) is a remarkable play which propounds the religious problem, but which avoids the racial confrontation that would have given it a prophetic reality. *Le Fanatisme ou Mahomet le prophète* (1741) constitutes an important landmark in the struggle for religious freedom, and is ranked by many critics as technically equal to *Zaïre*. In the classical context, it had the dramatically shocking scene of a son, Séide, killing his father, Zopire, on the stage. *Mérope* is the tragedy of a mother's love, contains no love-plot nor propaganda, and shows Voltaire at his best in its purity of style and simplicity of structure.

Sémiramis (1748) was written as part of Voltaire's campaign against Crébillon *père*. It has many striking scenes, though there is a substantiated story that when the ghost of Ninus rose, to the roll of thunder and the shaking of a tomb, some wag exclaimed 'Place à l'ombre', producing a sensation quite different from that envisaged by the author. The play is, however, judged to be the most horrific of the first half of the century.

After his English experience, Voltaire had admired Shakespeare greatly, and it was he who introduced him to the French; but he himself was too classical in mind and spirit to do more than adopt, and weaken, a few of the devices of the great English dramatist, in an attempt to add something to French tradition that would stimulate and widen the scope of tragedy. Later, as was to be expected, he grew critical of Shakespeare, whose full greatness he never realised as Diderot had done when he described him as 'un colosse entre les jambes duquel nous marcherions tous'. Yet Voltaire, as a critic of Shakespeare, compares very favourably with his English counterparts.

Voltaire's own excursion into social comedy, *Nanine ou Le Préjugé vaincu* (1749), was not particularly well received, and he returned henceforward to the writing of tragedies. *Oreste* was written to rival Crébillon's *Electre*. The interest of *L'Orphelin de la Chine* lies in its subject, in the large number of actors present on the stage at the same time, and in its thesis – the barbarity of primitive man, and the virtues of civilisation. It was Voltaire's answer to Rousseau's *Discours sur les sciences et les arts*. *Tancrède* (1760) has as its theme medieval courtly love, and was written in crossed rhymes, to make the flow of language more rapid and the style more conversational. It was the first play to make full use of the whole stage, following on Lauraguais'[8] success in clearing it of the privileged spectators who normally crowded the sides, by paying 12,000 livres to compensate for the loss of income from seats. Voltaire so thoroughly approved this clearance that in the same year he dedicated his satirical play *L'Ecossaise* to the beneficent Lauraguais.

According to Voltaire, *Olympe* (1762) was written in six days, so that he could rest upon the seventh – although he did in fact add two more acts afterwards, and eighty-three soldiers appeared on the stage. Voltaire increasingly pandered to the prevailing taste for dramatic and panoramic spectacle, following *Tancrède* with *Les Scythes*, and his fount of inspiration seemed never to dry up. He wrote seven more tragedies after the age of sixty, of which *Irène* was the work of his eighty-first year: he had twenty-seven plays performed over the years.

Voltaire's special talent for the genre, and his obstinate fidelity to its forms, prolonged the life of classical tragedy beyond its appointed time: after his death, no tragedies of any significance were written. He not only wrote his tragedies in verse, but rose to the defence of poetry against La Motte, who claimed the super-excellence of prose for all literary undertakings, and recommended

[8] L.-F. de Brancas, comte de Lauraguais (1733–1824), was a wealthy eccentric whose range of knowledge and interests was encyclopaedic, and who throughout his long life, which included periods of exile in England, was an opponent of the government of the day. A prolific writer, he is responsible for two poor tragedies, *Clytemnestre* and *Jocaste*. In recognition of his service to the stage of the Comédie Française, the *sociétaires* granted him a free seat for life.

that poetry be abandoned, since it was the lesser form. His *Discours sur la tragédie*, which served as a preface to *Brutus*, and his earlier preface to *Oedipe* must both be read and studied in order to understand and appreciate Voltaire's views on tragedy. He greatly admired the French dramatists Racine and Corneille, preferring them even to the great Greek playwrights, and his work shows every evidence of their conscious or unconscious influence. He greatly admired Shakespeare for the presentation on stage of tragic emotion inspired or released by violent and terrible action; but had no appreciation of the psychological insight in Shakespeare's plays. He recognised his appeal to the imagination, appreciated the advantages of a direct and natural speech, and realised that much could be gained from him; but he never became aware of his vivid poetic imagery and lyrical verbal torrent, nor his profound and universal awareness of the depths of the human heart, mind, and experience. Voltaire became in the end highly critical of Shakespeare, as an examination of *Lettres à l'Académie* (1776) will show. This change of opinion may have been influenced by the fact that La Place's translation of Shakespeare's works (1745), and the Letourneur version of 1759, together with Ducis' adaptations, not only showed some of Shakespeare's quality, but revealed Voltaire's indebtedness to him which the former repudiated. Yet it is clear that the indebtedness does in fact exist, for certain historical subjects, for greater realism, freedom, and crudity on stage; and for the introduction of Arabs, Chinese, Americans, and even Frenchmen of an earlier age into his plays.

Voltaire was himself responsible for innovations in the theatre of his day. Spectators having been once cleared from the actual stage by Lauraguais' handsome compensation, Voltaire saw to it that they never returned. He grew increasingly concerned with the actual staging of his plays, and learned how to meet the new demands made by an increasing number of supporting actors and walk-ons, and the consequent need for special grouping and movement, the type and extent of décor needed for the subjects being treated on the grand scale, the presentation of a ghost, the sounds of strife and warfare, the simulation of the noise of a distant cannon, and so forth. He was also in favour of costume changes, and the use of curtains.

Apart from revolutionary and impressive staging and an elementary form of direction, previously unknown, his excellence was to be found in the representation and expression of pathos, and in giving his ideas emotional support in dramatic form. His innovations, which in modern terms seem innocuous, shocked the public of his day: but in spite of this stimulant, classical tragedy became obsolescent, through the weakening of psychological interest, and moved in the same direction as the contemporary *drame*. Even Voltaire began to expound a moral lesson in his plays.

Voltaire's enormous and lasting passion for the theatre – he wrote some fifty plays over seventy years – is revealed in his correspondence, and he showed a life-long interest in the staging of plays, in acting, in directing actors and listening to their advice, in everything, in fact, which pertains to the theatre. He built private theatres in every one of his several properties – Cirey, Tournay, Les Délices, and Ferney – and he himself played the part of Lusignan in *Zaïre*. In his day, he eclipsed his rivals, Lagrange-Chancel, Marivaux, Campistron, Piron, and Crébillon.[9] He continued to be very popular throughout the early Romantic period, because of his exotic setting, and surface emotions, so typical of melodrama, which was then much in favour.

There was in all his work for the theatre an element of propaganda, discreet, but ever present, which prepared the way for the development of the theatre of ideas from the theatre of emotions.

IV. HISTORY

Voltaire's historical works rank second only to his *contes* as models of lucid prose and literary presentation. They combine dramatic with narrative qualities, reveal an exceptional and critical intelligence, a capacity to deal expertly with the sifting of material, and the objective probing into conflicting evidence. Voltaire has been hailed as the first modern historian of real consequence. It is certain that he was the first to evolve the method for the writing of history which endures to the present day. As Montesquieu had made politics into a science, so Voltaire made history into a science: he challenged those past historians who subordinated truth to prejudice, and broke away from those whose treatment of historical events was lifeless and tedious.

His own attitude to history was organic and dynamic, which made his work both reliable and readable. He demonstrated with his earliest work in that field his concern for accuracy, objectivity, and credibility, and an unerring instinct that enabled him to sift the more from the less important, the facts of history from its mythology. He was in total opposition to those historians whose views were coloured by religion, and in particular Bossuet, whose *Histoire universelle* was the standard history. Bossuet's whole attitude was consistently religious, with its literal interpretation of the Bible, his conception of Mohammedans as *ipso facto* barbarians,

[9] It may well be said that the superlative acting of Mlle Clairon and Le Kain, who frequently played for him added to the value of his tragedies.

of the lives of kings being of more significance than the lives of ordinary men, of the direct intervention of God to determine the results of battle, and of the glory of victory in battle as paramount over victory in terms of cultural progress, and the wellbeing of the people.

Voltaire, far from dwelling on military prowess, court pageantry, and diplomatic intrigues, approached history analytically, basing his studies on recorded facts, and assessing the reigns of monarchs using, according to the general good done to the people under their rule, their span of power as mere temporal landmarks. Every aspect was submitted to his acute critical sense; and his criteria are valid today. Against his better judgement and in accordance with the custom of his day, he indulged in more anecdotes than is to modern taste, but he seldom failed to stress their true and broad significance, relative to his study.

His knowledge of human psychology and his experience of the theatre assisted him in probing motives, and presenting issues with clarity and precision; and the philosopher and the rationalist were seldom absent from his text. He undertook extensive research, and if this is sometimes proved inadequate by modern standards, he nevertheless blazed a new trail, and one that has been followed ever since.

Voltaire had a scrupulous respect for truth, but believed that the task of the historian was to interpret the facts of the past, and that history held a lesson for the present. He held firmly to the principle of natural causation, without, however, discarding the element of chance in small issues that were not fundamental. By his new methods, he completely eclipsed such historians as Mézeray, who by and large confined himself to portraits of kings, having no capacity for the interpretation of historical events, and whose work was full of errors; and Daniel, the Jesuit historiographer, whose work contained no reference to the arts, customs, economics, or laws of any given period. Voltaire combined science with art in subtle harmony, and there is progression in his historical writings.

The *Histoire de Charles XII et de Pierre le Grand* (1731) is centred on the conflict of personality between his two exciting antagonists, the heroic military leader who set out to conquer, Charles XII of Sweden, and the despot with iron will, brute force, and unflagging energy, Peter the Great. From this conflict, and with due examination of Sweden's economy and her military strength, and the heroic grandeur, somewhat glamorised, of her leader, Voltaire draws his conclusions: that Sweden's greatness ended with the glory of Charles XII, mysteriously shot in battle; and that Russia's greatness began with the Battle of Poltava in

1709, and was achieved through travail and suffering, increased by the conflict with Charles XII.

Voltaire spent ten years on this book, and took trouble to contact Baron Fabrice, an eyewitness of the death of Charles XII. His purpose was to use only unimpeachable sources, to present only facts that were demonstrably true, or those with the highest degree of credibility attached to them, in a vital and arresting manner, and in this he succeeded. There were eight editions of the work in London alone; and it is in effect the foundation stone of scientific and secular analysis of events.

Le Siècle de Louis XIV (1751) offered a substantial and detailed account of the reign of the Sun King. Every aspect of life during that period is touched upon with faithful accuracy, from the intrigues of the *noblesse* to the soldier whose actual pay is recorded. The work was begun at Cirey, and in 1739 an early draft was seized by the police. It was under the influence of Frederick the Great that the scope of the work was enlarged, and it was in fact completed in Prussia. In undertaking his task, Voltaire examined 200 volumes of memoirs, as well as drawing on his own experience of the reign, and that of older people known to him. Although he was forced by the circumstances of the period to dwell at length on military history, he gave an overall picture of the age that has never yet been equalled in its detail, its brilliant analysis, its sharp commentary, and its intellectual detachment. He stressed the widespread misery, engendered by senseless wars, waged for reasons of conflicting dynastic ambitions, and complex political interests in no way concerned with common humanity. He was a great admirer of Machiavelli, whose type of mind and spirit he intuitively understood; and he probed deeply into the egomania of ambitious men in high places. His own ideal being consistently humanitarian and essentially moral, he condemned the scheming of the Cardinal de Retz. The work is centred round the majestic figure of Louis XIV, and the contrast between his early grandeur and the misery of his last years. Voltaire demonstrates the excesses of the Jesuits, and above all the consequences of the Revocation of the Edict of Nantes, and launches a great plea for tolerance. The work is crowned with an account of the literary, artistic, and intellectual greatness of the age. This short survey of French civilisation, with pride of place given to writers, was another innovation. It was also valid; and his observations on Corneille, Racine, Fénelon, Bossuet, and other great artists of the period are for the most part well balanced, generally substantiated, and always interesting. Voltaire's conclusion was that, in spite of weaknesses in government and politics, errors of policy, and examples of barbarism, in spite of senseless internecine wars such as those of the Fronde, upon which he dwelt at length, civilisation had made great progress under Louis XIV; and after the publication of this book, it was impossible to think of this age as anything but the Golden Age of modern times.

Le Siècle de Louis XIV is the work of a thinker concerned with the broad sweep of history, and relating events in the perspective of advancing civilisation. Voltaire was at once close enough to the period under review to know those who had lived within its span, or the still-living contemporaries of those men, and distant enough from it to be able to offer detached and intelligent assessment. These factors, combined with his acute political insight, gave a sharp edge to his interpretation of events, and of the movements of the time. Nor should it be forgotten that his praise of 'le siècle de Louis XIV' carried with it by implication 'la critique du siècle de Louis XV'.

The *Essai sur les mœurs* (1756), whose full title is the *Essai sur l'histoire générale et l'esprit des nations*, is a monumental work of even greater scope. Voltaire worked at it from 1745, and when Cramer edited it in 1756, it had 164 chapters. *La Philosophie de l'histoire*, dedicated to Catherine II and first published in 1765, was incorporated as as Introduction to the *Essai* in the edition of 1769, and the final addition of two chapters in 1775 brings the total number of chapters to 197.

The undertaking by one man of so vast and comprehensive a history demonstrates Voltaire's encyclopaedic mind, his unremitting intellectual activity, and the universal scope of his ambitions. Essentially, the work is on the lines of *Le Siècle de Louis XIV*, and there is the same care to ensure reliability and readability. R. Pomeau closely examined 150 pages in four sections of the *Essai*, checking 380 references:[10] of these, 319 were exact, 32 all but exact, 6 unidentified, 14 contained rearranged quotations, and only 9 were incorrect. Few scholars today would claim this degree of accuracy in so vast a project, which in any case they would not tackle without collaborators. The history is subjective in that it reveals Voltaire's innate horror of bloodshed, violence, and torture, his hatred of the secular power of the Church, and of all forms of religious fanaticism and persecution. This is not surprising in a man whose general philosophical views were those of a humanitarian, and whose sensibility was such that he took to his bed with a fever every year on the anniversary of the massacre of St Bartholomew's Day.

It is an easy game to fault Voltaire's documentation, and the picture he gives of the Middle Ages; to discover lapses, and to

[10] *Essai sur les mœurs et l'esprit des nations*, ed. R. Pomeau, 1963, p. xxiii.

point to fragmentation through an excess of anecdotes. Notwithstanding, the method of modern history is clearly outlined in this colossal enterprise; and it is by using his own criteria that he can best be faulted on several scores, a paradox that would have pleased him mightily.

V. PHILOSOPHY

Voltaire's definition of a philosopher was a man whose mind was turned to practical issues and to a consideration of the best way to live on this earth.

He eschewed metaphysics, the supernatural, the mystical, and the obscure. He avoided the esoteric jargon of his day in a determination to make himself intelligible to the masses. He subscribed to the Encyclopaedic ideal of popularising wisdom and his major philosophy was expressed in his *contes*, in which he gave vivid and entertaining life to his theories.

He had a poor opinion of metaphysics, but was careful to inform himself of existing attitudes, and the substance of past and contemporary work, before writing his *Traité de Métaphysique* which is directly concerned with the demolition of metaphysics. This *Traité*, which was written but not published in 1734, gives evidence of his wide erudition, the range of his sources, and his rationalist approach. The plan of the work encompasses a vast field, leading through disquisitions on the existence of God, citing arguments for and against belief, by means of a clear exposition of sensationalist philosophy, to questions of ethics and the liberty of man, the whole revealing Voltaire's philosophical and humanitarian preoccupations and priorities.

The main discernible influences up to the publication of the *Lettres philosophiques* in 1734 are Bayle and Fontenelle, Newton and English deism. Voltaire was studying science from 1734 to 1741, and his deism was further developed under the influence of the new physics. In 1738 he wrote his *Eléments de la philosophie de Newton*. In that same year he wrote his *Essai sur la nature du feu*; and also discussed such questions as the nature of human freedom, with Frederick the Great, and the philosophy of Leibniz, with Mme du Châtelet. From 1741 to 1750, during which years his major effort was centred on literature, he gathered material for his later propagandist work; and from 1750 to 1760 he grew more bitter, through the Prussian experience, the circumstances of his life generally, and the sorry state of the world: these elements combined to produce in him an urgent desire for the elucidation of his own philosophical position; and the following period, 1760 to 1778, was one of great philosophical activity, and polemical writing on behalf of scientific progress, and the ideals of the Enlightenment.

It was then that he produced his major philosophical works, the *Dictionnaire philosophique*, the *Questions sur l'Encyclopédie*, and the *Traité sur la tolérance*. He expounded his deism in somewhat different terms at different stages in his life. God is necessary to him as the creator of the world, the source of order and rationality in the universe; 'Je me range à l'opinion de l'existence de l'être suprême comme la plus vraisemblable et la plus probable,' but he was against all forms of organised religion, ritual, or dogma. He praised Jesus Christ for his sublime ethics, and was unable to accept Descartes' *idées innées*; he maintained his total distrust of metaphysics: 'Je ramène toujours autant que je peux la métaphysique à la morale', and preferred Locke to Descartes; and believed that there was in every man an instinct that made society possible.

In his *Traité de métaphysique* he had demonstrated the vacuum of metaphysical speculation, and had brought out the wealth of theories surrounding this speculation, also the consequential relativity of stated truth, which is so often seen to be merely enlightened self-interest. If Voltaire holds that on balance there are better reasons for believing in God than for disbelieving in him, he nevertheless refuses at first to acknowledge a moral God. For him, morality is expedient, and good and evil must be judged relative to social criteria of usefulness. The immortality of the soul is of little consequence if the whole man, good or bad, does not survive in the next world; but if his soul is to rejoin the community of heavenly angels unchanged, it would seem unreasonable that God did not give him immortality here on this earth. He believed in man's limited freedom, basing himself upon practical considerations and the human belief that man is in fact free and can act as if he were; and he concluded that, to all intents and purposes, we are free, within the necessary restrictions of a voluntary society. It is his sincere belief in a rational God that later led him to envisage a moral God and rendered so serious the problem of evil.

The philosopher of the eighteenth century is very much present in Voltaire's rationalist argument, based on practical wisdom and a desire to improve the lot of mankind, and not upon evolving complex, sophisticated systems ultimately harmful to mankind. His deism is at the root of his great concern with ethics and moral behaviour; God is often brought into his argument to lend support to his social and political theory. Throughout his writings he is seen as seeking what he calls the *flambeau de la physique* and the *bâton de l'expérience* to guide him through the maze of life and doctrine; and as discarding all conclusions based upon faith, prejudice, revelation, and the supernatural. It is for this attitude of mind that Voltaire, a moral philosopher and a deist, so often finds himself on the same intellectual side as atheists and free-thinkers, and is so often believed to share all their views.

His ethics are concerned primarily with the behaviour of man, and *l'homme de bien*, who is his ideal, must be a good father, a good citizen, and exercise charity towards his neighbour and justice towards all. Voltaire believed that *bienfaisance* was the ultimate virtue; and attached little value to the charms of the primitive state, because of his faith in the progress of civilisation. His concern for man in society did not lead him to reject natural passions, but to suggest that they be tempered and directed towards the general wellbeing of the community. He abhorred despotism, and agreed with Montesquieu in urging a strong government with respect for human rights, ready to prevent outside interests, religious or political, from usurping power beyond their own domain. For him, the monarchical was the best system of government, provided that the king were enlightened, and prepared to accept guidance from the philosophers. He never urged exact equality, realising that the abilities of men are unequal, but contented himself with seeking equality before the law. He never challenged the the idea of ownership of property, nor ever sought dramatically to overthrow the social order, for the patriarch of Ferney was no democrat. He accepted the idea of honours, and the hierarchy of intelligence if not of birth, and would have welcomed a *république des lettres*. He often expressed disdain for *la canaille*, the mob, but never considered it a negligible force – a mistake made by many aristocrats at that time – and he sincerely wished for better popular education.

All his life Voltaire fought for all freedoms – personal, political, and religious – for tolerance and the freedom of the press. He hated fanaticism, war, feudal rights, and serfdom; he worked for the fair distribution of taxes, and for punishment proportionate to, but not in excess of, the crime committed. These views are to be found in all his works, from the earliest to the very last: and nowhere so vividly and clearly enshrined as in the *Dictionnaire philosophique* and the *Traité sur la tolerance*, while the *Philosophe ignorant*, recently re-edited,[11] offers a rapid review of his deism and a comprehensive survey of its consequences.

His views changed with advancing years on the question of Providence, of evil, of the soul, and of free-will, which in 1736 he accepted, but which after 1750 seemed to him upon further consideration to be an illusion. His relative optimism changed to a relative pessimism, as can best be demonstrated by reading his *contes* in their chronological order of composition.

His views on practical considerations never changed. To the end

[11] Ed. J. L. Carr in *Textes français classiques et modernes*, 1965.

he insisted that there must be belief in Divine Providence, in freedom, in the immortality of the soul, and in God as a *Dieu rémunérateur et vengeur*, for the mass of people need the support of religion to maintain them in the paths of righteousness, even if philosophers are exempt from this necessity. In this he is in accord with Diderot, who believed that ultimately there must be two moral laws: one for the mob and one for the intelligent man. He made this manifest by challenging Roman Catholicism and the Church on all points: the celibacy of priests, asceticism, ritual of every kind, and unthinking obedience to rules; the whole summed up in his celebrated phrase: 'Ecrasez l'infâme!'

The *Lettres philosophiques*, followed by the *Remarques sur les Pensées de Pascal*, had an enormous success, and were frequently re-edited. They served to make England, and English thought, science, and literature available to the French for a number of generations. He had read Muralt's *Lettres sur les Anglois et les François et sur les voyages* (1728) and other works on English life, but relied chiefly on his own impressions, and his quick eye was most concerned with the reaction of the French public, to whom the work was addressed. The book is brilliantly written, covers diverse subjects, and is eminently readable.

Voltaire begins with letters on the Quakers, who gained his favour, as did the Anabaptists, since they came closer to deism than members of other sects, and because they concentrated on works of social reform. He then reviewed the Anglicans, the Presbyterians, and the Socinians, underlining by implication his own deism: and phrases such as 'L'Anglais va au ciel par le chemin qui lui plaît' and 'Qui boit du Tokay croit en Dieu' have become proverbial.

From the religious he moves to political and other fields, examining Parliament, government, trade, and modern medicine (by way of inoculation against smallpox). Then follow extremely important letters on Bacon, the great empirical philosopher Locke, and Newton, who is compared with Descartes, and whose scientific theories he sets out. Lastly he dealt with literature: tragedy – in which, according to Voltaire, the English show invention, but little good taste – comedy, the world of letters, and Pope and other celebrated contemporary poets; he exalts the status of the man of letters, and links this with the question of academies.

The unity of the work springs from Voltaire's general attitude and from his main contention, that France is the land of slaves and England the land of the free. In his ideal republic, every citizen would perform a useful task; and world peace would be based upon the development of commerce and technology, and secular and social values. He points out that in England thirty somewhat ridiculous sects co-exist peacefully; that the king is restrained by

Parliament, and the people have *Habeas Corpus*. Their freedom extends to philosophy, and to literature, where classical rules are ignored; and men of commerce as well as of letters are honoured.

Most of these themes are reiterated in his later philosophical works. Apart from his writings on Newton, the scientist and philosopher, there is a *Discours en vers sur l'homme* (1738); a *discours* entitled *De la Liberté*; a *Poème sur la loi naturelle* (written 1754), which expounds Voltaire's deism; and the *Poème sur le désastre de Lisbonne*, which considers the question of Providence, and of evil on earth; also the *Traité sur la tolérance* (1763) and the *Dictionnaire philosophique* (1764), to which were added in 1770–72 *Questions sur L'Encyclopédie*, a collection of articles destined for the *Encyclopédie* and the *Dictionnaire de l'Académie*, and which were also published separately in that same period; and a posthumous work, *L'Opinion par alphabet*.

This complete work forms a comprehensive inventory of religious, political, and social errors, written in a vivid style full of malice, and it oddly embodies many of the basic tenets, or myths, according to some critics, of the later nineteenth-century liberalism. Julien Benda has stressed its three major aspects: political, in which all men have equal rights; intellectual, with faith in science and practical development, and a distrust of metaphysics; and philosophical, with a belief in the possibility of progress.

VI. PHILOSOPHICAL TALES

Voltaire virtually created a new literary form with his *contes*, and one of which he has remained the acknowledged master. The philosophical views which form their core are those put forward in the *Lettres philosophiques*, in his *Correspondance*, and in his poems; but here they gain in clarity and effectiveness, stealing up on the reader enjoying a diverting story and catching him unawares.

The *conte*, with its narrative serving as a peg on which to hang ideas and commentary upon social attitudes, and its brilliant satire, appealed to the logic, realism, and natural critical sense of the average literate man, and led him by a subtle empathy to agree with certain of the author's views that might well have shocked or offended him, presented in another form. Voltaire's first *conte* has been traced to the *Voyages du Baron du Gangan* (1739), of which no copy has been discovered; but the comments of Frederick the Great, to whom the author described the work as a 'philosophical trifle', lead to the supposition that it foreshadowed *Micromégas*.

Zadig, written in 1747, is the prototype of the later tales, and lends confirmation to the statement that each of the *contes* reflects a stage in the intellectual development of the author. By the time *Zadig* was written, Voltaire had already shed his early optimism, expressed in *Le Mondain* and the somewhat complacent 'Si tout n'est pas bien, tout est passable' of the *Vision de Babouc* (1746). Now his optimism, inspired by Pope, Shaftesbury (through the intermediary Bolingbroke), and the implications of orderliness in Newtonianism, is qualified, and he is probing the nature of life and destiny. 'Il n'y a point de mal dont il ne naisse un bien' would not fall so easily from his pen. He was no longer so sure of a benêficent Providence, and highlights the caprice of destiny. Part of the pleasure of reading *Zadig* derives from its obliquity. After having carefully conditioned his reader to make the right responses, Voltaire flattered his intelligence by allowing him to read between the lines and begging him to draw his own conclusions. He assumed, or appeared to assume, that his readers accepted traditional attitudes, and then made use of these to serve his own ends; as when his generalisations about women feed the assumed prejudices of men, and flatter their acumen as his wit becomes more highly sophisticated, yet remaining within the grasp of the average intelligent man. The butt of Voltaire's satire is familiar throughout to his readers: the work is successful because of the way in which the tale unfolds, its irony, and above all its mordant style, 'pétillant de malice'.

The main theme is concerned with destiny and the evil of this world, as in *Micromégas* (1752), but in the later work Voltaire emphasised the relativity of man in the universe, coining the phrase 'le point de vue de Sirius', that is, life on this earth viewed as from a distant star. He once more introduced the absurdity of all metaphysical speculation and systems of philosophy. Man must realise his human limitations; and even men such as Leibniz, with his doctrine of pre-established harmony, Descartes, Maupertuis, and Fontenelle do not escape Voltaire's criticism. He satirises war and the manner in which men commonly fight without understanding why, a divagation more fully developed in *Le Monde comme il va* and reaching its finest expression in the third chapter of *Candide*, where Voltaire at his simplest offers an account of the horrific reality of war, with its arbitrary nature and its wasteful senselessness.

Candide, to which the *Histoire des voyages de Scarmentado* (1756) is seen as a curtain-raiser, reflects Voltaire's anguished questioning over a period of years, following upon the Lisbon earthquake, which led him to examine his own conscience, and which finally brought him to the meliorist position: 'Un jour tout sera bien, voilà notre espérance.'

Voltaire's troubled mind had been seeking solace from the first:

'Tout est bien aujourd'hui, voilà l'illusion', he wrote in his *Poème sur le désastre de Lisbonne.* In his copy of Pope's *Essay on Man* (1733), opposite the words 'One truth is clear. Whatever is, is right', he wrote in English 'What can I hope if all is right?', for he was deeply conscious of the desperate plight of the world.

The adventures of *Candide* may well be regarded as Voltaire's spiritual biography, as well as his commentary on notable philosophical attitudes of his day. He pours ridicule upon Leibniz's *Théodicée* (1710), and upon the optimism of his disciple Wolff. He destroys accepted clichés by the light of reason, with a cold detachment – 'Il n'y a rien de plus solide que la vertu et le plaisir de revoir Mademoiselle Cunégonde' – a juxtaposition which pricks the pretentious bubble of the first portentous statement, and of Candide's trivial conception of the absolute, learnt of his teacher.

When Candide arrives at Eldorado, an earthly Paradise woven from Voltaire's dreams, he finds he cannot live there endlessly, for no man can live without the spur of purpose and meaningful activity. Voltaire no doubt intended this section of the book to be a parody of the biblical Garden of Eden, expressing his own version of original sin; but in the event it offered a wider content, with an implied lesson for himself and for others. After many trials and tribulations, Candide reaches a measure of peace and contentment by letting the wider world go by, living among friends, and looking after his own garden, much in the same way that the patriarch of Ferney looked after his property, developed trade on it, and ensured the greater prosperity of all those who lived on it. At the end, none of the characters have changed fundamentally; but they have all grown wiser, and learned how to put their respective talents to good account. It is clear that, in Voltaire's view, cooperation and goodwill are the cardinal virtues, leading to a happy and useful life when they are translated into action.

The incredible activity of Candide as he hurtles through life is a projection of Voltaire's own experience and of his ability to resolve personal problems by exteriorising them, and then taking appropriate action with reason and not instinct as guide. This general philosophy is one so eminently wise and sanely balanced that it leads even the most fastidious to accept Voltaire's irreverence, indecency, and suggestiveness within the narrative.

After the publication of *Candide* Leibniz's philosophy of optimism never recovered its prestige; and a meliorism which allowed for reform and change through a conviction that things, however desperate, could in fact be improved, offered powerful support to the philosophical propaganda of the day.

The literary qualities of *Candide* are many, as if Voltaire poured into this one *conte* the great harvest of his active, questing, brilliant mind. The story has a superlative rhythm, obtaining dramatic and narrative effects by following swift-flowing passages pulsing with vitality, with elegiac moments of repose, peaks of excitement alternating with quiet tragedy, the whole singing like a ballad with its use of *leitmotiv* to make the reiterated refrain. *Candide* is a brilliant firework, sparkling with wit and with malice, mordant, sardonic, and filled brimful with zest and vitality. The element of parody in the fairy-tale setting with the happy ending, for a tale that is in effect the story of man's anguished and tortured travail to discover himself and the meaning of the universe, is not the least evidence of Voltaire's humour, which bites even as it entertains.

Beneath the gay fairy-tale lies a reality, an awareness of life in all its terrible and terrifying aspects, as well as its gay and joyous ones; beneath the *insouciance* and simplicity of Candide, the central figure, lurks a lost and desperate soul. And this duality is expressed in a supple and splendid prose, directed by an imagination powerful and precise enough to find the exact expression for every thought, every idea, every emotion, and then to embroider with wit and irony. If it were possible to single out one work, from his vast literary output in diverse forms, as being Voltaire's most representative work, and his masterpiece, then *Candide* is undoubtedly that work. His tale is that of a pilgrim's progress through a familiar world of trouble and folly. His pilgrim, unlike Bunyan's, is no idealist bent on reaching heaven, but a realist seeking heaven on earth, endowed only with commonsense and with reason. Voltaire's aim was to debunk the meaningless phrases of optimists and pessimists alike, to satirise the men and institutions of his own and former times. His last word, too often misquoted, epitomises his philosophy: 'il faut cultiver notre jardin'. This may be taken literally, as Voltaire did at Ferney. It may be taken to mean that man must cultivate his talents and selfishly look after his own interests, an interpretation which many of Voltaire's alleged disciples took as their own, especially during the period of the Third Republic.[12] But Voltaire certainly meant to imply that men should toil together for a common purpose, and for their greater common good, as he demonstrates by stressing *our* garden, and in an impersonal construction. It is man in society, not simply man as an individual, who must remain our chief concern, a message he had expressed at the very outset of his career, and one which he sustained with unswerving constancy.

L'Ingénu is basically a satire of social and political hypocrisy, announced in a letter to d'Alembert (1767): 'Il n'y a point d'Ingénu, je n'ai point fait d'Ingénu, je ne l'aurais jamais fait; j'ai

[12] See J. Benda's introduction to Voltaire's *Dictionnaire philosophique*, ed. J. Benda and R. Naves, 2 vols., 1935–36.

l'innocence de la colombe, et je veux avoir la prudence du serpent.' There could have been no clearer signature than this absolute denial with reservations. The work, written when Voltaire was seventy-four, is as youthful in tone as the better-known *Candide.* The vertiginous tempo of the latter is here slowed down, the story more probable, and the tone more earnest. The work as a whole is closer to ordinary life and its characterisation more developed. It lacks some part of the swift-flowing quality of the other tales, and their bubbling humour, but there is wit and mordant satire in it. Once more he attacks the Church as an institution, and the Jesuits in particular, showing how Christianity has unnecessarily increased suffering on earth through idle and over-subtle speculations. He writes favourably of the Jansenist Gordon, one of the characters in the story.

L'Ingénu has a noble ancestry, including the *Lettres persanes,* and owes something to the baron de la Hontan, to C.-Pinot Duclos' *Histoire de Madame de Luz,* to the *Lettres d'un sauvage dépaysé,* the *Lettres iroquoises,* and to the *Espion Américain en Europe ou Lettres Illinoises,* among the fashionable exotics of this and an earlier period.

Following in these unlikely footsteps, Voltaire takes as the hero of his story a Red Indian of the Huron tribe, who arrives in France, gets himself baptised, and endeavours to understand the new world into which he has fallen. The possibilities for satire in this confrontation of the outsider with what generally passes for civilisation are exploited to the full: yet in its more serious aspects the book offers Voltaire's version of that same Noble Savage who exercised the mind of Rousseau, and with whom Diderot was concerned in the *Supplément au Voyage de Bougainville.* All three agree on natural law as the only true law for man, since it is in accordance with the instinctive reason he possesses; but Voltaire does not accept that primitive society is wholly good, nor that the society evolved from it is wholly bad. As always, he urges moderation, understanding, and adaptability, and believes that primitive reason needs to be developed and enriched by civilisation. His ethics, based on universal values and totally independent of revealed religion, are founded on toleration and the willingness to promote socially desirable changes. The last words of *L'Ingénu* could well be used as Voltaire's testament of philosophy – 'Malheur est bon à quelque chose', says the good Jansenist Gordon, but the Ingénu has the final word: 'Malheur n'est bon à rien.'

The work had a topical side, for France had just renounced Canada, and also a polemical side, which ensured its immediate success, aided no doubt by Voltaire's celebrity as a controversial and audacious writer. Its lasting qualities, laced with wit, have made it rank second only to *Candide*. Similar stylistic qualities are to be found in *L'Homme aux quarante écus* (1768), which tackles the question of taxation and protests against inequalities in that field, and *La Princesse de Babylone*, published in the same year.

So protean an author must be a rich field for international study, and there are no signs yet that the field is exhausted. There have been important books in many languages on most aspects of Voltaire's work, including a major work on his taste, and another on his literary critical theories. Yet since he developed critical acumen in all fields of the human mind, there are as many studies still to be undertaken on the qualities of his art: his conciseness, compression, and telescoping of narrative and dialogue; his use of *leitmotiv*, flashback, and enumerative summaries producing a cumulative effect; his use of word order to point a phrase, and his exact placing of a word to add a subtle note of emphasis, and to lead on to the next thought; his awareness of the significance of sounds in the construction of vivid imagery; and his masterly use of understatement, irony, burlesque, contrast, bathos, paradox, and reiteration. This general perfection of style, language, and structure is to be found in all his *contes*, in the short stories scattered through his *Correspondance*, and in many of the shorter pieces known as *pistolets de poche*, a fact which a new anthology of his less well-known stories would make abundantly clear.

VII. CORRESPONDENCE

An appreciation of Voltaire would be singularly incomplete without reference to his correspondence, the very extent of which defeats attempts at analysis and synthesis. The number of letters has increased with every new edition. In Beuchot's edition of 1828 onwards there were 7,473 letters; in that of Moland (1877–82) there were 9,098; and by 1939 it was estimated that the number of extant letters written between 1711 and 1778, and addressed to 700 correspondents of many different nationalities and walks of life, amounted to 10,000. Today, thanks to Dr T. Besterman, we have over 20,000 letters: and a further 4,000 have come to light since the publication of the existing 107 volumes. It is certain that a large number of letters have been lost, but those we possess suffice to make Voltaire's collected letters the largest in world literature, and the most significant in historical importance. Thanks to them, a whole period comes to life with its serious and its frivolous preoccupations, its political, religious, and philosophical controversies, its scientific discussions and literary tastes. They provide a first-hand and well-informed commentary on the European scene which surpasses in general interest, range of topic, and breadth if not always depth, in lively intelligence and sheer literary merit, the substantial correspondence of Rousseau and of Diderot, which are ranked very high by all discerning critics. This voluminous correspondence is at least as significant for the littérateur and the psychologist as for the historian. In it Voltaire himself stands revealed, the whole man, with his acute brain and wit and his human foibles. We can follow his intellectual development from his early beginnings to the year of his death. We see a highly cultured and intelligent man, unexpectedly warm in his close personal relationships, a many-sided personality with marked prejudices, a disarming vanity, and a capacity for generosity and disinterested action oddly allied with a shrewd and calculating nature. His letters have the charm of a constant improvisation even when their effect upon his readers has been carefully estimated; and they have the appeal of a wit which is as natural to him as the style in which he writes. He illumines the world that mattered to him with his personality, his keen appreciation of life and events, his quick intelligence. He knows how to entertain his reader, often at his own expense, with sly remarks about his illness, his lean and decrepit appearance, the likely imminence of his death, turning his malice upon himself and so disarming all but the most prejudiced reader.

VIII. CONCLUSION

Today, two hundred and more years after producing his masterpiece, *Candide*, Voltaire, the intellectual leader of the eighteenth century in the great war for the liberation of humanity, is still a legendary figure. A *philosophe* rather than a philosopher in the eyes of the historians of philosophy, he must nevertheless rank with Socrates and Montaigne among the greatest thinkers the world has known in their particular tradition. His name is more often quoted than that of his great French contemporaries: Montesquieu, who gave us basic ideas on law; Diderot, whose philosophy and ethics and fiction are only now being truly understood; and Rousseau himself, whose part in shaping our spiritual, educational, and political theories need hardly be stressed.

Paradoxically enough, it was Voltaire, a cynic, an ironist, and a deist, who blasphemed against the Catholic religion, and not a leading churchman, who became the apostle of human justice and political freedom, and stood in the vanguard of human progress. He believed wholeheartedly in the republic of letters which would cut across all frontiers, in the lasting amity of nations brought together by trade and mutual interest, in scientific and technological advance which would improve the spiritual as well as the material lot of man. Whilst aware of the horror of war and pouring ridicule on the legions of mercenaries, he failed to foresee the modern conflagration of total war. But he certainly knew how to fight oppression, fanaticism, intolerance, injustice, and stupidity. His methods were those of an experienced journalist, a great publicist, and a successful propagandist, born before his time, as Jean Cocteau once pointed out. He knew how to beat the drum with vigour, clarity, and unfailing regularity. He was remarkably successful in educating a whole nation, and his technique, based on wit and logic, because it was so effective, could well be studied anew.

Chapter 9

ROUSSEAU

JEAN-JACQUES ROUSSEAU (1712–78) was one of the most influential thinkers and writers of his age. His way of life and peculiar emotionalism, his social and political theories, and his principles of education exerted a profound influence upon his own and subsequent generations; and he is still today one of the writers most widely read, criticised, and discussed.

Other writers and thinkers had previously shown a sensibility similar to his, and called with a similar sincerity for a return to idyllic nature, creating a climate of intellectual opinion that was favourable to the dissemination of Rousseau's major principles. The reaction against rationalism, and against excessive sophistication of manners and modes, that set in early in the century, was to his advantage; and although he was a renegade from the *Encyclopédie* camp, his friendship with Diderot, which lasted for fourteen years, inevitably left its mark upon him. Ultimately he stands alone; yet all his work shows a natural affinity of mind and spirit with the *philosophes*.

Many interpretations of his work and his character, the one so closely intertwined with the other, have been made. Critics have stressed at different times different aspects of this protean personality, dwelling upon French or Genevan characteristics; upon the Protestant or the Catholic Rousseau; upon the individualist or the totalitarian temper of his mind; and they have referred to the potential Surrealist, Existentialist, or Modernist lurking within him. The fact that emerges with crystal clarity from these conflicting studies is that Rousseau is uniquely Rousseau, and must be swallowed whole. His complexity is such that any approach to him or to his writings must be of some value; and even tendentious works have their place, if they throw new light on aspects of the genesis of Rousseau's work.

The unbiased reader would do well to begin a coherent study with Rousseau's *Confessions*, startling in their manifest over-all accuracy and sincerity, and in which he strips himself to the skin; and the importance of this key to his other works needs hardly to be stressed. Professor R. Grimsley has subtitled his important book on Rousseau[1] *A study in self-awareness*; this, and the recent biography by J. Guehenno,[2] who has been careful to correct minor inaccuracies on Rousseau's part, due no doubt to forgetfulness, and to offer explanation of events in the light of the most recent investigations, also serve to illuminate the *Confessions*.

Rousseau was the supreme egotist. Involved in controversy and conflict all his life, perpetually aware of the loyalty of his friends and the machinations of his foes, and deeply responsive to his environment, he was ultimately concerned only with himself, and this gives the *Confessions* their unique power of depth and detail, in a self-analysis that has never been equalled.

It is typical that his last works were not even consciously written for publication, but rather to clarify his own ideas, and give point to his life through a fuller understanding of its complexities. He then took little interest in a posterity that might not ever read his apologia. He ceased to be merely a littérateur, writing to express his feelings and ideas about the society of his time: instead he turned his great analytical powers inward upon himself, until the inmost recesses of his being were laid bare.

Herein lies the significance of Rousseau's work. It is so closely related to his total experience of life, so exact an expression of his personality, that apparently conflicting opinions expressed in juxtaposition can be reconciled by reference to his complex inner self. He was able to practise his own ideal way of life in a manner that is given to few. Whether he failed ultimately in his attempt to fulfil his dream, as most would have he did, or whether he succeeded, is still a fruitful subject for debate among scholars, and part of his continued appeal to his very wide public, who for their part are intrigued by the reasonable measure of success he obtained in practising what he preached.

Rousseau's fascination, exerted over diverse minds and emotions from the beginning, derives from his sensibility and from the power of his intellect, with its exceptional ability to analyse and to synthesise, and with its cogent logic, which, wherever it is misapplied, adds to the interest of his writing by forcing his readers to strive to understand its divagations and find an explanation for them. From his equally exceptional powers of expression he forged an instrument so supple and so accurate that he was able to convey, directly or by implication, the most delicate shades of feeling, the most subtle detail of thought, and *nuances* of sensibility so fine that they had remained beyond the scope of previous writers.

His work is so woven with the pattern of his life, and the importance of his work linked so closely with that pattern, that he can

[1] *Jean-Jacques Rousseau, a study in self-awareness*, 1961.
[2] *Jean-Jacques*, 3 vols., 1948–52.

be understood only imperfectly without recourse to his background.

Jean-Jacques Rousseau was born in Geneva on 28 June 1712, into a family that had been converted to Calvinism and taken refuge in Geneva in the middle of the sixteenth century. His mother died a few days after his birth, and for the first ten years of his life he was brought up by an affectionate, but unstable, irritable, erratic, and feckless father, a watchmaker by trade. The child Jean-Jacques received no proper schooling. His father read the sermons of Calvinist divines to him, the *Lives* of Plutarch, and French 'romanesque' novels of the previous century, among them *Le Grand Cyrus* by Mlle de Scudéry, and *Cléopâtre* by La Calprenède. These factors in his childhood serve to explain in part his lifelong search for, and detachment from, familial and marital love, his theories on parenthood, and his deep desire for affection oddly allied to the rejection of intimate contact. They explain the necessity that drove him to find a mother substitute in Mme de Warens, perhaps the only woman he truly loved, and whom, significantly, he called Maman.

In 1722 the father quarrelled with a fellow-citizen and fled to Nyon (Vaud), leaving his two sons, François and Jean-Jacques, then aged ten, in the care of a maternal uncle. François was apprenticed and Jean-Jacques sent to the Pastor J.-J. Lambercier at Bossey, near Geneva. Two years later, in September 1724, his schooling then deemed finished, he returned to his uncle and became clerk to the notary J.-L. Masseron for a short period. In April 1725 he was apprenticed to Abel du Commun, an engraver, and stayed with him until, on 14 March 1728, not yet sixteen years old, he decided to run away from du Commun and from Geneva.

These early years, as recounted by Rousseau in his *Confessions*, have a special fascination. The factual and emotional precision of his account is not only surprising, but revealing of the child who was indeed the father of the man, the deprived child of the social worker's case-book, abandoned by his mother through death, by his father in early childhood, brought up on the hard bread of charity in loveless surroundings. Wholly concerned with total self-analysis, Rousseau neither pities nor despises the child he was; he simply presents him, warts and all, exposing curious aspects of his personality and his early sexuality, as when he states that Mlle Lambercier ceased to beat him for his peccadilloes as soon as she discovered that he enjoyed the beatings too much. In his relationship with others he experienced deep humiliation, part of it caused by his resentment of his own dishonesty and idleness, which made him feel inferior. His assessment of du Commun as a harsh and brutal master reveals his lifelong feeling of revolt, present in the child, developed in the man, an intractable will, and a determined opposition to social ills.

Rousseau presents also an unusually vivid glimpse of life in eighteenth-century Geneva and its neighbouring districts, seen from the angle of the artisan and lower-middle class. Rousseau has often been accused of leading the life of a vagabond, but it should be noted that in the beginning he had very little option in the matter, and later submitted passively to his fate, rather than voluntarily choosing a peripatetic existence. After his departure from Geneva, he moved from job to job as a lackey.

His meeting on Palm Sunday 1728 with Mme de Warens, which he has described with charm and sincerity in the *Confessions*, is a key date, for it marks the beginning of his emotional life, and of his most formative years, from an intellectual point of view. Madame de Warens was a Vaudoise, who had left her husband and recently become a Catholic convert. She received financial support from the King of Sardinia for services rendered, and also from ecclesiastical authorities, to encourage her to make new converts. This she did in Rousseau's case by sending him to Turin's Hospice for Catechumens, which he entered on 12 April 1728. He abjured Calvinism on 21 April and was received into the Roman Catholic Church on 23 April. While he was in Turin he became an engraver, and also served as lackey to the comte de Gouvon. He was given lessons in Latin and in Tuscan, and acquired some knowledge of Italian music.

Although he was well treated, he decided to return to Mme de Warens after a year abroad, in the spring of 1729. He was then sent to a Lazarist seminary, but quickly discovered that he had no vocation for the priesthood. He next attended the choristers' school of the Cathedral at Annecy, where he furthered his knowledge of music. In 1730 he paid visits to Fribourg, Geneva, Lausanne, Vevey, and Neuchâtel (1730–31), where he taught music. He became involved with a Levantine adventurer describing himself as the Archimandrite of Jerusalem; Rousseau had to be rescued from him by the French ambassador at Solothurn.

After months of wandering, he visited Paris in the autumn of 1731, at the request of that same ambassador at Solothurn; but he stayed for only a few days, returning on foot to Mme de Warens, who was now settled at Chambéry. His need of her, from the moment of their meeting, is demonstrated by his quick decision to return to her from Turin, and his long trek from Paris to Chambéry on foot. Upon his return, at the age of twenty, they began their strange, and strangely moving, liaison. She, who was twelve years older than he, offered herself to him for his own good, and to save him from the possible moral dangers he might incur, and they became lovers, after she had given him time to make up his mind about this possible new relationship. It is clear that he accepted more as a son than as a lover, and was not disturbed to find himself sharing her favours with her steward, Claude Anet.

There has been a great deal of research into the life of Mme de Warens, and much has been written about her. The one fact of prime importance that emerges is Rousseau's love for her, which endured long after their liaison had come to an end. It is known that he, the misanthrope, the misogynist, sent her money when she had fallen into a state of great deterioration and was in dire need; and in the unfinished tenth *Rêverie*, the last pages he ever wrote, he refers to her in deeply moving terms.

The depth and persistence of his devotion is explicable. She offered a boy starved of normal family love, the birthright of every child, a warmth of affection, a security, and an interest in what he was, what he did, and what he thought, that served to fill the place left cold and vacant by his mother's early death, and by his father's feckless indifference. She soothed his constant feeling of humiliation and inferiority: for if she was his employer, and he her subordinate, she was also his mistress, and so he mastered her.

To his bedazzled eyes, she was a lady of quality, of a much higher social class than his own, so that in stooping to him, she raised him up. She gave him a rich and full experience of love and its attendant emotions; and she opened for him the door that led to another way of life, an entry into a society he had before known only as a lackey. She also gave him the freedom of her extensive library, gave him the opportunity to further his own sadly neglected education, and encouraged him to seize this opportunity with both hands. He suffered all the disadvantages of the self-taught, the slow and painful process of discovery, the struggle to understand things beyond his present depth; but because of the struggle to wrest learning from books, he was able to liberate and discipline his brilliant mind, and make that learning his for life, since there had been no shallow nor specious short cuts to its acquirement. Those years between the age of twenty-five and thirty-two were key years for Rousseau, illumined by the idyll at Les Charmettes (1736–37), which remained unforgettable when so much else in his life turned sour in the remembrance.

Apart from occasional trips to Switzerland or France, he remained with Mme de Warens at Chambéry or in her country house of Les Charmettes until 1740. Their relationship entered upon a difficult patch in the year 1738–39. He returned from a visit to Montpellier, taken for health reasons, to find that a new lover, Wintzenried, had supplanted him: Mme de Warens had made it clear that the idyll was over. Rousseau had been suffering from uraemia since 1737, his condition growing progressively worse, during which time she had shown no more than a maternal solicitude.

He left in May 1740 to become tutor to the children of Monsieur de Mably, provost of Lyons, the elder brother of Condillac and of the abbé de Mably; but he was not invited to stay on when the year for which he was contracted came to an end. In 1742 he moved to Paris, to hawk around a new system of musical notation, an opera, a comedy, and a collection of poems. He expounded his system to the Académie des Sciences, which remained unimpressed. From September 1743 to August 1744 he was in Venice as secretary to Monsieur de Montaigu, the French ambassador, with whom he quarrelled; and he left Venice for Paris. There he wrote a ballet, *Les Muses galantes*, which impressed the duc de Richelieu, but otherwise attracted little attention. He was commissioned by Richelieu to review *Les Fêtes de Ramire*, an opera by Rameau, with libretto by Voltaire. This led to correspondence with Voltaire, and a widening interest in poetry and drama.

The vicissitudes of his life in Paris at that period repeated those of his earlier years. He resented the fact that his name was not officially mentioned in connection with the opera. He declared his love for his protectress, Mme Dupin, who immediately forbade him her house. He earned his living by secretarial duties, and copying music. This last, and indeed copying his own manuscripts, was never an irksome task for Rousseau. He had the fine hand of an engraver, and had inherited the meticulous care of the watchmaker; and the work soothed his nerves and his perpetually agitated mind.

He was in frequent contact with socially exalted people; but it was his friendship with Diderot that brought him his greatest happiness. Once a week he dined at the Hôtel du Panier Fleuri with Diderot and with Condillac, and he valued highly these meetings with their subsequent discussions. Diderot commissioned Rousseau to write articles on music and political economy for the *Encyclopédie*.

In 1745 or 1746 Jean-Jacques took as his mistress Thérèse Le Vasseur, a servant at the hotel in which he was staying, and to whom he remained faithful for the rest of his life, marrying her on 30 August 1768. They had five children, in 1746, 1747, 1748, and 1751, all of whom, according to their father, were sent to an orphanage, the Enfants-Trouvés, which was a fairly common practice at the time in cases where the prospects of the children were very poor.

As the years went by, Rousseau developed an increasing sense of guilt on this score, so obsessional that it brought him near to insanity. He repeatedly refers to his conduct in his writings, and again in the *Rêveries* which he wrote a few months before his death. Some critics have questioned the truth of his statements concerning his children, since there is no contemporary evidence to prove them conclusively, except for the total sincerity and frankness of his *Confessions* on all demonstrable issues.

It is certain that in his mature years, he gave every evidence of a growing moral conscience; and his wrongful accusation of a serving-girl, Marion, of the theft of a ribbon is linked with the abandonment of his children as crimes for which he felt deep and lasting remorse. Many of the early readers of the *Confessions* were outraged by the relation of these actions and shocked by the nature of their author. Greater knowledge of human psychology and the workings of the subconscious mind have made contemporary readers more tolerant and less easily horrified.

Rousseau was thirty-seven before he began to make his mark as a writer, and to think of writing as a major activity in his life. Towards the end of July 1749 he was on his way to visit Diderot, imprisoned in Vincennes. He had just read in the *Mercure de France* that the Academy of Dijon was offering a prize for an essay debating whether the revival of the arts and sciences was liable to corrupt or to purify morals. He relates in the *Confessions* how, as a result of this, he had a vision and became another man. He arrived at the prison in a state of great excitement, and Diderot urged him to compete for the prize. He may have suggested the paradoxical line of approach which Rousseau in the event adopted; but he never claimed the ideas it contained as his own. Rousseau's later writings tend to show that his pent-up emotions had reached explosion-point at that moment. He released them then, and argued that science and art had corrupted morals.

At this time Rousseau was known mainly as a composer and writer on music, but he had literary aspirations as well. He had just finished his opera *Les Muses galantes*, and the revision of *Les Fêtes de Ramire*; also a comedy, *Narcisse*, and a tragedy *La Découverte du Nouveau-Monde* (1741); he had also written *L'Engagement téméraire*, *Arlequin amoureux malgré lui*, and a poem, *L'Allée de Sylvie*; and he was thinking of editing a journal, *Le Persifleur*. He had also shown some interest in science, through the lectures in chemistry of Rouelle, and from 1746 onwards he drafted his *Institutions chymiques*.

The *Discours* Rousseau submitted for the prize, a work of some twenty pages, contained an historical part, showing how developing culture was leading to political slavery and moral vice. He argued that primitive, ignorant people like the Persians, the

Scythians, the Germans, and the Spartans preserved their virtue, as indeed did the Romans before their decadence, a standpoint clearly demonstrated in a fine piece of rhetorical writing known as the *Prosopopée de Fabricius.* In a second part, Rousseau set out to prove that the arts and sciences must necessarily and logically be pernicious, since they create luxury; and luxury weakens the state. Here, Rousseau took up a standpoint in diametric opposition to that of Voltaire in his poem *Le Mondain.* Luxury, he argued, enhances the social position of woman to the detriment of manly virtues and genius; it destroys military prowess, is harmful to patriotism and religion, and sets talent above virtue. Philosophy is excellent in principle, but philosophers, by spreading dangerous maxims, do nothing but harm. Science in the hands of incompetent people is a menace; and the spreading of culture will not increase the number of great minds, of men like Cicero or Bacon, who are truly capable of leading society and uplifting mankind.

In July 1750, Rousseau's *Discours sur les sciences et les arts* was awarded first prize. At the end of the year the work was published, and Rousseau became famous overnight. He was favoured by high society, its members appreciating his paradox without being unduly worried by its implications. It is interesting to note that he never found himself at home in this milieu, through a consciousness of personal inadequacy, and because his need to justify to himself his association with the low-born Thérèse Le Vasseur inhibited him in the presence of the highly born. This unease may have reinforced his general stand against the values of society.

The *Discours* read like a clever academic exercise, and as such no doubt deserved its success. Rousseau continued to develop his interest in music and in drama. His comedy *Narcisse* was presented at the Comédie Française in that same year (1750) and in the following year he wrote a *Lettre sur la musique française,* expressing his preference for Italian music.

In 1754 he returned to Geneva, visiting the shores of the lake, and in particular Clarens, which was later to be used as a setting for *La Nouvelle Héloïse.* He received a warm welcome in his birthplace and was prompted to return to the Protestant faith, and to reacquire his rights as a citizen of Geneva. It was on this occasion that he paid what was to be his last visit to Mme de Warens, now in straitened circumstances and much deteriorated, in which they seem to have restored in some measure their mother–son relationship, for she gave Thérèse her ring.

In 1755 Rousseau published a *Discours sur l'origine de l'inégalité parmi les hommes,* which he entered for the Dijon competition, but which failed to gain an award, in spite of the elegance of its style. In contradiction to the ideas expressed in his first *Discours* concerning the nefarious effects of culture, Rousseau had continued his literary activities. The success of his opera *Le Devin du village*, which continued to be performed throughout 1753 both at court and at the Opéra, left him uneasy, and once again unable to reconcile principles with practice.

The problem of inequality is germane to the arts and the sciences, since both create social disturbances. The influence of Diderot impregnates the second *Discours*, and some of Rousseau's pages read as though they were the development of ideas expressed in Diderot's *Pensées sur l'interprétation de la nature*. It is clear that Rousseau had studied his subject with great care: there is ample evidence that he had read Condillac's *Essai sur l'origine des connaissances humaines* (1746), also Grotius, Puffendorf, Locke, and Hobbes, who had also considered the question of the natural state; and Buffon and others, who provided him with scientific data. Rousseau dedicated this second *Discours* to the republic of Geneva, perhaps in the hope of being asked to adjudicate in the conflict between the *Petit Conseil*, in whom executive power resided, and the *Grand Conseil*, who held their mandate from the people.

After a long preface dealing with questions of method, Rousseau, in a short preamble, distinguishes two forms of inequality: the natural, based upon diversity of force; and the moral, or political, inequality. Man is described in his physical condition, happy in his natural state, an animal fighting similar animals, without weapons other than his senses, until the urgent needs of survival provoked him into the creation of arms. Man, primitive morally, is endowed with intelligence as well as with instincts, is free and capable of improvement. Rousseau expands the idea of the innocent savage, a generalised character who becomes our ancestor, the prototype of primitive humanity. He offers an imaginative sketch of the evolution of man, subject to nature and to the influence of climate; and the formation of social groups indulging in the recreation of dance and conversation. In this intermediary stage, man passes from his primitive to his civilised form, and here the seed of inequality is found. Cultivation of the soil leads to property, and so to laws and institutions for the protection of property, and so civil law replaces natural law.

Man originally chooses his masters by a free and conscious act, but soon power becomes arbitrary, and each becomes the slave of his master, and in turn enslaves his inferior. Rousseau attacks the idea of property as being at the root of social trouble. Rousseau, in dealing with the birth of government, foreshadows his *Contrat Social*, which he had first conceived some ten years earlier, and later sought to publish under the title *Institutions politiques*. In the same year (1755) he wrote the *Discours sur l'économie politique*, which Diderot had commissioned for the *Encyclopédie*; and in April 1756 he moved to the Hermitage, near Montmorency, which Mme d'Epinay had made available to him, and where he worked at *Julie ou La Nouvelle Héloïse*.

Some of his inspiration for the book derives from the comtesse d'Houdetot, with whom he fell passionately and romantically in love. She was the sister of Mme d'Epinay, and some twenty years his junior. She herself was in love with the soldier-poet Saint-Lambert, whose mistress she was, and with whom she had a liaison that lasted until his death. Rousseau was aware that his love for her was unrequited, but hoped for her continued friendship, which soon proved to be impossible in the circumstances then obtaining. Much of the eloquence, the subtlety, and, it must be confessed, the absurdity, to be found in the situations and the attitudes of the chief characters in *Julie* is due to this strange and inconclusive relationship, which kindled Rousseau's imagination, and roused his latent romanticism.

In 1756 he wrote a *Lettre sur la Providence* addressed to Voltaire, with whom relations grew subsequently strained. He broke with Mme d'Epinay, owing to a misunderstanding with her lover, the baron Grimm, who had become Diderot's closest friend, and finally with Diderot himself. This catastrophic alienation from the circles he most valued brought on the persecution mania that grew within him for the rest of his life. Thérèse had always disliked country life, and it is much to her credit that she endured so many years of it for his sake; so now they moved to Montlouis, where they remained until June 1762, owing to his friendship with the gracious and tactful maréchal de Luxembourg and his wife, both of whom were devoted to Rousseau.

Rousseau was now relatively happy, working on *La Nouvelle Héloïse*, and thereby compensating himself for his lack of emotional success in his own life. It was written in the form of letters, and owes something to Richardson and to Prévost.

In October 1758 he wrote a *Lettre à M. d'Alembert*, usually referred to as *Lettre sur les spectacles*, in which he argued against the establishment of a theatre in Geneva, in opposition to the views expressed earlier in the year by d'Alembert, in the article 'Genève' of the *Encyclopédie*, and challenging Voltaire on the same subject. According to Rousseau, plays were immoral, and the theatre an artificial product born of idleness and vanity, which stirred the passions of men and led them into temptation and evil. Women became unfeminine and shameless, and the men enslaved by them became effeminate. Indirectly, he was attacking the theatre in Paris, with its peculiar values, and the sophisticated pattern of Parisian society, which had never been to his taste. But his primary concern was with Geneva, and he set himself against the opening of a theatre in that city. This resolution from a writer who had launched himself in the theatre and in opera with great success points not so much to inconsistency, as to the resurgence of Calvinism and the deepening preoccupation with moral issues that marked his intellectual development.

He saw Geneva as a small state still capable of the simplicity and innocence of the Greek communities of ancient days; and he was successful in his lifetime, as well as in that of Voltaire, in keeping the theatre away, by allying himself with the *Grand Conseil* in the struggle with the more aristocratic and broadminded *Petit Conseil.* His stand for increased democracy involved greater restriction of the liberty of the subject.

As a substitute for the theatre, the citizens of Geneva were invited to take part in public open-air festivities, guaranteed innocent, and balls organised and supervised by chaperones of unimpeachable morals, who could be forgiven for scheming to turn such occasions into marriage marts of the highest respectability. Rousseau's *Lettre sur les spectacles* gave great offence to Diderot, destroying the last shreds of relationship between them, and, together with factors of a personal kind, achieving a complete and final break, after a friendship that had lasted so many years.

La Nouvelle Héloïse, completed at Montmorency, was published early in 1761, and enjoyed an immediate and overwhelming success. The novel is concerned with passionate love and rigorous duty. Julie d'Etanges falls headlong in love with her tutor, Saint-Preux, much as Héloïse fell in love with Abélard. Her father refuses to allow her to marry a commoner, and she is eventually married to Monsieur de Wolmar. She seeks to atone for her past sin by confessing it to her husband, and by proving herself to be a model wife and mother. Monsieur de Wolmar, who has implicit faith in her, invites Saint-Preux to his home, and leaves the two former lovers together. They survive this moral test, Saint-Preux through his integrity and masculine virtue, Julie through her love for her children and the help of her religious principles. They discover, however, that the love between them still exists, unchanged, unadulterated, and that their present proximity causes them intense suffering. Julie saves her son from drowning, but as a result catches a chill from which she dies, a neat solution to a problem that could not otherwise be solved, and the surest possible way of securing Julie's absolute virtue.

The story line in all its absurdity is at once typical of Rousseau's worst excesses of sentimentality, and the least important part of the novel. It is lifted out of the novelette class by Rousseau's superb style, vivid word pictures, and the translation of his own frustrated love for Mme d'Houdetot into the Roman virtue of Julie and Saint-Preux. The descriptions of natural beauty, of Clarens and the Lake of Geneva, that abound in it reflect a new sensibility, and the life of the house in its rural setting, where Monsieur de Wolmar and his household, including his servants, shared in simple pleasures in perfect harmony, embodies Rousseau's dream of natural man in natural surroundings. There are brilliant digressions, disquisitions on Calvinism, on life in Paris (II, 14; 21), duelling (I, 57), class prejudice (II, 16; 27), the theatre and morality (II, 17; 23), suicide (III, 21; 22), music (I, 48), the education of children (VI, 12; and *passim*), and atheism (V, 5), subjects never until then treated in a novel, and of greater interest to his contemporaries than they are now, when digression is resolutely excluded from novel-writing.

La Nouvelle Héloïse has dated. The social conditions of the eighteenth century that brought the novel its great success have long since disappeared, and the modern reader finds little of interest in the moral and social theme of the novel, or its letter-form and its long disquisitions, which make it difficult for him to detach and appreciate the love story of Julie and Saint-Preux.

This core to the story is as valid as that of the *Confessions*, and stems from the same source. It is complementary to, and a continuation of, the same history of a strange, weak-willed, egotistical personality, in a different form. The intensely personal life of the author is revealed as absolutely the world of imaginative dreams, touched upon in the *Confessions*, in which Rousseau sought escape from the frustrations of reality: 'Les seuls retours du passé peuvent me flatter, et ces retours si vifs et si vrais dans l'époque dont je parle me font vivre heureux malgré mes malheurs', he wrote in the *Confessions*.

The romantic sensibility with which the novel is imbued offers marked contrast to the dialectical brilliance of the two *Discours*, the *Lettre à d'Alembert*, and later polemical writing, as if *La Nouvelle Héloïse* were a surprising and incongruous work to come from Rousseau's pen. Yet close reading of the *Confessions* leads to an opposite conclusion, that the novel was a more natural expression of his genius than his philosophical treatises; for his life reads like a picaresque novel with psychological undertones; Jean-Jacques was highly endowed with the powerful imagination necessary to the creative writer, and a fluid sense of style that inevitably lent itself to his purpose.

The *lettres d'amour*, which were the starting-point of *Julie*, sprang from this powerful imagination, from dreams and fantasies embroidered round youthful memories. Unlike *Adolphe*[3] and

[3] See P. E. Charvet, *A Literary History of France, the Nineteenth Century 1789–1870*, 1967, pp. 51 et seq.

Dominique,[4] love stories drawn from experience, *Julie* is a concept, a synthesis of all the author's imaginative dreams of which he was himself the hero. This is the essence of the novel which deeply moved readers bored with libertine excesses, through the purity of its idyllic love theme, although in its final version it had nevertheless changed course and become the statement of a social doctrine.

The work shows evidence of many influences in its presentation, among them, as noted above, certainly Prévost and Richardson. Topics widely discussed by the society of the day are evident throughout; and the influence of Mme d'Houdetot is paramount, as Rousseau made clear when he wrote in the *Confessions*: 'Je vis ma Julie en Madame d'Houdetot, et bientôt je ne vis plus que Madame d'Houdetot, mais revêtue de toutes les perfections dont je venais d'orner l'idole de mon coeur.'

This idealised version of his abortive association with Mme d'Houdetot, seen exclusively from his own angle and coloured with his imaginative wish-fulfilment, and his agony of renunciation, expressed through Julie, of a relationship he had never in fact enjoyed, illumines the romantic side of Rousseau's nature; and an exploration of his unrequited love for the lady and its transmogrification in *La Nouvelle Héloïse* serves to unravel the seeming contradiction within the author's mind, and the apparent antithesis between his life and his philosophical doctrine.

The novel has a dual theme, of passionate love, and of virtue. The first part is given to the first of the two themes through a succession of different emotional attitudes, rather than through an amorous progression: the novel of virtue begins with Julie's marriage to Monsieur de Wolmar. The religious ceremony operates upon her as though by magic, and she is converted by it to find great happiness in her marriage and in obeying the laws of God. There is some confusion over the definition of real virtue – and changing statements concerning the state of virtue can prove disturbing – but there can never be any doubt about the sincerity and the validity of Julie's conversion. Many ideas and principles are presented and elucidated in this second part, but special interest lies in the curious *ménage à trois* established therein. Julie, Saint-Preux, and Monsieur de Wolmar living happily together under one roof is a transposition of the Sophie d'Houdetot, Rousseau, and Saint-Lambert situation, with the signal difference that Sophie and Jean-Jacques were never in fact lovers. To this extent the triangular establishment is grafted on to the novel rather than an intrinsic part of it, and has no artistic nor psychological justification in the novel. It is in fact a continuation of the passage in the *Confessions* in which Rousseau states: 'Nous formâmes le projet

[4] Ibid., pp. 169, 185–6.

charmant d'une étroite société entre nous trois . . .', which he is free to create only in his imagination. His fictional *ménage à trois* may also be an extension of his own participation in a real one in the household of Mme de Warens, in which he shared the favours of his mistress with Claude Anet. Writing in the *Confessions*, he says: 'Ainsi s'établit entre nous trois une unité sans autre exemple peut-être sur la terre . . .'. This is a recurring pattern in his emotional life, real or imaginary; for when later he was supplanted by Wintzenreid in the affections of Mme de Warens, he once more had to contemplate a similar triangular relationship.

La Nouvelle Héloïse is a complex synthesis of the experiences, dreams, and philosophy of Rousseau, pervaded by the romantic sensibility, more fully revealed in the *Confessions* and the *Rêveries*, which was given full rein in some lyrical passages,[5] a foretaste of the prose-poem in the *Cinquième Rêverie*.

In April 1762 Rousseau published *Du Contrat Social*, one of the most remarkable treatises of political theory that has ever been written, largely based on his conception of government in ancient Rome, and concerned mainly with Geneva. A month later *Emile* appeared, written in the form of a novel, and destined to have a great impact in the field of education. Rousseau was not concerned with propounding a simple, workable new system of instruction, but with propounding new principles of education. Emile is to be taught by one person, whose whole thought and time must be given to the child's education. Rousseau's approach is a combination of theory and story-writing, as in his creation of Sophie, the predestined bride of Emile, and in the completion of his education: a contrived and arbitrary invention totally lacking in plausibility.

The work, nevertheless, has practical aspects. Rousseau never lost sight of the main purpose of real education, and expounded theories that were revolutionary in his day. He stressed the need to learn from experience; and although the *Leçons de choses* demonstrated in the novel are over-contrived, they foreshadow the best teaching of Pestalozzi and Maria Montessori, among the great educationists. His intention was to allow the child to develop freely and to grade the child's learning in accordance with his age and stage of development, and to make it meaningful for him. He owed something to earlier writers, from Plato and Aristotle to Montaigne and Locke; but he drew most from personal experience, and his own reflections upon that experience, gathering his ideas into a coherent philosophy of education to which modern pedagogues still turn.

Emile is an ordinary child, whom he wished to make morally and intellectually self-reliant, so that he would take no harm from

[5] Cf. *Oeuvres complètes*, II, 1961, 4e partie, XVII, pp. 518–20.

his entry into society. His aim was the aim of all real educationists – to help to develop a free and well-balanced personality in the pupil, and to make of him a good citizen.

Modern research has shown how Rousseau's educational precepts supplemented his views on government, and why they were so revolutionary in his own day. Contemporary civilisation was, to his mind, corrupt and decadent, its structures causing only harm to the individual and leading to his disorientation and misery. Man had become alienated from his original nature, and could no longer be himself. In his *Discours sur l'inégalité*, Rousseau opposed virtue, the solid moral strength derived from an honest heart and a purity of spirit, to the corrupt society that destroyed mankind. The only hope for the future, therefore, was to evolve a new political system; and in order to achieve that, there must be a new form of education. This antecedent thought serves to explain why so much of Emile's early education was negative, and why he was not allowed to mix with other children: he must be removed from all influences and learn only through his dependence upon things that surrounded him, whose nature and substance he must explore. This theoretical yet empirical approach to education explains why *Robinson Crusoe* was the only children's book to find favour in his eyes; and that one, it will be remembered, was written for adults. After learning from necessity, the child must learn from utility: his concern is with things, sensations, and feelings, not with words and abstractions. All Emile's instincts and passions are basically good, but they need discipline as well as fulfilment. And only when he is properly educated will he be fit to enter society. The nature of the society he should then enter is explained in Rousseau's political writings, for, as Professor Grimsley has stated: 'a new rational unity must replace the instinctive unity of the primitive state'.

Rousseau is naturally led to consider the philosophical basis of all legitimate governments, and it is at this point that the *Contrat Social*, on which he had been working at the same time, is wholly relevant.

The *Profession de foi du vicaire savoyard*, which embodies Rousseau's views on religion, is contained within the novel *Emile*. He reveals himself as highly critical of philosophical scepticism, and of Christianity as an institution. His belief is pragmatic and based largely on moral conscience; he does not, however, reject proofs of the existence of God based upon the existence of motion.

His doctrine of a Supreme Being is in fact a form of 'natural religion' or deism, founded upon the dictates of his heart, reinforced by reason, and not, as in Voltaire's case, founded upon essentially rationalistic convictions. In this manner Rousseau launched a new religious sensibility, destined to be of long-lasting appeal. He, who was persecuted for his beliefs, was in fact the most deeply religious of the great thinkers of his age, and may indeed have been the only one who was so in the broad sense of the term. He never abandoned his belief in God and in the immortality of the soul; and his last work, the *Rêveries du promeneur solitaire*, shows his awareness that he was soon to appear before the tribunal of God and plead his case.

In the *Contrat Social* Rousseau viewed religion from the social and institutional standpoint, as he had previously done in certain passages of the *Lettre sur les spectacles*. In the *Profession de foi du vicaire savoyard* he expounds the philosophical and instinctive basis of his faith. For him, God has made Nature just and good, and has brought order out of chaos. Man's deep feeling for Nature is a form of communion with God, and he listens to the divine voice of conscience. Intuition has its place in his understanding of the world; and happiness, the goal of man's living, can be achieved only through a natural simplicity which implies a relaxed existence, the prerequisite of ecstasy, mystical experience, and beatitude, the deep heart of religion. Rousseau admires Jesus Christ, but does not admit that he has redeemed mankind or washed away the sins of the world. Although he accepts the message of the Gospels he is no Christian. His deism, like that of Voltaire, becomes the platform for an ethical system; but unlike Voltaire's it has a Protestant austerity. He has no interest in ritual, the creed, or the Church; but only in individual man, and his discovery of the wonders of nature which he identifies with himself. Rousseau's vision of man becoming almost God-like, of man achieving his salvation unaided and of his own free-will, and of the transfiguration of human existence, was destined to change the spiritual outlook of countless men of the Romantic and post-Romantic period, and has proved attractive to widely diverse people, philosophers, critics, those with religious predispositions, but without any particular faith, and to poets of various schools, right up to the present day.

The *Contrat Social* starts with the premise that man is born free, and with equal rights: but to establish an ideal society man must alienate his freedom and subordinate it to the general will, whether the government under which he lives be democratic, aristocratic, or monarchical. Laws must be the same for all and made by general will for the security of all, and in this way they will be both good and absolute. Evil springs from the size and complexity of modern societies, and from differences in wealth. In spite of its theoretical nature, Rousseau's criticism of the contemporary social system was far-reaching, and brought about extraordinary consequences.

The *Contrat Social*, which started by advocating freedom, ended by advocating totalitarianism and state despotism: yet there is only an apparent inconsistency here, for in Rousseau's system, the state could do no wrong, since it incarnated the general good. His speculations have sometimes been condemned as sophistries: but largely by those who have failed to distinguish between theory and practice, or to acknowledge the part played by theory in the advancement of political systems. As Rousseau sees it, man needs to fear tyranny only in society, where right, and not might, must dominate the social order. Political society must therefore rest upon a contract, one more theoretical rather than real, made between free, intelligent men who choose a form of government. In the eighteenth century, the idea of a social contract was often considered as a rational and quasi-legal reality, but it may in fact be thought of as a tacit undertaking by the contracting parties. This pact, when it is ratified, justifies the state in assuming all rights. The alienation of the individual is total, to avoid inequality and injustice – 'Each one uniting with all obeys only himself and remains as free as before' – so there can be no question of tyranny, where all obey the general will, which is necessarily directed to the general good. Social man achieves true freedom by obeying a law which he has prescribed for himself, and finds fulfilment from living fraternally and equally with his fellows, all sharing the same ideals. This view, therefore, which seems to foreshadow totalitarianism, is in fact democratic, since all sovereignty lies with the people.

The *souverain*, defined as the community, may delegate executive powers to one man or to a government, its specific form being determined by historical, geographical, and other factors. It must be clearly distinguished from the legislator who, according to Rousseau, must be of exceptional excellence, in order to ensure the enactment of good laws, according to the *volonté générale* which is 'toujours droite', but alas, 'le jugement qui la guide n'est pas toujours éclairé.'[6]

The basic idea of a contract, which he made popular, served to focus attention on the fact that all forms of government are only relatively valid; and his readers were quick to see that if one party to the contract – in this case the government of the day – no longer filled its role of ideal legislator, working by common consent for the common good, then the contract became void, and therefore could, and should, be replaced. The whole conception of the Divine Right of Kings, and other arbitrary bases for authority, received in the *Contrat Social* a blow from which they never recovered.

[6] *Du Contrat Social*, book II, chapter vi.

Both *Emile* and the *Contrat Social* being deemed revolutionary and counter to the interests of the monarchy, Rousseau's arrest was ordered. He took refuge at Môtiers-Travers in the principality of Neuchâtel, then governed in the name of Frederick II of Prussia by Marshal Keith, a Jacobite in the Prussian service. The marshal became his friend, and he stayed there from July 1762 to September 1765. In 1763, in a *Lettre à Christophe de Beaumont*, the archbishop of Paris, who had attacked *Emile*, he upheld his *profession de foi*. He renounced his citizenship of Geneva and, in 1764, in his *Lettres écrites de la montagne*, he replied to J.-B. Tronchin, procurator-general of the Genevan Republic and partisan of the *Petit Conseil* of Geneva, who had ordered the burning of *Emile* and *Du Contrat Social*. In September 1764, Mathieu Buttafucco,[7] a friend of the Corsican Pasquale Paoli,[8] asked Rousseau to prepare a constitution for Corsica. This undertaking was never fully honoured, but Rousseau wrote in 1764–65 *Lettres à Buttafucco sur la législation de la Corse* and a *Projet de Constitution pour la Corse*. At the very end of 1764 Rousseau received an anonymous pamphlet, *Le Sentiment des citoyens*, in which he was branded as a hypocrite, a heartless father, and an ungrateful friend. This pamphlet, in fact written by Voltaire, shocked Rousseau deeply, and led him to undertake the writing of the *Confessions* to vindicate his good faith and good name. The *Lettres écrites de la montagne* had incensed the Protestant pastors of Geneva and Neuchâtel, and in September 1765 stones were thrown at his house. He was by now thoroughly disillusioned and his early persecution mania, given real cause, overwhelmed him, and caused him to seek escape. He left Môtiers, and spent two beatific months on the tiny Ile de Saint-Pierre, in the canton of Berne. This small lull left a lasting impression upon him, vividly and lengthily recorded in the *Confessions*, poetically and analytically in the *Cinquième Rêverie du promeneur solitaire*. For Rousseau, an island was the ultimate refuge, a symbolical return to the comfort and security of his mother's womb.

On the advice of his friend Marshal Keith, and with the help of David Hume, he moved on to England, stopping off at Strasbourg and Paris. He arrived in England, where he was to spend thirteen months, in January 1766, and began to work on the

[7] Matteo or Mathieu Buttafucco (1731–1806) favoured French intervention in Corsica. In 1781 he became *Maréchal de camp* and was later elected deputy for the nobility of Corsica to the *Etats-Généraux* of 1789. He became a royalist and emigrated in 1791, retiring to Corsica in 1803.

[8] Pasquale Paoli (1725–1807), a Corsican general and patriot, headed the Corsican government 1757–68, reorganising its administration and founding a university at Corte. After the French had broken down Corsican resistance, he took refuge in England in 1769.

Confessions. Although he was very well received in London, his English adventure was to turn out badly. He moved to Wootton, in Derbyshire, a house let to him at a nominal rental by Richard Davenport, a friend of Hume. Rousseau was in an abnormally emotional state, and his reaction to events, complicated by being in a foreign land, and by Thérèse's dislike of the country, was largely irrational.

It came to his knowledge that letters were being circulated in Paris, holding him up to ridicule, and generally believed to have been written by the King of Prussia, although in fact Horace Walpole was their author. Rousseau, with no real cause, suspected Hume of having participated in the affair, and he began to distrust him, driven by fear, by his persecution mania, and an hysterical desire to vindicate his good name. Hume promptly set out to justify himself at Rousseau's expense, and there was an open quarrel, news of which crossed the Channel, and occasioned much excitement and mirth throughout Europe.

In May 1767 Rousseau fled to France, where the order for his arrest, issued in 1762, was still in force. He spent a few days with the marquis de Mirabeau, then moved, under the name of Monsieur Renou, to Trye-le-Château, near Gisors, lent to him by the prince de Conti. He completed the first part of the *Confessions* at Trye, and published his *Dictionnaire de musique*. In June 1768, seized with a sudden panic, he left for Bourgoin, near Lyons, when he at last married Thérèse Le Vasseur, who had been with him for twenty-two or twenty-three years. He then moved on to Monquin, where he began work on the second part of the *Confessions*.

Early in June 1770, he travelled to Paris with the fixed intention of defending himself against his enemies, and remained there for the major part of his last eight years, mostly in a small apartment in the Rue Plâtrière (now the Rue J.-J. Rousseau), living on such pensions as he had, and by copying music, left in peace by a tolerant, or perhaps an indifferent, government. He resumed his own name, and upon completion of the *Confessions* in 1770, read extracts in the salons he attended, for purposes of self-justification. Madame d'Epinay, who had every reason to fear his revelations, asked the police to place an embargo on these readings, with no success.

In 1771 Count Wielhorski invited Rousseau to draw up a scheme of reforms for the Poles. He then drafted his *Considérations sur le gouvernement de la Pologne* to meet this request, and in the same year he composed his *Lettres sur la botanique*.

His unbalanced state of mind, deeply affected by the events of his life, and by his maniac terrors, was made manifest in his

Dialogue: Rousseau juge de Jean-Jacques (1772–76). These form a pathological document as riveting now as when they were composed. Written with all the vivid imagery of which Rousseau was master, they are marked by the brilliant but warped logic of the insane, the work of a man haunted day and night by the terror of a plot against him, which did not in fact exist. In these *Dialogues* a powerful imagination, combined with superlative logic, is brought to bear upon considerations so absurd that the work betrays its author.

The dialogue is between Rousseau, represented as a well-balanced man of independent views, who has read Jean-Jacques' works and is prejudiced against him, but nevertheless is striving for an objective assessment; and Le Français, who has not read a line of the works, but is totally prejudiced against Jean-Jacques, and is in effect the faceless enemy that haunted Rousseau, his unrelenting persecutor. There is a third character – the blameless Jean-Jacques, the innocent man who has done nothing in his life or in his work to justify the persecution he endures.

Lawyers, as well as psychologists, have found the work significant, for the exceptional clarity with which arguments are marshalled, and the brilliance of Rousseau's special pleading. There are pages of uncanny insight into his own nature, particularly in the second dialogue, that highlight his character and his way of life, and prepare for the final poetic illumination in the *Rêveries*. So, in the black depths of uncontrollable despair drawing near to the total collapse of his mind, Rousseau wrote this brochure in defence of himself, and he now went out into the streets to distribute a pamphlet, *A tout Français aimant la vérité*, among those whose looks appealed to him through their intelligence or their compassion. He tried to place a copy of this pamphlet and of the *Dialogues* upon the high altar of Notre Dame (24 February 1776), seeking the protection of God; but the grille surrounding the choir denied him access, and he knew that God had now forsaken him.

Towards the end of 1776 a sudden euphoria set in, and he began writing the *Rêveries du promeneur solitaire*, and continued in this work until two months before his death in 1778. These are reflective and descriptive essays, filled with reminiscences of childhood and maturity, seen through kindlier eyes than those that probed in the *Confessions*, the work of a tired man coming to the end of his life. The *Rêveries*, written in a minor key, have great freshness, beauty, poetry, and depth, and add another dimension to the *Confessions*. Here he expressed, with an absolute purity of style, his feeling for nature, his reverence for life, his search for happiness, and his ultimate philosophy. He began this work for his own inner satisfaction, and to clarify his life's experience for himself. He is totally indifferent to the reactions of a possible public, and was able to ignore his enemies by reflecting that to dismiss them from his mind was to deny their existence. His imagination, dimmed by age and weariness of spirit, was still powerful enough to bring moments of ecstasy and of peace. This, his last work, is at once a summary and a vindication of his life, his writings, and his philosophy; and one that has attracted a perpetual legion of readers and disciples.

Critics have stressed the reasons for his personal failure. He advocated the superimposition of the imaginary life upon the reality of people and events; and this is to mutilate life in its fullness. Yet the potentialities of his way of life, in which he persistently refused to face up to the reality of his psychic being by creating another persona for himself, captured the imagination of countless thousands, who had equal need of escape.

Rousseau spent his last years copying music, walking in the suburbs, sometimes accompanied by his disciple Bernardin de Saint-Pierre, and going on botanical expeditions. In May 1778 he moved into a *pavillon* at Ermenonville, belonging to the marquis de Girardin, so that he could more easily collect botanical specimens, and died there on 2 July of apoplexy. He was buried on the Ile des Peupliers in the lake at Ermenonville; and in 1794, during the Revolution, his remains were removed to the Panthéon.

For Rousseau, life was more important than literature, and his writing took up a relatively small part of his time, and served chiefly as a self-imposed catharsis.

Retrospectively, it can be seen that Rousseau's work in all its diversity – political, philosophical, polemic, fictional, and autobiographical – is one vast saga of himself; and its basic theme, that man is naturally innocent, a view which challenged the orthodox view of original sin, is fundamental because of his need to convince himself of his own personal goodness. The noble savage of whom he wrote so convincingly, under so many guises, was himself. Too intelligent to believe that there could be a reversion to the primitive condition of man, he sought to lead as natural a life as possible, to return to nature in the depths of his being, and so release his potentialities to the full; and to convince himself of his own righteousness, he sought to persuade others to accept his premises. For him, self-awareness leads to goodness; and his whole life was spent, and exhausted, in the struggle to reconcile his own self-assertion and inevitable disregard of others with his insatiable desire to come to terms with his fellow men. If in the end he failed and became a *promeneur solitaire*, then in his thinking this could only be the fault of the society that rejected him.

Unable to find his niche as he wandered through life, he concluded that contemporary society was ill-suited to true men. He turned to small closed communities, like that of Monsieur de Wolmar, in *La Nouvelle Héloïse*. But the dream turned sour whenever he sought to make it real, and he found himself the outsider again.

It is fitting to conclude this study of Rousseau by an evaluation of the *Confessions*, a unique book, as he himself understood: 'Je forme une entreprise qui n'eut jamais d'exemple et dont l'exécution n'aura point d'imitateur. Je veux montrer à mes semblables un homme dans toute la vérité de la nature; et cet homme, ce sera moi,' he wrote provocatively, and yet with sincerity, at the beginning of his monumental work. His challenge was never taken up until recently, for no other writer of autobiography has been so unflinching in detail; and those few who, like André Gide in *Si le grain ne meurt*, have claimed to be even franker in self-exposure, have failed to convey the rich diversity of a whole life's experience.

The *Confessions*, taken in conjunction with the *Correspondance*, offer the key to the philosopher, the political thinker, the writer, the musician, and the poet contained within the single framework of a deeply suffering man, who nevertheless touched upon moments of ecstasy. Conversely, the reading of Rousseau's other great works enables us to appreciate the *Confessions* more fully: and the publication of a critical edition of Rousseau's *Correspondance* in the coming years, containing many hitherto unknown letters, a monument to Rousseau scholarship, will shed fresh and complementary light on the man and his relationships.

Rousseau is often misquoted, for he never meant that man was born good, but that he was born innocent, that is, neither good nor evil. He distinguished between the wicked, who wilfully harm others, and the culpable, who sin through weakness or error. For him, to confess sincerely is to gain absolution and to become good: to listen to the inner voice of conscience is to find peace. This religious belief, together with a strong sense of guilt, is the motivating force which accounts for some of the very frank passages in the *Confessions*, which reveal the tormented but arrogant sinner, whose growing moral sense is accompanied by an increased awareness of impending death. Rousseau's desire to justify himself to posterity is less urgent than his desire to justify himself to God. Yet with God, as with his fellows, his pride led him to distort the truth a little, in spite of his avowed intention, when the truth was unbearable. It has been demonstrated, however, that there are few errors in the *Confessions*: but their greatest truth lies in the emotional atmosphere of the actions he describes, for he never mistakes his feelings.

His interpretation of the facts and events of his life has the ring of the essential truth of an unfolding personal drama, the inevitability of the strange happenings in his life, given his own deep passivity.

As he passes from his early childhood to the experiences of his slow maturity, and reaches those disturbing glimpses of the lover ailing in body and in mind, he kindles an almost unwilling sympathy for the lonely and self-absorbed pilgrim whose vivid imagination and graphic style enabled him to recreate the past, and to convey as well as anyone has ever done the very core of his own being. His personal magnetism, which drew many to him before he had made his mark, still operates today in his written work, whether it be used to absolve or to condemn him. Part of his tragedy was that in spite of this initial attraction his friends were all in turn alienated through his dark distrust and sense of persecution, until most of his intimates became his enemies.

Rousseau believed that through the *Confessions* he would be able to distinguish friend from foe; and it is true that even the modern reader is apt to take sides, although in fact Rousseau was neither saint nor monster. Hypersensitivity, introspection, egomania, neurosis, ill-health, and persecution may well have brought him to the borderland of the insanity his enemies maliciously foretold; and it is certain that he suffered from multiple delusions to the very end of his life. The miracle is that he did escape from himself, if only for brief periods of time, from his real and imaginary tormentors, and from the petty miseries of his life. The secret of his escape lies in the significant words: 'En me disant, j'ai joui, je jouis encore.' He had the power of total recall, and very few old men have dwelt so creatively on happy memories of the past, deliberately discarding unhappy obsessions, to fashion for himself a superstructure of perfect content, to which the *Rêveries* bear witness.

The *Confessions* mark a step in a metamorphosis by which, through the purification of past sensations and a poetic evocation, beatitude can at last be achieved. Through the power of Rousseau's pen and of his need comes a shared experience, a communion with nature, a journey through description and narrative to reach the man himself, and face the reality of human existence. Rousseau presents the anguish of a sinner seeking absolution, striving to achieve an impossible ideal in a world of relative values; or more simply trying only to perpetuate a moment of experience.

The *Confessions* have great unity of style and spirit. Rousseau never lost sight of his intention – to write his apologia. His faults, crimes, and peccadilloes are all recorded and self-judged, building a remarkable self-portrait. By the time he was writing the *Rêveries*, he had abandoned all hope of successful defence; but in the *Confessions* he is still eager to vindicate his reputation, his ideas, his philosophy, and his conception of nature, life, and God. For forty years he sustained the almost unendurable struggle to find himself and be himself. He followed in the footsteps of Montaigne – 'notre maître à tous' – whom he exceeded in self-love. For Pascal, the self is hateful, and religion requires a man to turn away from self: for Rousseau the self was the one reality. This search for himself, as Marcel Raymond has said,[9] was his true vocation; but his success, albeit very real at times, was intermittent, and his vision failed him at the last. Many have noted the sadness of the ultimate failure of a man who identified God with himself, rather than himself with God. Yet his success, relative or otherwise, was greater than most men achieve. Rousseau's great art as a narrator of varied and striking events, with the true voice of a poet, explains his lasting hold upon the imagination of all who have read him.

As yet there has been no specific study of the influence of the *Confessions* and the *Rêveries*, clearly detectable in all subsequent forms of autobiography – memoirs, personal journals, prose-poems, meditation, or *vies romancées*. The part played by Rousseau's work in shaping contemporary French thought, from Symbolism and Surrealism to Existentialism, has been no more than touched upon; and even books such as M. I. Markovitch's *J.-J. Rousseau et Tolstoï*, for all their wealth of detail on certain aspects, fail to convey the magnitude of Rousseau's contribution to world literature.

[9] Cf. *J.-J. Rousseau, La Quête de soi et la rêverie*, 1962.

Chapter 10

DIDEROT

DENIS DIDEROT straddles the eighteenth century like a colossus. He was a powerful genius; philosopher, thinker, critic, scientist, and artist; and an ardent, impetuous man, with a great gift for friendship and a personality so exuberant and so overwhelming that he made his mark not only upon the circles he frequented, but upon the century into which he was born, and subsequent centuries to the present day.

He was a Champenois, born at Langres on 5 October 1713, the son of a master cutler who was widely respected in his own milieu, and by his son as soon as he grew old enough to recognise his father's worth. The boy was educated by the Jesuits at Langres from the age of nine, since his father destined him for the Church. He was tonsured at the age of thirteen, by which time his extraordinary brilliance, his intellectual quality, and his bold and daring spirit had manifested themselves, together with athletic prowess equally remarkable. He did not in fact enter the Church. From 1729 to 1732 he studied in Paris at the Jansenist Collège d'Harcourt, or at the Jesuit Lycée Louis-le-Grand, or most probably at both these institutions, receiving the degree of Master of Arts at the University of Paris in 1732, after three years of progress and development that startled and sometimes dismayed his teachers, because of the precocity and audacity of his questing mind, and the tempestuous ardour of his personality.

He spent the following two years studying law as an articled clerk in the office of Maître Clément de Ris, during which time he brought all his scholar's enthusiasm to bear upon an increasing interest in languages, in literature and philosophy, and above all in mathematics, in all of which he showed exceptional ability. As Naigeon has stated, Diderot was drawn towards geometry and the abstract sciences all his life, because of their independence and generality.

It was by this time clear that he was not sufficiently interested in law to make it his career; and for the next ten years (1734–44), to the dismay of his father, he led a precarious existence earning his living by whatever means came to hand: as a tutor, and one who would spend the whole day on a brilliant pupil, and never return at all for a second brief session with a dull one; one who accepted payment in kind – food, furniture, linen – and in cash, or went without it if it pleased him; he worked also as a publisher's hack, and wrote sermons for missionaries at fifty *écus* each. He was a great frequenter of cafés, where the discussion of ideas and attitudes stimulated and excited him, and in which he played his full part, a well-known figure in the Régence, the Laurent, and most of all in the Procope, where he met Jean-Jacques Rousseau in 1741, establishing a friendship with him that lasted for fifteen years. There is evidence that Diderot planned to enter the Church in that same year; but none that he did in fact ever enter the seminary of Saint-Sulpice, perhaps because it was at this time that he met Antoinette, daughter of Mme Champion, a linen-draper, and fell in love with her. He had no career, no prospects; and his father, who had already suffered so much from watching his brilliant son apparently frittering his life away, thoroughly disapproved of the match. They were, however, secretly married in 1743, when Diderot was thirty, and had not yet published anything at all.

In spite of his estrangement from his father, he was strongly attached to his family, and it was possibly this attachment that had made him consider entering the Church in 1741, since he knew it to be the pious hope of his parents. Throughout his subsequent career, he showed an excellent grasp of religious principles and modes of thought, as well as considerable familiarity with the writings of the Fathers of the Church and of lesser divines, and with religious controversies through the centuries. There is no doubt also that his latent idealism and positive emotionalism prolonged his religious phase.

It was his marriage that first impelled him to undertake literary work, since now he had a wife to support. He became an experienced translator, rendering into French Temple Stanyan's *History of Greece* in 1743, the *Inquiry Concerning Virtue or Merit* of the third earl of Shaftesbury in 1745, and Robert James's *Medicinal Dictionary* in 1746–48.

His marriage, begun so romantically, showed itself almost immediately to be an unhappy failure, the union of two people who, once the first rapture had disappeared, proved to have nothing in common. Only one of their four children survived, a daughter Angélique, born in 1753, to whom Diderot was devoted all his life, attending personally to her education, both moral and academic, and in 1772 arranging a successful marriage for her with Caroillon de Vandeul. Madame de Vandeul later wrote extremely interesting and appreciative *Mémoires* of her father.

In 1745 the publisher André Le Breton approached Diderot with a view to bringing out an encyclopaedia. It was originally intended to be a translation in French of Ephraim Chambers's *Cyclopaedia*, drawing upon the *Dictionnaire de Trévoux*, and had been entrusted in 1743 to John Mills and Gottfried Sellius. Diderot soon changed the nature of the project, which in his hands became an important method of radical and revolutionary opinion. He seized upon every opportunity of broadening the scope of the encyclopaedia, gathering together a team of energetic and devoted workers, literary men, philosophers, scientists, and priests, some already well established, others just at the beginning of their careers, and all united in a common purpose – to extend the boundaries of knowledge, and by so doing to strike a resounding blow against reactionary forces in the Church and in the state.

As the responsibilities of a married man had impelled Diderot to launch himself as a translator, so the inadequacies of that marriage indirectly impelled him into the publication of his own works. Lacking any form of intellectual understanding from his wife, he turned to a certain Mme de Puisieux, who appeared to be an intelligent and witty woman. As soon as she became his mistress, however, she revealed herself as a harpy, and her demands for money were so incessant that Diderot could only meet them by publishing such works as *Les Bijoux indiscrets* (1748), a novel in the fashionable mode, held to be indecent, but with serious undertones of a philosophical and critical nature which have only recently been studied.

Les Pensées philosophiques, his earliest original work, already shows a strong current of anti-Christian thought, the first public expression of his growing religious perplexity that had held him back from entering the Church in 1741. It was an opuscule of some sixty pages, crammed with new and explosive ideas written down in a vivid and virile prose. There were some who went so far as to attribute it to Voltaire; an attribution which may have contributed in some measure to its sensational success, and its condemnation to burning. Diderot's revolt from orthodoxy sprang as much from his temperament as from his philosophical convictions, and from his protean character which caused comparisons to be drawn with Socrates on the one hand and the powerful, tempestuous, and full-blooded men born of the Renaissance on the other.

It is very probable that he led a modestly dissipated life in his twenties, and this, coupled with the moral laxity of the times, freed him from conventional ethics and left him to discover moral codes suited to his mind and his strong and fearless character. He was able throughout his life to distinguish prevailing modes of thought and behaviour from the intellectual speculation that marks his original thought; so managing to combine intellectual freedom with a relatively conventional life, led according to the shibboleths of the bourgeois society of his day. His knowledge of normal family life, the pattern of his relationship with his parents, and his life-long contacts with Langres, the place of his birth, his roots among ordinary people, even his unsatisfactory marriage to a woman who, though without malice, could not begin to share or even to understand his major preoccupations in life, but who yet gave him his adored daughter; all these factors enriched his human experience in a way unknown to his great contemporaries, and provided him with practical criteria of normal behaviour, to serve as a check and a corrective to uninhibited speculation.

In addition to his work on the *Encyclopédie*, and on his translations, Diderot followed the *Pensées philosophiques* with the *Promenade du sceptique* in 1747 (pub. 1830), which took his argument several steps further, and with the *Lettre sur les aveugles* in 1749, the most audacious of the three, in which he expounded the doctrine of materialist atheism, and which stressed human dependence on sense impressions. The *Lettre* is remarkable for its proposal to teach the blind to read through the sense of touch, preparing the way for Louis Braille in the following century; and for the presentation of the first step in his evolutionary theory of survival by superior adaptation.

Diderot was arrested for the irreligion and audacity of his work – and also because it gave offence to Mme Dupré de Saint-Maur, an intimate friend of d'Argenson, then Minister of Police – and imprisoned in Vincennes for three months. While there he began to question the extra-curricular activities of Mme de Puisieux, who was still dunning him for money; he climbed over the prison walls to follow her after a visit she made to him, so beautifully dressed that he grew suspicious, watched her with the lover who was consoling her in his absence, returned to prison, and severed all connections with her.

His imprisonment, his lost mistress, his diverse literary activities, his family and social life in no way interfered with the great work of his life. In 1750 he published his *Prospectus* of the projected *Encyclopédie*, which d'Alembert, his co-editor, expanded into a brilliant *Discours préliminaire* in 1751.

The *Encyclopédie* is the magnificent testament of the Age of Enlightenment, and one of the three or four great intellectual landmarks of the eighteenth century; and it is equally important both in its conception and in its realisation. Diderot was perhaps the only man in his century with the quality of mind and spirit, and the intellectual power to carry the weight of an undertaking that was intended to present knowledge as an organised whole, as a vast genealogical tree stressing the interconnections between the sciences. Its secondary purpose was to serve as a *dictionnaire raisonné*, to propound the essential principles and applications of every art and science known at that time. Its underlying philosophy, given the co-editors Diderot and d'Alembert, was rationalist, and based on faith in the progress of the human mind.

Eighteenth-century philosophy examined, following in the footsteps of Locke rather than of Descartes, some of the great questions of the age and of the modern society then evolving. Montesquieu, Voltaire, Rousseau, d'Alembert, Condillac, and d'Holbach all brought their encyclopaedic knowledge and their unparalleled range of interests to bear upon these problems; but of all these exceptionally brilliant men, Diderot alone had the breadth of mind and type of genius that made him able to interpret and synthesise the data at his disposal, to evolve the new methodology required for the intensive study of nature, and to foreshadow some of the major scientific discoveries of the following century. 'C'était', wrote Grimm, 'la tête la plus naturellement encyclopédique qui ait existé'; and even Voltaire, not easily given to praise of rival philosophers, said of him: 'Tout est dans la sphère d'activité de son génie.'

Diderot never oversimplified the issues with which he was dealing, whether they were concerned with the universe, life, man and human destiny, religion, the origin and government of the world, society, ethics, or aesthetics. His mind was wide, and powerful enough to allow him to accept the diversity of facts; his extraordinary talent for synthesis impelled him to try to account for this diversity; and with great intellectual integrity he never forced the facts to fit in with his theories, but instead enlarged and changed his theories to explain the facts. His approach, in all his writings, was undogmatic, empirical, and dialectical, and this was of particular value in his work, which lasted nearly thirty years, on the *Encyclopédie*: it also brought about many difficulties for him, and some of the real or apparent contradictions in his thought.

'Tout se tient dans la nature' (Assézat – Tourneux ed., II, p. iii) he wrote, and again, 'Tout ce qui est ne peut être ni contre nature ni hors de nature' (A–T, II, p. 189). He was deeply and constantly aware of the 'grande châine qui lie toutes choses', which is defined in the *Encyclopédie* as 'l'enchâinement des connaissances'. If the natural forces are all one, this will be reflected in the microcosm of man as well as in the macrocosm of the universe. 'Je suis porté à croire que tout ce que nous avons vu, connu, aperçu, entendu,' he wrote later in the *Eléments de physiologie*, 'jusqu'aux arbres d'une longue forêt . . . tous les concerts que nous avons entendus, tout cela existe en nous à notre insu' (A–T, IX, pp. 366–7). He concluded that the link between man and the world was very close. For Diderot, who believed in the objective reality of nature, there was a necessary parallel between the laws of the universe, and those that govern the working of the mind – 'Le type de nos raisonnements les plus étendus, leur liaison, leur conséquence, est nécessaire dans notre entendement comme l'enchaînement, la liaison des effets, des causes, des objets, des qualités des objets l'est dans la nature' (A–T, IV, p. 372). This is reasoning by analogy and it leads to an awareness of the link between the spiritual and the physical worlds and of the validity of thought whenever it is based upon fact.

It is the awareness of this link, allied with a refusal to accept the premise that the determinism of the physical world could be translated without modification into the world of the spirit, which made him draw back from the mechanical materialism of La Mettrie, as expressed in such works as *L'Homme-machine* and *L'Homme-plante*.

Diderot undertook to write articles on history, philosophy, and the mechanical arts for the *Encyclopédie*, as well as to edit, with d'Alembert, all the work of their collaborators; and an examination of his total output of work serves to show that this vast labour, over so many years, did not even begin to exhaust his vast mental and physical strength. But it was with this herculean task that he came most truly into his own, since each of his many aptitudes and talents – his naturally encyclopaedic mind, his protean knowledge of science and of the methodology of his time, his powers of intuition that enabled him to extend his already great store of learning with unusual speed and clarity – was called upon. To these factors must be added the power and rhythm of his writing – an inexhaustible fount of ideas – and an intellectual fertility and energy that has scarcely been equalled. There was no branch of human knowledge unknown to him – mechanics, geometry, mathematics, philosophy, theology, moral law, linguistics, the arts, music, drama, the sciences, metaphysics, philology, and politics.

Here clearly was the comprehensive genius, more than adequate in his physical and mental prowess, to bring so vast a conception as the *Encyclopédie* to full fruition. In his hands, and those of his co-editor d'Alembert, it became much more than a compendium of past and present knowledge. It became the mirror of advanced thought, embodying necessary social and political reforms, and pointing the way to a scientific and technological revolution. Diderot's passionate concern for mankind, projected into the *Encyclopédie*, was essentially revolutionary and philosophic, hostile to the *ancien régime* and to the inadequacies of the aristocracy in their exceptionally privileged position. The *Encyclopédie* contained a rehabilitation of honest labour and industry, until then mocked and despised. By making every effort to elevate, from their secular degradation, the backbone of the race, the vast mass of the middle and working classes, upon whom society does in fact depend, Diderot offered a calculated death-blow to the parasites within the aristocracy and the Church.

The publication of the *Encyclopédie*, with its seventeen volumes of text, and eleven volumes of plates, prepared over the period 1751–72, was the greatest publishing venture of the century. It provided Diderot with his chief occupation and source of income during those years. His work first as co-editor, and then as sole editor, suffered many vicissitudes. His enemies manoeuvred against him, and some of his friends deserted him. Publication was suspended in 1752, resumed in 1753, and suspended again in 1759, before it was brought to its splendid conclusion in 1772. There was a critical moment in 1758 when d'Alembert, alarmed at the way in which the *Encyclopédie* attracted trouble, resigned from his post as co-editor after the publication of the seventh volume, which brought Rousseau's attack on d'Alembert's 'Genève' article. There was to be an even more shattering experience in 1764, when Diderot discovered that Le Breton had secretly deleted compromising or dangerous material from the corrected proofs of some ten folio volumes. He was throughout bedevilled by both friends and enemies, forced to fight the increasing and splenetic opposition of Church and *parlement*, and to deal with the vacillations of government policy and censorship. Yet in spite of minor and major irritations and frustrations, he continued to be an energetic and conscientious general editor, revising all articles submitted, and giving his closest attention and detailed technical knowledge to the choice and presentation of the illustrations for 3,000 to 4,000 plates, of exceptional practical and historical interest. He also contributed innumerable articles in his own name, dealing mainly with the history of philosophy ('Eclectisme', a full-length study of the subject), with social theory ('Droit naturel'), with general aesthetics ('Beau'), and with the mechanical arts.

Diderot's rejection of Christianity, and the deepening of his materialist philosophy, provide the key to all his writing, and led him into the expression of some of his most interesting ideas. For his exhaustive work on the *Encyclopédie* miraculously left him with time, thought, and energy to spare for other writings. Yet his best work belongs to later years.

Those ideas he had first presented in the *Lettre sur les aveugles* (1749), adumbrating an evolutionary theory of survival by superior adaptation, challenging the existence of an intelligent God, and stating that the order we see in the universe is simply the human apprehension of the laws of motion in matter, were developed still further in the *Pensées sur l'interprétation de la nature* (1754), generally recognised as the *discours de la méthode* of the eighteenth century. Here emphasis was laid upon empiricism, and the inductive form of reasoning generally associated with the name of Francis Bacon; and Diderot offered examples of the sort of scientific results obtainable through scientific investigation and conjectures supported by evidence. His emphasis on the new experimental approach to science points to the failure of Cartesianism to explain reality, and his recourse to hypotheses demonstrates the inadequacy of contemporary scientific knowledge. As his evolutionary doctrine expanded, he took up his position beyond Democritus, Epicurus, and Lucretius, and close to that of Lamarck and Darwin.

Diderot published few other works in his lifetime,[1] though he never ceased to write. Special mention should be made of his *Lettre sur les sourds et muets* (1751), which deals with the function of language and the question of aesthetics. His manuscripts were known only to his intimates, among whom they were circulated, and to the privileged subscribers to Grimm's *Correspondance littéraire*, to which he contributed articles, following a friendship established between them in 1750.

Among his most noteworthy philosophical works, in which his monistic materialism was most brilliantly expressed, were *L'Entretien entre d'Alembert et Diderot* and the *Rêve de d'Alembert*, both written in 1769, but not published until 1830, and the *Eléments de physiologie* (1774–80). Diderot towers above the contemporary philosophers of his age, even above Voltaire, not only through his power and grasp of principles, and his direct and unremitting attack upon Church and state, on which they all were engaged; but also because he alone among them, having completed the negative and destructive aspects of attack, sought to discover and express the positive principle of a new philosophy. Before him, no one had attempted this major constructive effort: and Diderot was immediately suspect, dubbed leader of the new materialist movement, and subject to prolonged attack throughout the second half of the century.

In the works quoted above, Diderot not only developed his materialist philosophy, and foreshadowed the evolutionary doc-

[1] This is why few dates of publication have been given. In many cases dates of composition are uncertain, or can only be provided for drafts or revised drafts, even in the case of important texts. On the complex question of Diderot manuscripts, see H. Dieckmann, *Inventaire du fonds Vandeul et inédits de Diderot*, 1951, and P. Vernière, *Diderot, ses manuscrits et ses copistes*, 1967.

trine, but also evolved the first modern theory of the cellular structure of matter. He started from sensationalist premises, to give positive content to Leibniz's idealistic monad, following in the steps of Maupertuis, and tried to demonstrate that the passage from the inorganic to the organic may be achieved stage by stage. He saw matter as an entity lending itself to many forms and invariably endowed with *sensibilité*, active or kinetic. His molecular theory of the universe hinged on his non-Cartesian conception of motion inherent in matter: 'Le mouvement est également et dans le corps transféré et dans le corps immobile. Le repos est un concept abstrait qui n'existe point en nature.' (A–T, II, p. 106). Time is the factor underlying all changes, and an essential part of the evolutionary processes. As his thought progressed, he discarded the theory of pre-formation, leading to a mechanical and static conception of the universe, and replaced it by epigenesis, which explained organic formation in terms of juxtaposition and contiguity. He found himself in disagreement with Buffon and Needham, who had discovered infusoria, on the question of spontaneous generation, since such a hypothesis left unresolved the problem of the special sensitivity of living organisms. His knowledge of medicine led him to give a place of increasing importance to *organisation*.

In 1759, while his wife was away visiting his family, he had met and taken as mistress Sophie Volland, an attachment that lasted more than twenty years. For the first time in his life, as far as records show, and at the age of forty-six, he met a woman equal to being his companion. It was a liaison founded on common interests, natural sympathy, and a deepening friendship. She never disturbed his marriage or made claims on him, as Mme de Puisieux had done. With her he found the companionship lacking in his marriage with Antoinette, who could not appreciate his intellectual struggles and triumphs. His witty Sophie, with her alert, questing mind and wide culture, filled that vacuum in his life.

It was in a letter to her, dated October 1759, that he attempted to clarify the problem of the organisation of matter as he saw it – molecular combinations possessing specialised functions, with the autonomous working of the brain seen as a kingpin of neural mechanism, a kind of sixth sense of extraordinary power.

His speculations in these areas of science are of particular interest, but it is the dialectical brilliance of their presentation that is exceptional. Diderot successfully took over the method already used by Bernard de Fontenelle, but was himself more concerned with deepening and developing his thought for its own sake, and giving rein to his astonishing imagination, which allowed him to penetrate to the heart of mysteries as yet unsolved, than with popularising his views for the sake of the general reader. He often expressed his ideas in paradox, and invariably in dialogue form; they stem from a sense of reality, and a rare understanding of the complexities and contradictions inherent in human nature, the result of a prolonged examination upon which the whole of his exceptionally well-stocked and original mind was brought to bear.

Diderot's ideas on embryology were well in advance of his time, and in line with modern discoveries. While his contemporaries were still refusing to accept bi-parental heredity, he propounded his own theory to account for birth factors and inherited characteristics, foreshadowing the future scientific data concerning genes and chromosomes, explaining the phenomena occasioned by recessive genes, and stressing the fundamental role of chromosomes; incredibly enough, in view of the state of research into these matters at that time, he linked the production of monstrous or abnormal children to the unpairing of one or other of the pairs of chromosome 'threads' at the moment of generation. He was handicapped in his exposition by the lack of a vocabulary fitted to his new theories, and had to anticipate scientific verification, in view of inadequate laboratory facilities; and there is some confusion in his mind between cellular organisation and the nervous system. His hypotheses were confirmed, together with the soundness of his methodology, by the discovery of organic cells and the principle of cell division. His analysis of the old problem of which came first, the chicken or the egg, is masterly: 'Si la question de la priorité de l'oeuf ou de la poule vous embarrasse, c'est que vous supposez que les animaux ont été originairement ce qu'ils sont à présent' (A–T, II, 110); this leads him into the proposition that the problem is false, and one that is solved by the continuity and evolvement of the evolutionary pattern; this discussion is followed by some of his most remarkable pages on embryology.

In his attempts at breaking down the previously existing barrier between inorganic and organic nature, Diderot arrived astonishingly close to the modern molecular theory, and if, in view of his necessarily restricted vocabulary, the modern cell be substituted for his 'living molecule', and the atom for his 'dead molecule', then it will be seen that he expounded the complete chain, from the molecule to the universe, which is as all-embracing as that of any modern materialist philosophy. 'Le prodige, c'est la vie, c'est la sensibilité; et ce prodige n'en est plus un . . . . Lorsque j'ai vu la matière inerte passer à l'état sensible, rien ne doit plus m'étonner.' (A–T, II, pp. 133–4). He adumbrates the theories of Lamarck in his own century, and Darwin in the next, concerning the principles governing heredity and natural selection, and the necessary link between organs, functions, and needs, or, as he expresses it with great concision in the *Eléments de physiologie*, 'L'organisation détermine les fonctions et les besoins' (A–T, IV, p. 336).

Diderot made it clear that, as a living part of a living world, man could only be understood in his cosmological context. His genetic theory is particularly impressive, and takes him far beyond the sensationalist doctrine of Locke, Condillac, and Helvétius. In the *Suite de l'entretien*, a postscript to the *Rêve de d'Alembert*, he approaches the question of abnormality with the same insight and intuition he had shown in earlier aspects of his research. Starting from the premise 'Tout ce qui est ne peut être ni contre nature ni hors de nature', he denies that anything called monstrous or perverted is in fact outside the scope of nature. The large number of abortive species thrown up by nature argues against divine design, and may more properly be explained by genetics, or by a peculiar reaction to any given environment.

Diderot's main concern in the *Rêve de d'Alembert* is with physiology, with particular reference to monstrosity, deviation, and hybrids. As he had previously done in the *Lettre sur les aveugles*, he stresses the close connection between physiology and psychology, and the inter-reaction of responses. From this point he developed his theory of dreams, which was destined later to impress Sigmund Freud. In his later works, he gave increasing importance, within the framework of his monistic and energetistic materialism, to the power of the brain in the determination of life and events.

It is remarkable that Diderot was able, in the absence of scientific proof, to advance such accurate theories. This was partly due to the fact that he kept himself well informed concerning all recent scientific writings and discoveries. The reading list he drew up in preparation for the *Eléments de physiologie* proves this. He had read and annotated Haller's major work on physiology, the writings of Charles Bonnet, Bordeu, Robert Whytt, and of Buffon; and he knew of Malpighi's experiments, and of those of Needham. In the ordinary course of his extraordinary life he came into frequent and sustained personal contact with scientists and doctors. It was also due to his exceptional powers of logic, deduction, and synthesis, and to the power of his imaginative vision of the universe. He was moreover, a man with an intellect capable of encompassing and organising all the known knowledge of his time.

Accepting the evidence offered by men of science and of medicine, he had recourse to hypotheses only where necessary to account for the facts presented, bearing in mind the preservation of the essential unity of matter. 'La sensibilité, propriété générale de la matière' (A–T, II, p. 116) was one of such hypotheses, and by probing further he came to understand that this was a latent *sensibilité*, and significant only in living matter. This in turn led him to examine the organisation of matter, with sensitivity concentrated in specific organs, and so to establish a hierarchy between the brain and nerve centres, so that a full and simple explanation of the universe was made to include the mental processes of man.

Unlike Bonnet and Robinet, who believed that the fundamental unity of nature finds expression in forms determined by God, and is therefore fixed and lasting, Diderot envisaged an ever-changing world without God, in which forms are born of chance, and are then indefinitely and necessarily subject to change. We are therefore limited in our apprehension of nature, which must remain ultimately unknowable. As he had already written in 1753: 'Si l'état des êtres est dans une vicissitude perpétuelle; si la nature est encore à l'ouvrage, malgré la chaîne qui lie les phénomènes, il n'y a point de philosophie. Toute notre science naturelle devient aussi transitoire que les mots.' (A–T, II, p. 48). Diderot certainly had the power to select significant data, synthesise known facts, and interpret them. He used carefully chosen analogies, inductive as well as deductive reasoning, and his mind was able to seize upon hidden connections and correspondences. He also made use of his faculty of intuition, or *esprit d'observation*, which Spinoza called *scientia intuitiva*, the whole illumined by his creative and imaginative drive. Step by step he unfolded his new and majestic vision of life, building up a grandiose picture which he expressed with natural eloquence, sometimes bordering on lyrical ecstasy. In the *Rêve de d'Alembert*, there are mature passages which echo the new cosmic revelation of the blind Saunderson, where Diderot conveys a deep, almost mystical, communion with the very processes of nature. The excitement of gradual discovery is conveyed through the ebb and flow of discussion. He maintained that thought as well as life has its organic complexity, and becomes creative when, without ever denying the authenticity of facts, it goes beyond them, to reach a cosmic understanding of the universe. In the age of destructive criticism, Diderot's ability to synthesise appears extraordinary. He knew that experimental philosophy was destined to take the place of rational speculation, and that the question 'how?', and not the question 'why?', was the key to intellectual progress; and, since the one who knows and the knowable facts are of the same substance, conjectures that are well founded have validity.

The question whether the *Rêve de d'Alembert* in particular should be considered as a speculative essay, or as a reflection of Diderot's definitive opinion, has exercised many critics, but it focuses attention on the wrong point. On 2 September 1769,

Diderot wrote to Mlle Volland, referring to the *Rêve*: 'Il n'est pas possible d'être plus profond et plus fou' (*Corresp.*, ed. Roth, IV, p. 140). And again: 'Cela est de la plus haute extravagance, et tout à la fois de la philosophie la plus profonde' (ibid., p. 126). No one could improve upon this final comment by Diderot. It is certain that he was particularly attached to this work, whose peculiar quality lies not only in the merit of the scientific theory or the new and viable philosophy propounded, but in the author's ability to convey his satisfaction at having fulfilled an intellectual need, and his conviction that the literary form adopted matched the quality of the thought. He realised that, following in the footsteps of Fontenelle, he had enlarged even further the realm of literature, since the dialogue on scientific facts is presented as a real dialogue between known people, and this dialectical method coupled with Diderot's fine prose style combined the acquisition of scientific knowledge with literary entertainment. Diderot's humour and subtlety, as well as an incongruous schoolboyish sense of mischief, were put to good use in the text, where real names and transferred names, real and fictional people, rub shoulders in a comedy much enjoyed by the contemporary élite of close friends and acquaintances, the 'in-people' who would have caught every *nuance*, understood every transference, and enjoyed full awareness of the reasons for which Mlle de Lespinasse asked Diderot to suppress the work.

In several particulars the *Eléments de physiologie* takes Diderot's theories further than the *Rêve de d'Alembert*, but it does not enjoy the same literary interest or vitality, nor is it as convincing. But whether wholly successful or not, Diderot always has an active concern for literary values, concentrating on discovering the form of expression ideally suited for his thought. So philosophy and science become the subject of stylised dialogues, scenes from plays with an element of *marivaudage*. He broke down the idea of narrow genres, and evolved new and broader literary forms; so that his drama includes moral sermons, and his novels disquisitions on ethics and aesthetics.

The determinist materialism which he had evolved had grave bearing on the moral issues which were never far from his mind. If it is true that 'les êtres ne sont jamais ni dans leur génération, ni dans leur conformation, ni dans leur usage que ce que les résistances, les lois du mouvement et l'ordre universel les déterminent à être,' there can be no liberty, virtue must spring from a felicitous natural disposition, and *bienfaisance* and *malfaisance* must take the place of good and evil. At the time he wrote the *Lettre sur les aveugles*, he saw the world as one in which morality was almost entirely dependent on the senses, yet he was inwardly convinced of the need for morality, and in the absence of God he was unable to find a basis for virtue. Starting from Shaftesbury's standpoint in the *Essai sur le mérite et la vertu*, which he freely translated 'Point de vertu sans croire en Dieu, point de bonheur sans vertu' he vacillates, trapped, along with most contemporary thinkers, into the self-deception of believing, because he wanted to, that virtue necessarily produces happiness.

This is a point of view that is consistently expressed in his work for the theatre, and particularly stressed in his two major plays, *Le Fils naturel* (1757) and *Le Père de famille* (1758). Diderot, as might be expected from someone of his dramatic temperament, gift of dialogue, and didactic frame of mind, was from the beginning deeply interested in the theatre, and managed to find time for several plays, articles, and treatises on drama; yet he never brought off a resounding success in the theatre itself. The delightful *Est-il bon? Est-il méchant?* (1781) is a small masterpiece, but it was never given a public performance before the twentieth century, and even his major plays met with no success when they were staged.

The belief that virtue necessarily produces happiness lies behind his theory of *le drame*. 'On distingue dans tout objet moral un milieu et deux extrêmes: il semble donc que, toute action dramatique étant un objet moral, il devait y avoir un genre moyen et deux genres extrêmes', he wrote. Since comedy and tragedy offered the two extremes, Diderot concentrated, in theory and in practice, upon the genre half-way between them: the serious, bourgeois, real-life drama, written and presented for the moral welfare of its participants and spectators. It was deliberately didactic, with the intention of delivering moral sermons that would have wider appeal and greater emotional value than those delivered from the pulpits.

Diderot's theories on drama, to be found in the *Entretiens sur Le Fils naturel* (1757) and his *De la poésie dramatique* (1758), are important landmarks in the history of the theatre. Beginning with *comédie larmoyante*, a genre for which he had great admiration, he stressed the need for greater realism on the stage, and insisted that characters should be presented in their milieu, should belong to specific professions, and establish recognisable relationships, the better to add force to the moral and social implications of the play, which were, for him, of primary importance. He urged changes in stagecraft and décor, and showed a weakness for *tableaux vivants*, which he was convinced would profoundly affect audiences.

His theories exercised paramount influence over Lessing, whose *Hamburgische Dramaturgie* appeared in 1767–68; but it was not until the nineteenth century, with Emile Augier and Dumas *fils*, that certain of his suggestions were adopted. In his best-known writing on the theatre, the *Paradoxe sur le comédien* (1773–78, published 1830), presented in dialogue form, Diderot argues that great actors, like great poets, are insensitive, for sensibility would impede interpretation, and confuse the necessary judgement and penetration they must bring to bear upon it. His definition of the actor is of particular interest: 'un pantin merveilleux dont le poète tient la ficelle et auquel il indique la véritable forme qu'il doit prendre' – and offers scope for argument on the nature of acting.

Diderot's *drames* were in effect social theses expressed in dramatic form, and of remarkable moral power and eloquence. So also were his novels, bringing equal innovation to the current literary form.

In the preface to *Le Père de famille*, and in other writings on the theatre, Diderot argued that education holds the key to moral progress. From the standpoint of philosophic propaganda, this principle reinforced the cause of the Encyclopaedic movement, but it was more for the unthinking crowd than for the honest thinker. Diderot soon came to believe that the only thing to do with the *méchant*, that is the man born bad, whom nothing can modify, was to destroy him, a view he expressed as late as in the *Neveu de Rameau*, where, however, his admiration for genius as such leads him to wonder whether genius, which must take its course, does not carry its own justification. He now thought increasingly in terms of the individual, and not solely of society. It is 'Moi' (i.e. Diderot) and not 'Lui' (i.e. Le Neveu de Rameau) who is thankful for the genius of Racine, and is ready to endure his alleged wickedness because of it. His consideration of genius, of the nature of man in his social context, and his dissatisfaction with common, bourgeois, prejudiced morality prompts him to say: 'Il n'y a point de lois pour le sage' (A–T, v, p. 307), and to proclaim: 'Il est une doctrine spéculative qui n'est ni pour la multitude, ni pour la pratique et que si sans être fat on n'écrit pas tout ce qu'on fait, sans être inconséquent on ne fait pas tout ce qu'on écrit.' This being so, it is difficult to see how the problem of the *doctrine spéculative* – the establishment of moral law in an immoral society – may be achieved. Diderot's inner conflict was clearly shown in the *Neveu de Rameau* (written between 1761 and 1774, translated by Goethe in 1805, retranslated into French in 1823; first authentic text in 1891). The dialogue between Diderot and Rameau's nephew is spontaneous and witty, and the comments are pungent, bitter, and ironic. In essence, the work, which may properly be called a satire, challenges the cant of contemporary society and the hypocrisy of conventional morality. It offers, in the nephew, a vigorous and dramatic sketch of a parasite and an eccentric, a musician who is gifted yet unable to make his mark through insufficient talent, and who is shamelessly selfish and amoral. He is challenged up to a point by Diderot, and each antagonist scores in turn, each, however, remaining basically faithful to his views and to himself; and the debate is in the end inconclusive. This brilliantly conceived, highly original, and entertaining *divertissement* cuts deep. It has authenticity, and reveals the full complexity of Diderot's nature, and of his philosophical ideas. He argues that man may be devoid of meaning outside the context of society, since he must necessarily subordinate himself to the society of which he is an integral part. Yet man is unique, whether he be a genius or a *génie manqué* – great creative artist or an interpretative artist with some small element of creative power – thereby transcending the whole concept of man as predetermined. But perhaps the nephew, in his freedom from social convention, and from unquestioned belief in absolutes, may well owe his disposition to the *maudite fibre paternelle*, as he himself alleges, and to a natural reaction, given his nature, to the corrupt society in which he must fight for survival. From the philosophical standpoint, the work may be reconciled with determinism; it is the ethics that are ambivalent.

This inner conflict reached crisis point by 1773. Only a new work of fiction, superimposing on reality an imaginary story closely connected with, but not determined by, reality, could crystallise his new attitude. His novel, *Jacques le fataliste* (1773, published 1796), which owes something to Laurence Sterne, and which has been considered as a kind of 'anti-*Candide*', is in the tradition of the picaresque novel and of the *conte philosophique*. L. G. Crocker has seen in *Jacques le fataliste* a moral experiment leading to no final or decisive result, and in a sense this is true. All Diderot's important late literary works may be seen as investigations of the psycho-physiological condition of man, his moral behaviour and his relative independence, with a view to confirming or modifying his materialist philosophy. Jacques, who believes in Fate, is involved in an endless argument with his master, who does not. As they journey along together, they retell the story of their lives and loves and listen to those of others whom they chance to meet. H. Bénac and others believe that Jacques and his master incarnate two aspects of Diderot. Yet Jacques' popular fatalism has little in common with Diderot's scientific determinism; and his sardonic interest in others differs greatly from Diderot's normal attitude of profound interest in the value of other people as individuals. It is possible that Diderot underwent a kind of catharsis in writing this novel, for although he does not reject determinism, he perceives that it cannot be made to apply indiscriminately to every action in life, as Jacques so ridiculously asserts that it can. The moral world is not wholly and obviously dependent on the physical, as Jacques believes, since man in his actions is incalculable. But the master's championship of free-will is equally foolish. Diderot demonstrates the limitations of man's understanding, leaving him able to discover only partial truth, for the limitations of Jacques and his master are common to all mankind, and make it difficult to establish philosophical and ethical codes. Here it is the philosophical standpoint that is ambivalent, as was the ethical one in *Le Neveu de Rameau*.

In *La Religieuse* (1760, published 1798), a profoundly moving novel of the horrific experiences of a young girl without vocation immured as a nun, Diderot did not directly attack the Church, but opposed a man-made system running counter to nature, and vividly demonstrated some of the dangers of celibacy and of sexual repression. In the *Supplément au Voyage de Bougainville* (1772, published 1796), Diderot unfolded his dream of a free society based on tolerance and on sexual liberty in far-off Tahiti, without, however, indulging in Rousseau's form of primitivism, nor wishing to bring Tahiti to Paris. But in *Jacques*, as in many of his *contes* (*Les Deux Amis de Bourbonne*, 1773, *Ceci n'est pas un conte*, 1772, and *Mme de La Carlière*, 1773), he examined individual cases without assuming absolute moral standards. Jacques and his master are posturing mimes, just like the nephew, and remain pasteboard parodies of man. Their stories, with the countless but always significant digressions, nevertheless seem real to us; but they never illustrate the views of either the master or Jacques. The examination of one very long and constantly interrupted episode in the book – that of Mme de La Pommeraye – is enough to show the curious juxtaposition of psychological truth based on the facts of life, and of the ratiocination of would-be philosophers. Madame de La Pommeraye can scarcely be held to have been biologically determined either for good or evil, since her feelings can change from love to hate and revenge in a trice. Her transformation, like the change of heart of the prostitute d'Aisnon, is not predetermined but is presented as being possible in the circumstances. Side by side with such surprising transformations, the childish disputation of Jacques and his master forms a strange and seemingly irrelevant counterpoint. The conclusion reached is that there is no strict moral code even for ordinary people, and that man forced into a code of virtue is not necessarily happier. Punishment does not necessarily discourage wrongdoing: and it becomes clear that the easy morality Diderot had stressed so emotionally in the *drames* was founded upon unrealistic precepts. Each individual case has its *raison d'être*, for 'chacun apprécie l'injure et le bienfait à sa manière'. All mankind, like the characters in the book, protects itself with an artistic distortion of the truth, a simplification based on selection, which is part of the human creative force. When Jacques caused his master's saddle-strap to break and his master fell as a result, he thought he was proving the effects of cause and effect at the expense of free-will, whilst in fact he was simply demonstrating his own power. J. R. Loy [2] sees in this a demonstration of moral freedom, as opposed to unmotivated or pure free-will. It can, and should, however, be argued, that Diderot at no point invalidates his scientific determinism, nor closes the door on psychological determinism, since, unlike Condillac, he believes that the brain acts as a sixth sense and, unlike Helvétius, that heredity is stronger than environment in determining aptitudes and shaping a destiny. He also, unlike modern behaviourists, believed in the inheritance of acquired characteristics. In the *Réfutation de l'ouvrage d'Helvétius intitulé L'Homme* (published in 1875) and in the *Essai sur les règnes de Claude et de Néron* (1778), known as *Essai sur Sénèque* (which may be regarded as a late apologia), he revealed his new philosophical preoccupations, dissociating himself from the simpler theories held by his contemporaries, and modifying his own in the light of experience. At the personal level, he accepts a stoicism in which virtue is its own reward. At the philosophical level, it is the behaviour of man in his unpredictable creative life, whether it be ultimately determined or not, that fascinates him. His moral attitude, a *recherche du bonheur*, is founded on his monistic conception of the universe; so that society is seen as the union of mankind, and the solitary man remains condemned, as he was in the *Essai sur le mérite et la vertu*, as well as in the *Entretiens sur Le Fils naturel*.

Yet Diderot, whose life and works show constantly a deep-seated desire to belong, is aware of being an outsider; this serves to explain his interest in the genius, who is an exceptional creature striving to live among ordinary men, and in individual man who also, after his fashion, partakes of genius. Faced with an apparently insoluble philosophical problem, and one which he does not intend to try to solve in a novel in which he himself as author determines the limited terms of reference, he manages to avoid opting for one answer or jettisoning one of two opposing philosophies. He now finds solutions of no practical consequence from the humanist standpoint, which he has discovered to be the only one truly based on an observation of reality, and from this discovery stems the humorous and ironic tone of his writing. Neither science nor philosophy can provide the total explanation of man, who in some measure shares the creative power commonly attributed to

[2] *Diderot's Determined Fatalist*, 1950, pp. 128 et seq.

God, and who alone in the universe can seemingly make time itself stand still, as happens in moments of ecstasy and emotional stress. The apparent waywardness of Diderot's thought, if not of his reasoning, serves to prove the complexity of the exterior world it mirrors, and his method is not now simply the one he favoured in his *Pensées sur l'interprétation de la nature*, nor one that can be applied indiscriminately. It is the development of a personal form of apprehension and expression of reality. The dialogue form, which he made his own, can serve, as in the *Rêve de d'Alembert*, for the linear exposition of a thought, allowing pauses, for purposes of clarification, or as a springboard for a further development; it can also, as in *Jacques le fataliste*, prove even more exciting when a large number of characters, and we must include the author and the reader among them, bring out in lively conversation the strange complexity of human nature, the *pantomime des gueux*, which is the substance of the novel and summary of mankind.

Diderot, who had all the makings of a dramatist, and who sought to establish himself triumphantly in the theatre, achieved his ambition only by indirect means. For those of his plays that were presented brought no real success; and the most charming, *Est-il bon? Est-il méchant?*, is so closely related to Diderot's personality, experience, and situation in his own day that it has become esoteric, and has proved to be not wholly intelligible today. His best plays were those not specifically written in that form, nor for the theatre. In 1963, Pierre Fresnay and Jacques Bertheau proved superbly on the stage of the Michodière that *Le Neveu de Rameau* was outstandingly good theatre.

Some of his finest dramatic scenes are to be found in *Jacques le fataliste*, worthy of similar dramatic treatment to that accorded to *Le Neveu de Rameau*, in his *Correspondance* with Sophie Volland and also in his *Salons*.

His correspondence with Sophie, covering most of their long association, goes from May 1759 to September 1774, and forms one of the most fascinating revelations of a buoyant personality, an active mind incessantly reaching out towards new discoveries. To read that correspondence is to know intimately what manner of man Diderot was, in all his many parts – philosopher, artist, thinker, scientist, poet, dramatist, and wit; and to enjoy his ebullience, the anecdotes that pour from his ready pen, the hilarious juxtaposition of scabrous tales and moral dissertations, of joyous obscenities and prim judgements, of an incredible dialogue concerning the Grand Lama and a commentary on the arts. The personality emerging is gargantuan, admirable, and sympathetic: and the revelation so unaffected and so total that it leads to a more intimate understanding of his whole work. Apparent inconsistencies and contradictions disappear in the ample unfolding of his thought in all its diversity and all its unity.

Considerable light is also shed upon the milieu he frequented, and upon his social connections: Mme d'Epinay and her circle; his close friend the baron F.-M. Grimm; the baron d'Holbach; Abbé Ferdinando Galiani; and many other prominent people in his day. The letters are written in a vivid colloquial style, which is to be found in his essays, among them *Regrets sur ma vieille robe de chambre* (1792) and *Entretien d'un père avec ses enfants* (1773). These are the work of an exuberant conversationalist, an enthusiast, a gifted narrator, and an emotional warm-hearted lover: as indeed he was a warm-hearted friend, who must have suffered when his fifteen-year-long friendship with Rousseau came to an end in 1758, over an involved entanglement concerning J.-F. de Saint-Lambert, Mme d'Houdetot, and Rousseau, and his newly formed friendship with Grimm.[3]

In 1759, Diderot turned his attention to new problems and became an art critic, largely to help Grimm, to whose *Correspondance littéraire* he had already made notable contributions. Grimm had asked Diderot to cover for him the annual exhibition of paintings at the Louvre, and was at first dismayed, and then amazed and delighted, to receive a book instead of the article he had envisaged. For the three years 1765–67 in particular he covered most successfully the salon, and in so doing developed an insight into the minds and techniques of painters, and into the growth of his own taste. It is recorded that, in each of those years, he spent every night for a fortnight in assembling his ideas and writing his reports. These, now known as the *Salons* (1759–81), have set a standard for all subsequent art criticism, and although his approach is a literary one – it is the subject of the canvas, its meaning and message, that are of primary importance so far as he is concerned – he does frequently transcend the contemporary to grapple with the fundamentals of art. His vast enthusiasm for beauty and perfection, and his infallible instinct, led him to sound judgement far in advance of limited aesthetic considerations, and enabled him to arouse the delight he himself experienced in those who read his critical reviews; and to guide the public to look upon Chardin, Fragonard, Falconet, Vernet, Houdon, and above all, Greuze, with new eyes.

The aesthetic principle implied in his comments is sometimes at variance with his theories. Association with painters and artists, and his own observation, made him realise the inadequacy of the current theory of *le beau idéal*. He admired Greuze for his well-balanced pathos and bourgeois values; but he was equally appre-

[3] See above, pp. 192, 193, 196, 212.

ciative of the realism and gift for colour of Chardin, and the subtle technique of Vernet. He condemned the artificial in style, and the rococo associated with Boucher. The catholicity of his taste, and his instinctive understanding of technical matters, remarkable in one with no practical experience of painting, prompted him to write commentaries so illuminating that they affected the later schools of painting, the Impressionists, and even the Surrealists.

Diderot's aesthetic theories and his criticism are closely linked with his ethics. They are to be found in a number of works, in particular in the *Encyclopédie* article 'Beau' (1751), in his *Salons*, and in the *Essai sur la peinture*. His article 'Beau', based as it is on a careful perusal of the works of French and English writers on the subject, develops a theory of beauty defined as the perception of relationships, in accordance with sensationalist philosophy and the relativity of all things. The great artist is defined as the man who seizes on significant relationships and analogies. He needs to be fired with enthusiasm and to be able to communicate his vision through sounds, colours, lines, or words. Diderot had already stressed the importance of gesture and expression in communication in *Lettre sur les sourds et muets* (1751), which deals with words as signs and symbols, abstractions not to be confused with reality; and also at some length with the problem of language, especially inversion. The need for the close association of word and gesture, of sound and rhythm in the case of the poet, he stressed in the *Paradoxe sur le comédien*. Beauty springs from an awareness of harmonies of sound, colour, sense, rhythm, and structure, innumerable *correspondances*, to borrow Baudelaire's term, between sense impressions; and the quality of a work must depend upon the adequacy of the artist's power of expression. Art mirrors life, but cannot be equated with life: it is rather like the *clavecin oculaire* of Père Castel (A–T, II, p. 139), which Diderot found so fascinating. This clavichord had coloured ribbons, so that when it was played a 'symphony' of colour resulted.

The completion of the *Encyclopédie* had left Diderot without a regular source of income. To relieve him of financial worry, Catherine the Great first bought his library for a substantial sum, through an agent in Paris, with a request that he retain the books in Paris until she required them; she then appointed him librarian of them, with a yearly salary for the duration of his life. Diderot went to St Petersburg in 1773 to thank her, and was received with great honour and warmth. He wrote for her the *Plan d'une université pour le gouvernement de Russie* (first published in an abridged form 1813–14), but his political ideas were too radical for the empress. After his death, his books and copies of all his manuscripts were dispatched to Catherine the Great by his daughter, Mme de Vandeul. The set of manuscripts which the latter retained, with a view to their ultimate publication, and was allowed to moulder for many years, was preserved[4] and is now deposited in the Bibliothèque Nationale. It is only recently, through the availability of these and other texts, and the research that they have promoted, that a more exact impression of his thought has been achieved. In particular, it can now be shown that Diderot, in his later years, held more radical political views than was believed. The *Encyclopédie* was a major instrument in the war on existing social and political institutions: articles such as 'autorité politique', which stated that sovereignty rested with the people, and that on 'droit naturel', are of equal importance with those specifically aimed at abuses from which the people suffered, and in which he developed economic theories, discussing luxury, taxation, and population problems, as well as the principle of equality. Diderot stressed the need to divorce the powers of the state and Church and refused to subordinate political institutions to religious sanction. In *Observations sur les instructions de Catherine II à ses députés*, he went even further, in identifying sovereignty with the nation, which was invested with legislative power; and in voicing criticism of a benevolent despotism, as well as of tyranny. But although Diderot's political theories after 1765 are particularly interesting, it is the earlier ones that exercised some influence in shaping political opinion before 1789. These were not as conservative as has sometimes been stated: his suggested curbs on absolute power may appear Utopian, but they suggest a more democratic ideal than Rousseau's politics. They include natural law, and the inalienable civil liberty of the individual in society; the right to free speech transcending any reason of public security; and individual fulfilment in an open society. He has, however, little to say on structures of government or fundamental constitutional law. His theories are not always consistent, and vacillate between the idea that social controls are necessary, and the idea of anarchy. His politics spring from his ethics, and his philosophical determinism impedes his political thought, with which it appears to be at variance, though it is important to point out, as L. G. Crocker has done,[5] that belief in determinism does not logically exclude belief in political freedom, in individual rights, or in the action of will and reason in history. The weakness of his political thought lies rather in his failure to relate the self-centred, anarchical man to the moral and political structure of society.

[4] H. Dieckmann, *Inventaire du fonds Vandeul et inédits de Diderot*, 1951.

[5] *An Age of Crisis*, 1954, ch. 3, pp. 71–106; and *Nature and Culture*, 1963, ch. 7, pp. 430–95.

tired into the shell of his own personal and family life. The death of Sophie Volland in 1784 was a great grief to him, and he survived her by only five months, dying of coronary thrombosis on 30 July 1784, in the house in the Rue de Richelieu which Catherine the Great had put at his disposal.

It was through the intervention of his son-in-law that he was buried in consecrated ground at St Roch. Apocryphally his last words were: 'Le premier pas vers la philosophie, c'est l'incrédulité', a ghostly reiteration of a statement made in the early *Pensées philosophiques*.[6] His open-minded scepticism, always present, is also always provisional: scepticism is simply an avenue to truth, and should never lead to mere negativism. He thus stands with Montaigne and takes up a position of great consequence within the tradition of humanism. A new definition of the philosopher emerges from Diderot's deceptively simple statement: 'Si l'on voit la chose comme elle est en nature, on est philosophe.'

Diderot was essentially of his age, and he transcended that age; 'Nous sommes l'universe entier,' Diderot once wrote (*Corresp.*, ed. Roth, VI, p. 376) and he might have been writing his own epitaph; he elaborated his original philosophical ideas in the light of this intuitive truth, within the terms of reference of his own age. The great bulk of his literary production was written mainly for his friends and circulated among them, and yet it may also be said that he wrote for the hypothetical intelligent future reader, who somehow managed to be present as a character, and a confidant, in so much of his work.

Perhaps the greatest genius of a century of brilliant men, he fulfilled his total promise within his own lifetime, but it is only in our time that he has been understood.

[6] See *Œuvres complètes de Diderot*, ed. Assézat-Tourneux, 1875, I, p. 140, *pensée* XXXI.

Chapter 11

THE *ENCYCLOPÉDIE*, *PHILOSOPHES*, CRITICS, AND OTHER WRITERS

I. THE 'ENCYCLOPÉDIE'

THE *Encyclopédie*, a vast collective enterprise which was to popularise knowledge and new scientific discoveries, to point the way to future progress and to effect a revolution in the minds of unprejudiced readers, started from modest beginnings. Le Breton, the chief publisher, intended it to be little more than a translation and adaptation of the English *Cyclopedia*, or *Universal Dictionary of the Arts and Sciences* (1728), by Ephraïm Chambers. He first approached a German, Gottfried Sellius, and an Englishman, John Mills, but Sellius died and Mills quarrelled with Le Breton. The latter then got in touch with the Abbé Gua de Malves of the French Academy of Sciences, who suggested bringing the work up to date and broadening its scope. It was he who recruited Diderot, already known for his share in the translation of James's *Medicinal Dictionary*. Arrangements for publication were held up, and when, in 1745, Le Breton, who had meanwhile quarrelled with Gua de Malves, decided on a fresh start, he called Diderot in as chief editor in association with d'Alembert, who had already a considerable reputation as a mathematician. A new *privilège* was obtained on 21 January 1746. The work was now to be an original publication, owing something for its general inspiration to Bayle's *Dictionnaire historique et critique*, which, however, had left science and technology out of its terms of reference. It was to differ from other dictionaries, such as that by Moreri or that of Trévoux, by its hostility to the Catholic Church and to the political régime, and by the new spirit of scepticism it embodied. It favoured an independent line of enquiry in politics and philosophy, and sought to free people from prejudice, in the name of reason.

In one sense it was a work of vulgarisation, destined to develop interest in science and technology as well as the new philosophy. Numerous plates of great intrinsic beauty, describing the arts and crafts featured in the *Encyclopédie*, were one of its special features, of enormous practical value at the time, and still of considerable historical interest today. The intellectual justification for an *Encyclopédie* of this kind is to be found in Diderot's *Prospectus* (October 1750) and in d'Alembert's *Discours préliminaire* (1751), in which the dual function of the publication is clearly stated:

Comme Encyclopédie, il doit exposer, autant qu'il est possible, l'ordre et l'enchaînement des connaissances humaines; comme *Dictionnaire raisonné des sciences, des arts et des métiers*, il doit contenir sur chaque science et sur chaque art, soit libéral, soit mécanique, des principles généraux qui en sont la base, et les détails les plus essentiels qui en font le corps et la substance.

D'Alembert goes on to emphasise the great chain that links the arts and the sciences, and to establish the genealogy and filiation of knowledge by studying the origin and generation of ideas. This chart of human knowledge, which figures prominently in the first volume of the *Encyclopédie*, and which owes something to Francis Bacon, brings out the unity of man's varied activity.

The *Encyclopédie ou Dictionnaire raisonné des arts et métiers par une société de gens de lettres* had a basic, philosophical unity, in keeping with the enlightened views of the leading thinkers of the period; it is this that gives it a unique place among similar works. The first two volumes appeared in 1751 in quick succession. A curious incident then occurred which led to the suppression of these volumes by a decree of the *Conseil d'Etat* (7 February 1752), which, however, did not preclude work continuing on further volumes. The trouble arose on account of a thesis by the abbé de Prades (1720–62) which was successfully sustained in the Sorbonne (18 November 1751). Subsequently the Sorbonne had second thoughts and discovered ten propositions in the thesis that were held to be heretical. The abbé was threatened with *prise de corps* and had to flee to Holland and later to Prussia. He was known to be a friend of Diderot, who was believed to have had a hand in the work; and Diderot had in fact written an *Apologie de l'abbé de Prades* which incensed the opposition, and particularly the Jesuits, who saw in the *Encyclopédie* a rival to their own *Dictionnaire de Trévoux*. It was thanks to Malesherbes, who had the support of Mme de Pompadour and of d'Argenson in his efforts to protect the publication, that the *privilège* which had been granted was not revoked. Volumes III to VI then appeared quietly and without causing disturbance. The subscribers, at first 2,000, rose to 3,000 with Volume IV and to 4,000 with Volume VII.

The publication of the seventh volume (1757) caused a new storm. It contained the article 'Genève' by d'Alembert, which praised Protestant ministers of religion, thereby incensing the Jesuits; and, with some encouragement from Voltaire, lent support to the idea of establishing a theatre in Geneva. Rousseau replied by his *Lettre sur les spectacles*, which attacked the *Encyclopédie* and led to Rousseau's break with Diderot and the *coterie holbachique*. Nor were the Protestant ministers of Geneva pleased by d'Alembert's article; Fréron, in his *Année littéraire*, launched a virulent attack which Malesherbes could not restrain; Moreau, in a *Nouveau Mémoire pour servir à l'histoire des Cacouacs*, heaped ridicule on the Encyclopaedists, before Palissot attacked them in his play *Les Philosophes* (1760).[1] D'Alembert resigned his post as a co-editor, confining himself to contributing numerous articles on scientific subjects; Duclos and Marmontel also found it wise to defect.

In spite of the strength of the opposition, and against the advice of Voltaire, who wished to see the *Encyclopédie* continued outside France, Diderot, who was to have the staunch support of Jaucourt, decided to carry on, but, following the publication in July 1758 of *De l'Esprit*, by Helvétius, a work taken to represent the true views of the Encyclopaedists, and as such condemned to be burnt (10 August 1758), the Encyclopaedic venture was once again in jeopardy. On 8 March 1759 the *Conseil d'Etat* suppressed all volumes (A–H) that had so far appeared, and on 3 September Pope Clement XIII condemned the *Encyclopédie*: however, it continued to be written, edited, and printed in secret, under a fictitious name of Neuchâtel publishers, and with the tacit or verbal assent of the government.

Eleven volumes of plates were prepared and published between 1762 and 1772, under Diderot's personal supervision, while work proceeded on the remaining ten volumes of text. The latter were ready by 1765 and distributed in 1766. The *Encyclopédie* grew into a work of seventeen volumes in folio, with eleven volumes of plates. A further five volumes of supplements, which are not by Diderot, followed in 1777, and in 1780 there appeared two volumes of *Tables*.

Numerous pirate editions appeared abroad: Geneva, 28 vols. (1770–76); Lucca, 28 vols. (1758–76); and Leghorn, 33 vols. (1770–79). In 1768 Pancoucke obtained permission to publish his own edition, but was prevented from doing so by an *ordre supérieur* in 1770. Editions with the supplements embodied in the original text soon appeared: Geneva (1777); Neuchâtel (1778–81); Lausanne (1778–82); Yverdon (58 vols. 1770–80). It was refashioned according to another plan, appearing as an *Encyclopédie méthodique ou par ordre de matières, par une société de gens de lettres* (Paris, Pancouke, 1782–93, and Agasse, 1792–1832: in all, 166 volumes). Finally an *Abrégé de l'Encyclopédie* was established by R. Ollivier (1798–1800) in twelve volumes drawn from *L'Esprit de l'Encyclo-*

[1] The *Cacouacs* was a nickname given to the *philosophes*, likened to savages fiercer than the original inhabitants of the Caribbean islands.

pédie ou Choix des articles les plus agréables, les plus curieux et les plus piquants de ce grand dictionnaire (1768).[2] The public response was remarkable and suggests that the work answered a very real need. There is evidence to show that 4,225 sets of the original edition were sold at a price of 980 livres.[3]

The articles in the last ten volumes are more critical on matters concerning religion, politics, and economics, but are in fact less controversial than originally intended. The publisher Le Breton took it upon himself to effect cuts on the proof sheets which Diderot had marked. Diderot only discovered the deception in 1764, when it was too late to re-establish his text and, not unnaturally, never forgave Le Breton for his cowardice and dishonesty. A volume of proof sheets recently discovered has revealed the extent of the changes. The opponents, however, were not to be placated. Besides the Jesuits, Moreau, Palissot, and Fréron, the Jansenists never ceased to show hostility in *Les Nouvelles ecclésiastiques*, and Lefranc de Pompignan and Gilbert were confirmed opponents of the *philosophes.* Fortunately for the success of the enterprise, the opposition were seriously divided, and support came from some influential quarters. The comte d'Argenson, to whom the *Encyclopédie* was dedicated, Mme de Pompadour, who spoke to the king on behalf of the work, and Malesherbes, who was in charge of the *librairie* from 1750 to 1763, now proved invaluable allies. Malesherbes, who had to order the removal of the manuscripts, at one time went so far as to have them placed in his own custody for their safe protection. Malesherbes, who died on the scaffold in 1794, is the author of *Lettres sur la révocation de l'édit de Nantes*, *Observations sur l'histoire naturelle de Buffon*, and *Mémoires sur la librairie et la liberté de la presse*, works that show his sympathy with the new movement. The king's vacillating policy is explicable in terms of the strong conflicting influences that worked upon him. In the end the Encyclopaedists and their friends, with the help of powerful personalities intervening on their behalf in high places, won the day against the religious and political forces at work against them. It is in fact thanks to the government, with the support of enlightened public opinion, that they were able to overcome the persecution of Jesuits, Jansenists, pamphleteers, and the Parlement itself.

In their articles (often signed or easily attributable) the contributors, who were usually experts in their subject, revealed their

[2] The Abbé Joseph de La Porte undertook the edition of this work which ran to six impressions in four years. The *Histoire générale des dogmes et opinions philosophiques*, 3 vols., 1769, draws on articles by Diderot and others. On these editions see J. Lough, *Essays on the Encyclopédie of Diderot and d'Alembert*, 1968.

[3] The value of the livre being approximately 8/- ($1) in today's currency.

independence of authority, their liberal aspirations, and humanitarian preoccupations, but for the most part remained moderate in tone, and guarded in their expression, so much so that Duclos wrote: 'Ils en feront autant qu'ils finiront par m'envoyer à confesse.' This is certainly true of the articles by the Abbé Yvon on 'Ame', 'Athéisme', and 'Dieu', less so of those by the Abbé Mallet and the Abbé Morellet. Diderot himself was at times most circumspect, especially on religious matters,[4] and he often took refuge in irony, which would only be apparent to the more alert.[5] Cross-references provided an excellent opportunity for safely making one's real convictions known. In the article 'Cordeliers', for instance, priests are highly praised, but the reader is referred to 'Capuchon', where they are turned to ridicule.

There remain many unaccountable contradictions in the work. Ultimately, of course, the *Encyclopédie* must be judged whilst bearing in mind the date of its composition and the state of knowledge at the time, as well as in the light of the prevailing political situation. It is the general spirit of the work that is unmistakable, with its emphasis on science, on reason, and the idea of progress, its defence of nature and criticism of all abuses or prejudices and superstitions (including belief in supernatural phenomena) that run counter to reason or nature. The Encyclopaedists effectively challenged political, religious, and social institutions, and suggested a number of reforms. Such articles as 'Corvées', 'Chasse', 'Impôts', 'Epargne', 'Education' (in which d'Alembert inveighs against the custom of sending a baby to a foster-mother, and of wrapping him up in swaddling clothes), 'Collège', 'Inoculation', 'Fermiers', 'Grains', 'Crimes', 'Vingtième', and 'Privilège' all repay study. The Encyclopaedists may have been cautious in political matters, pinning their hopes on a liberal and limited monarchy resting on consent and on a first-class legislator, but they were outspoken in condemning torture as part of the process of justice. They condemned torture as being both ineffective as a means of revealing the truth and also as a violation of the rights of man. The articles 'Intolérance', 'Fanatisme', 'Réfugiés', 'Législateur', and 'Inquisiteurs' unambiguously call for a humanitarian outlook and for tolerance. Diderot in 'Paix' and Jaucourt in 'Guerre' wrote strongly against war. Diderot himself was responsible for more than one hundred articles on the history of philosophy, ethics, aesthetics, and the mechanical arts; he also redrafted the articles of others. His contribution includes: 'Agriculture', 'Art', 'Autorité politique', 'Aristotélisme', 'Beau' (making the perception of relationships the basis of the beautiful), 'Droit

[4] See articles 'Christianisme', 'Société', 'Providence', 'Chaos'.
[5] See article 'Caucase'.

naturel', 'Eclectisme' (48 columns), 'Epicuréisme', 'Hobbisme', 'Leibnizianisme', 'Platonisme', 'Pouvoir', 'Propriété', 'Pyrrhonienne', 'Souverain', and 'Tyran'. His philosophical articles show a careful reading of Jacob Brucker's *Historia Critica Philosophiae* (Leipzig, 1742–44), to whose thought he gave a materialist bias, which he combined with Locke's sensationalist psychology and epistemology.

Diderot applied his materialist conception of the world to politics, and the methods used for the study of science to the problems of society. He believed in a natural man, who is necessarily happy, and a universal man who is essentially sociable; virtue is that which allows the individual to subordinate his selfish good to the common good, and thereby ensures his ultimate happiness. For Diderot, authority rests on the consent of the people (in this he was following in the footsteps of Locke who, in 1690, had upheld the validity of this idea in his *Two Treatises of Government*), and government rests on a contract. Civil and natural law must equate, in order that the essential liberties of the individual should be protected. Education is seen as the great safeguard against abuse and exploitation. D'Alembert, in addition to writing the *Discours préliminaire*,[6] and articles on mathematics and physics, is responsible for the articles 'Collège' (which criticised current university education, openly attacking the methods employed by the Jesuits[7]), 'Cosmogonie', 'Cartésianisme' (which brings out the methodology of science), as well as the controversial 'Genève'.

The chevalier de Jaucourt (1740–80), a Protestant who gave up his fortune for the cause of the *Encyclopédie*, was to prove Diderot's right-hand man as from 1758. He had an encyclopaedic knowledge and wrote innumerable articles on politics, history, the physical and natural sciences. Voltaire for his part contributed 'les perles de l'Encyclopédie', which he later included in his *Dictionnaire philosophique*: 'Elégance', 'Eloquence', 'Esprit', 'Imagination', etc. Rousseau wrote on music and an important article 'Economie politique'; Montesquieu wrote the article 'Goût'; d'Holbach, articles on chemistry; Daubenton (1706–99), on natural history; Marmontel, on literature (his articles were later published under the title *Eléments de littérature*, 1787); Saint-Lambert, on 'Luxe', etc.; Beauzée, the Abbé Girard, and especially Dumarsais (1676–1756), author of a *Traité des tropes*, on grammar; Barthez, Louis, and Tronchin (his article on 'Inoculation', which he defended, was considered bold), on medical matters; Deslandes, on

[6] See above, pp. 243–4.

[7] On this issue and on the more general question of educational principles and methods in the eighteenth century, see R. Mortier, 'The "Philosophes" and public education', *Yale French Studies*, No. 40 (1968).

naval matters; Le Blond, on military art; Boucher d'Argis, on law; Goumier and Blondel, on architecture; Landois and Diderot, on art and painting; and Le Roy, on hunting. Turgot wrote five remarkable articles on 'Existence', 'Foires', 'Marchés', 'Fondations', and 'Etymologie'. 'Foires' and 'Marchés' can be taken with Quesnay's articles on 'Fermiers' and 'Grains', for their insight into the science of economics, which they virtually founded. 'Etymologie' has been heralded as a first expression of the principles of the new science of philology. In it Turgot deals with such matters as semantics, definition of terms, nomenclature, and the relationship between words and ideas. Thus political economics, statistics (called *arithmétique politique*), sociology (in such articles as 'Liberté', 'Modification', and 'Malfaisant', which bring out that man is educable and consequently can be modified), and philology owe some of their first steps to the *Encyclopédie*. The critical method adopted was turned to biblical exegesis (see the article 'Chronologie sacrée') and undermined religious belief to the greater advantage of science.

In spite of an obvious disorder in the presentation of their ideas, the Encyclopaedists did achieve a large measure of coherence. Their examination of knowledge and their interpretation of it was a first rational effort at establishing an ordered conception of the world. The science and the technological progress outlined is, of course, outdated; and the unexpected moderation of the writers on religious and political issues, which in fact reflects that of the majority of the readers, should not surprise us nor blind us to a great historical achievement, and to the lasting validity of many of the liberal positions adopted. A revolution in the minds of intelligent people was effected, and Diderot achieved his purpose as stated in his article 'Encyclopédie': 'changer la façon commune de penser'. The new outlook, a new approach to social, moral, and political problems, by-passing Christianity, a call for *humanité* and *bienfaisance*, a challenge to superstition and despotism, with constant appeals for toleration and justice, the enthroning of Nature in association with Science and Reason, heralded a new age in which the free critical spirit was turned to the spiritual and material betterment of mankind.

II. THE ENCYCLOPAEDISTS AND OTHER 'PHILOSOPHES'

The number of articles contributed by d'Alembert to the *Encyclopédie* was considerable and their quality was certainly high; and his exceptional intelligence, coupled with his high standing in the world of science and letters and in the salons he frequented, as well as his close connection with Voltaire in particular, gave him a prominent place in the Encyclopaedic movement, immediately after that of Diderot. He was for important years the co-director of the undertaking, the main purpose of which he outlined in his *Discours préliminaire*, situating it clearly in an historical and philosophical context.

Jean le Rond, called d'Alembert (1717–83), the illegitimate son of Mme de Tencin, was found on the steps of the Saint-Jean-le-Rond church, near Notre Dame, in November 1717. Some six months later he was placed with a certain Mme Rousseau, the wife of a glazier, in whose house he continued to live till he was forty-seven years old, without her realising his eminence. His father, Louis Camus, Chevalier Destouches, *lieutenant-général* in the artillery, was a friend of Fénelon, and may have shared some of the latter's views on the importance of education. Destouches never acknowledged paternity, but he arranged for his son to be sent to the Collège des Quatre Nations at the age of twelve, and on his death in 1726 left him an income of 1,200 livres per annum. The boy was enrolled at the Collège under the name of Jean-Baptiste Darembert, and claimed to be Jean Lerond, but he finally agreed to being known as d'Alembert. He was a brilliant pupil, an excellent Latinist and Hellenist, becoming Master of Arts at the age of eighteen. His Jansenist teachers encouraged him to study theology, but he chose to study law, and was called to the Bar in 1738. His preference, however, was for mathematics, and for years he led a retired life, leaving his room in Mme Rousseau's house only for visits to the theatre.

In 1739, at the age of twenty-one, he wrote a *Mémoire sur le calcul intégral* and was able to correct mistakes in P. Rainau's *L'Analyse démontrée*. In 1741 he wrote on *La Réfraction des corps solides*, and was elected a member of the Académie des Sciences and, in 1748, of the Royal Society. In 1743 appeared his *Traité de dynamique*, a major contribution which revolutionised the science of motion. In it he had already turned his attention to the philosophical issue of the degree of probability of all accepted truths. In 1744 there followed *Traité de l'équilibre des fluides*, and *Réflexions sur la cause générale des vents*, which he dedicated to Frederick II; and in 1749 appeared *Les recherches sur la précession des équinoxes et sur la mutation de l'axe de la terre*, a work of scientific consequence. It was with an established scientific reputation that he became co-editor of the *Encyclopédie*, now turning his attention to literature and frequenting the salon of Mme Geoffrin, who claimed to have discovered him, and who was highly amused by his gift of mimicry; he entertained her guests by 'taking off' the actors of the Comédie Française and of the Opéra, and many *savants*, not excluding her own *habitués*. Some time before October 1748 he became *petit ami* and *habitué* of Mme du Deffand, whom he had met at the home of Président Hénault. He visited her every day, and she called him 'le sublime géomètre, le dieu, le prodigieux, l'aimable d'Alembert.' The success of his *Discours préliminaire* (1751), recognised even by his opponents, further enhanced his reputation.

In April 1756, Mme du Deffand invited Mlle de Lespinasse to enter her household as *demoiselle de compagnie*. Like d'Alembert, she was an illegitimate child, some fifteen years younger than he. He fell in love with her, and at the age of forty-seven went to live in an apartment below hers, acting as her secretary. Mlle de Lespinasse, however, loved M. de Mora and M. de Guibert. When d'Alembert wrote her portrait in 1771, he accused her of a desire to please everyone and of being by nature cold, a reproach often levelled at his own head. She died in his arms in 1776, begging his pardon. He understood her meaning only when, as executor of her will, he proceeded to read the papers she had left behind, discovering her passionate love for M. de Mora, which had been unknown to him. He sustained so great a shock that he told M. de Guibert: 'Je n'ai plus qu'à mourir'.

His life is devoid of the incidents to be found in those of his contemporaries. A cautious man, who knew when to decline honours, such as an invitation from Catherine the Great, and the appointment as tutor to the son of the empress, he was called by Barruel 'le renard de l'Encyclopédie'. In 1752 he declined an invitation to go to Berlin, in spite of which Frederick II granted him a small pension. In 1754 he was elected to the French Academy through the good offices of Mme du Deffand. In 1755 he spent a few weeks with Frederick. In 1756 he spent five weeks in Geneva, staying with Voltaire at Les Délices, and in 1757 the seventh volume of the *Encyclopédie* appeared and with it his article 'Genève'. It was this article which led to the difficulties earlier referred to, and which, coupled with official action against the continued publication of the *Encyclopédie*, led to his withdrawing as co-editor.

In 1760 he had a first quarrel with Mme du Deffand, and by way of revenge organised a 4 p.m. reception in the home of Mlle de Lespinasse, prior to visiting Mme du Deffand. It was after the publication of *Opuscules mathématiques* (1761) and *Mémoires sur la théorie mathématique de l'inoculation* that Catherine II invited him to St Petersburg, and that he declined to go; he spent two months at Potsdam, however, in 1763. After the celebrated quarrel between Mme du Deffand and Mlle de Lespinasse had taken place, he became an *habitué* of the new salon Mlle de Lespinasse opened in the Rue de Bellechasse, where she entertained the Encyclopaedists; besides d'Alembert, such men as Condorcet, Turgot, Marmontel, Suard, and Morellet. It became known as the *laboratoire de l'Encyclopédie*. After the death of Mlle de Lespinasse, he frequented the salons of Mme Helvétius, Mme Necker, and Condorcet, and received three times a week at his own home at the Vieux-Louvre, where twenty-five to thirty coaches could usually be seen at his door. He died on 29 October 1783.

Since 1772 he had been *secrétaire perpétuel* of the Académie and resolved to write its history. His *Eloges des académiciens* who had died between 1700 and 1770 show considerable perspicacity (as for example that of Marivaux), but they are not full historical accounts of the life and the works of those he praises. He brought in many digressions which enabled him to develop themes found in his earlier works.

Apart from his *Traité de dynamique*, d'Alembert's claim to greatness lay in his *Discours préliminaire*, which achieved its obvious purpose of interesting public opinion and disarming official criticism by its inherent quality and dignified tone. It was only on a second reading that it was seen that religion was being subordinated to social and philosophical factors. The work is in three parts, the third reproducing the *Prospectus* by Diderot, which is primarily an advertisement. In the first part d'Alembert provided his genealogical tree of philosophical classification of knowledge. He pointed to the chain which unites the sciences and the arts and attempted to give the exact sciences the role of leadership formerly given to divine revelation. By so doing he adumbrated the official doctrine of the modern state, and exercised an undoubted influence on nineteenth-century thought.

In the second part, d'Alembert provided a general survey of the arts and the sciences from the Middle Ages, for which he and all his contemporaries had little respect. His main concern was to show the enormous progress that was being made in all spheres. His picture of the Renaissance is less incomplete and he has some excellent pages on humanism, on Descartes, to whom he was fairer than most of his contemporaries, on Newton, etc. His survey of science, as of letters and the arts, is very brief, and, rather surprisingly, his literary criticism derives directly from that of Boileau, and is consequently of little interest. The general philosophical introduction is remarkable for its clear and categorical statement of the current sensationalist philosophy, for its stress on the empirical approach to knowledge of Locke, and for its conception of a new philosophy and a new science working in harmony as the justification of the publication of the *Encyclopédie*. By its content, by its limpid, clear, condensed style, and the quality of its thought, it was worthy of an undertaking conceived as a challenge to reactionary accepted opinion and destined to mark an important step in the history of ideas.

The Jesuits attacked the *Encyclopédie* and d'Alembert personally in the *Journal de Trévoux*, and indirectly through an onslaught on the thesis of the abbé de Prades. They were responsible for many anonymous pamphlets against d'Alembert, who was virulently attacked on the very day he was received in the Académie Française, and for the continued satire of the *Cacouacs*. Moreau aimed at d'Alembert in particular in his *Nouveau Mémoire pour servir à l'histoire des Cacouacs*. Montenoy, a friend of Fréron, who had criticised d'Alembert's *Eloge de Montesquieu* in the *Année littéraire* and championed the *parti dévot*, published his ironic *Petites Lettres sur de grands philosophes*. P. Hayer in *La Religion vengée* (1756–63) wrote a refutation of the *Encyclopédie*. But in 1764 the Society of Jesus was suppressed in France by order of the king, and d'Alembert triumphed over his opponents in his *Mémoire sur la destruction des Jésuites* (1765). With important *Éclaircissements* (1759), his *Essai sur les éléments de philosophie ou sur les principes des connaissances humaines* constitutes a panegyric of the eighteenth century and of the philosophic movement, and a record of his intellectual development. His *Mélanges de philosophie, d'histoire et de littérature* (1753, final revision 1764) shows the wide range of his interests and knowledge.

Not all the Encyclopaedists were *philosophes*, nor were all the *philosophes* Encyclopaedists. Condillac and Helvétius were Encyclopaedists, but are more significant as philosophers. Etienne Bonnot de Condillac, abbé de Mureaux (1715–80), lived a simple, austere life, too much withdrawn to know much of men and society. But the dry, precise style in which he wrote, which was in keeping with his personality, was eminently suited for the expression of his philosophy. At first he confined himself to systematising the ideas of Locke, in his *Essai sur l'origine des connaissances humaines* (1746), followed in 1749 by his *Traité des systèmes*, a work in two volumes in which he examined the systems of Malebranche, Leibniz, Spinoza, and Boursier, and the general validity of hypotheses; and developed a devastatingly destructive attack on systematic metaphysics. His analysis is sound and this is perhaps his finest work.

The *Traité des sensations* (1754) derived its inspiration from Locke, but it is nevertheless an original contribution to sensationalist philosophy. Starting from sensory experience, and claiming that perception is the source of all knowledge, Condillac vindicated the experimental method. 'Le principal objet de cet ouvrage', he wrote, 'est de faire voir comment toutes nos connaissances et toutes nos facultés viennent des sens, ou pour parler plus exactement des sensations.' Attention and memory spring from the nature of the impression made on our senses. Comparison, reflection, and the power of abstraction necessarily follow, and imagination is merely reflection working with images. Condillac was right in believing with Locke that our faculties may be acquired, and result from habit, and in challenging Locke's opinion that this fact is not necessarily incompatible with the theory of innate ideas. In Condillac's view the hereditary does not necessarily involve the unchanging or eternal. He always reduced everything to sensation, which he found at the root of our very will.

He likened man to a statue to whom is granted five senses, and in his *Traité des animaux* (1754), he showed that his *homme-statue* had no idea of God or revelation and that he would feel ashamed of his gods of clay. He may, however, adore the forces of nature which have moulded him. In his later *Art de penser* (1780), he argued that the self is merely the sum of our sensations, and that there is no God, apart from the *idée d'infini*, which is none other than a material concept based on numbers. Ethics for him rested on the conformity of our actions and our laws, which are social habits. In his appendix to the *Traité des sensations* he showed that 'man-statue' can learn, through experience, to deliberate and may exercise free-will, and he defined his personal freedom as follows: 'La liberté n'est que le pouvoir de faire ce qu'on ne fait pas ou de ne pas faire ce qu'on fait.' That which satisfies the passions and the mind is deemed to be beautiful and good. By stressing the need to study the origins of our ideas and the nature of the operations of our mind, Condillac brought out the necessity for a new kind of education, and for a new society, change being the very essence of things. At birth we all receive impressions in the same manner, and it is the way in which our sensations are associated or transformed that determines our mental activity. He showed great interest in the young child and the early functioning of the mind. He was much interested in the problem of language and his ideas on the subject form the basis of his onslaught on metaphysics. He studied grammar and its origins and wrote an *Art d'écrire* and an *Art de raisonner*, as well as an *Art de penser*. His *Logique* was published in 1780 and a *Langue des calculs* in 1798. He lived a retired life and obtained the position of tutor to the infant duke of Parma, grandson of Louis XV, for whom he wrote thirteen volumes of a *Cours d'études*, providing his pupil with a very comprehensive curriculum. He also wrote *Le Commerce et le gouvernement considérés relativement l'un à l'autre* (1776), the subtitle of which indicates its purpose: *Notions élémentaires sur le commerce déterminées par des suppositions ou Principes de la science économique*; the general thesis of this work was attacked by the Physiocrats. His views on the right of property are very similar to those of Rousseau, of whom he had been a friend, and the influence of his thought on another friend, Diderot, was very great, as can be seen in the *Lettre sur les aveugles*, and in other works. His sensationalist philosophy was generally adopted by French contemporary philosophers and early materialists.

His elder brother, the Abbé G. Bonnot de Mably (1709–85), was introduced into society by the Cardinal de Tencin and Mme de Tencin, to whose family he was related. He was entrusted with the task of writing the Cardinal's speeches for the Conseil des Ministres, and thereby exercised a real influence at court, till he broke with the Cardinal over the latter's desire to nullify a Protestant marriage. He then retired into private life. In *Parallèle des Romains et des Français* (1740) he favoured a strong monarchy as best able to ensure progress and prosperity. After 1746 he turned his attention to Greece, studying Plutarch and Thucydides. He wrote *Le Droit public de l'Europe fondé sur les traités* (1748), *Observations sur les Grecs* (1749), and *Observations sur les Romains* (1751), which led him to conclude that happiness depends on *mores* and not on advance in knowledge. His *Entretiens de Phocion sur le rapport de la morale avec la politique* (1763), which reiterated this view, was at the time as popular as Rousseau's *Discours sur les lettres et les arts*. Other works include *De la Législation ou Principes des lois* (1771) and *Observations sur le gouvernement et les lois des Etats-Unis d'Amérique* (1784), in which he advised the United States to give up mercantilism if it wished to survive.

Having spent seventeen years of his life studying the Greeks and the Romans, he wished to apply to eighteenth-century France the principles of the Greek republics, and of Rome during its period of aristocratic domination. He visited Poland to draft a constitution for that country, staying there for one year, but growing increasingly discouraged and melancholy. *Du Gouvernement et des lois de la Pologne* appeared in 1781. His prophecies having failed to materialise, he was known as 'le Prophète de malheur', and it was ironic that he died four years before his prophecies became true. He had called for the convocation of the *Tiers Etat*, but he had little understanding of contemporary society, and of the emerging middle class based on industrial and commercial development. He was one of the first socialists, through his egalitarian principles, his love of humanity and of justice, and his distrust of wealth and luxury. He exercised an undoubted influence on Marat, Babeuf, and other revolutionary figures. *De l'Etude de l'histoire* appeared in 1783 and *Des Droits et des devoirs du citoyen* appeared posthumously.

Friedrich Melchior, Baron Grimm (1723–1807), one of the most famous critics of the eighteenth century, was born in Regensburg and educated at the University of Leipzig. Finding himself penniless, he accepted the post of preceptor of the children of the comte de Schomberg and went to France in 1749. There he met Rousseau, with whom he shared a taste for music, and who introduced him to his friends. In 1753 he published *Le Petit Prophète de Boehmischbroda*, a witty satirical work which was frequently reprinted and which provoked a number of rejoinders, as well as an anonymous *Au Petit Prophète de Boehmischbroda* (21 February 1753), which is held to be by Diderot. The controversy to which it gave expression centred around the Querelle des Bouffons, which opposed the partisans of French to those of Italian music. All the Encyclopaedists and their friends favoured the new Italian music.

Grimm now mingled in literary circles, frequenting the salon of the baron d'Holbach, and becoming involved in a lifelong liaison with Mme d'Epinay. He quarrelled with Rousseau, who became embittered against him, as is shown in the *Confessions*, and established a close friendship with Diderot, based in part on their contrasting natures. He became *Lecteur* to the duke of Saxe-Gotha and secretary to the count of Friesen, then *Secrétaire des Commandements* of the duc d'Orléans (1755). In 1753 he took over from the Abbé Raynal the task of providing foreign princes with information about activities in Paris, and edited the *Correspondance littéraire, philosophique et critique avec Catherine II et plusieurs princes d'Allemagne* between 1754 and 1773, when he handed over to Jakob Heinrich Meister. The journal was sent to the Queen of Sweden, the King of Poland, and many others, copies being supplied in manuscript form. An examination of surviving texts shows that they are not identical for any given number. Sometimes parts have been lost, more often they were never supplied. This correspondence includes a number of works by Diderot which were not printed in his lifetime. Grimm passed on to Diderot the task of reviewing the annual salon, or art exhibition, and the *Salons* which Diderot contributed mark the true beginning of art criticism.

The *Correspondance littéraire*, written in a vigorous and elegant style, provides the best record of literary events for thirty-seven years. Grimm was well informed and shrewd, and had no need to fear censorship by the French. He was made a baron of the Holy Roman Empire in 1772. In 1776 he was appointed by the Diet of Frankfurt as minister plenipotentiary at the court of Versailles and in 1777 he was appointed Russian Councillor of State. The events of the French Revolution led him to leave France in 1790, which he did with regret. He stopped in Brussels and then went on to St Petersburg, where Catherine the Great made him Russian minister to Saxony. His *Correspondance* covers the years 1754–90 and was first published in sixteen volumes in 1812–13, to which a supplement by Barbier was added in 1814. A highly intelligent man, he anticipated by twenty-five years some of the opinions of Goethe and sponsored a return to the classical models of antiquity and of England and France. He was cold and selfish, and held strong opinions; he exercised a considerable influence in the milieu in which he lived. He remains the best foreign judge of France and French life for the period he reviewed. He was always in the inner circle of philosophical activity and endorsed the aims and beliefs of his friends. He died impoverished and embittered in Gotha.

Paul-Henri Thiry, baron d'Holbach (1723–89), was born in the Palatinate, settling in Paris in 1749. He was a rich, kindly, well-educated man who kept an open house for free-thinkers. The Abbé Galiani called him 'le maître d'hôtel de la philosophie', a title he earned by giving famous dinners, to which were invited men such as Rousseau, Buffon, d'Alembert, Helvétius, Raynal, Grimm, Marmontel, Condillac, Turgot, and perhaps above all Diderot, who felt most at home in this circle, and who wrote some very vivid accounts of their forgatherings in his correspondence with Mlle Volland. D'Holbach had an encyclopaedic range of knowledge and took up an extreme position in philosophy, pushing sensationalist convictions to the point of complete materialism and atheism. He believed only in Matter and Motion, which he called Nature. In politics he favoured a liberal monarchy, for fear of democracy degenerating into domination by the superstitious masses of the people. But he inveighed against all forms of tyranny and passionately espoused the cause of political and religious liberty. His style is clear and eloquent, but at times long-winded and rhetorical. There is an undeniable harshness and lack of subtlety in his thought and a monotonous repetition of ideas, coupled with an intolerance of opposition, which makes his work unattractive to the average reader. He was an honest man, *simplement simple*, as Mme Geoffrin put it, and he exercised a great influence on his guests, on Diderot, on Naigeon, who worshipped him, and on many others.

His output supplements the *Encyclopédie*, for which he wrote over 450 articles. He began with translations from the German (1752–66): *L'Art de la verrerie*; *La Minéralogie*; *L'Introduction à La Minéralogie de Henckel*; *La Chimie métallurgique* (by Gellert); *Essai sur l'histoire des couches de la terre*; *L'Art des mines*; *Œuvres métallurgiques* (by Christian Orschall); and *Traité du Souffre* (by Stahl). He wrote articles on chemistry, pharmacology, physiology, and medicine for the *Encyclopédie*. These works supplied factual information that was to be of great service to the French. He then turned his attention to religion, which he virulently attacked, pointing out inconsistencies in the dogma of the Church, and the nature of the myths to which they had given rise. *Le Christianisme dévoilé ou Examen des principes et des effets de la religion chrétienne* was published under the name of Boulanger in 1766. In it Christian ethics were judged to be no better than any other and Christianity was presented as running counter to the true interest of the state, invariably impeding progress. The articles 'Prêtres', 'Représentants', 'Théocratie' are especially important.

In the same year d'Holbach published *Le Christianisme primitif vengé des entreprises et des excès de nos prêtres modernes*, and *De l'Imposture sacerdotale ou Recueil de pièces sur le clergé*; there followed in 1768 *La Contagion sacrée ou Histoire naturelle de la superstition*, and *Essai sur les préjugés* appeared in 1770. In the same year, under the name of Mirabaud, a writer no longer living, he brought out *Le Système de la nature ou des lois du monde physique et moral*. Man is seen as no more than a physical being, and there can be no moral man distinct from physical man. He drew bold conclusions from this view, and expressed in resounding terms his atheism and his materialism, categorically denying the immortality of the soul and the existence of free-will. He succeeded in appalling both Frederick the Great and Voltaire. In 1772, he published *Le Bon Sens ou Idées naturelles opposées aux idées surnaturelles*, which summarised his ideas and appeared to many as the Bible of atheism.[8] He applied to ethics and politics the ideas he had expressed in his *Système de la nature*, in *Système social ou Principes naturels de la morale et de la politique* (1773). *Les Eléments de la morale universelle ou Les Devoirs de l'homme fondés sur la nature* was more moderate in tone and was better received (1790). He translated from the English P. Annet's *The Life of David or the Man after God's own Heart*, which he entitled *David ou L'Histoire de l'homme selon le cœur de Dieu* (1768). He also redrafted the last chapter of *Militaire philosophe ou Difficultés sur la religion proposées au père Malebranche* (1767) with help from Naigeon; and wrote *Lettres à Eugénie ou Préservatif contre les préjugés* (2 vols., 1768) with notes by Naigeon, which was attributed to Fréret; *La Théologie portative* (1767); *Les Prêtres démasqués ou Les Intrigues du clergé chrétien* (1767) translated from the English; *De la Cruauté religieuse* (1769); *Essai sur les préjugés ou De l'Influence des opinions sur les mœurs et le bonheur des hommes*, par M. de M*** (1770); *Examen critique de la vie et des ouvrages de Saint Paul* (1770); *Histoire critique*

[8] It was republished in 1791 under the name of the Curé Meslier.

de Jésus-Christ ou Analyse raisonnée des Evangiles (1770); *La Politique naturelle ou Discours sur les vrais principes du gouvernement par un ancien magistrat* (1772, 2 vols.); *L'Ethocratie ou Le Gouvernement fondé sur la morale* (1776); and many other translations and essays. D'Holbach's publisher was Marc-Michel Rey of Amsterdam, and he was helped by Naigeon, who saw his works through the press.

The *Système de la nature* in two volumes, with a preliminary notice by Naigeon, is d'Holbach's most important work, one in which, according to Grimm, Diderot played some part. The Abbé N.-S. Bergier (1718–90), in *Examen du matérialisme ou Réfutation du système de la nature* (1771), attempted to refute d'Holbach's case without much success.[9] D'Holbach applied the sensationalist philosophy to a theory of the universe. According to him, there is no God, no spiritual beings, only Matter and Movement. Beings are only a combination of matter, and society is formed of animals brought together by a material need. The only possible ethic is one of self-interest. In his second part he claimed that man invented God so that God could deliver him from evil; evil is nothing else but ignorance. God is the cause of all phenomena for which we have no explanation, and will decrease in stature as knowledge grows and all that is mysterious disappears. He reiterates endlessly that man is *un être purement physique*. His actions are movements in him which come from the exercise of the will or from thought, and are the necessary and natural consequence of human mechanisms and impulses. The *Système de la nature* is a landmark in the struggles against the Church.

J.-A. Naigeon (1738–1810), a friend of d'Holbach and of Diderot, was a minor Encyclopaedist who contributed the articles 'Ame' and 'Unitaires'. He began his career by studying drawing, painting, and sculpture, but he soon abandoned the fine arts to find fulfilment in militant philosophical propaganda. Like d'Holbach, he was an avowed atheist, and also a simple, righteous, and studious man. He was a Latin scholar, concerning himself with Epictetus and with La Grange's translation of Seneca. A discriminating bibliophile, he acquired a fine collection of Latin books, which was sold to the publisher Firmin Didot and eventually dispersed. Apart from work in collaboration with d'Holbach, and notices on La Fontaine, Racine, and the *Essais* of Montaigne (1802), with autographed additions by the author, he is remembered for his part in *Le Militaire philosophe ou Difficultés sur la religion proposées au père Malebranche* and as editor of a *Recueil*

[9] The Abbé Bergier also wrote *Le Déisme réfuté par lui-même* (1765) and *Certitudes des preuves du Christianisme* (1768).

philosophique in two volumes and the *Encyclopédie méthodique*, which contain philosophical articles of an anti-religious nature, drawn from the Ancients and the Moderns. His edition of Diderot's works published in 1798 is a first attempt at a critical complete edition, and kindled a revival of interest in a man whom he proclaimed his master.

Claude-Adrien Helvétius (1715–71) was a sensationalist philosopher of greater distinction. He came from a Protestant German family which had settled in Holland. His grandfather, a doctor who popularised the use of ipecacuhana, was given a title by Louis XIV. His father, who was also a doctor, was successful in saving the life of the future Louis XV, and was appointed doctor to Queen Marie Leczinska. It was through the patronage of the queen that Helvétius obtained the post of *fermier-général* and acquired a great personal fortune. By his general theory of mankind he should have been an egotist, but in practice he was generous and warm-hearted. He resigned his office in 1750, marrying in the following year and settling down in his property at Voré in Perche. He purchased the office of *Maître d'Hôtel* to the queen, a useful sinecure, but he was seldom to be seen at court, preferring to live the life of a kindly philosopher at Voré for nine months of the year, promoting agriculture and industry on his estate; for the rest of the time he was to be found in Paris, where he opened his own salon.

Helvétius started his literary career by writing an unfinished poem in ten cantos, *Le Bonheur* (published in 1772), and a tragedy on the Fiesco Conspiracy. As a child he had read and admired Locke, and in 1758 he published anonymously *De l'Esprit*, a work taken to be a summary of the philosophy of the Encyclopaedists, which was condemned by Parlement, the Sorbonne, the Pope, the court, the Jesuits, and the Jansenists. Yielding to his mother's entreaties, he wrote three retractions, in spite of which his book was burnt, and he was forced to resign his post as *Maître d'Hôtel*. He would no doubt have been imprisoned or exiled had it not been for Malesherbes, Choiseul, and Mme de Pompadour. His social and political ideas, especially his attack on despotism, united the opposition against him, his metaphysics and his ethics attracting comparatively less attention. The main theme of the book seemed to be paradoxical. All our faculties may be reduced to physical sensibility, and we differ from animals only in the question of organisation of sense impressions. Our intelligence may thus be accounted for by an accidental conformation of our organs. If intelligence depends on our senses, ethics depends on social self-interest. As individuals we are solely motivated by self-interest, by love of pleasure and fear of pain. We are therefore unable to choose between right and wrong, and our notions of justice vary according to the customs of the country in which we live. Man is reduced to being nothing more than an organism. Much later, in 1772, appeared a supplement to *De l'Esprit*, entitled *De l'Homme, de ses facultés intellectuelles et de son éducation*, which is bolder and offers a more direct challenge to religion. Diderot wrote a *Réfutation* of the latter work, together with some observations on *De l'Esprit*, which are of considerable value in any effort to trace the evolution of Diderot's thought, in the light of a deepening of his practical experience of life; much of his criticism of Helvétius is valid.

Diderot and the majority of the Encyclopaedists accorded the first place in their thinking to the biological sciences, whilst Helvétius, a friend and great admirer of Fontenelle, held to Cartesian, mechanistic conceptions, and by so doing served as a useful link between Fontenelle and the *idéologues*. As a psychologist and sociologist, he overestimated the power of education and environment, whilst postulating a constant human nature. He relied on education to see political justice established, without realising that changes in an educational system are commonly effected by politicians to support their own new political structures. But of all the *philosophes* he probably comes closest to the Marxists by the attention he paid to the working classes, and by his conception of man, which is more abstract than that of Locke, whose thought he systematised.

Helvétius' wrong generalisations with regard to self-interest and the motivation of individuals would appear to be true for the Marxist when applied to collectivity, and Marxists would have approved of his request for the establishing of state schools to mould the future citizens. Y. Belaval, in a stimulating introduction to the 1969 reprint of Helvétius' *Complete Works*, for which G. Olms is responsible, has brought out the interest of Helvétius' collective psychology.

Helvétius was a kindly, disinterested man, who loved discussion, and was personally liked by Rousseau, Turgot, Voltaire, Buffon, Montesquieu (it is no longer believed that he wrote the famous letters to Montesquieu and to Saurin on *L'Esprit des lois*, but he had the latter title in mind when he determined his own), and Mme de Graffigny, whose niece he married in 1751. After his death, his wife, a beautiful and intelligent woman of fine character, and an excellent hostess, received in her salon Condillac, d'Holbach, Franklin, Turgot, Jefferson, Chamfort, Morellet, and Cabanis, to whom she gave her house at Auteuil. It is said that both Turgot and Franklin made her offers of marriage, but she preferred to lead a quiet, secluded life, undertaking many good works, and deeply attached to her dogs, her cats, her hens, and her canaries.

Little is known of Morelly beyond his works: *Essai sur l'esprit humain* (1745); *Essai sur le cœur humain* (1745); *Physique de la beauté ou Pouvoir naturel de ses charmes* (1748); *Le Prince, Les délices du cœur ou Traité des qualités d'un grand roi et systéme d'un sage gouvernement* (1751), in which we find an outline of his social ideas; *Naufrage des îles flottantes à la Basiliade* (1763), an allegorical heroic poem in fourteen cantos, which expounded a system of government based on communism, bolder than that in Thomas More's *Utopia*; and *Le Code de la nature* (1755), his most important work, which was wrongly attributed to Diderot.

Le Code de la nature ou Le Véritable Esprit de ses lois de tout temps négligé ou méconnu provided a full answer to the critics of his heroic poem. It expressed in dogmatic terms Morelly's communist principles, influenced Babeuf, Louis Blanc, and Cabet, and marked an important stage in socialist thinking before Karl Marx. According to Morelly, man is born good, his passions are legitimate, and society should ensure his wellbeing without allowing him to get depraved. Laws and institutions must be blamed if man is unhappy and if he is subject to restraint. Our ethics, based on prejudice, and our education are responsible for all our ills. He claimed that property, apart from what is needed for immediate use, pleasure, or work, should not be in the hands of individuals, that all artisans or workers should be a charge on the state, that all citizens must contribute to the public weal according to their strength, talent, and age, and that their duties should be determined according to distributive laws. This doctrine is a first expression of communism, for which Louis Blanc was later to find a formula: 'à chacun selon ses besoins, de chacun selon ses facultés (*L'Organisation du travail*, 1840). The distributive laws are economic laws, which determine the allocation of produce. In his ideal society, all forms of sale or barter would be forbidden. All men between the ages of twenty-four and twenty-five would have to undertake compulsory agricultural service. Marriage and family life would be compulsory and celibacy would be tolerated only after the age of forty. Divorce could be effected after ten years of marriage. Infants would be compulsorily breast-fed, and educated in a *gymnase* from the age of five. Professional training in *ateliers* would start at the age of ten. The study of metaphysics would be forbidden. Government would be on communist lines; the head of each tribe, who would be appointed for life, would serve as head of state by a system of rotation. The cities would be governed by a senate of fathers of over fifty, and by a magistrate appointed annually to exercise executive powers. Morelly believed that very few penal laws would be required; laws, he claimed, are the source of all evil, but he did not explain how, under his system, good laws only would be enacted.

André Morellet (1727–1819), who had become acquainted with Turgot, Loménie de Brienne, and the abbé de Prades whilst studying at the Sorbonne, met Diderot through de Prades and remained in the Encyclopaedic group till 1752, when he took up the post of tutor to the son of the chancellor of Lorraine. He wrote a *Petit Ecrit sur une matière intéressante, la tolérance* (1756), defending Protestants and Jansenists against the Roman Catholic Church, which filled Diderot and d'Alembert with delight. He contributed to the *Encyclopédie* with articles on theology and metaphysics ('Fatalité', 'Figures', 'Fils de Dieu', 'Foi', and 'Fondamentaux'). He then turned his attention to industry with *Réflexions sur les advantages de la fabrication et de l'usage des toiles peintes* (1758), which earned government approval. In 1762 he published, with the approval of Malesherbes, an extract of *Directorium Inquisitorum* under the title *Manuel des inquisiteurs.* He was now moving in salon circles, especially in that of Mme Geoffrin. He wrote a witty and biting *Préface de la Comédie des philosophes* which was directed against Palissot (1760), and in which there was some criticism of the princesse de Robecq, as a result of which he was incarcerated in the Bastille for two months, at the end of which time the maréchal de Luxembourg, prompted by Rousseau, secured his release. Henceforward he posed as a martyr. He became a close friend of d'Holbach, translated Beccaria's *Traité des délits et des peines* in 1766, and only the outbreak of the French Revolution brought to a halt the *Prospectus d'un nouveau dictionnaire du commerce* on which he had been engaged for twenty years.

In 1772 Morellet visited England and met members of the British government, and also Benjamin Franklin, who was in England at the time, and Lord Shelburne, in the course of a commercial mission with which he had been entrusted. In 1775 he went to Ferney, where he was received by Voltaire. He was on friendly terms with Marmontel, whose niece he married. In 1784 he received a pension of 4,000 livres from Louis XVI and was elected to the French Academy. In 1792, when the French Academy was suppressed, he was its director and had been placed in charge of the work on its dictionary. At first he supported the Revolution, writing *Objections sur la forme des états de 1614*, *Réflexions du lendemain*, and *Moyen de dispenser utilement les biens ecclésiastiques* (1789). But he soon became disillusioned and passed to the side of reaction. He held on to all the papers of the French Academy, only returning them in 1803. He was able to find a safe retreat and reappeared in the capital only after 9 *thermidor*. His dislike of the Revolution turned into hatred. He continued to write: *La Loi des familles*, *La Cause des pères*, *Supplément à La Cause des pères*, and *Dernière Défense, appel à l'opinion publique*. In order to earn his living he translated twenty novels and travel books from the English (1797–1800). In 1807 he was elected a member of the *Corps législatif*. In 1815, when eighty-eight, he had a fall which disabled him, yet in spite of this his four volumes of *Mélanges de littérature et de philosophie au XVIIIe siècle* were published in 1818. He was an intelligent but somewhat shallow thinker who had style, and knew how to popularise the ideas of his group on toleration, free-thought, inoculation, and so on. He upheld eighteenth-century philosophy and values till the end of his life.

The career of Ferdinando Galiani (1728–87), who became an intimate if the *coterie holbachique*, is interesting. He was an Italian statesman, littérateur, and economist, who had enjoyed the privilege of studying under famous teachers, and of meeting some of the most renowned Italian scientists and thinkers, including Giambattista Vico, in the archbishop's palace at Naples. He was intellectually precocious, and acquired an encyclopaedic knowledge, showing particular interest and competence in the fields of commerce, politics, and economics. He wrote *Della Moneta*, or *Grand Traité de la monnaie*, in 1750. In 1759 he was sent to Paris as secretary of the count of Castromonte and began to study French intensively. He became a close friend of Diderot, Grimm, and Mme d'Epinay. They were fascinated by this Neapolitan abbé, no more than four and a half feet tall, as portly as Punch, with a penchant for delivering monologues accompanied by lively gestures and mimicry. Some of his monologues, a compound of folly and wisdom, lasted for one hour. Marmontel, who became his friend, compared him to a Harlequin endowed with the mind of Machiavelli. He was for ever laughing and provoking laughter, and Voltaire appreciated his irony and paradoxes, which sprang from alternate bouts of faith and scepticism. His command of French became well-nigh perfect. His most important work is *Dialogue sur le commerce des blés*, published under a pseudonym in 1770, evolving a theory of value based on utility and scarcity. He became involved in a debate with the Abbé Morellet who was a spokesman of the Physiocrats and advocated complete freedom while he saw the necessity of regulations. He was a musician with a good voice, and a skilled player of the harpsichord. He was also an antiquarian who collected a fine musical library, coins, rocks, sculpture, and especially statues. He died of a stroke in Naples in 1787, saddened by the death of several of his Parisian friends. His two volumes of correspondence with Mme d'Epinay are interesting and well-written.

The Abbé Raynal (1717–96) is known for his *Histoire philosophique et politique des établissements et du commerce des Européens dans les deux Indes*, of which twenty editions appeared between the first in 1774 and the last in 1880. Diderot and others had a hand in the writing. The work attacked tyranny and superstition, and was condemned to be burnt in 1781. Raynal was compelled to go into exile, and he retracted the most daring views he or his friends had expressed.

III. THE PHYSIOCRATS

An important group of thinkers known as the Physiocrats, a term first used by J.-B. Say in 1829, was formed around 1750, and founded the science of economics. They were concerned with commerce and with agriculture. One of their number, Gournay (1712–59), was an apostle of free trade and coined the expression 'Laissez faire, laissez passer'. Quesnay (1694–1774), who contributed the articles 'Fermiers' and 'Grains' to the *Encyclopédie* and drafted articles on 'Hommes' and 'Impôts', was the founder of the school which saw in agriculture evidence of the power of nature and in the soil the sole source of true wealth. Only in agriculture was the net yield found to be greater than the effort put in. The Physiocrats noted that the peasant was the only worker to be charged rent and deemed that only the peasants were productive workers. Man had the right to use his capital and any challenge to this right was held to be manifestly unjust both to the individual and to society. It followed that trade must be free, and from an analysis of economic factors they concluded that there was need for political reforms. The Physiocrats became increasingly revolutionary in outlook and fostered the cause of democracy, detailing some of the social and administrative reforms which the Revolution was to carry out. They believed in a strong state government and found in greater and better education the sole guarantee against despotism.

Quesnay published *Extraits des économies royales de Sully* (1758), *Analyse du tableau économique* (1760), and *Maximes générales du gouvernement économique d'un royaume agricole* (1760). A volume of writings by Quesnay was published by Dupont de Nemours in 1767 under the title *Physiocratie ou Constitution naturelle du gouvernement le plus avantageux au genre humain.* The school of Physiocrats included Turgot, who wrote for the *Encyclopédie;* Victor Riquetti, marquis de Mirabeau (1715–89), called 'l'ami des hommes' after his publication of *L'Ami des hommes ou Traité sur la population* (1756), his *Théorie de l'impôt*

(1760), and *Philosophie rurale* (1763); Mercier de la Rivière, who wrote *L'Ordre naturel et essentiel des sociétés politiques* (1767); and Dupont de Nemours (1739–1817), who founded *Le Journal de l'agriculture, du commerce et des finances* in 1765, and published, under the title *Physiocratie*, the most important works of his friends, as well as Quesnay's, his own *Origine et progrès d'une science nouvelle* (1768), and *Abrégé des principes* (1773). The Abbé Baudeau who first attacked the economists in *Ephémérides du citoyen ou Chronique de l'esprit national* was converted by Dupont de Nemours and then wrote *Nouvelles Ephémérides économiques ou Bibliothèque raisonnée de l'histoire, de la morale et de la politique*. The Physiocrats were subject to many attacks by the *philosophes*: Voltaire in *L'Homme aux quarante écus* (1768), the Abbé Mably in *Doutes proposés aux philosophes économistes sur l'ordre naturel et essentiel des sociétés politiques* (1768), and the Abbé Galiani in *Dialogue sur le commerce des blés* (1770).

Their opinions, however, closely linked as they were with conditions prevailing in France, served to focus attention on economic factors generally neglected, which were seen to shape politics and history. They provided a remarkable *tableau* or inventory of conditions in rural France, and in the long run did much to improve the conditions of the peasants. Parmentier (1737–1813), a philanthropist, tackled the problem of starvation in a practical way by suggesting new foods in *Sur les végétaux nourrisseurs qui en temps de disette peuvent remplacer les aliments ordinaires*, a work which was crowned by the Académie de Besançon in 1772. Owing to the patronage of Louis XVI, he was able to spread the cultivation of the potato, called *la parmentière*, a vegetable first imported by Sir Walter Raleigh from America to Ireland, and which had become popular in England, Germany, and Flanders long before it was grown in France. It was thanks to Turgot that the Physiocrats exercised their greatest influence, but Morellet, Malesherbes, Trudaine, and especially Dupont de Nemours also popularised their theories and their projected reforms. Real famine, due to an increase in the price of wheat, had occurred in 1726, 1739, and 1740. The misery and poverty of the peasants, from the poor *métayer* to the small landholder, remained acute and was ignored by the clergy and the nobility, whilst the growing bourgeoisie and the intelligentsia became the allies of the peasants in their common hatred of the financiers and the privileged classes. The price of corn, which affected the price of bread, led to severe economic crises, which became ever more serious as the Revolution drew near. It has been argued that if the government had supported Turgot and implemented his proposed reforms, the French Revolution might have been averted.

IV. CONDORCET AND THE 'IDÉOLOGUES'

The last great eighteenth-century *philosophe* is M.-J.-A.-N. de Caritat, marquis de Condorcet (1743–94), who was also a mathematician of repute, and an economist. At the age of sixteen he brilliantly sustained a mathematical thesis before d'Alembert, Clairaut, and the geometer Fontaine. At seventeen he dedicated a work, *Une Profession de foi*, to Turgot, who became his friend. At nineteen he was received into society, thanks to the good offices of a relative, the duc de La Rochefoucauld. He then wrote a number of mathematical dissertations: *Essai sur le calcul intégral* (1765); *Sur le problème des trois corps* (1769); *Sur le calcul analytique*; and *Sur les séries récurrentes*. He accompanied d'Alembert on a visit to Voltaire at Ferney in 1770, and his correspondence with Voltaire is very friendly in tone. At sixteen he became a member of the Académie des Sciences, where he read his *éloge* of Buffon and his *éloge* of d'Alembert, both very favourably received. His *éloges* of academicians are all noteworthy for their perspicacity. In 1782 he was elected a member of the Académie Française, his *discours de réception* being on *Les Avantages que la société peut retenir de la réunion des sciences physiques aux sciences morales*. He frequented Buffon, Vaucanson, Franklin, and especially d'Alembert, who invited him to complete some scientific and literary work for the *Encyclopédie*, and who made him executor of his will. His scientific reputation was great, and won him a prize in 1777 for work on his *Théorie des comètes*, and for his experiments with d'Alembert and Bossut on the resistance of liquids. His *Essai sur l'application de l'analyse à la probabilité des décisions rendues à la pluralité des voix* (1785), the second edition of which is entitled *Eléments du calcul des probabilités, et son application aux jeux de hasard, à la loterie et aux jugements des hommes*, is an outstanding contribution to the subject. His articles in the *Encyclopédie*, written under the pseudonym Schwartz, dealt with political economy and philosophy, and are in the spirit of those of the Physiocrats. His *Réflexions sur l'esclavage des nègres* (1782), took up the cause of the American negro. At the age of forty-three he fell deeply in love with the niece of Condillac, who was the sister of Mme Cabanis and of the future Marshal Grouchy, and he married her in 1786. At first she thought him cold and aloof, but even though he became increasingly involved in politics, she grew devotedly attached to him, responding to the exceptional nobility of his character.

The American War of Independence first led him to take up politics, and turned him into a republican. He saw revolution as the culmination of a process of emancipation from bigotry and the dawn of an age of justice, equality, and reason. In 1789 he pinned his hopes on the constitutional party, and in 1791 he was made *commissaire de la trésorerie* and became a deputy, assuming the office of Secretary of the Legislative Assembly in October of that year. He seldom spoke in public, since he had a weak voice and was both timid and excitable; but his fellow deputies called upon him when fine, rhetorical speeches were required. He was made President in February 1792, and urged moderation, as, for instance, in requesting that the death penalty be carried out only in the case of *émigrés* caught with arms in their hands. He voted against the death penalty in the hope of saving the king, but he supported a resolution that Louis XVI be condemned to *les galères à perpétuité*, a fate worse than death, as all royalists knew. He took sides with the Girondins, sharing their aversion to violence. On 8 July 1793 he was arraigned and condemned to death on 3 October. He then wrote an *Adresse aux citoyens français sur la nouvelle constitution*. He went into hiding, staying with Mme Vernet for eight months. When it looked as if he would be jeopardising her safety, he left and called upon his friend Suard, who gave him a copy of the Epistles of Horace and turned him away from his door. He was soon caught and according to one story escaped from the guillotine only by taking some poison which his brother-in-law Cabanis had given him.[10]

Condorcet's greatest work is *Esquisse d'un tableau historique des progrés de l'esprit humain* (1794), which offers a synthesis of French philosophical thought of the century. It is a brilliant piece of writing. He begins with an account of the progress of science and civilisation from early beginnings to the threshold of the eighteenth century, and proceeds to express his admiration for the great contribution to mankind of the *philosophes*, and for their ideal, which he sums up in three words, *raison, tolérance, humanité*. In the last part of the book he expresses his confidence in the future, which he sees as based on equality between men and between nations, and on the continuous progress of civilisation, thanks to education and science. For his unshakeable idealism he was called *un mouton enragé*. His *Eloge et pensées de Pascal* (1776), his *Vie de Turgot* (1786–87), his *Vie de Voltaire* (1787), are justly famous in spite of an excess of rhetoric and some stylistic blemishes. He shared in the task of publishing the Kehl edition of Voltaire's works.

A whole group of philosophers called *idéologues* sprang up in the wake of Condillac, concerned with the science of ideas and the operations of the mind. P.-J.-G. Cabanis (1757–1808) was a

10 Some biographers hold that he died from exposure.

doctor as well as a philosopher. He learnt medicine from another doctor at a relatively late date, after returning from Poland, where, at the age of sixteen, he had gone to act as tutor in a Polish family. He was still in Poland at the time of the partition of that country in 1773. His *Observations sur les hôpitaux* appeared in 1789. His primary interest was in the philosophy, rather than in the practice, of medicine. He was a friend of Mme Helvétius, and of Mirabeau, to whom he supplied information regarding public education. He was wrongly accused of having poisoned Mirabeau, who died in his arms. Cabanis married Condorcet's sister-in-law, Charlotte Grouchy. Later he supported the policies of the Directoire, and was a member of the *Conseil des Cinq Cents*. Bonaparte made him a senator and a commander of the Légion d'honneur. In *Traité du physique et du moral de l'homme* (1792) he showed that he was both a physiologist and a philosopher. His aim was to complete the work of Condillac by studying the nature and origin of sensation. He was a convinced materialist, going so far as to move a resolution that the name of God should never be allowed in speeches at the Institut.

Destutt de Tracy (1754–1836) is the author of *Eléments d'idéologie*, in which an attempt is made to show that thought depends on the invention of language, that is to say, on a sign which may be spoken or the written word. His views were attacked by Reid and by Kant, but he maintained that there was no certitude apart from sensation, that the only authority was that of reason, and that thought and will were a product of the organisation of matter. Ideology thus became a part of zoology. Our intelligence depends ultimately on physiology. Lamarck (1744–1829), who expounded his transformist theory in *Philosophie zoologique* (1809), before Darwin's *Origin of Species*, is another materialist thinker, as also was Laromiguière (1756–1837), who published his Sorbonne lectures under the title *Leçons de philosophie*.

V. FRENCH PHILOSOPHERS AT THE COURT OF FREDERICK THE GREAT

Frederick the Great claimed to be 'enlightened' and with the help of Voltaire hoped to achieve some distinction as a writer. His *Anti-Machiavel* bears signs of Voltaire's influence, but in his *Matinées royales ou Entretiens sur l'art de régner*, published anonymously, we read an ominous passage, clearly reflecting his personal view: '... ne vous avisez plus de faire l'enfant, et sachez pour toujours, qu'en fait de royaume l'on prend quand on peut, et l'on n'a jamais tort, que quand on est obligé de rendre.' The *Mémoires et histoires de Frédéric II* were published in 1750, 1788, and 1805 and the *Œuvres du philosophe de Sans-Souci* became well known. He gathered around him at Potsdam, in his celebrated circle of Sans Souci, and as members of the reorganised Academy of Berlin, a number of prominent philosophers and writers, the greatest of whom was Voltaire,[11] and others like Maupertuis and La Mettrie, much disliked by most of the Encyclopaedists, yet who held views of some importance.

Pierre-Louis Moreau de Maupertuis (1698–1759) was a geometer as well as a philosopher. He began his career as a musketeer, rising to be captain of the dragoons, but he was more drawn to science than to a military career, and studied Newton's physics, to which he converted Voltaire. He was made a member of the Académie des Sciences in 1731, and became involved in a controversy over the true measurements of the earth. Maurepas invited him to direct an expedition to the Arctic Circle, from which he brought back data purporting to show that there was a flattening of the earth towards the Pole. He was given a great welcome on his return to Paris in 1737. He was elected a member of the Royal Society and of the French Academy in 1743, but his arrogance and conceit made him unpopular. He was, therefore, glad to accept Frederick's invitation to become president of the Berlin Academy. He now turned his interest to philosophy. At the Prussian court he made a number of enemies, including Koenig, and quarrelled with Voltaire soon after the latter's arrival in Berlin (1752). Voltaire satirised him in *Micromégas,* and in *Histoire du Docteur Akakia et du Natif de Saint-Malo* (1753), one of his most virulent pamphlets;[12] Voltaire covered him with such ridicule that he never recovered his credit, and he died, full of resentment, in Basle in 1759. Maupertuis' scientific work, much praised in certain quarters during his lifetime, is now considered second-rate, but he helped to introduce the Newtonian doctrine of gravitation. His philosophical ideas have recently attracted considerable attention. His *Vénus physique* (1745) and his *Essai de philosophie morale* (1751) stimulated thought, as did his treatise published under the name of Dr Bauman and included under the title *Système de la nature in Oeuvres de Maupertuis,* vol. I (1759). Maupertuis saw clearly that Cartesianism was inadequate in its account

[11] The group also included Jordan, a friend of d'Argens, who died in 1745, and Count Algarotti (1712–64), who popularised Newtonian optics and was an Italian connoisseur of arts and science of repute. He wrote essays on classical themes as well as on architecture and painting, and on the opera. He resided in Germany from 1740 to 1749.

[12] See the critical edition of this work, with an introduction and commentary by Jacques Tuffet, 1967, and also the earlier edition in *Studies on Voltaire,* XXX (1964), by C. Fleischauer.

of the origin of life and the organisation of matter, and he suggested that nature had properties unknown to Descartes, thereby foreshadowing a vitalist philosophy. He strove to transform Leibniz's spiritual monad into a material molecule, but he was unable to understand the evolutionary process, or to come to grips with genetics as Diderot did in the *Rêve de d'Alembert*. Diderot's own refutation of Dr Bauman was in reality a pretext to develop Maupertuis' most dangerous ideas without exposing himself to attack.

Julien Offray de La Mettrie (1709–51) was a physician as well as a philosopher. After qualifying as a doctor he went in 1733 to Leiden to study under Boerhaave, and after practising in his native town of Saint-Malo, he was appointed surgeon to the guards in Paris. He became convinced that psychological phenomena were the effects of organic changes in the brain and nervous system, a view which he developed in *Histoire naturelle de l'âme* (around 1745). There was an outcry against this work, which drove La Mettrie back to Holland, where he developed his doctrines more boldly and fully, in *L'Homme-machine* (1747–48, English translation 1750), *L'Homme-plante* (1748), and *Les Animaux plus que machines* (1750), all reflecting a consistent materialism which proved unacceptable to his contemporaries. He drew the ethical consequences of his philosophy in *Discours sur le bonheur ou L'Anti-Sénèque* (1748), *Système d'Epicure* (1750), and *L'Art de jouir* (1751). For him the purpose of life was to be found in the pleasure of the senses, and real virtue is none other than self-love; atheism alone could ensure man's happiness, at present jeopardised by the wars brought about by theologians. The soul is only the thinking part of the body and dies with it. When death comes, 'la farce est jouée', so life must be enjoyed to the full.

Frederick II appointed him court reader in 1748, when he had to leave Holland. He continued to lead a gay, carefree life in Berlin, where he died of tainted pheasant *pâté*. He was treated as a kind of court jester by his friends and abhorred by his enemies, the Catholics, the *philosophes*, and the doctors. But his collected *Œuvres philosophiques* (1751) mark an important date in the history of early materialism.

J.-H.-S. Formey (1711–97), who was a foundation member of the Académie de Berlin and became its *secrétaire perpétuel*, was born in Berlin of French Protestant refugees. He first became a minister of religion, but in 1737, after six years in the ministry, he accepted a chair of eloquence at the French College in Berlin, and later occupied its chair of philosophy. His erudition kept him in touch with the Encyclopaedists; and he avoided any serious quarrel with Voltaire. A member of the Grand Directoire of the refugee

Huguenot Church in Prussia, and author of 150 works, he enjoyed a favoured situation, and died whilst held in high esteem and showered with official honours. He is best known for his *Histoire de l'Académie des Sciences de Berlin* and his *Mémoires de l'Académie de Berlin* (1750) which contain a great number of *eloges* (including one of Maupertuis, 1761), *mémoires*, and *dissertations* (1746–93). His refutation of Diderot's *Pensées philosophiques* and of *Toussaint's Les Mœurs* appeared in 1749. He was an enthusiastic sponsor of Leibniz and Wolff. He published *La Belle Wolfienne* (with Chambrier) in 1746. He edited the *Bibliothéque Germanique*, etc., important as an organ of Wolffian propaganda in France and for the propagation of information on German literature and scholarship. His attack on Rousseau in the *Anti-Emile* (1763) was harsh. It was followed by *Emile chrétien, consacré à l'utilité publique* (1764). Other works include *Système du vrai bonheur* (1751); *Le Philosophe chrétien ou Discours moraux* (1752, 2 vols.); *L'Anti-sans-souci, ou La Folie des nouveaux philosophes naturalistes, déistes et autres impies, dépeints au naturel* (1761). He contributed articles to the *Encyclopédie française*, the *Nouvelles littéraires*, and the *Journal encyclopédique*. He left a vast correspondence of some 120,000 letters, largely unexplored, which is preserved in the archives of the Academy, now in East Berlin.

Baculard d'Arnaud, Le Guay de Prémontval, and Toussaint spent some years in Berlin. François-Vincent Toussaint (1715–72) was a Jansenist before becoming a *philosophe*. He was an early friend of Diderot, and was associated with him in the translation of James's *Medicinal Dictionary*. He shared with the young Diderot an emotional deism.

He extolled virtue, the passions, and 'enthusiasm', preferring the virtuous man to the *honnête homme* before Rousseau. In *Les Mœurs* (1748), which were completed by *Eclaircissements* (1762), we have one of the earliest expositions of a *morale naturelle* independent of any religious belief or cult. The Parlement of Paris condemned it to be burnt. He contributed articles on jurisprudence to the first two volumes of the *Encyclopédie* until he went to Belgium, where he edited the *Gazette française*. Although he had referred to Frederick the Great as 'le brigand du Nord', the latter invited him to fill the chair of logic and rhetoric at his Military Academy. Toussaint's publications include: *Lettre sur les avantages et les inconvénients de l'imprimerie* (1751), *Essai sur le rachat des rentes et des redevances* (1751), and *Histoire des passions ou Aventures du chevalier Shroop* (1751), a philosophical novel in two volumes.

Jean-Baptiste de Boyer, marquis d'Argens (1703 or 1704–71),

was a sceptical philosopher and free-thinker who moved to Holland so that he could write freely, and then to Prussia where Frederick II appointed him chamberlain, and where he remained for twenty-five years as literary factotum, editing and publishing for the king. He became one of the leading polemical writers of the philosophical party through the publication of bi-weekly *Lettres*, in the form of periodical *demi-feuilles* which were issued from The Hague. The *Lettres juives, chinoises et cabalistiques* (1736–40) are three distinct works, for which he himself suggested the collective title *Correspondance philosophique*, and comprise eighteen volumes of philosophical and social theory and gossip. He also wrote a *Philosophie du bon sens* (2 vols., 1737) and *Mémoires secrets de la république des lettres* (1737–48), which he revised and extended and incorporated in *Histoire de l'esprit humain* (14 vols., 1765–68). In the tenth volume will be found some information on the collaboration of the Abbé Yvon in the *Apologie de l'abbé de Prades* and on the life of de Prades in Prussia.

D'Argens' early work is the more interesting. He wrote *Réflexions sur le goût* (1743), a work of purely literary criticism; some translations, especially a *Défense du paganisme* by the Emperor Julian, whom he greatly admired; *Mémoires de M. le marquis d'Argens* (1735), which still hold the reader's interest; and *Songes philosophiques* (1746). Most of his works were frequently reprinted in the eighteenth century. He was loyal to Frederick II, who, in his later years, treated him badly. Their final break, which occurred in 1769, was due to a misunderstanding over a projected return to Berlin. There was never more than minor friction with Voltaire: the patriarch of Ferney had a certain affection for 'frère Isaac', as he called him, who had supported him against Maupertuis. In a letter dated 1 February 1771, Voltaire wrote to him: 'C'était un philosophe gai, sensible et vertueux.'

VI. THE ANTI-ENCYCLOPAEDISTS

There were a number of anti-Encyclopaedists, hopelessly outnumbered and outclassed, who stood by the teaching of the Church, and the traditional values. They were for the most part members of the clergy or of the privileged nobility. Those with power manifested their displeasure by having recourse to the courts or to forms of repression, or by appeals to the king. Few were writers and fewer writers of any distinction, for in a century that required wit for literary survival, they were singularly lacking in that quality.

The apologists of the Catholic Church have been the object of a detailed study by Albert Monod, in *De Pascal à Chateaubriand, les défenseurs français du christianisme de 1670 à 1802* (1916), who lists some 600 titles for the years 1740–90, and who has indicated the concessions made to the *philosophes* in Catholic theology on such issues as attitude towards nature and reason, morality, and original sin. More recently in *Catholics and Unbelievers in Eighteenth-century France* (1939) R. R. Palmer has endeavoured to redress the balance by examining most carefully the background of Catholic theology. But if the orthodox thinkers do not deserve quite so deep an oblivion as they have fallen into, they had neither the gift of expression of the leading *philosophes*, nor real originality of mind, nor were their utterances in keeping with the dominant spirit of the period, and the advances in scientific knowledge. The archbishops, and bishops, fulminated from the pulpit and in *mandements*, but there was among them no orator, nor any convincing champion of their cause. If the names of Nonotte (author of a *Dictionnaire philosophique de la religion*), of Chaumeix (author of *Préjugés légitimes contre l'Encyclopédie*, 8 vols., 1758, the most ambitious work directed against the *Encyclopédie*), of Lefranc de Pompignan, bishop of Puy (author of *Avertissement du clergé sur les dangers de l'incrédulité*, 1770), are remembered, it is thanks only to Voltaire's diatribes. Some virulent religious pamphlets appeared, but showed no originality of mind or talent, so that Voltaire's prayer: 'Mon Dieu! rendez nos ennemis bien ennuyeux!' was answered. None knew how to handle irony. Mention may be made of the Abbé Yvon, a simple man who contributed a number of orthodox articles to the *Encyclopédie* and wrote an *Histoire philosophique de la religion* (1779), of Barruel, the abbé de Crillon, of the Abbé Trublet,[13] the Abbé Houteville, the Abbé Bullet. They based their faith on revelation.

Berruyer in his *Histoire du peuple de Dieu* (1728–58) stressed the need for interpreting the scriptures in the light of contemporary belief, and held strongly to the Catholic contention that the Bible cannot be set up as an independent authority for the true faith, arguing with conviction against the Protestant standpoint. He claimed that the Church was not hidebound by tradition, but should assert at any given moment its interpretation of a changeless doctrine through the pronouncements of its spokesmen, thereby giving life to the creed. He carried little weight, however, with

[13] The Abbé Trublet (1697–1770) shared with Fontenelle and La Motte (on whom he published memoirs in 1759) a dislike of verse, and he incurred Voltaire's displeasure for his attack on *La Henriade*. His *Pensées choisies sur l'incrédulité* appeared in 1737. His *Panégyriques des saints suivis de réflexions sur l'éloquence* is no more than an exercise in style. His *Essais de morale et de littérature* (2 vols., 1735) is devoid of originality. He published in 1754 an edition of Maupertuis' *Essai sur la formation des corps organisés.*

the unbelievers, who ridiculed the rococo trappings he gave to his serious apologia of Catholicism. Dom Augustin Calmet (1672–1757), a distinguished Benedictine monk, was a better scholar. He taught philosophy and theology at the age of eighteen and rapidly acquired a knowledge of oriental languages. He founded in the abbey of Munster an academy devoted to the study of the Holy Scriptures. His *Commentaire littéral sur tous les livres de l'Ancien et du Nouveau Testament* (22 vols., 1707–16, reprinted in 9 vols., 1724–26) is a work of much learning which he summed up in his *Dictionnaire critique, historique et chronologique de la Bible* (4 vols., 1722–28). Other works include: *Histoire ecclésiastique et civile de la Lorraine* (1728); *Histoire généalogique de la maison du Châtelet, branche puînée de la maison de Lorraine* (1741); *Histoire universelle et profane* (9 vols., 1735–61); *Trésor d'antiquités sacrées et profanes* (3 vols., 1722). Dom Calmet was a disinterested man who refused a bishopric in order to pursue his research. His great erudition was not matched by a sound historical method or critical acumen. He and his fellow Benedictines, however, made a real contribution to scholarship, unlike controversialists such as the Jesuit P. Sennemaud (*Pensées philosophiques d'un citoyen de Montmartre*, 1756), or the Jansenist L. Troya d'Assigny (*Saint-Augustin contre l'incrédulité*, 1754; *Saint-Augustin en contraste avec les philosophes du siècle*, 1770).

Perhaps the best anti-Encyclopaedist was the Abbé Guénée (1717–1803) who showed flashes of wit in his *Lettres de quelques juifs portugais, allemands et polonais à M. de Voltaire, avec un petit commentaire extrait d'un plus grand* (1759), which quickly ran to five editions. The most famous and respected was the Abbé Bergier, whose style was ponderous and who wrote at very great length.[14] In his vast work *Certitude des preuves du Christianisme* (1773), a reply to the sceptical views of Fréret, he staked all on the truth of miracles, as does the Abbé G. Gauchat[15] who states that 'Les miracles évangéliques sont sensés', by which the *philosophes* were able to infer that Christian miracles are less miraculous than those of the pagans. The level of the debate was low. The archbishop of Paris insisted on the right of the Church to persecute its opponents because they were in the wrong, and consequently certain of eternal damnation, from which their souls had to be rescued by force if necessary. He asked Marmontel to retract formally a statement made in 1767 in favour of toleration: 'On

[14] His works include: *Examen du matérialisme* (1771); *Le Déisme réfuté par lui-même* (1771); and contributions on theology to the *Encyclopédie méthodique*.

[15] Author of *Lettres critiques, ou Analyse et réfutation de divers écrits modernes contre la religion* (1755–63).

n'éclaire pas les esprits avec les feux des bûchers.' The bishop of Puy wrote: 'Tout impie est, par cela seul, criminel d'Etat.'[16]

The Catholic critic Elie-Catherine Fréron (1718–76) was a vigorous opponent of the *philosophes* in another field. His opposition was political and literary. He went so far as to denounce the printers of the *Encyclopédie* to the police. His shrewd critical faculty found an outlet in the *Année littéraire* which he founded in 1754, and in which he reviewed the chief literary productions of the day. Fréron, who was imprisoned first at Vincennes in 1746, then in the Bastille in 1757, and who narrowly escaped a third term of detention in 1765, was an affable man in private life; but his vitriolic criticism and his genuine perspicacity and wit led him to incur the undying displeasure of Voltaire, who poured ridicule on him in satirical verse, and in *L'Ecossaise* (1760). Fréron left a son who took over *L'Année littéraire* at his death until 1790. His views were not those of his father, for he became a significant French revolutionary journalist, bringing out *L'Orateur du peuple* in 1789. He assumed the leadership of the *jeunesse dorée* during the Thermidorian reaction.

An interesting and enigmatical thinker is Dom Deschamps (1716–74), a Benedictine monk and yet an unbeliever whose general position closely parallels that of the Curé Meslier. In 1769 he wrote what purported to be an outspoken attack on the Encyclopaedists entitled *Lettres sur l'esprit du siècle*, but a close examination of the work reveals his latent materialism. He was in touch with Rousseau, Diderot, and many other *philosophes*, and Diderot, after meeting him, characterised him as an apostle of materialism. After reading d'Holbach's *Système de la nature* and Robinet's *De la Nature*, Dom Deschamps evolved a rational theology that is indistinguishable from materialism and the philosophical ideas that foreshadow some of Hegel's principles, and lead to a dialectical explanation of reality. His social ideas are to be found in his *Observations morales* (post–1770) which, together with a *Préface* and *Observations métaphysiques*, constitute *Le Vrai Système ou Le Mot de l'énigme métaphysique et morale*, which J. Thomas and F. Venturi edited in 1963. He lived in the château des Ormes, home of the family d'Argenson, and, a short time before his death, moved back to his own monastery which was in the vicinity. He was granted the last rites of the Church. Cases such as his, which hold a peculiar fascination for the state of mind

[16] For information on the position of the Church, see John McManners, *French Ecclesiastical Society under the Ancien Régime* 1969. Basil Guy, following Carl Becker and R. R. Palmer, has urged a reappraisal of the *abbé de cour*, often more enlightened than is thought, in 'Towards an appreciation of the *abbé de cour*', *Yale Studies*, 1968, pp. 77–90.

they reveal, bring out very clearly the main direction of contemporary thought, and the inherent weakness of the position of the anti-Encyclopaedists in an age of disbelief.

There were, of course, men who retained their faith, like the prince de Ligne, without allowing themselves to become involved in controversies. Charles-Joseph, prince de Ligne (1735–1814) was born in Brussels, the capital of the Austrian Netherlands. He was the son of Claude Lamoral, head of a family established in Hainault, ranking as princes of the Holy Roman Empire from 1601, and owned the château of Beloeil, near Mons, one of the great houses of Europe. He made his military reputation during the Seven Years War, rising to the rank of field-marshal (1808) in the Austrian forces, but he was also a diplomat and writer. He had a perfect command of the French tongue, and entered into a witty correspondence with Voltaire and others. He was liked and trusted by Marie-Antoinette and by Joseph II of Austria, whom he assisted at an otherwise private interview with Frederick the Great in 1770. He was received by Marie-Antoinette at Versailles, and by Catherine II (1782), who gave him a property in the Crimea. He was present at the siege of Ochakov, which was directed by Potemkin, and at the taking of Belgrade under Laudon (1789). The death of his son, killed in action in 1792, left him disconsolate and he retired to Vienna. There he received distinguished men and took some comfort in literature. He died during the Congress of Vienna in 1814. His works, all written in French, were published in thirty volumes between 1795 and 1809. They deal for the most part with military tactics, but contain some masterpieces of literary style and some perceptive comments on the great literary men of the age. He had a vivid style, and wrote with a singular charm and the studied negligence of a man of quality.

VII. SCIENTISTS

Science and philosophy were closely linked. The *philosophes* were often scientists who considered the methodology of science, and were not exclusively concerned with the benefits new scientific and technological discoveries would bring in their train. Scientific truth appeared to them as the one certainty, the absolute after which they were striving, and an adequate substitute for metaphysical speculations, which could only prove in the end to be abortive. They all stressed the empirical approach to knowledge, which they attributed to Locke and to Bacon, without, however, dismissing deductive reasoning or the need for hypotheses. Diderot in particular stressed the importance of intuition in the discovery of the secrets of nature, and made extensive use of analogy in his approach to understanding. Although his *Pensées sur l'interprétation de la nature* were not well understood by his contemporaries, they constitute the *discours de la méthode* of the century.

The strength of the new movement lay in the powers of observation of its leading figures, and in their ability to interpret their data on fruitful lines. They were helped by numerous works which popularised science, including translations of scientific works by English and German writers, many of which ran to a number of reprints. The following titles may be listed: the Abbé J.-A. Nollet (1700–37): *Leçons de physique expérimentale* (6 vols., 1743); *Essai sur l'électricité des corps* (1750); A. de Jussieu (1686–1758); the author of *Mémoires* on zoology, botany, anatomy, and the mercury mines of Almaden, published by the Académie des Sciences, and the first to make known the flower and fruit of the coffee plant. His brother, B. de Jussieu (1699–1777), enjoyed a high reputation as a botanist; his nephew popularised his natural method for the classification of plants. The Abbé N.-A. Pluche (1688–1761) wrote *Le Spectacle de la nature* (8 t. in 9 vols., 1732) which dealt with physics, natural history, etc.; this work, frequently reprinted, was translated into almost all languages. The Jesuit C. Buffier (1661–1737), a collaborator of the *Journal de Trévoux*, published in 1732 a *Cours des sciences*, and popularised the physics of Newton. The works of Malpighi, Boerhaave (1668–1738), van Musschenbroek (1682–1761), Hartsoeker, Nieuwentijdt (*De l'Existence de Dieu démontrée par les merveilles de la nature* appeared under this title in 1725), A. de Haller (1708–77), Akenside (1721–1770), were well known often through translations, as were William Denham's *Physico-Theology* (1713) and *Astro-Theology* (1715); and J. T. Needham's *An account of some microscopical discoveries* (1745; translated into French in 1747). Count F. Algarotti, whom Voltaire called his 'cher cygne de Padoue', is the author of *Newtonianismo per le dame*, translated into French as *Le Système de Newton mis à la portée des dames*. These men, and many others, provided information which the Encyclopaedists could digest, use, modify, and interpret, and disseminated new scientific data to a relatively large public, creating a climate of opinion favourable to scientific speculation. The intellectual approach which was to characterise the scientists is to be seen in Montesquieu, for instance, who examined particular institutions and *mores* before moving on to more ambitious and vaster, as well as more general, considerations; in Turgot and Condorcet, who examined local government before attempting to lay the foundations of a new political science; and in Voltaire who examined specific aspects of history before the broad sweeps of civilisation, and who evolved his critical method and defined his objectives only after making a detailed study of a limited period.

In the field of science, physics advanced very quickly and, after Voltaire's intervention, Newtonian physics became the most widely accepted theory and led to a renewal of interest in astronomy and geography. Scientific progress soon extended to mathematics, with d'Alembert, La Condamine, and others; geometry, with Lagrange and Monge; algebra, with Laplace; electricity, with Coulomb; chemistry, with Lavoisier who discovered oxygen and was the founder of this science: all made enormous strides, leading directly or indirectly to interest in new sciences, particularly the biological sciences, which developed in different ways.

Réaumur (1683–1757), a physicist well known for the thermometer he invented and which bears his name, showed even greater originality as a naturalist in his work on insects,[17] whose anatomy and social habits he examined, and proved conclusively that corals were not plants. The Académie des Sciences entrusted to Réaumur the *Description des divers arts et métiers*, and the range of expertise shown by the later Encyclopaedists in their scientific articles is remarkable. Diderot, writing on the problems of the blind, indicated before Braille a method by which the blind could be made to read. He speculated on the genesis of life and showed proficiency in mathematical subjects, in physics, in music, and in physiology (drafting *Eléments de physiologie* after reading Haller's work on the subject). He followed Fontenelle's example and broadened the whole range of science within the field of literature, by expounding scientific speculations through fictitious dialogues, and in a highly stylised literary form.

The development of biological sciences and medicine is particularly noteworthy, in view of its repercussions on the philosophy and social and political thought of the latter part of the eighteenth century, and of the whole of the nineteenth century. Trembley, a relative of Charles Bonnet, examined in 1740 the functions of the polyp and concluded that it was an animal. His findings were published in 1744, and this discovery, shattering as it did the usual division between the animal and the vegetable kingdom, affected diversely but deeply La Mettrie, Maupertuis, Buffon, Robinet, and Diderot. For Maupertuis living matter was composed of *molécules séminales*, whose activity could be accounted for by the force of attraction. In *La Vénus physique* he had already developed Leibniz's theory of monads, endowing his molecules with an internal principle of activity and an internal finality, and he adopted Leibniz's theory of continuity and change. Maupertuis, like Dr Bordeu and Diderot, believed in an organic sensitivity, a considerable step

[17] *Mémoires pour servir à l'histoire des insectes*, 6 vols., 1734–42.

forward on Locke's theory of sentient matter. It now became possible to see the universe as living, self-sufficient, and self-regenerating, perpetually reforming itself through a process of ordered change.

The completion of the Linnaean binomial system in 1753 posed a threat to traditional theology; but the speculative transformism of Maillet (as expressed in *Telliamed*), Robinet's belief in a process of trial and error as adequate to account for the creation of man, and Bonnet's, and especially Diderot's, evolutionary doctrine, went further by providing a firm basis for a truly dialectical materialism. Buffon seems to have hesitated over accepting the full consequences of evolution. He believed in indestructible organic molecules, but showed great caution, as when he spoke of 'une assez petite famille de souches principales desquelles il n'est pas impossible que toutes les autres soient issues'. Laplace for his part evolved a theory of planetary evolution; whilst Diderot extended the principle of evolution to the whole universe, live or allegedly dead.

At the turn of the century Lamarck, a pupil of Buffon who was much scoffed at by Cuvier (a devout Huguenot, who in fact succeeded Buffon), developed for the first time a thoroughgoing transformist theory in his *Philosophie zoologique*, even extending his evolutionary views on the origin of the species to the processes of the human mind. Medical speculation and research underpinned these theories. A new vitalism supplanted the mechanist speculations of medical men, who now saw illness as essentially a state of imbalance. Bordeu, Broussais, and Bichat laid the foundations of the modern science of medicine, establishing the study of physiology and anatomy on a new basis. The sciences of nature, i.e. biology and medicine, now determined the formulation of a new materialism. These developments soon led to the conception of a new science: sociology. The *idéologues* for their part believed that natural laws govern human relationships, as physical laws rule the universe. It followed that social organisation could become the subject of scientific investigation. In this sense men such as Monge, Berthollet, Bichat, Vicq-d'Azyr, and Cabanis may be held to be forerunners of socialism. Cabanis is particularly interesting in providing a link between the world of Condillac, Diderot, and the *philosophes*, especially Condorcet, and the philosophy of organism which Henri de Saint-Simon was to propound. But whereas in their philosophy Condillac and Cabanis had followed Locke's egalitarian concept of man, Saint-Simon, as did Diderot and Bichat, stressed the genetic inequality between men and the differences in their aptitudes. The existence of an élite, either biologically superior or better adapted to the needs of society, led Saint-Simon to commend technocracy as the best form of government.

The most widely respected scientist of the period who can lay claims to being a great writer was Buffon. George-Louis Leclerc (1707–88), who became comte de Buffon in 1772, was educated by the Jesuits. He travelled with his English friend the duke of Kingston, in the south of France, Italy, Switzerland, and especially in England; and on his return he undertook works on mathematics and physics. In 1733 he became a *membre adjoint* of the Académie des Sciences and in 1739 he was appointed *Intendant du Jardin et du Cabinet du Roi*, now the Jardin des Plantes. He continued, however, to spend eight months in the year at Montbard in Burgundy, and for forty years from 1744 he worked on his *Histoire complète et scientifique de la nature*, the first three volumes (*Terre, Histoire de l'homme*) appearing in 1749; there followed twelve volumes (*Quadrupèdes vivipares*) in 1753–78; nine volumes (*Oiseaux*) in 1770–83; five volumes (*Minéraux*) in 1783–88; and seven volumes of *Suppléments* in 1774–89, which include his *Discours sur le style* (1777) and *Epoques de la nature* (1778). His work was completed by Lacépède in 1789, after his death in 1788. In all the *Histoire naturelle* consists of thirty-six volumes. Buffon had as collaborators Daubenton, Guéneau de Montbéliard, the Abbé Bexon, and Faujas de Saint-Fond, but the work is essentially his own in conception and style.

Drawing on observation and personal experience, Buffon reacted against the arbitrary classifications of Linnaeus and others, stressing the unity of creation and establishing a gradation of species with man at the head of the universe. In some eloquent passages he shows his gift for philosophical generalities in the grand manner. He divided the history of the earth into seven epochs. The world, at first a mass of fire, became a continent covered by the sea. He boldly surveyed the great cataclysms of nature, mingling geology and scientific facts with imaginative poetry, as if he himself were present at the dramatic events he conjured up. The writing has grandeur and majesty, life and a lyrical movement. It conforms to his somewhat old-fashioned views on style as expressed in his *Discours sur le style*, originally his address to the French Academy, which had elected him to its membership in 1753. It contains much advice and many definitions, the best known of which, 'Le style est l'ordre et le mouvement qu'on met dans ses pensées', applies particularly well to his own writing. His harmonious prose takes us back to the rhetoric of Bossuet. These early volumes with their cult of science fired Diderot's imagination when he first read them during his detention at Vincennes (1749), and Diderot's subsequent excitement and sense of wonder at his own materialistic conception of the universe, which can be likened to the illumination of a deeply religious man, has a lyricism which echoes that of

Buffon, to whose stimulus it was in part due. Buffon gave the universe a new image, and his thought, evolving as the volumes succeed one another, echoes the scientific achievements of the period. In the early volumes, he shows his belief in the fixity of species individually created by God; he becomes increasingly anthropocentric, the ultimate purpose of God being the greater good of men. But the realisation that species were scattered in the world, and yet seemed to have a common ancestry, that those found in the New World argued in favour of some process of adaptation, led him to adopt transformist views, and ultimately to question any universal, permanent order of things. He never wavered in his anthropocentrism. In *Les Epoques de la nature,* however, which may be considered as marking the last stage in his thought, man is subordinated to nature. Buffon then turns visionary, and for him nature becomes God. He came very near to pantheism. His language matched the grandeur of his thought, and the majesty and power of his prose bear witness to his poetic genius. His descriptions, whether of epochs or of animals, are unforgettable, even though they are now judged to be unscientific, with demonstrable errors and lacunae. Even if his science is outdated, he has the merit of having seen the coming importance of geology and of palaeontology. He was the first scientist to try to deal scientifically with the problem of the origin of the species, and his predictions were remarkably accurate in a number of cases. He foresaw to some degree the Revolution which came to pass in 1789. He believed in the plurality of inhabited worlds; he envisaged the piercing of the Suez Canal; he guessed the coming importance of coal as a source of power; and put forward the possibility of an instrument capable of reproducing speech.

Buffon was not greatly in sympathy with the Encyclopaedists, for he was fastidious in his ways and lacked courage when it came to dealing with religion or politics, but the Encyclopaedists saw in him a useful ally, and rated his *Histoire naturelle* as one of the three or four great achievements of the century. His reputation in his own day was second only to that of Voltaire and Rousseau.

VIII. MORALISTS

The moralists – if we restrict the term to writers of maxims, detached thoughts, and portraits – were cradled in the salons: it was there that their reputation was made, and where they found their public. The stamp of the great moralists of the seventeenth century is to be found in the works of novelists from Lesage and Marivaux to Laclos, and in that of many playwrights, as well as in those of Rousseau and Diderot. Among those who have a claim to the title are two writers primarily known as historians: Rollin in his *Traité des études* (1726–28), which is the work of a pedagogue as well as of a moralist; and Duclos in his *Considérations sur les Mœurs de ce siècle* (1751). But the names of three writers stand out above all others: Vauvenargues, Chamfort, and Rivarol.

Luc de Clapiers, marquis de Vauvenargues (1715–47), began his career as a soldier, but during the army's retreat from Prague in the War of the Austrian Succession, in 1742, both his legs were seriously frostbitten. He returned to France in 1743 in very poor health, and with little else than the rank of captain to his credit. He resigned his commission in 1744 and came to live in Paris, where he became the friend of Marmontel and Voltaire. His misfortunes continued; he failed to obtain a post in the diplomatic service, and he caught smallpox, which left him disfigured and a chronic invalid. He lived on in great physical and mental pain, showing enormous fortitude in his suffering, till his death in 1747. In spite of his sad life and lack of recognition, his philosophy is optimistic and may properly be opposed to the pessimism of La Rochefoucauld and the melancholy of Chamfort. Vauvenargues believed in a kind nature, and in the beauty of an active life devoted to a good cause, even if it ended in apparent failure. He saw in such a life the *gloire* which inspired Corneille's heroes and heroines, and he paid tribute to the exaltation of the will and to all the stoical virtues. He glorified the passions, which he stated as fine in themselves, and as the prime motivating force of the will. Many of his maxims are justly famous for their content and their style:

> Les grandes pensées, viennent du coeur.
> La raison nous trompe plus souvent que la nature.
> C'est un grand signe de médiocrité de louer toujours modérément.

These and many others are to be found in his *Introduction à la connaissance de l'esprit humain* (1746), to which was appended *Réflexions sur divers sujets*, *Conseil à un jeune homme*, and *Réflexions critiques sur quelques poètes*. His ethics are founded on sentiment. He believed in altruism, in following nature, and in rehabilitating the instincts. His direct influence was slight, but his work reflects a shift from cold reason to sentiment, which Rousseau and Diderot, among others, were to illustrate more fully.

Whereas Vauvenargues was an incurable optimist in spite of the tragic circumstances of his life, Chamfort was a bitter misanthropist in spite of his success, and his wit had the biting irony of a sensitive and deeply wounded man.

Sébastien-Roch-Nicolas Chamfort (1741–94) had an attractive

personality and his charm led to his success in literary circles. Up to the French Revolution he spoke with enthusiasm of the *Tiers Etat*, and is credited with the words which head a pamphlet by Sieyès: 'Qu'est-ce que le Tiers-Etat? – Tout. – Qu'a-t-il? Rien.' – and also the much-quoted: 'Guerre aux châteaux! Paix aux chaumières!' But he was shocked at the violence and excesses of the Revolution, and sided with the moderates. To escape from the horrors of prison with which he was faced, he tried to kill himself with a razor and a pistol, but only succeeded in inflicting terrible wounds upon himself, from which he died soon after. As he lay dying he said to Sieyès: 'Ah! mon ami, je m'en vais enfin de ce monde, où il faut cœur se brise ou se bronze.' His *Maximes et Pensées, Caractères et anecdotes* were published posthumously by his friend Ginguené in 1795. They were part of a vast book which Chamfort never completed. The maxims are in the tradition of the eighteenth century, but reflect the melancholy mood prevailing at the time of the Revolution. The following may be quoted as examples:

> La plus perdue de toutes nos journées est celle où on n'a pas ri.
> Il y a une mélancholie qui tient à la grandeur de l'esprit.
> Il y a des redites pour l'oreille et pour l'esprit, il n'y en a point pour le cœur.

He knew how to tell an anecdote, as in the following passage:

> M. de Voltaire, passant par Soissons, reçut la visite des députés de l'Académie de Soissons, qui disaient que cette Académie était la fille aînée de l'Académie Française: 'Oui, Messieurs,' répondit-il, 'la fille aînée, fille sage, fille honnête, qui n'a jamais fait parler d'elle.'

or:

> On faisait une procession avec la châsse de sainte Geneviève, pour obtenir de la sécheresse. A peine la procession fut-elle en route, qu'il commença à pleuvoir. Sur quoi l'évêque de Castres dit plaisamment: 'Le sainte se trompe; elle croit qu'on lui demande de la pluie.'

He had a brilliant wit. When the revolutionaries came out with the slogan 'Fraternité ou la mort', he summed up their views in his own words: 'Sois mon frère, ou je te tue.'

Chamfort is also the author of two comedies, *La Jeune Indienne* (1764) and *Le Marchand de Smyrne* (1770), a tragedy, *Mustapha et Zéangir* (1776),[18] an *Eloge de Molière*, crowned in 1766 by the Académie Française, and an *Eloge de la Fontaine*, crowned in 1774 by the Académie de Marseille. Although he was a member of the French Academy he wrote a *Discours sur les Académies* which

[18] Published in 1777, a reworking of Belin's tragedy of the same name (1705).

strongly attacked them. This address was given by Mirabeau to the Assemblée Nationale, and published one month after the death of Mirabeau in 1791. In spite of rejoinders by Suard and Morellet, the *Discours* led to the suppression of all academies in 1793, but in 1795, with the founding of the Institut de France, they were re-established.

Like Chamfort, Antoine Rivarol (1755–1801) was a brilliant conversationalist, whose dazzling wit shone in the salons. He wrote a number of pamphlets, and a *Discours sur l'universalité de la langue française* which won him fame and a pension from Louis XVI. He made many enemies by publishing his *Petit Almanach des grands hommes pour l'année 1788*. During the Revolution he sided with the royalists, and wrote a *Petit Almanach des grands hommes de la Révolution*, which added politicians to his literary enemies. He was driven into exile in 1792, going first to Brussels, then to London and to Hamburg. He started work on a *Dictionnaire de la langue française*, publishing only its *Discours préliminaire* (1797). By the end of the year 1800 he was in Berlin, where he died a few months later.

Perhaps the most famous line of his *Discours sur l'universalité de la langue française*, which was crowned by the Berlin Academy, is the following: 'Ce qui n'est pas clair n'est pas français.' Many of his maxims, which were recorded in *Carnets*, are justly famous:

L'imprimerie est l'artillerie de la pensée.
Un livre qu'on soutient est un livre qui tombe.
Mirabeau était capable de tout pour de l'argent, même d'une bonne action.

Il y a grande distinction à faire entre la majorité arithmétique et la majorité politique d'un Etat.

Un peu de philosophie écarte de la religion, et beaucoup y ramène. Bacon a dit ceci de la religion, et il a voulu faire entendre que, lorsqu'on revient à elle, c'est qu'elle nous rappelle par son côté politique.

IX. HISTORIANS

Many *philosophes* were also known as historians, and their contributions combining a study of history with a philosophical or political commentary on contemporary events have been examined under other headings. Voltaire remains the only historian with a critical method that may be questioned in its detail and application, but which can be acknowledged as scientific. Other historians offer information, mostly uncritical, and are only examined today for their expression of eighteenth-century opinion and their relation to the philosophic movement as a whole. The following works may be listed:

Dom Bernard de Montfaucon (1655–1741): *procureur-général* of the Benedictine Congregation of Saint-Maur, famous for its scholars; published a monumental *Antiquité expliquée et réprésentée en figures*, in Latin and in French, in 10 volumes with a supplement in 5 volumes, during 1719–24. This work, of which 1,800 copies were sold in the first two months after publication, an unprecedented achievement for a study of this kind, was instrumental in developing a widespread interest in archaeology.

Rollin (1661–1714): *Histoire ancienne des Egyptiens, Carthaginois, Assyriens, Babyloniens, Mèdes, Perses, Macédoniens, Grecs* (12 vols., 1730); *Histoire romaine* (9 vols., 1738).

Rapin-Thoyras (1661–1723): *Histoire d'Angleterre depuis l'établissement des Romains jusqu'à la mort de Charles I* (8 vols., 1724).

The Abbé Dubos (1670–1742): *Histoire critique de l'établissement de la monarchie dans les Gaules* (1734).

J.-I. Berruyer (1681–1758): *Histoire du peuple de Dieu* (1728).

Président Hénault (1685–1770): *Abrégé chronologique de l'histoire de France* (1744).

Duclos (1704–72): *Histoire de Louis XI* (1745); *Mémoires secrets sur les règnes de Louis XIV et de Louis XV* (published 1791); *Considérations sur l'Italie* (1766–67, published 1791).

The Abbé Velly (1709–57): *Histoire de France depuis Clovis* (1755).

Président de Brosses (1709–77): *Histoire de la république romaine dans le cours du VIIe siècle* (1777).

The Abbé de Mably: *Observations sur l'histoire de France* (1765); *De la Manière d'écrire l'histoire* (1783).

The Abbé Raynal (1713–96): *Histoire philosophique et politique des établissements et du commerce des Européens dans les deux Indes* (1770).

The Abbé Barthélemy (1716–95): *Voyage du jeune Anacharsis en Grèce* (1788), which may be considered as a novel.[19]

Anquetil (1723–1806): *Louis XIV, sa cour et la Régence* (1789); *Précis d'histoire universelle* (1797).

Rulhière (1735–91): *Histoire de l'anarchie de Pologne* (1762).

Volney (1757–1820): *Les Ruines ou Méditations sur les révolutions des empires* (1791).[20]

All these writers, in so far as they were true historians, were completely outclassed by Voltaire.

19 See below, p. 354

20 Volney, who became a member of the Assemblée Constituante, is also the author of *Voyage en Egypte et en Syrie* (1787) and *La Loi naturelle ou Principes physiques de la morale déduite de l'organisation de l'homme et de l'univers* (1793).

X. CRITICS

The Querelle des Anciens et des Modernes gave rise to literary discussions on the subject of poetry, Mme Dacier upholding the classical ideal against La Motte in *Des Causes de la corruption du goût* (1714),[21] and theories on genres and on the various arts abound. Voltaire's literary theories expressed in *Le Temple du goût* (1738), *Commentaire sur Corneille* (1764), and elsewhere are essentially conservative and derive from the seventeenth-century classical tradition. He believed in the possibility of establishing criteria of taste, and his literary ideal is French classicism. Yet he modified his views to meet the general philosophical standpoint, as when he wrote in the article 'Goût' of the *Dictionnaire philosophique:* 'Le meilleur goût en tout genre est d'imiter la nature avec le plus de fidélité, de force et de grâce.' Marmontel's *Eléments de littérature* (6 vols., 1787) constitutes a first step towards a history of literature. The author, however, tends to make unsubstantial judgements and appears impressionistic. He shows at times considerable penetration and expresses himself with grace and elegance. His principles of criticism are close to those of Voltaire. Montesquieu, in his *Essai sur le goût*, developed an aesthetic based on humanism, underpinning his analysis of pleasure with general principles. These do not lead to a unique model which every artist must try to reproduce. Judgement is not formed *a priori*, but by a considered evaluation, based on psychology and historical experience.

Special mention of works on aesthetics may be made in view of the interest shown in this subject. The word 'aesthetic' was first used by A.-A. Baumgarten in 1735, and appeared as the title of a work *Aesthetica* in 1750; but earlier writers were groping towards a definition of beauty and the formulation of aesthetic principles generally applicable to all the arts or specific to each. The problem of the relationship between the arts interested most of the *philosophes*, and Condillac, Voltaire, Diderot, d'Alembert, Rousseau, Montesquieu, and Marmontel treated questions of aesthetics. Works of importance by other writers include:

Traité du beau (1715) by the Swiss writer J.-P. Crousaz, for whom beauty arises out of a relationship between an object and intellectual notions of personal approval associated with pleasant sentiment, i.e. with an individual's personal sense of reality.

Réflexions critiques sur la poésie et la peinture (2 vols., 1719),

[21] Later Louis Racine, in *Réflexions sur la poésie* (1747), and the Abbé N.-C.-J. Trublet (1697–1770) continued to support the aristocratic classical tradition.

by the Abbé J.-B. Dubos (1670–1742), is a more developed study with many interesting theories. He suggested the existence of a special sense which allows us to appreciate beauty, but he acknowledged the influence of external factors, thereby reintroducing the notion of the relativity of our aesthetic values.

Jacques Bonnet (1644–1724) wrote an *Histoire de la musique et de ses effets depuis son origine jusqu'à présent, et en quoi consiste sa beauté* (1715) and *Histoire générale de la danse sacrée et profane et le parallèle de la peinture et de la poésie, avec un supplément sur l'Histoire de la musique* (1723).[22]

Essai sur le beau (1741) by Père André marks a retrograde step, in that the author believes in an essential beauty independent of any criterion, and in a natural beauty independent of human opinions. He associated the beautiful with the true and the virtuous, and required a degree of unity for a work to justify being termed artistic.

The Abbé Batteux, in *Les Beaux-arts réduits à un seul principe* (1746), saw the fine arts as imitations of nature, and gives to reason the first and last word. His work was widely read but much criticised, in particular by Diderot. Aesthetic theories as expressed by Voltaire, by Montesquieu, in his *Essai sur le goût dans les choses de la nature et de l'art*, by Rousseau, in the *Lettre à d'Alembert*,[23] and by Condillac, in *Essai sur l'origine des connaissances humaines*,[24] are less important than those formulated in Germany by Winckelmann, Lessing, and Kant, and in England by Francis Hutcheson and Edmund Burke. Those of Diderot, however, which are to be found in the article 'Beau' of the *Encyclopédie* and developed more interestingly in the salons, and in the *Essai sur la peinture*, etc., have acquired a new importance in the light of a general revaluation of his philosophical, literary, and political ideas.

[22] M.-P.-G. de Chabanon (1730–92) is the author of *De la Musique considérée en elle-même et dans ses rapports avec la parole, les langues, la poésie et le théâtre* (1785), an important work for the comparative study of the various arts. He also wrote *Sur le sort de la poésie en ce siècle philosophe* (1764), and his best-documented work *Observations sur la musique et principalement sur la métaphysique de l'art* (1779).

The *Essai sur l'union de la poésie et de la musique* (1763) by F.-J. marquis de Chastellux follows the theories of Winckelmann in suggesting that art should improve upon nature. See also *Lettres sur les arts imitatifs en général et sur la danse en particulier* (1760) by J.-G. Noverre (1727–1810), a famous choreographer.

[23] C. Desprez de Boissy (1730–87), in *Lettres sur les spectacles avec une histoire des ouvrages pour et contre le théâtre* (1759, 1771), deals with the notion of the good and the beautiful in the theatre.

[24] Starting from Condillac's hypothesis of Phidias' statue, Charles Bonnet (1720–93), a Genevese naturalist and philosopher, evolved his own sensationalist philosophy, which makes room for inner observations and introspection side by side with pure analysis among the faculties of the mind, and foreshadowed in some respects Destutt de Tracy, and Maine de Biran in his *Essai analytique sur les facultés de l'âme* (1760).

XI. JOURNALS AND MEMOIRS

Family papers, letters, and state archives such as those of the Bastille, and the voluminous correspondence of Voltaire, Rousseau, and Diderot provide the reader with first-hand information. Another source is to be found in journals and memoirs.

The first daily to appear was *Le Journal de Paris ou Poste du soir* (1777–1811); but there were many weekly, fortnightly, and monthly journals. The literary historian will find most rewarding the *Correspondance littéraire* (1753–1813) first edited by Grimm,[25] a contributor being the Swiss J.-H. Meister (1744–1826), a man much influenced by Diderot and subsequently by Lavater who helped him regain his faith.[26] Meister, who started as Grimm's secretary, became editor of the *Correspondance littéraire* in March 1773. *Le Journal encyclopédique* (1756–93), a fortnightly, also spread the influence of the *Encyclopédie* to ever-widening circles. It was founded by Pierre Rousseau and printed at Bouillon. Among its contributors figure: Voltaire, Formey, Chamfort, Deleyre, Naigeon. In 1793 it merged with *L'Esprit des journaux*. P. Rousseau also founded and directed the Société Typographique which published: *Romans et contes* by Voltaire, *Essai sur les règnes de Claude et de Néron* by Diderot, *Analyse raisonnée de Bayle* by the abbé de Marsy, *Réflexions morales de Marc-Aurèle* and *Le Compère Mathieu* by Dulaurens. The *Journal politique, ou Gazette des gazettes* and the *Recueil philosophique et littéraire* (the first part of which is due to Robinet and to J.-L. Castillon) were also published at Bouillon. The contribution of Huguenot journalists publishing abroad deserves special mention. Apart from Formey's activities as editor and contributor to French journals to which reference has earlier been made, there is Michel de La Roche's *Bibliothèque anglaise, ou Histoire littéraire de la Grande Bretagne* (15 vols., 1717–28) and his *Mémoires littéraires de la Grande Bretagne* (1720–24), and sundry Dutch journals founded in the seventeenth century such as the *Histoire des ouvrages des savants*. The *Journal littéraire* (1713–22; 1729–36) published every two months at The Hague till 1715, then twice a year, is more of a literary journal than any other at the time. The weekly *Nouvelles littéraires* (1715–20) was also published at The Hague. There were also the *Journal britannique* (1750–57); *La Bibliothèque impartiale* (1750–58) directed by Elie Luzac *fils* and J.-H.-S. Formey; and the *Gazette de Leyde*, well known throughout Europe, which was published by members of the Luzac family.

[25] See above, p. 247.

[26] J.-H. Meister is the author of a translation from the German, *Nouvelles Idylles de Gessner* (1777), and of a great number of books.

Other journals include: d'Argens' *Lettres* and *Mémoires*;[27] *La Gazette de France*, a weekly, which started publication in 1688; *Le Mercure galant*, founded in 1672, which became *Le Mercure de France* in 1724, was reorganised by Marmontel in 1758 and continued till 1825; *Le Journal des savants* (1665–1792); *Le Journal de Trévoux* (1701–67), run by the Jesuits; *Les Nouvelles ecclésiastiques* (1728–1803), run by the Jansenists; *Le Spectateur français* (1722–23), *L'Indigent philosophe* (1728), *Le Cabinet du philosophe* (1734), all three produced by Marivaux; *Le Nouvelliste du Parnasse* (1730–32); *Les Observations sur les écrits modernes* (1735–43) and *Jugements sur quelques ouvrages nouveaux* (1744–45), produced by the Abbé Desfontaines; *Les Nouvelles littéraires de Londres* (1700–40); *Le Pour et Contre* (1733–40) by the Abbé Prévost; *Les cinq années littéraires* (1748–52) published by P. Clément at The Hague; *Bibliothèque raisonnée* (1728–53), to which Voltaire contributed reviews; *Bibliothèque germanique* (1720–41), also published in Amsterdam; the monthly *Bibliothèque française* (1723–42); *Bibliothèque italique* (1728–34); *Bibliothèque britannique* (1733–47); *Observations sur la littérature moderne* (1749–52), published every two months by the Abbé J. de La Porte; *Journal anglais* (1775–78); *Lettres sur quelques écrits de ce temps* (1749–54) and *L'Année littéraire* (1754–76) by Fréron, continued by his son and others till 1790; *L'Observateur littéraire* (1758–61) by the abbé de La Porte; *Le Journal économique* (1751–1752); *Le Journal étranger* (1754–62) and *Gazette littéraire de l'Europe* (1764–66), both edited by J.-P.-A. Suard and the Abbé Arnaud; *L'Avant-coureur* (1760–73); *Les Ephémérides du citoyen* (1765–72); *Le Journal de lecture* (1775–79); *Le Journal de littérature, des sciences et des arts* (1779–83); *Le Journal général de l'Europe* (1785–89); *Mercure Suisse* (1732–75); *Le Journal de politique et de littérature* (1777) by Linguet; *Les Annales politiques civiles et littéraires* (1777–92) by Linguet, except when the latter was detained in the Bastille when Mallet du Pan and Durey de Morsan took over (1780–83). With the proclamation in 1789 of the freedom to publish, which was reaffirmed in 1791, a large number of new journals saw the light of day and daily political newspapers were established. The ablest journalist of the Revolution was Camille Desmoulins (1760–94) who died on the scaffold. Madame Roland (1754–93), known for her 'liberal' salon and chief writer for the *Courrier de Lyon*, left letters, and memoirs of importance.

Another source of information on current literary, scientific, and political events is to be found in the memoirs of the times. In addition to those of the duc de Saint-Simon and others which have already been mentioned, reference should be made to those of

[27] See above, pp. 263–4.

Mathieu Marais (1664–1737), valuable for the study of the early years of the reign of Louis XV, and those of Louis Petit de Bachaumont (end of seventeenth century to 1771), published in six volumes under the title *Mémoires secrets pour servir à l'histoire de la république* in 1777, and continued by Mairobert and others who brought the total up to 36 volumes (1789). These were frequently re-edited in full or in an abridged form. Bachaumont, an amiable but indolent dilettante, picked up much of his information in the salon of a Mme Doublet, which specialised in literary, artistic, and political gossip, constituting a veritable newsgathering centre and also a centre for the distribution of news. Some of the items thus distributed were republished in the *Mémoires* (1777–89), which may thus be considered as a collective production. In political issues Bachaumont aligned himself with the parliamentarians, and was part of a philosophic set called the *patriots*, which was anti-clerical.

Bachaumont's work, often referred to as the *Journal de Bachaumont*, shows an undiscriminating taste and little critical acumen. He and his associates provided summaries of plays, reports on literary events, reviews of new publications, especially those printed in a clandestine manner or the sale of which was prohibited, many anecdotes, some previously unpublished texts, in prose and in verse, songs, *éloges académiques*, satires, sermons, etc., and more particularly *Salons* covering the biennial exhibitions from 1767 to 1787. He is the author of *Mémoires sur le Louvre, l'Opéra, la place Louis XV, les salles de spectacles, la bibliothèque du Roi* (1750), *Essai sur la peinture, la sculpture et l'architecture* (1751), and *Vers sur l'achèvement du Louvre* (1755). He was sometimes called 'la tête à perruque de M. de Voltaire', because he had adopted Voltaire's hairstyle. He also shared Voltaire's views on religion and his philosophical outlook.

The marquis d'Argens, who spent twenty-five years of his life in Frederick's circle, shared the king's cynicism and scepticism. He first came into prominence through the publication of *Lettres juives*, *Lettres chinoises*, *Lettres cabalistiques*. He wrote a *Philosophie du bon sens*, but it is his *Mémoires secrets de la république des lettres*, and *Mémoires du marquis d'Argens*, that are best remembered for their documentary value.

The *Journal et Mémoires de d'Argenson*, published by Rathery for the Société de l'Histoire de France (9 vols., 1859–67), is another valuable source of first-hand information. The *Correspondance littéraire secrète* (19 vols., 1775–93) and the *Correspondance secrète, politique et littéraire* (18 vols., 1787–90) by F. Métra is gossipy. J.-F. Marmontel's *Mémoires*, written in 1798, and A. Morellet's *Mémoires*, published in two volumes in 1821, are both favourable to Diderot and hostile to Rousseau.

The *Mémoires de Mme de Genlis* (1746–1831), which were published in 1825, are neither *confessions* in the sense Rousseau gave to the term, nor as objective as one would have liked. All those who admired her become great men in her own eyes. She disliked the *philosophes*, earning for herself the name 'Mère de l'Eglise', which M.-J. Chénier gave her. She could not draw a good portrait but she could tell amusing anecdotes and her remarks on Voltaire, Rousseau, Diderot, d'Alembert, Buffon, Saint-Lambert, Raynal, Marmontel, Bernardin de Saint-Pierre, La Harpe, and Palissot are not devoid of penetration. Most of her memoirs as recorded in *Souvenirs de Félicie* had appeared earlier in the *Bibliothèque des Romans*. She was a prolific writer on education, becoming the governess of the future King Louis-Philippe and writing charming books for children, and a *Théâtre d'éducation* (1799) on aesthetics; she was a *salonnière* and the author of a novel in letter-form, *Adèle et Théodore* (1782), another in the *genre troubadour*, *Les Chevaliers du Cygne* (1795, 3 vols.), of *Les Veillées du château*, and the *Dîners du baron d'Holbach* (1822). Her best novel, *Mademoiselle de Clermont*, although devoid of originality, illustrates her easy-flowing style, but of her eighty works only her *Mémoires* are consulted today. She played a dubious part during the French Revolution and after, being noted for her duplicity.

Chapter 12

THE THEATRE

I. GENERAL BACKGROUND

SOME knowledge of the general conditions prevailing in the French theatre during the century is a prerequisite for the understanding of the work of the playwrights. Since the publication in 1957 of J. Lough's *Paris Theatre Audiences in the Seventeenth and Eighteenth Centuries*, in 1967 of C. Alasseur's *La Comédie Française au XVIIIe siècle, étude économique*, and of other works dealing with the provincial theatre, a clearer picture of material conditions can be formed.[1]

The list of all plays put on at the Comédie Française during the period under review, together with the receipts derived from them, with an estimation of their value in real terms, are available, as are some incomplete registers of the Théâtre Italien. It is clear that in the course of the century the theatre in general became a more stable undertaking than heretofore, and its enjoyment an integral part of social life at all levels. The power of attraction exercised is well described in *La Nouvelle Héloïse*, part II, letter xxiii. The upper classes seem to have visited the Comédie Française twice a week regularly, and the Opéra once a week, for performances usually lasting from 6 p.m. to 9.30 p.m. They also invited reputable companies to act in their homes for private entertainment, and frequently joined with the professional actors to take part in the plays performed. Suitable halls, with stages designed by specialised architects, became an important and necessary addition at court, and in the palaces, castles, and town and country houses of the nobility and the wealthy.

At the end of his reign Louis XIV, now become devout and austere in his tastes, ceased to favour the Comédie Française; and in 1697 expelled the Italian players from their theatre. With the advent of Philippe, duc d'Orléans, however, there was a sudden change for the better in the fortunes of the theatre. It became

[1] See also: C. Brenner, *A Bibliographical list of plays in the French language, 1770-89*, 1947; A Joannidès, *La Comédie-Française de 1680 à 1920*, 1921; H. Carrington Lancaster, *The Comédie Française 1701–1774 (Plays, Actors, Spectators, Finances)*, 1951; Claude and François Parfaict, *Dictionnaire des théâtres de Paris*, 6 vols., 1756.

increasingly fashionable to go to the theatre, and all visiting monarchs and dignitaries would be invited to spend a gala evening there. The public was much the same as that of the previous century, with the aristocracy prominent in patronage and the best seats, while bourgeoisie, students, and artisans filled the *parterre*, where there were no seats, forming a vociferous group whose judgement authors grew increasingly to respect. Performances lasted anything from two to four hours, with two plays given nightly.

As conditions improved materially, particularly with the removal of the Comédie Française from the Jeu de Paume, Rue des Fossés Saint-Germain (now Rue de l'Ancienne Comédie), which it had occupied since 1687, to the Tuileries in 1770 and to the Odéon in 1782, authors complained more bitterly. They preferred the lively and critical *parterre* of students and artisans in the Ancienne Comédie to the cruder and less intelligent patrons of the Tuileries. As time went on, the vital part of the audience was increasingly to be found among the motley bourgeois crew crowding the *parterre*. These could afford to attend only by making considerable financial sacrifice; but the mass of the people were debarred by cost until towards the end of the century.

The old attitudes prevailed in the Church. All actors were still treated as a lower and vicious order of mankind. In 1730 Adrienne Lecouvreur, one of the greatest actresses the world has ever known, died and was refused Christian burial. All actors were automatically excommunicated; and the Italian players under Riccoboni never ceased to protest against an excommunication which was not the rule of Rome itself. They made such public show of their perfectly genuine religious principles and practice that they gradually swayed public opinion in favour of less arbitrary judgements. Prelates were sometimes seen at the theatre in Paris, but they remained basically hostile and suspicious. Yet even in Geneva, in spite of Calvinism and Rousseau, the theatre opened again; but Voltaire did not live to see this triumph of his views.

In view of the fact that a vast number of people were unable to attend the theatre, a few free performances were put on from time to time. Until 1753 only comedies were given free. In 1765 a tragedy, *Le Siège de Calais* by P.-L. Buyrette, called Dormont de Belloy, was played before a paper audience, perhaps because it had a patriotic theme. In 1778 *Zaïre* and in 1781 *Adélaïde du Guesclin* and *La Partie de chasse de Henri IV* were given free.

The Comédie Française had a company of sixteen to twenty-one actors and actresses, all of whom held full shares, and a smaller number of others who held half-shares; in all there were twenty-three shares. Admission to the company was on the recommendation of the members of the company, but subject to the approval of the four Gentlemen of the Chamber, or of the king, who could request an actor to retire. The company received from the state an annual subsidy of about 12,000 livres or francs. If it played at Versailles the actors were entertained to supper and received a fee – 6 francs a day in 1734. According to David Garrick, each French actor when playing at court received a bottle of wine per day, a pair of silk stockings, and the right to hire a coach free. In 1763 the company received 650 francs per day for performances either at Fontainebleau or at Versailles. Actors without a part and left behind on such occasion received 2 to 5 francs per day by way of compensation. Every new actor joining the Comédie had to invest 13,000 francs in the company, which he recovered upon his retirement. He was also entitled to a pension. If he had to purchase his own costume and wigs, unlike the artistes at the Opéra, he could spend as much as 30,000 livres on clothes, or thirty times as much as the annual salary of a *Directeur de la Monnaie*, such as Marivaux's father. It will be seen that the *Comédiens* had status and considerable security and that the present system of administration of the state-run Comédie Française evolved logically and in a straightforward manner from the situation it enjoyed under the *ancien régime*.

For the eighteenth century as a whole, the total potential yearly attendance at the Comédie Française has been estimated as 200,000, when the population of Paris was 600,000.[2] The most successful play between 1701 and 1774 is *Inès de Castro*.[3] There was no clear correlation between success and financial profit, if a year's working is taken into consideration. Sometimes plays which knew little success continued to be performed, either because none other was immediately available, or in answer to various forms of pressure, or to meet the personal wishes of the actors. The Comédie Française enjoyed a greater success after 1750, partly no doubt on account of the talent of great actors like Mlle Clairon, Le Kain, Préville, Brizard, and Molé. In the earlier period Adrienne Lecouvreur, Mlle Dumesnil, Mlle Dangeville, and Mlle Gausin all had their supporters, but after the elderly Baron had given up there were no good male leads until Le Kain. Seats continued to be expensive. If we take a labourer's pay as a guide, the cheapest seat works out at about two pounds, the dearest eight or ten pounds. The *petite loge* rented by the duc d'Orléans cost 6,000 livres per

[2] According to the statistics of the Ville de Paris, the population of Paris may err on the conservative side. See C. Alasseur, *La Comédie Français* audience for any given play is calculated as 8,000 to 14,000 between 1720 and 1740, and 10,000 to 18,000 between 1740 and 1774, but these figures may err on the conservative side. See C. Alasseur, *La Comédie Française au XVIIIe siècle, étude économique*, 1967, p. 66.

[3] See below, p. 295.

annum in 1767, equal to eight months of an actor's pay. The real jump in attendance, however, occurs after 1750, when the enriched bourgeoisie seeks to fill the theatre. This later period, together with the short period of the regency, are the highlights of financial success. The stipends of the actors, even the most highly paid, remained inadequate, and to maintain the sort of establishment that Adrienne Lecouvreur insisted upon, recourse had to be made to patrons. The much advertised immorality of the acting profession was in part a product of its social dependence and professional requirements.

The most original theatre of the period is generally considered to and had a large stage, three tiers of boxes, and a *parterre* in which spectators stood; behind the *parterre* there was an amphitheatre. There were spectators on the stage or *plateau* until 1759, when the comte de Lauraguais, a keen patron of the theatre, had the *banquettes* removed by paying an indemnity of 12,000 livres to the Comédie Française. Above the stage were *balcons*. There were at first 2,000 seats. In 1756 the passage to the raised amphitheatre was narrowed to allow for a *petite loge* on either side; these were let by the month or the year. In 1757 further *petites loges* were constructed above the *second balcon* and above the first two boxes of the second tier. In all there were at least fifteen *petites loges*. The success of this innovation was so great that more *petites loges* were built at the expense of the sides of the amphitheatre, then of the circles and the *second balcon*. When the spectators were refused accommodation on the stage, an additional *balcon* was constructed. The aristocracy favoured the *petites loges* since they recalled a salon. These, however, blocked the view for people in the amphitheatre, and exposed those in the *parterre* to receiving falling objects on their heads. There was neither ventilation nor general facilities, and the lighting by smoking candles was poor, although the *lustres* looked magnificent. The theatres at Lyons and at Bordeaux were better. We find no figures for repairs or maintenance in the accounts. The *sociétaires* could count on the prestige of their theatre, but incidents occurred in the *parterre* and, for *Le Barbier de Séville*, in addition to the ordinary *gardes*, 184 soldiers were in attendance to ensure against trouble. No women were allowed in the *parterre*, a fact which emphasised social divisions.

The most original theatre of the period is generally considered to be that of the Théâtre Italien. Catherine de Medicis introduced the Italian players into France in the sixteenth century, and their special form of *commedia dell'arte*, improvised comedy performed by masked players in traditional costume, became a feature of the theatre scene in France for nearly three centuries. In 1665 the Italian players were honoured by the title *Comédiens du Roi*; and in 1697 they were expelled from their theatre and exiled from Paris by that same king, who accused them of satirising Mme de Maintenon in a scenario they planned to put on, *La Fausse Prude*.

Their exile was not rescinded until 1716, by which time Louis XIV had died (Mme de Maintenon dying in 1719), and the regent, interested in all matters theatrical, invited a distinguished company of players under the patronage of the duke of Parma. Antonia Farnese, to come to Paris. The company was led by Luigi-Riccoboni (1674–1753), known as Lelio because he played the Lover, and included Mme Riccoboni,[4] known as Flaminia, as the Lady, her brother Giuseppe Balleti as second Lover, and their young cousin Zanetta Benozzi[5] to play second lead to Flaminia. Their Arlecchino, key figure in *commedia dell'arte*, was Tomasso Antonio Vicentini (1683–1739), known as Thomassin.

The company gave a first and outstanding performance on 18 May 1716 at the Palais Royal, then moved to the Hôtel de Bourgogne. As time went on, the company acquired an excellent command of French; and Marivaux wrote his plays expressly for them. The delightful young Zanetta incarnated his enchanting Silvia, and Thomassin became the many-faceted Arlequin of Marivaux's delicate comedies.

After a long run of success, the Italian players suffered from a waning interest in their specialised comedy, and lost support in spite of every effort to catch the public eye. The last great Italian Arlequin was Carlo Antonio Bertinazzi (1710–83), known as Carlin, who continued to perform on occasion in Italian, and in the true tradition of *commedia dell'arte*.

The Opéra, sited in the Palais Royal from 1673 to 1763, moved to the Tuileries, but had returned to the Palais Royal by 1770. Lully (1672) was the first director of the Opéra; and it was in this theatre that Rameau achieved success, and where a liking for opera developed throughout the century. It is interesting to note that the members of the Académie Royale de Musique et de Danse, numbering some 200 persons, were not subject to excommunication, as were all other actors, because their institution had been founded by the king.

From the literary standpoint, the history of the Comédie Française, the Comédie Italienne, the Opéra, and the Théâtre de la Foire in Paris is of paramount importance, since from their mutual hostilities and guerrilla warfare, waged throughout the century, new theatre forms evolved, and greater scope was given to dramatists.

[4] She was a scholar, linguist, and musician, reputed also for her charm and wit.

[5] She was fifteen years old when she joined the company. See above, pp. 96-7.

The Théâtre de la Foire would probably never have served as catalyst if Louis XIV had not expelled his Italian players from the Hôtel de Bourgogne in 1697. The major players returned to Italy, but others, who had no future there or who for their own reasons preferred to remain in Paris, in spite of the edict, went to the fairgrounds of Saint-Germain for the winter season and Saint-Laurent[6] in summer, where they either joined with other fairground companies, or formed their own, performing peculiar variants of the traditional *commedia dell'arte*. This infiltration proved fruitful, and over the years the *forains* evolved a new type of fairground theatre that attracted not only the plebs but also the patricians, as well as a number of dramatists of quality.

The success of the *forains* was such that both the *Grands Comédiens* of the Comédie Française and members of the Opéra became involved in lasting conflict with them, exerting their royal privilege and exclusive right of performance. In 1703 the *forains* were debarred from performing scenes in dialogue form; so they gave their shows in impertinent monologues. Speech was then forbidden to them; they used mime, supplemented by scrolls on which the dialogue was written large. In 1719 the *Comédiens* managed to suppress them, but they were allowed by the regent, who resettled them in a *jeu de paume* where they produced such successes as *Achmet et Almanzine*, an *opéra-comique* by Lesage, Fuselier, and d'Orneval, which had 125 consecutive performances. This particular company was again suppressed in 1745, but reopened its doors in 1752, with Monet and later Favart as director. This fusion of genres and players, generated in the fairground theatres from a mixture of French and Italian comedy, together with modifications and innovations due to the continued embargoes of the *Comédiens*, became a new form, light opera of a special kind, housed in what came to be known as the Opéra-Comique, which merged with the Théâtre Italien in 1762, settling at first in the Hôtel de Bourgogne but moving in 1783 to approximately its present site.

From modest beginnings, *opéra-comique* at first was only concerned with parodying opera, but soon presented spectacles with dancing and music which scarcely differ from some of those then presented by the *forains* or the Italian players, now restored to Paris under Luigi Riccoboni. Favart and Sedaine wrote specifically for this theatre, as Lesage[7] had done earlier in the century for the Théâtre de la Foire.

[6] A varied bill was offered at the great fairs, including performances by clowns, acrobats, puppets, and mimes; shows offering parodies, satire, song, and dance; and circus turns with lions, monkeys, hares beating drums, etc.

[7] His *Arlequin, roi de Serendib* (1713) is a good example of the type of play that led to success in the Théâtre de la Foire.

There were several private theatres in operation at this time, notably one at the court of Sceaux in the palace of the duchesse du Maine, one at Cirey in the home of Mme du Châtelet, and similar ones in other aristocratic milieux; special mention may be made of that at Les Délices and that at Ferney in the houses of Voltaire. In these theatres professional and amateur companies performed, and some spectacles included both. Marivaux's plays were often given (in somewhat truncated form), because they were found to be original and because of the practical consideration that they required only small casts. Italian comedy, improvised in the traditional manner on familiar scenarii, was another feature of these private theatres, and occasionally tragedy held the floor.

Towards the end of the century, *parades*,[8] often in the genre *poissard*, full of crude puns and obscenities, and *proverbes*, such as those by Carmontelle, became popular in literary circles, and continued to influence writers in the nineteenth century, Musset in particular. Colleges, too, put on special performances, the Jesuits more especially staging lavish productions of Latin tragedies at the Collège Louis-le-Grand; but these were brought to an end by a decree of the Parlement de Paris in 1759, as a result of Jansenist persuasion. Late in the century, a fairly large number of new theatres opened their doors: the Théâtre Nicolet, Boulevard du Temple, which became in 1772 the Théâtre des Grands Danseurs du Roi; the Ambigu Comique, founded by Audinot in 1769, which specialised in mime and *féeries*; the Théâtre des Associés (1774); and the Variétés Amusantes (1778), which was moved to the Palais Royal. In 1791 the Assemblée Nationale proclaimed the freedom of the theatres, abolishing the privilege of the *Comédiens du Roi*, and maintaining as a matter of principle that plays could only be performed by permission of the author. Beaumarchais, who had taken an active part in establishing a Société des Auteurs Dramatiques in 1777, intervened in person to secure at last an author's right to royalties. Prior to this, by an order of 1697, authors were entitled to one-ninth of receipts, less expenses, but if a play's receipts fell below 1,200 livres in winter, and 800 livres in summer, it became the property of the theatre in which it was shown. As a result, from time to time efforts were directed towards securing

[8] The *parades* were originally a short extract or advertisement designed to entice the public into the hall. The regent and other aristocrats enjoyed fraternising with the *plèbe* and this kind of crude humour was transferred to private places such as that of Lenormand d'Etioles, the husband of Mme de Pompadour. The humour was coarse and the style adopted involved faulty speech *liaisons*, called *cuirs*. The characters are traditional, often drawn from Italian comedy or children's fairy-tales – Isabelle, Léandre, Gilles, Arlequin – and presented in an obscene way. Charles Collé (1709–1793) was the best exponent of the genre, which ladies of quality particularly enjoyed.

the immediate failure of certain plays, which became money-making successes once they fell into the ownership of the theatre. Accounts in any case were badly and irregularly kept, demonstrably false, and open to all abuses.

Throughout a century of change and internecine warfare among the major companies in Paris, the Comédie Française, in spite of reverses and the rivalry of the Théâtre Italien, triumphantly kept its individuality and maintained an unbroken tradition. On the other hand, the Théâtre Italien was driven by changing tastes and changing times to accept the merger with the Opéra-Comique and the *forains*, and this altered the traditions of all three. It is against this background that the impact on French society of tragedies, comedies, and *drames*, their part in philosophical and pre-revolutionary propaganda, and in fostering a new sensibility, as well as in preaching the gospel of reason, must be judged. Awareness of the limited audience that could be reached, and of the nature of that audience, leads to a minimising of the role of the theatre in the intellectual origins of the French Revolution, as does a close study of the content of the plays produced. It is certainly as a mirror of social change and current values that it is intellectually most significant, apart from two or three outstanding playwrights whose particular gifts lift them into another category.

II. TRAGEDY

Tragedy in the eighteenth century, as performed on the stage of the Théâtre Français, enjoyed the highest status. It was patronised by the aristocracy and intellectual élite, and made the reputation of Adrienne Lecouvreur, Mlle Dumesnil, Mlle Clairon, and Le Kain, some of the finest actors of France. It inherited the classical tradition so dazzlingly illustrated in the seventeenth century with the great tragedies of Corneille and Racine, whose penetrating analyses of character and motives and the quality of whose verse all remained unquestioned and seemed to augur well for the genre. When, in 1716, the public saw for the first time on the stage Racine's *Athalie*, his pre-eminence was confirmed and the opening-up of new vistas could be detected. *Athalie* was unusual in its inspiration, which was neither Greek nor Roman, and it had an unwonted spectacular element to whet new appetites.

In fact, the eighteenth century witnessed the decline of tragedy, and, had it not been for Voltaire, it might have witnessed its death. Carrington Lancaster, in endeavouring to pinpoint the cause of this decline, has shown[9] that it is not due to any dearth of drama-

[9] *French Tragedy in the Time of Louis XV and Voltaire, 1715-74*, 2 vols., 1950.

tists, for between 1715 and 1774 there were sixty-nine authors for the 145 tragedies actually performed; moreover, they seem to have come from every region of France, and from almost every kind of social background. It can hardly be due to a change in the composition of the audience, which in fact grew in size with the opening of a larger theatre and only assumed very slowly a truly bourgeois character. The real cause of decline is in its very success in the previous age, and the consequent anxiety to renew the theatre on different lines and in accordance with the prevailing spirit of the age. The latter was not conducive to great tragedy: it was more concerned with ideas than with characters moving spectators to awe, horror, or pity. Furthermore, the age was not one of belief, neither belief in the Christian religion, nor in the Greek gods, nor in Providence, their modern counterpart. It can be argued that the essence of tragedy lies in a hero larger than life, facing an inevitable but unjust doom: there can be no tragedy where characters are not struggling with destiny. Certainly Voltaire and other playwrights, whether their source of inspiration was Roman,[10] Greek, biblical,[11] or even drawn from French history or recent events, introduced the necessary deity with appropriate lyricism and apostrophes, but without conviction. It is not only that as individuals they had private doubts; their very public had also greatly changed in outlook. So the playwrights substituted chance for fate, and multiplied the number of accidents or coincidences in their plots, in order to help on the action. In *Zaïre*, perhaps the best tragedy of the century, if Nérestan had used the words 'ma Sœur' in a letter, instead of 'Zaïre', disaster would have been averted; and in Act V, scene ix of the same play, if Zaïre had exclaimed: 'O mon frère, est-ce vous?', instead of 'Est-ce vous, Nérestan?', she would not have been killed. From the days of Crébillon, the number of recognition scenes grew excessively. They can be criticised as being artificially contrived, or as being a by-product of a superficial rationalistic approach to the problem. There was a marked reluctance to accept the notion of tragic fate, except academically. This fact may, conversely, explain why the century gave birth to brilliant writers of comedy. Certainly a belief in man and in his ability to make his own destiny, so akin to belief in human freedom and in the idea of human progress, is one close to the heart of the *philosophes*. This is what gave depth to the character of Figaro in both of Beaumarchais' masterpieces.

[10] Lefranc de Pompignan's *Didon et Enée* (1734) exemplifies this point.

[11] Tragedies drawn from the Bible all come early in the century and though Duché, Nadal, Genest, and others wrote on biblical themes, only Longepierre had a modest success. His *Electre*, however, performed in 1702 and published only in 1730, won him most fame, appearing as it did before Crébillon's *Electre* (1709).

Tragedy in the classical sense is best represented in the early part of the century by a writer already well known in salon society in the seventeenth century, Prosper Jolyot de Crébillon (1674–1762), who was in his day considered by many as the equal of Voltaire as a dramatist, and who is still recognised as the second ablest writer of tragedies of the century. His tragedies, their subjects taken from Greek mythology, are in five acts and written in alexandrines, as were all other tragedies of the time (with the possible exception of *Beverley* (1768) by Saurin, which is in *vers libres* and which most critics would prefer to call a *drame*). What renders them remarkable are the innovations of the author. Crébillon introduces disguises, recognition scenes, abductions, mistaken identities, *coups de théâtre*, and similar devices in a manner hitherto unknown to tragedy. It is claimed that he brought in a *romanesque* element, which he borrowed from the novels of the seventeenth century, as is implied by the very term, and that this fostered a new realism. But the devices he used were already to be found in seventeenth- and eighteenth-century comedy; in any case they complicate to little advantage the simple structure of a classical plot, and in practice undermined the real basis of tragedy.

More important perhaps was his introduction of horror, or more precisely the terrible, which was intended to awaken pity, and was quickly imitated by dramatists such as Pellegrini and Danchet. But he soon had to tone down the terrible to suit the sensibility of his public. His innovation, however, was destined to prove popular in the end. It paved the way for melodrama, earning for Crébillon the title of 'père du mélodrame', and for Romantic drama. His first tragedy, *La Mort des enfants de Brutus*, was turned down by the Comédie Française, and never published. *Idoménée* (1705) and *Atrée* (1707) already show his concern with terror as a mainspring of tragedy. *Rhadamiste et Zénobie* (1711) is his masterpiece, for its successful characterisation and fine style, but his later tragedies are not without merit. *Xerxès* (1714) and *Sémiramis* (1717) were unsuccessful, and Voltaire had little trouble in eclipsing his rival with his own *Sémiramis* in 1748. Crébillon met with greater success with *Pyrrhus* (1726). He was elected to the French Academy in 1731, and in 1733 was named royal censor. In 1735 he was given the further appointment of police censor, and these positions he held till his death in 1762, at the ripe age of eighty-eight.

It is as censor that he kindled Voltaire's ire and, prompted by jealousy and a spirit of emulation, Voltaire decided to borrow the themes of a number of his rival's plays.[12] Crébillon, however, very wisely refused to be drawn into open conflict and stopped pro-

[12] *Sémiramis* (1748), *Oreste* (1750), *Rome sauvée* (1752), *Octave et le jeune Pompée* (1764), and *Les Pélopides* (1771).

ducing plays for twenty-two years. He now moved in court circles, and was granted a pension by the king, who made him one of his librarians and had his works published in 1750 at his own expense. In 1748, when seventy-five, Crébillon produced *Catilina,* which was lavishly staged with the help of the royal treasury. It is a well-constructed play, without any special merit, which Voltaire sought to cap by producing *Rome sauvée* (1752) on the same subject. Crébillon's last play, *Le Triumvirat ou La Mort de Cicéron* (1755), a kind of sequel to *Catilina,* had a *succès d'estime* on 23 December when it was performed. It is hardly inferior to Voltaire's *Octave et le jeune Pompée ou Le Triumvirat,* which was badly received in 1764. Crébillon, who had failed to distinguish between the terrible and the horrible, and thereby set a fashion which popular audiences were later to approve, revealed the contemporary taste for the spectacular and its desire for a drama more removed from the classical form than that which it knew. Both he and Voltaire were well aware of the excellence of the classical tradition they had inherited, but their own preoccupations, as well as the taste of their public, were pulling them in new directions. They fought a rearguard action in defence of classical tragedy and effected an uneasy compromise between their aesthetic ideal, the spirit of the times, and their own desire for innovation.

Voltaire, as well as Crébillon, gave a larger place to sentiment, which sometimes wholly replaced passion in the tragedies of both writers. Dramatists increasingly drew on medieval and modern themes, and introduced minor changes in technique. But the main difference between their works and those of the seventeenth century lies in the stress they laid on philosophical, political, religious, or social ideas, already to be found in Voltaire's *Œdipe,* but manifest increasingly up to the time of the Revolution. One might have expected even more propaganda in the tragedies of the period. Voltaire in particular showed taste in not underlining the element of propaganda in *Mahomet* for instance, in which he could have indulged to the full his hatred of fanaticism. He saw the need for a study of character and of motives, and never lost sight of the need to arouse emotions as well as interest the mind. But propaganda can be all the more effective for being disguised, or subordinated to aesthetic considerations. Lesser dramatists all too often confined themselves to presenting issues of 'philosophical' significance, and so wrote bad plays.

There can be no doubt the theatre served as an instrument of propaganda. In the case of Voltaire this has been analysed very carefully by R. S. Ridgway,[13] and even where propaganda is not

[13] R. S. Ridgway, 'La propagande philosophique dans les tragédies de Voltaire', *Studies on Voltaire and the Eighteenth century,* XV, 1961.

Voltaire's main concern, none of the basic assumptions in his plays run contrary to his philosophical beliefs, whether religious, social, or political. But lesser dramatists also presented issues of philosophical interest from their personal standpoints. La Motte, in *Inès de Castro* (1723), whose heroine foreshadows 'La dame aux camélias', is decidedly anti-clerical. Houdar de la Motte (1672–1731) started to write tragedies at the age of fifty – *Les Machabées* (1722), *Romulus* (1722), *Œdipe* (completed before 23 July 1725, performed 18 March 1726, published 1730, and parodied by Legrand in *Le Chevalier errant*) – but it is *Inès de Castro* that brought him fame as a dramatist. It is one of the best-known plays of the century, and from 1719 to 1729 no tragedies could rival its success, and that of *Œdipe*. Possibly influenced by Rotrou's *Laure persécutée* and Corneille's *Théodore*, La Motte turned for inspiration and effect to sentiment, so successfully that the fifth act led Voltaire to weep. The combination of sentiment and anti-clericalism leading away from true tragedy to tragi-comedy makes *Inès de Castro* probably the most striking play of a period which extends from *Rhadamiste et Zénobie* to *Zaïre*. Chaligny de Paline's play *Coriolan*[14] was suppressed by the censor because it criticised the foreign policy of the government. Louis de Boissy in *Admète et Alceste* (1738) challenges Christianity through paganism, attacking the priest who:

> Va semer l'épouvante et la rébellion,
> Sous le voile sacré de la Religion.

and contains passages which remind one of Voltaire's *Brutus*.

Other dramatists take up a different stand. Sauvigny upholds monotheism and a belief in immortality, as does Gresset in *Edouard III*. Religion itself is seldom the object of a frontal attack, but is usually subordinated to the higher law of nature, and its ministers are shown up as cruel in Voltaire's *Alzire* and in Nadal's *Machabées*. P.-F.-A. Lefèvre in *Cosroès* (1767) suggests that man makes God in his own image.[15] Lagrange-Chancel's (1677–1758) best plays are tragi-comedies: *Amasis* (1701) borrows its plot from *Le Grand Cyrus*, La Chapelle's *Téléphonte*, and possibly *Athalie*. He had the ability to create interesting situations and resisted efforts to provide a more elaborate scenery. His other plays are less good: *Alceste* (1704), *Ino et Mélicerte* (1713), *Sophonisbe* (1716), which was performed but whose text was later lost, *Les Jeux olympiques* (1729). Although Lagrange-Chancel ranks with Crébillon as one of the two best dramatists of the first fifteen years of the

[14] This subject also inspired La Harpe, whose *Coriolan* was staged in 1784.

[15] Lefèvre is also the author of a tragedy, *Zuma*, performed in 1777.

century, it is perhaps only his eloquent pleas for tolerance that save him from total oblivion. Piron did not hesitate to stage Indians in *Fernand Cortez* and *Montézuma* (1744). François Tronchin, a Protestant from Geneva, in *Marie Stuart, reine d'Ecosse* (1734) failed to raise the religious question, as one might have expected. Morand, F.-M.-C. Deschamps, and Le Blanc especially may be mentioned. The latter, in *Aben-Saïd, empereur des Mogols* (1735), writes:

> Le zèle des Autels est toujours redoutable.
> Il arme les esprits d'un courage indomptable
> Et l'intérêt du Ciel, animant chaque Etat.
> Fait du soldat un prêtre et du prêtre un soldat.

As a whole these playwrights are little else but imitators of Voltaire. Bernard Saurin (1706–81), who wrote his first and most horrific tragedy, *Aménophis*, at the age of forty-four, indulged in an anti-clerical vein and showed the social preoccupation of the times, as in:

> Si celui qui n'en est que le dépositaire
> En fait des maux publics l'instrument arbitraire,
> Né pour les maintenir, s'il viole les lois,
> Le peuple devient libre et rentre en tous ses droits.

But soon Saurin became more guarded in his criticism of the clergy, acting on the advice of Voltaire. In the grand manner of Corneille, he wrote *Spartacus* (1760), which contains a plea for internationalism, and *Blanche et Guiscard* (1764), an adaptation of James Thomson's play *Tancred and Sigismunda*, which goes back to a story in *Gil Blas*. His best work, however, is certainly *Beverley* (1768), inspired by *The Gamester* by Edward Moore. Towards the end of the century Lemierre in *Guillaume Tell* (1767) had some success through exploiting the patriotic feeling aroused by the Seven Years War. Lemierre (1723–93) was an able writer who wrote poems as well as plays. His best play is perhaps *Hypermnestre* (1759). *Térée* (1787) and *Idoménée* (1761) show evidence of the influence of *Télémaque*, and especially of Crébillon, in their subject. *Barneveldt* (1791) is centred on the execution of a Dutch statesman in 1619, and presents a picture of family dissension as well as of horror. *Artaxerce* (1768) was taken from Metastasio. But in spite of a relative failure in 1770, it was *La Veuve du Malabar*, revived with great success in 1780, that captured the imagination. It ran to 104 performances. The play dwelt on the theme of Hindu *suttee* and showed a widow about to be burnt alive to satisfy a Brahmin's religious convictions. The public was delighted to find priests unmasked and put to shame, and the spectacle of a flaming Indian funeral pyre filled it with pleasurable horror. The play pointed to a new conception of tragedy, and preached tolerance. Meister spoke of the play's 'sensibilité touchante'.

Another playwright, Dormont de Belloy (1727–75), whose real name was Pierre-Laurent Buyrette, and who is sometimes ranked with Lemierre as second only to Voltaire, wrote a patriotic play *Le Siège de Calais*, which proved highly successful. He traded on the need to arouse French patriotism after the disastrous Seven Years War, and remembering Mme de Tencin's novel *Le Siège de Calais* (1739), to which he refers, he produced a work which commended itself to Louis XV, who gave him a gold medal and 1,000 *écus*. The play was given the honour of a free performance on 12 March 1765 for the benefit of the people of the Halles, and in 1773 was acted at the request of the Dauphin and Marie-Antoinette. It was revived again in 1790 and in 1814. The chief figure was the heroic mayor of Calais, a bourgeois, and not Edward the greedy sovereign. In it occur such lines as:

> C'est mon Pays, mon Roi, la France qui m'appelle.
> Tremblez; faibles Sujets, qui trahissez vos Maîtres,
> Un Roi punit toujours ceux qu'il a rendus traîtres.

His other plays, *Titus* (1759), *Zelmire* (1762), *Gabrielle de Vergy* (written 1765, published 1770, performed 1777), and *Pierre le Cruel* (1772), are disappointing. He wrote mostly historical plays which scarcely deserve the title of tragedies. *Le Siège de Calais*, and indeed *Guillaume Tell*, were, however, disliked for their patriotic panache by the group of d'Holbach and his friends, who were more concerned with attacking the monarchy than with galvanising the people into heroic efforts to save their country. In fact, this patriotic wave was ineffective in stemming the tide against the institution of monarchy, but it did serve to inflame republican ardour when the latter had to face the *émigrés* and foreign invaders during and after the Revolution. Other historical plays include *Les Druides* (1763, performed 1772) by Le Blanc du Guillet, in which fanaticism is attacked; *Richard III* by Rosoy, who defended the monarchy and was executed in 1792; and four plays by La Harpe (1739–1803) which were all failures: *Le Comte de Warwick* (1763), *Timoléon* (1764), *Pharamond*, and *Gustave Wasa* (1766).[16] *Le Comte de Strafford* (1789, published 1795) by Lally-Tollendal was written in memory of his father, beheaded in 1766.

Rousseau's disciples are surprisingly few on the stage. Louis de Cahusac[17] in *Zarès* and Bauvin in *Arminius ou Les Chérusques* praise the virtue of primitive man, and Sauvigny in *La Mort de*

16 He also wrote *Menzikoff* (1781), *Jeanne de Naples* (1781), *Philoctète* (1781), *Les Brames* (1783), but he made his reputation as an academic critic.

17 De Cahusac also wrote a treatise on the history of dancing, an opera with music by Rameau, a *comédie-ballet*, and a comedy entitled *Zénaïde*.

Socrate defended Rousseau, but in *Hirza ou Les Illinois* (1766), which deals with French expansion in the New World, with the beauty of the Niagara as background and with the love of freedom of the Indians, it is civilisation that triumphs.[18] Both in *L'Orphelin de la Chine* and *Les Scythes*, Voltaire emphasises primitive cruelty, which must yield to more humane practices. This stressing of the social virtues is not so surprising if one thinks of the nature of the theatre as an essentially social institution. To sum up: even if *Œdipe*, *Brutus*, *Mahomet*, and *Guillaume Tell* foreshadow at their respective dates the kind of philosophical *tirades* we find in Beaumarchais' *Tarare*, even more than in *Le Mariage de Figaro*, the fact remains that philosophical propaganda in the tragedies of the time seems remarkably superficial. Religion is seen from without, and with no specific names attached; fanaticism and despotism remain anonymous. Their philosophical ideas are very slight if they are compared with their counterpart in the prose writings of the great thinkers. The dramatist sought easy success: and it was Fréron who pointed out that a dramatist was certain of applause if he attacked the clergy. The best propagandist remains Voltaire, because he was the most intelligent and also the most daring, as when, in *Agathocle*, he proposed abdication of the king as the solution to the political problem. But this play was never performed on the stage of the Comédie Française.

Voltaire's admirer Marmontel (1723–99), famous for his *contes moraux*, *Bélisaire* and *Les Incas*, for his literary criticism, and for his *Mémoires*, aroused the enthusiasm of the *parterre* with his *Denys le tyran* (1748), so much so that he had to make a personal appearance on the stage, but the critics, unlike the public, were far colder in their appraisal, and his other plays, *Aristomène* (1750), *Cléopâtre* (1750), *Les Héraclides* (1753), and *Egyptus* (see p. 74) were failures, in spite of the anti-clerical propaganda they contained.

One drawback to propagandist plays is that they date very quickly, especially when the cause they preach has been won; and in any historical evaluation it is most important to date them. War is condemned in Chaligny's *Coriolan* (1722),[19] but more strongly in Saurin's *Spartacus* (1770), and in Voltaire's *Les Scythes* (1767), both very much around the same date. Appeals in favour of commerce and prosperity abounded in Lemierre's tragedies, and fell upon willing ears. On the other hand, it was rather facile of Lemierre in his *La Veuve du Malabar* (1770), and of Sedaine in his *Philosophe sans le savoir*, to condemn duelling, since the practice

[18] He also wrote *Vashington ou La Liberté du Nouveau Monde*, performed in 1791.

[19] There are plays by Mauger, Balze (1776), and P.-P. Gudin de la Brenellerie (1776) on the same subject.

no longer had any strong advocates. The general stress on ideas in tragedy had decided drawbacks. As Carrington Lancaster has stated: 'Political, religious and humanitarian ideas are of interest to the historian, but they do not by themselves make fine plays. They may rather render a tragedy ineffective, especially after the cause has been won for which the authors fought.'[20]

New outside influences were also at work, broadening the conception of tragedy. P.-A. de La Place (1707–93) published in 1745 *Le Théâtre anglais*, which contained ten translations of plays by Shakespeare, Ben Jonson, Otway, Dryden, Rowe, and Congreve, and produced a *Venise sauvée* (1747) freely translated from Otway's *Venice Preserved*, and a *Jeanne d'Angleterre*, imitated from Rowe's *Lady Jane Grey* (1748, unpublished).[21] Ducis successfully adapted Shakespeare's plays, and *Hamlet* and *Romeo and Juliet* were well received and impressed the public by their novelty and difference from accepted French taste.[22] Shakespeare may be said to have contributed to the liberalising tendency which was to free tragedy from the tyranny of the unities, of the proprieties, and of noble language, and helped to make it possible for murders to be enacted on stage. But he also speeded on the now inevitable decline of classical drama. Dubuisson's only successful tragedy was *Nadir ou Thamas-Kouli-Kan* (1780), based on Jonas Hanway's *Revolution of Persia* (1754). Other foreign playwrights exercised their influence, such as J. E. Schlegel, Maffei, and Metastasio.

Tragedy was the subject of continued experimentation. The subject of the plays might be drawn from the Middle Ages or from contemporary fact, and the setting might be in a palace in Peru or Zanzibar, in Mexico or by the Niagara Falls, in China, Mecca, or the Malabar coast. The exotic became the rage, but there remained surprisingly little local colour. A funeral pyre, a corpse on a bed, 320 supernumerary soldiers, as in Dorat's *Régulus* (1765), the firing of cannon, the clap of thunder, the hissing of serpents; all provided drama of a new kind without increasing true realism.

It is perhaps in costume that the greatest progress was made. Le Kain and Mlle Clairon went to some pains to acquire more historically acceptable dress; and senators in red robes provided an unwonted touch of colour. It is, of course, after 1759, when the stage was cleared of spectators, that new possibilities emerged. Voltaire soon took advantage of them, as when in *Tancrède* he

[20] op. cit., p. 623.

[21] Rowe's *Fair Penitent* is the source of two tragedies entitled *Caliste*.

[22] In *Le Roi Léar* (1783) he was able for the first time to make use of Le Tourneur's translation instead of relying upon La Place. His *Macbeth* was performed in 1784. He wrote also an *Othello ou Le More de Venise* (1783), *Jean sans-Terre ou La Mort d'Arthur* (1791), and *Œdipe chez Admète* (1780), which grafted Euripides upon Sophocles.

introduced an army of knights. The staging of pageants and *tableaux*, of processions of soldiers, priests, and senators, changed the very nature of drama. Pathos took the place of passion and a mother's love for her children that of the love of heroes of old. Often love itself was left out. The public certainly showed that it was weary of kings and would accept a mayor or Swiss peasants as substitutes for the royal heroes. They showed a preference for different forms of realism and enjoyed most the interplay of ideas, so that the best dramatists had to have something of the *philosophe* about them. The degeneration of classical tragedy into *le drame* hardly calls for any expression of surprise. Many of the tragedies reviewed are tragedies only in name. Some listed by Carrington Lancaster in his work on eighteenth-century tragedy appear also on F. Gaiffe's long list of *drames*. The distinction between the genres has become so blurred that contemporaries lost interest in it and the fact that twenty-one new tragedies were performed between April 1782 and June 1789 with Ducis, La Harpe, and Maisonneuve[23] as the most popular playwrights has little significance. Even Voltaire, the greatest defender of the bastion of tragedy, wrote: 'Tout est permis, hormis le genre ennuyeux.' Too many of his contemporaries adopted, without knowing it, the only genre he had rightly proscribed.

III. COMEDY

Comedy, unlike classical tragedy, is not commonly concerned with the eternal verities of human nature, nor the noble or ignoble deeds of kings and heroes of history, with splendid or villainous characters, but rather with the manners of men, their foibles and vices, and the peculiarities of individuals. Molière had indeed presented at once individual and universal types, but few new subjects remained for plays on similar lines. His successors at first imitated him, and strove to write plays even more in accordance with the narrow classical ideal. They wrote in verse and in five acts, and offered the form, if not the core, of the classical ideal. The most successful playwrights were those who developed their own originality in their own manner, without emulating Molière, whose greatness they recognised without wishing to continue writing in his pattern. The two greatest writers of comedies of the eighteenth century, Marivaux and Beaumarchais, who rank only after Molière in public estimation today, owed practically nothing to their predecessor; and the comparisons often drawn between them are mis-

[23] Author of *Roxelane et Mustapha* (1785), *Odmard et Zulna* (1788).

leading and have proved singularly fruitless. Both Marivaux and Beaumarchais belong essentially to a different tradition.

The case of Regnard (1656–1710) appears at first sight to be special, for he borrowed some of his subjects, situations, and perhaps characters, from Molière. *Les Folies amoureuses* has been compared to *L'Ecole des femmes*, and *Le Légataire universel* to *Monsieur de Pourceaugnac*, *Les Fourberies de Scapin*, and *Le Malade imaginaire*. Moreover, some of his characters, such as *le joueur* and *le distrait*, at first sight strike the spectator as *types* that might be developed in the fashion of Molière. In fact his play *Le Joueur* is centred on gaming, and not on the presentation of character, and comedy arises out of the hero's alternate movements, towards gaming when he is in funds, and towards his beloved when he is out of luck. Regnard was a great playwright who brought to his dramatic work his own gift for laughter, his sense of theatre and fun, and his own inimitable style. He may have been superficial, but he had wit and a liberal mind. He took delight in using the most implausible situations, and in speeding up the action in his comedies. He experimented with the Molière tradition, as indeed with that of the Italian comedy, to which his *Folies amoureuses* owes so much; and his fine flow of language and sensitivity reflect the wealthy man of the world, the unrepentant hedonist, the gifted amateur with all the qualities as well as the defects that the term conjures up. Above all, he gave much more place to *peinture de moeurs* and social conditions than Molière had done, pointing the way to a new style of comedy. His play *Le Joueur* might be compared with that by Dufresny of the same date, or the latter's *La Joueuse*: this characteristic theme of the age can be followed through Edward Moore's *The Gamester* (1753), Diderot's adaptation of it in 1760 (published in 1819) which he passed on to Saurin, who produced *Beverley* in 1768. Bruté de Loirelle, for his part, had translated Moore's play in 1762 and d'Alembert adapted a monologue, toning it down to make it more acceptable to his audience. The latter plays are meant to edify and to point a moral lesson. Regnard's gay tone is unequalled until Beaumarchais, even if he evokes amusement rather more than laughter. In all such respects Regnard heralds the regency and not the later manner of the mid-century.

Dufresny, a gifted descendant of Henri IV, and much loved by Louis XIV, had flashes of genius and originality. He produced *Les Bourgeoises à la mode* in 1692, but *L'Esprit de contradiction* (1710) is no doubt his most interesting play. He could not sustain a brilliant beginning, and although his dialogue is superb, his style is generally careless. He was inventive and probably thought of the subject of *Le Joueur* before Regnard, but his play on the same theme is decidedly weaker. He is now better known for his *Amusements sérieux et comiques d'un Siamois à Paris* (which may have influenced Montesquieu at the time he wrote *Les Lettres persanes*) and as director of the *Mercure galant*.

Florent Carton Dancourt (1661–1725) is another author at the turn of the century who may be considered as writing in the wake of Molière, whom he replaced, so to speak, on the stage of the Comédie Française. An actor and director, he wrote in all some sixty plays. He turned away from portraying universal man to focusing attention on the manners and customs of the bourgeoisie; and his plays, which he continued to produce up to the time of the regency, have great documentary value. He drew on current events for his subjects, depicting the *demi-monde* and the world of money before Lesage. He was a man of the theatre who knew how to link scenes, but his technical ability cannot blind present readers to his facile manner, his indifferent style, and his superficiality. His best play is *Le Chevalier à la mode* (1687), which may be linked with Baron's *L'Homme à bonne fortune* and Regnard's *Arlequin, homme à bonne fortune* (1690), as presenting early examples of a new character, who strives in an immoral society to gain advancement in life by deceiving women. With Dancourt we are indeed moving rapidly into a dubious world that earned for the comedies of the period the title of *comédies de mauvaises mœurs*. We find signs of disintegration already before the death of Louis XIV, in the rising of moneyed men at the expense of the aristocracy, and of intriguers everywhere. The documentary value of his work is further enhanced by his portrayal of peasants, which is very rare on the contemporary French stage. He was able to make them speak in their own idiom, and his dialogue is lifelike and well sustained, although his general style is flat. *Le Chevalier à la mode* was revived with success in 1706. *Le Tuteur* (1695) is also well known. Others are remembered only for their titles: *La Désolation des joueuses*, *La Maison de campagne*, *L'Eté des coquettes* (1690), *La Femme d'intrigue*, *Les Bourgeoises à la mode*, *La Parisienne*, *La Loterie*, *L'Opérateur Barry*, *La Famille à la mode*, *Le Retour des officiers* (1697), *Le Galant Jardinier*, *Les Fêtes nocturnes du cours*, *La Foire de Besons* (1695), *La Foire Saint-Germain* (1696), and *Les Enfants de Paris* (1699).

Dancourt's shrewd powers of observation were trained upon the financial plight of the upper classes, and he transcribes with realism the bourgeoisie and lower classes. Lesage, whose work has already been examined,[24] in a play such as *Turcaret*, was more satirical. It was he who transformed a comedy of character into a comedy of manners. He combined, in his portrayal of the money-grasping

[24] See above, pp. 78 et seq.

tax-farmer, depth of satire with realism, and a fine dramatic sense with convincing stage dialogue. In one sense it can be claimed that *Turcaret* is a play of the seventeenth century, as is the character portrayed. But it is certainly not a refined play for a sophisticated aristocratic audience, nor has it the glitter and slapstick of Italian comedy. Its originality from the historical standpoint is that it is a serious comedy, not intended to make the spectator laugh, except uncomfortably; and that it presents a grave satire of contemporary society more akin to works intended for a bourgeois audience.

Marivaux, too, has a serious undertone in his plays, and his social comedies reveal a taste for philosophical speculation. But his most typical work, closely associated with the Italian company of Luigi Riccoboni, reflects in style and content the salon circles in which he moved and the spirit of the *fêtes galantes*. In his comedies, which are basically concerned with love, he reveals himself as a moralist. We have brought out elsewhere the originality of this drama and its unique merit.[25] Historically, it has to be seen in the perspective of Italian comedy, as Lesage can be seen in that of the Théâtre de la Foire. In the general evolution of eighteenth-century comedy, it marks a step towards psychological realism and greater sensibility.

Riccoboni, who himself preferred tragic roles and waged a long battle for the reform of the stage and for raising its status, as indeed for greater morality on the part of actors, wrote a comedy, *La Femme jalouse*, well within the scope of the Italian technique, although a comedy of character. He wrote a *tragédie burlesque* entitled *Arcagambis*, and his wife Flaminia a French comedy entitled *Le Naufrage*. At first (in 1716) he put on plays in Italian, and then such plays as Regnard's *Le Joueur* and Corneille's *Le Menteur*; in all, he put on sixty plays in six months at the Hôtel de Bourgogne. As he abandoned the Italian language and put on plays in French, he staged parodies, especially parodies of tragedies, such as *Œdipe travesti* by Legrand and Dominique (1720, a parody of Voltaire's *Œdipe*) and *Agnès de Chaillot* (a parody of La Motte's *Inès de Castro*). Voltaire remained hostile to the Italians and equally disliked Lelio, Marivaux, and Watteau. There was a polemic over parody in which La Motte and Fuzelier, a purveyor of farces for the Foire, were involved. The Italian players soon found their own authors. Gueulette, who has recorded their history, wrote *Arlequin Pluton* (1719), *Le Trésor supposé* (1720), and *L'Amour précepteur*. Saint-Jorry collaborated with Riccoboni to write *Le Philosophe trompé par la nature* (1719); C.-A. Coypel *le jeune* wrote *Les Amours à la chasse* (1718); and Autreau *L'Amante*

[25] See above, pp. 90 et seq.

romanesque ou La Capricieuse (1718), *Les Amours ignorants* (1720; this may have inspired Marivaux in *Arlequin poli par l'amour*) and *Le Besoin d'aimer*. F. Delisle de La Drévetière also wrote for this theatre. His *Arlequin sauvage* (1723), with its dialogue between the savage and the civilised man, was a great success and was frequently revived. His *Timon le misanthrope* (1722) shows him as a precursor of Rousseau, and contains much social satire. *Arlequin au banquet des sept sages* (1723) is a parody of *Le Banquet ridicule*. *Le Faucon et les oies de Bocace* was performed in 1725. In the wake of Marivaux and Delisle, d'Allainval wrote *L'Embarras des richesses*. Other plays staged by the Italian players whilst directed by Riccoboni include *Le Dédain affecté* by Monucault, *La Capricieuse* by Jolly, *La Veuve à la mode* by Saint-Foix, and *Le Jaloux*, *Le Portrait*, *Les Effets du dépit*, and *Les Amants réunis* (1727) by Beauchamps. Lelio put on *L'Italien marié à Paris*, *comédie française* in 1728 but shortly after, on 25 April 1729, Riccoboni and his family were requested to leave. Marivaux's *La Colonie*, Flaminia's play, and Delisle's *Abdilly* had all proved failures.

Later performances at the Comédie Italienne are less clearly comedies. Marivaux stands out in retrospect as the culmination of what was best in Italian comedy in France, even though his plays appear at a moment of decadence from the standpoint of *commedia dell'arte*. For he brought to his theatre many complex and personal elements which show him as a highly original playwright. If Marivaux had incarnated the spirit of the *fêtes galantes* and the elegance of the aristocratic world, he had also refined sentiment, moving away from the tradition of laughter common to Italian comedy and to Molière. He thus took a decided step towards a new type of comedy, at once psychological and serious.

Lesage, whilst seemingly within the orbit of Molière, in *Turcaret* had, as we have seen, turned his back on true comedy, and had evolved a serious comedy of manners involving satire. He was in fact taking an important step towards a new type of comedy, called *comédie larmoyante*, which in turn led to the *drame*.

As early as 1728 Piron, in *Les Fils ingrats* (the theme of which recalls that of *King Lear* and of *Le Père Goriot*), had mingled the serious and the sentimental, but he had subordinated the serious element to a comic background. He had, however, been concerned with the pattern of family relationships, one of the main preoccupations of the writers of *drames*. In *La Métromanie* (1738) he wrote an excellent play of its kind which had a considerable and lasting success. It is well written and amusing and has been held as deriving from Molière, for the chief character, who has a passion for writing verse, is a monomaniac like so many in Molière's comedies; but his craze is a passing phase rather than a permanent characteristic, and the general theme, as well as the indifferent characterisation, turned the work into a superficial comedy in spite of the author's lively talent. The fact that *La Métromanie* was written in verse, inescapable in view of the subject, did not endear it to a new generation of dramatists seeking greater realism in the theatre.

It was Destouches who really set the fashion for serious, moralising comedy. The general direction he gave comedy was reinforced by the propaganda of the *philosophes* and in keeping with their aspirations as reformers. The need was felt to satirise the social evils of the day and especially to elevate the public by appealing to their finer sensibilities and by teaching them virtue; the stage was clearly the best medium for reaching such a large audience. It became vulgar to laugh and good form to weep. Men indulged in touchingly sentimental scenes and shed tears in public. Philippe Néricault Destouches (1680–1754) launched himself into a military career, mixing in the best circles and being first noticed by M. de Puysieux, the French ambassador to Switzerland. On the latter's recommendation, he was sent to England by the regent in 1717, where he was appointed *chargé d'affaires*, staying till 1723. He had shown talent in writing comedies of character from an early date, and his first plays, up to 1717, are chiefly comedies of character and intrigue: *Le Curieux impertinent* (1710), *L'Ingrat*, and *L'Irrésolu* (1712), all in five acts and in verse. These works show a real sense of comedy, *L'Irrésolu* in particular (the theme is also the subject of a play, *L'Inconstant*, by Collin d'Harleville). After a long period of hesitation which the spectator would naturally expect to lead to some positive attitude, the hero exclaims, to everyone's general amusement:

> J'aurais mieux fait, je crois, d'épouser Célimène.

Le Médisant (1715) is less good than Gresset's *Le Méchant*. *Le Triple Mariage* (1716) is based on an amusing incident in the life of the marquis de Saint-Aulaire. *L'Obstacle imprévu* appeared in 1717. It is clear that Destouches was naturally drawn to this type of comedy, and his experiments along other lines are therefore particularly significant, in that they reflect the change in general taste rather than in his own. He wrote 'tearful' comedies scarcely distinguishable from Nivelle de La Chaussée's *comédies larmoyantes*. He was no doubt under the influence of his English wife, of the plays of Cibber and Steele, and of Marivaux's moralising manner in his *Spectateur français*, as well as of the sentimental ethics of Shaftesbury. He was, moreover, aware of the wind of change blowing through all forms of literature. His best play is *Le Glorieux* (1732).

It lacks the wit of plays by Regnard or Dufresny, the realism of those by Dancourt, and the depth of Lesage at his best, but it is a competent, well-observed, cold comedy, which still retains something of Molière's classical pattern in its hero, the comte de Tubières, who is degraded by his overweening vice till the dénouement, when he is defeated by love. Essentially a sentimental comedy, it presents virtue with an oratorical flourish and with approbation. The last two lines of the play illustrate its moralising manner:

> Et je sens que la gloire et la présomption
> N'attirent que la haine et l'indignation.

Le Philosophe marié (1727) presents the same subject as *Le Préjugé à la mode* (1735), which is Nivelle de La Chaussée's best work, and reveals his concern with social and moral problems. Other plays are less interesting: *Les Philosophes amoureux* (1730), *L'Ambitieux*, *L'Enfant gâté*, *L'Amour usé*, *Le Trésor caché*, *La Force du naturel*, *Le Dissipateur* (based on *Timon of Athens*), *Le Tambour nocturne* (taken from Addison), and *La Fausse Agnès* (which may be compared with Molière's *L'Ecole des femmes* and Regnard's *Les Folies amoureuses*). Their titles alone, however, reveal the new trend. But in the case of Destouches, there is little more than an emphasis on a new approach, and his work lacks the drastic pruning of all that might arouse laughter and the relegation of character to a quite secondary role, which became the deliberate policy of later dramatists. It is not till Figaro appears on the stage that there is a return to personality as a dominant element, such as we find in *Le Glorieux*.

Pierre-Claude Nivelle de La Chaussée (1692–1754) came of a rich family and mingled with members of high society, for the most part *libertins*. He knew Caumartin, a prominent man of the robe, through whom he met Voltaire, around 1711. He went on business to Amsterdam in 1720, but became bored with his career and returned to Paris. Although he lost a fortune in the Law bankruptcy, he was still able to live comfortably and to cut a figure in society. In 1719 he wrote an unsigned attack on the *Fables* of La Motte under the title *Lettres de Mme la Marquise de L.*, and during 1720–30 he wrote *contes* for the licentious society which came into being during the regency. In 1731 he published a defence of poetry which was directed against La Motte, *L'Epître de Clio à M. de B.*, and other poems. He was a member of the *bande joyeuse* that made the *parade* fashionable. It is for his plays of a moralising kind, however, that he won recognition and he was elected to the French Academy in 1736. Sometimes called 'le Révérend Père La Chaussée' because of the edifying character of his comedies, he was in fact branded as a *méchant* for his behaviour towards women, and his appeal to the emotions seems to be a striking example of a systematic appeal to the prevailing taste for the pathetic and the romantic. He cannot be said to have originated sentimentality in the theatre, which is also to be found in Piron and Destouches, as well as in La Motte, Fénelon, Marivaux, and others, but he helped to popularise *comédie larmoyante* and to focus attention on the new aesthetic idea implied in his work. He himself was no conscious innovator and evolved no doctrine, rules, or theories, but his plays, by their consistent presentation of scenes drawn from domestic life and of family relationships, and by their constant appeal to emotions, enshrined *sensibilité* as the cardinal factor in the new set of human and aesthetic values that was being evolved. His best play is *Le Préjugé à la mode* (1735) on a subject suggested by Mlle Quinault. The prejudice he attacks – and which Regnard had endorsed in a very funny play, *Démocrite, ou Le Rieur* – is that it is unthinkable for a man of quality and taste to be in love with his wife or to show his feelings without becoming an object of ridicule. La Chaussée's plot is improbable, his style pretentious, and his poetry dull, yet the public flocked to see the play, and shed tears over it. *L'Ecole des mères* (1744), and particularly *Mélanide* (1741) and *La Gouvernante* (1747), proved exceptionally successful.

The quarrel over the *mélange des genres* lasted for some years. It was taken up by Diderot, and in Germany by Lessing, and *comédie larmoyante* was defended by d'Alembert, chiefly because it had proved successful. With the advent of moral comedy, the eclipse of Molière's type of comedy was complete; sentimentality had triumphed over laughter, and the stage was set for *Cénie* by Mme de Graffigny and *Nanine* (1749) by Voltaire, works that come close to Diderot's definition of *drames*.

Jean-Baptiste-Louis Gresset (1709–77), a novitiate pupil and apprentice teacher in Jesuit colleges, started his literary career as a poet, publishing first a collection of poems (1731), then *Vert-Vert* (1734), for which he was relegated to La Flèche and eventually expelled from the society in 1735. He wrote *Le Carême impromptu*, *Le Lutrin vivant*, and a number of *épîtres* and *contes* in verse. He had become interested in Plautus, Terence, Molière, and Regnard whilst still at school at the Collège Louis-le-Grand and wrote for the stage a tragedy *Edouard III*, which was a complete failure (1740), a sentimental comedy *Sidney* (1745), set in England, which portrayed a sombre and melancholy hero with suicidal tendencies, who provided an early incarnation of English spleen, *Les Bourgeois* (1747), *Les Parvenus* (1748), *L'Esprit à la mode*, and *L'Ecole de l'amour-propre* (1751). But his best play is undoubtedly

Le Méchant (1747). The latter presents a composite character, Cléon, who embodies all too many different kinds of wickedness. He is a cold, calculating, mean, selfish, and vain man, with a marked resemblance to *Le Médisant* of Destouches. It is the presentation of the social background which distinguishes the play: a refined, witty, slanderous, and malicious society so accurately portrayed that, according to Rousseau, it could see no wickedness in the character with the title part. This play may in fact be the last comedy of character of the period, but its real interest lies in the new ethical code it adopts, for Gresset's *méchant* is in fact the *malfaisant* and stands condemned, not in terms of any Christian ethics, but in terms of a practical social morality. The latter in this instance, as in so many *drames*, is based on sentiment and on an appeal to the finer instincts in man. The play ends with the following lines:

> Malgré tout le succès de l'esprit des méchants,
> Je sens qu'on en revient toujours aux bonnes gens.

This Rousseau-ish conception of the fundamental goodness of men flattered the public and seemed comforting to the few true believers in an inner voice of conscience, and the far greater number anxious to see a new ethical code established, which could stand without God. It is this general tone and underlying philosophical attitude which makes *Le Méchant* a forerunner of many *drames*. In 1741 Gresset had published *L'Abbaye*, directed against the monks. He was elected a member of the Academy of Berlin and in 1748 of the French Academy. He married and settled down in Amiens in 1749, renouncing the stage, with a view to devoting his life to religion. He destroyed several of his comedies and published a critical *Lettre sur la comédie*, which was the object of sarcasm both from Voltaire and Piron.

If Gresset's *Sidney* is a *comédie larmoyante*, so is Voltaire's *Nanine ou Le Préjugé vaincu* (1749), the *préjugé* being that of social status. It is a tearful but not a dull play, dealing with philosophical and social theory. Chevrier's *L'Epouse suivante* (1755) and Voisenon's *La Jeune Grecque* (1756) are in the same hybrid genre and the growing use of prose, as being more natural than verse, may be detected in plays of this period. As for *Silvie ou Le Jaloux* (1742) by Landois, it antedates Diderot by the dramatic principles it implies, as does *Cénie* (1750) by Mme de Graffigny, which is styled a tragedy, but is written in prose.

Tragedy was becoming an instrument of philosophical propaganda and tragedy and comedy were about to fuse. It is at this interesting moment that Diderot evolved the theory of *drame* which he illustrated in two of his plays. Diderot himself named

Silvie and *Cénie* as models of what he wished to see realised on a grand scale. However, before considering the *drame*, reference must be made to one true comedy which was presented in 1760 and which satirised violently the leading thinkers of the age. Palissot's play, *Les Philosophes*, by its very subject cannot be fitted into the general evolution of the new genre whose theorist it derided. The play is very superficial, but at the time it was found funny and it created such a stir and so many cabals that it may be said to have achieved something of its aim. It has the distinction of being the only play of any consequence whatever to run counter to the philosophical tide. It incensed Voltaire, whose riposte was *L'Ecossaise* (1760), and Sedaine had it in mind when countering with his play *Le Philosophe sans le savoir*. Diderot was sensitive to the attack on him, but abstained from replying except in the *Neveu de Rameau*, which was not destined for general publication. All the characters in Palissot's comedy were real people. Cidalyse was said to be Helvétius, though some thought of Mme Geoffrin, Mme de La Marck, Mme Riccoboni, or Mme d'Epinay. Le Petit Prophète was identified with Grimm, Théophraste with Duclos, and Dortidius with Diderot. Rousseau did not escape attack, nor did Mlle Clairon, the well-known actress. The struggle around the play illustrates the conflict of the social, religious, and political ideas of the period and as such has some interest; but there is little inherent merit in the text of the play.

Charles Palissot (1730–1814) was an exceptionally precocious and gifted pupil, who completed his courses in rhetoric and philosophy and became Master of Arts at eleven years of age. Four years later he finished his theological studies and entered the Oratoire in Paris, where he stayed two months. At seventeen he wrote a tragedy, which was turned down, but before even finishing this play he wrote *Apollon mentor ou Le Télémaque moderne* (1748). A number of minor works failed to bring him fame, so he turned to satire, first writing a short comedy, *Le Cercle*, which allegedly contained references to Rousseau and to Mme du Châtelet, and led d'Alembert to request King Stanislas to expel him from the Academy of Nancy. In 1757 he published *Petites Lettres sur de grands philosophes*, directed against the *philosophes* and more particularly against Diderot's theory of *drame*. He never wholly lost the favour of persons in positions of influence and later became a friend of Napoleon. His literary judgements were categorical and unsound. His tragedy *Zarès* (1751) is devoid of quality. His later works include *La Dunciade ou La Guerre des sots* (1764), a satire imitated from Pope.

The satirical vein, well exploited by Lesage at the beginning of the century, and brilliantly utilised by Voltaire and others in their fiction, now found expression on the stage only in minor works, parodies for popular or private entertainment, and it is only with Beaumarchais that it regains stature. By 1757 the prevailing mood was one of earnest reappraisal and unqualified seriousness.

IV. 'LE DRAME'

It has been contended that it was a desire to create new theatre forms which gave rise to the *drame*, but it would appear that a greater aesthetic change was involved. The seriousness of everyday reality could not find expression in classical drama, which had developed a special idiom of its own. Classicism had evolved canons of taste and a rigid set of rules which, in tragedy, are reflected in the unities, the play in five acts and in verse, and especially in the creation of a distinctive form of expression, highly sophisticated and unnatural, which gave a sense of timelessness to the great tragedies; the fine and highly stylised poetry it evolved is far removed from the language of everyday life. Erich Auerbach in *Mimesis* has referred to the 'seclusion and isolation of the tragic process', rooted in a 'very complicated and multilayered tradition', which is in fact highly artificial and can be seen as reasonable only in terms of its own perspective. To a lesser extent this would be true of classical and of Italian comedy.

The historical significance of *le drame*, a new form of bourgeois theatre half-way between tragedy and comedy, is the step it marks towards a greater realism. To quote Auerbach once more:

> They [the realist novelists of the nineteenth century, especially Balzac and Stendhal] broke with the classical rule of distinct levels of style, for according to this rule, everyday practical reality could find a place in literature only within the frame of a low or intermediate kind of style, that is to say, as either grotesquely comic or pleasant, light, colourful and elegant entertainment. They thus completed a development which had long been in preparation (since the time of the novel of manners and the *comédie larmoyante* of the eighteenth century, and more pronouncedly since the *Sturm und Drang* and early romanticism). And they opened the way for modern realism, which has ever since developed in increasingly rich forms, in keeping with the constantly changing and expanding reality of modern life.

Whatever its failings, the *drame*, which for this purpose may be said to include the *comédie larmoyante*, has provided a milestone in this evolution.

The term *drame* is technically applied in France to plays of the second half of the eighteenth century constructed according to canons of taste enunciated by Diderot in his *Entretiens sur Le Fils naturel* (1757), which accompanied his play *Le Fils naturel*. In the *troisième entretien* he pleads his case for a new genre. He called it first *comédie*, then *tragédie domestique et bourgeoise*, and finally *drame*. In his list of diverse types of plays he maintained that *burlesque*, at one extreme of comedy, and *merveilleux*, at the other extreme of tragedy, are outside the scope of nature, thereby underlining that his general aesthetic theory is based on his philosophy of nature. Although he soon learnt that art was not merely imitation of nature, but involved the translation of an ideal model present in the mind of the artist, and that in the theatre everything must be larger than life, he saw the need for conveying the illusion of reality, which is at the root of the creation of the *drame bourgeois*. Since man is not always in a state of grief or joy, there must be a point in between these extremes that is properly the province of drama based on real life. This half-way house may be termed *comédie sérieuse* or *tragédie bourgeoise* at will. What is more important is to turn to realism, to well-selected subjects drawn from everyday life, to simple plots, and to dialogue written in prose. Social conditions naturally have their place in this conception of drama and are given priority over analysis of character, which is the basis of classical drama. Hence the insistence on depicting men in their professions rather than of a given character. So the dramatist will stage, not misers or hypocrites, but either professional persons or else those linked by family relationships. These were to be studied not so much as individuals, but as representatives of clearly defined occupations. One curious result of this way of thinking has been the successful rehabilitation on the stage, if not elsewhere, of the soldier, the innkeeper, and the servant. A question such as 'Parce qu'ils sont nos valets, ont-ils cessé d'être des hommes?' leads us directly to Figaro, stout upholder of the rights of the *Tiers Etat*. No longer is the bourgeois to be exposed to ridicule, as he so often was in the comedies of Molière. Society, according to Diderot, should be depicted in its generality. It is tempting but dangerous to oversimplify Diderot's thought and, to do justice to his projected reforms, it should be pointed out that he does not seek to abolish character study, but to derive it from occupational circumstance. Hence the stress is laid upon the professions followed by his characters, for he is really urging, as his *Discours de la poésie dramatique* brings out quite clearly, that the *drame* should be a serious, not a frivolous, comment on contemporary society. Given the axiom that the theatre lends itself to all forms of art which make a special appeal to the senses, Diderot welcomes the possible creation of hybrid forms of art, mixing the resources of plastic art, *tableaux*, décors, mime, gesture, and voice. It is of interest to note that in his writings he anticipated grand opera, romantic ballet, and the use of simultaneous sets, in his search for an increased range of theatrical experience.

He laid part of the blame for contemporary shortcomings on the influence of the classical tradition. He saw sense in Aristotle's much-criticised and ill-applied dramatic unities, only challenging the unity of place on the grounds that swift, efficient scene-changing could render it unnecessary; above all he insisted on what he calls the *unité de discours*, i.e. the need for an overriding unity of production in keeping with the internal unity of the text. However, authors must feel free to break the unities if they can do so without impairing dramatic illusion. The essential law of artistic composition is to respect *vraisemblance*.

It is in the light of this principle that blind imitation of classical drama must lead to failure. The laws of classical drama arose out of the conditions of the time, and cannot therefore be applied without modification to a different civilisation and a different form of theatre. These theories of *vraisemblance*, the unities, and *tableaux* are discussed in the first section of *Entretiens sur Le Fils naturel*. In the second, Diderot deals with eloquence, mime, and good acting, deploring the rhetorical style still favoured by the actors of the Comédie Française, and stressing the need for *tableaux* or stage pictures to enhance realism, and for actors to behave naturally on the stage. It is in the third part that he adumbrates his full theory.

There is a salient feature of the *drame bourgeois* with which we have not dealt and which Diderot himself omitted from his own summary of reforms: the moral significance of the play. It is no doubt this didactic preoccupation which mars his own dramatic works. Diderot is always first and foremost a moralist. 'Voulez-vous être auteur? Voulez-vous être critique?' he asks, 'Commencez par être homme de bien.' His *homme de bien* is, of course, *un homme sensible* in the first instance. In the age of *sensibilité*, speeches on virtue, and sentimental apostrophes to nature, *bienfaisance* and the like became the order of the day. In wishing to make the new theatre serve as a great moralising force, an instrument of philosophical propaganda, Diderot is far from alone. He was trying to do for the theatre what Greuze was doing for painting. It can be argued that the countless *drames* of the late eighteenth century were appreciated and enjoyed as vehicles of propaganda and cheap emotionalism; yet it remains true that the Church would have maintained a virtual monopoly in moral values had it not been for the theatre. And many plays, by their veiled anti-clerical speeches, provided an effective counterblast to propaganda from the pulpit. In Diderot's Utopia, the theatre would take the place of the Church, and actors that of the priests:

'Tous les peuples ont leurs sabbats, et nous aurons aussi les nôtres.'[26] The *drame* as a vehicle for popularising a new gospel must not be underestimated.

Diderot was subordinating art to an overriding ethical purpose, and his disciples followed his advice to the letter. Moral preoccupations often determine the subject and very structure of their plays: every opportunity is taken to exalt the good in man and to revile his wickedness. The main purpose of theatre becomes to purge man of evil, not primarily through argument, logic, or discussion, but through emotional impact. Those who today would seek to subordinate art to politics and misuse drama for purposes of propaganda would do well to apply themselves to Diderot's precept: 'Qu'un auteur intelligence instruise et qu'il plaise, mais que ce soit y penser. Si l'on remarque son but, il le manque, il cesse de dialoguer, il prêche.'[27]

Yet Diderot himself as a dramatist failed to carry out his own precepts as a theorist. His plays are overloaded with moral strictures that inevitably defeat his purpose. Both *Le Fils naturel* (first performed 1771) and *Le Père de famille* are intended as *drames*. They are studies in human relationships, the plots are largely shaped by the apparent social differences between the characters, and both plays contain much moralising. They both are filled with emotional rhetoric and theatrical devices of all kinds, and show little psychological insight. Neither play does justice to his talent as a dramatist, as shown in his later play *Est-il bon? Est-il méchant?* or in *Le Neveu de Rameau*. Neither play does justice to his dramatic theories, partly because they are the work of a man without practical theatre experience – his stage directions, for example, are all extraneous to the action of the play. His mediocre plots fail to convey any social or psychological message of consequence, since they are, oddly enough in view of his avowed intentions, set in a milieu of well-to-do people of a non-professional type. It must be admitted that *Le Philosophe sans le savoir* (1765), by Sedaine, whom Diderot greatly admired, is an incomparably better example of the *drame* than either of Diderot's plays. Yet both achieved considerable notoriety and both have their place in the history of French drama.

The theory of the *drame* was also formulated by Beaumarchais in his *Essai sur le genre dramatique sérieux* (1767), and by Mercier in his *Du Théâtre ou Nouvel Essai sur l'art dramatique* (1773), but neither writer adds materially to Diderot's original presentation. There were foreign influences, primarily English, at work. Lillo's *The London Merchant* (1731), showing the effect of debauchery

[26] *Œuvres complètes de Diderot*, ed. Assézat-Tourneux, VIII, p. 109.
[27] Ibid., VII, pp. 345–6.

on a weak character, had been translated into French in 1748, and *The Gamester* by Edward Moore was translated in 1762, having been earlier adapted into French by Diderot. Both *The London Merchant* and *The Gamester* were first defined as *drames* by Diderot; both are mirrors of the bourgeoisie and both have a moral aim in view. Adaptations for the French stage of Shakespeare, Fielding, and Richardson in particular increased the range of French theatrical experience. German influence is less easily assessed. *Miss Sara Sampson* by Lessing was performed in 1755, before *Le Fils naturel*, and Professor H. Dieckmann has found a translation of this work among Diderot's manuscript pages, but Lessing, who rendered Diderot's *Entretiens* into German, has acknowledged Diderot's work as his chief inspiration. There is ample evidence that by this time a major movement in the theatre was under way. Later Goethe, Schiller, and Gessner were to exercise some considerable influence.

F. Gaiffe in his monumental study of *le drame*[28] has somewhat arbitrarily limited it to those plays which appeared in France between *Le Fils naturel* in 1757 and the proclamation of the freedom of the theatres in 1791, and has endeavoured to establish strict criteria. It is perhaps wiser, and certainly simpler, to consider the writers of *drames* as a heterodox group who shared from the very beginning a feeling of involvement in the diffusion of a moral propaganda destined to supplement the philosophical propaganda. Without neglecting religious and political propaganda, the writers give most attention to social questions, the excellence of human nature and above all of primitive man; the glorification of passions, of the natural instincts of the savage as opposed to the corruption of civilised man, of the superiority of the simple rustic life over the city life, and of merchants and other workers over the privileged classes. Commerce is extolled, as are the weak and the oppressed. Equality before the law is stressed as an ideal and the social condition of women deplored. War is declared on fanaticism, priests, and prejudices. Pleas in favour of natural religion abound, which enable an attack on forced monastic vocations, and, under the guise of honouring Henri IV, Louis XV is attacked.

This propaganda became more daring as the century progressed. The reaction of the public deserves closer study than it has yet received. It remembered little of the theory of the *drames*, but enjoyed long lectures in dialogue form when it heard them on the stage, and what shocks our sense of theatre today is sometimes what ensured the success of the play in its time. But such was the tide that swept the world that even early failure could not halt the ultimate success of quite mediocre plays. Nothing ever checked

[28] *Le Drame en France au XVIIIe siècle*, 1910.

Mercier who, after failing at the Théâtre Français, fell back on performances in the provinces and on private stages before making a comeback on the Parisian stage.

The relative failure of Diderot's *Le Père de famille* did not prevent the work from setting the tone for the *drame*. Young dramatists felt prompted to accept the new aesthetic doctrine and adopted similar themes. Sedaine's *Le Philosophe sans le savoir*, still calling itself a comedy, was immediately considered the model of the genre. Excellently constructed, it answered the new ideal in that bourgeois virtues and commerce were upheld, sincerity and pathos exploited to the full, and the style adopted was suitably moral in tone. The plot, however, was already outmoded, centring as it did upon duelling. Surprisingly, it required the bourgeois M. Vanderk, protagonist of the *Philosophes*, to be in reality a man of noble birth. Sedaine was not in advance of his timid public. This excellent play, now considered as a museum piece, suffered immediately from the fact that its propaganda, as all propaganda, has dated. Furthermore, the philosophical ideas expounded were, as they always are in drama, simpler than those of the more advanced thinkers. It illustrates Diderot's official ethics, rather than his deep-seated beliefs. The apologia of nature becomes *de rigueur*. In the plays of this period, pastorals and *paysanneries* had already accustomed the public to some of the pseudo-simplicities of nature. Now these were presented in association with the theory of the goodness of man in nature, offering virtuous love in an idyllic setting and suggesting social and political reforms. Countless *drames* sing the praises of domestic bliss, real love as a basis for marriage, and the cult of primitive emotions and manners. Delisle with his *Arlequin sauvage* (1723) had known a great success, even before Marmontel had staged Voltaire's Huron (*Le Huron*, 1768, with music by Grétry). We find echoes in the theatre of the journal of Bougainville and other seafaring men, of Rousseau's hypotheses concerning primitive men, and even of Diderot's presentation of moral problems in *Le Supplément au Voyage de Bougainville*, a work which they could not have read. Chamfort in *La Jeune Indienne* (1764) indulges in long dissertations on the barbarism of civilised society, for the marriage of the fickle Englishman Belton and the dusky Betti offered a good pretext for glorifying mixed marriages, for showing a warm heart, as well as for extolling the benefits of commerce, the curse of gold, and the beauty of the savage state. Love within marriage is now seen as deeply moving and best calculated to ensure happiness. Fathers love their sons and mothers suckle their own children. Never had there been so many children on the stage and never were there so many scenes reminiscent of paintings by Greuze.

The list of Florian's plays, *Le Bon Ménage* (1783), *La Bonne Mère* (1785), *Le Bon Fils* (1785), and *Le Bon Père* (1790), is evidence enough. These themes became conventional long before Mercier, and are to be found also in Fabre d'Eglantine's *Les Précepteurs* (1799), which sings the praises of a rational and philosophical education, after the pattern of Rousseau. The essential goodness of man becomes an axiom. Thus Mercier wrote:

Si je croyais l'homme né méchant je briserais la plume et laisserais mon encrier se dessécher . . . Qui es-tu? ô toi! qui oses dire que l'homme est né méchant! Monstre, qui t'a élevé? Ce pernicieux blasphème où l'as-tu puisé? . . . Vis dans l'innocence de l'enfance, la confiance et la simplicité de la jeunesse, l'amour des pères et des mères pour leurs enfants; vois s'il est un seul homme inaccessible à la pitié . . . les hommes naissent véritablement frères . . .

All this theatrical verbiage, a mixture of sincerity and hypocrisy, finds a parallel in English literature at the time of Queen Victoria. Great success attended the presentation of the rehabilitation of seduced girls, criminals, and traitors acknowledging the wickedness of their ways, and conversions of all kinds, except to the Church. Beaumarchais may be commended for not falling too readily for this kind of cheap and unconvincing morality. Lovelace, almost attractive in the novels of the period, is satirised in plays such as Voltaire's *Le Droit du seigneur*, the works of Mercier, and Beaumarchais' *Eugénie*. Favart stands out for having preserved the satirical vein of the earlier regency together with a desire to return to nature. *Bergeries* certainly remain fashionable. *Bastien et Bastienne* and *Le Devin du village* (1752) by Rousseau met with great success, and Favart in *Les Moissonneurs* and Mercier in *Le Campagnard ou Le Riche désabusé* (published 1779) exploit the theme of an Eldorado or new Golden Age suited to the sentimental and social aspirations of a whole generation.

Social and political propaganda hinged on the cult of the primitive in man. It became incumbent on a playwright to express pity for the poor, the Protestants wrongly condemned to the galleys, deserters who are victims of military regulations and prejudice, and nuns forcibly locked up in convents. It may be said that the Calas affair paved the way for many *drames*, such as those by Lemierre d'Argy, Laya, and M.-J. Chénier. If a good priest is placed on the stage it is to condemn more surely the vast majority who are automatically branded as wicked. Mercier appealed to the public conscience of the spectators more than to their aesthetic taste. He defended the deserter, and democracy as well, in *La Brouette du vinaigrier* (1776), in which Dominique, the old *vinaigrier*, is seen as a better man than Delomer, the rich man. He presented, too, scenes from provincial life and from foreign countries. But he had to bide his time, for the public was hardly ripe for such a crude social commentary. It preferred for a time personal satire, as in *Les Philosophes* by Palissot, and *L'Ecossaise* by Voltaire, plays given in the popular theatre of the boulevards, of Audinot and Nicolet. Mercier's fame dates from 1781, when his *Tableau de Paris* began to appear, and as the French Revolution draws near his works gain in appeal and significance.

The political attitudes of eighteenth-century dramatists were very diverse. But it was generally held that all political systems or ideas rest on natural law, social man must be natural man, and laws must be nature codified; they are not immutable, but should encourage virtue and ensure greater happiness. Tyrants are exposed. Reason must govern man. By 1789 anti-clericalism is commonplace, and the challenge to authority grows specific. Thus Mercier in *Jean Hennuyer* writes: 'Qui ne parle plus en homme, ne peut plus commander en roi.' A bitter irony pervades plays of sinister implications, and the idea of kingship is brought down. The popularity of patriotic plays such as de Belloy's *Le Siège de Calais* must be counterbalanced by the international humanitarian crusade of the *philosophes*, who show the people as decimated by war and famine and stress universal peace, the brotherhood of man, and all the ideas of Voltaire, Rousseau, and the Abbé Raynal. By 1789 new plays are essentially topical, clear calls to struggle, but often technically defective.

The connection between these plays, so full of propaganda, and the new dramatic theories needs to be brought out. The frequent reiteration of the theories contributed greatly to the success of the propaganda and led the public to accept the new spirit. Undoubtedly Diderot, rather than Voltaire, exercised the greatest influence, through his *Entretiens sur Le Fils naturel* and his *Essai sur la poésie dramatique*. Diderot more clearly than any other stressed the need for a philosophical theatre, essentially moral, which would take the place of the Church. The *philosophe*, who may be an atheist, is an *homme de bien* and an excellent citizen. This attitude is better expressed by long tirades or sermons than by pieces of dialogue, by *tableaux* or dramatic situations reminiscent of theurgical or liturgical dramas. Invocations to nature are like prayers. The new virtue is essentially non-Christian, and the new religion rests preferably on the goodness of man and never admits of original sin. This religion, which is very simple and proved popular for a time, is in no wise comparable in intellectual content with the religion of science inaugurated by Diderot in his *Lettre sur les aveugles*, his *Pensées sur l'interprétation de la nature*, and in the *Encyclopédie*.

The *drames* seem to have been designed to supplement the

general political activity of the *philosophes*. Diderot in particular was led to distinguish between ethics for the masses and the more subtle ethics of the enlightened. The dramatic merit of his novel *Le Neveu de Rameau* springs precisely from the conflict between the two ethics, a conflict with social and psychological overtones, which is never found in the theatre of the period. The great weakness of the *drames* lay in their poor psychology and inability to probe into the complexity of the subconscious. It is as an expression of an historical moment and as a document of pre-revolutionary preoccupations that the *drame* has its place in the history of ideas; and for its liberating general attitude and specific efforts towards a new bourgeois realism that it has its place in the history of the theatre.

F. Gaiffe in his exhaustive list of *drames*[29] includes fifty-two plays of consequence, by various playwrights, the following perhaps deserving mention here: *Le Fabricant de Londres* by Falbaire (1771); *Les Fautes sont personnelles* and *Sa Mère l'allaita* by Restif (1784–90); *Gabrielle d'Estrées* by Sauvigny; *L'Honnête Criminel ou L'Amour filial* by Falbaire (1768); *Jeannot et Colin* by Florian; *Joachim ou Le Triomphe de la piété filiale* by Blin de Sainmore; *Mélanie ou La Religieuse by* La Harpe (1772 and 1791, published 1770); *Le Partie de chasse de Henri IV* by Collé (1774); *Fanfan et Colas* by Mme de Beaunoir (1784, with a sequel in 1785); *Sylvain* by Marmontel; *Tom Jones* by Poinsinet (with music by Philidor, 1765); *Les Victimes cloîtrées* by Monvel (1791); *Barneveldt* by La Harpe (1778); *L'Ecole de la jeunesse ou Le Barneveldt français* by Anseaume (music by Duni, 1765); *Jenneval ou Le Barneveldt français* by Mercier (1776); *Bélisaire* by Moissy (1769); *Bélisaire* by d'Ozicourt (1769); and *Béverley, tragédie bourgeoise* by Saurin (1767). There are also four plays, by Monnier, d'Abancourt, Berquin, and Florian, all entitled *Le Bon Fils; Calas ou Le Fanatisme* by Lemierre d'Argy (1790); *Les Calas* by M. de Brumore; *Jean Calas*, a tragedy by Laya (1790); *Jean Calas, ou L'Ecole des Juges* by Chénier (1791); *Le Déserteur* by Sedaine (music by Monsigny, 1769); *Le Déserteur* by Mercier (1771); *Les Ennemis réconciliés* by Bruté de Loirelle (1766); and *L'Erreur d'un moment ou La Suite de Julie* by Monvel.

Of these dramatists, Sedaine, Baculard d'Arnaud, and Sébastien Mercier stand out. Sedaine (1719–97) started life as a stonecutter, and was eventually employed by Buron, the architect, who noticed his talent and found him a patron. In 1752 he published some songs and short poems which won him a measure of success, and he felt encouraged to write operas and *vaudevilles*. His comic opera *Le Diable à quatre* (1756) set the style of his later work. His best-

[29] op. cit., pp. 557–77.

known works are a one-act comedy, *La Gageure imprévue* (1768), a delightful piece of *marivaudage*, and *Le Philosophe sans le savoir*, which he saw as a serious rejoinder to Palissot's satirical comedy *Les Philosophes*. Between 1756 and 1761 Sedaine provided the Opéra-Comique with *comédies à ariettes*. His work was much appreciated by the *forains* and he was considered as the virtual founder of the *opéra-comique*, inspiring Monsigny, Philidor, and Grétry. Plays include *Le Diable à quatre*, *Blaise le savetier*, *L'Huître et les plaideurs*, *Les Trocqueurs dupés*, and *Le Jardinier et son seigneur*, which show borrowings from La Fontaine. He also wrote *On ne s'avise pas de tout* (1761), and *Le Roi et le fermier* (borrowed from Dodsley); *Rose et Colas, a bergerie*, his favourite play; *Maillard ou Paris sauvé* (first performed in 1777 but stopped by the censor); *Le Déserteur* (1769), *Aucassin et Nicolette*, and *Les Mœurs du bon vieux temps*; and *Richard Cœur de Lion* (1784), which has a famous *romance* by Grétry, 'Mon coeur brûle. . . .' The excellent public response to this last play led to his election to the French Academy, after fourteen unsuccessful attempts. He married in 1769 and had four children. His last days were sad, and he had the macabre pleasure of reading his own very favourable obituary notices, which appeared prematurely. He espoused the revolutionary cause, but broke with the extremists David and the Jacobins, and suffered greatly from the dispersal of his friends, and from the suppression of the Académie Royale and of his own pension. A rather withdrawn and cold man, he was acclaimed by Diderot as an *observateur*, and *homme de génie*, as a proud, brilliant conversationalist, caustic but without bitterness, and with exceptional self-possession. Diderot regretted that Sedaine was too old in years to prove a suitable match for his daughter.

Le Philosophe sans le savoir, which was an instant success in spite of stylistic blemishes, is a study of the qualities developed by trade and profession, showing the broadening of the mind through trade and awareness of the solidarity of mankind. M. Vanderk is the ideal *philosophe*, if we accept the definition of the word as it stands in the *Encyclopédie*: 'Le philosophe est un homme qui se gouverne par la raison, ouvert à toutes les meilleures influences de la vie, jaloux de son honneur, remplissant ses devoirs sociaux et familiers.' The theme is the glorification of the enlightened bourgeoisie, but the author is somewhat inconsistent, since his plot requires the *philosophe*, who turns out to be after all a nobleman who has renounced his title, to send his son to fight in a duel. The duel in fact led the play to be censored and Sedaine to change a scene in his original draft. The characters as a whole belong to an aristocratic milieu and speak the idiom natural to the *philosophes*, discussing ideas and social problems as well as their feelings. The over-all impression is of a lifelike presentation of pleasant people. The play can be fully appreciated only when it is staged, and its occasional revival is invariably successful. There are moments of melancholy, as when Vanderk junior awaits his supreme test at dawn before the duel. But soon the prevailing mood of gaiety returns, and an optimistic note creeps in with the advent of the musicians. Love is relegated to a secondary role, but we are offered the convincing picture of a young and innocent girl. Family scenes are touching, like those depicted by Greuze. In *Turcaret* all the characters were evil; here they are all good. The scenario of the play was taken up in the Romantic period by George Sand, in her comedy *Le Mariage de Victorine*. Its main purpose in the eighteenth century was to vindicate the term *philosophe*, badly battered by Palissot, and to illustrate by a convincing success the dramatic possibilities of Diderot's theories.

F.-T.-M. Baculard d'Arnaud (1718–1805) first became known to Voltaire through his verse. Voltaire recommended him to Frederick the Great and he went to Berlin, but he soon returned to Paris where he lived in poverty. His writings cover a wide range of works, including *Les Epreuves du sentiment*, *Les Nouvelles historiques*, *Les Délassements de l'homme sensible*, *Les Loisirs utiles*, and some mediocre sacred odes entitled *Les Lamentations de Jérémie* (1752). But it is his four plays that are most noteworthy, especially *Le Comte de Comminge ou Les Amants malheureux*, based on a novel by Mme de Tencin, and the only one to be performed. The play is in verse, and was published in 1765, but was not put on the stage of the Comédie Française till 1790. In spite of the author's strong Catholic beliefs, most unusual among fellow playwrights, his work illustrates well an exaggerated sensibility coupled with a sense of horror which paved the way for Romantic melodrama. *Euphémie* (1768) is set in a crypt and the heroine, stumbling over a slab, nearly falls into the tomb. *Fayel* is a medieval tragedy based on the story of the châtelain de Coucy, presenting still *tableaux* in medieval costume and suitable trappings. The Lady of Fayel is supposed to eat the heart of de Coucy, but the corpse is kept off-stage and the spectator is spared a gruesome final scene. Baculard, in spite of such scenes of tragic horror, failed to affect his audience as much as he wished owing to his lack of dramatic imagination, and his plays remain cold, dull, and clumsy in style and presentation.

Louis-Sébastien Mercier (1740–1814) also began with verse. He wrote twenty *héroïdes*, which met with no success, and thereafter he affected to despise all verse. He was professor of rhetoric at the Collège de Bordeaux, and after a career as politician, journalist, and dramatist, he occupied the chair of history at the Ecole Centrale for some time after the Revolution. His early *drames* were imitated from the German and the English. He formulated his aesthetic ideas in his *Essai sur l'art dramatique*, which, however, adds little to Diderot's theories. He is credited with coining the word *dramaturge*, which alone perhaps survives of the 3,000 new words to enrich the French language that he proposed in a work entitled *Néologismes*. He illustrated his dramatic theories in a number of plays which had no success in Paris, but were acclaimed in the provinces, and this fact, together with a change in mood, led in due course to their return to the capital. He had derived his inspiration from the people and shown disdain for the classics, Homer, Plautus, and especially Racine and Boileau, whom he called 'les pestiférés de la littérature.' He wrote in all thirty-one plays including *L'Habitant de la Guadeloupe*, *La Brouette du vinaigrier*, and *Le Déserteur*, which was much applauded and earned for him a pension of 800 livres from Marie-Antoinette. His plays were published in four volumes in 1778–84, and included, in addition to those mentioned, *Jenneval ou Le Barneveldt français*, *Natalie*, *Olinde et Sophronice*, *L'Indigent*, *La Maison de Molière*, *Jean Hennuyer, évêque de Lisieux*, *Childéric Ier*, *Louis XI*, *Philippe II*, etc. But it is his *Tableau de Paris*, the first two volumes of which appeared in 1781 to be followed by twelve written at Neuchâtel, where he had taken refuge (1782–89), and *Le Nouveau Paris* (1797) in six parts, enlarged to six volumes in 1800, which made his reputation and still provide a source of information on contemporary life. He sided with the Girondins during the Revolution, contributing to the *Chronique du mois*, a Girondin publication. He was elected to the Convention for Seine-et-Oise and remained a moderate, voting for the banishment of the king. He was incarcerated after the fall of the Girondins, and after *9 thermidor* he returned to the Convention. In a strange work which contains much folly and some good ideas, *L'An 2440 ou Rêve s'il en fut jamais* (1770), he outlined political reforms to be adopted 670 years later. This led him to consider himself as the true prophet of the Revolution. But soon, disillusioned and increasingly reactionary, he began to attack the ideas of Voltaire and voted against popular education, a fact which earned him the nickname 'Le singe de Jean-Jacques'. He was a member of the Cinq-Cents,[30] but his eccentricity became increasingly pronounced and weakened his influence. He was antagonistic to whatever government was in power, favouring the Republicans once again under the Empire, and calling Napoleon a 'sabre organisé'. He had little commonsense and less taste – the only painter he liked was Greuze.

[30] Created, under the Directoire, by the constitution of 1795, forming with the Conseil des Anciens the legislative body.

He attacked the views of Locke and Condillac, as also those of Copernicus and Newton. He was constantly challenging the authorities who, however, reluctantly decided to let him speak his mind freely. With Brizard he edited J.-J. Rousseau's works, and on his death left the manuscript of a *Cours de littérature,* as well as the early sections of a dictionary. His total output is enormous and earned for him the title of 'le plus grand livrier de France'. Apart from his *Tableau de Paris,* his *drames* alone survive as a dated monument to a genre which was not destined to develop without a complete transformation, and as a stepping-stone in the search for realism.

V. BEAUMARCHAIS (1732–99)

Pierre-Augustin Caron, who derived the title de Beaumarchais from a property owned by his first wife, wrote comparatively little for the theatre, and in his case literary activity took second place to the business of living. His life and temperament are the key to his work, and his ability to portray them one reason for his success. His life-story, however, is so complex that a summary of salient features can scarcely do it justice. The son of a clockmaker, he started by inventing a useful watch-escapement at the age of twenty, acquiring the title of *horloger du roi.* Perhaps something of his training in craftsmanship may be detected in the construction of his *Barbier de Séville* and his understanding of the intricate mechanism of complicated plots. He had a gift for music, being an accomplished harp-player, and for poetry, and was early noted for his wit.

His social advancement was rapid and he became music-master to the daughters of Louis XV. His first marriage, which ended in his wife's death after only a few months, gave him his title and his social standing. He became the friend of a great financier, Pâris-Duverney, who initiated him into the world of speculation and the considerable profits to be derived out of supplies to the army. He was able to acquire the post of *Secrétaire du Roi,* which ennobled him, and in 1763 he became *Lieutenant-général de la Varenne du Louvre,* that is to say, a magistrate empowered to try offences such as poaching. In 1764 he went to Madrid, ostensibly to avenge the honour of his sister Lisette, who had been deserted by her fickle fiancé, Clavijo y Faxardo. In his fourth *Mémoire* (1774) against Goëzman he retold the story of his adventures in Spain, which Goethe was to present in his play entitled *Clavigo.*

Beaumarchais had now an acknowledged place in society and frequented the salons. He entertained and wrote poetry and short plays, or *parades*, two of which still exist: *Les Bottes de sept lieues* and *Jean-Bête à la Foire*, besides two scenes, *Colin et Colette*, a *paysannerie*, and *Les Députés de la Halle et du Gros-Caillou*, in the style called *poissard*. He decided to try his hand at writing *drames*, and on 25 February 1767 he produced *Eugénie ou La Vertu malheureuse*, a play in five acts, the first to bear the official title of *drame*, which failed on the first night, but which he promptly cut down to four acts, after which amputation it obtained some success. The play was published with a manifesto, *Lettre sur le genre dramatique sérieux*, which has little intrinsic originality, apart from embodying Beaumarchais' cherished beliefs, his conviction as a thinker that the future lay with *drames*, a view which is echoed in his last play, *L'Autre Tartuffe, ou La Mère coupable*, first performed in 1792. His defence of the *drame*, which runs counter to his own talent and temperament, and is not in accordance with his personal success as a playwright, points to the strong prevailing tide in intellectual and artistic quarters and to Beaumarchais' own natural adaptability.

Beaumarchais has been likened to Voltaire for his style, wit, and cleverness, but Voltaire fought battles in major causes, which went to the root of some of the greatest issues of his day, while Beaumarchais remained a self-seeker (though one not incapable of great generosity in private relations): a spy in the king's pay working for dubious causes, he was at best an *éminence grise*, and if in later life he helped materially the insurgents of America by supplying them with arms, he never lost sight of the financial reward to which he was entitled and which Congress omitted to pay him. *Eugénie* was followed in 1770 by another *drame*, *Les Deux Amis, ou Le Négociant de Lyon*, which, although better written, was a complete failure, possibly owing to its feeble plot. The writing of these two *drames* left their mark on Beaumarchais' later masterpieces. They explain his inclusion of moralising and sentimental passages and his frequent references to philosophical, often anticlerical, ideas. They show, too, a concern for realism in dialogue and an awareness of social problems and natural feelings throughout the social classes, which the glitter of his later irony and sharp ripostes do not disguise. His attention to setting, décors, costume, and stage directions, as well as to the spectacular quality of the entertainment to be provided, may also owe something to his conception of *drame* as the most worthwhile form of theatre.

1770 was a bad year for Beaumarchais. His second wife died in November. Earlier on, in July, Pâris-Duverney, aged eighty-seven, had also died – but left him a large sum of money. The will was challenged by the heir, Comte Falcoz de La Blache. Legal proceedings dragged on till February 1772, when the courts decided in Beaumarchais' favour. La Blache, however, appealed and the case went to the *Grand Conseil*, and thence to the tribunal of Aix-en-Provence. La Blache wrote pamphlets against Beaumarchais, who replied with such great ferocity that he was condemned to pay a fine of 1,000 *écus* for the virulence of his attack. It was not till 21 July 1778 that Beaumarchais won his case. The verdict ensured his material prosperity, but the protracted struggle left its mark on Beaumarchais and on his work.

Early in 1773 the outlook, however, seemed promising again. He wrote a comic opera, *Le Barbier de Séville*, which was, however, turned down by the Comédie Italienne. He then converted it into a comedy which the Comédie Française agreed to put on. But in February he became involved in a quarrel with the duc de Chaulnes over an actress, Mlle Mesnard, to whom he openly offered his protection. He was incarcerated and only allowed out of gaol to attend the hearing of the La Blache case on 5 April, and to present his own case to the *rapporteur du tribunal*, an Alsatian called Goëzman. In the fashion customary at the time he offered some money and a watch studded with diamonds to Mme Goëzman, and fifteen *louis* to the secretary. In spite of this Beaumarchais lost his case and found himself ruined. Mme Goëzman returned the money and the watch, but not the fifteen *louis*, which the secretary denied having received. Goëzman alleged an attempt at corruption. This in turn led Beaumarchais to write the first of his famous *Mémoires* (5 September 1773), in which he set himself up as the champion of liberty against the corrupt Parlement Maupeou. This was followed by three other *Mémoires*, which turned the tables on Goëzman, who was indicted. These *Mémoires* are among the most brilliant pieces of French polemic writing, only yielding first place to the *Provinciales* by Pascal, largely because the issues Beaumarchais aired are basically personal and have not the same wide intellectual consequence. They are masterpieces of literary style, especially the fourth, which provoked the admiration of Voltaire. They contain exceptionally fine scenes of comedy equal to those in his best plays. In 1774 the courts condemned Mme Goëzman, and her husband was deprived of his office, but Beaumarchais too was reprimanded and lost his civic rights and his office of magistrate, with the financial emoluments it carried with it. His *Mémoires* were condemned to be burnt by the public executioner.

Beaumarchais' popularity was greatly increased by the injustice he suffered and by his published statement. He offered the government his services as secret agent, and went to London, in the company of a blackmailer, to try to have a pamphlet against Mme du Barry, favourite of the king, suppressed. The king, however, died and his mission lost all point. Beaumarchais was then entrusted with the task, which came to nothing, of pursuing an enemy of France, diversely called Angelucci or Atkinson, in London, Holland, Germany, and Vienna, where he was arrested, but released on the intervention of the French court. The story of his strange adventures, widely spread, did his credit little good. But he had the support of the authorities, after the abolition of the Parlement Maupeou in 1774, and of the court.

It is at this point that he asked for the censor's approval for his play *Le Barbier de Séville, ou La Précaution inutile*, which was at last performed on 23 February 1775. The play, enlarged to five acts, contained much extraneous matter directed against his enemies and was a dismal failure. Three days later Beaumarchais produced the play as we now know it, in four acts, but still close to the text of the earlier draft. Thus revised, it was an instant and lasting success. Professor E.-J. Arnould, in his scholarly edition,[31] has reproduced all five known versions of the text, with a detailed commentary. An examination reveals above all Beaumarchais' intelligence and dexterity, and his main concern with success, not simply the vindication of his *amour-propre* as a writer. In his attitude to his craft he may be likened to Voltaire, who was always willing to listen to advice, and he realised that for a dramatist success must be achieved in the theatre and not in the library.

In April 1775, he moved back to London to settle a case of political blackmail instigated by the chevalier d'Eon, formerly a French ambassador in Russia, but now a refugee in London, where he was seen dressed as a woman, who was threatening to reveal secret documents with which he had been entrusted. Beaumarchais met John Wilkes, Lord Mayor of London and supporter of the American insurgents. He sought to align France with the insurgents against England in the War of Independence, and drafted a memorandum for Louis XVI to this effect. With help from the government he set up a company, Rodrigue Hortalez et Cie, to send munitions to the insurgents and to arm vessels, and he entered into secret negotiations with American agents. The operations were on a large scale, involving the Spanish as well as the French government. In 1778 France officially recognised the independence of the United States, and broke off diplomatic relations with England. Thanks to the intervention of the king and other Ministers, the verdict of the Goëzman trial was set aside and Beaumarchais fully reinstated on 6 September 1776. He now led a feverish existence, deeply committed to traffic in arms, without receiving any financial return for his labour. He turned his attention to the question of a dramatist's copyright, and fought a campaign,

[31] *La Genèse du Barbier de Séville*, 1965.

prompted by the inadequate return for his *Barbier de Séville*, which eventually led to the establishment of copyright by a decree of 23 June 1791.

In the teeth of opposition he launched an edition of Voltaire's complete works, called the Kehl edition, in connection with which he set himself up as printer and papermaker, but he lost many millions in this venture. He next became involved unsuccessfully in polemics with Mirabeau, and it is during this sombre period that he put the finishing touches to *La Folle Journée, ou Le Mariage de Figaro*, which he had begun in 1778. It was read with approval by the actors of the Comédie Française on 29 September 1781. A first censor passed it, the queen enjoyed it, but Louis XVI took exception to many things, especially to the famous monologue in which occur adverse references to the state prison. He is reputed to have declared: 'il faudrait détruire la Bastille pour que la représentation de cette pièce ne fût pas une inconséquence dangereuse'. It should be stated that in his first draft Beaumarchais had referred to the Bastille by name, and had criticised the Church and the censorship in more open terms than in the text as we now know it. Beaumarchais revised his text and read it in the salons. A second censor, Suard, reported unfavourably. Nevertheless, the play was about to be performed by the actors of the Comédie Française at the Théâtre des Menus-Plaisirs, for the benefit of the comte d'Artois, brother of the king, when orders were given to have it stopped.

The consequent publicity enhanced Beaumarchais' popularity and kindled widespread curiosity, which Beaumarchais exploited to the full. He had a third censor give his approval, and the play was at last performed for the first time on 18 September 1783. It was a resounding personal triumph. After being submitted to three further censors, the first of whom questioned its morality, he was given the full right to have it performed, and on 27 April, in the new Théâtre Français, the success of the play was so great that it was hailed as the author's apotheosis. In spite of opposition from various interested quarters, it had a very long run. Beaumarchais, however, could not restrain his tongue in an exchange of pleasantries with Suard, in which he described the latter, by inference, as a flea. Louis XVI then had him sent ignominiously to the prison of Saint-Lazare, but after four days the comte d'Artois secured his release, Louis XVI finally agreeing to give him 800,000 livres as compensation for the requisitioning of Beaumarchais' merchant fleet, and as a reward for his activities over the American transactions.

Le Barbier de Séville was presented before the court in 1776 both at Versailles and at Trianon and was performed with the comte d'Artois in the role of Figaro, and the queen, Marie-Antoinette, in that of Rosine on 19 August 1785. In 1786 Beaumarchais married Mlle de Willermaula, with whom he had been on intimate terms for twelve years, and in spite of his widely reported infidelities, the union proved to be a happy one. In 1787 he sought to avenge the honour of an abandoned wife, Mme Kornmann, and was bested by a lawyer called Bergasse, whom the courts, however, condemned for libel. On 8 June 1787 his opera in five acts, *Tarare*, was performed at the Théâtre de l'Académie Royale de Musique (or Opéra). This is a mediocre work, intended as a *grand spectacle* as well as a *tragédie philosophique*. The setting was pseudo-oriental, the shepherds were dressed in court taffeta, and Tarare, the honest and intelligent soldier who leads the fight against tyranny, is crowned king, to public acclamation. He makes his entry from above, descending from the clouds by a silk ladder. The last lines were painted in the clouds in letters of fire:

> Mortel, qui que tu sois, prince, brahme, ou soldat,
> Homme, ta grandeur sur la terre
> N'appartient point à ton état,
> Elle est tout à ton caractère.

Beaumarchais intended to strike a blow in favour of natural equality, but the sad fact remains that the opera is in fact a string of platitudes. Even so, the censor asked for changes. In 1795, however, when the opera was revived, the language became more violent and changes in the opposite direction were effected. The opera had thirty-three performances, but did not come up to Beaumarchais' expectations, nor did it change the course of opera by reducing the part of music to the advantage of the libretto, as he sincerely hoped. Three editions of the work, however, appeared in 1787.

At the outbreak of the Revolution, Beaumarchais became very unpopular, largely for having had a sumptuous residence built opposite the Bastille. He was incarcerated and made destitute, but escaped the guillotine and fled abroad, only returning to France in July 1796. In 1792, however, *L'Autre Tartuffe, ou La Mère coupable*, a *drame* in five acts, which, with the *Barbier* and the *Mariage* constitutes the trilogy of plays staging Figaro, was performed. It had been accepted by the Comédie Française in February 1791, but owing to Beaumarchais' quarrel with that institution over the question of copyright, the performance was deferred. Eventually it was a second-rate company, the Comédiens du Marais, that provided the *première* on 16 June 1792. It is a *drame larmoyant*, without fire, which reflects Beaumarchais' own disillusion. His purpose he stated as 'faire étouffer de sanglots avec les mêmes personnages qui nous firent rire aux éclats'. It did serve, however, as one critic has pointed out, to pave the way for Scribe, Augier, and Dumas. Beaumarchais continued a fully active life until his sudden death at the age of sixty-seven.

A man of intrigue, resource, and wit, he is the prototype of his own Figaro whom he has bequeathed to posterity. Figaro is the last of the valets, the inheritor of countless generations of clowns, but the first incarnation of the man of the Revolution, the individual bent on self-betterment and without prejudice or scruple, the challenger of the establishment, and the shining apostle of the free man who makes his own destiny as best he can. A man of infinite resource, he appears to be dangerous, yet is deeply human and ultimately attractive. In the *Barbier* he is young and has some illusions, in the *Mariage* he is more bitter. In spite of the Spanish airs and graces, which adorn the *Barbier* more than the *Mariage* (from which in an early version they were wholly absent), the real terms of reference are French: the intellectual, psychological, and emotional climate is that of eighteenth-century France. The Spanish trappings free the imagination to accept any fantasy or improbability within the highly involved action of exceptionally swift-moving plays.

Figaro's philosophy of life is totally hedonistic and he makes it clear that servants as well as masters have a way of life, and seek to attain strangely similar ends. There is nothing of the serf in his attitude of mind. He is a man at liberty, so that he may become the willing accomplice of a former master without becoming his servant and losing his dignity, or become the courageous rival when his love is at stake. But it would be wrong to see in him the mere mouthpiece of the *Tiers Etat*, a figure of political propaganda. He has a greater stature. The power and danger of Figaro within the society of his time is that he is a manifestly free man. In his two masterpieces Beaumarchais returns to comedy and laughter, but not in fact to the tradition of Molière. We see traces of all the influences of the time: Italian comedy, *parades*, *drames*, comic opera, and Voltaire, whom he had read with care and understanding, and whose wit he endorsed. Critics have listed a very large number of plays bearing on similar subjects, and his plots can be shown to be unoriginal; his characters, too, are merely interesting modifications of known theatrical characters, his philosophical ideas are derivative and simple, and his moral ideas dubious or commonplace.

The deep originality of his best works lies in their style, and in their presentation of a remarkable personality. Technically the *Barbier* is the better constructed. But both have the outstanding quality of a breathtaking pace, coupled with verve. The *Barbier* contains forty-four scenes, as against the twenty-one in Molière's *Le Misanthrope*, all closely linked and so superbly integrated that they move like a surge of a sunlit sea. The details can be studied as the interpolation of inventive *lazzi*; the skilful moves and countermoves of the chief protagonists; the minor variations in a fast general tempo; the pleasures of complications and perplexities; and the ingenious unwinding of plot. In the *Mariage* even the inconsistencies that have been spotted by the critics pale into insignificance as the play quickens pace. It is as if we were watching some superb conjuring trick, or indeed, as the famous actress Mme Dussane once said, the perfection of a ballet in which every step has been marked out and needs to be perfectly timed. Beaumarchais has offered in his masterpieces of unwonted complexity, assembling as they do so many different currents, an entertainment that combines undoubted realism with pure theatre, topical commentary with enduring values, and ambiguity within a pattern of social change. Perhaps next to his personality, his stupendous vitality involved in countless intrigues and many improbable situations, it is his unique command of language, his eighteenth-century wit coupled with an unwonted freedom of expression, matching the new freedom of thought, which is the key to his continued success. Although today we are insensitive to some of his ploys and fail to appreciate the point of many allusions,[32] we see perhaps more clearly than in the past the basic greatness and originality of the two plays on which Beaumarchais' fame most assuredly rests. They mark at once the culmination of life under the *ancien régime*, a turning-point, and a signpost to a still uncertain future.

VI. THEATRE OF THE REVOLUTION

The theatre of the Revolution in a sense completed the work of the earlier *drames*. It sets aside completely the classical tradition and the aristocratic society and subordinates all aesthetic consideration to politics and often to journalistic activity. It reflects stages of the Revolution itself remarkably well and can be judged primarily as propaganda. Certainly plays of an earlier date, including the old classical plays, were put on, but they were refurbished so as to conform with the political aspirations of the day. Marie-

[32] In *Le Mariage de Figaro*, for instance, Figaro was seen as Beaumarchais, Brid'Oison as Goëzman, Bazile as the censor Marin, etc. Even the disturbing character of Chérubin, a thirteen-year-old *polisson*, one of Beaumarchais' most remarkable creations, whose presence is hardly required by the plot, had many counterparts in real life, and especially in *Heureusement*, a play by Rochon de Chabannes. Yet one may suspect that Beaumarchais drew on his own early experiences for his characterisation of Chérubin.

Joseph Chénier's (1764–1811) tragedy *Charles IX, ou L'Ecole des rois* (1789) may be said to have started the new era. It was written before the events, and modified in the light of changed circumstances. Naturally, it ran into trouble with the censorship, but Chénier made an issue of this opposition and was successful in securing the abolition of censorship. In spite of public approval, the play was frowned upon by the actors of the Comédie Française, but the reformers were successful in securing the proclamation of the liberty of the theatres on 13 January 1791, and the great actor Talma, who had taken sides with the revolutionaries and had moved with members of the company to a truly national theatre in the Rue de Richelieu, ensured its performance.[33]

Monvel's *Les Victimes cloîtrées* (1791) is violently anti-clerical; Cousin Jacque's *Nicodème dans la lune* (1791) points to the failure of constitutional government; Laya's *L'Ami des lois* (1793), judged the best of all these plays, is a strong plea for moderation against extremism, courageously staged just before the Terror; Maréchal's *Le Jugement dernier des rois* (1793) shows the revolutionary fervour at its peak; Ducancel's *L'Intérieur des comités révolutionnaires* (1795) gives voice to a reaction after the Reign of Terror; and Maillot's famous *Madame Angot ou La Poissarde parvenue* (1795)[34] brings out social upheaval at the time of the Revolution. Népomucène Lemercier (1771–1840),[35] Gabriel Legouvé (1764–1812),[36] Bouilly (1763–1842), author of a tragedy *Jean-Jacques Rousseau à ses derniers moments*, Fabre d'Eglantine (1750–94),[37] Arnault (1766–1834), Ronsin (1752–94), Drigny, André-Meurville wrote tragedies, and N. Lemercier, Fabre d'Eglantine, Collin d'Harleville (1755–1806), L.-E. Carron de Flins des Oliviers, and Ducancel wrote comedies which were staged during the Revolution. Jean-Louis Laya (1761–1833) may be singled out for special attention. He began his career with a comedy written in collaboration with Legouvé, *Le Nouveau Narcisse*, and together they published a volume of elegies, *Essais de deux amis*. In 1790 Laya had performed at the Comédie Française *Les Dangers de l'opinion* and a tragedy, *Jean Calas*, inspired by the success of M.-J. Chénier's *Charles IX*.[38] In 1793 he gave *L'Ami des lois*, the

[33] Other plays include: *Azémire* (1786), *Henri VIII*, *Jean Calas ou L'Ecole des juges* (1791), *Caïus Gracchus* (1792).

[34] The well-known *opérette*, *La Fille de Madame Angot* (1872) by Lecocq, is based on this play.

[35] His first play, *Méléagre*, was performed in 1788. The best known of his many plays are *Agamemnon* and *Pinto*.

[36] Author of *La Mort d'Abel* (1792).

[37] His best-known play is the *Philinte de Molière*.

[38] Interest in Jean Calas is seen also in Lemierre d'Argy's *drame*, *Calas ou Le Fanatisme* (1790), and may have been prompted in part by Falbaire's *Honnête Criminel* (1790).

moderation of which led to his prosecution, and he had to hide during the Terror. Later he wrote for various journals and produced three plays, *Les Deux Stuarts* (1797), *Falkland* (1799), and *Une Journée du jeune Néron* (1799). He succeeded Delille to the chair of literary history and French poetry at the Sorbonne in 1813, and was elected to the French Academy in 1817.

L'Ami des lois was performed on 2 January 1793, nineteen days before the execution of the king, and was seen as a political manifesto. It aroused great controversy, and its plea for moderation showed its author's courage. The play was so dangerously successful that performance had to be stopped. Many thought that Nomphage was Robespierre and Duricrâne Marat. The Convention then granted permission for one day, after which the performance of all plays was stopped by decree, for fear of public disorder. It was revived in 1795, but it had already dated. It shows signs of haste in composition, as do all the revolutionary plays, for dramatists were little concerned with questions of technique.

With the advent of Napoleon, censorship was restored, and classical plays regained their popularity, but melodramas were highly favoured in the theatres of the boulevards. The stage was set for the Romantic drama.

The various forms of drama practised in the eighteenth century all achieved success, then faded from the stage. They left, however, their mark on the history of the theatre in a multiplicity of ways, which will readily be detected by the historian; and even if there is no continuous pattern of evolution, there is a constant change and adaptation to the new requirements of a growing audience.

Eighteenth-century French drama left a few great names, the greatest being Marivaux and Beaumarchais. It aired issues of general philosophical and aesthetic importance which concerned the art of drama, as well as others of narrower scope affecting only playwrights and actors. The abiding interest in the theories propounded by Diderot in his critical works and in his *Paradoxe sur le comédien*, which deals with the psychology and status of the actor, is evidence of the importance of the matters raised, and, in the pattern of change which the century offers, is to be found not only a clear reflection of the temper of the times and of contemporary society and manners, but the formulation of a new aesthetic principle which bifurcated into romanticism and realism.

Chapter 13

THE NOVEL

HISTORICAL event, mythology, legend, the epic poem, and the narrative of minstrels and troubadours are all woven into the remote past of the history of the novel; but the forms known to the seventeenth, eighteenth, nineteenth, and extended into the twentieth, centuries have no precise model in antiquity or the Middle Ages. In France, they have been developed chiefly from prose works of the seventeenth century.[1]

In that century, novels grew increasingly popular among a growing number of readers, particularly among women of culture and the frequenters of salons in Paris and in the provinces. It may be said that, foreign influences apart, sentiment was represented by Nervèze and d'Urfé, adventure by Gomberville, the heroic by Mlle de Scudéry, and the historical by Segrais. Yet at the same time authors of fiction were held to be in some sort morally dubious: this serves in part to explain the prefaces, essentially sober and moral in tone, with which novelists of the seventeenth century, and their successors in the eighteenth, opened their works, and which were more frequently given to self-justification than to appraisal of their theme.

Two main trends are to be discovered in the evolution of the novel during the seventeenth century: the epic or heroic, dealing with characters of more than common stature whose grandeur is such that they invariably triumph in love and in battle over those lesser mortals who oppose them; and the popular, comic vein that yielded a rich harvest.

In the first category are to be found works in the tradition of the seventeenth century previously mentioned: chronicles of military exploits, real or imaginary, and *romanesque* adventures, often associated with historical events such as the Fronde, and which predictably incorporated disquisitions on love, *galanterie*, and similar manifestations of preciosity. These works enshrined the cardinal virtues of the age. *L'Astrée* (1607–27) by d'Urfé, ostensibly depicting the love of a shepherd and a shepherdess, but in fact representing known people and known situations, set a pattern that was quickly imitated, and one that enjoyed general popularity. *Le Grand Cyrus* (1649–53) and *Clélie* (1654–60) were widely read in their own

[1] Cf. Yarrow, op. cit., pp. 42–9, 166–9, 289–303, 386–92.

day by people aware of their historical and social interest. Their authors, whilst providing chronicles of contemporary society, and refining the French language as an instrument for the conveying of subtle nuances of meaning, feeling, and emotion, wrote novels which, as Richardson pointed out, 'dealt so much in the marvellous and improbable, or were so unnaturally inflaming to the passions and so full of love and intrigue, that most of them seemed calculated to fire the imagination rather than to inform the judgement'. Yet even these long, historical biographies marked an effort towards greater realism, and fostered the vogue of memoirs and pseudo-memoirs of the seventeenth and eighteenth centuries.

The second tradition, that of the popular and satirical novel, goes back to the *fabliaux* of the Middle Ages and the picaresque genre. It is represented in France by Sorel, Scarron, and Furetière, whose writings, deemed unworthy, were considered failures by the élite of their day. In fact, the *Histoire comique de Francion* (1623–33), *Le Roman Comique* (1651, 1657), and *Le Roman bourgeois* (1666) soon seemed more real than the works of La Calprenède and of Scudéry, which were mainly concerned with high society; they dealt with the trivialities of everyday life, and expressed in a less restrained vernacular language a different kind of realism. Some of these works may even be termed *anti-romans*, featuring *anti-héros*, whilst others, exploiting burlesque, were openly satirical. In the name of realism, and by appealing to commonsense, these writers derided the insipid conversations of shepherds and the romantic exploits of fictional heroes. Furetière declared: 'Au lieu de vous tromper par ces vaines subtilités, je vous raconterai sincèrement et avec fidélité plusieurs historiettes et galanteries...' However, in setting up anti-heroes indulging in anti-exploits, these novelists often reveal themselves as superficial as the heroes they caricature. Scarron, Furetière, and Sorel may be good storytellers, but their works lack many of the essential ingredients of fiction as we know it. It is a far cry from Furetière to Lesage and Marivaux.

Daniel Huet as early as 1670 found a succinct definition of the novel: 'Les romans sont des fictions de choses qui ont pu être et qui n'ont point été.' (*De l'Origine des romans*). Huet, however, failed to see the true justification for bringing ordinary bourgeois characters into novels, and it was only by so doing that the ordinary bourgeois reader could be led to identify himself with the fictional characters depicted.

Both currents, the aristocratic and the popular, are reflected in the novels of the eighteenth century, but even though this was not immediately apparent,[2] it is the popular form that exercised the greater influence. It is difficult and certainly artificial to define and

[2] *Les Liaisons dangereuses* by Laclos is an example in point

to measure influences, a task rendered even more difficult when foreign sources are involved. Certainly Cervantes, Defoe, and, in particular, Richardson contributed considerably to the new forms that emerged in France, but in varying proportions and usually as minor aspects of new and highly original work. Perhaps, if we take the novel as forming one gigantic whole, it is best considered as the epic of modern society, the sum total of individual experiences, much more than the mere *fil de vive narration* of which Fénelon spoke. In the early type of narrative we are presented, however ambiguously, with the autobiography of one man, then with the several biographies of many, and ultimately with the picture of an age, of mankind itself, reflected through the experience of the writer. The early novelists found themselves in an obvious dilemma. They felt impelled to tell unusual stories and to recount heroic events, in order to rivet the attention of their readers, but it was also necessary to make their stories appear to be true if their purpose was to be achieved. This is what led the more interesting writers to examine closely questions of technique and to experiment with new fictional devices.

Fiction continued to be identified with history, or to be considered as nothing but lies, for a long time. Rousseau in his fourth *Rêverie*[3] must be commended for his perspicacity in distinguishing fiction from falsehood, even if the main purpose of his analysis was to justify his own alleged lies. Before Voltaire the historian did not observe absolute fidelity to recorded facts, and self-styled pseudo-memoirs often contained more accurate data than allegedly true histories. In an interesting article, 'L'Histoire a-t-elle engendré le roman?',[4] G. May observes that when one passes from authentic memoirs, such as those of Commynes or La Rochefoucauld, through apocryphal memoirs or pseudo-historical works, such as those of Courtilz de Sandras and Hamilton, to novels in memoir-form, such as *Gil Blas* (1715–36), one has the feeling that a significant development has taken place, and that this evolution is fundamental to the understanding of the history of the French novel. The outstanding advantage of the autobiographical form is that it renders it difficult for the reader to reject even improbable facts, since he knows he cannot challenge the author's apparent first-hand experience. The literary technique required by the apocryphal autobiography is the same as that of the true autobiography. The first person is used in both cases as the more natural form, in contrast with true history, which uses indirect speech. Occasionally, as when the memoirs are said to have been discovered by accident

[3] *Rêveries du promeneur solitaire*, in *Œuvres complètes*, 1962, vol. I, pp. 1024–39.

[4] *Revue d'Histoire littéraire de la France*, lv, p. 156.

and published by another person, the third person is employed. Sometimes writers became confused or careless, as happened in the case of the *Mémoires du Sieur de Pontis* (1678), and varied their practice within the same work. In their efforts to secure greater verisimilitude, they were over-concerned with literal belief, and with making claims for an authenticity which could not be sustained. They failed to understand the technique of imaginative processes by which, as Coleridge put it, there can be on the reader's part a willing suspension of disbelief. Further, the conception of a serious novel written in the third person, postulating in effect an omniscient writer, was not entertained till very late in the century, after much experimentation. The eighteenth-century novelist for the most part found himself caught in a trap: he must strive for verisimilitude and at the same time embellish the truth if he wished to succeed. He must not be caught out in a lie nor appear fanciful. In such a context, the very cynicism prevalent in indecent or libertine novels may be taken, not as a fantasy, but as a realistic portrayal of society. When Baculard d'Arnaud asked the writer to 'embellir la vérité', he was really calling his attention to the need for a basis of truth. Miss V. Mylne, who has dealt with these questions in detail and with insight,[5] may rightly claim that the realistic description of the shipwreck in *Paul et Virginie* is a necessary foil to the tragic denouement of that romantic tale.

Various efforts have been made to categorise the French eighteenth-century novels. One may distinguish the psychological novel, the novel of manners, the philosophical tale, the romantic or sentimental novel, the libertine novel, and the oriental tale. But critics cannot agree on the appropriateness of the divisions, nor even on which element is dominant in any given novel. A work such as Prévost's *Cleveland*, for example, is in fact a sentimental story presented as history, and one providing a social commentary. One should perhaps fall back on a chronological arrangement, studying the production of a given decade, but this is rendered difficult when the date of composition is different from that of publication, or stretches over a long period of years. Moreover, in the case of authors such as Lesage and Marivaux, who wrote other works besides novels, the critic is reluctant to take in isolation part of their total output. Henri Coulet, in his very full and recent study,[6] has adopted a combination of chronology and genres, using sub-genres as recurring headings. But his varied categories remain rather arbitrary, and are in any case confusing and too numerous to prove helpful to any but the specialist.

It is the intention in this instance to adhere to very broad cate-

[5] *The Eighteenth-century French Novel, Techniques of Illusion*, 1965.
[6] *Le Roman jusqu'à la Révolution*, 1967.

gories, referring to labels only when relevant, in the hope of focusing attention on the works and their authors, pinpointing their salient features, and finally leaving it to the reader to effect his own provisional synthesis from the tentative observations provided.

It is now generally agreed that Robert Chasles is a precursor of modern realism in the novel, and as such deserves special consideration here, although he belongs essentially to an earlier period and his work cannot easily be labelled under any of the commonly accepted headings. Robert Challes or Chasles (1659 to some time after 1721) is the author of an interesting *Journal de voyages aux Indes orientales* (written 1690–91, published 1721); of *Mémoires* on French colonial politics (1716), first published by A. Augustin-Thierry in 1831; of the sixth volume of a translation of *Don Quixote* by Thomas Amaulry; and of a correspondence with writers of the *Journal Littéraire* (1713–18), recently found at Leyden and edited by F. Deloffre.[7] He is, however, best known for the seven stories that comprise *Les Illustres Françoises* (1713).[8] This work was given as 'histoires véritables' and published anonymously. Its success was immediate and lasting. It had twenty editions between 1713 and 1756. It was translated into English by Mrs Aubin under the title *The Illustrious French Lovers* in 1727 (new edition 1739), and into German by J. F. Riederer in 1728. H. Roddier[9] has demonstrated its influence on Prévost, and F. Deloffre that on Marivaux. The episode *L'Histoire de Des Frans et de Silvie* also inspired Landois in *Sylvie* (1741), which dealt with the social upheaval engendered by a similar *mésalliance*. Although Champfleury drew attention to the work in 1857, it remained virtually unknown, owing in part to its anonymity and in part to a failure to understand its originality. Chasles' *Illustres Françoises*, which antedates *Gil Blas*, is a landmark in the development of realism. He scorned the pseudo-shepherds of *L'Astrée*, the false orientalism of La Calprenède and Gomberville, the mock heroes of antiquity to be found in Scudéry, Mme de Villedieu, and Fénelon, as also the pseudo-historical characters of Saint-Réal, Courtilz, and Mme de La Fayette. He gave his characters the names of real people and introduced people of lowly station into his narrative, provided their strong passions singled them out for attention. He depicted social conditions without recourse to satire

[7] *Annales Universitatis Saraviensis, Philosophie-Lettres*, 1954.

[8] F. Deloffre has brought out a critical edition in two volumes, Société d'Editions 'Les Belles Lettres', 1959. See Yarrow, op. cit., pp. 388–9, for a detailed account of the work.

[9] H. Roddier, 'Robert Challes, inspirateur de Richardson et de l'abbé Prévost', *Revue de Littérature comparée*, Jan.–March 1947, stresses the place of the work in the history of the sentimental novel of the eighteenth century.

or caricature, and saw in them a determining factor in human conduct. He introduces more pen-portraits than either Marivaux or Prévost were to do and, stressing the role of individual temperament, presented the workings of the subconscious mind objectively. His seven stories can be read singly, but they have greater unity than the *Heptameron* by Marguerite de Navarre, with which they have been compared for their narrative technique, since many characters reappear in different focus, much as in Balzac's *Comédie humaine* of later date. There is realism in the setting, in references to the time of year, to the weather, and to actual time; and, according to F. Deloffre, there is occasionally poetic realism. Above all else, Chasles demonstrated that a realistic novel is neither history nor fantasy. He informs his reader in no uncertain terms that he will forgo historical accuracy and make use of anachronisms in order to prevent the reader getting at the truth, thereby ensuring in the reader's mind the over-all historicity of recorded events, but leading him unerringly to consider the truth of fiction as a transposition of an immediate reality into a work of art. Of course, Chasles utilises the fictional devices of his predecessors, including those in Sorel's *Francion*, to which he specifically refers, but these proved acceptable in their context. He adopted a conversational and disjointed style, which was to leave its mark on the novels of the century, and his dialogue was often taken *verbatim* from real life, sometimes heightened by a sense of drama. He was refreshingly free from cant and had an earnest sincerity which some critics miscalled cynicism. Before Diderot, he showed the relativity of moral values; and in Mme de Londé, for instance, he portrays a woman who preaches and practises free love, and has the courage to stand by her moral decision; and, before Diderot's *Pensées philosophiques*, he vindicated strong passions. A detailed comparison with *Jacques le fataliste*, one which would prove singularly rewarding, would lead to a reassessment of the basic assumptions of realism in the novel; of the value of a structure which consists of episodes and digressions; and of the nature of the relationship between characters, environment, storytelling, dialogue, and the whole range of fictional techniques. But *Les Illustres Françoises* lacks depth. Chasles, although no true libertine, had the superficiality of the cynic. He wrote in the first person, yet avoided personal commentaries and moral observations, such as are to be found in Marivaux and so many others, and, more important, he never intervened as author in the shaping of the plot. But he failed to probe into the motives and actions of his characters and his realism remains crude. Although he gave consideration to such questions as freedom, grace, fatality, and human responsibility, in common with the great eighteenth-century novelists, he does not truly face up to what H. Coulet has called 'the anguished metaphysical questions' posed by his successors.

The apocryphal autobiography was the main form until 1750,[10] when the true novel in letter form was evolved, without, however, displacing in weight of numbers the earlier form. The pseudo-memoir as a literary form is best studied in the works of Courtilz de Sandras. As Vivienne Mylne has said: 'Courtilz provides an extraordinarily clear illustration . . . of the progress from biography to pseudo-memoirs in a single author's work.' He was a journalist anxious to convey his own vision of the world, and has been likened to that other professional journalist, Daniel Defoe. He transcended the purely personal by leading his reader to become identified with his characters. In his *Mémoires de d'Artagnan*, popularised by Alexandre Dumas in *Les Trois Mousquetaires*, he presented a hero who is the very antithesis of Gil Blas, the picaro. D'Artagnan and Gil Blas are as two sides of a diptych. Lesage, however, unlike Courtilz, remains wholly absent from his story, leaving it to his hero Gil Blas to point the moral of his tale. This transposition of personal comment from author to fictional character led to considerable experimentation. This is one reason why Diderot, in *Jacques le fataliste*, introduced as characters both the author and the reader. In this work the over-all coherence of the narrative is maintained, in spite of numerous so-called realistic digressions, their chief purpose being to establish a truer realism. Lesage, for his own fictional purposes, utilised a characteristic of the autobiographical novel, the time lag between action and narrative, which has disadvantages as well as advantages, as can be seen in many eighteenth-century works, including *La Religieuse* by Diderot. Lesage distinguished between the narrator and the protagonist in his novel, and also between Gil Blas the elder and Gil Blas the younger. He developed the technique of what has been called the naïve hero, thereby paving the way for the self-conscious analysis to be found in Marivaux's *Vie de Marianne*, and opening the door to irony and satire as we see it in *Candide* and other *contes* by Voltaire. The reader finds it easy to identify himself with an innocent young man experiencing life and facing up to its struggles, so that the hero becomes approachable and the distance between the views of the younger and the older man who tells the story lends objectivity and authenticity to the novel. The device by which another man tells the story, so as to involve the reader more surely, also enables the storyteller to bring out the amusing side of an incident. There is, for example, the irony of the older Gil Blas laughing at the expense of the younger, and this allows the possibility of creating an environment, and setting a tone more con-

[10] Between 1700 and 1750 200 novels of this kind have been listed.

ducive to intimacy with the reader, who witnesses the morality or immorality of the writer's world as if he were part of it. Lesage went further than Courtilz de Sandras with such techniques, as he did also in ensuring that the cadre he adopted determined the ingenuity of the tale. In a similar manner Marianne, at the beginning of the story of her life, writes to a friend, setting an intimate tone from which she never departs. With *Gil Blas* we have then the fusion of the two earlier kinds of novel. Gil Blas is the hero but also at the same time the anti-hero. He incarnates perhaps a new type of character, a bourgeois hero with bourgeois values, a man set on self-advancement and on making his personal fortune. He may seem as anti-social as the wolf of the fable or as the noble conqueror. In either case, the weaker man perishes. He is ultimately the hero of his own life, a quintessential individualist. Lesage, who allied the picaresque tradition of Quevedo and Cervantes to French sources, broadened the conception of the novel by presenting his readers with a whole world. He offered 'peintures de mœurs en action' objectively, without strong satire, and with good humour. Moreover, he covered a wide span of life's experience, since his *Gil Blas* was written over a long period of time, and this is reflected in the temper of the work. The early chapters of *Gil Blas* are gay and lighthearted in tone. Scenes worthy of figuring in a comedy abound, whilst the later chapters mark a greater seriousness, and a slowing down which corresponded to the new way of life in France. *Gil Blas* is not truly realistic but it is rather a 'transposition fantaisiste d'une expérience', like all French novels till 1760. Ultimately, it presents the figure of a selfish man eager to rise to the top of the social ladder, even though he owns nothing but a broken-down mule. Gil Blas is the French forerunner of Jacob, the *paysan parvenu*, and has undoubtedly affinities with Candide, Jacques le Fataliste, and such libertine figures as Valmont in *Les Liaisons dangereuses*, Gaudet d'Arras in the works of Restif de La Bretonne, and with numerous characters in less-well-known productions.

Marivaux also started his career as novelist in the burlesque tradition of Sorel's *Francion*, with his *Télémaque travesti* (probably written in 1714), his *L'Iliade travestie* (1711), and satirical works such as *Le Bilboquet* (1714). He also wrote pseudo-memoirs in the picaresque manner, before turning with his *Vie de Marianne* to a new type of pseudo-autobiographical novel. 'C'est une femme qui raconte sa vie' he began and thereby allowed himself scope for a psychological study of unexcelled depth. The life presented is that of a thinking as well as a feeling woman. 'C'est une femme qui pense' might have been an equally appropriate beginning, suggests H. Coulet. In this book the inner world of the mind is explored in depth, and the outside world is only subjectively perceived, therefore there is little if any objective comment. With Jacob in *Le Paysan parvenu*, there is progress from the technical standpoint, in that the chief character is independent. He moves in his own right in the light of events and he retains his freedom of action in his relations with the persons he meets. These relations are convincing to the reader, because they change him and he changes them. Superficially, the form of the novel marks a return to the picaresque, but allows for the retention of a far greater psychological content and the stressing of human motivation. Jacob can even react negatively to events, as for instance on the occasion of his first visit to Paris, which, unlike Marianne, he finds most disappointing. He shapes his destiny, according to his past, his own volition, and his own acts. He is negative in appearance only, adapting himself to circumstances as did Marianne. In practice, he transforms passivity into a self-revealing and potent force. The seducer who uses friendship, then love, to obtain the hand and fortune of his victim is a type we find throughout the period, in England as well as in France. The variants of Don Juan are infinite and are fully exploited in the literature of the period. Here, with Jacob, the figure is associated with that of the social climber; and it is worth noting that in all cases he is a manifestation of anti-social tendencies. It comes interestingly from Marivaux's pen, he who was a frequenter of the salon of Mme de Lambert and that of Mme de Tencin, whom he in fact represented in the character of Mme Dorsin; and whose novels are situated in a sophisticated and superficially urbane setting at a particular moment of history. In his novels of manners there are indeed cabmen and cloistered nuns, as well as countless indices of a disturbing and realistic background. His sense of pathos, his dwelling on emotion and on moralising, his preoccupation with social problems, his probing analyses, and his particular subtlety combine to add a new dimension to the novel, and the serious, moral tone he adopted is already that of the second half of the century. His acute sensibility antedated Richardson and Rousseau. The framework to this new conception of the novel remained, however, the memoir. If on the one hand this prevented his finishing his novel, since a writer of memoirs cannot recount his own death, it served in his skilful hands to enrich his analyses, his awareness of the complexity of human character (and here playing with time appears as a prerequisite for study of character in depth), of himself in the role of author as well as vicariously through his characters, and of the presence and personality of his reader. His expertise in the handling of the memoir-form and the long letter-form according to new fictional techniques greatly enriched the novel.

L'Abbé Prévost also adopted the memoir-form, as is obvious from the title of his principal work: *Mémoires et aventures d'un homme de qualité qui s'est retiré du monde* (1728–31). Unlike Lesage, he claimed that his stories were based on authentic manuscripts, but in Paris if not in the provinces this statement would not have been seriously entertained. His work is in the tradition of pseudo-memoirs, for he often revealed himself as author to the attentive reader, and spoke of 'ouvrage d'imagination' when referring to *Cleveland*. He no doubt maintained the fiction of conventional memoirs because the readers preferred it so, tacitly endorsing in a literal sense Steele's ironical comment: 'The word memoir is French for a novel' (22 October 1709). The myth died very slowly, for it had the peculiar advantage of disarming censorship. Its very success in early days tended to prolong its life, since it was judged to be a recipe for success, and it also had the unexpected advantage of fostering analysis of feeling. Prévost wished his works to have the *truth* of the memoir and the analytical scope of the genre. He therefore referred to historical facts (the deportation of prostitutes in *Manon Lescaut*) and historical figures such as Cromwell in his works. The framework of his tales is consistently realistic, for the narrator claims to be drawing on memoirs; and he avoids as far as possible those chance encounters and unlikely coincidences that destroy verisimilitude in a work like *Gil Blas*. By a stroke of luck or genius, in *Manon Lescaut* he did not underline the role of the primary narrator, and the links between this volume and the others in the series of which it is a constituent part are tenuous. The story unfolds as a biography, but plunges straight into the main subject and is presented with the classical simplicity of structure of *La Princesse de Clèves*. And like *La Princesse de Clèves* it poses a moral problem that can be resolved only in ambiguous terms. Manon may be excused because of her youth, her natural goodness, her 'innocent' love, and her sensibility: yet she must be considered guilty by Jansenist moralists and other religious pundits. This ambiguity, brilliantly exploited and expressed in a sustained poetic language, enhances the impression of depth in the analysis. The characters, too, are basically consistent, as they show development with time and changing circumstances, and they add a feeling of realism, in spite of the romanticism of the theme. The work provides a study of the relationship of personality to action as well as to events, and the reader has the illusion of seeing a real life unfold. The significance of *Manon Lescaut*, which was not seen at the time of publication, should not be underestimated by critics who now praise very highly Prévost's other novels.

Rousseau's *La Nouvelle Héloïse* is a still greater landmark, not only because of its presentation of a straightforward yet complex love affair in an idyllic setting, and because it answered the secret dreams of a generation that found in it an exciting new way of life; but because the novel, albeit still in letter-form, became clearly the vehicle for the expression of man in his whole being, his character, his relationship with others and his environment, and his intellectual, social, and moral preoccupations. The digressions which interrupt the story may well be justified in this broad perspective. Many unusual factors in this novel ensured its lasting influence, yet it stands a little outside the normal development of the novel. In some ways the *Confessions*, already unique in their revelatory power, were to prove his greatest novel, and to mark a decisive point in the development from true or pseudo-memoir to fiction. For the very sincerity of his purpose, together with his creative force, led Rousseau inevitably and paradoxically to build the portrait of a fictional man based upon the quintessence of his own being. In this context the *Confessions* appear as the ideal form of literature for the revelation of the whole man.

With Voltaire, the novel became the *conte philosophique*, belonging to a somewhat different tradition, often parodying the oriental tale from which it purports to derive, but incorporating realism and also pseudo-realism in the manner of Lesage, a bogus psychology that springs from a real, if somewhat haphazard, knowledge of man and woman in general, and of the mainspring of human motivation. It adopted and emended the picaresque tradition and depended for much of its satire on a brilliantly incisive style, outstanding even in an age when most authors were stylists. Essentially, however, his novels are philosophical propaganda, and depend for their effect on the ideas expressed or suggested.

Diderot, like Voltaire, is in a world of his own, partly because of the range of his mind, partly because of historical circumstance, which prevented the publication and diffusion of his best works before the nineteenth century and so denied them any possible influence on contemporary writers, and partly because of their complexity, which has only been revealed in the twentieth century. In *Les Bijoux indiscrets*, he wrote the masterpiece of the libertine novel. Although judged immoral, the work contained much serious thought and telling satire. *La Religieuse*, with its dramatic scenes and incidents brilliantly chosen and handled, is a masterpiece of the pseudo-memoir, in spite of a somewhat lame and abrupt conclusion. Diderot's difficulty was no doubt that which faced Marivaux when he failed to conclude his *Vie de Marianne*, and is inherent in the genre. *Le Neveu de Rameau* is a kind of dialogue with a little narrative and some description, and once again the end is inconclusive, though in this case true to life and artistically satisfying. Diderot's fictional masterpiece, however, is *Jacques le fataliste*, because of the issues it raises and the technical problems it attempts to resolve. To convince his reader that he is writing the truth – when, as everyone must realise, he is telling a story – he reiterates to the point of monotony that were he writing a novel he would be free to make his characters behave in a way different from the one he describes them as adopting. In this way he seeks to convince his reader that he for once is telling the truth. His handling of all conceivable devices to foster this belief is technically remarkable and amazingly complex. *Jacques le fataliste* is brilliantly effective and must be judged significant for any novelist bent on understanding his craft and seeing the results of a technique developed to its furthest extent. We are led to examine the question of the relationship between life and art, the nature of illusion in art, the problem of creativity and its limitations, and to examine matter and reality, mind and matter. Historically, Diderot's general theories and philosophy, and his ideas on the *drames* and on emotional relationships, influenced his contemporaries. Certainly Restif de La Bretonne wrote under the shadow of Diderot, as well as of Rousseau. But Restif, as also Laclos and Sade, the other outstanding figures in the French novel not as yet referred to, belong decidedly to the latter part of the century and are best considered after the examination of the production of lesser writers, whose influence in their day was great and in whom there has been a growing interest since the last war.

These writers are for the most part in the tradition of the writers of pseudo-memoirs and letters, many contributing their own small quota of technical accomplishment. More often they recount stories of seductions, human peculiarities, and odd relationships in strange situations, and the emerging pattern is one of *galanterie*, with an unrelenting war between the sexes as background. What fascinates the present-day reader, living in a so-called 'permissive' society with no clear set principles of behaviour or moral code, is precisely the picture of moral anarchy presented. Man is trapped between conflicting urges that require satisfaction at different levels; and in the eighteenth century his desires are shown as being mutually incompatible. Thus we see the supreme egotist, the self-assertive vain seducer bent on cheating the woman he alleges he loves, who is in fact caught in an absurd trap, in which sensuality is at odds with emotion and intellect. This can also be seen in the plays of the period, which reflect this same prevailing trend, but it is most fully developed in the novel. Laclos has given us the masterpiece of the libertine novel in which sex is in the mind, but in which conflicting emotions still continue to destroy the intellectual fabric and reassert the rights of nature, albeit a perverted nature.

Professor Etiemble has largely contributed[11] to the revived interest in the *Mémoires du comte de Grammont* by Hamilton (1645 or 1646–1720), one of a select band of foreigners who contributed to French letters, and which includes the prince de Ligne, Horace Walpole, the Abbé Galiani, Frederick II of Prussia, Catherine II, Grimm and Lord Chesterfield, Beckford and Casanova, whose command of the French language is extraordinarily complete. Hamilton's *Mémoires*, written in 1703–04 and published in 1713, deal with events which took place some fifty years earlier, and are ostensibly written by Grammont, Hamilton's brother-in-law. They were considered by Voltaire to be a novel as entertaining as the burlesque genre of Scarron, although of a different kind. In these memoirs the years 1639 to 1669 are covered in a cynical fashion, satirising events at the court of St James and at the court of Savoy, but the work is guardedly silent about events at Versailles, an omission which incurred the disdain of the duc de Saint-Simon. The work deserves the title of novel, since events are seen through the eyes of a central character, who, seemingly innocent at first, soon becomes involved in what may be called the war of the sexes, and the *galanterie* depicted is itself subject to social conventions and formulae, which are vividly expressed. These *Mémoires* are already typical of many novels of the eighteenth century in form and substance, and the elegant style in which they are written is a model of its kind; but in spite of touches of true comedy and realism they lack the penetration of Saint-Simon and the insight of the great analysts of the human heart that were to follow.

Hamilton sheltered under another name, as did later Mme d'Epinay in her *Histoire de Madame de Montbrillant*, remarkable for its portrayal of contemporary society, and Crébillon *fils*, whose *Les Egarements du cœur et de l'esprit* is presented as *Mémoires de Monsieur de Meilcour*, although the *Epître* is signed Crébillon.

Crébillon *fils* (1707–77) was the son of the Crébillon who rivalled Voltaire as a dramatist. He was a hedonist, yet a man whose rectitude makes the allegations of indecency and immorality which he had to face the more ironic. He was imprisoned for political reasons in 1734. (*L'Ecumoire, ou Tanzaï et Néadarné, histoire japonaise* (1734) contained thinly veiled satirical allusions to the bull *Unigenitus*, to Louis XV and the duchesse du Maine, and caricatured Cardinal Dubois whilst referring to God as 'Le Grand Singe'.) He was exiled from Paris at the instigation of Mme de Pompadour on the grounds of his immorality. Yet on reading his novels Lady Henrietta Maria Stafford became so interested in him that she offered him her hand in marriage. After living to-

[11] *Romanciers du XVIIIe siècle*, 2 vols., 1960–65.

gether for four years they were married in 1748. Although she was a plain woman with a squint, Crébillon seems to have remained deeply attached to her till her death in 1756. In 1759 he was made Royal Censor, a post which his father had held before him, and which he exercised with tact. *Le Sopha, conte moral* (1742) is an oriental tale like *L'Ecumoire*, allowing scope for imagination and licence and reputed to be highly immoral, for which he was exiled for three months. The story is told by a Hindu whose soul transmigrates from one sofa to another until it discovers one on which two virgins enjoy the first fruits of their love. He was manifestly attracted to the oriental tale which his public greatly appreciated, but he feared that the triviality of the subject matter would detract his readers' attention from the attempted depth of his analysis of sentiment. Earlier in *Le Sylphe* (1730) and *Lettres de la marquise de M*** au comte de R**** (1732) he exploited, before Richardson, the possibilities of the letter-form, also used in *Lettres athéniennes* and *Lettres de la duchesse de *** au duc de ****. The *Lettres de la marquise*, given as authentic, number seventy and serve as pretext for an exploration of libertine behaviour. They contain digressions of psychological interest, and especially an analysis in depth of remorse, but the novel fails as a whole, for its plot cannot be satisfactorily developed since the letters are not dated and there is consequently little possibility of relating psychological analysis to events. It is, however, successful in depicting aspects of French life and in conveying gradations in the expression of love. It is this last aspect of his work which has prompted Rayner Heppenstall to see in him a sentimental amoralist who established a hierarchy of sentiments with *amour* the more highly valued. But love is not divorced from gallantry and is part of a complex game, as can be seen in *Les Egarements du cœur et de l'esprit, ou Mémoires de Monsieur de Meilcour* (1736–38) which paves the way for *Les liaisons dangereuses* by Laclos. *Les Egarements* is technically less significant, but more interesting. Etiemble, rightly defining the substance of the book as 'le dépucelage d'un adolescent par une femme de quarante ans', but more questionably commending its pedagogical qualities, is fascinated by Crébillon's lack of moral prejudice, and it is clear that Crébillon *fils* was a nonconformist in matters of ethics as well as politics and religion. Miss Mylne, for her part, observes that for the first time an author of memoirs acknowledges that he has invented his story. An omniscient author describes actions that take place, analysing them and explaining them without the reader being expected to infer what goes on in the mind of the characters portrayed. The psychology of M. de Meilcour is well brought out in his different responses to three women: Mme de Lursay who is forty, Hortense de Théville, a pretty, virtuous girl whom Meilcour loves and idealises, and Mme de Sénanges, an old coquette of whom Mme de Lursay is jealous. Meilcour is directed by Versac, a man who knows all the answers in the game Meilcour is invited to play. Crébillon's characters do not behave wholly consistently and sometimes reflect too closely their author's own intelligence; there is little probing in depth, nor is the interaction of his characters clearly expressed. The tale is diffuse, there are too many hasty generalisations about men and women, and too much moralising. There are, too, drawbacks to the first-person narrative adopted, which renders it more difficult to accept interpretations suggested for the actions taking place. But Crébillon has style and wit, imagination and a certain finesse, and the classical simplicity of his plot, which takes only fifteen days to unfold, coupled with very lengthy analyses, gives an unwonted illusion of endless time. Not unnaturally, he was as much appreciated by his Spanish and English readers as by the French: Sterne went so far as to say that it was only after reading Rabelais and Crébillon that he ventured to take up the pen. Crébillon was a pessimist who had no illusions about the goodness of nature: he saw man as a libertine, sensual and libidinous, vicious and unhappy, forever seeking an enjoyment he cannot find. For him, love, or desire, thrives on opposition and its non-satisfaction alone can ensure its continuity. Men are incapable of resisting the 'surprise des sens' and women, essentially weak, are doomed to yield. Crébillon is particularly interested in characters who have lost their innocence and are learning to be cynics: his knowledge of the mind and heart is certainly great, and, no doubt, as H. Coulet has suggested, he has projected into his best work his own profound disquiet. He sees that love can be born under absurd conditions, and honest women be drawn to libertines: he examines causes of sexual impotence, which help to bring out the peculiar relationship of physical and sentimental love. He challenges the myth of free-will, the myth of conscience, and believes that 'cœur, corps et esprit' are never at one: regretfully he concludes that sentiment is insincere, and subordinated to sensuality. In spite of intelligent experimentation in the form of his novels, he did not succeed in writing a definitive work, embodying the several aspects of his thought and experience. Among his numerous writings may be listed *La Nuit et le moment, ou Les Matines de Cythère* (1775); *Les Heureux Orphelins, histoire imitée de l'anglais* (perhaps by his wife); *Le Hasard du coin du feu, dialogue moral* (1763); *Ah! quel conte!*. Much is suggestive in his works, but these are no longer considered mere pornography on account of their flashes of real insight and their high literary merit. His use of dialogue is particularly successful. He enjoyed the company of his own circle of friends and presided over the Sunday dinners of the Caveau which he instituted in 1752, and sometime after the death of his wife he founded a club, the Pelletier, where he must have met Sterne, Garrick, and Wilkes. He died poor at seventy.

Duclos (1704–72) was less successful than Crébillon, possibly because he transposed too directly his own personal experience into his works. His *Histoire de la baronne de Luz* (1740) is a story of the time of Henri IV. His *Confessions du comte de* *** (1741), as Voltaire wrote on 19 January 1742, is at first sight little more than a journal without a plot, the facts recorded being all too readily forgotten, in spite of an alleged portrait of Mme de Tencin under the name of Tonin. It achieved, however, considerable notoriety, for the main adventure was considered to be the story of his own licentious life. In fact the image of society it evokes is that of vice rampant. The novel is interesting for its moral disquisitions on love, and for its portrayal of a sensitive, unusually *complaisante* woman in love with a man who discusses with her his mistresses and his amorous exploits. He finally places her esteem above sexual satisfaction, and they marry when their capacity for love is exhausted. The marriage, cemented in friendship, leads to happiness in a rural retreat. This unexpected moral ending is praised by Etiemble as the triumph of commonsense in human relations: it certainly has the merit of originality and of showing a certain perspicacity.

Duclos' career and his varied activities show his position in eighteenth-century society. He started as an exceptionally gifted pupil at the Collège d'Harcourt and frequented early literary circles and cafés, as well as showing an interest in the theatre. His scholarly pursuits led him to be elected to the Académie des Inscriptions et Belles Lettres (1739), and to write a *Mémoire sur l'origine et les révolutions des langues celtiques et françaises* in 1740, followed by a second *Mémoire* in 1741. In 1744 he was elected mayor of Dinan, which office he held till 1749. He became *député* of the Tiers Etat de Bretagne, which office he held till 1754. In 1746 he was elected a member of the Académie Française, and through Mme de Pompadour was charged with the task of cataloguing the French and Latin manuscripts of the Bibliothèque du Roi. In 1750 he was appointed Historiographer of the King in succession to Voltaire, no doubt for writing an *Histoire de Louis XI*. In 1751 appeared his important work on *Considérations sur les mœurs*, with a supplement in novel-form, *Mémoires sur les mœurs du XVIIIe siècle*. In 1755 he was elected *secrétaire perpétuel* of the French Academy, on whose dictionary he worked from 1761. In 1763 we find him in England, where he was received by George III, and in 1766 he travelled to Italy, being received by the Pope in 1767. His *Considérations sur l'Italie* were published posthumously in 1791. He was writing his autobiography when he died in Paris on 26 March 1772. Rousseau said of him that he was 'un homme droit et adroit'. He had led a dissipated youth, but he had studied sufficiently well to have laid a solid foundation for his later work (his complete works appeared in ten volumes in 1806, and were re-edited in 1821). The comtesse de Rochefort summed up his character well when she said: 'Pour vous, Duclos, il ne vous faut que du vin, du fromage et la première venue.' He is best remembered as a novelist for his *tableaux de mœurs*, but lately he is being reconsidered as a forerunner of Laclos and Sade. He shows a thrice-raped virtuous woman as defenceless when faced by a determined libertine. The seducer's monotonous succession of conquests strikes a modern reader as mechanical and therefore boring, but it is part of a tradition of cynicism which is represented also in La Morlière's lighthearted satire *Angola, histoire indienne* (1746), the Abbé Voisenon's licentious *Le Sultan Misapouf* (1746) and *Zulmis et Zelmaïde* (1745), Fougeret de Monbron's *Margot la ravaudeuse* (1750), *Le Cosmopolite, ou Le Citoyen du monde* (1750), mentioned as a source of *Candide*, and of the *Voyages de Scarmentado* by Voltaire, P.-J.-B. Nougaret's *Lucette ou Les Progrès du libertinage* (2 vols., 1765, vol. 3, 1766) and *La Capucinade* (1765). Other *romans libertins* include Mirabeau's *Le Libertin de qualité* (1783), Abbé Dulaurens' *Imirce ou La Fille de la nature* (1765), and especially *Le Compère Mathieu* (1766), which owes something to Rabelais as well as to Diderot. The latter work borrows also from *Candide*. It is basically concerned with a disputation between Mathieu, a disciple of Rousseau and an apostle of freedom, the unintellectual savage who finally discovers man's wickedness and becomes a Manichaean, and Jérôme, a third party to the discussion, who becomes a deist and liberal Christian. The author's intention is obscure. Whilst he obviously detests all priests, Catholics, and saints, whom he brands as hypocrites, he nevertheless accepts the traditional mask of society. His *L'Arrétin ou La Débauche de l'esprit en fait de bon sens* (1763) is an expression of incredulity that leaves his readers equally perplexed as to his private views. With Durosoi's *Clairval philosophe, ou La Force des passions, Mémoires d'une femme retirée du monde* (2 parts, 1765), we find an apologia of 'libertinage vertueux'.[12] Among the more interesting writers of this kind are Denon, Louvet, and Nerciat.

Baron Dominique Vivant de Non or Denon (1747–1825) was a

[12] B. Farmian du Rosoy, called Durosoi or Durosoy (1745–92), founded the *Gazette de Paris* (1789–92) which he edited till his death by the guillotine. He wrote *Lettres de Cécile à Julie* (1764) and a number of plays: *Les Devins français ou Le Siège de Calais* (1765); *Richard III* (1781); *Henri IV ou La Bataille d'Ivry, drame lyrique* (1774); *L'Amour filial* (1786).

diplomat, a courtier, and an artist as well as a writer, and achieved renown in his lifetime as a Lovelace. In court circles ladies called him 'Le Faune', and among actors he was known as 'le petit-jeune-homme couleur-de-rose', following the unsuccessful performance of his play *Julia ou Le Bon Père*. He frequented Boucher and Caylus, the art connoisseur. After a visit to Ferney, he published a witty but harsh portrait of Voltaire which created a scandal. He was a member of the Académie Royale de Peinture, and has left many engravings, chiefly of drawings, to illustrate his *Voyage pittoresque de Naples et de Sicile*. His name appeared on the list of *émigrés*, and he was only saved from the scaffold through the intervention of the painter David. He then worked on models for civil uniforms and became a national engraver. He met Robespierre, frequented the salon of Mme de Beauharnais, and became a friend of Bonaparte, whom he had first met at a ball given by Talleyrand. He accompanied Napoleon to Egypt and his *Voyage dans la Basse et la Haute Egypte pendant les campagnes du général Bonaparte* did much to reveal Egyptian art to the West, for he illustrated his text with drawings. He became director-in-chief of the National Museums, and is responsible for the plan to erect the Vendôme column in Paris, and to have the Chevaux de Venise erected on the Petit Arc de Triomphe of the Carrousel. Louis XVIII maintained him in office, but requested him to make restitution of artistic treasures stolen by Napoleon. He declined to do so, and retired to write an *Histoire de l'art depuis les temps les plus reculés jusqu'au commencement du XIXe siècle*. He left 325 plates, which show to advantage his not inconsiderable talent as an engraver. His literary reputation rests chiefly on a very short story, *Point de lendemain*, published in June 1777 in *Mélanges littéraires ou Journal des dames* and signed M.D.G.C.D.R. *Point de lendemain* is the story of an affair lasting one night which has no past and no future. The man feeds on a dream, and the woman, deceiving her husband and her lover, deliberately seeks sensual and intellectual pleasure in a chance and necessarily short encounter. The author exploits his subject, and the hearts and minds of his characters, with wit and cynicism, but behind the façade, as Etiemble has suggested, there lurks mystery, obscurity, the cool silence of nature, and a pre-Romantic sensibility in which *paysage* is shown as *état d'âme*.

Louvet de Couvray (1760–97) was an important personage during the French Revolution, voting for the death of the king, not from conviction but, as he said, out of respect for majority government and democratic principle. He joined the Club des Jacobins following the publication of his brochure *Paris justifié* (1789), which was received with acclaim. His *Sentinelle*, financed by Dumouriez, was posted on the walls of Paris, and his articles in the *Journal des débats du Club des Jacobins* (10 August 1791–10 March 1793), written in his capacity as director and chief editor, showed to advantage his talent for irony. An eloquent speaker and an effective pamphleteer, he was elected deputy of the Loiret and joined the Girondins. His virulent attack on Robespierre, whom he branded as a tyrant, *Robespierre, je t'accuse d'avoir évidemment marché au suprême pouvoir*, is written in an elevated and incisive style, but it was mistimed, as was his attack on Marat, and in fact it served to strengthen Robespierre's position.

His refutation of Saint-Just's attack on the Girondins, a later publication, is to be found in his *Mémoires*. He was proscribed along with the Girondins, and took refuge first in Normandy and then in the Jura, where he led the life of a hunted man. He recounted the circumstances in *Quelques notices pour l'histoire et le récit de mes périls depuis le 31 mai 1793*. He returned to Paris after *9 thermidor* (27 July 1794), having made no concessions to his enemies. He was elected President of the Assembly and member of the *Comité du salut public*, and he was naturally abhorred by the *émigrés*. He became disillusioned with republican policies, exclaiming shortly before his death: 'Grâce à Dieu, je finis avant la République.' In 1793, during the years of his proscription, he had married a childhood friend, who had left her husband to rejoin him in May 1789, but had been unable to secure a divorce before 1792. He called her Lodoïska, after the Polish heroine in his novel *Faublas*. He was never parted from her till his death, when his disconsolate wife took poison, and only agreed to take an antidote when her child was brought to her. Louvet's life begins with trivial *amours*, moves on to that of a prominent politician at a key moment in French history, and ends in tired desperation tinged with fortitude, a biography no doubt more interesting than his own *Faublas* which, however, enjoyed a considerable reputation for two decades, although it is now almost forgotten. *Une année de la vie du chevalier de Faublas* appeared in 1787, *Six Semaines de la vie du chevalier de Faublas* in 1788, and *La Fin des amours du chevalier de Faublas* in 1790. The novel as a whole is licentious, and its *histoires d'alcôve* form a strange prelude to the author's subsequent revolutionary career. At first sight it seems to reflect no more than an aristocratic way of life, but a closer examination reveals in the hero Faublas a future Jacobin, deeply conscious of social injustice. The novel is entertaining and well written, the numerous episodes following one another with speed. There are a very large number of disguises and accidental meetings, and the villains receive their just deserts. Digressions abound, which make tedious reading. Faublas, who is essentially the author's *alter ego*, is a French rake given to appearing in women's dress. The author writes without prejudice, without humour, or any trace of scepticism. He confuses pleasure with virtue. Philarète Chasles summed up the work very well in 1827:

En somme, l'invention de Faublas est gracieuse et féconde: le style pur, élégant, souple et facile, un peu vulgaire en certaines pages; peu de force, beaucoup d'agréments; plus de grâce que d'esprit; plus d'esprit que de volupté; plus de volupté que d'observation; encore plus de légèreté que tout cela; enfin un singulier mélange de tendresse volage, d'ivresse des sens, d'imagination follement plaisante, en font un ouvrage aussi dangereux que remarquable.

The danger has receded as the character has increasingly appeared shallow. This novel, however, coupled with *La Revue des années blanche et noire*, in which the clergy and the nobility were attacked, and *Emilie de Varmont ou Le Divorce nécessaire et les amours du curé Sévin* (1791), a social work which recommends the marriage of priests, as well as the establishment of divorce, helped him to begin his political career under favourable auspices; but ultimately hastened his political demise.

André-Robert Andrea de Nerciat (1739–1800) was a poet of little consequence who achieved notoriety as a writer of obscene books. He testifies to the contemporary success of Louvet, for in 1788 he published *Les Galanteries du jeune chevalier de Faublas ou Les Folies parisiennes* (in four volumes). Other works include *Contes nouveaux* (1777); *Félicia ou Mes Fredaines* (1775), with a sequel in two volumes entitled *Monrose* (1795); *Mon Noviciat* (1792); *Le Diable-au-corps* (first part of *Les Ecarts du tempérament ou Le Catéchisme de Figaro*, 1785); and *Les Aphrodites* (1793).[13]

Casanova, whose expurgated *Mémoires* were published in twelve volumes at Leipzig in 1826–32, and in five volumes in Paris in 1843,[14] may be fittingly considered in the context of the novels in memoir form that have been reviewed. These confessions of an aged sensualist devoid of shame or regret, recounting his amorous adventures with cynicism but without distaste, underlie the close connection between the two genres, for Casanova's true story has been embellished in keeping with prevailing taste, and written in the witty, effective style that characterises the literary age, often as rococo in literature as in painting. Giacomo Girolamo Casanova de Seingalt, born in Venice in 1725, is the most famous of three

[13] *Félicia*, reputedly immoral, was to have appeared in M. Etiemble's two-volume anthology of eighteenth-century novels, but had to be excluded for reasons of space. This is to be regretted, since the work reflects a characteristic aspect of literary output of the time, imperfectly covered by other recent publications.

[14] Brockhaus, which owns the original manuscript, has brought out a complete edition in six volumes (1960–62; with Plon of Paris).

gifted brothers, one of whom, François (1727–1805), is best known for his war-paintings. The son of actors who were not renowned for their strict morality, Jean-Jacques had eclipsed them in sexual prowess by the age of fifteen. He had inherited the looks of his mother and soon acquired the manners of a *petit-maître*. He combined a precocious intellect (he is known to have sustained a thesis in law at the age of sixteen) with a deep sensuality and a considerable personal magnetism. He was expelled from a seminary following a scandal, and turned adventurer, publicist, diplomat, and fortune-hunter, as well as preacher and abbé. He may be likened to a Gil Blas unable to grow up, or an even more corrupt Don Juan. It is claimed that he seduced two or three thousand women of all ages, classes, and nationalities. In 1755, when in Venice, he was gaoled, but contrived a hair-raising escape which won him the acclaim of all Europe. He met Rousseau, Voltaire, Suvarov, Frederick the Great, Catherine II, Louis XV, Mme de Pompadour, and M. de Bernis. His memoirs shed an illuminating light on the age, its underlying decadence and corruption, and provide as well a testimony to his excesses as amorist and his extravagances. His lascivious life and tainted loves brought him close to crime: he was a libertine, a cardsharper, and a cutthroat, whom Jules Janin called a 'fille de joie faite homme', and whom another critic likened to a hermaphrodite, the unsavoury chevalier d'Eon. He was also an illuminist, a *grand cophte*, but was essentially a cheat and deceiver. In spite of all this he was showered with honours; in his time he wore the Papal cross and the orders of knighthood of a number of Italian princes. He became involved in a duel in Warsaw which led him to flee to Paris, Madrid, and eventually to Venice. The French Revolution made him cautious, so he assumed the duties of librarian to Count Waldstein, who at the time was without a library. Casanova had the gift of a brilliant storyteller and conversationalist, and his account of his escape from gaol won him instant recognition as a writer and has been acknowledged as a literary masterpiece. His special aptitude, monotonously exploited, lies in conveying in fluent style the fumblings of a halting memory awakened by the sight of some long-forgotten memento of a past love. The memoirs are thus for their author a melancholy way of reliving some of the enjoyments of the past and of recreating his own reality, somewhat after the fashion later adopted by Proust. In addition to his *Mémoires*, written in French, Casanova has left some historical tales in Italian, an account of his captivity (Prague, 1788), and a verse translation of the *Iliad*. He died in Bohemia in 1798.

Many *romans de mœurs* have close affinities with *romans libertins*, introducing similar characters or reflecting similar mental attitudes. De Mouhy, an ex-cavalry officer, provides a good portrait of the *fermier-général* in his *Paysanne parvenue* (1735–37), and of a venal *grand vicaire* in *Mémoires d'une fille de qualité*. G. de la Bataille wrote *Jeannette Seconde ou La Nouvelle Paysanne parvenue* (1744) to show up conventual intrigues, and Fromaget, in *Promenade de Saint-Cloud* (1736), attacked the director of conscience. Anti-clericalism is evident in Brunet de Brou's *La Religieuse malgré elle* (1720) and in Mouhy's *Mémoires d'Anne-Marie de Moras* (1739). Saint-Foix in *Lettre d'une Turque* (1730) satirises gambling and immorality as well as forced religious vocations. D'Argens in *Le Législateur moderne* is equally critical. Mauvillon in *Le Soldat parvenu* (1735) brings out the arrogance and the immorality of the military. Magny in *Spectacles nocturnes* (1756) offers a sincere and shrewd picture of the decadence of polite society. The class-structure as it affects marriage comes under fire in Sainte-Colombe's *Mémoires du baron de Puineuf*, and in *Les Plaisirs d'un jour* (1764) he provides a detailed account of stage life.

The numerous oriental or pseudo-oriental tales are commonly satirical and libertine in intent. They go back to the *Thousand and One Nights*, first partially translated into French in 1704. In *Grigri* (1739), an allegorical novel of manners in a pseudo-Japanese setting, Cahusac satirised the court at Versailles. Other allegorical novels include: *Zelinga* (1749) by Palissot, *Ma-gakou* (1752) by Chevrier (also author of *Mémoires d'une honnête femme*, 1753), and *Mirza et Fatmé* (1754) by Saurin. The oriental tale hardly forms an independent category, apart from the fact of its basic theme. The *contes*, too, as a genre, reflect many currents, one of the most characteristic being the *contes moraux*. Marmontel, who derived much inspiration from Voltaire, wrote a great number that describe manners and serve to edify. He believed that he was fostering virtue when he depicted characters imbued with the fine sentiments of nature in such works as *La Mauvaise Mère*, *Le Bon Mari*, *La Bergère des Alpes*, etc. Happiness and virtue, sentimentally linked, were an unfailing recipe for success. Many of his tales were turned into plays and bear witness to the prevailing mood. His longer novels were also instruments of philosophical propaganda, as is evident in *Bélisaire*[15] (1767) and *Les Incas*. But his appeals to tolerance and his particular expression of the basic ideas of the *philosophes* were banal in his own time and cannot be read with enthusiasm today. It is his style that is now most highly commended and one critic has found the masterly technique we associate with the name of Maupassant in individual passages by Marmontel.

[15] *Bélisaire* was translated into Russian by Catherine II.

There are many *romans à thèse*. The Abbé Gérard in *Le Comte de Valmont, ou Les Egarements de la raison* (1774) wrote a public-spirited book, filled with piety and virtue, which was intended to provide a suitable textbook for young aristocrats. In effect this work is in the tradition of Fénelon's *Télémaque*, as is the better-known work of the Abbé Barthélemy, *Voyage du jeune Anacharsis en Grèce dans le milieu du IVe siècle avant l'ère vulgaire* (1788), a learned introduction to Greek culture, which has served many generations of young *lycéens*. J.-J. Barthélemy (1716–95) was also a numismatist, an archaeologist, and an author of antiquarian works, but it is on his well-documented and fluently written introduction to Hellenic culture, started in 1757, that his fame rests. The *Voyage du jeune Anacharsis* met with some success in England, when translated into English in 1794. L.-S. Mercier in *L'Homme sauvage* (1767) marshals an exceptional case for the civilised world against barbarism, and this work has been cited as a source for Chateaubriand's *René*. Mercier, better known for his plays and his *Tableau de Paris* (1781–90), also wrote novels on historical themes.

One wonders whether Restif de La Bretonne's novel *La Découverte australe par un homme volant ou Le Dédale français* (1781), which foreshadows Jules Verne, is a *roman philosophique* or a *roman didactique*. There are, too, *contes fantastiques*, fairy-tales that dabble in the occult. Jacques Cazotte (1719–92), remembered today only as the man who sat on a school-bench with Rameau's nephew and later provided some information on the character whom Diderot made famous, has some claim to recognition as the first writer to introduce mysticism or illuminism into the novel. *Le Diable amoureux* (1762), admired by Gérard de Nerval, became a model for the fantastic novel. It shows an unbridled imagination. Every conceivable scheme is conjured up to lead his unfortunate hero into temptation. Cazotte really believed in his devils – *Le Lord impromptu* (1767) also contains magic – yet his novel lacks depth which did not prevent it from enjoying instant success. Cazotte, an *illuminé*, is known to have received a visit from Martinez Pasqualis, the Portuguese theosophist, to have been initiated into demonology, and to have joined a lodge of *martinistes*. His interest in the occult was extended to the Kabbala, but his knowledge of the subject was superficial and has been questioned by Etiemble and Castex. Cazotte may have been doing no more than exploit a new vein with a certain grace, to which he added a little personal emotion, tinged with sensuality. He had an unusual life. From 1741 to 1743 he moved in literary and salon circles, writing *La Patte du chat, conte zinzimois* (1741), *Mille et une fadaises* (1742), consisting of Arabian tales, and others in the fashion of the time.

He then went to Martinique (1747–52, and again 1754–59), and on his first return to France in 1752, he wrote two ballads, *Les Prouesses inimitables d'Ollivier, marquis d'Edesse*, which is a source for his later novel *Ollivier* (1763), and *La Veillée de la bonne femme ou Le Réveil d'Enguerrand*. He became involved in the Querelle des Bouffons, writing two pamphlets, *La Guerre de l'Opéra* and *Observations*. He then composed a comic opera in one night, *Sabots*, which had some success, and a poem, *La Guerre de Genève*, in the seventh canto of which is to be found a clever pastiche of Voltaire. During the Revolution he sided with the royalists, and entered into a fairly innocuous correspondence with Pouteau, to whom he sent plans for the escape of the royal family. His letters were seized and he was gaoled on 18 August 1792. On 29 and 30 August he was interrogated by Fouquier-Tinville, and on 1 September was sentenced to death for having corresponded with the *émigrés*. His daughter, showing extraordinary courage and devotion, joined him in gaol and as he was dragged from prison the crowd pleaded for his pardon, which was then granted. Later in the same month a new order for his arrest was issued, and on 24 September, after a public hearing in which the seventy-three-year-old man conducted himself with great dignity, he was once more condemned and this time executed, on the Place du Carrousel. The judge paid tribute to his courage and probity. Cazotte's last words are on record: 'Je meurs comme j'ai vécu, fidèle à mon Dieu et à mon roi.' The following line of verse, often quoted, has served to perpetuate the memory of his last days:

> Des bourreaux l'ont absous, des juges l'ont frappé.

Tales by other writers are more horrific. Beckford, who wrote in French, is responsible for an immoral and melancholy tale, *Vathek* (French text 1787), in which the heroes triumph in their villainy, only to discover that they hate themselves. In *Pauliska ou La Perversité moderne* (1798) Révéroni Saint-Cyr describes a secret and evil society, in which the new discoveries of science are put to monstrous purposes, and prisons and torture are commonplace. Other novelists share this taste for perversity, gloom, and melodrama. Among them, Baculard d'Arnaud indulged in the *genre sombre* in *Epreuves du sentiment* (5 vols., 1770–80), but the horrific experiences he was able to stage successfully fail to rouse interest or emotion in his novels, no doubt because he had no imagination.[16] Loaisel de Tréogate, author of *Dolbreuse* (1783), *Florello*, *Valinore*, and *Les Soirées de mélancolie* (1777), is more original. He has a Breton sensibility and writes of feudal castles, cemeteries, lonely woods, and chapels in ruins. In

[16] See above, p. 320, for information on Baculard d'Arnaud's *drames*.

these respects he foreshadows the romanticism of Chateaubriand, without the talent to exploit new forms; H. Coulet has aptly described his work as 'rococo tardif'.

The sentimental romance is the dominant type of novel from Rousseau to the Revolution. There were earlier prototypes and before Rousseau the following works may be listed: *Les Mémoires de milédi B**** (1760), attributed to Mlle de la Guesnerie; *Confessions du comte de**** (1741) by Duclos; *Mémoires d'une fille de qualité* (1742) by Guillot de La Chassagne; *Les Epoux malheureux* (1746) by Baculard d'Arnaud; *Les Confessions d'un fat* (1749) by chevalier de Bastide; and *Les Cent Nouvelles nouvelles* (36 parts in 19 vols. 1732–39) by Mme de Gomez.

The best of the early sentimental novels were undoubtedly by women writers. Madame de Tencin's *Mémoires du comte de Comminge* (1735) has love as its main theme, with striking scenes built on *romanesque* situations, and moments of pathos. There is a Romantic sensibility in certain passages of despair, death, sadness, and passion, presented against a sombre backcloth of dark forests and of dungeons, and throughout she has succeeded in conveying an impression of sincerity. Françoise d'Issembourg d'Happoncourt, dame de Graffigny (1695–1758), is worthy of special mention. A great-grand-niece of J. Callot, she entered the literary world only at the age of forty-three, after being received by Voltaire at Cirey. Her *Vie privée de Voltaire et de Mme du Châtelet* was not published until 1820, but the letters of which it consists were circulated at the time and won her notoriety. She had to leave Cirey after Mme du Châtelet had alleged that she had despatched to friends at Nancy a canto of *La Pucelle*. She first wrote a short story, *Recueil de ces messieurs* (1745), which was severely criticised, whereupon she decided to learn her craft. In 1747 she published her *Lettres d'une Péruvienne*, which achieved an immediate and lasting success. It owes something to the *Lettres persanes* and to *Pamela*, and also to the *Lettres d'une religieuse portugaise*. The style is precious but not without charm, and it was this work which led Turgot to draft his observations on French institutions and manners. Mme de Graffigny, who lived separated from a brutal and violent husband who eventually died in gaol, ran her own salon. It was there that Helvétius met her niece, whom he eventually married. Inspired by Nivelle de La Chaussée's attempts at *comédie larmoyante*, she wrote an interesting play, *Cénie*, which Diderot praised as an early example of *drame*, and another, *La Fille d'Aristide*, which was a failure in the theatre. This fact prompted the abbé de Voisenon to state: 'Elle me lit sa pièce; je la trouvai mauvaise, et elle me trouva méchant. La pièce fut jouée; le public mourut d'ennui et l'auteur de chagrin.' Her

Lettres d'une Péruvienne, the first sentimental novel to be written in letter-form in France, earn her her place in literature. The Peruvian Zilia is taken from her home and wanders in our Western hemisphere like some lost and tragic soul. She places her ideal happiness in a marriage of heart and reason, but society shatters the mainspring of her life. She comes to grips with a new and horrible reality which leads to her betrayal by her fiancé Aza. She finds eventual salvation by renouncing passion and returning to the bosom of Mother Nature to lead a placid existence. The novel has sensibility, sincerity, and authenticity, but lacks the pungent philosophical satire of Voltaire's *L'Ingénu*, or even that of the *Lettres iroquoises*. Madame de Graffigny, who drew her own self-portrait in her heroine, certainly thought of herself as a *femme philosophe*. She was a feminist, and attacked the prevailing pattern of education for women, in particular that provided by nuns. Her emotional power and eloquence and her feeling for nature make her a forerunner of *La Nouvelle Héloïse*.

The outstanding woman novelist is Marie-Jeanne Laboras de Mézières, dame Riccoboni (1714–92), the actress wife of A.-F. Riccoboni, an actor-playwright and son of the famous Lelio-Luigi Riccoboni. She gave up the stage in 1761, having achieved considerable success playing the part of the *amoureuse*. Madame Riccoboni was popular both in England and in France: she translated Fielding's novel *Amelia* in 1762, and showed a predilection for English titles from 1757, when she published *Lettres de mistress Fanni Butlerd à Milord Charles Alfred Caitombridge* as a translation from the English. Many of her novels are similarly written in letter-form. In 1759 *Lettres de milady Juliette Catesby à milady Henrietta Campley, son amie* appeared, but it is a work which is not so engaging as her earlier *Histoire de M. le marquis de Cressy* (1758), an elegantly phrased and sensitive novel in which the hero Cressy recalls Versac and Lovelace. Madame Riccoboni showed taste and discretion in presenting an innocent woman betrayed and about to commit suicide; the work is simple yet strong and for this reason[17] is to be preferred to *Clarissa*. *Histoire de Miss Jenny* in four parts (1764) is less good, as are the *Lettres d'Adélaïde de Dammartin, comtesse de Sancerre* (1766), the *Lettres d'Elisabeth-Sophie de Vallière* (1772), and the *Lettres de mylord Rivers* (1777), in which the epistolary form interferes with the development of the action. Her feminism is less militant than that of Mme de Graffigny. She can present love and suffering, but not passion, as Prévost had done, nor the sustained characterisation of a woman in love as found in Marivaux's *La*

[17] According to F. C. Green, *French Novelists, Manners and Ideas from the Renaissance to the Revolution*, 2nd ed. 1964.

Vie de Marianne, for which she provided a conclusion. She adopted an increasingly moralising and sententious style. From a realistic beginning she indulged increasingly in the *romanesque*, and in 1779–80 she wrote four stories in the so-called *troubadour* style of the marquis de Tressan. She stood firm against the sinister characterisation we find in Laclos, and at first she wrote with elegance and wit, and was noted for her delicacy of feeling. Later she became repetitious and over-emphatic in style, a fact ascribed to her experience as an actress on the stage. Her language was increasingly studded with epithets and exclamation marks.[18] The epistolary novel which Mme Riccoboni so worthily exemplifies became fashionable in 1761, holding its own with surprising constancy during each successive decade (roughly 50 out of 350 titles for each decade) till 1790. Mme Le Prince de Beaumont's *Lettres de Montier* (1753) went into seven editions before 1775. They are 'sensibles' and didactic.

The *Lettres d'une religieuse portugaise* (1669) by Guilleragues exercised a considerable influence on the genre, but between 1741 and *La Nouvelle Héloïse* (1761) little appeared. Dorat's *Les Sacrifices de l'amour, ou Lettres de la vicomtesse de Senanges et du chevalier de Versenai* (1771), in which the two lovers are at last united thanks to the fortunate death of the husband, is typical of the later period and shows the influence of *La Nouvelle Héloïse*. By 1760, however, the vogue had been established. The basic idea, that of publishing an exchange of letters, is not very different from that of publishing a personal diary and one can see how the form developed naturally out of the memoir, the principal difference being in the perspective of time which it offers. The letter-form allows the writer, and therefore the reader, to come closer to events; its weakness lies in the necessary length of the letters, which tend to amount to monologues and can seem unnatural. Success in the genre is rare. In France its vogue owes much to *Pamela*, later French novelists refining on Richardson's technique. Its attraction lay in the possibilities for greater realism and more detailed analysis of feelings and motives from different standpoints. Often the novelists merged the technique of the memoir and that of the

[18] Mention should be made of the novels by Mme de Genlis: the *Chevaliers du Cygne* (1795), in the *genre troubadour*, and *Adèle et Théodore* (1782), in letter-form (see above, p. 283). Sophie Ristaud, dame Cottin (1773–1807), is another woman novelist who combined the *romanesque* with a melancholy note and whose stories of unhappy love proved popular at the end of the century. *Claire d'Albe* (1791), *Malvina*, *Amélie de Mansfield*, and especially *Mathilde* (1805), the story of a sister of Richard the Lion-heart, have a personal and often an epic quality. She wrote also a prose poem, *Prise de Jéricho*, *Elizabeth ou Les Exilés de Sibérie* (1806), and an unfinished work, *La Religion chrétienne prouvée par le sentiment*, which expresses ideas to be found in Chateaubriand.

letter, as is shown by the provision of editorial footnotes to letters. There was, moreover, the need to explain excessive correspondence. Clumsily and all too often writers claim that their characters could not resist the call of the pen and paper lying conveniently within reach, or they are made to travel unnecessarily so as to justify letter-writing; sometimes they have to be ill and confined to their own room, so as to be in a position to write plausibly to people staying under the same roof. Long conversations are recorded word for word, extending to whole pages, and inner monologues abound, as do exclamation marks. The public, however, welcomed these novels for their superficially greater authenticity, and this obliged the novelists to try to remain within the bounds of credibility. The technical difficulties of the genre seemed insurmountable until the appearance of Laclos' masterpiece.

The sentimental novel, which had English and French roots well before the appearance of *La Nouvelle Héloïse*, gained in strength, depth, and sense of direction thanks to Rousseau. One of the main expressions of post-Rousseau sensibility in the novel is to be found in the long popular *Paul et Virginie* by Bernardin de Saint-Pierre. Jacques-Henri-Bernardin de Saint-Pierre (1737–1814) first studied engineering, but early in his life dreamed of founding an ideal republic. He went to Madagascar and then spent two years in Mauritius, years that stimulated his imagination. In 1772 he met Rousseau and became his friend: they shared a common love of nature and hatred of society. With the encouragement of Rousseau, in 1773, he began the great work of his life, *Etudes de la nature*, the first three volumes of which appeared in 1784, and the fourth, including *Paul et Virginie*, in 1788. During the Revolution, he was made *Intendant* of the Jardin des Plantes and professor of ethics at the Ecole Normale Supérieure. In 1795 he was elected a member of the *Institut*.

The *Etudes de la nature* were intended to demonstrate the bounty of God and the wonders of his Providence. For this author, the world revolved wholly around Man, whom God created as the ultimate manifestation of his purpose. The enthusiasm with which this work was greeted is a sign of the secret longing for belief of an over-rationalistic society, but the *Etudes de la nature* are built on naïve and rationally unacceptable premises and have today only curiosity value. Outside its historical context the reasoning is puerile and borders on the absurd, for Bernardin de Saint-Pierre was certainly no thinker or theologian. But he was sincere, and above all he had an extraordinary gift for conveying feeling and depicting nature. *Paul et Virginie* is a charming, romantic tale of two lovers, told by a kindly old man, and concerns two French families who dwell in two cabins in Mauritius. A young widow,

Mme de la Tour, has a daughter, Virginie. A Breton lady lives with her son Paul, and both children grow up together as brother and sister. They are naturally good, pure, charming, and ignorant of the world. They live virtuous, happy lives in a wonderful tropical setting. Paul plants a few fruit-trees, whilst Virginie feeds the gulls by a stream. As she reaches the age of fifteen she experiences the first stirrings of love. She is, however, called back to France by an aunt, but the young people have had time to acknowledge their love. In his despair at the separation, Paul turns to study. Eighteen months later, Virginie sends a letter in which she depicts her misery in the midst of plenty. Soon, disinherited by her aunt, she decides to return, only to suffer shipwreck and death by drowning, within sight of the shore, in a storm over Mauritius, in spite of Paul's heroic efforts to save her. She dies with great dignity, refusing the help of a sailor, and preserving her modesty as she is swallowed up by the sea. Paul loses consciousness but is rescued, only to die of grief two months later. Marguerite, Mme de la Tour, and the unsympathetic aunt all die in turn. Paul and Virginie lie side by side in their tropical grave, next to their mothers and slaves, and only the two huts in ruins are left standing.

The plot, subordinated to didactic purposes, is slight and the story, especially in the second part, incorporates many moral sermons. The merits of the work, however, are great. There is realism of a new kind in the details, and in the outline of the plot, which is based on a true incident. The novel illustrates Rousseau's theories, for in Bernardin de Saint-Pierre's conception of things man is born good and, whilst evil is not denied, the tone is one of optimism, even if the conclusion is the romantic one of true love associated with death. The opposition of corrupt civilisation and innocent nature could not be more effectively exploited; and we can understand that the attraction of pure, simple, naïve love to very many people who had never known it must prove irresistible. Numerous passages have the charm and truth of dream sequences, well related as they are to a typically adolescent mind. Primitive society, through Bernardin de Saint-Pierre's travels, dreams, and general sensibility, transcends the myth created by Rousseau to become a truth, and seems to present innocence as it was before the Fall, in settings of exotic and previously unknown glamour. Bernardin de Saint-Pierre takes us well beyond Rousseau and close to Chateaubriand, who revealed the New World to his readers. Saint-Pierre's world, however, is that of Rousseau's in the Ile de Saint-Pierre, for it is similarly circumscribed by an island; it is at once as safe for the author as the womb of a mother for a child, yet surrounded by the terrors of the deep. In *Paul et Virginie* the shipwreck which brings about the final tragedy is described with unsurpassed evocative power, full of emotion based upon realism and a sense of awe. At an intellectual level the death of Virginie is gratuitous and absurd, as indeed are those of Manon Lescaut and Atala, but this sense of what is mere chance or purely fatuous prudishness is tempered by a growing awareness of an overriding Fate. The situation is in the romantic orbit of *Julie*. Yet in the final analysis, it is neither the subject matter nor the characterisation, nor the splendour of descriptive passages, which ensures Bernardin de Saint-Pierre's place in literature, but the composite picture the work offers of a new and intense way of feeling, the gravity of simple emotional life presented in a wonderfully full and melodious style:

> Cependant, l'heure du souper étant venue, on se mit à table, où chacun des convives, agité de passions différentes, mangea peu, et ne parla point. Virginie en sortit la première, et fut s'asseoir au lieu où nous sommes. Paul la suivit bientôt après, et vint se mettre auprès d'elle. L'un et l'autre gardèrent quelque temps un profond silence. Il faisait une de ces nuits délicieuses, si communes entre les tropiques, et dont le plus habile pinceau ne rendrait pas la beauté. La lune paraissait au milieu du firmament, entourée d'un rideau de nuages, que ses rayons dissipaient par degrés. Sa lumière se répandait insensiblement sur les montagnes de l'île et sur leurs pitons, qui brillaient d'un vert argenté. Les vents retenaient leurs haleines. On entendait dans les bois, au fond des vallées, au bout des rochers, de petits cris, de doux murmures d'oiseaux qui se caressaient dans leurs nids, réjouis par la clarté de la nuit et la tranquillité de l'air. Tous, jusqu'aux insectes, bruissaient sous l'herbe. Les étoiles étincelaient au ciel et se réfléchissaient au sein de la mer, qui répétait leurs images tremblantes. Virginie parcourait avec des regards distraits son vaste et sombre horizon distingué du rivage de l'île par les feux rouges des pêcheurs. Elle aperçut à l'entrée du port une lumière et une ombre: c'était le fanal et le corps du vaisseau où elle devait s'embarquer pour l'Europe, et qui, prêt à mettre à la voile, attendait à l'ancre la fin du calme. A cette vue, elle se troubla et détourna la tête pour que Paul ne la vit pas pleurer.

La Chaumière indienne (1791), like *Paul et Virginie*, illustrated the so-called return to nature, but it lacks the fine style of the earlier work and has proved to be far less popular. Both these exotic novels influenced Chateaubriand. His immediate disciples never captured the music of the master. Florian (1755–94), poet, dramatist, and writer of fables, is the author of two novels in the *style chevaleresque*, *Numa Pompilius* (1786) and *Gonzalve de Cordoue* (1791), but is better known for his pastoral novel *Estelle* (1788), an ingenuous and tender story which recalls *Paul et Virginie* but is too insipid to endure. Berquin (1747–91) wrote in a similarly naïve style, chiefly for children, and for readers looking for further manifestations of *sensibilité*.

In the novels of the three great writers whose works remain to be examined, traces are to be found of the influence of Rousseau and of Diderot, and an expression of the changing social and political pattern of the century.

N.-A.-E. Restif de La Bretonne (1734–1806) relived his life in his writings – one long and richly documented autobiography. In this he follows in the wake of the *Confessions*, rather than in that of *La Nouvelle Héloïse*. Paul Valéry has rated him higher than Rousseau, the English critic G. Saintsbury compared him with Defoe, Havelock Ellis saw in him a forerunner of Proust, and Marc Chadourne, his latest biographer, has likened him to André Gide. He remains a remarkable and much debated figure in the history of literature and ideas, and his reputation seems likely to grow through the reprinting of selected works. He produced about 200 volumes, many of which were printed by his own hand, and his writings cover a whole range of subjects with astonishing frankness. Born at Sacy (Yonne), he had a varied experience of life, moving to Paris where he worked as a journeyman printer and where he met Anne (or Agnès) Lebègue, whom he married in 1760. He has been heralded by Chadourne as a prophet who foreshadowed the atom, the sputnik, flying men, and air squadrons, the missile that shoots into interplanetary and interstellar space, bacteriology, atomic energy, the Superman, dictatorship, totalitarianism, the United States of Europe, social security, and communism: on the other hand, he has also been called 'the Casanova of the stews', 'the Rousseau of the gutter', and 'Balzac's caveman'. His life and loves, real or fancied, gave him notoriety. It is not known certainly whether he was a fetishist or a pervert in the technical sense; but it is certain that his vindication of incest was no mere rationalist exercise, for it is known that after the age of forty-five he appears to have felt the need to believe that he was the father of the women he took as his mistresses. In 1772 he announced his desire to become intimate with a certain Louise in order to have the pleasure of regretting her later. His eroticism, which is tinged with mysticism and emotional lucidity, is best revealed in his autobiography, *Monsieur Nicolas* (1794–97), in sixteen volumes, for the most part set in the Parisian underworld of the period. His accounts of his peregrinations in the Ile Saint-Louis, where he prowled during the night, being familiarly called Le Hibou, are especially vivid. It is this portrayal of eighteenth-century society which has led to his being referred to as the Zola of his age; but he believed naïvely that he could himself build up a real world of his own in which daughters of past mistresses figure as present ones. All the women he meets fall automatically into this category; and so he ends by living his own novel. He is known to have exaggerated his weaknesses and invented his own remorse and regrets for faults he had not committed, in order to give greater moral reality to his account. His remorse is merely the measure of his inordinate vanity. *Monsieur Nicolas ou Le Cœur humain dévoilé* is thus more of a novel than a true autobiography. *Les Nuits de Paris* (1788–94) *ou Le Spectateur moderne* (1788), however picturesque they may be, are bizarre and deal with chance meetings and anecdotes, and so do not provide the full picture of society claimed by the author. Gérard de Nerval, who thought of himself as the reincarnation of Restif, has retold in *Les Illuminés* (1852) the story of Sara, one of the more striking episodes in *Monsieur Nicolas*. But Nerval, in spite of much research, failed to distinguish fact from fiction, a task which Restif's vivid imagination has rendered difficult, as for instance when dealing with the story of the actress La Belle Guéant. Restif's work includes *La Famille vertueuse* (1767); *Lucile, ou Les Progrès de la vertu*; *Le Pied de Fanchette* (1769); *La Fille naturelle* (1769); *Le Pornographe*[19] (1769; a plan for regulating prostitution said to have been carried out by the Emperor Joseph II, and to have influenced authorities in other countries); *Le Paysan perverti* (1775) and *La Paysanne pervertie* (1784), recast and republished as *Le Paysan et la paysanne pervertis* (1787), largely autobiographical, which with *La Dernière Aventure d'un homme de quarante-cinq ans* (1783), are considered by some to be his best novels, the latter work reappearing in its entirety in *Monsieur Nicolas*; *La Vie de mon père* (1779), which deservedly brought fame to the author, since it presents an unusually detailed picture of peasant life in Burgundy and is the only one of his works free from salacity; *Mes Inscriptions*, a journal for 1780–87, discovered in 1887; *Les Contemporaines* (43 volumes, 1780–85) to which we may add the 23 volumes of *Les Françaises* (1786–); *Les Parisiennes* (1787–91), of great documentary value for the study of women of all classes, especially the middle class, in which figure booksellers, booth-keepers, pork butchers, etc., and for data on 200 crafts practised by women. His liaison with the perfidious Sara, whom he knew in 1780–82, is recorded in *Monsieur Nicolas*, his relationship with his wife, Agnès Lebègue, is to be found in *La Femme infidèle* (1786), and *Ingénue Saxancour* (1789) is the story of his eldest daughter, who was married to a sadistic maniac. *L'Anti-Justine* (1798) is a perverted fantasy.

Restif is always lucid and often prolix, although at times he can be laconic. His general ideas are naïve, but commonplace at the time he wrote. 'C'est être vertueux que de faire des enfants,' he unhesitatingly declares, as a worthy devotee of nature. Thanks to

[19] This is the first of his works which he himself set up in type. It forms the first volume of *Idées singulières*, which includes: *La Mimographe*, *Les Gymnographes*, *L'Andrographe*, *Le Thesmographe*, and *Le Glossographe*.

his prodigious memory, and his powers as a creative and descriptive artist, he has created and analysed one thousand characters, successfully presenting a world of bourgeois, artisans, and peasants, whether he felt drawn to it or not. Above all, he has imagination and force. Like Zola he has been criticised for lacking in taste, but he makes up for this by sheer vigour of expression and vividness of presentation. His character Gaudet d'Arras, who prefigures Vautrin in his desire for power over the minds of men, in his having recourse to second sight, and in his excessive friendship for the young Edward, stands out in the reader's memory. Gaudet d'Arras is an ex-priest, a renegade, an apostle of corruption (Vautrin in another incarnation), and a satanic character of epic dimensions, whose natural passions nothing can be allowed to check, presented against a realistic background of stews and brothels, visually close to Hogarth and sometimes to Greuze.[20] Restif has been categorised as a libertine writer on the strength of his eroticism, and as a social novelist for the picture of the world he has conjured up; but in his work different elements co-exist, to the point of defeating the systematic critic. The general term 'memoirs' seems to cover most adequately his varied production.

Les Liaisons dangereuses (1782), by Pierre-Ambroise Choderlos de Laclos (1741–1803), was judged scandalous when it first appeared, but is now acknowledged as a masterpiece. The novel, in letter-form, deals with two unscrupulous seducers, Valmont and Mme de Merteuil, who have had a liaison which Valmont has broken, to Mme de Merteuil's secret chagrin. They keep up a correspondence and a kind of partnership in crime, exchanging their views on the technique of seduction for seduction's sake, and for the gratification of their respective vanity. Mme de Merteuil, who surpasses Valmont in wickedness and *libertinage*, is wholly emancipated and presents hypocrisy as a science. She has been wounded in her vanity and must have her revenge on Valmont, which she obtains with diabolical subtlety, never making a false move until the very end. She is completely ruthless and believes herself to be superior in resolution to all men. Valmont is equally ruthless and enjoys the agonies of passion and remorse of Mme de Tourvel, whom he wishes to conquer for the sole pleasure of rejecting her and thereby satisfying his perverted mind. He is, however,

20 Gaudet d'Arras, who plays a leading part in *Le Paysan perverti* and in the fourth period in the life of Monsieur Nicolas, is such a vivid character that great efforts have been made to identify him with known characters. His name recalls *La Chandelle d'Arras*, a mock-heroic poem by Abbé Dulaurens, and his life that of *Compère Mathieu*, by the same unfrocked priest; but he is more probably a projection of one of Restif's selves, a personal devil whom he could render responsible for his perversion and all his faults and vices.

caught in his own snare and the reader feels that, had it not been for his inordinate vanity, he might have weakened in the end. It is Mme de Merteuil who sets the plot in motion and determines events from the start. She engineers the seduction of a young girl Cécile, the death of Mme de Tourvel, the devout lady whom she makes Valmont seduce, and the death in a duel of Valmont, whom she really 'loves', at the hands of Danceny whom she refuses to release. All her efforts are to no avail, for she herself develops smallpox, thereby becoming disfigured, and loses her lawsuit, thereby achieving her financial ruin. The revelation of her true character, as a result of Valmont's showing her letters to Danceny, leads to her final downfall. So retribution finally overcomes the wicked, even if in the process the good have perished. Even the vindication of their ego leads to a sense of futility. Laclos, who was a happily married soldier,[21] denounced *malfaisance* and *libertinage aristocratique*, and no doubt imagined that he had succeeded in the moral aim he set out in the preface of his book; but if good triumphs therein it is thanks only to a kind of accidental Providence strangely out of keeping with the psychological mechanism he has been at pains to describe. Moreover, the reader, through the novelist's art, is drawn to the masterly wicked characters Laclos has created, and his sympathy becomes involved to the point of wishing for Valmont's success. He is fascinated by the evil pact between Valmont and Mme de Merteuil, and the *éternelle rupture* that follows from their common, parallel destiny. 'Conquérir est notre destin', they write. As villains they are on a par with Gaudet d'Arras and hold us equally spellbound. For Mme de Merteuil and for Valmont, to be free is to impose one's will on others. There is a similarity to the case of the immoral *Neveu de Rameau* whose wickedness, however, is shown against the true picture of a corrupt society, which Diderot had evoked as background to his tale. The unavowed morality of *Les Liaisons dangereuses* is that against the superior experience and cunning of the truly bad, the innocent have no recourse but to flee. Laclos' psychological lucidity, his remorseless working-out of the action in terms of inevitable moves by the antagonists, who are good chess players, master-minded by an exponent who knows all the rules of the game, create an un-

[21] His life from 1759, when he entered the Ecole d'Artillerie of La Fère, is one of slow promotion from second lieutenant in 1762 to *Général d'artillerie* in 1800. In 1790 he was a member of the Club des Jacobins and in 1793 he was incarcerated at the Abbaye, then placed under house arrest, released and rearrested, but finally allowed to return to active service. There is little in Laclos' known life-story that can be linked with his great novel and this has led some writers to wonder whether after all the letters in *Les Liaisons dangereuses* may not be authentic. A close study of the letters, however, shows too great an artistic merit to have been written by more than one presiding hand and mind.

forgettable tale. Man is reduced to a clockwork mechanism, a compound of intellect, emotion and sensuality which can be accurately gauged. It was this theory that fascinated Stendhal, who was presented to Laclos in January 1800, at La Scala in Milan. One key to Laclos' understanding of life is to be found in his treatise *De l'Education des Femmes* (written 1783, published 1903) which analyses woman's subordinate position in society, and brings out as its inevitable consequence the development of her refined cunning in order to overcome her disability and enslavement. For Laclos, natural woman, like natural man, is born free, but in society she can only overcome her handicap by ruthless intelligence and cunning. He shows even in this early work his belief in laws governing the minds of men, and strives to illustrate the rules by presenting characters who are in fact types.

Laclos' analysis of the libertine is thorough. He may be defined as the man who is unshackled by love; he must seduce, but never be seduced. He chooses and hunts his prey, who must be allowed the same calculating chance of escape as the fox in fox-hunting; and the similar climax is the kill. He must invariably take the initiative, and act in full knowledge of the situation, as well as be widely experienced in distinguishing false from true virtue. He must not allow himself to be attracted by a pretty face, but must always choose his victim with deliberation. His life is an arduous one, requiring constant practice if perfection of *libertinage* is to be achieved.[22] With Laclos the epistolary novel has made great strides. The opening letters are masterly in that they introduce the subject of the novel in a natural manner, and we learn all we need to know about Cécile, her future marriage, the designs on her of Mme de Merteuil, and the role of Valmont, the intended seducer. The organic structure of the work becomes apparent, and the plot is tightly knit. None of the letters is gratuitous, and they are all couched in the language appropriate to the writer. Some letters are accidentally crossed: some serve to point the irony of the situation. The same events may be recorded differently by different pens. Often the correspondent reveals facts he alone could have known. We witness the unfolding of a complex play as though through reflecting mirrors, and as the action progresses, so does our understanding of the motives of the antagonists. As M. Seylaz has said of Mme de Tourvel: 'Ainsi la réalité de Mme de Tourvel se compose de ce qu'elle dit à sa correspondante, de la façon dont elle le dit, et aussi de ce qu'elle ne dit pas et que nous apprenons par ailleurs, de ce qu'elle fait et de ce que les autres

[22] The different stages in the career of the *libertin* have been analysed by R. Vailland in *Laclos par lui-même* (1953).

disent d'elle.[23] This might equally well apply to the other characters.

The main lines of the plot may be simple, as are the ideas expressed, but the multiplicity of points of view add a dimension to the work. The letter-form is justified in that the actions and reactions reported bring out the true nature of things, even if we think we are dealing with monomaniacs motivated by vanity and the desire to dominate. The device of the interrupted letter continued shortly after, and the clumsiness of such statements as that by Cécile: 'Mon Dieu, que vous êtes bonne, Madame! comme vous avez bien senti qu'il me serait plus facile de vous écrire que de vous parler.' (Letter 27), which Vivienne Mylne has pointed out,[24] are rare blemishes on a remarkable achievement. The letters follow one another out of logical necessity. They are truly dated and it is impossible to shuffle them – a prodigious advance on earlier techniques. The subtlety of Laclos' letter-writing is even greater when the reader is put in a position to read between the lines even more than was intended by the experienced correspondents who were accustomed to write for the benefit of people intelligent enough to do so. *Les Liaisons dangereuses* may be considered as the last great *roman d'analyse* of the century, as a work presenting a rarefied picture of an important element in society on the eve of the Revolution, and stylistically as the culmination of earlier attempts at technical perfection in the letter-form. It may also be viewed as offering the last stage in the long history of the seducer indulging in inhuman, intellectual libertinism. The variant of the libertine which Laclos has depicted is the female seducer, essentially a woman in revolt against the tyranny of men and therefore at one level an unwitting disciple of Rousseau.

Donatien-Alphonse-François, marquis de Sade (1740–1814), who bequeathed his name to a well-defined form of perversion, interests medical historians and students of psychology as well as students of literature. He was educated at the Lycée Louis-le-Grand, but at the age of fourteen was already in the *chevaux-légers* becoming a sub-lieutenant; he was then a lieutenant in the carabiniers, and later a captain in a cavalry regiment. He married in 1763 the elder daughter of the Président of the *Cour des Aides* in Paris, and launched himself upon a life of debauchery. Mme du Deffand has told how in 1768 he indulged in horrific affairs with two *filles de joie* at a house at Arcueil. His life is one long story of orgies, flagellation, and perversions which ended with the participant in a drunken stupor, and frequently in imprisonment. On one occasion,

[23] *Les Liaisons dangereuses et la création romanesque chez Laclos*, 1958, p. 73.

[24] op. cit., p. 242.

Louis XV intervened on his behalf, so that he was gaoled for only six weeks. At Marseilles in 1772 he was involved in a squalid adventure, as a result of which two persons died, and he was condemned for sodomy and poisoning. His wife helped him escape from the fortress in which he was incarcerated in August 1778. Later she visited him at Vincennes prison, but then decided to retire to a convent and declined to meet him again after the Revolution. In 1784 he was incarcerated in the Bastille by *lettre de cachet*, but released by the Assemblée Constituante, following a general amnesty. He wrote plays and novels in prison, in particular *Justine ou Les Malheurs de la vertu*. He became secretary of the *Société populaire de la section des piques*, and was able to save many people from the guillotine, including his father and mother-in-law. He was arrested by the Comité de Sûreté générale in 1793, and freed in October 1794. He then produced a new enlarged edition of *Justine* with engravings, and a work *Juliette* in six volumes, both of which were judged obscene, but which he nevertheless sent to Bonaparte. He was arrested again in 1801, placed in Sainte-Pélagie, and transferred in 1803 to the asylum of Charenton, being judged incurably mad. He then spent many years in confinement, a fact which may have exacerbated his mental peculiarities. He was a polite, soft-spoken person who uttered his obscenities in a quiet voice. In gaol he set up a theatre where his own plays were enacted in front of an outside public. He pushed his own ethical nihilism to its logical conclusion and turned the practice of crime into a doctrine. As a writer he delighted in the presentation of orgies, the drinking of blood and wine, and in scenes of violence in which children were torn away from their mother and women strangled as a climax to torture. With evident pleasure he depicted smashed skulls, men being skinned alive, heartrending cries and blasphemies, hearts being drawn out of breasts, incest, and shocking crimes. Many of his comedies and short stories were seized by the police and burned, and other works, still in manuscript form, are only now seeing the light of day through the publication by Gallimard of the *Oeuvres complètes*; but much may never be published. We do possess his journal from 1777 to 1790 and the *cahiers* he wrote at Charenton in his old age. Among his works are: *La Philosophe dans le boudoir*; *Aline et Valcourt ou Le Roman philosophique*[25] (written 1785–88, published 1795), a less obscene but equally immoral book in which Sade presents the tragic love story of an engaged couple and gives

[25] From which the episode *Histoire de Sainville et de Léonora* has been extracted and published separately in 1963 in the series *Le monde en 1018*. Léonora, a proud, lascivious woman, has traits which link her with Juliette.

a portrait of himself under the name of Valcourt; *Paulin et Belval ou Les Victimes d'un amour criminel* (1798); and *Les Crimes de l'amour ou Le Délire des passions* (1800). He wrote *Oxtiern ou Les Malheurs du libertinage*, a drama in three acts (1800, performed in 1791 and 1799), and a few comedies: *Le Misanthrope par amour*, in five acts, accepted by the Théâtre Français (1790), but never performed, and *Le Prévaricateur*; and ten or eleven other plays, *drames*, comic operas, and vaudevilles. He left also two historical novels.

Such a vast output renders generalisations difficult. Basically he was a frustrated man whose sensuality was exacerbated by incarceration. His imagination became his refuge and provided him with a possible escape. Always an egoist, anti-social, and early a pervert, he transformed his sexual needs into a system. He developed a philosophy which has made the word 'sadism' commonplace. He upheld the anti-social tendencies in man, which he believed to be fundamental and in accordance with nature, nor would he tolerate any form of self-restraint. Hence his defence of crime and of torture which could provide pleasure. For him, nature, an amoral, impersonal force which made life dependent on destruction for the creation of further life, was responsible for this state of affairs, so that murder and perversions, all part of nature, have to be accepted. Man, wholly conditioned by his environment, is therefore morally irresponsible. There can be no true freedom, only the satisfaction of desire to the greatest extent possible in society, where the destructive forces at work must ultimately triumph. Hence Sade's fundamentally anti-Christian attitude, and his contempt for any virtue involving self-denial. Charity for him is nothing more than a form of self-indulgence and an insult to others. The corruption of man, which he accepts, leads him to nihilism in all ethical matters. The relationship between the sexes is that of torturer and tortured. The need to inflict pain is necessarily present as a means of establishing a gulf between the two parties. The traditional libertine is wasting his time in his senseless sophistication. *Justine* (1791) is a typical work. It shows us a virtuous girl becoming the victim of evil people, and depicts orgies of perversion in a monastery. Often Sade's literary work turns into a treatise of sexual pathology. But his ideas are mostly expressed in his novels, and too frequently reiterated. His narrative is commonly disjointed, his characterisation poor, but his style has vigour, and he can build up a sense of mounting horror and violence in surprisingly pure prose. In life and in fiction his influence has proved to be enormous and has been exercised not only on those who have read his books, but on countless people who know him only by hearsay or repute, largely false.

This survey of the eighteenth-century novel can fittingly be brought to a close with Gabriel Sénac de Meilhan (1734–1803), since his work is the best of that written during the Revolution, and his novel *L'Emigré* combines the technique of the writer of memoirs with that of the emergent novelist. Meilhan was an intelligent, ambitious, and attractive libertine. The son of a doctor of Louis XV, he came into close touch with Mme de Pompadour, the duchesse de Grammont, sister of the duc de Choiseul, and the marquise de Créqui, with whom he exchanged long and intimate letters. He once addressed a poem to Voltaire which the latter acknowledged by calling him the 'favori d'Apollon'. Known to the comte d'Argenson, Maupeou, Bernis, and Duclos, he gained promotion in the service of the administration, becoming *Conseiller au Grand Conseil*, the Court of Appeal under the *ancien régime*, and *Intendant-général de la guerre et des armées du Roi* in 1775. Even when out of favour, he remained faithful to the *émigré* cause.

He wrote his novel *L'Emigré* (1794, pub. 1797) in exile at Brunswick, and A. Thibaudet has rated it the only important novel between *Paul et Virginie* (1788) and *Valérie* (1802) by Mme de Krüdener. This cosmopolitan work, in four volumes, provides an excellent picture of the life and ideas of the *émigrés*, and in some ways it is to be preferred to that of Mme de Staël's *Corinne*. It tells the love story of a young German woman married to a young *émigré* who is wounded, and effectively combines the technique of the novel in letter-form with that of history as written at that time. Characteristic of the author's standpoint are the two following quotations cited by Etiemble: 'Celui qui n'est pas heureux avec de la santé et de l'argent est un fou,' and 'Le plus grand des biens est la volupté des sens; l'art le plus nécessaire au bonheur est de savoir jouir, et de savoir s'abstenir pour jouir mieux et plus longtemps.' Meilhan expressed some very shrewd views on contemporary events, and on the Revolution itself. In politics, he was a counter-revolutionary, full of admiration for Montesquieu and Voltaire. The letters which comprise *L'Emigré* are given as having been written in 1793, and in his preface Meilhan writes: 'L'ouvrage qu'on présente au public est-il un roman, est-il une histoire? Cette question est facile à résoudre. On ne peut appeler roman un ouvrage qui renferme des récits exacts de faits avérés.' He was the first to realise that history at certain times reads like a novel. 'Tout est vraisemblable et tout est romanesque dans la révolution de la France' he wrote, with much truth. His life took him to London, to Aix-la-Chapelle, to St Petersburg, and to Moscow. Catherine the Great gave him a pension of 6,000 roubles and invited him to write a history of Russia and the story of her reign, but she liked neither him nor his humour. In 1794 he settled in Brunswick, where he wrote *L'Emigré*. In 1795 we find him in Vienna, where he became the close friend of the prince de Ligne and where he spent the last months of his life. In common with the prince de Ligne he had both wit and style, but little depth, and his numerous works are only of secondary interest. They include: *Mémoires d'Anne de Gonzagues, princesse palatine* (1786); *Considérations sur le luxe et les richesses* (1787), in which he disagrees with the views expressed by Necker; *Considérations sur l'esprit et les mœurs* (1787), which give a vivid picture of the corruption in the milieu in which he moved (a fuller version appeared in *Œuvres philosophiques et littéraires*, 1795); *Mélanges de philosophie et d'histoire* (1789); *Des Principes et des causes de la Révolution* (1790); *Les Deux Cousines* (1790), a *conte philosophique*; *Lettre à Mme de **** (1792), an interesting account of his first meeting with Catherine II; *Du Gouvernement, des mœurs et des conditions en France avant la Révolution* (1797); *Portraits et caractères des personnages distingués de la fin du XVIIIe siècle* (1813). These last two works are of considerable interest, bitter in tone, but containing finely drawn portraits which show great penetration. Both, like *L'Emigré*, combine the technique of the novelist with that of the historian.

The French novelists of the eighteenth century are seen at their best when translating into an artistic form the sense of a destiny being accomplished, and in relating fictional devices to a meaningful expression of human experience. Later, new methods were found to be appropriate to a somewhat different conception of the novel, but there had first to be a period of consolidation and experimentation. The myth of the memoir served to disarm censorship and to extend verisimilitude through a mixture of publicly known historical facts and private unknowable details.

It should not be inferred that by situating these eighteenth-century novels in the evolution of the genre, we need necessarily subscribe to the view that the later works are finer. In their own way, the great novels of the French eighteenth century have each their own perfection, and can scarcely be excelled for depth of human psychology and brilliance of style. Nor is it surprising that after the unparalleled success in the nineteenth century of masterpieces technically written from the standpoint of the omniscient writer and reader, we should witness the disintegration of the novel and the challenging of most of the assumptions on which it rested.

The newly found freedom of the twentieth century has led to a recrudescence of interest in French eighteenth-century works, written according to patterns with which we are no longer familiar, but which still hold interesting possibilities. The autobiographical form at least, so often practised, is unlikely ever to suffer more than temporary eclipse. From the autobiographical pseudo-memoirs of Mme de Villedieu's *Mémoires de la vie de Henriette-Sylvie de Molière* (1672), through Courlitz de Sandras' mixture of *histoire anecdotique*, *histoire secrète*, and *histoire tout court*, and Mme de Tencin's dwelling on suffering and love in the *Comte de Comminge*, through Marianne and Manon to Suzanne Simonin, the road is long. And even if a *biographie romancée* such as Restif's *La Vie de mon père* cannot compare for depth with Rousseau's *Confessions*, nevertheless it has the ring of authenticity. If one had to single out the outstanding novels of the age the following would need to be included: *La Nouvelle Héloïse* and the *Confessions*; *Les Lettres persanes*; *Candide* and other tales; *Le Neveu de Rameau*, *Jacques le fataliste* and *La Religieuse*; *Gil Blas*, *La Vie de Marianne*, and *Le Paysan parvenu*; Manon *Lescaut* and *Les Liaisons dangereuses*. Immediately after would come *Paul et Virginie*, *Les Egarements du cœur et de l'esprit*, *Monsieur Nicolas*, and *Justine*. Between them, they cover an enormous range of human experience and examine man as a sensual, feeling, and thinking being. Perhaps the only serious gap in the over-all picture is the failure to convey the reality of religious experience, with the possible exception of Rousseau.

Some 3,000 works of fiction were written in France during the century. Even the lesser known had some success, and were often translated into other tongues. The novelists' main effort was directed towards greater realism. They perfected the ability to describe accurately and well; they illustrated a changing social order and voiced a great diversity of ideas and feelings. They learnt early how to use dialogue effectively, and how to interest readers in the characters they sought to portray. They had a great sense of drama, and took trouble to build up their efforts, to develop their plots, and to explore in depth some of the recesses of the human mind and heart. They drew upon the resources of language for the expression of their ideas. At times they underestimated the critical acumen of the reader or his faculty of suspending disbelief; at other times they overestimated his intelligence and sensitivity; but all in all they were fortunate in having an enlightened, cosmopolitan public. The very diversity of the works reviewed, coupled with the briefest outline of the circumstances of the lives of the novelists concerned, prompts one to draw somewhat different conclusions from those usually held by critics who take into consideration only the significant landmarks of literature, which are also the more aesthetically satisfying. Not only are the usual classifications shown as inadequate, but facile generalisations cannot stand the light of scrutiny. We can see that sentiment and sensibility are features of the novel before Rousseau, and we can note the influence of very different authors on one and the same work. The character of the libertine existed in France before Lovelace. It is to be found in sentimental novels, as well as merged with other influences in the so-called libertine novels, highly popular in their day. The latter have been seen as a product of an aristocratic, salon society; and superficially this would appear to be true. But even after the Revolution they are still to be found, albeit in a new guise. Moreover, the salon society itself is but one manifestation of a way of life dependent on many factors, and became increasingly bourgeois as the century progressed. One can argue that the civilised, pastoral, or noble novels of the seventeenth century gave rise to the libertine novel; but one can also argue that the tradition of the bourgeois or vulgar novel, which reinforced the current of realism, also had its part to play in the evolution of this genre. The picaresque way of life, as seen in *Gil Blas* and in real life, is in the background of many a novelist's mind and continues until Figaro appears upon the stage. *Les Liaisons dangereuses* presented in Valmont an aristocratic mould which Laclos detested, but today he seems closer to the tradition of realism than to that of *L'Astrée* and its derivatives. The kind of love portrayed in these novels, base coin in the vindication of self and not an ennobling experience, is not in the heroic tradition. But the novels have a meaning and a literary value quite apart from the question of fitting them into an evolution or classifying them by subject matter, or by the nature of the devices they illustrate.

The most recent French critic, H. Coulet, combines an approach on the lines of that of Etiemble and of V. Mylne, with their emphasis on memoirs, pseudo-memoirs, and novels in letter-form, with a complex scheme of subheadings indicating sub-genres in defined phases of the social and political life of the period. But he can only avoid the arbitrariness of his new scheme of classification by frequent qualifications of most of his general statements under the headings he has himself adopted.

But whatever the system adopted and whatever the gaps it leaves, the point never to be forgotten is that the novel as a whole presented in its fullness the true picture of eighteenth-century man.

Chapter 14

THE AGE OF THE ENLIGHTENMENT

THE *Encyclopédie*, which underwent many vicissitudes from the time of its conception in 1746 to the appearance of the last volume some twenty-five years later, should be considered not only as an intellectual venture, but as a commercial enterprise involving the investment of very substantial capital and a great technical effort. In spite of what J. Proust has said in *Diderot et l'Encyclopédie*, it is fairly clear that the editors, d'Alembert and Diderot, were in fact responsible for the change in scope of the publication, from the five volumes with 120 plates foreseen in 1746 to the ten volumes, two of which were to consist of 600 plates, as advertised in the 1750 *Prospectus*; and the seventeen volumes, plus eleven volumes of plates, finally brought out. J. Proust has stressed the scope of the undertaking, with its 150 contributors and 4,000 subscribers, and the attribution of many articles is still in dispute. He is right in drawing our attention to the fact that the sheer business of finding contributors and subscribers, controlling the paper supply, the printing, the proof correcting, the binding and engraving of the volumes over a period of twenty-five years necessarily turned the publication from a relatively modest publishing venture into one of the most ambitious capitalist projects in the second half of the century. According to Voltaire,[1] whose figures have been found remarkably accurate, there was a turnover of 7,650,000 livres, which eclipses that for the entire trade between the East and the West Indies and France. We are in fact confronted by a major concern, with an expenditure of some 1,158,958 livres and an estimated profit for the publishers of 2,400,000 livres. The capital invested in the printing of the *Encyclopédie* provided a thousand artisans, paper-makers, printers, binders, and engravers with an income for twenty-five years. Many of the contributors, some of whom were also subscribers, received no payment for their articles. It was the support of public opinion and of certain vested interests, in what became a national enterprise, that rendered publication possible and profitable. This fact must

[1] Cf. *Questions sur l'Encyclopédie*, in *Oeuvres*, ed. Moland, vol. XVII, p. 4; see also J. Proust, *Diderot et l'Encyclopédie*, p.47.

never be lost sight of in any close examination of the story of the publication of the *Encyclopédie*. For just as government and official opposition were divided, so there was division in the ranks of the Encyclopaedists. The interests of the rich capitalist publishers and their friends were not always identical with those of the editors; it is known that Le Breton deleted passages presumed too dangerous after the proofs had been corrected by Diderot. The threat to continue publication abroad disturbed officials in high quarters: and the necessary compromises and inevitable complications served to promote the liberalism enshrined in the *Encyclopédie*, which was also fostered in such supplements as the *Encyclopédie méthodique*, the *Journal encyclopédique*, and the *Correspondance littéraire de Grimm*. For twenty-five critical years Le Breton's business house was the focal point of all information, of all literary, cultural, scientific, technological, and political curiosity. The editors were in touch with writers, scientists, industrialists, technologists, artisans and artists, and men of action; a bourgeois élite as much attached to social order as to reform, preparing unwittingly the Revolution to come, deeply involved in the industrial, rather than in the political, transformation. It is this aspect of the history of the period that needs now to be examined; and individual studies of collaborators and others involved should follow J. Proust's more general survey. But we may already surmise what the editing of the *Encyclopédie* did for Diderot, the man and the thinker. It provided him with a first-class education in breadth and in depth, with connections of an exceptionally interesting kind; and left him with a determining political and intellectual role as the leader of the most enlightened part of the nation. He was also in the best position conceivable for effecting as a *philosophe* the vast synthesis of all knowledge, which d'Alembert, in his *Discours préliminaire*, was also eager to promulgate for the greater benefit of mankind.

Following on the often biased studies of Soboul, Jean Luc, Momjian, Volguine, and others concerned with the social background of the *Encyclopédie*, J. Proust points to the fundamental antagonism between the Encyclopaedists and the government, which is very often obscured by the turn of events, or persons involved in somewhat ambiguous attitudes. The contributors, who were often privileged and endowed with private means, belonged for the most part to the upper and middle bourgeoisie and the professional classes. They had all one thing in common: they were the intellectuals, part of an enlightened élite, well informed and bent on reform, liberal in outlook and involved in the elaboration of a new economic and social order. An enormous industrial and technological revolution was afoot, and the need to increase national productivity was seldom far from the minds of the chief contributors. Historically, this loosely formed group or party – which Voltaire appropriately termed 'la séquelle encyclopédique' – triumphed after the *9 thermidor* (1794), during the last period of the Convention and under the Directory, when the bourgeoisie turned away from the lower classes and assumed power on its own account. Most of the publishing houses were by then directed by former Encyclopaedists. The Ecoles Centrales, the Ecole Normale Supérieure, the Ecole Polytechnique, and the *Institut* were established, and the universities, as indeed all other grades of education, were reorganised on modern lines. Under the Convention, the Girondins were for the most part disciples of the Encyclopaedists; and Diderot's works were once again brought to public notice through the Naigeon edition of them which appeared in 1798. A few former Encyclopaedists achieved positions of distinction, others positions of importance to the state or in the corridors of power, but none of real political consequence. They remained, however, well placed for moulding opinion and upholding the Encyclopaedist ideals. Daubenton, for example, the distinguished writer of articles on natural science, was appointed to a chair at the Ecole Normale Supérieure; Deleyre was put in charge of the *écoles normales*; Desmarets was appointed to teach natural history at the Ecole Normale de la Seine. Because of their exceptional competence, all made their mark as teachers and administrators, and a careful study of the careers of those whom they taught might yield surprising results. One contributor is known to have been guillotined, and a number fled the country with the aristocrats.

Many misconceptions, due to prejudice, about the diverse attitudes taken up during and after the French Revolution, and to sheer ignorance, still need to be swept away. It is, for instance, no longer possible to make Diderot responsible, as contemporaries believed, for Babeuf and the abortive *babouviste* plot. For Babeuf was inspired in his communist leanings by Morelly's *Code de la nature*, wrongly attributed to Diderot, and included in the first volume of Diderot's *Œuvres philosophiques*, published at Amsterdam in 1773. Indeed, it was partly to rectify this and similar errors that in 1789 Naigeon undertook his monumental edition of Diderot's works. Men like Fontanes and La Harpe feared that the Encyclopaedist policies would subvert the social order: and even in our time, Barrès and Maurras opposed the celebration of the bicentenary of Diderot's birth because of his alleged influence on the development of anarchist tendencies. The interpretation of history that is slowly unfolding pays particular attention to social and economic factors underlying political action. J. Proust has been in a position to show that the Encyclopaedists were largely middle-class landowners of some substance, many of whom, like Buffon, d'Holbach, Quesnay, Rollier des Ormes, the noted parliamentarian, Voltaire, and Diderot himself, enjoyed bourgeois comfort, and at times considerable wealth, from the exploitation of their properties, or through skilful modern investment in business and industrial or agricultural production. The purpose, policy, and significance of Danton, who was more directly influenced by Diderot than he knew, through the passages in Raynal that are in fact by Diderot, are more readily understood in this context. Even though Diderot chose his collaborators solely for their capacity, actual or potential, and their ability to play an active part in reviewing the economy of the nation, its ideology, and its very structure, he was what we now term class-conscious in his private life, and drawn to the hierarchy of wealth. It is significant that he married his daughter, whom he loved, to a man of substance from his own home town. There is a great difference between Voltaire with 200,000 livres income and the poorer Diderot, whom Rousseau, however, berates for having 'bons bas drapés, bons souliers, bonne camisole'. But, nevertheless, stress on intellectual activity as the main social activity of the Encyclopaedists was necessary, if an editor like Diderot was to cut across the old social conventions and class distinctions, and this led him, at times, to cut across the new ones based on money which were fast developing. Today, and since J. Proust's work, we are more concerned with a re-examination of the historical background to politics and thought than with a philosophical reappraisal, and any fresh information on matters of detail may well lead us to modify earlier generalisations.

The main contribution of French eighteenth-century thought to the history of ideas remains of course unchallenged. The *philosophes*' basic opposition to the fundamental conceptions underlying the dominant current of thought of the previous age, and indeed of earlier times, needs no emphasis; and their main theories, constantly reiterated – acceptance of nature, as opposed to asceticism; of reason, as opposed to a naïve faith in the supernatural; of tolerance, as opposed to religious persecution; and the vindication of the rights of man and the need to establish a better world on earth – herald the beginning of modern times. The Age of the Enlightenment has been contrasted with that of the Crusades. If one accepts this basic contention, one may trace the development of eighteenth-century rationalism from the Renaissance, which rehabilitated nature, dwelling on the part played by Rabelais, Erasmus, and humanism, and stressing that of Montaigne who incarnated for many the new man, essentially un-Christian, a man of nature without the grace of God. Montaigne, although a believer, taught his disciples how to doubt, and perfected a technique, later adopted by Voltaire and others, of killing by ridicule, or leading the intelligent reader to deduce rationally the true implications of a statement. Thus when Montaigne writes: 'C'est un grand ouvrier de miracles que l'esprit humain', taking care not to say 'que l'esprit païen', he implicitly undermines belief in Christian miracles themselves. And one may trace the development of the 'encyclopaedic spirit' through Descartes, Fontenelle, and Bayle to articles in the *Encyclopédie*. What, however, is holding the attention of present-day critics is the modifications in this over-all picture that need to be made in the light of what we now know about the minds of individual writers, and the continued effect of their upbringing on their mode of thought. We find in the case of many eighteenth-century advanced thinkers that what was true of Bayle is true of them: their knowledge of metaphysics and their familiarity with metaphysical concepts remain great, and survive in the recesses of their mind even when they have discarded what they came to look upon as religious prejudice. A close study of the texts shows that they could not opt out of the prevailing climate of opinion of their day, nor eschew discussion with their adversaries, sometimes more present in their own minds than in the flesh. The religious issue, whether dealt with from the Protestant, the Catholic, the deist, or the atheist standpoint, remained one of the most lively, as evidenced by the continued circulation of anonymous tracts by *colporteurs*, and by the considerable output of 'refutations' of works of alleged freethinkers, such as the anonymously published *Pensées philosophiques* by Diderot.

In spite of research, and important publications, mostly centred around the more significant figures, the polemical history of religious thought is still imperfectly known, but we can trace the survival of early preoccupations and interests in the mature thinking of writers such as Diderot. The detailed picture involves much shading of the over-all picture, and the nuances now emphasised must in the end change our attitude. There is no doubt that when Henry Vyverberg in *Historical Pessimism in the French Enlightenment* attacks the notion that the *philosophes* were optimists imbued with a simple faith in progress, he overstates his case; but he is right in challenging our preconceptions, and in providing a needed corrective.

Uncertainty and conflicting viewpoints also face the present-day critic when determining precisely the politics of the Encyclopaedists, and their true role in foreshadowing the French Revolution, nineteenth-century liberalism, and certain of the political assumptions, perhaps even myths, of our own age. It is agreed that for a long time the *philosophes* pinned their hopes of reform on an ideal legislator, who would ensure happiness and virtue, then on an enlightened despot, and only reluctantly, at a late stage and out of despair, turned away from the monarchy to espouse republican ideals, that were often inspired by Rousseau, whom few really understood at the time. For the most part, they were more concerned with practical reforms, affecting commerce and industry, and civil reforms, by which man would be allowed to do all that the laws were prepared to sanction. They did not ask for political freedom, as is clear from the perusal of the article 'Liberté' in the *Encyclopédie*. They did not wish to see all forms of censorship abolished, but rather the appointment of censors favourable to their cause. They unfailingly attacked inequalities in the social system, and the idea of a social contract as the basis of society gained ground, with its implication that if the ruler breaks the tacit agreement between himself and his subjects, he may be removed. Rousseau's insistence on the need for popular consent provided a rational basis for a Revolution that sprang from a multiplicity of causes, many of which were irrational. In the main, the peculiar contribution of eighteenth-century political thought can be summed up as follows: the conception of a state of nature which antedates organisation into society. The *philosophes*, especially Rousseau, presented an idyllic picture of primitive man, born innocent, that is to say neither good nor bad, which was not acceptable to all – witness Montesquieu's presentation of such a man in his *Histoire des Troglodytes* – and Voltaire, in spite of the naïve Candide or the occasional *bon Huron*, sees men essentially as 'des insectes se dévorant les uns les autres sur un petit tas de boue' (*Zadig*). But clearly the idea of natural man had the advantage of placing the responsibility for man's misery and crime on society itself, thereby justifying change. Man is readily convinced of the truth of ideas that help him in his despair, even when they do not stand up to objective analysis. From the polemical point of view, the doctrine of the original goodness of man had the advantage of directly challenging a cardinal tenet of the Roman Catholic Church, original sin. Of course, in their analyses of natural man and social evolution, and in their attitude to natural law (to which Rousseau is hostile and which Diderot favours), the *philosophes* held divergent views. This is one reason why Cobban's stimulating *In Search of Humanity* (1960) strikes many critics as old-fashioned and an over-simplification. It is in detailed studies of the writings of Voltaire, Rousseau, Montesquieu, and Diderot that the political issues have been or will be most satisfactorily clarified. The bringing to light of new data on Diderot's political opinions is a case in point. J. Proust has shown that the political theory evolved by

Diderot during the years 1750–65 was daring, but that he remained timid and eclectic on the subject of political reform. He was opposed to the revolutionary theories of Rousseau, which he nevertheless always kept in mind. He advocated in the *Encyclopédie* an enlightened monarchy, which later he opposed. His theory, untrammelled by concern with its practical application, sprang logically from his materialistic monism, his determinism, and his rationalism. His system of a monarchy, politically absolutist yet liberal in thought and economy, as expounded in the *Encyclopédie*, was well suited to an élite of landowners seeking order and security, and to the Encyclopaedist group as a whole. Historically, in spite of their obvious moderation, it is Diderot and his fellow materialists who attacked both the existing monarchy and the Church, whilst Voltaire and the deists wished to preserve the monarchy, and Rousseau wished to preserve religion. Diderot's role in the preparation of the Revolution is, therefore, the more comprehensive. Newer interpretations, based on greater knowledge of late writings, show that he was not a firm partisan of enlightened despotism, nor the dupe of Frederick II, nor the obsequious flatterer of Catherine the Great, to whom he wrote: 'Il n'y a de vrai souverain que la nation,' in a work which enshrined his claim that a monarch owed allegiance to the constitution, and which Catherine II burnt in anger in 1784. He was not truly a Physiocrat. His political ideas were taken over by the *idéologues* and the contributors to *La Décade*. In his *Mémoires*, addressed to Catherine, he outlined in eighteen points the reforms he thought that France required; and in the 1780 edition of Raynal's *Histoire des deux Indes*, under the title *Apostrophe à Louis XVI*, appears a passage which Raynal borrowed from Diderot, and which was published in the form of a tract in 1789. It is one of the first manifestos of the *Tiers Etat*.

Ernst Cassirer begins his study of the *Philosophy of the Enlightenment* by quoting d'Alembert, who stated in his *Essai sur les éléments de philosophie*:

> Pour peu qu'on considère avec des yeux attentifs le milieu du siècle où nous vivons, les événements qui nous occupent, ou du moins qui nous agitent, nos mœurs, nos ouvrages, et jusqu'à nos entretiens, on aperçoit sans peine qu'il s'est fait à plusieurs égards un changement bien remarquable dans nos idées; changement qui par sa rapidité semble nous en promettre un plus grand encore. C'est au temps à fixer l'objet, la nature et les limites de cette révolution, dont notre postérité connaîtra mieux que nous les inconvénients et les avantages.
>
> Tout siècle qui pense bien ou mal, pourvu qu'il croie penser, et qu'il pense autrement que le siècle qui l'a précédé, se pare du titre de *philosophe*; comme on a souvent honoré de *sages* ceux qui n'ont eu d'autre mérite que de contredire leurs contemporains. Notre siècle s'est donc appelé par excellence *le siècle de la philosophie*; plusieurs écrivains lui en ont donné le

nom, persuadés qu'il en rejaillirait quelqu'éclat sur eux; d'autres lui ont refusé cette gloire dans l'impuissance de la partager.

Si on examine sans prévention l'état actuel de nos connaissances, on ne peut disconvenir des progrès de la philosophie parmi nous. La science de la nature acquiert de jour en jour de nouvelles richesses; la géométrie, en reculant ses limites, a porté son flambeau dans les parties de la physique qui se trouvaient le plus près d'elle; le vrai système du monde a été connu, développé et perfectionné; la même sagacité qui s'était assujetti les mouvements des corps célestes, s'est portée sur les corps qui nous environnent; en appliquant la géométrie à l'étude de ces corps, ou en essayant de l'y appliquer, on a su apercevoir et fixer les avantages et les abus de cet emploi; en un mot depuis la terre jusqu'à Saturne, depuis l'histoire des cieux jusqu'à celle des insectes, la physique a changé de face. Avec elle presque toutes les autres sciences ont pris une nouvelle forme, et elles le devaient en effet. Quelques réflexions vont nous en convaincre.

L'étude de la nature semble être par elle-même froide et tranquille, parce que la satisfaction qu'elle procure est un sentiment uniforme, continu et sans secousses et que les plaisirs, pour être vifs, doivent être séparés par des intervalles et marqués par des accès. Néanmoins l'invention et l'usage d'une nouvelle méthode de philosopher, l'espèce d'enthousiasme qui accompagne les découvertes, une certaine élévation d'idées que produit en nous le spectacle de l'univers; toutes ces causes ont dû exciter dans les esprits une fermentation vive; cette fermentation agissant en tout sens par sa nature, s'est portée avec une espèce de violence sur tout ce qui s'est offert à elle, comme un fleuve qui a brisé ses digues. Or les hommes ne reviennent guère sur un objet qu'ils avaient négligé depuis longtemps, que pour réformer bien ou mal les idées qu'ils s'en étaient faites. Plus ils sont lents à secouer le joug de l'opinion, plus aussi, dès qu'ils l'ont brisé sur quelques points, ils sont portés à la briser sur tout le reste; car ils fuyent encore plus l'embarras d'examiner, qu'ils ne craignent de changer d'avis; et dès qu'ils ont pris une fois la peine de revenir sur leurs pas, ils regardent et reçoivent un nouveau système d'idées comme une sorte de récompense de leur courage et de leur travail. Ainsi, depuis les principes des sciences profanes jusqu'aux fondements de la révélation, depuis la métaphysique jusqu'aux matières de goût, depuis la musique jusqu'à la morale, depuis les disputes scolastiques des théologiens, jusqu'aux objets de commerce, depuis les droits des princes jusqu'à ceux des peuples, depuis la loi naturelle jusqu'aux lois arbitraires des nations, en un mot depuis les questions qui nous touchent davantage jusqu'à celles qui nous intéressent le plus faiblement, tout a été discuté, analysé, agité du moins. Une nouvelle lumière sur quelques objets, une nouvelle obscurité sur plusieurs, a été le fruit ou la suite de cette effervescence générale des esprits, comme l'effet du flux et reflux de l'océan est d'apporter sur le rivage quelques matières, et d'en éloigner les autres.[2]

It would be difficult to find a more apposite expression of contemporary intellectual life. Thirst for knowledge and intellectual curiosity were directed towards the external world. Awareness of the history, languages, and religions of people from foreign countries, and the new developments in science, especially in physics, mathematics, the natural sciences, and medicine, were changing the climate of opinion throughout Europe. Attention was drawn to the ethics, politics, and economics of social man; but it centred upon

[2] Ed. R. N. Schwab, 1965, pp. 8–12.

individual man, his nature, his happiness, his relationship to the cosmos, and the processes of his mind and their validity. The obvious parallel that can be established with the preoccupations of our own age has focused interest once more on the intellectual contribution of the Enlightenment, and on the personality and thought of its leading figures. Many of the most significant critical studies on the eighteenth century seek to provide, more or less consciously, a clarification of certain burning issues, if not a key to the solution of some of our most pressing intellectual problems today. Herein lies their strength, for their preoccupations lend reality and a sense of urgency to their arguments, and also their weakness, for the authors can speak, as did their predecessors, only for their own generation, and commonly only the fraction of their own generation they happen to belong to.

Although many of the earlier critics of the Enlightenment have pertinent things to say on a wide variety of questions, few in fact have a substantial contribution to make for the serious student of today. L. G. Crocker in a recent study[3] makes the point that before 1945 hardly any attempt was made to understand the Enlightenment as a whole, or to interpret its character and significance. He readily concedes that books and articles of value were written on individual writers, and that specific questions were explored to good purpose – luxury (by A. Morize), primitivism and exoticism (by G. Chinard and others), the extraordinary journey (by G. Atkinson). But even studies on individual writers were expressions of personal opinion, condemnations, or apologies. Irving Babbitt's *Rousseau and Romanticism* and L. I. Bredvold's *The Brave New World of the Enlightenment* are cited in evidence.

In his rapid survey of critical works published before the Second World War, L. G. Crocker praises wholeheartedly only R. Hubert's *Les Sciences sociales dans l'Encyclopédie* (1923), which remains a solid and impressive panorama of the various general problems that concerned the Encyclopaedists. Kingsley Martin's *French Liberal Thought in the Eighteenth Century* (1929) is extolled for its analyses, but criticised for the limitations of its perspective and for errors in interpretation of Rousseau and Helvétius. Carl Becker's *The Heavenly City of the Eighteenth-Century Philosophers* (1932) is described as a 'magnificent failure' since his thesis, which oversimplifies the facts, rests on an historical analogy between the Enlightenment and thirteenth-century Christianity. R. R. Palmer's *Catholics and Unbelievers in Eighteenth-Century France* (1939), whilst providing us with a much-needed study of Jesuit and Jansenist thought, is tinged with prejudice and coloured

[3] 'Recent Interpretations of the French Enlightenment', *Journal of World History*, vol. VIII, No. 3, 1964, pp. 426–56.

by facile generalisations; and above all ignores the current of illuminists, theosophists, and mystics who opposed rationalism and paved the way for the Romantic reaction against the Enlightenment. Even Daniel Mornet's monumental work on *Les Origines intellectuelles de la Révolution française* (1933) is now generally considered as little more than a reference work, a mine of information, with a negative thesis barren of ideas, failing to provide an evaluation of the problems and attempted solutions or of the various currents of thought indicated, and unable to show how the 'esprit de réforme' became between 1787 (Mornet's terminal point) and 1789 an 'esprit révolutionnaire'.[4] In practice only two pre-war publications stand out clearly as of intellectual significance: Ernst Cassirer, *Die Philosophie der Aufklärung* (1932), which was published in an English translation in 1951 under the title *The Philosophy of the Enlightenment* and was thereby given a new lease of life in all Anglo-Saxon countries; and Paul Hazard, *La Crise de la conscience européenne* (1935), completed in 1946 by *La Pensée européenne au XVIIIe siècle.*

Cassirer approached the Enlightenment as a philosopher and offered his readers a new and still valid perspective. Errors in detail may be forgiven, since they can be corrected, and serious omissions such as ethics and social thought may be rectified by new studies; but his main fault lies in a failure to take into account the true complexity of the Enlightenment because of his over-systematic approach, which involves a linear development of ideas leading up to Kant and Goethe. He was certainly not equipped to deal with the protean quality of Diderot's thought.[5] Yet this work will continue to be studied for its informed philosophical approach, its clarity, the brilliance of the exposition, and for having singled out the truly important issues in our eyes.

P. Hazard's finely written work has the merit of presenting a fuller panorama of eighteenth-century thought, embracing in his survey the lesser as well as the better-known figures, and stressing very properly the role of Christian forces, which had been generally overlooked. It has been criticised for being descriptive rather than analytical, for neglecting socio-economic factors, i.e. the rise of the middle classes, and for failing to do justice to scientific development. Moreover, although Hazard deals intelligently with the intellectual crisis, which he placed between 1680 and 1715, he does not provide any data on the diffusion or the import of the new ideas. In his later work, whilst rightly stressing the search for happiness as the mainspring of eighteenth-century thought, he is

[4] See A. Meynial, rev. *Révolution Française*, 87, 1934, pp. 5–17.
[5] See H. Dieckmann's review article, 'An interpretation of the eighteenth century', *Modern Language Quarterly*, 15, 1954, pp. 295–311.

too apt to oversimplify his vast canvas by spotlighting its most obvious stages. It is precisely this theme of happiness which gave R. Mauzi the title of his voluminous thesis, *L'Idée du bonheur au XVIIIe siècle* (1960). Mauzi's method of singling out one central theme around which to organise his material is fairly new in eighteenth-century studies, and foreshadows a number of works on similar lines.[6] L. G. Crocker has pointed out that, invaluable as Mauzi's book is as a work of erudition, it fails somewhat as a general study because the conceptual unity provided leads to serious omissions. Since eighteenth-century thought and feeling involved more than happiness, Mauzi's perspective cannot be quite sound. His survey ignores the political antagonism of the age between three conflicting moral positions, religious, humanistic, and anarchic. On the other hand, Mauzi has brought out clearly one of the main *idées-forces* of the age, the search for absolutes, and the hidden malaise and anguish. Preoccupation with ethics is also the main subject of L. G. Crocker, *An Age of Crisis* (1959) and *Nature and Culture: ethical thought in the French Enlightenment* (1963). In these vast works he shows how the concepts of morality that then obtained develop and culminate in moral nihilism. His study is based on the examination of a large number of secondary, as well as leading, *philosophes*, Christians and *anti-philosophes*, in France, England, and other countries. *An Age of Crisis* deals with the metaphysical problem and the psychological conditions of ethical theory, bringing out the eighteenth-century conception of character and human motivation. It shows how the 'natural law of human behaviour', seen as the counterpart of the physical law of gravitation, evolved and led ultimately to a moral nihilism which the *philosophes* dreaded. They pinned their hopes on meliorism, i.e. the possibility that men could be made to obey moral laws despite contrary instincts, 'indeed, we may even say, because of them'. L. G. Crocker concludes *An Age of Crisis* by surveying the nature of the impasse in which the analysis of human nature left ethics and the problem of values, and its significance for the present day. *Nature and Culture* deals with ethical theory itself. After discussing natural law and the nature of moral experience, the author devotes a long section to the 'utilitarian synthesis' which leads ultimately to nihilism. The main theme in the exploration of human nature, social life, and moral values is seen as the tension or polarity between nature and culture. This study brings out well the complexity and unity of the period, the nature of the ever-present dialogue in the minds of the writers as well as between the thinkers themselves. Crocker sees the organic development of ideas not as

[6] In this category may be placed: Jean Ehrard, *L'Idée de nature en France dans la première moitié du XVIIIe siècle*, 2 vols., 1963.

linear but as concentric waves. He is quick to seize on factors that foreshadow nineteenth- and twentieth-century developments from liberalism to totalitarianism. This may well be why he labours the role of authors such as Sade, which enables him to focus attention on the ultimate stage of nihilism, rather than the in-between stage reached by some of the most inherently interesting thinkers he discusses.

Mauzi in *L'Idée du bonheur* also touches on all the ethical theories of the age, showing the wide variety of sources from which they severally derive, noting the *philosophes*' effort rationally to deduce their ideas on happiness from a systematic knowledge of man, and their awareness of the implications of *libertinage* and eroticism. Like H. Vyverberg who, in *Historical Pessimism in the French Enlightenment*, attacked the notion that the *philosophes* were imbued with a simple faith in progress, Mauzi sees in pessimism the main characteristic of this happiness-obsessed culture. The Christian way of life and *le bonheur mondain* impinge one on the other, and are to be distinguished from *le bonheur philosophique*. This approach leads him to emphasise the illusory nature of eighteenth-century relativism, and the provisional nature of scepticism, in face of what Crocker calls the real search for universals. But while searching for new certainties, many, like Voltaire, remain obstinately in the world of the relative, and do so with a kind of desperate intensity. The very notion of truth as a matter of degree of credibility, to which Voltaire clung, does in fact dominate his deism and sets his very belief in God within the framework of the relative. Crocker is more illuminating than Mauzi in his own examination of the evolution from a feeling for the concrete and the individual to the unfolding of rationalistic programmes concerned with an abstract 'Man', 'general welfare', or public happiness, *la félicité publique*. Crocker, too, is more aware than Mauzi of the need to consider self-interest as part of the same complex, for *amour-propre* well understood can be seen as the source of all virtues. He is close to the truth when he sees the eighteenth century as identifying virtue and happiness, and believing somewhat blindly that general welfare would also provide individual happiness. He has understood Sade and Laclos as products of an evolution, rather than as individual thinkers standing out of their context; just as elsewhere he has pinpointed Diderot's nihilism side by side with his defence of social morality. He would appear to believe that these attitudes are coherent, on the assumption that the demands of culture are more valid and more important than the demands of the rebellious individual bent on self-affirmation. But one may prefer to see here an ambivalence which is typical of Diderot, and which can be extended to other *philosophes.* The reconciliation of natural immorality with social morality presents the unbeliever and the determinist philosopher with a problem that is best solved in practice, by the consideration of individual cases on their merits, rather than by abstract philosophy. If this be so, we may then see the eighteenth century as at once social and anti-social, posing rather than resolving the problem of morality without God. We can understand better the anguish of Voltaire having to reject Providence and other 'certitudes', still clinging to God to avoid moral chaos, and making man's need a measure of the truth, that is, the relative truth of an idea, as also Diderot's deep disquiet in face of his own cherished materialism.

It is perhaps our better understanding of earlier writers such as Bayle and Fontenelle, and of the anonymous freethinkers of clandestine literature, that is providing us with the necessary background to revaluations. The work of Mme E. Labrousse on Bayle and of I. O. Wade[7] and J. S. Spink[8] on clandestine French literature brings out the manifold complexities of the earlier age, and the ferment of ideas inherited by the generations of *philosophes.* If we have learned to avoid facile generalisations, we can also note the general trend and the extraordinary impact of the great works which came at the right time and gave body to much needed reforms, data on which to plan for the future, vitality to inchoate ideas, and style to formless notions. Work done on individual writers has provided a wealth of new material and interpretations which must lead to new and more accurate syntheses. New light on Voltaire has been shed by the publication of his correspondence by T. Besterman, R. Pomeau's fundamental contribution on Voltaire's religion, and the successful publication of *Studies on Voltaire and the Eighteenth Century*; knowledge of Rousseau has been stimulated by the publication of his works in the Pléiade edition, an earnest of his correspondence edited by R. A. Leigh, important studies by J. Starobinski, M. Raymond, R. Grimsley, L. G. Crocker, and others, and the publication of the *Annales J.-J. Rousseau*; of Diderot, through the biography by A. Wilson, the edition of many texts including the correspondence, as a forerunner of a new general edition of his complete works, the publications of H. Dieckmann, J. Seznec, L. G. Crocker, G. May, Y. Belaval, J. Lough, and many others, as well as the numerous volumes of *Diderot Studies*; of Montesquieu, thanks to the works of J. Crethe de la Gressaye, A. Masson, R. Shackleton, and P. Vernière; of d'Alembert, whose correspondence needs to be published; of

[7] I. O. Wade, *The Clandestine Organisation and Diffusion of Philosophic Ideas in France from 1700 to 1750*, 1938.

[8] J. S. Spink, *French Free-thought from Gassendi to Voltaire*, 1960.

d'Holbach, La Mettrie, Morelly, Abbé Galiani, and their contemporaries. Because of these, we are gathering a different and richer idea of intellectual life up to the time of the French Revolution.

From the historical standpoint, and for a general perspective, studies on the *Encyclopédie* and the Encyclopaedists are of singular importance. J. Le Gras' brief *Diderot et l'Encyclopédie* (1928) has now little to offer, and P. Grosclaude's *Un Audacieux Message, l'Encyclopédie* (1951) restates the well-known facts. Arthur Wilson in *The Testing Years, 1713–1759* (1957), has outlined the facts even more succinctly and satisfactorily, but for new information on the *Encyclopédie* itself, its contributors, their social background, and the underlying political issues, we must turn to J. Proust, *Diderot et l'Encyclopédie* (1962). We can now see more clearly the role of the *Encyclopédie* and the Encyclopaedists in the elaboration of political ideas and the shaping of events, in determining a new climate of opinion, and in forming an élite as well as a public. This does not, however, invalidate the general view that ideological conflicts have their origin in economic and social pressures, and that revolutions are never more than partly due to intellectual causes. The *Encyclopédie* is important not because it was necessarily read by a large public, but because it was the epitome of the age. It synthesised the scientific knowledge of the period, rendering it accessible to the non-specialist but educated man; and this is of particular consequence to the historian of science of today. It formulated a number of new hypotheses to account for facts, suggested new techniques, and above all, because of this basic activity, it was an instrument of war against all the prejudices of the *ancien régime*. The growing daring of the contributors reflected the spirit of the times; yet they remained original interpreters of public opinion. They formed the most powerfully intellectual body of men, and their differences on many points merely serve to bring out the intensity of the conflicts that underlay society in their day. It is through a detailed study of the *Encyclopédie*, and the full career and works of the Encyclopaedists, that we shall get really close to the living forces of the age and understand better the complex originality of the five or six great French thinkers whose names stand out so clearly today.

The new view of the eighteenth century comes therefore from detailed study of the social and political background of the age, and a closer scrutiny of articles in the *Encyclopédie* and of the works of the great and the minor writers. It comes, too, from our ability to cut across the divisions established by genres and disciplines. Thus science, the history of science, and philosophy are now seen as enriching literature and the history of ideas; and the need is for the synthesising of ever more complex data. Recently R. Mortier[9] has reminded us that we can no longer accept that rationalism and sensibility are exclusive – Diderot's and Rousseau's own works refute this. We no longer find it profitable to speak of pre-Romanticism in connection with any author of the period. We are not so certain of the old, and indeed sometimes of the new, generalisations. The works of Trahard, Monglond, Mornet, Van Tieghem, Hazard, and even Cassirer are now being questioned on matters of principle as well as of detail. Critics such as Werner Krauss,[10] Yvon Belaval, J. Proust, R. Mauzi, L. G. Crocker, H. Dieckmann, P. Gay,[11] and R. Mortier envisage a broadening of the whole concept of the Enlightenment, partly by placing it in its international context, relating, for example, a philosophical enthusiasm derived in some measure from Shaftesbury to the *Sturm und Drang* movement in Germany, so different from nineteenth-century romanticism, which R. Mortier has described as 'idealistic, reactionary, fantastic and mystical'. He has reminded us that the eighteenth century was certainly interested in dreams: those of Diderot and Rousseau, those of the abbé de Saint-Pierre on everlasting peace, of Père Castel on the hidden relationship between the arts, of Restif de La Bretonne, etc.; and with the possible exception of Rousseau and Diderot, which Mortier has ignored in this connection, it was united in rejecting the supernatural, and all transcendental experience; but it was only towards the end of the century, with Sade and Bernardin de Saint-Pierre, that it dissociated the two dominant tendencies of *reason* and *sensibility* which it had striven to harmonise into a coherent pattern. Certainly the capacity to receive emotions, the *uneasiness* of which Locke spoke, and which Condillac translated into *inquiétude* and considered the basis of psychic life, is not opposed to reason and intelligence, but its life force.

Thus philosophy, the philosophical and critical spirit, can no longer be separated from science, history, jurisprudence, and politics, nor confined to the realm of abstract speculation. Reason and nature must go hand in hand, since there is a close connection between the processes of the mind and the outside world it reflects; Diderot wrote:

[9] *Studies on Voltaire and the Eighteenth Century*, vol. XXVI, 1963, 'Unité ou Scission', pp. 1207–21. For the titles of works by the critics cited, see Bibliography, pp. 391–4.

[10] *Studien zur deutschen und französischen Aufklärung*, 1963.

[11] *The Enlightenment: an Interpretation*, vol. I: *The Rise of Modern Paganism* (1966) deals primarily with the intellectual origins of the movement. Vol. II, *The Science of Freedom* (1969), reappraises the programme of the Enlightenment, providing an important contribution to the social history of the period.

Le type de nos raisonnements les plus étendus, leur liaison, leur conséquence est nécessaire dans notre entendement comme l'enchaînement, la liaison des effets, des causes, des objets, des qualités des objets l'est dans la nature.[12]

In the quest for happiness, sentiment and reason combine to reconcile anarchical man and social man. If the majority of the *philosophes* clung to the bourgeois dream of reconciling happiness and virtue, at least they recognised man as an authentic individual, as well as a social and political animal, conditioned by education, economic, social, and political factors. It is the power of reason in individual man, whatever the nature of the factors that can lead it astray or distort it, that is the condition of his very real if limited freedom. For only the man who thinks can feel free and therefore be free.[13] And in spite of the determinist belief of many of the *philosophes*, it is the constant awareness of this personal freedom so manifest in practice that enabled them to step into new pastures and to lay the foundations of much progressive thought in the nineteenth and twentieth centuries.

The Age of Enlightenment is the Age of Reason and the Age of Sensibility in one. This truth is reflected in all the cultural activities of the period, in art and in music, in literature and in thought, in philosophy and the way of life; and although the emphasis changed in the course of the century, and from author to author, no careful critic can afford to neglect either element. In this respect, P. Trahard's *Les Maîtres de la sensibilité française au XVIIIe siècle* needs to be complemented by studies more concerned with French thought if a correct perspective is to be obtained. For with the eighteenth century, philosophy, criticism, science, and what we know as the history of ideas, all enter into literature, leading to that broadening of its concept which is a characteristic of the age. New systems of the universe are expounded in fine prose, for the better understanding of the intellectual, intelligent, educated public. Propaganda itself becomes literature, and achieves a growing status. The main preoccupation of the greatest writers was with philosophy and social action, not simply with *belles-lettres*. The *philosophes* directed their attention primarily to the social, political, and human problems of the day, and not to the entertainment of the many, or the aesthetic delight of the few. Yet they proved to be great stylists, moulding the language to their new needs, and experimenting in many directions. They were aware of the fact that ideas are valid only in so far as they can be conveyed with vigour and vividness, for they knew

[12] Diderot, *Oeuvres*, A.-T. IX, p. 372.
[13] Cf. Voltaire, *Traité de métaphysique*, ed. H. Temple Patterson, 1937, pp. 42–9.

that they had to convince and win readers over to their side. These urgent requirements led to a great diversity of style and refinement of language, from the mellifluous Latin periods of Buffon to the clipped and pungent style of Voltaire, a compound of total self-expression, obliquity, statement and understatement, logic and irony, and the jerky, vivid, apparently conversational and subtly diversified writing of Diderot. In this general climate of change in thought, values and style, of general scepticism and love of paradox, playwrights and novelists blossomed; but poets, in the sense in which the later Romantics and Symbolists have accustomed us to accept them, did not flourish. The achievements of the novelists in particular were fraught with great promise for the future. The littérateurs as a body mixed the traditional with the new, and, without being great innovators, they experimented in a variety of modes, as we have previously pointed out. But since the main current of the age was towards philosophy, the theatre and the novel tend in the main to provide an illustration and an accurate record of the preoccupations of the authors and readers of the time. The period is one of transition, with a peculiar flavour and exceptional attraction which time has not dimmed. Goethe's oft-quoted aphorism, 'Avec Voltaire un siècle finit, avec Rousseau un siècle commence', can no longer be accepted. Both writers are of their time, and both transcend their time. Endless speculation must attend their presentation of the basic problems of the individual and of society. They continue to attract and to repel, and they invariably stimulate: the quality of mind and the power of expression of these two great opponents stand out in spite of the animadversions of the most prejudiced commentator. With these two giants should be coupled the names of Montesquieu and Diderot, but lesser men who were yet great artists – Lesage, Marivaux, Prévost, Restif de La Bretonne, Laclos, Beaumarchais, and a host of others – all contributed through their diverse originality to the life and charm of a period two hundred years past, which yet still offers untold riches relevant to our contemporary social situation.

BIBLIOGRAPHY

Fuller bibliographies are contained in:

D. C. Cabeen, *A critical bibliography of French Literature*, vol. IV, *The Eighteenth Century*, ed. G. R. Havens and D. F. Bond, 1951; *Supplement*, ed. R. A. Brooks, 1968.

O. Klapp, *Bibliographie der französischen Literaturwissenschaft*, vols. I–VI, 1963–68.

G. Lanson, *Manuel bibliographique de la littérature française moderne, XVIIIe siècle*, 1923 ed., pp. 531–923. Supplement, pp. 1620–60. Continued by Jeanne Giraud, *Manuel de bibliographie littéraire pour les XVIe, XVIIe, et XVIIIe siècles français*, 1921–35, 1939; reprinted 1958.

R. Rancœur, *Bibliographie de la littérature française moderne (XVIe–XXe siècles)*. Published annually since 1963.

The Year's Work in Modern Language Studies. Published annually since 1931.

GENERAL WORKS[1]

Anthologies and Collective works

The Age of Enlightenment, An Anthology of Eighteenth Century French Literature, ed. Otis E. Fellows and Norman L. Torrey, 1942.

Les Philosophes du XVIIIe siècle, ed. J. Dedieu, 1952.

The Age of Enlightenment, ed. Isaiah Berlin, 1956.

Histoire des littératures, ed. R. Queneau, vol. 3, 1958 (Encyclopédie de la Pléiade).

Les Philosophes, ed. N. L. Torrey, 1960.

R. Desné, *Les matérialistes français de 1750 à 1800*, 1965 (extracts from a great number of writers with biographical and bibliographical notes, etc.).

J. Thoraval, C. Pellerin, M. Lambert, J. Le Solleuz, *Les Grandes Etapes de la civilisation française*, 1967.

[1] See also Chapter 14 for a review of some of the outstanding contributions to the field of eighteenth-century studies.

The Age of the Enlightenment, Studies presented to Theodore Besterman, St Andrews University Publications, No. LVII, 1967.

French Literature and its background, ed. J. Cruickshank, *3*, *The Eighteenth Century*, 1968.

L. G. Crocker, *The Age of Enlightenment*, 1969 (Introduction, editorial notes, and texts in translation).

Eighteenth Century French Studies, Literature and the Arts, ed. E. T. Dubois, E. Ratcliff, P. J. Yarrow, 1969.

Studies on Voltaire and the Eighteenth century, ed. Th. Besterman, 66 v. to 1969. Vols. XXIV–XXVII (1963) consist of the Transactions of the First International Congress on the Enlightenment; vols. LV–LVII (1967) of the Second.

A. Adam, G. Lerminier, E. Morot-Sir, *La Littérature française*, 2 vols., vol. I: *Des origines à la fin du XVIIIe siècle*, 1968.

P. Abraham and R. Desné, *Histoire littéraire de la France*, t. III (*De 1715 à 1789*), 1969.

New Cambridge Modern History, 1969, vols. VI, VII, VIII.

Dix-huitième Siècle, No. 1, 1969 (Annual publication, Garnier ed.)

General Studies

Jules Barni, *Histoire des idées morales et politiques au XVIIIe siècle, 1715–73*, 3 vols., 1865–73.

C. L. Becker, *The Heavenly City of the Eighteenth-century Philosophes*, 1932.

E. Bréhier, *Histoire de la philosophie*, 2 vols., 1929.

E. Cassirer, *Die Philosophie der Aufklärung*, Tübingen, 1932; English translation, 1951.

G. Chinard, *L'Amérique et le rêve exotique dans la littérature française aux XVIIe et XVIIIe siècles*, 2nd ed. 1934.

A. Cobban, *In Search of Humanity*, 1960.

——, ed., *The Eighteenth Century: Europe in the Age of Enlightenment*, 1969.

H. Cordier, *La Chine en France au XVIIIe siècle*, 1910.

A. Cresson, *Les Courants de la pensée philosophique française*, 2 vols., 1927.

L. G. Crocker, *An Age of Crisis*, 1959; *Nature and Culture: ethical thought in the Enlightenment*, 1963.

A. Dupront, *Les Lettres, les sciences, la religion et les arts dans la société française de la deuxième moitié du XVIIIe siècle* (Cours de la Sorbonne), 1963.

J. Ehrard, *L'Idée de nature en France dans la première moitié du XVIIIe siècle*, 2 vols., 1963.

J. Fabre, *Lumières et Romantisme*, 1963.

C. Frankel, *The Faith of Reason*, 1948.

B. Faÿ, *La Franc-Maçonnerie et la Révolution intellectuelle du XVIIIe siècle*, 1935.

Peter Gay, *The Enlightenment: An Interpretation*, vol. I: *The Rise of Modern Paganism*, 1966; vol. II, *The Science of Freedom*, 1969.

E. et J. de Goncourt, *La Femme au XVIIIe siècle*, 1862.

R. Gonnart, *La Légende du bon sauvage*, 1946.

F. C. Green, *Minuet: a critical survey of French and English literary ideas in the XVIIIth century*, 1935.

Basil Guy, *The French image of China before and after Voltaire*, in *Studies on Voltaire and the Eighteenth Century*, XXII, 1963.

G. R. Havens, *The Age of Ideas, from reaction to revolution in eighteenth-century France*, 1955.

P. Hazard, *La Crise de la conscience européenne*, 2 vols., 1935.

——, *La Pensée européenne au XVIIIe siècle, de Montesquieu à Lessing*, 3 vols., 1946.

Paul Janet, *Histoire de la science politique dans ses rapports avec la morale*, 1887.

Werner Krauss, *Studien zur Deutschen und Französischen Aufklärung*, 1963.

C.-E. Labrousse, R. Mousnier, M. Bouloiseau, *Le XVIIIe siècle, révolution intellectuelle, technique et politique, 1715–1815* (*Histoire générale des civilisations*, vol. V), 1953.

H. J. Laski, *The Rise of Liberalism*, 1936.

R. Laufer, *Style rococo, style des lumières*, 1963.

M. Launay and J. Goulemot, *Le Siècle des lumières*, 1968.

A. Lichtenberger, *Le Socialisme au XVIIIe siècle*, 1895.

M. Leroy, *Histoire des idées sociales en France*, vol. I: *de Montesquieu à Robespierre*, 1946.

A. Lortholary, *Le Mirage russe en France au XVIIIe siècle*, 1951.

J. Lough, *An Introduction to Eighteenth-century Thought*, 1960.

A. O. Lovejoy, *The Great Chain of Being, a study of the history of an idea*, 1953.

Kingsley Martin, *French Liberal Thought in the Eighteenth Century, a study of political ideas from Bayle to Condorcet*, 1929, 2nd ed. 1954.

P. Martino, *L'Orient dans la littérature française au XVIIe et au XVIIIe siècle*, 1906.

R. Mauzi, *L'Idée du bonheur dans la littérature et la pensée française du XVIIIe siècle*, 1960.

Gita May, *Madame Roland and the Age of Revolution*, 1970.

A. Monglond, *Histoire intérieure du préromantisme français de l'abbé Prévost à Joubert*, 1929.

D. Mornet, *Le Sentiment de la nature en France de J.-J. Rousseau à B. de Saint-Pierre*, 1907; *Les Sciences de la nature en France au XVIIIe siècle*, 1911; *Le Pensée française au XVIIIe siècle*, 1926; *Les Origines intellectuelles de la Révolution française, 1715–1787*, 1933.

R. Mortier, *Clartés et ombres du siècle des lumières*, 1960.

H. Nicolson, *The Age of Reason (1700–1789): Bayle, Voltaire, les Salons, 'l'Encyclopédie', Jean-Jacques Rousseau*, 1960.

V. Pinot, *La Chine et la formation de l'esprit philosophique en France*, 1932.

G. Poulet, *Etudes sur le temps humain*, 1950.

E. Préclin and V.-L. Tapié, *Le XVIIIe siècle*, 1952.

J. Roger, *Les Sciences de la vie dans la pensée française du XVIIIe siècle*, 1964.

P. Sagnac, *La Formation de la société française moderne*, 2 vols., 1945–46.

V. L. Saulnier, *La Littérature française du siècle philosophique (1715–1802)*, 1948.

J. Starobinski, *L'Invention de la liberté*, 1964.

J. L. Talmon, *The Rise of Totalitarian Democracy*, 1952.

P. Trahard, *Les Maîtres de la sensibilité française au XVIIIe siècle*, 4 vols., 1931–33.

H. Trevor-Roper, *The Historical Philosophy of the Enlightenment*, in *Studies on Voltaire and the Eighteenth Century*, XXVII, 1963.

P. Van Tieghem, *Le Préromantisme*, 1947.

C. E. Vaughan, *Studies in the History of Political Philosophy before and after Rousseau*, 1925.

J. Vier, *Histoire de la littérature française, XVIIIe siècle*, 1965.

H. Vyverberg, *Historical Pessimism in the French Enlightenment*, 1958.

J. G. Weightman, *Critical Judgment and Eighteenth-century Literature*, in Australian Universities Modern Language Association, 18, 1962.

B. Willey, *The Eighteenth-Century Background, studies on the idea of nature in the thought of the period*, 1940.

BIBLIOGRAPHIES TO PARTICULAR CHAPTERS

Chapter 1

Louis de Rouvroy, duc de Saint-Simon, *Mémoires de Saint-Simon*, ed. A. de Boislisle, 1879–1928, 41 vols. Also ed. by G. Truc in 7 vols., 1947–61.

R.-L. de Voyer de Paulmy, marquis d'Argenson, *Journal et mémoires*, ed. E.-J.-B. Rathery, 9 vols., 1859–69.

A. Morellet, *Mémoires inédits sur le XVIIIe siècle et la Révolution*, 1821.

C. B. A. Behrens, *The Ancien Régime*, 1967.

M. Bloch, *Les Caractères originaux de l'histoire rurale française*, 3rd ed., 1960.

T.-F. Bluche, *Les Magistrats du Parlement de Paris au XVIIIe siècle*, 1960.

H. Carré, *La Noblesse de France et l'opinion publique au XVIIIe siècle*, 1920.

A. Cobban, *A History of Modern France*, vol. I: *Old Régime and Revolution, 1715–99*; Penguin rev. ed. 1961.

P. Gaxotte, *Le Siècle de Louis XV*, 1935.

F. C. Green, *The Ancien Régime – A manual of French institutions and social classes*, 1958.

C.-E. Labrousse, *La Crise de l'économie française à la fin de l'Ancien Régime et au début de la Révolution*, 1943.

E. Lavisse, *Histoire de France*, vol. 8 (Part 2): *Le Règne de Louis XV (1715–74)*, 1909; vol. 9 (Part 1): *Le Règne de Louis XVI (1774–89)*, 1911.

M. Marion, *Dictionnaire des institutions de la France aux XVIIe et XVIIIe siècles*, 1923; reprinted 1968.

J. B. Perkins, *France under the Regency*, 1892; *France under Louis XV*, 1897.

E. Préclin, *Les Jansénistes du XVIIIe siècle et la constitution civile du clergé; le développement du richérisme; sa propagation dans le bas clergé*, 1928.

H. Sée, *Les Idées politiques en France au XVIIIe siècle*, 1920; *l'Evolution commerciale et industrielle de la France sous l'Ancien Régime*, 1925; *La France économique et sociale au XVIIIe siècle*, 1925; *La Vie économique et les classes sociales en France au XVIIIe siècle*, 1924; *L'Evolution de la pensée politique en France au XVIIIe siècle*, 1925.

H. Taine, *Les Origines de la France contemporaine*, vol. I: *L'Ancien Régime*, 16th ed., 1876.

A. de Tocqueville, *L'Ancien Régime et la Révolution*, in *Œuvres complètes*, 1952, 8th ed. vol. II.

Chapter 2

France in the eighteenth century, Royal Academy of Arts in London, 1968. Catalogue of the Winter exhibition 1968.

Diderot, *Salons*, ed. J. Seznec (and J. Adhémar for the first two vols.), 4 vols., 1957–67.

H. Dieckmann, *Esthetic Theory and Criticism in the Enlightenment, from examples of modern trends* (Fontenelle, Condillac, Diderot) in *Introduction to Modernity*, 1965.

W. Folkierski, *Entre le classicisme et le romantisme, Etude sur l'esthétique et les esthéticiens du XVIIIe siècle*, 1925.

A. Fontaine, *Les Doctrines d'art en France, peintres, amateurs, critiques, de Poussin à Diderot*, 1909.

Edmund et Jules de Goncourt, *L'Art au dix-huitième siècle, 1856–1875*. Tr. in part by R. Ironside, 1948.

Louis Hautecœur, *Littérature et peinture en France du XVIIe au XXe siècles*, 2nd ed., 1963.

Gita May, *Diderot et Baudelaire, critiques d'art*, 1957.

G. Pelles, *Art, Artists and Society; origins of a modern dilemma; painting in England and France, 1750–1850*, 1963.

Vassily Photiades, *Eighteenth Century Painting*, The Contact History of Art, English translation by Frances Partridge, 1964.

S. Rocheblave, *French painting in the Eighteenth Century*, tr. by G. F. Lees, 1937.

V. W. Topazio, *Art Criticism in the Enlightenment*, in *Studies on Voltaire and the Eighteenth Century*, XXVII, 1963.

R. H. Wilenski, *French Painting*, 1949.

B. S. Brook, *La Symphonie française dans la seconde moitié du XVIIIe siècle*, 1962.

B. Champigneulle, *L'Age classique de la musique française*, 1946.

J. Ecorcheville, *De Lulli à Rameau, 1690–1730, L'esthétique musicale*, 1906.

C. M. Girdlestone, *J.-P. Rameau, his life and work*, 1957.

D. J. Grout, *A Short History of Opera*, 2nd ed., 1965.

I. E. Lowinsky, *Taste, Style and Ideology in Eighteenth-century Music*, in *Aspects of the Eighteenth Century*, ed. Earl R. Wasserman, 1965.

R. Rolland, *Musiciens d'autrefois*, 2nd ed., 1908.

E. Vuillermoz, *Histoire de la musique* (Livre de Poche encyclopédique, 393–4), 1949.

Chapter 3

Histoire de Madame de Montbrillant; les pseudo-mémoires de Madame d'Epinay, ed. G. Roth, 1951.

Letters to and from Mme du Deffand and Julie de Lespinasse, ed. Warren Hunting Smith, 1938.

Letters of Mlle de Lespinasse, with notes on her life and character by d'Alembert, Marmontel, de Guibert, etc., and an introduction by C.-A. Sainte-Beuve, tr. by K. P. Wormeley, 1902.

J. Bertaut, *La Vie littéraire au XVIIIᵉ siècle*, 1954.
Helen Clergne, *The Salon: a Study of French Society and Personalities in the Eighteenth Century*, 1907.
L. Ducros, *La Société française au XVIIIᵉ siècle*, 1922.
G. P. Gooch, *Four French Salons*, 1951.
J. C. Herold, *Love in Five Temperaments*, 1961. (Essays on Mme de Tencin, Mlle Aïssé, Mme de Staal, and Mlle de Lespinasse.)
G. Mongrédien, *La Vie de société aux XVIIᵉ et XVIIIᵉ siècles*, 1950.
Sir Harold G. Nicolson, *The Salons (1660–1789)*, in *The Age of Reason*, 1960.
R. Picard, *Les Salons littéraires et la société française, 1610–1789*, 1943.

J. Drouet, *L'Abbé de Saint-Pierre, l'homme et l'œuvre*, 1912.
Merle L. Perkins, *The Moral and Political Philosophy of the Abbé de Saint-Pierre*, 1959.

R. Dauvergne, *La Marquise de Lambert à l'Hôtel de Nevers (1698–1773)*, 1947.
Suzanne Delorme, *Le Salon de la marquise de Lambert, berceau de l'Encyclopédie* in *Revue d'Histoire des sciences et de leurs applications*, 1951.
P.-M. Masson, *Une Vie de femme, Madame de Tencin*, 1909.
Janet Aldis, *Madame Geoffrin, Her Salon and Her Times, 1750–1777*, 2nd ed., 1906.
E. Pilon, *Le Salon de Madame Geoffrin et le sentimentalisme philosophique*, 1904.
A. Tornezy, *Un Bureau d'esprit au XVIIIᵉ siècle: le salon de Madame Geoffrin*, 1895.
L. Duisit, *Madame du Deffand épistolière*, 1963.
C. Ferval, *Mme du Deffand*, 1933.
G. Rageot, *Mme du Deffand*, 1937.
Lytton Strachey, *Madame du Deffand*, in *Books and Characters*, 1922.
J. Bouissounouse, *Julie de Lespinasse, ses amitiés, sa passion*, 1958.
M. Mitchiner, *A Muse in Love: Julie de Lespinasse*, 1962.
N. Royde-Smith, *The Double Heart: a Study of Julie de Lespinasse*, 1931.
Marquis de Ségur, *Julie de Lespinasse*, 1905 (English translation 1907).
H. Valentino, *Mme d'Epinay, 1726–1783; une femme d'esprit sous Louis XV*, 1952.

Chapter 4

Anthologie poétique française, ed. M. Allem, republished by Garnier-Flammarion, 1966.
L'Art poétique, ed. J. Charpier and P. Seghers, 1956.

M. M. Cameron, *L'Influence des Saisons de Thomson sur la poésie descriptive en France (1759–1810)*, 1927.
P. Citron, *La Poésie de Paris dans la littérature française de Rousseau à Baudelaire*, 1961.
R. Etiemble, *La Poésie au XVIIIe siècle*, in *Histoire des littératures*, vol. 3, ed. R. Queneau, 1958.
R. Finch, *The Sixth Sense; individualism in French poetry, 1686–1760*, 1966.
M. Gilman, *The Idea of Poetry in France; from Houdar de La Motte to Baudelaire*, 1958.
D. Mornet, *L'Alexandrin français dans la deuxième moitié du XVIIIe siècle*, 1907.
A. Thérive, *La Poésie au XVIIIe siècle, La Muse Française*, 1925.

P. Dimoff, *La Vie et l'œuvre d'André Chénier jusqu'à la Révolution française*, 1936.
J. Fabre, *André Chénier, l'homme et l'œuvre*, 1955.
F. Scarfe, *André Chénier. His Life and Work, 1762–1794*, 1965.
H. A. Grubbs, *Jean-Baptiste Rousseau; his life and works*, 1941.

Chapter 5

Lesage

Le Diable boiteux, in *Romanciers du XVIIIe siècle*, ed. Etiemble, 2 vols., 1960–65. The preface deals excellently with both *Le Diable boiteux* and *Gil Blas*.
Histoire de Gil Blas de Santillane, ed. M. Bardon, 2 vols., Garnier, 1942, reprinted 1955.

R. Alter, *The Incorruptibility of the Picaresque Hero*, in his *Rogue's Progress: studies in the picaresque novel*, 1964.
V. Barberet, *Lesage et le Théâtre de la Foire*, 1887.
F. Brunetière, *Les Epoques du Théâtre Français, 8e Conférence; Autour de Turcaret*, 1891–92.
L. G. Crocker, *Human Nature in the Novel*, in his *An Age of Crisis*, 1959.
C. Dédéyan, *A.-R. Lesage: Gil Blas* (Les Cours de Sorbonne), 1956.

H. C. Lancaster, *Sunset*, 1945.
C. Lenient, *La Comédie en France au XVIIIe siècle*, 1888.
E. Lintilhac, *Lesage*, 1893; *Histoire du théâtre en France*, t. IV (*XVIIIe siècle*), 1909.
M. Spaziani, *Il Teatro minore di Lesage. Studi e Ricerche*. Rome, 1957.

Marivaux

Marcel Arland, *Marivaux*, 1950. See also M. Arland's introduction to the Pléiade edition of Marivaux's plays and novels, 1949.
G. Attinger, *L'Esprit de la Commedia dell'arte dans le théâtre français*, 1950.
Xavier de Courville, *Un Apôtre de l'art du théâtre au XVIIIe siècle: Luigi Riccoboni, dit Lelio*, 2 vols., 1942–45. See especially vol. II.
F. Deloffre, *Une Préciosité nouvelle, Marivaux et le marivaudage, étude de langue et de style*, 1955, 2nd rev. ed., 1967; also introductions to his editions of the novels, the theatre, and the journals of Marivaux in the Classiques Garnier.
P. Gazagne, *Marivaux par lui-même*. Coll. 'Ecrivains de toujours', 1954.
E. J. H. Greene, *Marivaux*, 1965.
G. Larroumet, *Marivaux, sa vie et ses œuvres*, 1882.
K. N. McKee, *The Theatre of Marivaux*, 1958.
Thelma Niklaus, *Harlequin Phoenix, or the Rise and Fall of a Bergamask Rogue*, 1956.
C. Roy, *Lire Marivaux*, 1947.
P. Trahard, *Les Maîtres de la sensibilité française au XVIIIe siècle (1715–1789)*, t. I., 1931.

Abbé Prévost

L'Abbé Prévost (Actes du colloque d'Aix-en-Provence, 20 et 21 décembre, 1963). Aix-en-Provence, 1965.
F. Deloffre and R. Picard, introduction to their edition of *Manon Lescaut* in Classiques Garnier, 1965.
Claire-Elaine Engel, *Le Véritable Abbé Prévost*. Monaco, 1958.
H. Roddier, *L'Abbé Prévost, l'homme et l'œuvre*. Paris, 1955.
M. Rose de Labriolle Rutherford, articles on *Le Pour et Contre* in *Revue d'histoire littéraire de la France*, 1962; *Studies on Voltaire and the Eighteenth Century*, XXXIV–XXXV, 1965; *Revue d'histoire du théâtre*, vol. 14, 1962; *Revue de littérature comparée*, vol. 33, 1959.
J. Sgard, *Prévost romancier*, 1968.

Chapter 6

W. H. Barber, *Leibniz in France, from Arnauld to Voltaire; a study in French reactions to Leibnizianism 1670–1760*, 1955.
J.-P. Belin, *Le Commerce des livres prohibés à Paris de 1750 à 1789*, 1913.
E. R. Briggs, *L'Incrédulité et la pensée anglaise en France au début du XVIII*e *siècle*, in *Revue d'histoire littéraire de la France*, 1934.
P. Brochon, *Le Livre de colportage en France depuis le XVI*e *siècle, sa littérature, ses lecteurs*, 1954.
Y. Z. Duborg, *Le Livre français et son commerce en Hollande de 1750 à 1780*, 1925.
J. E. de la Harpe, *J.-P. de Crousaz et le conflit des idées au siècle des lumières*, 1955.
E. Hatin, *Les Gazettes de Hollande et la presse clandestine aux XVII*e *et XVIII*e *siècles*, 1865.
Peter Gay, *The Enlightenment: An Interpretation*, vol. I: *The Rise of Modern Paganism*, 1966.
G. Lanson, *Origines et premières manifestations de l'esprit philosophique dans la littérature française de 1675 à 1748*, in *Revue des Cours et Conférences*, 1907–10; *Questions diverses sur l'histoire de l'esprit philosophique en France avant 1750*, in *Revue d'histoire littéraire de la France*, 1912.
R. R. Palmer, *Catholics and Unbelievers in Eighteenth-century France*, 1939.
R. H. Popkin, *Scepticism in the Enlightenment*, in *Studies on Voltaire and the Eighteenth Century*, 1963.
Rt. Hon. J. M. Robertson, *A History of Free-thought ancient and modern to the period of the French Revolution*, 1899, 4th rev. ed., 1936, vol. II: *Pioneer Humanists*, 1907.
J. S. Spink, *French Free-thought from Gassendi to Voltaire*, 1960.
A. Vartanian, *Diderot and Descartes*, 1953.
P. Vernière, *Spinoza et la pensée française avant la Révolution*, 2 vols., 1954.
I. O. Wade, *The Clandestine Organization and Diffusion of Philosophic Ideas in France from 1700 to 1750*, 1938.

P. Brunet, *L'Introduction des théories de Newton en France au XVIII*e *siècle avant 1738*, 1931.
E. Sayous, *Les Déistes anglais et le christianisme, principalement depuis Toland jusqu'à Chubb (1696–1738)*, 1882.
D. B. Schlegel, *Shaftesbury and the French Deists*, 1956.

Leslie Stephen, *English Thought in the Eighteenth Century*, 2 vols., 1876, rev. 1902, repr. 1963.
N. L. Torrey, *Voltaire and the English Deists*, 1930.

Saint-Simon, Mémoires, ed. A. de Boislile, 41 vols. plus 5 vols. of appendices, 1879–1928. Also ed. G. Truc in 7 vols., Bibliothèque de la Pléiade, 1947–61.
F.-R. Bastide, *Saint-Simon par lui-même*, 1953.
Selections from Bayle's Dictionary, ed. E. A. Beller and M. du P. Lee-Ir, 1952. Also anthologies by M. Raymond (1954) and E. Labrousse (1965); and Pierre Bayle, *Œuvres diverses*, 4 vols., 1964–68.
Pierre Bayle, le philosophe de Rotterdam, ed. P. Dibon and R. H. Popkin, 1959.
A. Adam, *Pierre Bayle* in his *Histoire de la littérature française au XVII*[e] *siècle*, 1956.
E. Labrousse, *Pierre Bayle*, 2 vols., 1963–64; *Pierre Bayle et l'instrument critique*, 1965.
H. T. Mason, *Pierre Bayle and Voltaire*, 1963.
W. Rex, *Essays on Pierre Bayle and Religious Controversy*, 1965.
Annie Barnes, *Jean Le Clerc (1657–1736) et la république des lettres*, 1938.
Fontenelle, Entretiens sur la pluralité des mondes, Digression sur les Anciens et les Modernes, ed. R. Shackleton, 1955.
J.-R. Carré, *La Philosophie de Fontenelle ou Le Sourire de la raison*, 1932.
J. Dagen, *Pour une histoire de la pensée de Fontenelle*, in *Revue d'histoire littéraire de la France*, 1966.
F. Grégoire, *Fontenelle, une philosophie désabusée*, 1947.
Renée Simon, *Henry de Boulainviller*, 1939.
R. Simon, *Nicolas Fréret, académicien, 1688–1749*, in *Studies on Voltaire and the Eighteenth Century*, XVII, 1961.
Jean Meslier, *Testament*, 3 vols., Amsterdam, 1864; *Œuvres complètes*, ed. J. Deprun, R. Desné, and A. Soboul, 3 vols., 1969–70.
Articles *Boulainvilliers* and *Clandestine Philosophical Literature in France* in *Encyclopedia of Philosophy*, 1967.

Chapter 7

Editions

Œuvres complètes, by A. Masson, 3 vols., 1950–55.
Pléiade edition, by R. Caillois, 2 vols., 1949–51.
Intégrale edition, by D. Oster, Seuil, 1964.

L'Esprit des lois, crit. ed. by J. Brethe de La Gressaye. Les Textes Français, 4 vols., 1950–61.
Les Lettres persanes, by P. Vernière in Classiques Garnier, 1960.

Criticism

Actes du Congrès Montesquieu (with Introduction by L. Desgaves), 1956.
P. Barrière, *Un Grand Provincial: Charles-Louis de Secondat, baron de La Brède et de Montesquieu*, 1946.
G. Benrekassa, *Montesquieu*, 1968.
J. Dedieu, *Montesquieu*, 1913; *Montesquieu, l'homme et l'œuvre*, 1943, rev. ed., 1966.
Politique de Montesquieu, ed. J. Ehrard, Coll. U. Colin, 1965.
F. T. H. Fletcher, *Montesquieu and English Politics*, 1939.
J. R. Loy, *Montesquieu*, 1968.
Robert Shackleton, *Montesquieu, A Critical Biography*, 1961.
A. Sorel, *Montesquieu*, 1887, tr. M. B. & E. P. Anderson, 1888.
J. Starobinski, *Montesquieu par lui-même*, 1953.
M. H. Waddicor, *Montesquieu and the Philosophy of Natural Law*, 1970.

Chapter 8

Editions

See G. Bengesco, *Voltaire: Bibliographie de ses œuvres*, 1882–90. 6 vols. of a critical ed. of Voltaire's *Œuvres complètes* have appeared, by Th. Besterman, W. Barber, and others, published in Geneva by the Institut et Musée Voltaire, 1968–69. The best available edition of Voltaire's *Complete Works* is that by Moland, 1877–85; but the earlier ones by Beaumarchais and others, 1784–89, and by Beuchot, 1828–40, may still be used.
Correspondance, ed. Th. Besterman, 107 vols., 1953–65; also in Pléiade ed., 1964– .
Voltaire's Notebooks, ed. Th. Besterman, 1952; revised 1958.
La Henriade, ed. O. R. Taylor, 1965.
Œuvres historiques, ed. R. Pomeau, 1957.
Lettres philosophiques, ed. G. Lanson, 1906, 1909, rev. 1964; and ed. O. R. Taylor; and ed. R. Naves in Classiques Garnier.
Lettres d'amour de Voltaire à sa nièce, ed. Th. Besterman, 1957.
Traité de métaphysique, ed. H. Temple Patterson, 1937.
Micromégas: A study in the fusion of Science, Myth and Art, ed. I. O. Wade, 1950.
Essai sur les mœurs, ed. R. Pomeau, 1963.

Candide, ou L'Optimisme, ed. A. Morize, 1913, R. Pomeau, 1963, O. R. Taylor, 1941, L. G. Crocker, 1958, J. H. Brumfitt, 1968, and C. Thacker, 1968.
Dictionnaire philosophique, ed. J. Benda and R. Naves, 1935–36.
La Philosophie de l'histoire, ed. J. H. Brumfitt, 1963.
Le Philosophe ignorant, ed. J. L. Carr, 1965.
L'Ingénu, ed. W. R. Jones, 1936, 1957; *L'Ingénu and Histoire de Jenni*, ed. J. H. Brumfitt and M. Gerard Davis, 1960.
Poème sur la Loi Naturelle, ed. F. J. Crowley, 1938.
Le Temple du goût, ed. E. Carcassonne, 1938.
Le Taureau blanc, ed. R. Pomeau, 1957.
Zadig ou La Destinée, edition critique, by G. Ascoli, 2 vols., 1929, revised by J. Fabre, 2 vols., 1962.

Criticism

W. H. Barber, *Voltaire's 'Candide'*, 1960.
A. Bellessort, *Essai sur Voltaire*, 1926.
Th. Besterman, *Voltaire*, 1969.
W. F. Bottiglia, *Voltaire's 'Candide'; analysis of a classic*, 1st ed., 1957, 2nd ed., 1964, in *Studies on Voltaire and the Eighteenth Century*, VII and VIIa.
H. N. Brailsford, *Voltaire*, 1935.
J. H. Brumfitt, *Voltaire Historian*, 1958.
H. Carrington Lancaster, *French Tragedy in the Time of Louis XV and Voltaire, 1715–1774*, 2 vols., 1950.
G. Desnoiresterres, *Voltaire et la Société au XVIIIe siècle*, 8 vols., 1869–76.
P. Gay, *Voltaire's Politics, the Poet as Realist*, 1959.
J. Van den Heuvel, *Voltaire dans ses contes*, 1967.
G. Lanson, *Voltaire*, 1906, revised 1965.
H. Lion, *Les Tragédies et les théories dramatiques de Voltaire*, 1895.
T. R. Lounsbury, *Shakespeare and Voltaire*, 1902.
N. Mitford, *Voltaire in Love*, 1957.
J. Morley, *Voltaire*, 1872, repr. 1913.
B. L. de Muralt, *Lettres sur les Anglois et les François et sur les Voyages* (1827), ed. C. Gould, 1933.
R. Naves, *Voltaire, l'homme et l'œuvre*, 1942; *Le Goût de Voltaire*, 1938.
G. Pellissier, *Voltaire philosophe*, 1908.
R. Pomeau, *La Religion de Voltaire*, 1965, revised 1969; *Voltaire par lui-même*, 1955.
R. S. Ridgway, *La Propagande philosophique dans les tragédies de*

Voltaire, 1961, in *Studies on Voltaire and the Eighteenth Century*, XV.

N. Torrey, *The Spirit of Voltaire*, 1938; *Voltaire and the English Deists*, 1930.

V. W. Topazio, *Voltaire, A Critical Study of his Major Works*, 1967.

I. O. Wade, *Voltaire and Mme du Châtelet, an essay on the intellectual activity at Cirey*, 1941; *Studies on Voltaire*, 1947; *The Search for a new Voltaire*, 1958; *Voltaire and Candide*, 1959.

R. Waldinger, *Voltaire and Reform in the Light of the French Revolution*, 1959.

J. C. Weightman, *The Quality of Candide*, in *Essays presented to C. M. Girdlestone*, 1960.

See *La Table Ronde*, Feb. 1958, and all numbers of *Studies on Voltaire and the Eighteenth Century*, ed. Th. Besterman. 66 volumes have appeared between 1955 and 1969. See also M.-M. Barr, *Quarante années d'études voltairiennes* (1926–65), 1968, adding over 2,184 items to her bibliographies of 1929, 1933, 1941.

Chapter 9

Editions

Œuvres complètes, ed. B. Gagnebin and M. Raymond, Bibliothèque de la Pléiade, 1959–68, 4 vols. to 1969.

A la rencontre de J.-J. Rousseau, ed. B. Gagnebin, 1962.

Discours sur les sciences et les arts, ed. G. R. Havens, 1946.

Du Contrat Social, ed. C. E. Vaughan, 1918; G. Beaulavon, 1903.

La Nouvelle Héloïse, ed. D. Mornet, 4 vols., 1925; ed. J. Pomeau, 1960.

Emile, ed. Garnier.

La Profession de foi du Vicaire savoyard, ed. P.-M. Masson, 1914.

Du Contrat Social, including the *Discours & Lettre à d'Alembert*, ed. Garnier.

Rêveries du promeneur solitaire, ed. R. Niklaus, 1943, ed. M. Raymond, 1948; ed. J. S. Spink, 1948.

Correspondance Générale, ed. Th. Dufour and P. P. Plan, 20 vols., 1924–34.

Correspondance, vols. 1–8, ed. R. A. Leigh, 1965–69 (to date).

Lettre à M. D'Alembert sur les spectacles, ed. M. Fuchs, 1948.

Discours sur l'inégalité, ed. J. Lecercle, 1968.

The Political Writings of J.-J. Rousseau, ed. C. E. Vaughan, 1915.

Criticism

P. Burgelin, *La Philosophie de l'existence de Jean-Jacques Rousseau*, 1952.
J. H. Broome, *Rousseau, a Study of his Thought*, 1963.
E. Cassirer, *The Question of J.-J. Rousseau*, tr. P. Gay, 1962.
A. Cobban, *Rousseau and the Modern State*, 1934.
L.-J. Courtois, *Chronologie critique de la vie et des œuvres de J.-J. Rousseau*, 1924.
L. G. Crocker, *J.-J. Rousseau: The Quest, 1712–1758*, vol. I, 1968.
R. Derathé, *La Rationalisme de J.-J. Rousseau*, 1948; *J.-J. Rousseau et la science politique de son temps*, 1950.
F. C. Green, *J.-J. Rousseau*, 1955.
R. Grimsley, *Jean-Jacques Rousseau, a Study in Self-Awareness*, 1961; *J.-J. Rousseau and the Religious Quest*, 1968.
B. Groethuysen, *Jean-Jacques Rousseau*, 1949.
J. Guéhenno, *Jean-Jacques*, 3 vols., 1948–52.
H. Guillemin, *Un homme, deux ombres (Jean-Jacques, Julie, Sophie)*, 1943.
C. W. Hendel, *J.-J. Rousseau, Moralist*, 1934.
P. Jimack, *La Genèse et la rédaction de l'Emile de Jean-Jacques Rousseau*, 1960.
M. Launay, *Rousseau*, 1968.
P.-M. Masson, *La Religion de J.-J. Rousseau*, 3 vols., 1916.
G. May, *Rousseau par lui-même*, 1961.
D. Mornet, *Rousseau, l'homme et l'œuvre*, 1950.
M. Raymond, *J.-J. Rousseau, La Quête de soi et la rêverie*, 1962.
H. Roddier, *J.-J. Rousseau en Angleterre au XVIIIe siècle*, 1950.
A. Schinz, *La Pensée de J.-J. Rousseau*, 2 vols., 1929.
J. S. Spink, *J.-J. Rousseau et Genève*, 1934.
J. Starobinski, *Jean-Jacques Rousseau, la transparence et l'obstacle*, 1957.
J. Voisine, *J.-J. Rousseau en Angleterre à l'époque romantique, les écrits autobiographiques et la légende*, 1956.
C. E. Vulliamy, *Rousseau*, 1931.

Annales de la Société J.-J. Rousseau, 36 vols., 1905–65.
J.-J. Rousseau, by S. Baud-Bavy and others, 1962.

Chapter 10

Editions

On Diderot's manuscripts, see: H. Dieckmann, *Inventaire du fonds Vandeul*, 1951; P. Vernière, *Diderot, ses manuscrits et ses copistes*, 1967.

A critical edition of Diderot's complete works is in preparation; another, less scholarly, is in course of publication in Le Club Français du livre, 1970.

Diderot, *Œuvres complètes*, ed. Assézat–Tourneux, 20 vols., Paris, 1875–77, to be used in conjunction with the following critical editions:

Pensées philosophiques, 1950, *Lettre sur les aveugles*, 1951, ed. R. Niklaus.

Lettre sur les sourds et muets, ed. P. H. Meyer, 1966 (*Diderot Studies*, vii).

Le Rêve de d'Alembert, etc., ed. P. Vernière, 1951, J. Varloot, 1961, J. Roger, 1965.

Le Neveu de Rameau, ed. J. Fabre, 1950.

Le Supplément au Voyage de Bougainville, ed. H. Dieckmann, 1955.

Contes, ed. H. Dieckmann, 1963.

Quatre Contes, ed. J. Proust, Geneva, 1964.

Est-il bon? Est-il méchant?, ed. J. Undank (*Studies on Voltaire and the Eighteenth Century*, XVI, 1961).

La Religieuse, ed. J. Parrish, *Studies on Voltaire and the Eighteenth Century*, XXII, 1963.

Eléments de Physiologie, ed. J. Mayer, 1964.

Salons (1769–81), vols. 1–3, ed. J. Seznec and J. Adhémar; vol. 4, ed. J. Seznec, 1957–68.

Correspondance de Diderot, 14 vols. (to 1776), ed. M. Roth, vols. 13 and 14 with the collaboration of J. Varloot, 1955–69.

The five volumes of Diderot's works in the *Classiques Garnier* include all essential texts and will be found adequate for general purposes. They have been edited by P. Vernière, except for *Oeuvres romanesques*, ed. H. Bénac.

Criticism

Y. Belaval, *L'Esthétique sans paradoxe de Diderot*, 1950. See also Y. Belaval's articles in *Critique*, vol. viii, no. 58 (March 1952); vol. xii, nos. 100–101 (Sept.–Oct. 1953); vol. xiv, nos. 107–108 (April–May 1956).

A. Vartanian, *Diderot and Descartes*, 1953.

Arthur M. Wilson, *Diderot, The Testing Years (1713–1759)*, 1957. (A further volume is in preparation.)

M. T. Cartwright, *Diderot critique d'art et le problème de l'expression*, 1969 (*Diderot Studies*, xiii).

L. G. Crocker, *Two Diderot Studies: Ethics & Esthetics*, 1952; *The Embattled Philosopher, a biography of Denis Diderot*, 1954, rev. 1965.

H. Dieckmann, *Cinq Leçons sur Diderot*, 1959.
J. Doolittle, *Rameau's Nephew*, 1960.
A. G. Fredman, *Diderot and Sterne*, 1955.
P. Hermand, *Les Idées morales de Diderot*, 1923.
R. Kempf, *Diderot et le roman*, 1964.
J. R. Loy, *Diderot's Determined Fatalist*, 1950.
G. May, *Diderot et La Religieuse*, 1954; *Quatre Visages de Diderot*, 1951.
J. Meyer, *Diderot, homme de science*, 1959.
John (Lord) Morley, *Diderot and the Encyclopaedists*, 2 vols., 1878; repr. 1923.
D. Mornet, *Diderot*, 1941.
R. Mortier, *Diderot en Allemagne (1750–1850)*, 1954.
R. Pomeau, *Diderot, sa vie, son œuvre avec un exposé de sa philosophie*, 1967.
J. Pommier, *Diderot avant Vincennes*, 1939.
J. Proust, *Diderot et l'Encyclopédie*, 1962.
J. Seznec, *Essais sur Diderot et l'antiquité*, 1957; *Sur l'art et les artistes*, 1968.
J. Thomas, *L'Humanisme de Diderot*, 1932, rev. 1938, 1942.
F. Venturi, *Jeunesse de Diderot (1713–1753)*, 1939.
Cahiers de l'Association Internationale des Etudes Françaises, vol. 13, 1961.
Europe, No. 405–406 (Jan.–Feb. 1963).
Thirteen volumes of *Diderot Studies* (in English and in French), edited by Otis Fellows, have appeared between 1949 and 1970.

Chapter 11

Encyclopédie, etc. is available in a photographic reprint, 35 vols., 1966–67. Diderot, Denis, *Pictorial Encyclopedia of Trades and Industry*, 2 vols., 1959, reproduces 485 of the original engravings.
D. H. Gordon and L. N. Torrey, *The Censoring of Diderot's Encyclopédie and the Re-established Text*, 1947.
Louis Moreri, *Le Grand Dictionnaire historique, ou Le Mélange curieux de l'histoire sacrée et profane*, 6 vols., 1732, with a supplement in 1735. (The first edition was in 1675.)
R.-A. Farchault de Réaumur, *Recueil des planches sur les sciences, les arts libéraux et les arts mécaniques, avec leur explication*, 11 vols., 1762–72.
See also P. Bayle's *Dictionnaire historique et critique*, Chambers's *Cyclopedia*, and the *Dictionnaire de Trévoux*.
J. Lough, *The Encyclopédie of Diderot and d'Alembert*, 1954. (Selected articles.)

L. Ducros, *Les Encyclopédistes*, 1900.

P. Grosclaude, *Un Audacieux Message. L'Encyclopédie*, 1951; *Malesherbes, témoin et interprète de son temps*, 1961.

R. Hubert, *Les Sciences sociales dans l'Encyclopédie*, 1923.

F. A. Kafker, *A list of contributors to Diderot's Encyclopedia*, in *French Historical Studies*, vol. 3, 1963–64.

J. Le Gras, *Diderot et l'Encyclopédie*, 1928.

J. Lough, *Luneau de Boisjermain v. the publishers of the Encyclopédie* in *Studies on Voltaire and the Eighteenth Century*, XIII, 1963; *Essays on the Encyclopédie of Diderot and d'Alembert*, 1968.

J. (Lord) Morley, *Diderot and the Encyclopaedists*, 2 vols., 1878, repr. 1923.

J. N. Pappas, *Berthier's Journal de Trévoux and the Philosophes*, in *Studies on Voltaire and the Eighteenth Century*, III, 1957.

J. Proust, *Diderot et l'Encyclopédie*, 1962; *L'Encyclopédie dans le Bas-Languedoc au XVIIIme siècle*, 1968.

F. Venturi, *Le Origini dell'Enciclopedia*, 2nd ed., 1963.

A. M. Wilson, *Diderot: the Testing Years, 1713–1759*, 1957; Article on *Encyclopédie* in the *Encyclopedia of Philosophy*, 1966.

A.-N. Marquis de Condorcet, *Eloge de d'Alembert*, in his *Œuvres*.

J. Bertrand, *D'Alembert*, 1889.

R. Grimsley, *Jean d'Alembert*, 1963.

M. Muller, *Essai sur la philosophie de Jean d'Alembert*, 1926.

Marta Rezler, *The Voltaire–d'Alembert correspondence: an historical and bibliographical re-appraisal*, in *Studies on Voltaire and the Eighteenth Century*, XX, 1962.

G. Le Roy, *Introduction à l'œuvre philosophique de Condillac*, in *Œuvres philosophiques de Condillac, Corpus général des philosophes français*, 1947; *La Psychologie de Condillac*, 1937.

G. Baguenault de Puchesse, *Condillac: sa vie, sa philosophie, son influence*, 1910.

J. Knight, *The Geometric Spirit. The Abbé de Condillac and the French Enlightenment*, 1968.

R. Lefèvre, *Hommage à Condillac*, in *Cahiers d'Histoire*, I, 1956.

E. A. Whitfield, *Gabriel Bonnot de Mably*, 1930.

A. Cazes, *Grimm et les encyclopédistes*, 1933.

E. Scherer, *Melchior Grimm*, 1887.

R. Hubert, *D'Holbach et ses amis*, 1928.

P. Naville, *Paul Thiry d'Holbach et la philosophie scientifique au XVIIIe siècle*, 1943.

J. Lough, *Essai de bibliographie critique des publications du baron d'Holbach*, in *Revue d'histoire littéraire de la France*, 1939 and

1947; *Le Baron d'Holbach; quelques documents inédits ou peu connus*, in *Revue d'histoire littéraire de la France*, 1957.
V. W. Topazio, *D'Holbach's moral philosophy; its background and development*, 1956.
J. Lough, *Helvétius and d'Holbach*, in *Modern Language Review*, 1938.
Ian Cumming, *Helvétius, his Life and Place in the History of Educational Thought*, 1955.
D. W. Smith, *Helvétius, a Study in Persecution*, 1965.
A. Mazure, *Les Idées de l'abbé Morellet, membre de l'Académie française, 1727–1819*, 1910.
A. Feugère, *Un précurseur de la Révolution: l'abbé Raynal* (*1713–96*), *documents inédits*, 1922.
J. Rossi, *The Abbé Galiani in France*, 1930.
Condorcet, *Esquisse d'un tableau historique des progès de l'esprit humain*, ed. O. H. Prior, 1933. Tr. J. Barraclough, 1955.
J. Bouissounousse, *Condorcet, le philosophe de la Révolution*, 1962.
J. Cahen, *Condorcet et la Révolution française*, 1904.
A. Guillois, *La Marquise de Condorcet, sa famille, son salon, ses amis, 1764–1822*, 1897.
Abbé Augustin Barruel, *Abrégé des mémoires pour servir à l'histoire du jacobinisme*, 1798.
B. Faÿ, *L'Esprit révolutionnaire en France et aux Etats Unis à la fin du XVIIIe siècle*, 1925.
La Mettrie, *L'Homme machine*, ed. A. Vartanian, 1960.
R. Boissier, *La Mettrie*, 1931.
P. Lemée, *Julien Offray de La Mettrie*, 4 pt. (1925–37).
Maupertuis, *Œuvres*, ed. G. Tonelli, 4 vols., 1965.
Maupertuis, le savant et le philosophe, ed. E. Callot, 1964.
P. Brunet, *Maupertuis*, 1929.
M.-L. Dufrenoy, *Maupertuis et le progrès scientifique*, in *Studies on Voltaire and the Eighteenth Century*, XXV, 1963.

D. Dakin, *Turgot and the Ancien Régime in France*, 1939.
Mélanges Cain, 7, 1968 (art. on Turgot).
Quesnay, *Textes* in *François Quesnay et la Physiocratie*, vol. 2., 1958 (Institut National d'Etudes Démographiques). Jean Sutter's article on *Quesnay et la médecine* is particularly interesting.
L. Cheinisse, *Les Idées politiques des physiocrates*, 1914.
H. Higgs, *The Physiocrats*, 1897.
R. L. Meek, *The Economics of Physiocracy; Essays and Translations*, 1963.
T. P. Neill, *Quesnay and Physiocracy*, in *Journal of the History of Ideas*, 1948.

G. Schelle, *Du Pont de Nemours et l'école physiocratique*, 1888.

G. Weulersse, *Le Mouvement physiocratique en France de 1756 à 1770*, 2 vols., 1910; *La Physiocratie à la fin du règne de Louis XV, 1770–1774*; *La Physiocratie sous les Ministères de Turgot et de Necker, 1774–1781*, 1950.

R. J. White, *The Anti-Philosophers: a Study of the Philosophies in Eighteenth-Century France*, 1970.

E. Callot, *La Philosophie de la vie au XVIIIe siècle*, 1965 (for La Mettrie, Maupertuis); *Six philosophes français du XVIIIe siècle*, 1963 (Diderot, Fontenelle, Maupertuis, La Mettrie, d'Holbach, Rivarol).

J. Roger, *Les Sciences de la vie dans la pensée française du XVIIIe siècle*, 1963.

A. Sayous, *Charles Bonnet* in *Le Dix-Huitième Siècle à l'étranger*, 1861.

Buffon, *Œuvres philosophiques*, ed. J. Piveteau, 1954, in *Corpus général de philosophes français*.

——, *Les époques de la nature*, ed. J. Roger, 1962.

F. Bourdier, *Principaux Aspects de la vie et de l'œuvre de Buffon*, in *Buffon*, ed. L. Bertin and F. Bourdier, 1952.

G. Lanson, *Le Marquis de Vauvenargues*, 1930.

F. Vial, *Une Philosophie et une morale du sentiment: Luc de Clapiers, marquis de Vauvenargues*, 1938.

May Wallas, *Luc de Clapiers, Marquis de Vauvenargues*, 1928.

M.-F.-A. de Lescure, *Rivarol et la société française pendant la révolution et l'émigration (1753–1801)*, 1883.

A. Le Breton, *Rivarol, sa vie, ses idées, son talent, d'après des documents nouveaux*, 1895.

G. Saintsbury, *Chamfort and Rivarol* in his *Miscellaneous essays*, 1892.

R.-L. de Voyer de Paulmy, marquis d'Argenson, *Journal et mémoires*, ed. E.-J.-B. Rathery, 9 vols., 1859–69.

R. N. Stromberg, *History in the Eighteenth Century*, 1951.

A. Lombard, *L'Abbé Du Bos, un initiateur de la pensée moderne*, 1913.

E. Hatin, *Bibliographie historique et critique de la presse française . . .*, 1866.

G. Bonn, *Liste chronologique des périodiques français du XVIIIe siècle*, in *Modern Language Review*, v (March 1944).

J. H. Broome, *Pierre Desmaizeaux, journaliste; les Nouvelles littéraires de Londres entre 1700 et 1740*, *Revue de littérature comparée*, 1955.

Chapter 12

Eighteenth-Century French Plays, ed. C. D. Brenner and N. A. Goodyear.

Petitot, *Répertoire du Théâtre français*, 25 vols., 1817–19; *Suite du Répertoire*, 81 vols., 1822; *Fin du Répertoire*, 45 vols., 1824–1825; *Théâtre des Auteurs du premier et du second ordre*, 67 vols., 1818; *Répertoire du Théâtre du troisième ordre*, 8 vols., 1819–20.

C. D. Brenner, *A Bibliographical List of Plays in the French Language, 1700–1815*, 1947.

Frères Parfaict (François and Claude), *Histoire du Théâtre Français depuis son origine jusqu'à présent*, 1745–49 (vols. 14 and 15); *Dictionnaire des théâtres de Paris*, 7 vols., 1756.

C. Alasseur, *La Comédie Française au XVIIIe siècle* (*Civilisations et Sociétés*, 3), 1967.

M. Albert, *Les Théâtres des boulevards*, 1902.

G. Attinger, *L'Esprit de la commedia dell'arte dans le théâtre français*, 1950.

M. Carlson, *The Theatre of the French Revolution*, 1966.

X. de Courville, *Un apôtre de l'art du théâtre au XVIIIe siècle, Luigi Riccoboni dit Lélio*, 3 vols., 1943–45.

G. Desnoiresterres, *La Comédie satirique au XVIIIe siècle*, 1885.

J. Fabre, *Le Théâtre au XVIIIe siècle*, in *Histoire des Littératures*, vol. III, 1958.

L. Fontaine, *Le Théâtre et la philosophie au XVIIIe siècle*, 1878.

G. Gaiffe, *Le Drame en France au XVIIIe siècle*, 1910.

A. Joannidès, *La Comédie Française de 1680 à 1920*, 1921.

H. C. Lancaster, *Sunset; a History of Parisian Drama in the Last Years of Louis XIV, 1701–1715*, 1945.

——, *French Tragedy in the time of Louis XV and Voltaire, 1715–74*, 2 vols., 1950.

——, *The Comédie Française 1701–1774 (Plays, Actors, Spectators, Finances)*, 1951.

——, *French Tragedy in the Reign of Louis XVI and the Early Years of the French Revolution, 1774–1792*, 1953.

G. Lanson, *Esquisse d'une histoire de la tragédie française*, 1920.

C. Lenient, *La Comédie en France au XVIIIe siècle*, 1888.

E. Lintilhac, *Histoire générale du théâtre en France*, 1909 (vol. IV deals with eighteenth-century comedy).

M. Lioure, *Le Drame*, 1963.

J. Lough, *Paris Theatre Audiences in the Seventeenth and Eighteenth Centuries*, 1957.

L. Moland, *Le Théâtre de la Révolution, choix de pièces*, 1877.

J. Morel, *La Tragédie*, 1964.

T. Niklaus, *Harlequin Phoenix, or the Rise and Fall of a Bergamask Rogue*, 1956.

P. Voltz, *La Comédie*, 1964.

H. Welshinger, *Le Théâtre de la Révolution, 1789–99*, 1880.

A. Calame, *Regnard, sa vie, son œuvre*, 1960.

G. Lanson, *Nivelle de La Chaussée et la comédie larmoyante*, 1887.

D. Delafarge, *La Vie et l'œuvre de Palissot (1730–1814)*, 1912.

F. Gaiffe, *Le Mariage de Figaro*, 1928.

E.-F. Lintilhac, *Beaumarchais et ses œuvres*, 1887.

L. de Loménie, *Beaumarchais et son temps*, 2 vols., 1826 and 1880.

R. Pomeau, *Beaumarchais, l'homme et l'œuvre*, 1956.

J. Scherer, *La Dramaturgie de Beaumarchais*, 1954.

E.-J. Arnould, *La Genèse du Barbier de Séville*, 1965.

R. Niklaus, *Beaumarchais: Le Barbier de Séville*, 1968.

Le Mariage de Figaro, ed. J. B. Ratermanis, in *Studies on Voltaire and the Eighteenth Century*, LXIII, 1968.

A. R. Pugh, *Beaumarchais: Le Mariage de Figaro*, 1968 (a critical commentary).

L. Béclard, *Sébastien Mercier, sa vie, son œuvre, son temps, d'après des documents inédits*, 1903.

H. Temple Patterson, *Poetic Genesis; Sébastien Mercier into Victor Hugo*, in *Studies on Voltaire and the Eighteenth Century*, XI, 1960.

A. J. Bingham, *Marie-Joseph Chénier, Early Political Life and Ideas (1789–1794)*, 1939.

Chapter 13

Romanciers du XVIIIe Siècle, ed. Etiemble (Bibliothèque de la Pléiade), 2 vols., 1960–65.

Quatre Romans dans le goût français, ed. C. Roy, 1959 (*Mademoiselle de Clermont*, by Mme de Genlis; *Mémoires du Comte de Comminge*, by Mme de Tencin; *Madame de Selves*, by Duclos; *Point de lendemain*, by Vivant Denon).

Henri Coulet, *Le Roman jusqu'à La Révolution*, 2 vols., 1967.

M.-L. Dufrenoy, *L'Orient romanesque en France, 1704–89*, 1946–1947.

R. Etiemble, *Prosateurs du XVIIIe siècle* in *Histoire des littératures*, 1958.

S. Etienne, *Le Genre romanesque en France depuis l'apparition de la 'Nouvelle Héloïse' jusqu'aux approches de la Révolution*, 1922.

F. C. Green, *French Novelists, Manners and Ideas from the Renaissance to the Revolution*, 1929 and 1964; *La Peinture des mœurs de la bonne société dans le roman français de 1715 à 1761*, 1924; *The Novel* in his *Minuet, A Critical Survey of French and English Literary Ideas in the Eighteenth Century*, 1935.

A. Le Breton, *Le Roman français au XVIIIe siècle*, 1898.

G. May, *Le Dilemme du roman au XVIIIe siècle*, 1963.

J. Merlant, *Le Roman personnel de Rousseau à Fromentin*, 1905.

Max Milner, *Le Diable dans la littérature française de Cazotte à Baudelaire, 1772–1861*, vol. I, 1960.

P. Morillot, *Le Roman au XVIIIe siècle*, in his *Le Roman en France depuis 1610 jusqu'à nos jours*, 1892.

Vivienne Mylne, *The Eighteenth-Century French Novel, Techniques of Illusion*, 1965.

M. Ratner, *Theory and Criticism of the Novel in France from L'Astrée to 1750*, 1938.

J. Rousset, *Une Forme littéraire: le roman par lettres*, in his *Forme et signification: essais sur les structures littéraires de Corneille à Claudel*, 1962.

G. Saintsbury, *History of the French Novel*, 2 vols., 1917–19.

J. Texte, *Jean-Jacques Rousseau et les origines du cosmopolitisme littéraire, étude sur les relations littéraires de la France et de l'Angleterre au XVIIIe siècle*, 1895.

Ruth Clark, *Anthony Hamilton, His Life and Works and His Family*, 1921.

G. Duhamel, *Vues sur Hamilton*, in *Mercure de France*, 1949.

S. Lenel, *Un Homme de lettres au XVIIIe siècle: Marmontel, d'après des documents nouveaux et inédits*, 1902.

E. A. Crosby, *Une Romancière oubliée: Madame Riccoboni; sa vie, ses ouvrages; sa place dans la littérature anglaise et française du XVIIIe siècle*, 1924.

M. Defourneaux, *Les Lettres péruviennes en Espagne*, in *Mélanges offerts à Marcel Bataillon*, 1962.

J.-H. Maubert de Gouvet, *Les Lettres iroquoises*, ed. Enea Balmas, 1962.

C. Cherpack, *An Essay on Crébillon fils*, 1962.

A. Parreaux, *William Beckford, auteur de Vathek (1760–1844); étude de la création littéraire*, 1960.

P. Castex, *Le Précurseur français*, in his *Le Conte fantastique en France de Nodier à Maupassant*, 1951 (deals with Cazotte).

H. Juin, *Un Portrait d'Andréa de Nerciat*, in his *Chroniques sentimentales*, 1962.

M. Souriau, *Bernardin de Saint-Pierre d'après ses manuscrits*, 1905.

J. Simon, *Bernardin de Saint-Pierre, ou le Triomphe de Flore*, 1967.
G. Saillard, *Florian, sa vie, son œuvre*, 1912.
P. Meister, *Charles Duclos, 1704–72*, 1956.
A.-M. Schmidt, *Duclos, Sade et la littérature féroce* in *Revue des sciences humaines*, 1951.
C. R. Dawes, *Restif de la Bretonne*, 1946.
A. Bégué, *Etat présent des études sur Rêtif de la Bretonne*, 1948.
J. Rives Childs, *Restif de La Bretonne, témoignages et jugements, bibliographie*, 1948.
Marc Chadourne, *Restif de La Bretonne ou Le Siècle prophétique*, 1958.
A. Marton, *Restif de la Bretonne devant la critique*, 1950–63, in *Studi Francesi*, 1965.
E. Dard, *Un Acteur caché du drame révolutionnaire; le général Choderlos de Laclos, auteur des Liaisons dangereuses (1741–1803)*, 1905.
R. Vailland, *Laclos par lui-même*, 1958.
J.-J. Seylaz, *Les Liaisons dangereuses et la création romanesque chez Laclos*, 1958.
R. Grimsley, *Don Juanism in Les Liaisons dangereuses*, in *French Studies*, Jan. 1960.
D. R. Thelander, *Laclos and the Epistolary Novel*, 1963.
A.-A. and Y. Delmas, *A La Recherche des Liaisons dangereuses*, 1964.
B. Guy, *The Prince de Ligne, Laclos and the Liaisons dangereuses: two notes*, in *Romanic Review*, 1964.
L. Versini, *Essai sur les sources et la technique des 'Liaisons dangereuses': Laclos et la tradition*, 1968.
J. Dutourd, *Le fond et la forme; essai alphabétique sur la morale et le style*, 1958 (contains an appreciation of *Faublas*).
L. C. Sykes, *Madame Cottin*, 1949.
V. Wyndham, *Madame de Genlis, a biography*, 1960.
C. R. Dawes, *The Marquis de Sade, his life and works*, 1927.
G. Dupé, *Le Marquis de Sade*, 1957.
G. Gorer, *The Marquis de Sade*, rev. ed. 1963.
L. G. Crocker, *Sade and the Fleurs du mal*, in his *Nature and Culture*, 1963.
Centre Aixois d'études et de recherches sur le XVIIIe siècle, *Le Marquis de Sade*, 1968 (Papers of the colloquium of 1965).
Tel Quel, 28, 1967 (on Sade).
H. Stavan, *Gabriel Senac de Meilhan, 1736–1803, moraliste, romancier, homme de lettres*, 1968.

INDEX

D

E

F

Q

R

S

W

Y

Z

DIDEROT, ROUSSEAU, VOLTAIRE

Printed in Great Britain
by Western Printing Services Limited
Bristol